Welcome to CodeKey!

CodeKey is Prentice Hall's online, interactive tutorial for users learning a new programming language. You can complete selected programming exercises taken directly from your textbook and receive automated feedback on the code you write. The online exercises will tell you how to improve your code when you modify existing programs from the book. **CodeKey** will allow you to test your programs before submitting them for class assignments. You can use **CodeKey** for programming practice.

To use CodeKey you must first register online.

You will need a valid email address and the student access code that is printed beneath the silver coating below. Use a coin to scratch it off and reveal your access code.

Important: This code is for use by only one student and cannot be shared. If your secret code has already been used, you must purchase a new access code at www.prenhall.com/codekey

To register online:

1. Go to www.prenhall.com/codekey
2. Find the title of your textbook.
3. Click **Access CodeKey** and follow the on-screen instructions.
4. Enter your student access code (provided beneath the silver scratch-off coating above).
5. Follow the on-screen instructions.
6. During registration, you will select your own username and password. Choose something you will remember and keep it confidential.

After you register, you can access **CodeKey** anytime by going directly to
www.prenhall.com/codekey

Java, Java, Java ™

Object-Oriented Problem Solving

Third Edition

Ralph Morelli
Ralph Walde
Trinity College

PEARSON

Prentice Hall

Upper Saddle River, New Jersey 07458

Library of Congress Cataloging-in-Publication Data

Morelli, R. (Ralph)
  Java, Java, Java : object oriented problem solving / R. Morelli and R. Walde. – 3rd ed.
    p. cm.
  ISBN 0-13-147434-0
  1. Object-oriented programming (Computer science) 2. Java (Computer program
language I. Walde, R. (Ralph) II. Title.

QA76.64.M64 2006
005.13'3–dc21   2005054959

Vice President and Editorial Director, ECS: *Marcia J. Horton*
Executive Editor: *Tracy Dunkelburger*
Editorial Assistant: *Christianna Lee*
Executive Managing Editor: *Vince O'Brien*
Managing Editor: *Camille Trentacoste*
Production Editor: *Rose Kernan*
Director for Creative Services: *Paul Belfanti*
Creative Director: *Juan Lopez*
Cover Designer: *Bruce Kenselaar*
Managing Editor, AV Management and Production: *Patricia Burns*
Art Editor: *Xiaohong Zhu*
Manufacturing Manager: *Alexis Heydt-Long*
Manufacturing Buyer: *Lisa McDowell*
Marketing Manager: *Robin O'Brien*
Marketing Assistant: *Barrie Reinhold*

PEARSON
Prentice
Hall

© 2006 Pearson Education, Inc.
Pearson Prentice Hall
Pearson Education, Inc.
Upper Saddle River, New Jersey 07458

Pearson Prentice Hall™ is a trademark of Pearson Education, Inc.

Java™ is a trademark of Sun Microsystems, Inc. 4150 Network Circle, Santa Clara, CA 95054.

Printed in the United States of America

10 9 8 7 6 5 4 3 2 1

ISBN 0-13-147434-0

Pearson Education Ltd., *London*
Pearson Education Australia Pty. Ltd., *Sydney*
Pearson Education Singapore, Pte. Ltd.
Pearson Education North Asia Ltd., *Hong Kong*
Pearson Education Canada Inc., *Toronto*
Pearson Educatíon de Mexico, S.A. de C.V.
Pearson Education—Japan, *Tokyo*
Pearson Education Malaysia, Pte. Ltd.
Pearson Education, *Upper Saddle River, New Jersey*

To the Memory of Our Colleague
Bronzell Dinkins

Contents

3   Methods: Communicating with Objects   103

4   Input/Output: Designing the User Interface   149

5   Java Data and Operators   195

6   Control Structures   249

7   Strings and String Processing   305

8   Inheritance and Polymorphism 349

9   Arrays and Array Processing 405

10   Exceptions: When Things Go Wrong   471

11   Files and Streams: Input/Output Techniques   511

15   Sockets and Networking   707

16   Data Structures: Lists, Stacks, and Queues   767

Preface

We have designed this third edition of *Java, Java, Java* to be suitable for a typical Introduction to Computer Science (CS1) course or for a slightly more advanced Java as a Second Language course. This edition retains the "objects first" approach to programming and problem solving that was characteristic of the first two editions. Throughout the text we emphasize careful coverage of Java language features, introductory programming concepts, and object-oriented design principles.

The third edition retains many of the features of the first two editions, including:

- Early Introduction of Objects
- Emphasis on Object Oriented Design (OOD)
- Unified Modeling Language (UML) Diagrams
- Self-study Exercises with Answers
- Programming, Debugging, and Design Tips
- *From the Java Library* Sections
- *Object-Oriented Design* Sections
- End-of-Chapter Exercises
- Companion Web Site, with Power Points and other Resources

The *In the Laboratory* sections from the first two editions have been moved onto the book's Companion Web Site. Table 1 shows the Table of Contents for the third edition.

What's New in the Third Edition?

The third edition has the following substantive changes:

- Although the book retains its emphasis on a "running example" that is revisited in several chapters, the CyberPet examples have been replaced with a collection of games and puzzle

Table 1. Table of Contents for the Third Edition.

Chapter	Topic
Chapter 0	Computers, Objects, and Java (revised)
Chapter 1	Java Program Design and Development
Chapter 2	Objects: Defining, Creating, and Using
Chapter 3	Methods: Communicating with Objects (revised)
Chapter 4	Input/Output: Designing the User Interface (new)
Chapter 5	Java Data and Operators
Chapter 6	Control Structures
Chapter 7	Strings and String Processing
Chapter 8	Inheritance and Polymorphism (new)
Chapter 9	Arrays and Array Processing
Chapter 10	Exceptions: When Things Go Wrong
Chapter 11	Files and Streams
Chapter 12	Recursive Problem Solving
Chapter 13	Graphical User Interfaces
Chapter 14	Threads and Concurrent Programming
Chapter 15	Sockets and Networking (expanded)
Chapter 16	Data Structures: Lists, Stacks, and Queues (revised and expanded)

examples. The CyberPet examples from earlier editions will be available on the Companion Web Site.

- Chapters 0 (Computers, Objects, and Java) and 1 (Java Program Design and Development) have been substantially reorganized and rewritten. The new presentation is designed to reduce the pace with which new concepts are introduced. The treatment of object-oriented (OO) and UML concepts has also been simplified, and some of the more challenging OO topics, such as polymorphism, have been moved to a new Chapter 8.
- The new Java 1.5 `Scanner` class is introduced in Chapter 2 and is used to perform simple input operations.
- Chapter 4 (Input/Output: Designing the User Interface) has been completely rewritten. Rather than relying primarily on applet interfaces, as in the second edition, this new chapter provides independent introductions to both a command-line interface and a graphical user interface (GUI). Instructors can choose the type of interface that best suits their teaching style. The command-line interface is based on the `BufferedReader` class and is used throughout the rest of the text. The GUI is designed to work with either graphical applications or applets. Both approaches are carefully presented to highlight the fundamentals of user-interface design. The chapter concludes with an optional section that introduces file I/O using the new `Scanner` class.
- Much of the discussion of inheritance and polymorphism, that was woven through the first five chapters in the second edition, has been integrated into a new Chapter 8.
- An optional *graphics track* is woven throughout the text. Beginning with simple examples in Chapters 1 and 2, this track also includes some of the examples that were previously presented in Chapter 10 of the second edition.
- Chapter 15, on Sockets and Networking, is expanded to cover some of the more advanced Java technologies that have emerged, including servlets and Java Server Pages.
- Chapter 16, on Data Structures, has been refocused on how to use data structures. It makes greater use of Java's Collection Framework, including the `LinkedList` and `Stack` classes and the `List` interface. It has been expanded to cover some advanced data structures, such as sets, maps, and binary search trees.
- **CodeKey is integrated with chapter exercises!** CodeKey is an online, interactive programming tutorial designed to reinforce key Java programming concepts and techniques. The CodeKey icon in the margin next to the exercise number identifies end-of-chapter exercises that include a CodeKey component. Using CodeKey, students can receive automated feedback on the code they write and instructors can easily manage code assignments and student progress. The online CodeKey exercises give students the ability to test their programs before handing in their class assignments. Instructors can easily track individual and class coding attempts and performance online at any time. CodeKey provides hints on how to improve code and how to debug it, if necessary. Students will be alerted to errors and will receive programming tips on how to fix them. CodeKey is just another way Morelli and Walde make programming exercises easy, fun, and manageable!

Why Start with Objects?

The third edition still takes an *objects-early* approach to teaching Java, with the assumption that teaching beginners the "big picture" early gives them more time to master the principles of object-oriented programming. This approach seems to have gained in popularity as more and more instructors have begun to appreciate the advantages of the object-oriented perspective.

Object Orientation (OO) is a fundamental problem-solving and design concept, not just another language detail that should be relegated to the middle or the end of the book (or course). If OO concepts are introduced late, it is much too easy to skip over them when push comes to shove in the course.

The first time we taught Java in our CS1 course, we followed the same approach we had been taking in teaching C and C++. We started with the basic language features and structured programming concepts and then, somewhere around midterm, introduce object orientation. This approach was familiar, because it was taken in most of the textbooks then available in both Java and C++.

One problem with this approach was that many students failed to get the big picture. They could understand loops, if-else constructs, and arithmetic expressions, but they had difficulty decomposing a programming problem into a well-organized Java program. Also, it seemed that this procedural approach failed to take advantage of the strengths of Java's object orientation. Why teach an object-oriented language if you're going to treat it like C or Pascal?

I was reminded of a similar situation that existed when Pascal was the predominant CS1 language. Back then the main hurdle for beginners was *procedural abstraction*—learning the basic mechanisms of procedure call and parameter passing and learning how to **design** programs as a collection of procedures. *Oh! Pascal!*, our favorite introductory text, was typical of a "procedures early" approach. It covered procedures and parameters in Chapter 2, right after covering the assignment and I/O constructs in Chapter 1. It then covered program design and organization in Chapter 3. It didn't get into loops, if-else, and other structured programming concepts until Chapter 4 and beyond.

Today, the main hurdle for beginners is the concept of *object abstraction*. Beginning programmers must be able to see a program as a collection of interacting objects and must learn how to decompose programming problems into well-designed objects. Object orientation subsumes both procedural abstraction and structured programming concepts from the Pascal days. Teaching objects-early takes a top-down approach to these three important concepts. The sooner you begin to introduce objects and classes, the better the chances that students will master the important principles of object orientation.

Java is a good language for introducing object orientation. Its object model is better organized than C++. In C++ it is easy to "work around" or completely ignore OO features and treat the language like C. In Java there are good opportunities for motivating the discussion of object orientation. For example, it's almost impossible to discuss GUI-based Java applications without discussing inheritance and polymorphism. Thus, rather than using contrived examples of OO concepts, instructors can use some of Java's basic features—the class library, Swing and GUI components—to motivate these discussions in a natural way.

Organization of the Text

The book is still organized into three main parts. Part I (Chapters 0–4 introduces the basic concepts of object orientation and the basic features of the Java language. Part II (Chapters 5–9) focuses on the remaining language elements, including data types, control structures, string and array processing, and inheritance and polymorphism. Part III (Chapters 10–16) covers advanced topics, including exceptions, file I/O, recursion, GUIs, threads and concurrent programming, sockets and networking, data structures, servlets, and Java Server Pages.

The first two parts make up the topics that are typically covered in an introductory CS1 course. The chapters in Part III are self-contained and can be selectively added to the end of a CS1 course if time permits.

Table 2. A One-semester Course.

Weeks	Topics	Chapters
1	Object Orientation, UML	Chapter 0
	Program Design and Development	Chapter 1
2–3	Objects and Class Definitions	Chapter 2
	Methods and Parameters	Chapter 3
	Selection Structure (if-else)	
4	User Interfaces and I/O	Chapter 4
5	Data Types and Operators	Chapter 5
6–7	Control Structures (Loops)	Chapter 6
	Structured Programming	
8	String Processing (loops)	Chapter 7
9	Inheritance and Polymorphism	Chapter 8
10	Array Processing	Chapter 9
11	Recursion	Chapter 12
12	Advanced Topic (Exceptions)	Chapter 10
13	Advanced Topic (GUIs)	Chapter 11
	Advanced Topic (Threads)	Chapter 15

The first part (Chapters 0–4) introduces the basic concepts of object orientation, including objects, classes, methods, parameter passing, information hiding, and a little taste of inheritance, and polymorphism. The primary focus in these chapters is on introducing the basic idea that an object-oriented program is a collection of objects that communicate and cooperate with one another to solve problems. Java language elements are introduced as needed to reinforce this idea. Students are given the basic building blocks for constructing Java programs from scratch.

Although the programs in the first few chapters have limited functionality in terms of control structures and data types, the priority is placed on how objects are constructed and how they interact with one another through method calls and parameter passing.

The second part (Chapters 5–9) focuses on the remaining language elements, including data types and operators (Chapter 5), control structures (Chapter 6), strings (Chapter 7), and arrays (Chapter 9). It also provides thorough coverage of inheritance and polymorphism, the primary mechanisms of object orientation (Chapter 8).

Part three (Chapters 10–16) covers a variety of advanced topics (Table 1). Topics from these chapters can be used selectively depending on instructor and student interest.

Throughout the book, key concepts are introduced through simple, easy-to-grasp examples. Many of the concepts are used to create a set of games, that are used as a running example throughout the text. Our pedagogical approach focuses on design. Rather than starting off with language details, programming examples are carefully developed with an emphasis on the principles of object-oriented design.

Table 2 provides an example syllabus from our one-semester CS1 course. Our semester is 13 weeks (plus one reading week during which classes do not meet). We pick and choose from among the advanced topics during the last two weeks of the course, depending on the interests and skill levels of the students.

RALPH MORELLI
RALPH WALDE

0

Computers, Objects, and Java

OBJECTIVES

After studying this chapter, you will

- Understand basic computer terminology that will be used throughout the book.
- Become familiar with the notion of programming.
- Understand why Java is a good introductory programming language.
- Become familiar with Java objects and classes.
- Know some of the principles of the object-oriented programming approach.

OUTLINE

0.1 Welcome

Welcome to *Java, Java, Java*, a book that introduces you to object-oriented programming using the Java language. When considering the purpose of this text, three important questions might come to mind: Why study programming? Why study Java? What is object-oriented programming? This chapter will address these questions. First, we provide a brief introduction to computers and the Internet and the World Wide Web (WWW). Then, we address why someone would study programming and we examine types of programming languages. We introduce the Java programming language and conclude the chapter by exploring object-oriented programming principles and how Java is an object-oriented programming language.

0.2 What Is a Computer?

A *computer* is a machine that performs calculations and processes information. A computer works under the control of a computer program, a set of instructions that tell a computer what to do. *Hardware* refers to the electronic and mechanical components of a computer. *Software* refers to the programs that control the hardware.

A *general-purpose computer* of the sort that we will be programming can store many different programs in its memory. That is what gives it the ability to perform a wide variety of functions, from word processing to browsing the Internet. This is in contrast to a *special-purpose computer*, such as the one that resides in your microwave oven or the one that controls your digital watch or calculator. These types of computers contain control programs that are fixed and cannot be changed.

A computer's hardware is organized into several main subsystems or components (Fig. 0.1).

- *Output devices* provide a means by which information held in the computer can be displayed in some understandable or usable form. Common output devices include printers, monitors, and audio speakers.
- *Input devices* bring data and information into the computer. Some of the more common input devices are the keyboard, mouse, microphone, and scanner.
- *Primary memory* or *main memory* of a computer is used to store both data and programs. This type of memory, which is often called *RAM*, short for *Random Access Memory*, is built entirely out of electronic components—integrated circuit chips—which makes it extremely

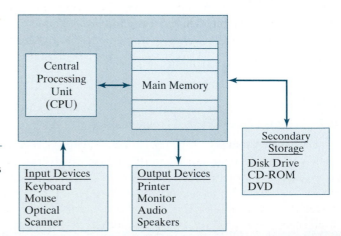

Figure 0.1 A diagram of the main functional components in a computer system. The arrows indicate the flow of information between various components.

fast. A computer's main memory is *volatile*, which means that any information stored in it is lost when the computer's power is turned off. In a sense, main memory acts as the computer's scratch pad, storing both programs and data temporarily while a program is running.

- *Secondary storage* devices are used for long-term or permanent storage of relatively large amounts of information. These devices include hard drives or magnetic disks, compact disks (CDs), digital video disks (DVDs), and magnetic tapes. All of these devices are *non-volatile*, meaning that they retain information when the computer's power is turned off. Compared to a computer's primary memory, these devices are relatively slow.

- The *central processing unit* (*CPU*) is the computer's main engine. The CPU is the computer's *microprocessor*, such as the Intel Pentium processor, which serves as the foundation for most Windows PCs, or the Power-PC processor, which serves as the foundation for Macintosh computers. The CPU is designed to perform the *fetch-execute cycle*, whereby it repeatedly gets the next machine instruction from memory and executes it. Under the direction of computer programs (software), the CPU issues signals that control the other components that make up the computer system. One portion of the CPU, known as the *arithmetic-logic unit* (*ALU*), performs all calculations, such as addition and subtraction, and all logical comparisons, such as when one piece of data is compared to another to determine if they are equal.

Fetch-execute cycle

There are two main types of software:

- *Application software* refers to programs designed to provide a particular task or service, such as word processors, computer games, spreadsheet programs, and Web browsers.
- *System software* includes programs that perform the basic operations that make a computer usable. For example, an important piece of system software is the *operating system*, which contains programs that manage the data stored on the computer's disks.

An operating system assists application software in performing tasks that are considered *primitive* or low-level, such as managing the computer's memory and its input and output devices.

Another important thing that the operating system does is to serve as an interface between the user and the hardware. The operating system determines how the user will interact with the system, or conversely, how the system will look and feel to the user. For example, in *command-line* systems, such as Unix and DOS (short for Disk Operating System), a program is run by typing its name on the command line. By contrast, in graphically based systems, such as Windows and Macintosh, a program is run by clicking on its icon with the mouse. Thus, this "point-and-click" interface has a totally different "look and feel" but does the same thing.

0.3 Networks, the Internet, and the World Wide Web

Most personal computers contain software that enables them to be connected to various-sized *networks* of computers. Networks allow many individual users to share costly computer resources, such as a high-speed printer or a large disk drive or *application server* that is used to store and distribute both data and programs to the computers on the network. Networks can range in size from *local area networks* (*LANs*), which connect computers and peripherals over a relatively small area, such as within a lab or a building, through *wide area networks* (*WANs*), which can span large geographic areas, such as cities and nations.

Processors Then and Now

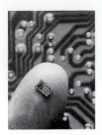

Photograph courtesy of Roger Duboisson, The Stock Market

To give you some idea of how rapidly computer hardware technology has advanced, let's compare the first digital processor with one of today's models.

The *ENIAC* (which stood for Electronic Numerical Integrator and Calculator) was developed in 1946 at the University of Pennsylvania primarily for calculating ballistic trajectories for the U.S. Army. ENIAC occupied more than 640 square feet of floor space and weighed nearly 30 tons. Instead of the *integrated circuits* or chip technology used in today's computers, ENIAC's digital technology was based on over 17,000 vacuum tubes. ENIAC, which could perform around 300 multiplications per second, ran more than 500 times faster than other computing machines of that day and age. To program the ENIAC, you would have to manipulate hundreds of cables and switches. It took two or three days for a team of several programmers, most of whom were young women, to set up a single program that would then run for a few seconds.

One of today's most advanced and powerful processors for desktop computers is Intel's Pentium IV processor. This chip contains 42 million transistors and runs at speeds over 3 GHz (3 gigahertz or 3 billion cycles per second). The Pentium processor is small enough to fit in a space the size of your pinky finger's fingernail. Despite its size, it executes millions of instructions per second, thereby enabling it to support a huge range of multimedia applications, including three-dimensional graphics, streaming audio and video, and speech-recognition applications. To write programs for the Pentium, you can choose from a wide range of high-level programming languages, including the Java language.

Client/server computing

Application servers are just one example of *client/server computing*, a computing approach made possible by networks. According to this approach, certain computers on the network are set up as *servers*, which provide certain well-defined services to *client* computers. For example, one computer in a network may be set up as the *e-mail server*, with the responsibility of sending, receiving, and storing mail for all users on the network. To access their e-mail on the e-mail server, individual users employ *client application software* that resides on their desktop computers, such as Outlook Express or Eudora or Pine. Similarly, another server may be set up as a *Web server*, with the responsibility of storing and serving up Web pages for all the users on the network. Users can run Web browsers, another type of client software, to access Web pages on the server. Java is particularly well suited for these types of *networked* or *distributed* applications, where part of the application software resides on a server and part resides on the client computer.

The *Internet* (with a capital *I*) is a network of networks whose geographical area covers the entire globe. The *World Wide Web (WWW)* is another example of distributed, client/server computing. The WWW is not a separate physical network. Rather it is a subset of the Internet that uses the *HyperText Transfer Protocol (HTTP)*. A *protocol* is a set of rules and conventions that govern how communication takes place between two computers. HTTP is a multimedia protocol, which means that it supports the transmission of text, graphics, sound, and other forms of information. Certain computers within a network run special software that enables them to play the role of HTTP (or Web) servers. They store Web documents and are capable of handling requests for documents from client browser applications. The servers and clients can be located anywhere on the Internet.

The documents stored on Web servers are encoded in a special text-based language known as *HyperText Markup Language*, or *HTML*. Web browsers, such as Netscape's Navigator and Microsoft's Internet Explorer, are designed to interpret documents coded in this language. The language itself is very simple. Its basic elements are known as *tags*, which consist of certain keywords or other text contained within angle brackets, < and >. For example, if you wanted to italicize text on a Web page, you would enclose it between the *<I>* and *</I>* tags. Thus, the following HTML code

```
<I>Italic font</I> can be used for <I>emphasis</I>.
```

would be displayed by the Web browser as

Italic font can be used for *emphasis*.

When you use a Web browser to surf the Internet, you repeatedly instruct your browser to go to a certain location and retrieve a page that is encoded in HTML. For example, if you typed the following *URL* (*Uniform Resource Locator*)

```
http://www.prenhall.com/morelli/index.html
```

into your browser, the browser would send a message to the Web server www located in the `prenhall.com` domain—the `prenhall` portion of this address specifies Prentice Hall, and the `com` portion specifies the commercial domain of the Internet—requesting that the document named `index.html` in the `morelli` directory be retrieved and sent back to your computer (Fig. 0.2). The beauty of the Web is that it is possible to embed text, sound, video, and graphics within an HTML document, making it possible to download a wide range of multimedia resources through this (relatively) simple mechanism.

The Web has begun to change business, entertainment, commerce, and education. The fact that it is possible to download computer games and other application software from the Web is changing the way software and other digital products are purchased and distributed. Similarly, as noted earlier, many businesses have begun to organize their information systems into *intranets*—private networks that implement the HTTP protocol. Currently, one of the biggest

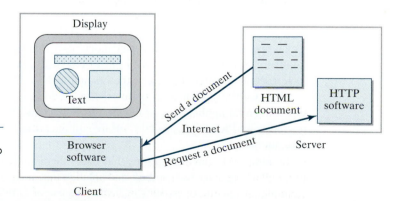

Figure 0.2 WWW: The client's browser requests a page from a Web server. When the HTML document is returned, it is interpreted and displayed by the browser.

areas of development on the Web is commerce. As consumers become more comfortable with the idea that credit-card information can be securely transmitted over the Web (as it can over a telephone), the Web will explode as a marketing medium as powerful, perhaps, as television is today. Because Java has been designed to support secure, distributed, networked applications, it is ideally suited to be used as the language for these types of applications.

0.4 Why Study Programming?

A **computer program** is a set of instructions that directs the computer's behavior. *Computer programming* is the art and science of designing and writing programs. Years ago it was widely believed that entrance into the computer age would require practically everyone to learn how to program. But this did not prove to be true. Today's computers come with so much easy-to-use software that knowing how to use a computer no longer requires programming skills.

Another reason to study programming might be to enter into a career as a computer scientist. However, although programming is one of its primary tools, computer science is a broad and varied discipline, which ranges from engineering subjects, such as processor design, to mathematical subjects, such as performance analysis. There are many computer scientists who do little or no programming as part of their everyday work. If you plan to major or minor in computer science, you will certainly learn to program, but good careers in the computing field are available to programmers and nonprogrammers alike.

One of the best reasons to study programming is that it is a creative and enjoyable problem-solving activity. This book will teach you how to develop well-designed solutions to a range of interesting problems. One of the best things about programming is that you can actually see and experience your solutions as running programs. As many students have indicated, there's really nothing like the kick you get from seeing your program solving a problem you've been struggling with. Designing and building well-written programs provides a powerful sense of accomplishment and satisfaction. What's more, Java is a language that makes programming even more fun, because once they're finished, many Java programs can be posted on the World Wide Web (WWW) for all the world to see!

0.5 Programming Languages

Most computer programs today are written in a **high-level language**, such as Java, C, C++, or FORTRAN. A programming language is considered high level if its statements resemble English-language statements. For example, all of the languages just mentioned have some form of an "if" statement, which says, "if a certain condition holds, then take a certain action."

Computer scientists have invented hundreds of high-level programming languages, although relatively few of these have been put to practical use. Some of the widely used languages have special features that make them suitable for one type of programming application or another. COBOL (COmmon Business-Oriented Language), for example, is still widely used in commercial applications. FORTRAN (FORmula TRANslator) is still preferred by some engineers and scientists. C and C++ are still the primary languages used by operating system programmers.

In addition to having features that make them suitable for certain types of applications, high-level languages use symbols and notation that make them easily readable by humans. For example, arithmetic operations in Java make use of familiar operators such as "+" and "−"

and "/," so that arithmetic expressions look more or less the way they do in algebra. Thus, to take the average of two numbers, you might use the expression

```
(a + b) / 2
```

The problem is that computers cannot directly understand such expressions. In order for a computer to run a program, the program must first be translated into the computer's *machine language*, which is the language understood by its CPU or microprocessor. Each type of microprocessor has its own specific machine language. That's why when you buy software it runs either on a Macintosh, which uses the Power-PC chip, or on a Windows machine, which uses the Pentium chip, but not on both. When a program can run on just one type of chip, it is known as *platform dependent*.

Platform dependent

In general, machine languages are based on the *binary code*, a two-value system that is well suited for electronic devices. In a binary representation scheme, everything is represented as a sequence of 1's and 0's, which corresponds closely to the computer's electronic "on" and "off" states. For example, in binary code, the number 13 would be represented as 1101. Similarly, a particular address in the computer's memory might be represented as 01100011, and an instruction in the computer's instruction set might be represented as 001100.

The instructions that make up a computer's machine language are very simple and basic. For example, a typical machine language might include instructions for ADD, SUBTRACT, DIVIDE, and MULTIPLY, but it wouldn't contain an instruction for AVERAGE. In most cases, a single instruction, called an *opcode*, carries out a single machine operation on one or more pieces of data, called its *operands*. Therefore, the process of averaging two numbers would have to be broken down into two or more steps. A machine language instruction itself might have something similar to the following format, in which an opcode is followed by several operands, which refer to the locations in the computer's primary memory where the data are stored. The following instruction says ADD the number in LOCATION1 to the number in LOCATION2 and store the result in LOCATION3:

Opcode	Operand 1	Operand 2	Operand 3
011110	110110	111100	111101
(ADD)	(LOCATION 1)	(LOCATION 2)	(LOCATION 3)

Given the primitive nature of machine language, an expression like $(a + b)/2$ would have to be translated into a sequence of several machine language instructions that, in binary code, might look as follows:

```
011110110110111100111101
000101000100010001001101
001000010001010101111011
```

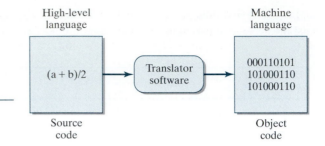

Figure 0.3 Translator software translates high-level *source code* to machine language *object code*.

In the early days of computing, before high-level languages were developed, computers had to be programmed directly in their machine languages, an extremely tedious and error-prone process. Imagine how difficult it would be to detect an error that consisted of putting a 0 in the preceding program where a 1 should occur!

Fortunately, we no longer have to worry about machine languages, because special programs can be used to translate a high-level or **source code** program into machine language code or **object code**, which is the only code that can be *executed* or run by the computer. In general, a program that translates source code to object code is known as a *translator* (Fig. 0.3). Thus, with suitable translation software for Java or C++ we can write programs as if the computer could understand Java or C++ directly.

Source code translators come in two varieties. An **interpreter** translates a single line of source code directly into machine language and executes the code before going on to the next line of source code. A **compiler** translates the entire source code program into *executable* object code, which means that the object code can then be run directly without further translation.

There are advantages and disadvantages to both approaches. Interpreted programs generally run less efficiently than compiled programs, because they must translate and execute each line of the program before proceeding to the next line. If a line of code is repeated, an interpreter would have to translate the line each time it is encountered. By contrast, once compiled, an object program is just executed without any need for further translation. It is also much easier to refine compiled code to make it run more efficiently. But interpreters are generally quicker and easier to develop and provide somewhat better error messages when things go wrong. Some languages that you may have heard of, such as BASIC, LISP, and Perl, are mostly used in interpreted form, although compilers are also available for these languages. Programs written in COBOL, FORTRAN, C, C++, and Pascal are compiled. As we will see in the next section, Java programs use both compilation and interpretation in their translation process.

0.6 Why Java?

Originally named "Oak" after a tree outside the office of its developer, James Goslin, Java is a relatively young programming language. It was initially designed by Sun Microsystems in 1991 as a language for embedding programs into electronic consumer devices, such as microwave ovens and home security systems. However, the tremendous popularity of the Internet and the World Wide Web led Sun to recast Java as a language for embedding programs into Web-based applications. As you will recall, the Internet is a global computer network, and the WWW is the portion of the network that provides multimedia access to a vast range of information. Java has become one of the most important languages for Web and Internet applications.

Java has also generated significant interest in the business community, where it has proved to have tremendous commercial potential. In addition to being a useful tool for helping businesses to promote their products and services over the Internet, Java is also a good language for distributing software and providing services to employees and clients on private corporate networks or intranets.

Because of its original intended role as a language for programming microprocessors embedded in consumer appliances, Java has been designed with a number of interesting features:

- Java is **object oriented**. Object-oriented languages divide programs into separate modules, called objects, that encapsulate the program's data and operations. Thus, *object-oriented programming (OOP)* and *object-oriented design (OOD)* refer to a particular way of organizing programs, one which is rapidly emerging as the preferred approach for building complex software systems. Unlike the C++ language, in which object-oriented features were grafted onto the C language, Java was designed from scratch as an object-oriented language.

  Object-oriented languages

- Java is *robust*, meaning that errors in Java programs don't cause system crashes as often as errors in other programming languages. Certain features of the language enable many potential errors to be detected before a program is run.

- Java is *platform independent*. A *platform*, in this context, is just a particular kind of computer system, such as a Macintosh or Windows system. Java's trademark is "Write once, run anywhere." This means that a Java program can be run without changes on different kinds of computers. This is not true for other high-level programming languages. This *portability*—the ability to run on virtually any platform—is one reason that Java is well suited for WWW applications.

  Platform independence

- Java is a *distributed* language, which means that its programs can be designed to run on computer networks. In addition to the language itself, Java comes with an extensive collection of *code libraries*—software that has been designed to be used directly for specific types of applications—that make it very easy to build software systems for the Internet and the WWW. This is one of the reasons why Java is so well suited for supporting applications on corporate networks.

- Java is a *secure* language. Designed to be used on networks, Java contains features that protect against *untrusted code*—code that might introduce a virus or corrupt your system in some way. For example, once they are downloaded into your browser, Web-based Java programs are prevented from reading and writing information from and to your desktop computer.

Despite this list of attractive features, perhaps the best reason for choosing Java as an introductory programming language is its potential for bringing fun and excitement into learning how to program. There are few other languages in which a beginning programmer can write a computer game or a graphically based application that can be distributed on a Web page to just about any computer in the world. The simplicity of Java's design and its easily accessible libraries bring such accomplishments within reach of the most novice programmers.

For example, we will work on projects throughout the text that involve games and puzzles. We start out in Chapter 2 by designing very simple games that involve storing and retrieving data. As we learn more sophisticated programming techniques, we gradually build more complexity into the games and puzzles. For example, we learn how to create interactive, two-person games in Chapter 4. In Chapter 8, we develop some games and puzzles that are played on virtual gameboards. Finally, in Chapter 14 we learn how to introduce games with multiple players on different computers. To get a look at where we are headed, you might want to visit the authors' companion Web site to try out some examples:

```
http://starbase.trincoll.edu/~jjjava/games/
```

0.7   What Is Object-Oriented Programming?

Java is an object-oriented (OO) language, and this book takes an object-oriented approach to programming. So before beginning our discussion of Java, it is important that we introduce some of the underlying concepts involved in object-oriented programming. We need to talk about what an object is, how objects are grouped into classes, how classes are related to each other, and how objects use messages to interact with and communicate with each other.

0.7.1   Basic Object-Oriented Programming Metaphor: Interacting Objects

A Java program, and any object-oriented program, is a collection of interacting objects that models a collection of real-world objects. Think of the model that a kitchen designer might use to lay out your new kitchen (Fig. 0.4). It will contain objects that represent the various kitchen appliances and cabinets. Each object in the model is a simplified version of the corresponding real object. For example, a rectangle might be used to represent the refrigerator.

A kitchen model is mostly *static*. It doesn't change. Once put into place, its various objects just stand there in a certain relation to each other. By contrast, a computer program is *dynamic*. It changes. It does things and performs certain actions. The objects in a computer program communicate with each other, and they change over time. In this respect, the objects that make up our computer programs are very *anthropomorphic*, a big word that means "like people." If we are eating together and I want you to pass me the salt, I say, "Please pass me the salt," and you invariably comply. Similarly, when you (Student X) put your ATM card into an ATM machine, the ATM object asks the bank's database object, "Give me Student X's bank account object," and the database invariably complies. If you tell the ATM you want to withdraw $100, it tells your bank account object to deduct $100 from your current balance. And so it goes. Both you and your bank account are changed objects as a result of the transaction.

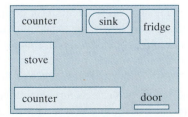

Figure 0.4   A model of a kitchen.

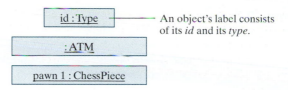

Figure 0.5   In UML, objects are represented by rectangles that are labeled with a two-part label of the form *id:Type*. The object's label is always underlined.

0.7.2   What Is an Object?

So what is an object? Just as in the real world, an **object** is any thing whatsoever. An object can be a physical thing, such as a `Car`, or a mental thing, such as an `Idea`. It can be a natural thing, such as an `Animal`, or an artificial, human-made thing, such as an ATM. A program that manages an ATM would involve `BankAccounts` and `Customer` objects. A chess program would involve a `Board` object and `ChessPiece` objects.

Throughout this text, we will use the notation shown in Figure 0.5 to depict objects and to illustrate object-oriented concepts. The notation is known as the **Unified Modeling Language**, or **UML** for short, and it is a standard in the object-oriented programming community. As the diagram shows, an object is represented by a rectangle whose label consists of the object's (optional) id and its type. An object's *id* is the name by which it is referred to in the computer program. In this case we show an ATM object whose id is not given and a `ChessPiece` object named `pawn1`. An object's label is always underlined.

0.7.3   Attributes and Values

Just as with real objects, the objects in our programs have certain characteristic **attributes**. For example, an ATM object would have a current amount of `cash` that it could dispense. A `ChessPiece` object might have a pair of `row` and `column` attributes that specify its position on the chessboard. Note that an object's attributes are themselves objects. The ATM's `cash` attribute and the chess piece's `row` and `column` attributes are `Numbers`.

Figure 0.6 shows two ATM objects and their respective attributes. As you can see, an object's attributes are listed in a second partition of the UML diagram. Note that each attribute has a value. So the `lobby:ATM` has a $8650.00 in `cash`, while the `drivethru:ATM` has only $150.00 in `cash`.

We sometimes refer to the collection of an object's attributes and values as its *state*. For example, the current state of the `lobby:ATM` is $8650.00 in cash. Of course, this is a gross simplification of an ATM's state, which would also include many other attributes. But it illustrates the point for you.

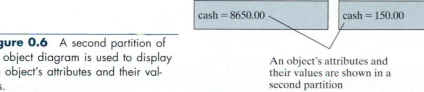

Figure 0.6   A second partition of an object diagram is used to display the object's attributes and their values.

An object's attributes and their values are shown in a second partition

Figure 0.7 Messages in UML are represented by labeled arrows. In this example,
we are telling a pawn to move from its current
position to row 3 column 4.

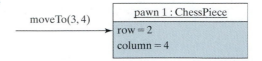

0.7.4   Actions and Messages

In addition to their attributes, objects also have characteristic **actions** or behaviors. As we have
already said, objects in programs are dynamic. They do things or have things done to them.
In fact, programming in Java is largely a matter of getting objects to perform certain actions
for us. For example, in a chess program the `ChessPiece`s have the ability to `moveTo()` a
new position on the chessboard. Similarly, when a customer pushes the "Current Balance"
button on an ATM machine, this is telling the ATM to `report()` the customer's current bank
balance. (Note how we use parentheses to distinguish actions from objects and attributes.)

The actions that are associated with an object can be used to send messages to the objects and
to retrieve information from objects. A **message** is the passing of information or data from one
object to another. Figure 0.7 illustrates how this works. In UML, messages are represented by
arrows. In this example, we are telling `pawn1:ChessPiece` to `moveTo(3,4)`. The numbers
3 and 4 in this case are arguments that tell the pawn what square to move to. (A chess board has
eight rows and eight columns, and each square is identified by its row and column coordinates.)
In general, an **argument** is a data value that specializes the content of a message in some way.
In this example we are telling the pawn to move forward by one row. If we wanted the pawn
to move forward by two rows, we would send the message `moveTo(4,4)`.

The diagram in Figure 0.8 depicts a sequence of messages representing an idealized ATM
transaction. First, an ATM customer asks the ATM machine to report his current balance. The
ATM machine in turn asks the customer's bank account to report the customer's balance. The
ATM receives the value $528.52 from the bank account and passes it along to the customer.
In this case, the message does not involve an argument. But it does involve a result. A **result**
is information or data that is returned to the object that sent the message.

Obviously, in order to respond to a message, an object has to know how to perform the
action that is requested. The pawn has to know how to move to a designated square. The ATM
has to know how to find out the customer's current balance. Indeed, an object can only respond
to messages that are associated with its characteristic actions and behaviors. You can't tell an
ATM to move forward two squares. And you can't ask a chess piece to tell you your current
bank balance.

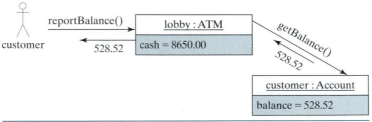

Figure 0.8 This UML diagram illustrates an ATM transaction in which
a customer asks the ATM machine for his current balance. The ATM
gets this information from an object representing the customer's bank
account and passes it to the customer.

Responding to a message or performing an action sometimes causes a change in an object's state. For example, after performing moveTo(3,4), the pawn will be on a different square. Its position will have changed. On the other hand, some messages (or actions) leave the object's state unchanged. Reporting the customer's bank account balance doesn't change the balance.

0.7.5   What Is a Class?

A **class** is a template for an object. A class encapsulates the attributes and actions that characterize a certain type of object. In an object-oriented program, classes serve as blueprints or templates for the objects that the program uses. We say that an object is an **instance** of a class. A good analogy here is to think of a class as a cookie cutter and its objects, or instances, as individual cookies. Just as we use the cookie cutter to stamp out cookies of a certain type, in an object-oriented program, we use a definition of a class to create objects of a certain type.

Writing an object-oriented program is largely a matter of designing classes and writing definitions for them in Java. Designing a class is a matter of specifying all of the attributes and behaviors that are characteristic of that type of object.

For example, suppose we are writing a drawing program. One type of object we would need for our program is a rectangle. A Rectangle object has two fundamental attributes, a length and a width. Given these attributes, we can define characteristic rectangle actions, such as the ability to calculate its area and the ability to draw itself. Identifying an object's attributes and actions is the kind of design activity that goes into developing an object-oriented program.

Figure 0.9 shows a UML diagram of our Rectangle class. Like the symbol for an object, a UML class symbol has up to three partitions. Unlike the UML object symbol, the label for a UML class only gives the class's name and is not underlined. The second partition lists the class's attributes, and the third partition lists the class's actions. Our rectangle has four attributes. The first two, x and y, determine a rectangle's position on a two-dimensional graph. The second two, length and width, determine a rectangle's dimensions. Note that the attributes have no values. This is because the class represents a general *type* of rectangle. It specifies what all rectangles have in common, without representing any particular rectangle. Like a cookie cutter for a cookie, a class gives the general shape of an object. The content is not included.

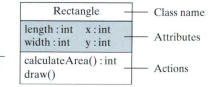

Figure 0.9   A UML diagram of the Rectangle class.

0.7.6   Variables and Methods

Up to this point we have been using the terms *attribute* and *action* to describe an object's features. We will continue to use this terminology when talking in general about objects or when talking about an object or class represented by a UML diagram.

However, when talking about a programming language, the more common way to describe an object's features is to talk about its variables and methods. A **variable**, which corresponds to an attribute, is a named memory location that can store a certain type of value. You can think of a variable as a special container that can only hold objects of a certain type. For example, as Figure 0.9 shows, `Rectangle`'s `length` and `width` are variables that can store a certain type of numeric value known as an `int`. An `int` value is a whole number, such as 76 or −5.

A **method**, which corresponds to an action or a behavior, is a named chunk of code that can be called upon, or *invoked*, to perform a certain predefined set of actions. For example, in our `Rectangle` object, the `calculateArea()` method can be called upon to calculate the rectangle's area. It would do this, of course, by multiplying the rectangle's length by its width. Similarly, the `draw()` method can be invoked to draw a picture of the rectangle. It would take the actions necessary to draw a rectangle on the console.

0.7.7   Instance versus Class Variables and Methods

Variables and methods can be associated either with objects or their classes. An **instance variable** (or **instance method**) is a variable (or method) that belongs to an object. By contrast, a **class variable** (or **class method**) is a variable (or method) that is associated with the class itself. An example will help make this distinction clear.

An instance variable will have different values for different instances. For example, individual `Rectangle`s will have different values for their `length`, `width`, `x`, and `y` variables. So these are examples of instance variables. The `calculateArea()` method is an example of an instance method because it uses the instance's current length and width values in its calculation. Similarly, the `draw()` method is an instance method because it uses the object's length and width to draw the object's shape.

An example of a class variable would be a variable in the `Rectangle` class that is used to keep track of how many individual `Rectangle`s have been created. (Our drawing program might need this information to help manage its memory resources.) Suppose we name this variable `nRectangles`, and suppose we add 1 to it each time a new `Rectangle` instance is created.

An example of a method that is associated with a class is a special method known as a **constructor**. This is a method used to create an object. It is used to create an instance of a class. Calling a constructor to create an object is like pressing the cookie cutter into the cookie dough: the result is an individual cookie (object).

Figure 0.10 illustrates these concepts. Note that class variables are underlined in the UML diagram. We have modified the `Rectangle` class to include its constructor method, which is named `Rectangle()`. It takes four arguments, representing the values that we want to give as the rectangle's *x*, *y*, length, and width respectively. The `Rectangle` class's `nRectangles` variable has a value of 2, representing that two `Rectangle` instances have been created. These are shown as members of the `Rectangle` class.

Rectangle
nRectangles = 2
length : int   x : int   width : int   y : int
Rectangle(x : int, y : int, l : int, w : int)   calculateArea() : int   draw()

Figure 0.10 The `Rectangle` class and two of its instances. The class variable, nRectangles, is underlined to distinguish it from `length` and `width`, the instance variables.

rect1 : Rectangle
length = 25   x = 100   width = 10   y = 50

rect2 : Rectangle
length = 30   x = 125   width = 20   y = 75

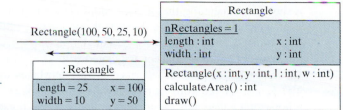

Figure 0.11 Constructing a Rectangle instance.

It won't be obvious to you at this point, but nRectangles is a value that has to be associated with the Rectangle class, not with its instances. To see this, let's imagine what happens when a new Rectangle instance is created. Figure 0.11 illustrates the process. When the Rectangle() constructor is invoked, its arguments (100, 50, 25, 10) are used by the Rectangle class to create a Rectangle object located at *x=100*, *y=50* and with a length of 25 and width of 10. The constructor method also increases the value of nRectangles by 1 as a way of keeping count of how many objects it has created.

0.7.8 Class Hierarchy and Inheritance

How are classes related to each other? In Java, and in any other object-oriented language, classes are organized in a class hierarchy. A **class hierarchy** is like an upside-down tree. At the very top of the hierarchy is the most general class. In Java, the most general class is the Object class. The classes below Object in the hierarchy are known as its **subclasses**. Since all of the objects we use in our programs belong to some class or other, this is like saying that all objects are Objects.

Figure 0.12 illustrates the concept of a class hierarchy using the classes that we have described in this section. As you can see, the Object class occurs at the top of the hierarchy. It is the most general class. It has features that are common to all Java objects. As you move down the hierarchy, the classes become more and more specialized. A Rectangle is an Object, but it contains attributes (length and width) that are common to all rectangles but not to other objects in the hierarchy. For example, an ATM object does not necessarily have a length and a width. Note that we have added a Square class to the hierarchy. A Square is a special type of Rectangle, one whose length equals its width.

To introduce some important terminology associated with this kind of hierarchy, we say that the Rectangle class is a subclass of the Object class. The Square class is a subclass of both Rectangle and Object. Classes that occur above a given class in the hierarchy are said to be its **superclasses**. Thus the Rectangle class is a superclass of the Square class. The Object class is also a superclass of Square. In general, we say that a subclass *extends*

Superclass and subclass

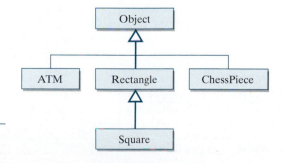

Figure 0.12 A hierarchy of Java classes.

a superclass, meaning that it adds additional elements (attributes and/or methods) to those contained in its superclasses. We saw this in the case of the `Square` class. It adds the feature that its length and width are always equal.

Class inheritance

Another important concept associated with a class hierarchy is the notion of **class inheritance**, whereby a subclass inherits elements (attributes and/or methods) from its superclasses. To take an example from the natural world, think of the sort of inheritance that occurs between a horse and a mammal. A horse is a mammal. So horses inherit the characteristic of being warm-blooded by virtue of also being mammals. (This is different from the kind of individual inheritance whereby you inherit your mother's blue eyes and your father's black hair.)

To illustrate how inheritance works, let's go back to our chess program. There are several different types of `ChessPiece`s. There are `Pawn`s, and `Knight`s, and `Queen`s and `King`s. Figure 0.13 illustrates the chess piece hierarchy. A pair of attributes that all chess pieces have in common is their `row` and `column` position on the chessboard. Because all chess pieces have these attributes in common, they are located at the top of the `ChessPiece` hierarchy and inherited by all `ChessPiece` subclasses. Of course, the `row` and `column` attributes are given different values in each `ChessPiece` object.

One of the actions that all chess pieces have in common is that they can `moveTo()` a given square on the chessboard. But different types of chess pieces have different ways of moving. For example, a `Bishop` can only move along the diagonals on the chessboard, whereas a `Rook` can only move along a row or column on the chessboard. So, clearly, we can't describe a `moveTo()` method that will work for all `ChessPiece`s. This is why we put the `moveTo()` method in all of the `ChessPiece` subclasses. The `ChessPiece` class also has a `moveTo()` method, but note that its name is italicized. This indicates that it cannot be completely defined at that level.

Finally, note that in chess, the king has certain special attributes and actions. Thus only the king can be put *in check*. This means that the king is under attack and in danger of being captured, thereby ending the game. Similarly, only the king has the ability to castle. This is

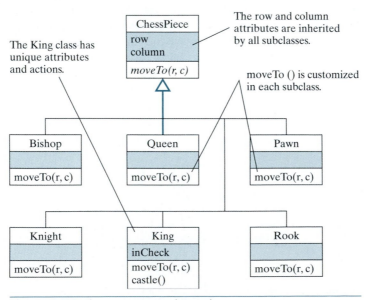

Figure 0.13 The `ChessPiece` hierarchy.

a special move that a king can make together with one of its rooks under certain conditions. Thus, the reason we show the `inCheck` attribute and `castle()` action in the `King` class is because these are characteristics that are particular to `Kings`.

In this way, a class hierarchy represents a *specialization* of classes as you move from top to bottom. The most general class, `ChessPiece`, is at the top of the hierarchy. Its attributes and methods are passed on to (inherited by) its subclasses. However, in addition to the attributes and methods they inherit from their superclasses, the subclasses define their own special attributes and methods. Each of the subclasses, `Pawn`, `Bishop`, and so on, represents some kind of specialization of the superclass. In this example, each of the subclasses has its own distinctive way of moving. And the `King` subclass has unique attributes and actions, `inCheck` and `castle()`.

0.7.9 Principles of Object-Oriented Design

As we have discussed, an object-oriented program is composed of many objects communicating with each other. The process of designing an object-oriented program to solve some problem or other involves several important principles:

- **Divide-and-Conquer Principle.** Generally, the first step in designing a program is to divide the overall problem into a number of objects that will interact with each other to solve the problem. Thus, an object-oriented program employs a *division of labor* much like the one we apply in organizing many of our real-world tasks. This *divide-and-conquer* approach is an important problem-solving strategy.

- **Encapsulation Principle.** Once the objects are identified, the next step involves deciding, for each object, what attributes it has and what actions it will take. The goal here is to encapsulate within each object the expertise needed to carry out its role in the program. Each object is a self-contained module with a clear responsibility and the tools (attributes and actions) necessary to carry out its role. Just as a dentist encapsulates the expertise needed to diagnose and treat a toothache, a well-designed object contains the information and methods needed to perform its role.

- **Interface Principle.** In order for objects to work cooperatively and efficiently, we have to clarify exactly how they are to interact, or *interface*, with one another. An object's interface should be designed to limit the way the object can be used by other objects. Think of how the different interfaces presented by a digital watch and an analog watch determine how the watches are used. In a digital watch, time is displayed in discrete units, and buttons are used to set the time in hours, minutes, and seconds. In an analog watch, the time is displayed by hands on a clock face, and time is set, less precisely, by turning a small wheel.

- **Information-Hiding Principle.** In order to enable objects to work together cooperatively, certain details of their individual design and performance should be hidden from other objects. To use the watch analogy again, in order to use a watch we needn't know how its time-keeping mechanism works. That level of detail is hidden from us. Hiding such implementation details protects the watch's mechanism but does not limit its usefulness.

- **Generality Principle.** To make objects as generally useful as possible, we design them not for a particular task but rather for a particular *kind* of task. This principle underlies the use of software libraries. As we will see, Java comes with an extensive library of classes that specialize in performing certain kinds of input and output operations. For example, rather than having to write our own method to print a message on the console, we can use a library object to handle our printing tasks.

- **Extensibility Principle.** One of the strengths of the object-oriented approach is the ability to extend an object's behavior to handle new tasks. This also has its analog in the everyday world. If a company needs sales agents to specialize in hardware orders, it would be more economical to extend the skills of its current sales agents instead of training a novice from scratch. In the same way, in the object-oriented approach, an object whose role is to input data might be specialized to input numeric data.

- **Abstraction Principle.** Abstraction is the ability to focus on the important features of an object when trying to work with large amounts of information. For example, if we are trying to design a floor plan for a kitchen, we can focus on the shapes and relative sizes of the appliances and ignore attributes such as color, style, and manufacturer. The objects we design in our Java programs will be abstractions in this sense because they ignore many of the attributes that characterize the real objects and focus only on those attributes that are essential for solving a particular problem.

These, then, are the principles that will guide our discussion as we learn how to design and write object-oriented Java programs.

CHAPTER SUMMARY

Technical Terms

action	instance variable
argument	interpreter
attribute	message
class	method
class hierarchy	object
class inheritance	object code
class method	object oriented
class variable	result
compiler	source code
computer program	subclass
constructor	superclass
high-level language	Unified Modeling Language (UML)
instance	variable
instance method	

Summary of Important Points

- A computer system generally consists of input/output devices, primary and secondary memory, and a central processing unit. A computer can only run programs in its own *machine language*, which is based on the *binary code*. Special programs known as *compilers* and *interpreters* translate *source code* programs written in a *high-level language*, such as Java, into machine language *object code* programs.

- *Application software* refers to programs designed to provide a particular task or service; *systems software* assists the user in using application software.

- The *client/server* model is a form of *distributed computing* in which part of the software for a task is stored on a *server* and part on *client* computers.

- HyperText Markup Language (HTML) is the language used to encode WWW documents.

- A Java program is a set of interacting objects. This is the basic metaphor of *object-oriented programming*.

- An *object* in a Java program encapsulates the program's *attributes* (or *variables*) and *actions* (or *methods*). A variable is a named memory location where data of an appropriate type can be stored. A method is a named section of code that can be called (or invoked) when needed.

- An object's methods are used to pass messages to it.

- A *class* is an abstract template that defines the characteristics and behaviors of all objects of a certain type.

- An object is an *instance* of a class. An object has *instance methods* and *instance variables*. A *class method* (or *class variable*) is a method (or variable) that is associated with the class itself, not with its instances.

- A *constructor* is a special method that is used to construct objects.

- Java classes are organized into a *class hierarchy*, with the `Object` class at the top of the hierarchy. For a given class, classes that occur below it in the hierarchy are called its *subclasses*, while classes that occur above it are called its *superclasses*.

- Classes *inherit* attributes and methods from their superclasses. This is known as *class inheritance*.

- The main principles of the object-oriented programming approach are as follows:

  - Divide and Conquer: Successful problem solving involves breaking a complex problem into objects.

  - Encapsulation and Modularity: Each object should be assigned a clear role.

  - Public Interface: Each object should present a clear public interface that determines how other objects will use it.

  - Information Hiding: Each object should shield its users from unnecessary details of how it performs its role.

  - Generality: Objects should be designed to be as general as possible.

  - Extensibility: Objects should be designed so that their functionality can be extended to carry out more specialized tasks.

  - *Abstraction* is the ability to focus on certain important features of an object while ignoring other features.

EXERCISES

EXERCISE 0.1 Fill in the blanks in each of the following statements.

(a) Dividing a problem or a task into parts is an example of the _____ principle.

(b) Designing a class so that it shields certain parts of an object from other objects is an example of the _____ principle.

(c) Java programs that can run without change on a wide variety of computers are an example of _____.

(d) The fact that social security numbers are divided into three parts is an example of the _____ principle.

(e) To say that a program is robust means that _____.

(f) An _____ is a separate module that encapsulates a Java program's attributes and actions.

EXERCISE 0.2 Explain the difference between each of the following pairs of concepts.

(a) *hardware* and *software*

(b) *systems* software and *application* software

(c) *compiler* and *interpreter*

(d) *machine language* and *high-level language*

(e) *general-purpose* computer and *special-purpose* computer

(f) *primary* memory and *secondary* memory

(g) *CPU* and *ALU*

(h) *Internet* and *WWW*

(i) *client* and *server*

(j) *HTTP* and *HTML*

(k) *source* code and *object* code

EXERCISE 0.3 Fill in the blanks in each of the following statements.

a. A _____ is a set of instructions that directs a computer's behavior.

b. A disk drive would be an example of a _____ device.

c. A mouse is an example of an _____ device.

d. A monitor is an example of an _____ device.

e. The computer's _____ functions like a scratch pad.

f. Java is an example of a _____ programming language.

g. The Internet is a network of _____.

h. The protocol used by the World Wide Web is the _____ protocol.

i. Web documents are written in _____ code.

j. A _____ is a networked computer that is used to store data for other computers on the network.

EXERCISE 0.4   Identify the component of computer hardware that is responsible for the following functions.

    a. executing the *fetch-execute cycle*
    b. arithmetic operations
    c. executing instructions
    d. storing programs while they are executing
    e. storing programs and data when the computer is off

EXERCISE 0.5   Explain why a typical piece of software, such as a word processor, cannot run on both a Macintosh and a Windows machine.

EXERCISE 0.6   What advantages do you see in platform independence? What are the disadvantages?

EXERCISE 0.7   In what sense is a person's name an abstraction? In what sense is any word of the English language an abstraction?

EXERCISE 0.8   Analyze the process of writing a research paper in terms of the divide-and-conquer and encapsulation principles.

EXERCISE 0.9   Analyze your car by using object-oriented design principles. In other words, pick one of your car's systems, such as the braking system, and analyze it in terms of the divide-and-conquer, encapsulation, information-hiding, and interface principles.

EXERCISE 0.10   Make an object-oriented analysis of the interaction between a student, a librarian, and a library database when a student checks a book out of a college library.

Photograph courtesy of Ken Reid, Getty Images, Inc. - Taxi.

1

Java Program Design and Development

OBJECTIVES

After studying this chapter, you will

- Know the basic steps involved in program development.
- Understand some of the basic elements of the Java language.
- Know how to use simple output operations in a Java program.
- Be able to distinguish between different types of errors in a program.
- Understand how a Java program is translated into machine language.
- Understand the difference between a Java application and a Java applet.
- Know how to edit, compile, and run Java programs.

OUTLINE

1.1 Introduction

This chapter introduces some of the basic concepts and techniques involved in Java program design and development. We begin by identifying the main steps in designing an object-oriented program. The steps are illustrated by designing a program that "asks" and "answers" riddles. As an example of a riddle, consider the question "What is black and white and read all over?" The answer, of course, is a newspaper. Following the design phase, we then focus on the steps involved in coding a Java program, including the process of editing, compiling, and running a program. Because Java programs come in two varieties, applications and applets, we describe how the coding process differs for these two varieties.

Next we begin to familiarize ourselves with Java's extensive class library by studying its `PrintStream` and `System` classes. These classes contain objects and methods that enable us to print output from a program. By the end of the chapter you will be able to design and write a Java application that "sings" your favorite song.

1.2 Designing Good Programs

Programming is not simply a question of typing Java code. It involves a considerable amount of planning and careful designing. Badly designed programs rarely work correctly. Even though it is tempting for novice programmers to start entering code almost immediately, one of the first rules of programming is

JAVA PROGRAMMING TIP: The sooner you begin to type code, the longer the program will take to finish, because careful design of the program must precede coding. This is particularly true of object-oriented programs.

In other words, the more thought and care you put into designing a program, the more likely you are to end up with one that works correctly. The following subsections provide a brief overview of the program development process.

1.2.1 The Software Engineering Life Cycle

Software engineering is the process of designing and writing software. The *software life cycle* refers to the different phases involved in the design and development of a computer program. Our presentation of examples in the book will focus on four phases of the overall life cycle. In the *specification* phase we provide a statement of the problem and a detailed description of what the program will do. In the *design* phase we describe the details of the various classes, methods, and data that will be used in the program. The *implementation* phase refers to the actual coding of the program into Java. In the *testing* phase we test the program's performance to make sure it is correct, recoding it or redesigning it as necessary.

Figure 1.1 gives a more detailed overview of the program-development process, focusing most of the attention on the design phase of the software life cycle. It shows that designing an object-oriented program is a matter of asking the right questions about the classes, data, and methods that make up the program.

Overall, the program-development process can be viewed as one that repeatedly applies the divide-and-conquer principle. That is, most programming problems can be repeatedly

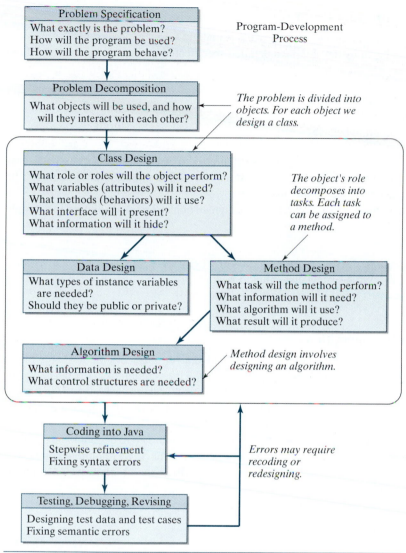

Program-Development
Process

Problem Specification

What exactly is the problem?
How will the program be used?
How will the program behave?

Problem Decomposition

What objects will be used, and how
will they interact with each other?

*The problem is divided into
objects. For each object we
design a class.*

Class Design

What role or roles will the object perform?
What variables (attributes) will it need?
What methods (behaviors) will it use?
What interface will it present?
What information will it hide?

*The object's role
decomposes into
tasks. Each task
can be assigned to
a method.*

Data Design

What types of instance variables
are needed?
Should they be public or private?

Method Design

What task will the method perform?
What information will it need?
What algorithm will it use?
What result will it produce?

Algorithm Design

What information is needed?
What control structures are needed?

*Method design involves
designing an algorithm.*

Coding into Java

Stepwise refinement
Fixing syntax errors

*Errors may require
recoding or
redesigning.*

Testing, Debugging, Revising

Designing test data and test cases
Fixing semantic errors

Figure 1.1 An overview of the program-development process.

divided until you have a collection of relatively easy to solve subproblems, each of which can be handled by an object. In this way the program is divided into a collection of interacting objects. For each object we design a class. During class design, each object is divided further into its variables and methods.

*Divide and
conquer*

When should we stop subdividing? How much of a task should be assigned to a single object or a single method? The answers to these and similar questions are not easy. Good answers require the kind of judgment that comes through experience, and frequently there is more than one good way to design a solution. Here again, as we learn more about object-oriented programming, we'll learn more about how to make these design decisions.

1.3   Designing a Riddle Program

The first step in the program-development process is making sure you understand the problem (Fig. 1.1). Thus, we begin by developing a detailed specification, which should address three basic questions:

- What exactly is the problem to be solved?
- How will the program be used?
- How should the program behave?

In the real world, the problem specification is often arrived at through an extensive discussion between the customer and the developer. In an introductory programming course, the specification is usually assigned by the instructor.

To help make these ideas a little clearer, let's design an object-oriented solution to a simple problem.

> **Problem Specification.** Design a class that will represent a riddle with a given question and answer. The definition of this class should make it possible to store different riddles and to retrieve a riddle's question and answer independently.

1.3.1   Problem Decomposition

Divide and conquer

Most problems are too big and too complex to be tackled all at once. So, the next step in the design process is to divide the problem into parts that make the solution more manageable. In the object-oriented approach, a problem is divided into objects, where each object will handle one specific aspect of the program's overall job. In effect, each object will become an expert or specialist in some aspect of the program's overall behavior.

Note that there is some ambiguity here about how far we should go in decomposing a given program. This ambiguity is part of the design process. How much we should decompose a program before its parts become "simple to solve" depends on the problem we're trying to solve and on the problem solver.

One useful design guideline for trying to decide what objects are needed is the following:

> **EFFECTIVE DESIGN: Looking for Nouns.**   Choosing a program's objects is often a matter of looking for nouns in the problem specification.

Again, there's some ambiguity involved in this guideline. For example, the key noun in our current problem is *riddle*, so our solution will involve an object that serves as a model for a riddle. The main task of this Java object will be simply to represent a riddle. Two other nouns in the specification are *question* and *answer*. Fortunately, Java has built-in `String` objects that represent strings of characters such as words or sentences. We can use two `String` objects for the riddle's question and answer. Thus, for this simple problem, we need only design one new type of object—a riddle—whose primary role will be to represent a riddle's question and answer.

Don't worry too much if our design decisions seem somewhat mysterious at this stage. A good understanding of object-oriented design can come only after much design experience, but this is a good place to start.

1.3.2   Object Design

Once we have divided a problem into a set of cooperating objects, designing a Java program is primarily a matter of designing and creating the objects themselves. In our example, this means we must now design the features of our riddle object. For each object, we must answer the following basic design questions:

- What role will the object perform in the program?
- What data or information will it need?
- What actions will it take?
- What interface will it present to other objects?
- What information will it hide from other objects?

For our riddle object, the answers to these questions are shown in Figure 1.2. Bear in mind that although we talk about designing an object, we are really talking about designing the object's class. A class defines the collection of objects that belong to it. The class can be considered the object's *type*. This is the same as for real-world objects. Thus, Seabiscuit is a horse—that is, Seabiscuit is an object of type horse. Similarly, an individual riddle, such as the newspaper riddle, is a riddle. That is, it is an object of type Riddle.

The following discussion shows how we arrived at the decisions for the design specifications for the Riddle class, illustrated in Figure 1.2.

The role of the Riddle object is to model an ordinary riddle. Because a riddle is defined in terms of its question and answer, our Riddle object will need some way to store these two pieces of information. As we learned in Chapter 0, an instance variable is a named memory location that belongs to an object. The fact that the memory location is named makes it easy to retrieve the data stored there by invoking the variable's name. For example, to print a riddle's question we would say something like "print question," and whatever is stored in *question* would be retrieved and printed.

What is the object's role?

In general, instance variables are used to store the information that an object needs to perform its role. They correspond to what we have been calling the object's attributes. Deciding on these variables provides the answer to the question "What information does the object need?"

What information will the object need?

- Class Name: Riddle
- Role: To store and retrieve a question and answer
- Attributes (Information)
  - question: A variable to store a riddle's question (private)
  - answer: A variable to store a riddle's answer (private)
- Behaviors
  - Riddle(): A method to set a riddle's question and answer
  - getQuestion(): A method to return a riddle's question
  - getAnswer(): A method to return a riddle's answer

Figure 1.2   Design specification for the Riddle class.

Next we decide what actions a `Riddle` object will take. A useful design guideline for actions of objects is the following:

> **EFFECTIVE DESIGN: Looking for Verbs.** Choosing the behavior of an object is often a matter of looking for verbs in the problem specification.

What actions will the object take?

For this problem, the key verbs are *set* and *retrieve*. As specified in Figure 1.2, each `Riddle` object should provide some means of setting the values of its question and answer variables and a means of retrieving each value separately.

Each of the actions we have identified will be encapsulated in a Java method. As you will recall from Chapter 0, a method is a named section of code that can be *invoked*, or called upon, to perform a particular action. In the object-oriented approach, calling a method (method invocation) is the means by which interaction occurs among objects. Calling a method is like sending a message between objects. For example, when we want to get a riddle's answer, we would invoke the `getAnswer()` method. This is like sending the message "Give me your answer." A special method known as a constructor is invoked when an object is first created. We will use the `Riddle()` constructor to give specific values to the riddle's question and answer variables.

What interface will it present, and what information will it hide?

In designing an object, we must decide which methods should be made available to other objects. This determines what interface the object should present and what information it should hide from other objects. In general, those methods that will be used to communicate with an object are designated as part of the object's interface. Except for its interface, all other information maintained by each riddle should be kept "hidden" from other objects. For example, it is not necessary for other objects to know where a riddle object stores its question and answer. The fact that they are stored in variables named `question` and `answer` rather than variables named `ques` and `ans` is irrelevant to other objects.

> **EFFECTIVE DESIGN: Object Interface.** An object's interface should consist of just those methods needed to communicate with or to use the object.

> **EFFECTIVE DESIGN: Information Hiding.** An object should hide most of the details of its implementation.

Taken together, these various design decisions lead to the specification shown in Figure 1.3. As our discussion has illustrated, we arrived at the decisions by asking and answering the right questions. In most classes the attributes (variables) are private. This is represented by a minus sign ($-$). In this example, the operations (methods) are public, which is represented by the plus sign ($+$). The figure shows that the `Riddle` class has two hidden (or private) variables for storing data and three visible (or public) methods that represent the operations it can perform.

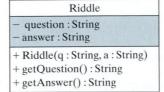

Riddle
− question : String − answer : String
+ Riddle(q : String, a : String) + getQuestion() : String + getAnswer() : String

Figure 1.3 A UML class diagram representing the `Riddle` class.

1.3.3   Data, Methods, and Algorithms

Among the details that must be worked out in designing a riddle object is deciding what type of data, methods, and algorithms we need. There are two basic questions involved:

- What type of data will be used to represent the information needed by the riddle?
- How will each method carry out its task?

Like other programming languages, Java supports a wide range of different types of data, some simple and some complex. Obviously a riddle's question and answer should be represented by text. As we noted earlier, Java's `String` type, which is designed to store text, can be considered a string of characters.

What type of data will be used?

In designing a method, you have to decide what the method will do. In order to carry out its task, a method will need certain information, which it may store in variables. In addition, it will have to carry out a sequence of individual actions to perform the task. This is called its **algorithm** which is a step-by-step description of the solution to a problem. And, finally, you must decide what result the method will produce. Thus, as in designing objects, it is important to ask the right questions:

How will each method carry out its task?

- What specific task will the method perform?
- What information will it need to perform its task?
- What algorithm will the method use?
- What result will the method produce?

Methods can be thought of as using an algorithm to complete a required action. The algorithm required for the `Riddle()` constructor is very simple but also typical of constructors for many classes. It takes two strings and assigns the first to the `question` instance variable and then assigns the second to the `answer` instance variable. The algorithms for the other two methods for the Riddle class are even simpler. They are referred to as *get* methods that merely *return*, or produce, the value that is currently stored in an instance variable.

Not all methods are so simple to design, and not all algorithms are so simple. Even when programming a simple arithmetic problem, the steps involved in the algorithm will not always be as obvious as they are when doing the calculation by hand. For example, suppose the problem were to calculate the sum of a list of numbers. If we were telling a classmate how to do this problem, we might just say, "Add up all the numbers and report their total." But this description is far too vague to be used in a program. By contrast, here's an algorithm that a program could use:

Algorithm design

1. Set the initial value of the sum to 0.
2. If there are no more numbers to total, go to step 5.
3. Add the next number to the sum.
4. Go to step 2.
5. Report the sum.

Each step in this algorithm is simple and easy to follow. It would be relatively easy to translate it into Java. Because English is somewhat imprecise as an algorithmic language, programmers frequently write algorithms in the programming language itself or in **pseudocode**, a

Pseudocode

hybrid language that combines English and programming language structures without being too fussy about programming-language syntax. For example, the preceding algorithm might be expressed in pseudocode as follows:

```
sum = 0
while (more numbers remain)
    add next number to sum
print the sum
```

Of course, it is unlikely that an experienced programmer would take the trouble to write out pseudocode for such a simple algorithm. But many programming problems are quite complex, and careful design is required to minimize the number of errors in the program. In such situations, pseudocode could be useful.

Another important part of designing an algorithm is to *trace* it—that is, to step through it line by line—on some sample data. For example, we might test the list-summing algorithm by tracing it on the list of numbers shown here.

Sum	List of Numbers
0	54 30 20
54	30 20
84	20
104	–

Initially, the sum starts out at 0 and the list of numbers contains 54, 30, and 20. On each iteration through the algorithm, the sum increases by the amount of the next number, and the list diminishes in size. The algorithm stops with the correct total left under the sum column. While this trace didn't turn up any errors, it is frequently possible to find flaws in an algorithm by tracing it in this way.

1.3.4   Coding into Java

Once a sufficiently detailed design has been developed, it is time to start generating Java code. The wrong way to do this would be to type the entire program and then compile and run it. This generally leads to dozens of errors that can be both demoralizing and difficult to fix.

Stepwise refinement

The right way to code is to use the principle of **stepwise refinement**. The program is coded in small stages, and after each stage the code is compiled and tested. For example, you could write the code for a single method and test that method before moving on to another part of the program. In this way, small errors are caught before moving on to the next stage.

The code for the Riddle class is shown in Figure 1.4. Even though we have not yet begun learning the details of the Java language, you can easily pick out the key parts in this program: the instance variables question and answer of type String, which are used to store the riddle's data; the Riddle() constructor and the getQuestion() and getAnswer() methods make up the interface. The specific language details needed to understand each of these elements will be covered in this and the following chapter.

```
/*
 * File: Riddle.java
 * Author: Java, Java, Java
 * Description: Defines a simple riddle.
 */
public class Riddle extends Object          // Class header
{                                           // Begin class body
  private String question;                  // Instance variables
  private String answer;

  public Riddle(String q, String a)         // Constructor method
  {
    question = q;
    answer = a;
  } // Riddle()

  public String getQuestion()               // Instance method
  {
    return question;
  } // getQuestion()

  public String getAnswer()                 // Instance method
  {
    return answer;
  } // getAnswer()
} // Riddle class                           // End class body
```

Figure 1.4 The `Riddle` class definition.

1.3.5 Syntax and Semantics

Writing Java code requires that you know its syntax and semantics. A language's **syntax** is the set of rules that determines whether a particular statement is correctly formulated. As an example of a syntax rule, consider the following two English statements: Syntax

```
The rain in Spain falls mainly on the plain.    // Valid
Spain rain the mainly in on the falls plain.    // Invalid
```

The first sentence follows the rules of English syntax (grammar), and it means that it rains a lot on the Spanish plain. The second sentence does not follow English syntax, and, as a result, it is rendered meaningless. An example of a Java syntax rule is that a Java statement must end with a semicolon.

However, unlike in English, where you can still be understood even when you break a syntax rule, in a programming language the syntax rules are very strict. If you break even the slightest syntax rule—for example, if you forget just a single semicolon—the program won't work at all.

Similarly, the programmer must know the **semantics** of the language—that is, the meaning of each statement. In a programming language, a statement's meaning is determined by what effect it will have on the program. For example, to set the `sum` to 0 in the preceding algorithm, an assignment statement is used to store the value 0 into the memory location named `sum`. Thus, we say that the statement Semantics

```
sum = 0;
```

assigns 0 to the memory location `sum`, where it will be stored until some other part of the program needs it.

Learning Java's syntax and semantics is a major part of learning to program. This aspect of learning to program is a lot like learning a foreign language. The more quickly you become fluent in the new language (Java), the better you will be at expressing solutions to interesting programming problems. The longer you struggle with Java's rules and conventions, the more difficult it will be to talk about problems in a common language. Also, computers are a lot fussier about correct language than humans, and even the smallest syntax or semantic error can cause tremendous frustration. So try to be very precise in learning Java's syntax and semantics.

1.3.6   Testing, Debugging, and Revising

Coding, testing, and revising a program is a repetitive process, one that may require you to repeat the different program-development stages shown in Figure 1.1. According to the stepwise-refinement principle, the process of developing a program should proceed in small, incremental steps, where the solution becomes more refined at each step. However, no matter how much care you take, things can still go wrong during the coding process.

Syntax errors
A *syntax error* is an error that breaks one of Java's syntax rules. Such errors will be detected by the Java compiler. Syntax errors are relatively easy to fix once you understand the error messages provided by the compiler. As long as a program contains syntax errors, the programmer must correct them and recompile the program. Once all the syntax errors are corrected, the compiler will produce an executable version of the program, which can then be run.

When a program is run, the computer carries out the steps specified in the program and produces results. However, just because a program runs does not mean that its actions and results are correct. A running program can contain *semantic errors*, also called *logic errors*.
Semantic errors
A semantic error is caused by an error in the logical design of the program causing it to behave incorrectly, producing incorrect results.

Unlike syntax errors, semantic errors cannot be detected automatically. For example, suppose that a program contains the following statement for calculating the area of a rectangle:

```
return length + width;
```

Adding length and width instead of multiplying them will give an incorrect area calculation. Because there is nothing syntactically wrong with the expression `length + width`, however, the compiler won't detect an error in this statement. Thus, the computer will execute this statement and compute the incorrect area.

Semantic errors can only be discovered by testing the program, and they are sometimes very hard to detect. Just because a program appears to run correctly on one test doesn't guarantee that it contains no semantic errors. It might only mean that it has not been adequately tested.

Fixing semantic errors is known as *debugging* a program, and when subtle errors occur this can be the most frustrating part of the whole program-development process. The examples presented in this text will occasionally provide hints and suggestions on how to track down *bugs*, or errors, in your code. One point to remember when you are trying to find a very subtle bug is that no matter how convinced you are that your code is correct and the bug was caused by an error in the computer, the error will almost certainly turn out to be caused by your code!

1.3.7   Writing Readable Programs

Becoming a proficient programmer goes beyond simply writing a program that produces correct output. It also involves developing good *programming style*, which includes how readable and understandable your code is. Our goal is to help you develop a programming style that satisfies the following principles:

Programming style

- **Readability.** Programs should be easy to read and understand. Comments should be used to document and explain the program's code.
- **Clarity.** Programs should employ well-known constructs and standard conventions and should avoid programming tricks and unnecessarily obscure or complex code.
- **Flexibility.** Programs should be designed and written so that they are easy to modify.

1.4   Java Language Elements

In this section we will introduce some of the key elements of the Java language by describing the details of a small program. We will look at how a program is organized and what the various parts do. Our intent is to introduce important language elements, many of which will be explained in greater detail in later sections.

The program we will study is a Java version of the traditional HelloWorld program—"traditional" because practically every introductory programming text begins with it. When it is run, the HelloWorld program (Fig. 1.5) displays the greeting "Hello World!" on the console.

Grace Hopper and the First Computer Bug

Rear Admiral Grace Murray Hopper (1906–1992) was a pioneer computer programmer and one of the original developers of the COBOL programming language, which stands for *CO*mmon *B*usiness-*O*riented *L*anguage. Among her many achievements and distinctions, Admiral Hopper also had a role in coining the term *computer bug*.

In August 1945, she and a group of other programmers were working on the Mark I, an electro-mechanical computer developed at Harvard that was one of the ancestors of today's electronic computers. After several hours of trying to figure out why the machine was malfunctioning, someone located and removed a two-inch moth from one of the computer's circuits. From then on whenever anything went wrong with a computer, Admiral Hopper and others would say "it had bugs in it." The first bug itself is still taped to Admiral Hopper's 1945 log book, which is now in the collection of the Naval Surface Weapons Center.

In 1991, Admiral Hopper was awarded the National Medal of Technology by President George H.W. Bush. To commemorate and honor Admiral Hopper's many contributions, the U.S. Navy recently named a warship after her. For more information on Admiral Hopper, see the Web site at

Photograph courtesy of Naval Visual News Service

```
http://www.chips.navy.mil
```

```
/*
 * File: HelloWorld.java
 * Author: Java Java Java
 * Description: Prints Hello World greeting.
 */
public class HelloWorld extends Object        // Class header
{                                             // Start class body
  private String greeting = "Hello World!";
  public void greet()                         // Method definition
  {                                           // Start method body
      System.out.println(greeting);           // Output statement
  } // greet()                                // End method body
  public static void main(String args[])      // Method header
  {
    HelloWorld helloworld;                    // declare
    helloworld = new HelloWorld();            // create
    helloworld.greet();                       // Method call
  } // main()
} // HelloWorld class                         // End class body
```

Figure 1.5   The `HelloWorld` application program.

1.4.1   Comments

The first thing to notice about the `HelloWorld` program is the use of comments. A **comment** is a nonexecutable portion of a program that is used to document the program. Because comments are not executable instructions, they are ignored by the compiler. Their sole purpose is to make the program easier for the programmer to read and understand.

The `HelloWorld` program contains examples of two types of Java comments. Any text contained within /* and */ is considered a comment. As you can see in `HelloWorld`, this kind of comment can extend over several lines and is sometimes called a *multiline* comment. A second type of comment is any text that follows double slashes (//) on a line. This is known as a *single-line comment* because it cannot extend beyond a single line.

When the compiler encounters the beginning marker (/*) of a multiline comment, it skips over everything until it finds a matching end marker (*/). One implication of this is that it is not possible to put one multiline comment inside of another. That is, one comment cannot be *nested*, or contained, within another comment. The following code segment illustrates the rules that govern the use of /* and */:

```
/* This first comment begins and ends on the same line. */
/* A second comment starts on this line ...
   and goes on ...
   and this is the last line of the second comment.
*/
/* A third comment starts on this line ...
   /* This is NOT a fourth comment. It is just
      part of the third comment.
   And this is the last line of the third comment.
*/
*/  This is an error because it is an unmatched end marker.
```

As you can see from this example, it is impossible to begin a new comment inside an already-started comment because all the text inside the first comment, including /*, is ignored by the compiler.

> **JAVA LANGUAGE RULE**   **Comments.** Any text contained within /* and */, which may span several lines, is considered a comment and is ignored by the compiler. Inserting double slashes (//) into a line turns the rest of the line into a comment.

Multiline comments are often used to create a *comment block* that provides useful documentation for the program. In HelloWorld, the program begins with a comment block that identifies the name of the file that contains the program and its author, and provides a brief description of what the program does.

For single-line comments, double slashes (//) can be inserted anywhere on a line of code. As a result, the rest of the line is ignored by the compiler. We use single-line comments throughout the HelloWorld program to provide a running commentary of its language elements.

Single-line comment

> **JAVA PROGRAMMING TIP: Use of Comments.** A well-written program should begin with a comment block that provides the name of the program, its author, and a description of what the program does.

1.4.2   Program Layout

Another thing to notice about the program is how neatly it is arranged on the page. This is done deliberately so that the program will be easy to read and understand. In Java, program expressions and statements may be arranged any way the programmer likes. They may occur one per line, several per line, or one per several lines. But the fact that the rules governing the layout of the program are so lax makes it all the more important that we adopt a good programming style, one that will help make programs easy to read.

So look at how things are presented in HelloWorld. Note how beginning and ending braces, { and }, are aligned, and note how we use single-line comments to annotate ending braces. Braces are used to mark the beginning and end of different blocks of code in a Java program. It can sometimes be difficult to know which beginning and end braces are matched up. Proper indentation and the use of single-line comments make it easier to determine how the braces are matched up.

Similarly, indentation is used to show when one element of the program is contained within another element. Thus, the elements of the HelloWorld class are indented inside the braces that mark the beginning and end of the class. And the statements in the main() method are indented to indicate that they belong to that method. Use of indentation in this way, to identify the program's structure, makes the program easier to read and understand.

> **JAVA PROGRAMMING TIP: Use of Indentation.**   Indent the code within a block, and align the block's opening and closing braces. Use a comment to mark the end of a block of code.

Table 1.1. Java keywords.

abstract	continue	for	new	switch
assert	default	goto	package	synchronized
boolean	do	if	private	this
break	double	implements	protected	throw
byte	else	import	public	throws
case	enum	instanceof	return	transient
catch	extend	int	short	try
char	final	interface	static	void
class	finally	long	strictfp	volatile
const	float	native	super	while

1.4.3 Keywords and Identifiers

The Java language contains 50 predefined **keywords** (Table 1.1). These are words that have special meaning in the language and whose use is reserved for special purposes. For example, the keywords used in the HelloWorld program (Fig. 1.5) are: `class`, `extends`, `private`, `public`, `static`, and `void`.

Because their use is restricted, keywords cannot be used as the names of methods, variables, or classes. However, the programmer can make up names for the classes, methods, and variables that occur in a program, provided that certain rules and conventions are followed.

Identifier syntax   The names for classes, methods, and variables are called identifiers, and they follow certain syntax rules:

> **JAVA LANGUAGE RULE**   **Identifier.** An **identifier** must begin with a capital or lower-case letter and may be followed by any number of letters, digits, underscores (_), or dollar signs ($). An identifier may not be identical to a Java keyword.

Names in Java are *case sensitive*, which means that two different identifiers may contain the same letters in the same order. For example, `thisVar` and `ThisVar` are two different identifiers.

Identifier style   In addition to the syntax rule that governs identifiers, Java programmers follow certain style conventions in making up names for classes, variables, and methods. By convention, class names in Java begin with a capital letter and use capital letters to distinguish the individual *Java naming conventions* words in the name—for example, `HelloWorld` and `TextField`. Variable and method names begin with a lowercase letter but also use capital letters to distinguish the words in the name— for example, `main()`, `greeting`, `greet()`, `getQuestion()`, and `getAnswer()`. The advantage of this convention is that it is easy to distinguish the different elements in a program— classes, methods, variables—just by how they are written. (For more on Java style conventions, see Appendix A.).

Another important style convention followed by Java programmers is to choose descriptive identifiers when naming classes, variables, and methods. This helps to make the program more readable.

JAVA PROGRAMMING TIP: Choice of Identifiers.   To make your program more readable, choose names that describe the purpose of the class, variable, or method.

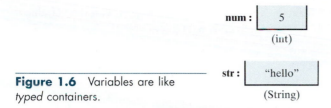

Figure 1.6 Variables are like *typed* containers.

1.4.4 Data Types and Variables

A computer program wouldn't be very useful if it couldn't manipulate different kinds of data, such as numbers and strings. The operations that one can do on a piece of data depend on the data's type. For example, you can divide and multiply numbers, but you cannot do this with strings. Thus, every piece of data in a Java program is classified according to its **data type**.

Broadly speaking, there are two categories of data in Java: various types of objects and eight different types of built-in **primitive data types**. In addition to new types of objects that are created by programmers, Java has many different types of built-in objects. Two types that we will encounter in this chapter are the `String` and `PrintStream` objects. Java's primitive types include three integer types, three real-number types, a character type, and a boolean type with values true and false. The names of the primitive types are keywords like `int` for one integer type, `double` for one real-number type, and `boolean`.   *Primitive types*

As we noted in Chapter 0, a variable is a named storage location that can store a value of a particular type. Practically speaking, you can think of a variable as a special container into which you can place values, but only values of a certain type (Fig. 1.6). For example, an `int` variable can store values like 5 or −100. A `String` variable can store values like "Hello." (Actually, this is not the full story, which is a little more complicated, but we will get to that in Chapter 2.)

In the `HelloWorld` class, the instance variable `greeting` (line 8) stores a value of type `String`. In the `main()` method, the variable `helloworld` is assigned a `HelloWorld` object (line 16).

A **literal value** is an actual value of some type that occurs in a program. For example, a string enclosed in double quotes, such as "Hello World!," is known as a `String` literal. A number such as 45.2 would be an example of a literal of type `double`, and −72 would be an example of a literal of type `int`. Our HelloWorld program contains just a single literal value, the "HelloWorld!" `String`.

1.4.5 Statements

A Java program is a collection of statements. A **statement** is a segment of code that takes some action in the program. As a program runs, we say that it *executes* statements, meaning that it carries out the actions specified by these statements. In our `HelloWorld` program, statements of various types occur on lines 8, 11, 15, 16, and 17. Note that all of these lines end with a semicolon. The rule in Java is that statements must end with a semicolon. Omitting the semicolon would cause a syntax error.   *Executing a program*

A **declaration statement** is a statement that declares a variable of a particular type. In Java, a variable must be declared before it can be used in a program. Failure to declare it would cause a syntax error. In its simplest form, a declaration statement begins with the variable's type, which is followed by the variable's name, and ends with a semicolon:

Type VariableName ;

A variable's type is either one of the primitive types we mentioned, such as `int`, `double`, or `boolean`, or, for an object, it is the name of the object's class, such as `String` or `HelloWorld`. A variable's name may be any legal identifier, as defined earlier, although the convention in Java is to begin variable names with a lowercase letter. In our `HelloWorld` program, an example a simple declaration statement occurs on line 15:

```
HelloWorld helloworld;
```

This example declares a variable for an object. The variable's name is `helloworld`, and its type is `HelloWorld`, the name of the class that is being defined in our example. To take another example, the following statements declare two `int` variables, named `int1` and `int2`:

```
int int1;
int int2;
```

As we noted, an `int` is one of Java's primitive types and the word *int* is a Java keyword.

Without going into too much detail at this point, declaring a variable causes the program to set aside enough memory for the type of data that will be stored in that variable. So in this example, Java would reserve enough space to store an `int`.

An **assignment statement** is a statement that stores (assigns) a value in a variable. An assignment statement uses the equal sign (=) as an assignment operator. In its simplest form, an assignment statement has a variable on the left-hand side of the equals sign and some type of value on the right-hand side. Like other statements, an assignment statement ends with a semicolon:

VariableName = Value ;

When it executes an assignment statement, Java will first determine what value is given on the right-hand side and then assign (store) that value to (in) the variable on the left-hand side. Here are some simple examples:

```
greeting = "Hello World";
num1 = 50;          // (a) Assign 50 to num1
num2 = 10 + 15;     // (b) Assign 25 to num2
num1 = num2;        // (c) Copy num2's value (25) into num1
```

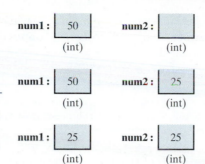

Figure 1.7 This illustrates how the state of the variables num1 and num2 changes over the course of the three assignments, (a), (b), (c), given in the text.

In the first case, the value on the right-hand side is the string literal "Hello World!," which gets stored in greeting. Of course, greeting has to be the right type of container—in this case, a String variable. In the next case, the value on the right-hand side is 50. So that is the value that gets stored in num1, assuming that num1 is an int variable. The situation after this assignment is shown in the top drawing in Figure 1.7. In the third case, the value on the right-hand side is 25, which is determined by adding 10 and 15. So the value that gets assigned to num2 is 25. After this assignment we have the situation shown in the middle drawing in the figure. Of course, this assumes that num2 is an int variable. In the last case, the value on the right-hand side is 25, the value that we just stored in the variable num2. So 25 gets stored in num1. This is the bottom drawing in the accompanying figure.

The last of these examples

```
num1 = num2;    // Copy num2's value into num1
```

can be confusing to beginning programmers, so it is worth some additional comment. In this case, there are variables on both the left and right of the assignment operator. But they have very different meaning. The variable on the right is treated as a value. If the variable is storing 25, then that is its value. In fact, whatever occurs on the right-hand side of an assignment operator is treated as a value. The variable on the left-hand side is treated as a memory location. It is where the value 25 will be stored as a result of executing this statement. The effect of this statement is to copy the value stored in *num2* into *num1*, as illustrated in Figure 1.8.

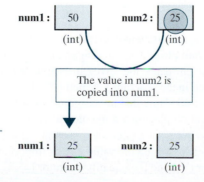

Figure 1.8 In the assignment *num1 = num2;*, *num2*'s value is copied into *num1*.

Java has many other kinds of statements, and we will be learning about them in subsequent examples. The following examples from the `HelloWorld` program are examples of statements in which a method is called:

```
System.out.println(greeting);  // Call println() method
helloworld.greet();            // Call greet() method
```

We will discuss these kinds of statements in greater detail as we go along. One final type of statement that should be mentioned at this point is the **compound statement** (or **block**), which is a sequence of statements contained within braces {}. We see three examples of this in the `HelloWorld` program. The body of a class definition extends from lines 7 through 19. The body of the `greet()` method is a block that extends from line 10 through line 12. The body of the `main()` method is a block that extends from line 14 to 19.

1.4.6 Expressions and Operators

The manipulation of data in a program is done by using an *expression* of some kind that specifies the action. An **expression** is Java code that specifies or produces a value in the program. For example, if you want to add two numbers, you would use an arithmetic expression, such as *num*1 + *num*2. If you want to compare two numbers, you would use a relation expression, such as *num*1 < *num*2. As you can see, these and many other expressions in Java involve the use of special symbols called **operators**. Here we see the addition operator (+) and the less-than operator (<). We have already talked about the assignment operator (=).

Java expressions and operators have a type that depends on the type of data that is being manipulated. For example, when adding two `int` values, such as 5 + 10, the expression itself produces an `int` result. When comparing two numbers with the less than operator, *num*1 < *num*2, the expression itself produces a `boolean` type, either true or false.

It is important to note that expressions cannot occur on their own. They occur as part of the program's statements. Here are some additional examples of expressions:

```
num = 7          // An assignment expression of type int
num = square(7)  // An method call expression of type int
num == 7         // An equality expression of type boolean
```

The first of these is an assignment expression. It has a value of 7, because it is assigning 7 to `num`. The second example is also an assignment expression, but this one has a method call, `square(7)`, on its right-hand side. (We can assume that a method named `square()` has been appropriately defined in the program.) A method call is just another kind of expression. In this case, it has the value 49. Note that an assignment expression can be turned into a standalone assignment statement by placing a semicolon after it.

The third expression is an equality expression, which has the value `true`, assuming that the variable on its left is storing the value 7. It is important to note the difference between the assignment operator (=) and the equality operator (==).

> **JAVA LANGUAGE RULE**   **Equality and Assignment.** Be careful not to confuse =
> and ==. The symbol = is the assignment operator. It assigns the value on its right-hand side
> to the variable on its left-hand side. The symbol == is the equality operator. It evaluates
> whether the expressions on its left- and right-hand sides have the same value and returns
> either `true` or `false`.

SELF-STUDY EXERCISES

EXERCISE 1.1   What is stored in the variable `num` after the following two statements are executed?

```
int num = 11;
num = 23 - num;
```

EXERCISE 1.2   Write a statement that will declare a variable of type `int` called `num2`, and store
in it the sum of 711 and 712.

1.4.7   Class Definition

A Java program consists of one or more class definitions. In the `HelloWorld` example, we
are defining the `HelloWorld` class, but there are also three predefined classes involved in the
program. These are the `Object`, `String`, and `System` classes all of which are defined in the
Java class library. Predefined classes, such as these, can be used in any program.

As the `HelloWorld` program's comments indicate, a class definition has two parts: a *class*
header and a *class body*. In general, a class header takes the following form, some parts of
which are optional (*opt*):

> *ClassModifiers*~opt~   `class`   *ClassName*   *Pedigree*~opt~

The class header for the `HelloWorld` class is:

> `public class HelloWorld extends Object`

The purpose of the header is to give the class its name (`HelloWorld`), identify its accessibility
(`public` as opposed to `private`), and describe where it fits into the Java class hierarchy (as
an extension of the `Object` class). In this case, the header begins with the optional access
modifier, `public`, which declares that this class can be accessed by any other classes. The
next part of the declaration identifies the name of the class, `HelloWorld`. And the last part
declares that `HelloWorld` is a subclass of the `Object` class. We call this part of the definition
the class's pedigree.

As you will recall from Chapter 0, the `Object` class is the top class of the entire Java hierarchy. By declaring that `HelloWorld extends Object`, we are saying that `HelloWorld` is
a direct *subclass* of `Object`. In fact, it is not necessary to declare explicitly that `HelloWorld`
extends `Object` because that is Java's default assumption. That is, if you omit the extends
clause in the class header, Java will automatically assume that the class is a subclass of `Object`.

The class's body, which is enclosed within curly brackets {}, contains the declaration and
definition of the elements that make up the objects of the class. This is where the object's
attributes and actions are defined.

Class header

Class body

1.4.8   Declaring an Instance Variable

There are generally two kinds of elements declared and defined in the class body: variables and methods. As we described in Chapter 0, an instance variable is a variable that belongs to each object, or instance, of the class. That is, each instance of a class has its own copies of the class's instance variables. The `HelloWorld` class has a single instance variable, (`greeting`), which is declared as follows:

```
private String greeting = "Hello World!";
```

In general, an instance variable declaration has the following syntax, some parts of which are optional:

$$Modifiers_{opt} \quad Type \quad VariableName \quad InitializerExpression_{opt}$$

Thus, a variable declaration begins with optional modifiers. In declaring the `greeting` variable, we use the access modifier, `private`, to declare that `greeting`, which belongs to the `HelloWorld` class, cannot be directly accessed by other objects. The next part of the declaration is the variable's type. In this case, the `greeting` variable is a `String`, which means that it can store a string object. The type is followed by the name of the variable, in this case (`greeting`). This is the name that is used to refer to this memory location throughout the class. For example, the variable is referred to on line 11, where it is used in a `println()` statement.

Information hiding

    The last part of the declaration is an optional initializer expression. In this example, we use it to assign an initial value, "Hello World!," to the `greeting` variable.

1.4.9   Defining an Instance Method

Recall that a method is a named section of code that can be called or invoked to carry out an action or operation. In a Java class, the methods correspond to the object's behaviors or actions. The `HelloWorld` program has two method definitions: the `greet()` method and the `main()` method.

    A method definition consists of two parts: the method header and the method body. In general, a method header takes the following form, including some parts which are optional:

$$Modifiers_{opt} \quad ReturnType \quad MethodName \quad (ParameterList_{opt})$$

As with a variable declaration, a method definition begins with optional modifiers. For example, the definition of the `greet()` method on line 9 uses the access modifier, `public`, to declare that this method can be accessed or referred to by other classes. The `main()` method, whose definition begins on line 13, is a special method, and is explained in the next section.

    The next part of the method header is the method's return type. This is the type of value, if any, that the method returns. Both of the methods in `HelloWorld` have a return type of `void`. This means that they don't return a value of any kind. Void methods just execute the sequence of statements given in their bodies. For an example of a method that does return a value, take a look again at the declaration of the `getQuestion()` method in the `Riddle` class, which returns a `String` (Fig. 1.4).

The method's name follows the method's return type. This is the name that is used when the method is called. For example, the `greet()` method is called on line 17.

Following the method's name is the method's parameter list. A **parameter** is a variable that temporarily stores data values that are being passed to the method when the method is called. Some methods, such as the `greet()` method, do not have parameters, because they are not passed any information. For an example of a method that does have parameters, see the `Riddle()` constructor, which contains parameters for the riddle's question and answer (Fig. 1.4).

The last part of method definition is its body, which contains a sequence of executable statements. An **executable statement** is a Java statement that takes some kind of action when the program is run. For example, the statement in the `greet()` method,

```
System.out.println(greeting);    // Output statement
```

prints a greeting on the console.

1.4.10 Java Application Programs

The HelloWorld program is an example of a Java **application program**, or a Java application, for short. An application program is a standalone program—"standalone" in the sense that it does not depend on any other program, like a Web browser, for its execution. Every Java application program must contain a `main()` method, which is where the program begins execution when it is run. For a program that contains several classes, it is up to the programmer to decide which class should contain the `main()` method. We don't have to worry about that decision for the HelloWorld program because it contains just a single class.

Because of its unique role as the starting point for every Java application program, it is very important that the header for the main method be declared exactly as shown in the `HelloWorld` class:

```
public static void main(String args[])
```

It must be declared `public` so that it can be accessed from outside the class that contains it. The `static` modifier is used to designate `main()` as a class method. As you might recall *Class method* from Chapter 0, a class method is a method associated directly with the class that contains it rather than with the objects of the class. A class method is not part of the class's objects. Unlike instance methods, which are invoked through a class's objects, a class method is called through the class itself. Thus, a class method can be called even before the program has created objects of the class. The special role of `main()` as the program's starting point requires that it be a class method because it is called by the Java runtime system before the program has created any objects.

The `main()` method has a `void` return type, which means that it does not return any value. Finally, note that `main()`'s parameter list contains a declaration of a `String` parameter named *args*. This is actually an array that can be used to pass string arguments to the program when it is started up. We won't worry about this feature until Chapter 9.

1.4.11   Creating and Using Objects

The body of the main() method is where the HelloWorld program creates its one and only object. Recall that when it is run, the HelloWorld program just prints the "Hello World!" greeting. As we noted earlier, this action happens in the greet() method. So in order to make this action happen, we need to call the greet() method. However, because the greet() method is an instance method that belongs to a HelloWorld object, we first need to create a HelloWorld instance. This is what happens in the body of the main() method (Fig. 1.5).

The main() method contains three statements:

```
HelloWorld helloworld;              // Variable declaration
helloworld = new HelloWorld();      // Object instantiation
helloworld.greet();                 // Method invocation
```

The first statement declares a variable of type HelloWorld, which is then assigned a HelloWorld object. The second statement creates a HelloWorld object. This is done by invoking the HelloWorld() constructor method. Creating an object is called **object instantiation** because you are creating an instance of the object. Once a HelloWorld instance is created, we can use one of its instance methods to perform some task or operation. Thus, in the third statement, we call the greet() method, which will print "Hello World!" on the console.

Default constructor

If you look back at the HelloWorld program in Figure 1.5 you won't find a definition of a constructor method. This is not an error because Java will provide a default constructor if a class does not contain a constructor definition. The **default constructor** is a trivial constructor method—"trivial" because its body contains no statements. Here is what the default HelloWorld() constructor would look like:

```
public HelloWorld() { }  // Default constructor
```

For most of the classes we design, we will design our own constructors, just as we did in the Riddle class (Fig. 1.4). We will use constructors to assign initial values to an object's instance variables or to perform other kinds of tasks that are needed when an object is created. Because the HelloWorld object doesn't require any startup tasks, we can make do with the default constructor.

Interacting objects

The HelloWorld program illustrates the idea that an object-oriented program is a collection of interacting objects. Although we create just a single HelloWorld object in the main() method, there are two other objects used in the program. One is the greeting, which is a String object consisting of the string "Hello World!" The other is the System.out object, which is a special Java system object used for printing.

1.4.12   Java Applets

A Java **applet** is a program that is executed by a Web browser and whose output is embedded within a Web page. Figure 1.9 shows a Java applet named HelloWorldApplet. This

```
    /** HelloWorldApplet program */
import java.applet.Applet;                    // Import class names
import java.awt.Graphics;

public class HelloWorldApplet extends Applet  // Class header
{                                             // Start of body
    public void paint(Graphics g)             // The paint method
    {
        g.drawString("Hello World!",10,10);
    }                                         // End of paint
}                                             // End of HelloWorld
```

Figure 1.9 `HelloWorldApplet` program.

program does more or less the same thing as the `HelloWorld` application—it displays the "Hello World!" greeting. The difference is that it displays the greeting within a Web page rather than directly on the console.

As in the case of the `HelloWorld` application program, the `HelloWorldApplet` consists of a class definition. It contains a single method definition, the `paint()` method, which contains a single executable statement:

```
g.drawString("Hello World!",10,10);
```

This statement displays the "Hello World!" message directly on a Web page. The `draw-String()` method is one of the many drawing and painting methods defined in the `Graphics` class. Every Java applet comes with its own `Graphics` object, which is referred to here simply as `g`. Thus, we are using that object's `drawString()` method to draw on the applet window. Don't worry if this seems a bit mysterious now. We'll explain it more fully when we take up graphics examples again.

The `HelloWorldApplet` also contains some elements, such as the `import` statements, that we did not find in the `HelloWorld` application. We will now discuss those features.

1.4.13 Java Library Packages

Recall that the `HelloWorld` application program used two predefined classes, the `String` and the `System` classes. Both of these classes are basic language classes in Java. The `HelloWorldApplet` program also uses predefined classes, such as `Applet` and `Graphics`. However, these two classes are not part of Java's basic language classes. To understand the difference between these classes, it will be necessary to talk briefly about how the Java class library is organized.

A **package** is a collection of interrelated classes in the Java class library. For example, the `java.lang` package contains classes, such as `Object`, `String`, and `System`, that are central to the Java language. Just about all Java programs use the classes in this package. The `java.awt` package provides classes, such as `Button`, `TextField`, and `Graphics`, that are used in graphical user interfaces (GUIs). The `java.net` package provides classes used for networking tasks, and the `java.io` package provides classes used for input and output operations.

All Java classes belong to some package, including those that are programmer defined. To assign a class to a package, you would provide a `package` statement as the first statement in the file that contains the class definition. For example, the files containing the definitions of the classes in the `java.lang` package all begin with the following statement:

```
package java.lang;
```

If you omit the `package` statement, as we do for the programs in this book, Java places such classes into an unnamed default package.

Thus, the full name of any Java class includes the name of the package that contains it. For example, the full name for the `System` class is `java.lang.System`, and the full name for the `String` class is `java.lang.String`. Similarly, the full name for the `Graphics` class is `java.awt.Graphics`. In short, the full name for a Java class takes the following form:

package.class

In other words, the full name of any class provides its package name as a prefix.

Of all the packages in the Java library, the `java.lang` package is the only one whose classes are available by their shorthand names to all Java programs. This means that when a program uses a class from the `java.lang` package, it can refer to it simply by its class name. For example, in the `HelloWorld` program we referred directly to the `String` class rather than to `java.lang.String`.

1.4.14   The `import` Statement

The `import` statement makes Java classes available to programs under their abbreviated names. Any public class in the Java class library is available to a program by its fully qualified name. Thus, if a program was using the `Graphics` class, it could always refer to it as `java.awt.Graphics`. However, being able to refer to `Graphics` by its shorthand name makes the program a bit shorter and more readable.

The `import` statement doesn't actually load classes into the program. It just makes their abbreviated names available. For example, the import statements in `HelloWorldApplet` allow us to refer to the `Applet` and `Graphics` classes by their abbreviated names (Fig. 1.9).

The `import` statement takes two possible forms:

import *package.class*

import *package.*

The first form allows a specific class to be known by its abbreviated name. The second form, which uses the asterisk as a wildcard character (`'*'`), allows all the classes in the specified package to be known by their short names. The `import` statements in `HelloWorldApplet` are examples of the first form. The following example,

```
import java.lang.*;
```

allows all the classes in the `java.lang` package to be referred to by their class names alone. In fact, this particular `import` statement is implicit in every Java program.

1.4.15   Qualified Names in Java

In the preceding subsections we saw several examples of names in Java programs that used *dot notation*. A **qualified name** is a name that is separated into parts using Java's dot notation. Examples include package names, such as `java.awt`, class names, such as `java.applet.Applet`, and even method names, such as `helloworld.greet()`.

Just as in our natural language, the meaning of a name in a Java program depends on the context. For example, the expression `helloworld.greet()` refers to the `greet()` method, which belongs to the `HelloWorld` class. If we were using this expression from within that class, you wouldn't need to qualify the name in this way. You could just refer to `greet()` and it would be clear from the context which method you meant.

This is no different than using someone's first name ("Kim") when there's only one Kim around, but using a full name ("Kim Smith") when the first name alone would be too vague or ambiguous.

One thing that complicates the use of qualified names is that they are used to refer to different kinds of things in a Java program. But this is no different, really, than in our natural language, where the same names ("George Washington") can refer to people, bridges, universities, and so on. Here again, just as in our natural language, Java uses the context to understand the meaning of the name. For example, the expression `java.lang.System` refers to the `System` class in the `java.lang` package, whereas the expression `System.out.print()` refers to a method in the `System.out` object.

How can you tell these apart? Java can tell them apart because the first one occurs as part of an `import` statement, so it must be referring to something that belongs to a package. The second expression would only be valid in a context where a method invocation is allowed. You will have to learn a bit more about the Java language before you'll be able to completely understand these names, but the following provide some naming rules to get you started.

> **JAVA LANGUAGE RULE**   **Library Class Names.** By convention, class names in Java begin with an uppercase letter. When referenced as part of a package, the class name is the last part of the name. For example, `java.lang.System` refers to the `System` class in the `java.lang` package.

> **JAVA LANGUAGE RULE**   **Dot Notation.** Names expressed in Java's *dot notation* depend for their meaning on the context in which they are used. In qualified names—that is, names of the form X.Y.Z—the last item in the name (Z) is the *referent*—that is, the element being referred to. The items that precede it (X.Y.) are used to qualify or clarify the referent.

The fact that names are context dependent in this way certainly complicates the task of learning what's what in a Java program. Part of learning to use Java's built-in classes is learning where a particular object or method is defined. It is a syntax error if the Java compiler can't find the object or method that you are referencing.

> **DEBUGGING TIP: Not Found Error.** If Java cannot find the item you are referring to, it will report an "X not found" error, where X is the class, method, variable, or package being referred to.

1.5   Editing, Compiling, and Running a Java Program

In this section we discuss the nuts and bolts of how to compile and run a Java program. Java programs come in two different varieties, applications and applets, and the process differs slightly for each of them. We have already discussed some of the main language features of Java applications and applets, so in this section we focus more on features of the programming environment itself. Because we do not assume any particular programming environment in this book, our discussion will be somewhat generic. However, we do begin with a brief overview of the types of programming environments one might encounter.

1.5.1   Java Development Environments

A Java programming environment typically consists of several programs that perform different tasks required to edit, compile, and run a Java program. The following description will be based on the software development environment provided by Sun Microsystems, the company that developed Java. It is currently known as the *Java2 Platform, Standard Edition 5.0* (*J2SE 5.0*). Versions of J2SE are available for various platforms, including Unix, Windows, and Macintosh computers. Free downloads are available at Sun's Web site at `http://java.sun.com/j2se/`. (For more details about the J2SE, see Appendix B.)

In some cases, the individual programs that make up the J2SE are available in a single program-development environment known as an *integrated development environment* (*IDE*). Some examples include MetroWerk's Codewarrior, Borland's JBuilder, and Sun's own NetBeans IDE. Each of these provides a complete development package for editing, compiling, and running Java applications and applets on a variety of platforms, including Linux and Windows.

Figure 1.10 illustrates the process involved in creating and running a Java program. The discussion that follows assumes that you are using J2SE as your development environment to edit, compile, and run the example program. If you are using some other environment, you will need to read the documentation provided with the software to determine exactly how to edit, compile, and run Java programs in that environment.

1.5.2   Editing a Program

Any text editor may be used to edit a program by merely typing the program and making corrections as needed. Popular Unix and Linux editors include `vi` and `emacs`. Macintosh editors include `SimpleText` and `BBEdit`, and the `WinEdit` and `NotePad` editors are available for Windows.

As we have seen, a Java program consists of one or more class definitions. We will follow the convention of placing each class definition in its own file. (Normally in Java a source file should contain only one `public` class definition.) The files containing these classes' definitions must be named *ClassName.java* where *ClassName* is the name of the `public` Java class contained in the file.

> **JAVA LANGUAGE RULE**   **File Names.** A file that defines a `public` Java class named `ClassName` must be saved in a text file named `ClassName.java`. Otherwise an error will result.

User types program into a file
using a standard text editor.

Correct the syntax errors

text editor

HelloWorld.java ← Editor creates the **source program** in a disk file.

javac → syntax errors ? → Y → **javac** generates a list of error messages

N

HelloWorld.class ← **javac** creates the **bytecode** in a disk file.

Hello.html

appletviewer or Web browser

Applets require an HTML file.
Applet Programming

java

The Java Virtual Machine loads the class file into memory and interprets and runs the bytecode.

Figure 1.10 Editing, compiling, and running `HelloWorld.java`.

For example, in the case of our `HelloWorld` application program, the file must be named `HelloWorld.java`, and for `HelloWorldApplet` it must be named `HelloWorldApplet.java`. Java is *case sensitive*, which means that it pays attention to whether a letter is typed uppercase or lowercase. So it would be an error if the file containing the `HelloWorld` class were named `helloworld.java` or `Helloworld.java`. The error in this case would be a semantic error. Java would not be able to find the `HelloWorld` class because it would be looking for a file named `HelloWorld.java`.

JAVA LANGUAGE RULE   **Case Sensitivity.** Java is case sensitive, which means that it treats `helloWorld` and `Helloworld` as different names.

1.5.3 Compiling a Program

Recall that before you can run a Java source program you have to compile it into the Java bytecode, the intermediate code understood by the Java Virtual Machine (JVM). Source code for applets and applications must be compiled. To run a Java program, whether an applet or an application, the JVM is then used to interpret and execute the bytecode.

J2SE comes in two parts, a runtime program, called the *Java Runtime Environment* (*JRE*) and a development package, called the *Software Development Kit* (*SDK*). If you are just going to run Java programs, you need only install the JRE on your computer. In order to run Java applets, our browser, such as Internet Explorer and Netscape Navigator, must contain a plug-in version of the JRE. On the other hand, if you are going to be developing Java programs, you will need to install the SDK as well.

The Java SDK compiler is named `javac`. In some environments—such as within Linux or at the Windows command prompt —`HelloWorld.java` would be compiled by typing the following command at the system prompt:

```
javac HelloWorld.java
```

As Figure 1.10 illustrates, if the `HelloWorld.java` program does not contain errors, the result of this command is the creation of a Java bytecode file named `HelloWorld.class`—a file that has the same prefix as the source file but with the suffix `.class` rather than `.java`. By default, the bytecode file will be placed in the same directory as the source file. If `javac` detects errors in the Java code, a list of error messages will be printed.

1.5.4 Running a Java Application Program

In order to run (or execute) a program on any computer, the program's *executable code* must be loaded into the computer's main memory. For Java environments, this means that the program's `.class` file must be loaded into the computer's memory, where it is then interpreted by the Java Virtual Machine. To run a Java program on Linux systems or at the Windows command prompt, type

```
java HelloWorld
```

on the command line. This command loads the JVM, which will then load and interpret the application's bytecode (`HelloWorld.class`). The "HelloWorld" string will be displayed on the command line.

On a Macintosh system or within an IDE, neither of which typically has a command-line interface, you would select the compile and run commands from a menu. Once the code is compiled, the run command will cause the JVM to be loaded and the bytecode to be interpreted. The "HelloWorld!" output would appear in a text-based window that automatically pops up on your computer screen. In any case, regardless of the system you use, running the `HelloWorld` application program will cause the "HelloWorld" message to be displayed on a standard output device of some kind (Fig. 1.11).

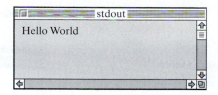

Figure 1.11   Running the `HelloWorld.java` application program.

1.5.5   Running a Java Applet

To run a Java applet, you need to use either a Web browser or the SDK's `appletviewer`, a stripped-down Web browser for running applets. The Web browser (or appletviewer) uses an HTML (HyperText Markup Language) document to locate the applet's bytecode files on the Web (or directly on your computer's hard drive). The HTML file must contain an `<applet>` tag, as shown in Figure 1.12, which tells the browser where to locate the applet's bytecode. (See Appendix B for more details about the appletviewer and the `<applet>` tag.)

If the applet tag is correctly specified, the Web browser (or appletviewer) will locate the Java bytecode file on the Web (or on your system's hard drive). It will then load the JVM, which will load the applet's code into memory and interpret and execute it.

The code in Figure 1.12 would be placed in a file named with an `.html` suffix to indicate that it is an HTML file. The name of the file in this case is not important, but let's suppose we give it the name `Hello.html`. What is important is to specify the `<applet>` tag correctly, designating the name of the Java bytecode that is to be executed, for example, `HelloWorld-Applet.class`. It is also necessary for the HTML file to be stored in the same directory or folder as the class file. (There are ways to get around this, but we'll deal with them later.)

Given the correctly coded HTML file, `Hello.html`, the `appletviewer` can be used to load and run the applet by typing the following command on the command line:

```
appletviewer Hello.html
```

If you are using a Web browser to run the applet, you would use the browser's menu to load `Hello.html` into the browser, either across the Internet by supplying its *URL* (*Uniform*

```
<html>
...
<applet code="HelloWorldApplet.class" width= 200 height=200>
</applet>
...
</html>
```

Figure 1.12   An example of an HTML file containing an `<applet>` tag. This specification will run the Java program named `HelloWorldApplet.class`.

Figure 1.13 Running HelloWorl-dApplet.java applet.

Resource Locator) or from your local disk by supplying the HTML file's full path name. (You can use the browser's *Open File* command to located the HTML file.) In any case, the appletviewer or the browser will load the program's bytecode into the computer's main memory and then verify, interpret, and execute the program. The result, as shown in Figure 1.13, is that the "Hello World!" message will be displayed within the browser or appletviewer window.

1.6 From the Java Library: `System` and `PrintStream`

java.sun.com/docs

JAVA COMES with a library of classes that can be used to perform common tasks. The Java class library is organized into a set of packages, where each package contains a collection of related classes. Throughout the book we will identify library classes and explain how to use them. In this section we introduce the `System` and `PrintStream` classes, which are used for printing a program's output.

Java programs need to be able to accept input and to display output. Deciding how a program will handle input and output (I/O) is part of designing its *user interface*, a topic we take up in detail in Chapter 4. The simplest type of user interface is a *command-line interface*, in which input is taken from the command line through the keyboard, and output is displayed on the console. Some Java applications use this type of interface. Another type of user interface is a *Graphical User Interface* (*GUI*), which uses buttons, text fields, and other graphical components for input and output. Java applets use GUIs, as do many Java applications. Because we want to be able to write programs that generate output, this section describes how Java handles simple console output.

In Java, any source or destination for I/O is considered a *stream* of bytes or characters. To perform output, we insert bytes or characters into the stream. To perform input, we extract bytes or characters from the stream. Even characters entered at a keyboard, if considered as a sequence of keystrokes, can be represented as a stream.

There are no I/O statements in the Java language. Instead, I/O is handled through methods that belong to classes contained in the `java.io` package. We have already seen how the output method `println()` is used to output a string to the console. For example, the following `println()` statement

```
System.out.println("Hello World");
```

prints the message "Hello World" on the Java console. Let's now examine this statement more carefully to see how it makes use of the Java I/O classes.

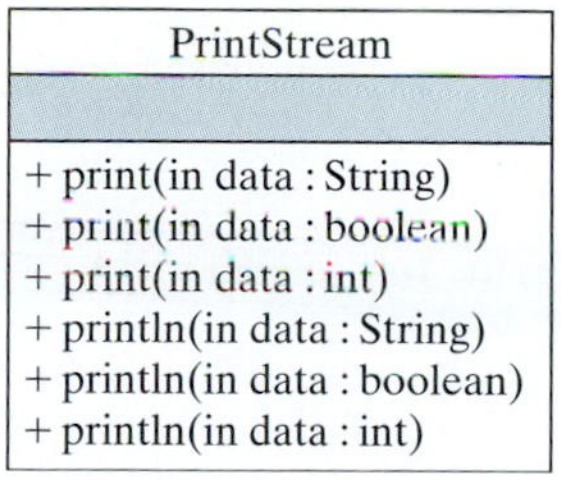

PrintStream
+ print(in data : String)
+ print(in data : boolean)
+ print(in data : int)
+ println(in data : String)
+ println(in data : boolean)
+ println(in data : int)

Figure 1.14 A UML class diagram of the PrintStream class.

The `java.io.PrintStream` class is Java's printing expert, so to speak. It contains a variety of `print()` and `println()` methods that can be used to print all of the various types of data we find in a Java program. A partial definition of `PrintStream` is shown in Figure 1.14. Note that in this case the `PrintStream` class has no attributes, just operations or methods.

Because the various `print()` and `println()` methods are instance methods of a `PrintStream` object, we can only use them by finding a `PrintStream` object and "telling" it to print data for us. As shown in Figure 1.15, Java's `java.lang.System` class contains three predefined streams, including two `PrintStream` objects. This class has public (+) attributes. None of its public methods are shown here.

Both the `System.out` and `System.err` objects can be used to write output to the console. As its name suggests, the `err` stream is used primarily for error messages, whereas the `out` stream is used for other printed output. Similarly, as its name suggests, the `System.in` object can be used to handle input, which will be covered in Chapter 2.

The only difference between the `print()` and `println()` methods is that `println()` will also print a carriage return and line feed after printing its data, thereby allowing subsequent output to be printed on a new line. For example, the following statements

```
System.out.print("hello");
System.out.println("hello again");
System.out.println("goodbye");
```

would produce the following output:

```
hellohello again
goodbye
```

Now that we know how to use Java's printing expert, let's use it to "sing" a version of "Old MacDonald Had a Farm." As you might guess, this program will simply consist of a sequence of `System.out.println()` statements each of which prints a line of the verse. The complete Java application program is shown in Figure 1.16.

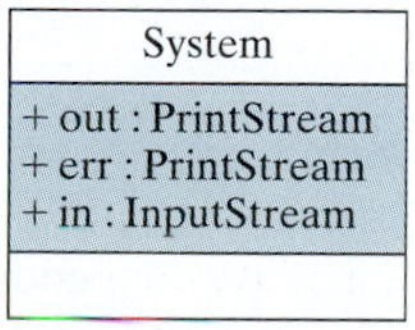

System
+ out : PrintStream
+ err : PrintStream
+ in : InputStream

Figure 1.15 The System class.

```
public class OldMacDonald
{
  public static void main(String args[])                    // Main method
  {
    System.out.println("Old MacDonald had a farm");
    System.out.println("E I E I O.");
    System.out.println("And on his farm he had a duck.");
    System.out.println("E I E I O.");
    System.out.println("With a quack quack here.");
    System.out.println("And a quack quack there.");
    System.out.println("Here a quack, there a quack,");
    System.out.println("Everywhere a quack quack.");
    System.out.println("Old MacDonald had a farm");
    System.out.println("E I E I O.");
  }                                                          // End of main
}                                                            // End of OldMacDonald
```

Figure 1.16 The `OldMacDonald.java` class.

This example illustrates the importance of using the Java class library. If there's a task we want to perform, one of the first things we should ask is whether there is already an "expert" in Java's class library that performs it. If so, we can use methods provided by the expert to perform the task in question.

EFFECTIVE DESIGN: Using the Java Library. Learning how to use classes and objects from the Java class library is an important part of object-oriented programming in Java.

SELF-STUDY EXERCISES

```
*********
* ** ** *
*   **   *
* *    * *
* ****   *
*********
```

EXERCISE 1.3 One good way to learn how to write programs is to modify existing programs. Modify the `OldMacDonald` class to "sing" one more verse of the song.

EXERCISE 1.4 Write a Java class that prints the design shown on the left.

CHAPTER SUMMARY

Technical Terms

algorithm	assignment statement
applet	comment
application program	compound statement (block)

data type	package
declaration statement	parameter
default constructor	primitive data type
executable statement	pseudocode
expression	
identifier	qualified name
keyword	semantics
literal value	statement
object instantiation	stepwise refinement
operator	syntax

Summary of Important Points

- Good program design requires that each object and method have a well-defined role and a clear definition of what information is needed for the task and what results will be produced.
- Good program design is important; if you start coding too soon, without allowing the time to design it properly, the longer the program will take to finish. Good program design strives for readability, clarity, and flexibility.
- Testing a program is very important and must be done with care, but it can only reveal the presence of bugs, not their absence.
- An algorithm is a step-by-step process that solves some problem. Algorithms are often described in pseudocode, a hybrid language that combines English and programming-language constructs.
- A syntax error occurs when a statement breaks a Java syntax rules. Syntax errors are detected by the compiler. A semantic error is an error in the program's design and cannot be detected by the compiler.
- Writing Java code should follow the stepwise refinement process.
- Double slashes (//) are used to make a single-line comment. Comments that extend over several lines must begin with /* and end with */.
- An *identifier* must begin with a letter of the alphabet and may consist of any number of letters, digits, and the special characters _ and $. An identifier cannot be identical to a Java keyword. Identifiers are case sensitive.
- A *keyword* is a term that has special meaning in the Java language (Table 1.1).
- Examples of Java's *primitive data types* include the `int`, `boolean`, and `double` types.
- A variable is a named storage location. In Java, a variable must be declared before it can be used.
- A literal value is an actual value of some type, such as a `String` ("Hello") or an `int` (5).
- A declaration statement has the form: Type *VariableName*;
- An assignment statement has the form: *VariableName = Expression*; When it is executed it determines the value of the *Expression* on the right of the assignment operator (=) and stores the value in the variable named on the left.
- Java's operators are type dependent, where the type is dependent on the data being manipulated. When adding two `int` values (7 + 8), the + operation produces an `int` result.
- A class definition has two parts: a class header and a class body. A class header takes the form of optional modifiers followed by the word `class` followed by an identifier naming the class, followed, optionally, by the keyword `extends` and the name of the class's superclass.

- There are generally two kinds of elements declared and defined in the class body: variables and methods.
- Object instantiation is the process of creating an instance of a class using the **new** operator in conjunction with one of the class's constructors.
- Dot notation takes the form *qualifiers.elementName*. The expression System.out.print ("hello") uses Java dot notation to invoke the print() method of the System.out object.
- A Java application program runs in standalone mode. A Java applet is a program that runs in the context of a Java-enabled browser. Java applets are identified in HTML documents by using the <applet> tag.
- A Java source program must be stored in a file that has a .java extension. A Java bytecode file has the same name as the source file but a .class extension. It is an error in Java if the name of the source file is not identical to the name of the public Java class defined within the file.
- Java programs are first compiled into bytecode and then interpreted by the Java Virtual Machine (JVM).

SOLUTIONS TO SELF-STUDY EXERCISES

SOLUTION 1.1   The value 12 is stored in num.

SOLUTION 1.2   int num2 = 711 + 712;

SOLUTION 1.3   The definition of the OldMacDonald class is:

```java
public class OldMacDonald
{
  public static void main(String args[])                  // Main method
  {
    System.out.println("Old MacDonald had a farm");
    System.out.println("E I E I O.");
    System.out.println("And on his farm he had a duck.");
    System.out.println("E I E I O.");
    System.out.println("With a quack quack here.");
    System.out.println("And a quack quack there.");
    System.out.println("Here a quack, there a quack,");
    System.out.println("Everywhere a quack quack.");
    System.out.println("Old MacDonald had a farm");
    System.out.println("E I E I O.");

    System.out.println("Old MacDonald had a farm");
    System.out.println("E I E I O.");
    System.out.println("And on his farm he had a pig.");
    System.out.println("E I E I O.");
    System.out.println("With an oink oink here.");
    System.out.println("And an oink oink   there.");
    System.out.println("Here an oink, there an oink,");
    System.out.println("Everywhere an oink oink.");
    System.out.println("Old MacDonald had a farm");
    System.out.println("E I E I O.");
  }                                                       // End of main
}                                                         // End of OldMacDonald
```

SOLUTION 1.4   The definition of the `Pattern` class is:

```
public class Pattern
{
  public static void main(String args[])      // Main method
  {
    System.out.println("*********");
    System.out.println("* **   ** *");
    System.out.println("*    **    *");
    System.out.println("* *      * *");
    System.out.println("*   ****   *");
    System.out.println("*********");
  }                                            // End of main
}                                              // End of Pattern
```

EXERCISES

EXERCISE 1.1   Fill in the blanks in each of the following statements.

  a. A Java class definition contains an object's _____ and _____.
  b. A method definition contains two parts, a _____ and a _____.

EXERCISE 1.2   Explain the difference between each of the following pairs of concepts.

  a. *Application* and *applet*.
  b. *Single-line* comment and *multiline* comment.
  c. *Compiling* and *running* a program.
  d. *Source code* file and *bytecode* file.
  e. *Syntax* and *semantics*.
  f. *Syntax error* and *semantic error*.
  g. *Data* and *methods*.
  h. *Variable* and *method*.
  i. *Algorithm* and *method*.
  j. *Pseudocode* and *Java code*.
  k. *Method definition* and *method invocation*.

EXERCISE 1.3   For each of the following, identify it as either a syntax error or a semantic error.
Justify your answers.

  a. Write a class header as `public Class MyClass`.
  b. Define the `init()` header as `public vid init()`.
  c. Print a string of five asterisks by `System.out.println("***");`.
  d. Forget the semicolon at the end of a `println()` statement.
  e. Calculate the sum of two numbers as `N — M`.

EXERCISE 1.4 Suppose you have a Java program stored in a file named `Test.java`. Describe the compilation and execution process for this program, naming any other files that would be created.

EXERCISE 1.5 Suppose *N* is 15. What numbers would be output by the following pseudocode algorithm? Suppose *N* is 6. What would be output by the algorithm in that case?

```
0. Print N.
1. If N equals 1, stop.
2. If N is even, divide it by 2.
3. If N is odd, triple it and add 1.
4. Go to step 0.
```

EXERCISE 1.6 Suppose *N* is 5 and *M* is 3. What value would be reported by the following pseudocode algorithm? In general, what quantity does this algorithm calculate?

```
0. Write 0 on a piece of paper.
1. If M equals 0, report what's on the paper and stop.
2. Add N to the quantity written on the paper.
3. Subtract 1 from M.
4. Go to step 1.
```

EXERCISE 1.7 **Puzzle Problem**: You are given two different-length ropes that have the characteristic that they both take exactly one hour to burn. However, neither rope burns at a constant rate. Some sections of the ropes burn very fast; other sections burn very slowly. All you have to work with is a box of matches and the two ropes. Describe an algorithm that uses the ropes and the matches to calculate when exactly 45 minutes have elapsed.

EXERCISE 1.8 **Puzzle Problem**: A polar bear that lives right at the North Pole can walk due south for one hour, due east for one hour, and due north for one hour, and end up right back where it started. Is it possible to do this anywhere else on earth? Explain.

EXERCISE 1.9 **Puzzle Problem**: Lewis Carroll, the author of *Alice in Wonderland*, used the following puzzle to entertain his guests: A captive queen weighing 195 pounds, her son weighing 90 pounds, and her daughter weighing 165 pounds, were trapped in a very high tower. Outside their window was a pulley and rope with a basket fastened on each end. They managed to escape by using the baskets and a 75-pound weight they found in the tower. How did they do it? The problem is that anytime the difference in weight between the two baskets is more than 15 pounds, someone might get hurt. Describe an algorithm that gets them down safely.

EXERCISE 1.10   Puzzle Problem: Here's another Carroll favorite: A farmer needs to cross a river with a fox, a goose, and a bag of corn. There's a rowboat that will hold the farmer and one other passenger. The problem is that the fox will eat the goose if they are left alone on the riverbank, and the goose will eat the corn if they are left alone on the riverbank. Write an algorithm that describes how he got across without losing any of his possessions.

EXERCISE 1.11   Puzzle Problem: Have you heard this one? A farmer lent the mechanic next door a 40-pound weight. Unfortunately, the mechanic dropped the weight and it broke into four pieces. The good news, according to the mechanic, is that it is still possible to use the four pieces to weigh any quantity between 1 and 40 pounds on a balance scale. How much did each of the four pieces weigh? (*Hint*: You can weigh a 4-pound object on a balance by putting a 5-pound weight on one side and a 1-pound weight on the other.)

EXERCISE 1.12   Suppose your little sister asks you to show her how to use a pocket calculator so that she can calculate her homework average in her science course. Describe an algorithm that she can use to find the average of 10 homework grades.

EXERCISE 1.13   A Caesar cipher is a secret code in which each letter of the alphabet is shifted by N letters to the right, with the letters at the end of the alphabet wrapping around to the beginning. For example, if N is 1, when we shift each letter to the right, the word *daze* would be written as *ebaf*. Note that the z has wrapped around to the beginning of the alphabet. Describe an algorithm that can be used to create a Caesar-encoded message with a shift of 5.

EXERCISE 1.14   Suppose you received the message "sxccohv duh ixq," which you know to be a Caesar cipher. Figure out what it says and then describe an algorithm that will always find what the message said regardless of the size of the shift that was used.

EXERCISE 1.15   Suppose you're talking to your little brother on the phone and he wants you to calculate his homework average. All you have to work with is a piece of chalk and a very small chalkboard—big enough to write one four-digit number. What's more, although your little brother knows how to read numbers, he doesn't know how to count very well so he can't tell you how many grades there are. All he can do is read the numbers to you. Describe an algorithm that will calculate the correct average under these conditions.

EXERCISE 1.16   Write a *header* for a public applet named `SampleApplet`.

EXERCISE 1.17   Write a *header* for a public method named `getName`.

EXERCISE 1.18   Design a class to represent a geometric rectangle with a given length and width, such that it is capable of calculating the area and the perimeter of the rectangle.

EXERCISE 1.19   Modify the `OldMacDonald` class to "sing" either "Mary Had a Little Lamb" or your favorite nursery rhyme.

EXERCISE 1.20 Define a Java class called `Patterns`, modeled after `OldMacDonald`, that will print the following patterns of asterisks, one after the other heading down the page:

```
*****        *****      *****
 ****        *   *      *  *  *
  ***        *   *         *  *
   **        *   *      *  *  *
    *        *****      *****
```

EXERCISE 1.21 Write a Java class that prints your initials as block letters, as shown in the example in the margin.

EXERCISE 1.22   Challenge: Define a class that represents a `Temperature` object. It should store the current temperature in an instance variable of type `double`, and it should have two `public` methods, `setTemp(double t)`, which assigns `t` to the instance variable, and `getTemp()`, which `returns` the value of the instance variable. Use the `Riddle` class as a model.

EXERCISE 1.23   Challenge: Define a class named `TaxWhiz` that computes the sales tax for a purchase. It should store the current tax rate as an instance variable. Following the model of the `Riddle` class, you can initialize the rate using a `TaxWhiz()` method. This class should have one `public` method, `calcTax(double purchase)`, which `returns` a `double`, whose value is `purchases` times the tax rate. For example, if the tax rate is 4 percent, 0.04, and the purchase is $100, then `calcTax()` should return 4.0.

EXERCISE 1.24 What is stored in the variables `num1` and `num2` after the following statements are executed?

```
int num1 = 5;
int num2 = 8;
num1 = num1 + num2;
num2 = num1 + num2;
```

EXERCISE 1.25 Write a series of statements that will declare a variable of type `int` called `num` and store in it the difference between 61 and 51.

UML Exercises

EXERCISE 1.26 Modify the UML diagram of the `Riddle` class to contain a method named `getRiddle()` that would return the riddle's question and answer.

EXERCISE 1.27 Draw a UML class diagram representing the following class: The name of the class is `Circle`. It has one attribute, a `radius` represented by a `double` value. It has one operation, `calculateArea()`, which returns a `double`. Its attributes should be designated as private and its method as public.

EXERCISE 1.28   To represent a triangle we need attributes for each of its three sides and operations to create a triangle, calculate its area, and calculate its perimeter. Draw a UML diagram to represent this triangle.

EXERCISE 1.29   Try to give the Java class definition for the class described in the UML diagram shown in Figure 1.17.

Figure 1.17   The Person class.

Photograph courtesy of Russ Lappa, Prentice Hall School division.

2

Objects: Using, Creating, and Defining

OBJECTIVES

After studying this chapter, you will

- Be familiar with using variables to store and manipulate simple data.
- Be familiar with creating and using objects.
- Understand the relationship between classes and objects.
- Understand the difference between objects and data of primitive type.
- Understand the difference between static and instance elements of a class.
- Be able to understand and design a simple class in Java.
- Understand some of the basic principles of object-oriented programming.

OUTLINE

2.1 Introduction

This chapter introduces some more of the basic principles of object-oriented programming. We begin by looking at some examples of creating and using objects of type String and Graphics. Then we examine how user-defined classes are used by doing a detailed walk-through of the Riddle class we saw in Chapter 1. We focus on the basic Java language elements involved. By the end of these sections, you should know how to identify the key elements that make up a Java program.

We then present a detailed example of the program-development process by designing and implementing a class that models a certain two-person game. The design is represented using UML notation.

2.2 Using String Objects

A Java program is a collection of interacting objects, where each object is a module that encapsulates a portion of the program's attributes and actions. Objects belong to classes, which serve as templates, or blueprints, for creating objects. Think again of the cookie-cutter analogy. A class is like a cookie cutter. Just as a cookie cutter is used to shape and create individual cookies, a class definition is used to shape and create individual objects.

Programming in Java is primarily a matter of designing and defining class definitions, which are then used to construct objects. The objects perform the program's desired actions. To push the cookie-cutter analogy a little further, designing and defining a class is like building a cookie cutter. Obviously, very few of us would bake cookies if we first had to design and build the cookie cutters. We'd be better off using a pre-built cookie cutter. By the same token, rather than designing our own classes, it will be easier to get into "baking" programs if we begin by using some predefined Java classes.

The Java library contains many predefined classes that we will use in our programs. So let's begin our study of programming by using two of these classes, the String and Graphics classes.

2.2.1 Creating and Combining Strings

Strings are very useful objects in Java and in all computer programs. They are used for inputting and outputting all types of data. Therefore, it essential that we learn how to create and use String objects.

Figure 2.1 provides an overview of a very small part of Java's String class. In addition to the two String() constructor methods, which are used to create strings, it lists several

Figure 2.1 A partial representation of the String class.

```
                String
        ─────────────────────
        − value
        − count
        ─────────────────────
        + String()
        + String(in s : String)
        + length() : int
        + concat(in s : String) : String
        + equals(in s : String) : boolean
```

useful instance methods that can be used to manipulate strings. The String class also has two instance variables. One stores the String's *value*, which is a string of characters such as "Hello98," and the other stores the String's *count*, which is the number of characters in its string value.

Recall from Chapter 0 that in order to get things done in a program we send messages to objects. The messages must correspond to the object's instance methods. Sending a message to an object is a matter of calling one of its instance methods. In effect, we use an object's methods to get the object to perform certain actions for us. For example, if we have a String, named str and we want to find out how many characters it contains, we can call its length() method, using the expression str.length(). If we want to print str's length, we can embed this expression in a print statement:

```
System.out.println(str.length()); // Print str's length
```

In general, to use an object's instance method, we refer to the method in dot notation by first naming the object and then the method:

Dot notation

   objectName.methodName() ;

The *objectName* refers to a particular object, and the methodName() refers to one of its instance methods.

As this example makes clear, instance methods belong to objects, and in order to use a method, you must first have an object that has that method. Thus, to use one of the String methods in a program, we must first create a String object.

To create a String object in a program, we first declare a String variable.

```
String str; // Declare a String variable named str
```

We then create a String object by using the new keyword in conjunction with one of the String() constructors. We assign the new object to the variable we declared:

```
str = new String("Hello"); // Create a String object
```

This example will create a String that contains, as its value, the word "Hello" that is passed in by the constructor. The String object that this creates is shown in Figure 2.2.

Figure 2.2 A String object stores a sequence of characters and a count giving the number of characters.

str : String
value = "Hello"
count = 5

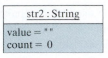

Figure 2.3   The empty string has a value of "" and its length is 0.

We can also use a constructor with an empty parameter list. Note that in this case we combine the *variable declaration* and the *object creation* into one statement:

```
String str2 = new String(); // Create a String
```

This example will create a `String` object that contains the empty string as its value. The **empty string** has the literal value ""—that is, a pair of double quotes that contain no characters. Because the empty string has no characters, the `count` variable stores a zero (Fig. 2.3).

Note that we use a constructor to assign an initial value to a variable of type `String` (or of a type equal to any other class). This differs from how we assign an initial value to variables of primitive type, for which we use a simple assignment operator. This difference is related to an important difference in the way Java treats these two types of variables. Variables of primitive type are names for memory locations where values of primitive type are stored. As soon as they are declared they are assigned a **default value** of that primitive type. The default value for `int` is 0, and the default value for `boolean` is `false`. On the other hand, variables declared to be of a type equal to a class name are designed to store a **reference** to an object of that type. (A reference is also called a **pointer** because it points to the memory address where the object itself is stored.) A constructor creates an object somewhere in memory and supplies a reference to it that is stored in the variable. For this reason, variables that are declared as a type equal to a class name are said to be variables of reference type, or **reference variables**. Reference variables have a special default value called `null` after they are declared and before they are assigned a reference. It is possible to check whether or not a reference variable contains a reference to an actual object by checking whether or not it contains this **null pointer**.

Once you have constructed a `String` object, you can use any of the methods shown in Figure 2.1 on it. As we have already seen, we use dot notation to call one of the methods. Thus, we first mention the name of the object followed by a period (dot), followed by the name of the method. For example, the following statements print the lengths of our two strings:

```
System.out.println(str.length());
System.out.println(str2.length());
```

Another useful `String` method is the `concat(String)` method which can be used to *concatenate* two strings. This method takes a `String` argument. It returns a `String` that combines the `String` argument to the `String` that the method is called on. Consider this example:

```
String s1 = new String("George ");
String s2 = new String("Washington");
System.out.println(s1.concat(s2));
```

In this case, the `concat()` method adds the `String` *s2* to the end of the `String` *s1*. The result, which gets printed, will be the `String` "George Washington."

Because strings are so important, Java allows a number of shortcuts to be used when creating and concatenating strings. For example, you don't have to use `new String()` when creating a new string object. The following code will also work:

```
String s1 = "George ";
String s2 = "Washington";
```

Similarly, an easier way to concatenate two `String` objects is to use the plus sign (+), which serves as a *concatenation operator* in Java:

```
System.out.println(s1 + s2);
```

Another useful `String` method is the `equals()` method. This is a `boolean` method that is used to compare two `String`s. If both `String`s have the same characters, in the same order, it will return true. Otherwise it will return false. For example, consider the following code segment:

```
String s1 = "Hello";
String s2 = "Hello";
String s3 = "hello";
```

In this case, the expression `s1.equals(s2)` will be true, but `s1.equals(s3)` will be false.

It is important to note that the empty string is not the same as a `String` variable that contains `null`. Executing the statements:

```
String s1;
String s2 = "";
System.out.println(s1.equals(s2));
```

will not only not print out `true`; it will cause the program to terminate abnormally. It is an error to use the method of a `String` variable, or any other variable whose type is a class, before it has been assigned an object. When the preceding code is executed, it will report a **null pointer exception**, one of the most common runtime errors. When you see that error message, it means that some method was executed on a variable that does not refer to an object. On the other hand, the empty string is a perfectly good `String` object which just happens to contain zero characters.

Figure 2.4 on the next page shows a program that uses string concatenation to create some silly sentences. The program declares a number of string variables, named `s`, `s1`, and so on, and it instantiates a `String` object for each variable to refer to. It then prints out a top-five list using the concatenation operator to combine strings. Can you figure out what it prints without running it?

```
public class StringPuns
{
  public static void main(String args[])
  { String s = new String("string");
    String s1 = s.concat(" puns.");
    System.out.println("Here are the top 5 " + s1);
    String s2 = "5. Hey baby, wanna ";
    String s3 = s + " along with me.";
    System.out.println(s2 + s3);
    System.out.println("4. I've got the world on a " + s + ".");
    String s4 = new String("two");
    String s5 = ". You have more class than a ";
    System.out.print(s4.length());
    System.out.println(s5 + s + " of pearls.");
    System.out.print("2. It is ");
    System.out.print(s.equals("string"));
    System.out.println(" that I am no " + s + " bean.");
    String s6 = " quintet.";
    System.out.println("1. These puns form a " + s + s6);
  } // main()
} // StringPuns class
```

Figure 2.4   A program that prints silly string puns.

SELF-STUDY EXERCISES

EXERCISE 2.1   What is the output to the console window when the following Java code fragment
is executed:

```
String s = "ing";
System.out.println("The s" + s + s + " k" + s + ".");
```

2.3   Drawing Shapes with a Graphics Object (Optional)

All of the instance methods of the String class that we have examined return values. The
length() method returns an int value, and the concat() method returns a String. Classes
also very commonly define instance methods that perform actions but do not return a value.
The Graphics object, g, that appears in Chapter 1's HelloWorldApplet is one example.
The program is reproduced in Figure 2.5.

At this point we will not worry about the language features that enable the paint() method
to draw on the applet window when the applet is executed by a Web browser. We will focus
instead on the information needed to make good use of the g.drawString() method. The
first thing you should know is that, when the paint() method is executed, its parameter, g,
refers to an instance of the Graphics class. Unlike our other examples involving variables
that refer to objects, in this case there is no need to use a constructor to create an object of type
Graphics. We can assume that g already refers to such an object.

```
/*
 * HelloWorldApplet program
 */
import java.applet.Applet;              // Import the Applet class
import java.awt.Graphics;               //   and the Graphics class

public class HelloWorldApplet extends Applet // Class header
{                                       // Start of body
  public void paint(Graphics g)         // The paint method
  {
    g.drawString("Hello World",10,10);
  }                                     // End of paint
}                                       // End of HelloWorld
```

Figure 2.5   `HelloWorldApplet` program.

We already know that the statement

```
g.drawString("Hello World",10,10);
```

displays the `String` "Hello World" in the applet window. More generally, if `str` is a literal `String` value or a reference to a `String` object, and `x` and `y` are literal `int` values or `int` variables, then

```
g.drawString(str,x,y)
```

displays the `String` `str` from left to right in the applet window, beginning at a point which is `x` pixels from the left edge of the window and `y` pixels down from the top edge of the window. In an applet window, the point with coordinates (0,0) is at the top-left corner. The horizontal axis grows positively from left to right. The vertical axis grows positively from top to bottom (Fig. 2.6). (A *pixel* is a dot on the console window that can be set to a certain color.) Note that increasing the value of `y` will cause `str` to be displayed lower. This is the opposite of the usual *x* and *y* coordinate system used in mathematics, where increasing the *y* value designates a higher point.

Figure 2.6   Coordinate system of a Java window.

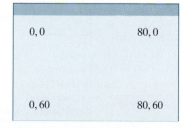

| 0,0 | 80,0 |
| 0,60 | 80,60 |

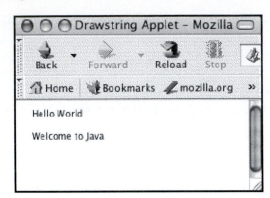

Figure 2.7 "Hello World" is drawn at coordinate (10, 10) and "Welcome to Java" at (10, 35) in the applet window.

With this information about `g.drawString()`, we can calculate where to display any message in the applet window. For example, if we wish to display the message "Welcome to Java" 25 pixels below where "Hello World" is displayed, we could use the statements

```
g.drawString("Hello World",10,10);
g.drawString("Welcome to Java",10,35);
```

in the body of `HelloWorldApplet`'s `paint()` method. The result of these statements would appear as shown in Figure 2.7.

2.3.1 Graphics Drawing Methods

The `Graphics` class discussed in the preceding section also has methods that can be used to draw geometric shapes in different colors. These methods can be used to create graphical user interfaces that are more interesting or to give a visual representation of data, such as a pie chart or a bar graph.

There are two `Graphics` methods for drawing rectangles, `fillRect()` and `drawRect()` (Fig. 2.8). The first draws a rectangle and fills it with the current drawing color, and the second just draws the outline of the rectangle. Using the `Graphics` object, `g`, each of these is called in the same way as the `drawString()` method from the previous example. Each of these methods takes four `int` arguments, which specify the rectangle's location and size. Thus, a call to `fillRect()` would take the form

```
g.fillRect(x,y,width,height);
```

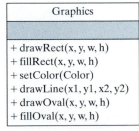

Graphics
+ drawRect(x, y, w, h)
+ fillRect(x, y, w, h)
+ setColor(Color)
+ drawLine(x1, y1, x2, y2)
+ drawOval(x, y, w, h)
+ fillOval(x, y, w, h)

Figure 2.8 Some of the drawing methods in the `Graphics` class.

where x and y arguments specify the location of the upper-left corner of the rectangle as x pixels from the left edge of the window and y pixels down from the top edge of the window. The width and height arguments specify the width and height of the rectangle in pixels. The drawRect() method also takes the same four arguments.

A Graphics object stores a single color for use in drawing shapes or displaying strings with drawString(). If we wish to draw an interesting scene in the applet window, we need to understand how to use colors.

For a given Graphics object, such as g, the setColor() method will set its color for all subsequent drawing commands. The setColor() method takes, as an argument, an object of type Color. All we need to know about the Color class is that it is contained in the java.awt package and that it contains 13 constant Color objects corresponding to 13 common colors. Table 2.1 lists the 13 Color constants. Each name corresponds to the color it will represent in the program.

Table 2.1. Predefined color constants in the Color class.

Color.black	Color.green	Color.red	Color.blue	Color.lightGreen
Color.white	Color.cyan	Color.magenta	Color.yellow	Color.darkGray
Color.orange	Color.gray	Color.pink		

To demonstrate how the new Graphics methods can be used for creating more interesting applets, let's develop a plan for displaying the messages "Hello World" and "Welcome to Java" on an applet, but this time we will draw the first message inside a colored rectangle and the second inside a colored oval. For the rectangle, let's use the drawRect() method to create its border. We can choose colors arbitrarily, say, cyan for filling the rectangle, blue for its border, and black for the string itself. In order to have the message visible, we should fill a rectangle with the color cyan first, then draw the border of the rectangle in blue, and, finally, display the message in black.

Drawing and filling a Graphics oval is very similar to drawing and filling a rectangle. Note in Figure 2.8 that the fillOval() and drawOval() methods take the same four arguments as the corresponding rectangle methods. An oval is inscribed within an enclosing rectangle. The x and y arguments give the coordinates of the enclosing rectangle's top-left point. And the width and height arguments give the enclosing rectangle's dimensions.

All that remains is to choose the location and dimensions of the rectangles. We could specify one rectangle as having its upper-left corner 25 pixels to the right of the left edge of the applet window and 25 pixels down from the top edge. A medium-sized rectangle could have a width of 140 pixels and a height of 40 pixels. The statement

```
g.fillRect(25, 25, 140, 40);
```

will fill this rectangle with whatever color happens to be g's current color. A location 25 pixels to the right of the left edge of the rectangle and 25 pixels down from the top edge of the rectangle would have coordinates x = 50 and y = 50. Thus, the statement

```
g.drawString("Hello World", 50, 50);
```

```
import java.awt.*;
import java.applet.*;

public class HelloWorldGraphic  extends Applet
{ public void paint(Graphics g)
  { g.setColor(Color.cyan);                        // Set color
    g.fillRect(25, 25, 140, 40);                   // Fill rectangle
    g.setColor(Color.blue);                        // Set color
    g.drawRect(25, 25, 140, 40);                   // Outline rectangle
    g.setColor(Color.black);                       // Set color
    g.drawString("Hello World", 50, 50);           // Display string
    g.setColor(Color.yellow);
    g.fillOval(25, 75, 140, 40);                   // Fill oval
    g.setColor(Color.red);
    g.drawOval(25, 75, 140, 40);                   // Outline oval
    g.setColor(Color.black);
    g.drawString("Welcome to Java", 50, 100);
  } // paint()
} // HelloWorldGraphic class
```

Figure 2.9 The HelloWorldGraphic class is an applet that shows how to use color and drawing methods.

will display "Hello World" inside the rectangle. We can use similar planning to locate the oval and its enclosed message.

Thus, we now have sufficient information to finish the paint() method for accomplishing our plan. The completed program is displayed in Figure 2.9. Note how we repeatedly use the g.setColor() method to change g's current color before drawing each element of our picture.

Figure 2.10 shows what this applet looks like when run in a browser. To experiment with this applet, download its source code and its corresponding HTML file from the book's Web

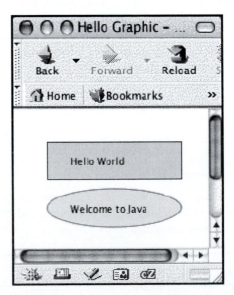

Figure 2.10 This is how the HelloWorldGraphic applet will look when run in a browser.

site, and compile and run it on your computer. If you've forgotten how to run an applet, review Section 1.5.5. Additional drawing capabilities will be explored throughout the text in sections that can either be covered or skipped.

2.4   Class Definition

To program in Java, the main thing you do is write class definitions for the various objects that will make up the program. A class definition *encapsulates* its objects' data and behavior. Once a class has been defined, it serves as a *template*, or blueprint, for creating individual *objects* or instances of the class.

The class as template

A class definition contains two types of elements: variables and methods. *Variables* are used to store the object's information. *Methods* are used to process the information. To design an object you need to answer five basic questions:

Variables and methods

1. What role will the object perform in the program?
2. What data or information will it need?
3. What actions will it take?
4. What interface will it present to other objects?
5. What information will it hide from other objects?

2.4.1   The `Riddle` Class

Our definition of the `Riddle` class from Chapter 1 is summarized in the UML diagram in Figure 2.11. A `Riddle` has two attributes, `question` and `answer`. Each of these variables stores a string of characters, which Java treats as data of type `String`. The `Riddle` class contains three methods. The `Riddle()` constructor method assigns initial values (q and a) to its `question` and `answer` variables. The `getQuestion()` and `getAnswer()` methods return the data stored in `question` and `answer` respectively.

The instance variables `question` and `answer` are designated as `private` (−), but the `Riddle()`, `getQuestion()` and `getAnswer()` methods are designated as `public` (+). These designations follow two important object-oriented design conventions, whose justification will become apparent as we discuss the `Riddle` class:

EFFECTIVE DESIGN: Private Variables. Instance variables are usually declared `private` so that they cannot be directly accessed by other objects.

Riddle
− question : String − answer : Sting
+ Riddle(q : String, a : String) + getQuestion( ) : String + getAnswer ( ) : String

Figure 2.11 The `Riddle` class.

```
public class Riddle
{ private String question;              // Instance variables
  private String answer;

  public Riddle(String q, String a)     // Constructor
  { question = q;
    answer = a;
  }                                     // Riddle constructor

  public String getQuestion()           // Instance method
  { return question;
  } // getQuestion()

  public String getAnswer()             // Instance method
  { return answer;
  } // getAnswer()
} // Riddle class
```

Figure 2.12 Definition of the `Riddle` class.

EFFECTIVE DESIGN: Public Methods. An object's `public` methods can be used by other objects to interact with the object. The `public` methods and variables of an object make up its **interface**.

Figure 2.12 shows the Java class definition that corresponds to the design given in the UML diagram. It contains the two `private` instance variables and defines the three `public` methods listed in the UML diagram. In a Java class definition, access to a class element, such as a variable or a method, is controlled by labeling it with either the `private` or the `public` *Access modifier* access modifier. An **access modifier** is a declaration that controls access to a class or one of its elements. Note that the `Riddle` class itself is declared `public`. This lets other classes have access to the class and to its public variables and methods.

Recall that a class is like a blueprint or a cookie cutter. The `Riddle` class defines the type of information (attributes) that each individual `Riddle` has, but it doesn't contain any actual values. It defines the methods (operations) that each `Riddle` can perform, but it doesn't actually perform the methods. In short, a class serves as a template, providing a detailed *Class as blueprint* blueprint of the objects (or instances) of that class.

2.4.2 The `RiddleUser` Class

Now that we have defined the `Riddle` class, we can test whether it works correctly by creating `Riddle` objects and "asking" them to tell us their riddles. To do this we need to define a `main()` method, which can be defined either within the `Riddle` class itself or in a second class named something like `RiddleUser`.

One advantage of using a second class is that it gets us in the habit of thinking about the need for a separate class to serve as a user interface, with a separate set of tasks from the *User interface* `Riddle` class. A **user interface** is an object or class that handles the interaction between a program's user and the rest of the program's computational tasks. This concept is illustrated in Figure 2.13. Note that we use the general term *computational object* to distinguish the rest of the program's computations from the user interface. Obviously, the exact nature of the computation will vary from program to program, just as will the details of the user interface.

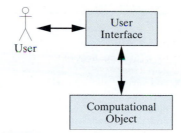

Figure 2.13 The user interface handles interactions between the user and the rest of the program.

The computation done by our `Riddle` class is just the storing and displaying of a riddle's question and answer.

By separating user interface tasks from riddle tasks, this design employs the divide-and-conquer principle: the `RiddleUser` class will create `Riddle` objects and handle interactions with the user, and the `Riddle` class will handle the storing and transmission of riddle information. Thus, as shown in Figure 2.14, this particular Java program will involve interaction between two types of objects: a `RiddleUser` and one or more `Riddles`. Note that we characterize the relationship between `Riddle` and `RiddleUser` with a one-way arrow labeled "Uses." This is because the `RiddleUser` will create an instance of `Riddle` and use its methods to display (for the user) a riddle.

Because almost all of our programs will involve some form of a user interface, we can generalize this design approach and follow it throughout the book. One way to think about this approach is as a division of labor between a user interface class and a second *computational* class, which performs whatever computations are needed by the particular program. In this case the computations are the simple `Riddle` methods that we have defined. In subsequent programs the computations will become more complex, which will make all the more clear that they should be separated from the user interface.

2.4.3   Object Instantiation: Creating `Riddle` Instances

Figure 2.15 shows the complete definition of the `RiddleUser` class, which serves as a very simple user interface. It creates two `Riddle` objects, named `riddle1` and `riddle2`. It then asks each object to request each riddle's question and answer, and displays them on the console.

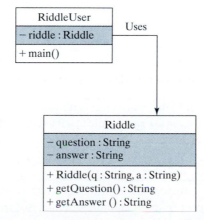

Figure 2.14 This UML class diagram represents an *association* between the `RiddleUser` and `Riddle` classes. The `RiddleUser` class will *use* one or more objects of the `Riddle` class.

```
public class RiddleUser
{
  public static void main(String argv[])
  { Riddle riddle1 = new Riddle(
      "What is black and white and red all over?",
      "An embarrassed zebra.");
    Riddle riddle2 = new Riddle(
      "What is black and white and read all over?",
      "A newspaper.");
    System.out.println("Here are two riddles:");
    System.out.println(riddle1.getQuestion());
    System.out.println(riddle2.getQuestion());
    System.out.println("The answer to the first riddle is:");
    System.out.println(riddle1.getAnswer());
    System.out.println("The answer to the second is:");
    System.out.println(riddle2.getAnswer());
  } // main()
} // RiddleUser class
```

Figure 2.15   The RiddleUser class.

We will now discuss the statements that make up RiddleUser's main() method. The following statements use the Riddle() constructor to create, or *instantiate*, two instances of the Riddle class:

```
Riddle riddle1 = new Riddle(
    "What is black and white and red all over?",
    "An embarrassed zebra.");
Riddle riddle2 = new Riddle(
    "What is black and white and read all over?",
    "A newspaper.");
```

Note how the constructor gives each object a pair of Strings that serve as the values of their two instance variables. Each object has its own question and its own answer, and each object has its own unique name, riddle1 and riddle2.

2.4.4   Interacting with Riddles

Once we have created Riddle instances with values assigned to their question and answer instance variables, we can ask each riddle to tell us either of its values. The following expression is an example of a *method call*:

```
riddle1.getQuestion()
```

Calling (or invoking) a method is a means of executing its code. The preceding method call just gets the `String` value that is stored in the `question` instance variable of `riddle1`.

Method call

> **JAVA PROGRAMMING TIP: Method Call versus Method Definition.** Don't confuse method calls with method definitions. The definition specifies the method's actions. The method call takes the actions.

If we want to display the value of `riddle1`'s `question`, we can embed this method call within a `println()` statement

```
System.out.println(riddle1.getQuestion());
```

This tells the `System.out` object to execute its `println()` method, which displays the string given to it by `riddle1` on the console. Thus, the output produced by this statement will be

```
What is black and white and red all over?
```

2.4.5   Define, Create, Use

As our Riddle example illustrates, writing a Java program is a matter of three basic steps:

- Define one or more classes (class definition).
- Create objects as instances of the classes (object instantiation).
- Use the objects to do tasks (object use).

The Java class definition determines what information will be stored in each object and what methods each object can perform. Instantiation creates an instance and associates a name with it in the program. The object's methods can then be called as a way of getting the object to perform certain tasks.

SELF-STUDY EXERCISES

EXERCISE 2.2   Identify the following elements in the `Riddle` class (Fig. 2.12):

- The name of the class.
- The names of two instance variables.
- The names of three methods.

EXERCISE 2.3   Identify the following elements in the `RiddleUser` class (Fig. 2.15):

- The names of two `Riddle` instances.
- All six method calls of the `Riddle` objects in the program.
- Two examples of qualified names.

2.5 CASE STUDY: Simulating a Two-Person Game

In this section, we will design and write the definition for a class that keeps track of the details of a well-known two-person game. We will focus on the details of designing the definition of a class in the Java language. Our objective is to understand what the program is doing and how it works, without necessarily understanding why it works the way it does. We will get to "why" later in the book.

The game we will consider is played by two persons with a row of sticks or coins or other objects. The players alternate turns. On each turn a player must remove one, two, or three sticks from the row. The player who removes the last stick from the row loses. The game can be played with any number of sticks, but starting with 21 sticks is quite common. This game is sometimes called "Nim," but there is a similar game involving multiple rows of sticks that is more frequently given that name. Thus we will refer to the game as "One-Row Nim."

2.5.1 Designing a OneRowNim Class

Problem Specification

Let's design a class named OneRowNim that simulates the game of One-Row Nim with a row of sticks. An object constructed with this class should manage data that corresponds to having some specified number of sticks when the game begins. It should keep track of whose turn it is, and it should allow a player to diminish the number of sticks remaining by one, two, or three. Finally, a OneRowNim object should be able to decide when the game is over and which player has won.

Problem Decomposition

Let's design OneRowNim so that it can be used with different kinds of user interfaces. One user interface could manage a game played by two persons who alternately designate their moves to the computer. Another user interface could let a human player play against moves made by the computer. In either of these cases we could have a human player designate a move by typing from the keyboard after being prompted in a console window or, alternatively, by inputting a number into a text field or selecting a radio button on a window. In this chapter, we will be concerned only with designing an object for managing the game. We will design user interfaces for the game in subsequent chapters.

Class Design: OneRowNim

As we saw in the Riddle example, class definitions can usually be broken down into two parts: (1) the information or attributes that the object needs, which must be stored in variables, and (2) the behavior or actions the object can take, which are defined in methods. In this chapter, we will focus on choosing appropriate instance variables and on designing methods as blocks of reusable code. Recall that a parameter is a variable that temporarily stores data values that are being passed to a method when the method is called. In this chapter, we will restrict our design to methods that do not have parameters and do not return values. We will return to the problem of designing changes to this class in the next chapter after an in-depth discussion of method parameters and return values.

What data do we need?

The OneRowNim object should manage two pieces of information that vary as the game is played. One is the number of sticks remaining in the row, and the other is which player has the next turn. Clearly, the number of sticks remaining corresponds to a positive integer that can be stored in a variable of type int. One suitable name for such a variable is nSticks. For this chapter, let us assume that the game starts with seven sticks rather than 21, to simplify discussion of the program.

Data designating which player takes the next turn could be stored in different ways. One way to do this is to think of the players as player 1 and player 2 and store a 1 or 2 in an int variable. Let's use player as the name for such a variable and assume that player 1 has the first turn.

The values of these two variables for a particular OneRowNim object at a particular time describe the object's state. An object's state at the beginning of a game is a 7 stored in nSticks and a 1 stored in player. After player 1 removes, say, two sticks on the first turn, the values 5 and 2 will be stored in the two variables.

Method Decomposition

Now that we have decided what information the OneRowNim object should manage, we need to decide what actions it should be able to perform. We should think of methods that would be needed to communicate with a user interface that is both prompting the human players and receiving moves from them. Clearly, methods are needed for taking a turn in the game. If a message to a OneRowNim object has no argument to indicate the number of sticks taken, there will need to be three methods corresponding to taking one, two, or three sticks. The method names takeOne(), takeTwo(), and takeThree() are descriptive of these actions. Each of these methods will be responsible for reducing the value of nSticks as well as for changing the value of player.

What methods do we need?

We should also have a method that gives the information a user needs when considering a move. Reporting the number of sticks remaining and whose turn it is to the console window would be an appropriate action. We can use report() as a name for this action.

Figure 2.16 is a UML class diagram that summarizes this design of the OneRowNim class. Note that the methods are declared public (+) and will thereby form the interface for a OneRowNim object. These will be the methods that other objects will use to interact with it. Similarly, we have followed the convention of designating that an object's instance variables— OneRowNim's instance variables—are to be kept hidden from other objects, and so we have designated them as private (−).

2.5.2   Defining the OneRowNim Class

Given our design of the OneRowNim class as described in Figure 2.16, the next step in building our simulation is to begin writing the Java class definition.

OneRowNim
− nSticks : int = 7
− player : int = 1
+ takeOne()
+ takeTwo()
+ takeThree()
+ report()

Figure 2.16 A UML class diagram for OneRowNim.

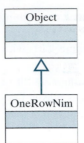

Figure 2.17 By default, OneRowNim
is a subclass of Object.

The Class Header

We need a *class header*, which will give the class a name and will specify its relationship to
other classes. Like all classes designed to create objects that could be used by other objects
or classes, the class OneRowNim should be preceded by the public modifier. Because the
class OneRowNim has not been described as having a relationship to any other Java class, its
header can omit the extends clause, and therefore it will be a direct subclass of Object
(Figure 2.17). Thus, the class header for OneRowNim will look like:

```
public class OneRowNim    // Class header
{                         // Beginning of class body

} // End of class body
```

The Class's Instance Variables

*Variables and
methods*

The body of a class definition consists of two parts: the class-level variables and the method
definitions. A **class-level variable** is a variable whose definition applies to the entire class in
which it is defined. Instance variables, which were introduced in Chapter 1, are one kind of
class-level variable.

In general, a class definition will take the form shown in Figure 2.18. Although Java does
not impose any particular order on variable and method declarations, in this book we will define
the class's class-level variables at the beginning of the class definition, followed by method

*Class-level vs.
local variables*

definitions. Class-level variables are distinguished from local variables. A **local variable** is
a variable that is defined within a method. Examples would be the variables q and a defined

```
public class ClassName
{ // Instance and class variables
    VariableDeclaration1
    VariableDeclaration2
    ...
  // Instance and class methods
    MethodDefinition1
    MethodDefinition2
    ...
} // End of class
```

Figure 2.18 A template for constructing a Java class definition.

Table 2.2. Java's accessibility rules.

Element	Modifier	Rule
Class	public	Accessible if its package is accessible.
	by default	Accessible only within its package.
Instance variable or instance method	public	Accessible to all other objects.
	protected	Accessible to its subclasses and to other classes in its package.
	private	Accessible only within the class.
	by default	Accessible only within the package.

in the `Riddle(String q, String a)` constructor (Fig. 2.12). As we will see better in Chapter 3, Java handles each type of variable differently.

A declaration for a variable at class level must follow the rules for declaring variables that were described in Section 1.4.8 with the added restriction that they should be modified by an access modifier, either `public`, `private`, or `protected`. The rules associated with these access modifiers are:

- A `private` class-level variable cannot be accessed outside the class in which it is declared.
- A `public` class-level variable can be referenced and modified by any other class.
- A `protected` class-level variable can only be accessed by subclasses of the class in which it is declared or by other classes that belong to the same package.

When a class, instance variable, or method is defined, you can declare it `public`, `protected`, or `private`. Or you can leave its access unspecified, in which case Java's default accessibility will apply.

Java determines accessibility in a top-down manner. Instance variables and methods are contained in classes, which are contained in packages. To determine whether an instance variable or method is accessible, Java starts by determining whether its containing package is accessible, and then whether its containing class is accessible. Access to classes, instance variables, and methods is defined according to the rules shown in Table 2.2.

Recall the distinction we made in Chapter 0 between class variables and instance variables. A class variable is associated with the class itself, whereas an instance variable is associated with each of the class's instances. In other words, each object contains its own copy of the class's instance variables, but only the class itself contains the single copy of a class variable. To designate a variable as a class variable it must be declared `static`.

The `Riddle` class that we considered earlier has the following two examples of valid declarations of instance variables:

```
private String question;
private String answer;
```

Class-Level Variables for OneRowNim

Let's now consider how to declare the class-level variables for the `OneRowNim` class. The UML class diagram for `OneRowNim` in Figure 2.16 contains all the information we need. The variables `nSticks` and `player` will store data for playing one game of One-Row Nim, so they should clearly be private instance variables. They both will store integer values, so they should be declared as variables of type `int`. Because we wish to start a game of One-Row Nim using seven sticks, with player 1 making the first move, we will assign 7 as the initial value for `nSticks` and 1 as the initial value for `player`. If we add the declarations for our instance variable declarations to the class header for the `OneRowNim` class, we get the following:

```
public class OneRowNim
{
  private int nSticks = 7;
  private int player = 1;

  // Method definitions go here
} // OneRowNim class
```

To summarize, despite its apparent simplicity, a class-level variable declaration actually accomplishes five tasks:

1. Sets aside a portion of the object's memory that can be used to store a certain type of data.

2. Specifies the type of data that can be stored in that location.

3. Associates an identifier (or name) with that location.

4. Determines which objects have access to the variable's name.

5. Assigns an initial value to the location.

OneRowNim's *Methods*

Designing and defining methods is a form of abstraction. By defining a certain sequence of actions as a method, you encapsulate those actions under a single name that can be invoked whenever needed. Instead of having to list the entire sequence again each time you want it performed, you simply call it by name. As you will recall from Chapter 1, a method definition consists of two parts, the method header and the method body. The method header declares the name of the method and other general information about the method. The method body contains the executable statements that the method performs.

```
public void methodName()     // Method header
{                            // Beginning of method body
} // End of method body
```

The Method Header

The method header follows a general format that consists of one or more *MethodModifiers*, the method's *ResultType*, the *MethodName*, and the method's *FormalParameterList*, which is enclosed in parentheses. Table 2.3 illustrates the method header form, and includes several examples of method headers that we have already encountered. The method body follows the method header.

Table 2.3. Method headers.

MethodModifiers	ResultType	MethodName	(FormalParameterList)
`public static`	`void`	`main`	`(String argv[])`
`public`	`void`	`paint`	`(Graphics g)`
`public`		`Riddle`	`(String q, String a)`
`public`	`String`	`getQuestion`	`()`
`public`	`String`	`getAnswer`	`()`

The rules on method access are the same as the rules on instance variable access: `private` methods are accessible only within the class itself, `protected` methods are accessible only to subclasses of the class in which the method is defined and to other classes in the same package, and `public` methods are accessible to all other classes.

EFFECTIVE DESIGN: Public versus Private Methods. If a method is used to communicate with an object, or if it passes information to or from an object, it should be declared `public`. If a method is intended to be used solely for internal operations within the object, it should be declared `private`. These methods are sometimes called *utility methods* or *helper methods*.

Recall from Chapter 0 the distinction between instance methods and class methods. Methods declared at the class level are assumed to be instance methods unless they are also declared `static`. The **static modifier** is used to declare that a class method or variable is associated with the class itself rather than with its instances. Just like `static` variables, methods that are declared `static` are associated with the class and are therefore called *class methods*. As its name implies, an instance method can only be used in association with an object (or instance) of a class. Most of the class-level methods we declare will be instance methods. Class methods are used only rarely in Java and mainly in situations where it is necessary to perform a calculation of some kind before objects of the class are created. We will see examples of class methods when we discuss the `Math` class, which has such methods as `sqrt(N)` to calculate the square root of N.

JAVA PROGRAMMING TIP: Class versus Instance Methods. If a method is designed to be used by an object, it is referred to as an instance method. No modifier is needed to designate an instance method. Class methods, which are used infrequently compared to instance methods, must be declared `static`.

All four of the methods in the `OneRowNim` class are instance methods (Fig. 2.19). They all perform actions associated with a particular instance of `OneRowNim`. That is, they are all used to manage a particular One-Row Nim game. Moreover, all four methods should be declared `public`, because they are designed for communicating with other objects rather than for performing internal calculations. Three of the methods are described as changing the values of the instance variables `nSticks` and `player`, and the fourth, `report()`, writes information to the console. All four methods will receive no data when being called and will not return any values. Thus they should all have `void` as a return type and should all have empty parameter lists.

```
public class OneRowNim
{ private int nSticks = 7;        // Start with 7 sticks.
  private int player = 1;         // Player 1 plays first.

  public void takeOne(){ }        // Method bodies need
  public void takeTwo(){ }        // to be defined.
  public void takeThree(){ }
  public void report(){ }
} // OneRowNim class
```

Figure 2.19   The Instance variables and method headers for the OneRowNim class.

Given these design decisions, we now can add method headers to our class definition of OneRowNim, in Figure 2.19. The figure displays the class header, instance variable declarations, and method headers.

The Method Body

Designing a method is an application of the encapsulation principle.

The body of a method definition is a block of Java statements enclosed by braces,{}, which are executed in sequence when the method is called. The description of the action required of the takeOne() method is typical of many methods that change the state of an object. The body of the takeOne() method should use a series of assignment statements to reduce the value stored in nSticks by 1 and change the value in player from 2 to 1 or from 1 to 2. The first change is accomplished in a straightforward way by the assignment:

```
nSticks = nSticks - 1;
```

This statement says: subtract 1 from the value stored in nSticks and assign the new value back to nSticks.

Deciding how to change the value in player is more difficult because we do not know whether its current value is 1 or 2. If its current value is 1, its new value should be 2; if its current value is 2, its new value should be 1. Note, however, that in both cases the current value plus the desired new value is equal to 3. Therefore, the new value of player are equal to 3 minus its current value. Writing this as an assignment we have:

```
player = 3 - player;
```

One can easily verify that this clever assignment assigns 2 to player if its current value is 1 and assigns 1 to it if its current value is 2. In effect, this assignment will toggle the value off player between 1 and 2 each time it is executed. In the next chapter we will introduce the if-else control structure, which will allow us to accomplish the same toggling action in a more straightforward manner. The complete definition of takeOne() method becomes:

```
public void takeOne()
{
  nSticks = nSticks - 1;    // Take one stick
  player = 3 - player;      // Change to other player
}
```

```
public class OneRowNim
{ private int nSticks = 7;                          // Start with 7 sticks.
  private int player = 1;                            // Player 1 plays first.

  public void takeOne()
  { nSticks = nSticks - 1;
    player = 3 - player;
  } // takeOne()

  public void takeTwo()
  { nSticks = nSticks - 2;
    player = 3 - player;
  } // takeTwo()

  public void takeThree()
  { nSticks = nSticks - 3;
    player = 3 - player;
  } // takeThree()

  public void report()
  { System.out.println("Number of sticks left: " + nSticks);
    System.out.println("Next turn by player " + player);
  } // report()
} // OneRowNim1 class
```

Figure 2.20 The OneRowNim class definition.

The `takeTwo()` and `takeThree()` methods are completely analogous to the `takeOne()` method, with the only difference being the amount subtracted from `nSticks`.

The body of the `report()` method must merely print the current values of the instance variables to the console window with `System.out.println()`. To be understandable to someone using a `OneRowNim` object, the values should be clearly labeled. Thus the body of `report()` could contain:

```
System.out.println("Number of sticks left: " + nSticks);
System.out.println("Next turn by player " + player);
```

This completes the method bodies of the `OneRowNim` class. The completed class definition is shown in Figure 2.20. We will discuss alternative methods for this class in the next chapter. In Chapter 4, we will develop several One-Row Nim user interface classes that will facilitate a user by indicating certain moves to make.

2.5.3   Testing the OneRowNim Class

Recall our *define, create, and use* mantra from Section 2.4.5. Now that we have defined the `OneRowNim` class, we can test whether it works correctly by creating `OneRowNim` objects and using them to perform the actions associated with the game. At this point, we can test `OneRowNim` by defining a `main()` method. Following the design we used in the riddle example, we will locate the `main()` method in a separate user-interface class named `OneRowNimTester`.

The body of `main()` should declare a variable of type `OneRowNim` and create an object for it to refer to. The variable can have any name, but a name like `game` would be consistent with the function of recording moves in a single game. To test the OneRowNim class, we should make a typical series of moves. For example, three moves taking three, three, and one sticks respectively would be one way that the seven sticks could be removed. Also, executing the report() method before the first move and after each move should display the current state of the game in the console window so that we can determine whether it is working correctly.

The following pseudocode outlines an appropriate sequence of statements in a main() method:

1. Declare a variable of type OneRowNim named game.
2. Instantiate a OneRowNim object to which game refers.
3. Command game to report.
4. Command game to remove three sticks.
5. Command game to report.
6. Command game to remove three sticks.
7. Command game to report.
8. Command game to remove one stick.
9. Command game to report.

It is now an easy task to convert the steps in the pseudocode outline into Java statements. The resulting main() method is shown with the complete definition of the OneRowNimTester class:

```java
public class OneRowNimTester
{ public static void main(String args[])
  { OneRowNim1 game = new OneRowNim();
    game.report();
    game.takeThree();
    game.report();
    game.takeThree();
    game.report();
    game.takeOne();
    game.report();
  } // main()
} // OneRowNimTester class
```

When it is run, OneRowNimTester produces the following output:

```
Number of sticks left: 7
Next turn by player 1
Number of sticks left: 4
Next turn by player 2
Number of sticks left: 1
Next turn by player 1
Number of sticks left: 0
Next turn by player 2
```

This output indicates that player 1 removed the final stick and so player 2 is the winner of the game.

SELF-STUDY EXERCISES

EXERCISE 2.4   Add a new declaration to the `Riddle` class for a `private String` instance variable named `hint`. Assign the variable an initial value of "`This riddle is too easy for a hint`".

EXERCISE 2.5   Write a header for a new method definition for `Riddle` named `getHint()`. Assume that this method requires no parameters and simply returns the `String` value stored in the `hint` instance variable. Should this method be declared `public` or `private`?

EXERCISE 2.6   Write a header for the definition of a new `public` method for `Riddle` named `setHint()` which sets the value of the `hint` instance variable to whatever `String` value it receives as a parameter. What should the result type be for this method?

EXERCISE 2.7   Create a partial definition of a `Student` class. Create instance variables for the first name, last name, and an integer student identification number. Write the headers for three methods. One method uses three parameters to set values for the three instance variables. One method returns the student identification number. The last method returns a `String` containing the student's first name and last name. Write only the headers for these methods.

2.5.4   Flow of Control: Method Call and Return

A program's **flow of control** is the order in which its statements are executed. In an object-oriented program, control passes from one object to another during the program's execution. It is important to have a clear understanding of this process.

In order to understand a Java program, it is necessary to understand the **method call and return** mechanism. We will encounter it repeatedly. A method call causes a program to transfer control to a statement located in another method. Figure 2.21 shows the method call and return structure.

In this example, we have two methods. We make no assumptions about where these methods are in relation to each other. They could be defined in the same class or in different classes. The `method1()` method executes sequentially until it calls `method2()`. This transfers control to the first statement in `method2()`. Execution continues sequentially through the statements in `method2()` until the `return` statement is executed.

JAVA LANGUAGE RULE   Return Statement. The `return` statement causes a method to return control to the *calling statement*—that is, to the statement that called the method in the first place.

Figure 2.21 The method call and return control structure. It is important to realize that `method1()` and `method2()` may be contained in different classes.

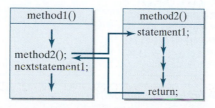

Default returns

Recall that if a void method does not contain a return statement, then control will automatically return to the calling statement after the invoked method executes its last statement.

2.5.5 Tracing the OneRowNim Program

To help us understand the flow of control in OneRowNim, we will perform a trace of its execution. Figure 2.22 shows all of the Java code involved in the program. In order to simplify our trace, we have moved the main() method from OneRowNimTester to the OneRowNim class. This does not affect the program's order of execution in any way. But keep in mind that the code in the main() method could just as well appear in the OneRowNimTester class. The listing in Figure 2.22 also adds line numbers to the program to show the order in which its statements are executed.

Execution of the OneRowNim program begins with the first statement in the main() method, labeled with line number 1. This statement declares a variable of type OneRowNim named game and calls a constructor OneRowNim() to create and initialize it. The constructor, which in this case is a default constructor, causes control to shift to the declaration of the instance variables nSticks and player in statements 2 and 3, and assigns them initial values of 7 and 1 respectively. Control then shifts back to the second statement in main(), which has the

```
     public class OneRowNim
2 {   private int nSticks = 7;          // Start with 7 sticks.
3      private int player = 1;           // Player 1 plays first.

       public void takeOne()
20     { nSticks = nSticks - 1;
21        player = 3 - player;
       } // takeOne()
       public void takeTwo()
       { nSticks = nSticks - 2;
          player = 3 - player;
       } // takeTwo()

       public void takeThree()
8,14   { nSticks = nSticks - 3;
9,15      player = 3 - player;
       } // takeThree()
       public void report()
5,11,17,23 { System.out.println("Number of sticks left: " + nSticks);
6,12,18,24   System.out.println("Next turn by player " + player);
       } // report()

       public static void main(String args[])
1      {  OneRowNim1 game = new OneRowNim1();
4         game.report();
7         game.takeThree();
10        game.report();
13        game.takeThree();
16        game.report();
19        game.takeOne();
22        game.report();
23      } // main()
     } // OneRowNim1 class
```

Figure 2.22 A trace of the OneRowNim program.

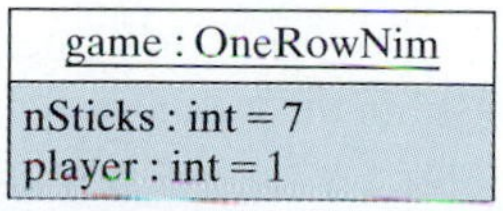

Figure 2.23 The initial state of game, a OneRowNim object.

label 4. At this point, game refers to an instance of the OneRowNim class with the initial state shown in Figure 2.23. Executing statement 4 causes control to shift to the report() method where statements 5 and 6 use System.out.println() to write the following statements to the console.

```
Number of sticks left: 7
Next turn by player 1
```

Control shifts back to statement 7 in the main() method, which calls the takeThree() method, sending control to the first statement of that method. Executing statement 8 causes 3 to be subtracted from the int value stored in the instance variable nSticks of game, leaving the value of 4. Executing statement 9 subtracts the value stored in the player variable, which is 1, from 3 and assigns the result (the value 2) back to player. The state of the object game, at this point, is shown in Figure 2.24. Tracing the remainder of the program follows in a similar manner. Note that the main() method calls game.report() four different times so that the two statements in the report() method are both executed on four different occasions. Note also that there is no call of game.takeTwo() in main(). As a result, the two statements in that method are never executed.

2.5.6 Object-Oriented Design: Basic Principles

We complete our discussion of the design and this first implementation of the OneRowNim class with a brief review of some of the object-oriented design principles that were employed in this example.

- **Encapsulation.** The OneRowNim class was designed to encapsulate a certain state and a certain set of actions. It was designed to simulate playing the One-Row Nim game. In addition, OneRowNim's methods were designed to encapsulate the actions that make up their particular tasks.
- **Information Hiding.** OneRowNim's instance variables, nSticks and player, are declared private so that other objects can only change the values of these variables with the public methods of a OneRowNim instance. The bodies of the public methods are also hidden from users of OneRowNim instances. An instance and its methods can be used without any knowledge of method definitions.

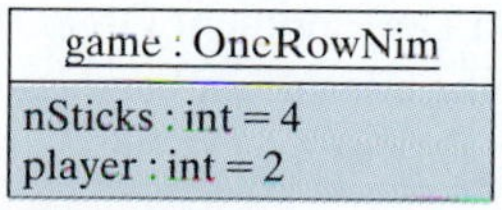

Figure 2.24 The state of game after line 9 is executed.

- **Clearly Designed Interface.** OneRowNim's interface is defined in terms of the public methods. These methods constrain the way users can interact with OneRowNim objects and ensure that OneRowNim instances remain in a valid state. These are the main purposes of a good interface.
- **Generality and Extensibility.** There is little in our design of OneRowNim that limits its use and extensibility. Moreover, as we will see later, we can create several different kinds of user interfaces to interact with OneRowNim objects.

The OneRowNim class has some obvious shortcomings that are a result of our decision to limit the design to methods without parameters or return values. These shortcomings include:

- A OneRowNim object cannot communicate to another object the number of remaining sticks, which player makes the next turn, or whether the game is over. It can only communicate by writing a report to the console window.
- The takeOne(), takeTwo(), and takeThree() methods all have similar definitions. It would be a better design if a single method could take away a specified number of sticks.

Alan Kay and the Smalltalk Language

Although *Simula* was the first programming language to use the concept of an object, *Smalltalk* was the first pure object-oriented language. Smalltalk was developed by Alan Kay in the late 1960s. Kay is an innovative thinker who has had a hand in the development of several advances, including windowing interfaces, laser printing, and the client/server model, all of which are commonplace today.

One of the abiding themes throughout Kay's career has been the idea that computers should be easy enough for kids to use. In the late 1960s, while still in graduate school, Kay designed a computer model that consisted of a notebook-sized portable computer with a keyboard, screen, mouse, and high-quality graphics interface. He had become convinced that graphics and icons were a far better way to communicate with a computer than the command-line interfaces that were prevalent at the time.

In the early 1970s Kay went to work at the Xerox Palo Alto Research Center (PARC), where he developed a prototype of his system known as the *Dynabook*. Smalltalk was the computer language Kay developed for this project. Smalltalk was designed along a biological model, in which individual entities, or "objects," communicate with each other by passing messages back and forth. Another goal of Smalltalk was to enable children to invent their own concepts and build programs with them—thus, the name *Smalltalk*.

Xerox's management was unable to see the potential of Kay's innovations. However, during a visit to Xerox in 1979, Steve Jobs, the founder of Apple Computer, was so impressed by Kay's work that he made it the inspiration of the Macintosh computer, which was first released in 1984.

Kay left Xerox in 1983 and became an Apple Fellow in 1984. In addition to working for Apple, Kay spent considerable time teaching kids how to use computers at his Open School in West Hollywood. In 1996 Kay became a Fellow (an "Imagineer") at Walt Disney Imagineering's Research and Development Organization, where he continues to explore innovative ways to enhance the educational and entertainment value of computers.

- There is no way to play a `OneRowNim` game starting with a number of sticks other than seven. It would be nice to have a way of playing a game that starts with any number of sticks.
- In order for a user to play a `OneRowNim` game, a user-interface class would need to be developed that would allow the user to receive information about the state of the game and to input moves.

As we study other features of Java in the next two chapters, we will modify the `OneRowNim` class to address these identified shortcomings.

2.6 From the Java Library: `java.util.Scanner`

IF WE WISH to write useful interactive programs, we must be able to receive information from users as well as send information to them. We saw in the preceding chapter that output from a program can be sent to the console window by simply using the `System.out.print()` and `System.out.println()` statements. In this section we describe two simple ways that Java can handle keyboard input. Receiving input from the keyboard, together with sending output to the console window, creates one of the standard user interfaces for programs.

java.sun.com/docs

Recall that in Java, any source or destination for I/O is considered a stream of bytes or characters. To perform keyboard input, we will extract characters from `System.in`, the input stream connected to the keyboard. Getting keyboard input from `System.in` involves two complications that are not present in dealing with `System.out.println()`. First, the normal keyboard input data requested of a user consists of a sequence of characters or digits that represent a word, phrase, integer, or real number. Normally, an entire sequence of characters typed by the user will represent data to be stored in a single variable, with the user hitting the return or enter key to signal the end of a piece of requested data. Java has a special class, `Buffered Reader`, that uses an input stream and has a method that collects characters until it reads the character or characters that correspond to hitting the return or enter key. A second complication for reading input involves the problem of how to handle receiving data that is not in the same format as expected. The `BufferedReader` class handles this problem by using certain *exceptions*, a special kind of error message that must be handled by the programmer. Chapter 10 is devoted to exceptions, and we will avoid their use, as far as possible, until that time.

There is an alternative way to handle keyboard input in the Java 2 Platform Standard Edition 5.0 (J2SE 5.0). A `Scanner` class has been added to the `java.util` package which permits keyboard input without forcing the programmer to handle exceptions. We introduce the `Scanner` class in the next subsection and then describe how a user-defined class introduced in Chapter 4 can function in an equivalent fashion to permit simple keyboard input.

2.6.1 Keyboard Input with the `Scanner` Class

A partial definition of `Scanner` is shown in Figure 2.25. Note that the `Scanner` methods listed are but a small subset of the public methods of this class. The Scanner class is in the `java.util` package, so classes that use it should import it with the following statement:

```
import java.util.Scanner;
```

Scanner
+ Scanner(in InputStream st)
+ next() : String
+ nextInt() : int
+ nextDouble() : double
+ useDelimiter(in String pat) : Scanner

Figure 2.25   The Scanner class, with a partial list of its public methods.

The Scanner class is designed to be a very flexible way to recognize chunks of data that fit specified patterns from any input stream. To use the Scanner class for keyboard input, we must create a Scanner instance and associate it with System.in. The class has a constructor for this purpose, so the statement

```
Scanner sc = new Scanner(System.in);
```

declares and instantiates an object that can be used for keyboard input. After we create a Scanner object, we can make a call to nextInt(), nextDouble(), or next() to read, respectively, an integer, real number, or string from the keyboard. The program in Figure 2.26 demonstrates how an integer would be read and used. When the nextInt() method is executed, no further statements are executed until an int value is returned by the method. Normally this does not happen until the user has typed in the digits of an integer and hit the return or enter key. Thus, executing the main() method of the TestScanner class will result in the output

```
Input an integer:
```

to the console window, and the program will wait for the user to type in an integer and hit the return or enter key. After this has been done the output will look something like:

```
Input an integer:123
123 squared = 15129
```

```java
import java.util.Scanner;

public class TestScanner
{
  public static void main(String[] args)
  {                                                  // Create Scanner object
    Scanner sc = new Scanner(System.in);
    System.out.print("Input an integer:");           // Prompt
    int num = sc.nextInt();                          // Read an integer
    System.out.println(num + " squared = " + num*num);
  } // main()
} // TestScanner class
```

Figure 2.26   A very brief program with a Scanner object used for keyboard input.

Keyboard input of real numbers and strings is handled in a similar manner.

Keyboard input will allow us to create examples of command-line interfaces for interactive programs. For example, the code

```
Scanner sc = new Scanner(System.in);
Riddle riddle = new Riddle(
   "What is black and white and red all over?",
   "An embarrassed zebra.");
System.out.println("Here is a riddle:");
System.out.println(riddle.getQuestion());
System.out.print("To see the answer, ");          // Prompt
System.out.println("type a letter and enter.");
String str = sc.next();                           // Wait for input
System.out.println(riddle.getAnswer());
```

will display a riddle question and prompt the user to type a letter and hit the enter key to see the answer. In the next chapter, we will develop new methods for the `OneRowNim` class that will be able to use `int` values input from the keyboard for the next move.

Since the `Scanner` class is designed as a flexible tool for recognizing chunks of data from any input stream, it has some properties that may be unexpected and not totally compatible with simple keyboard input. A `Scanner` object has a set of character strings that separate, or **delimit**, the chunks of data it is looking for. By default, this set of delimiters consists of any nonempty sequence of *white space* characters, that is, the space, tab, return, and newline characters. This will allow a user to input several integers separated by spaces before hitting the enter key. This might be handled by code like:

```
System.out.print("Input two integers and an enter:");
int num1 = sc.nextInt();
int num2 = sc.nextInt();
```

White space as delimiters also means that the `next()` method cannot return an empty string, nor can it return a string that contains any spaces. For example, consider the code:

```
System.out.print("Input the first president of the USA:");
String str = sc.next();
```

If one types "George Washington" and hits the enter key, the string `str` will store only "George." In order to get a `Scanner` object to read strings that contain spaces, we must use the `use-Delimiter()` method to define the set of delimiters as just that character string generated by hitting the enter key. For example, for some Windows operating systems, the statement

```
sc = sc.useDelimiter("\r\n");
```

will result in the `next()` method returning the entire string of characters input from the keyboard, up to but not including those generated by hitting the enter key.

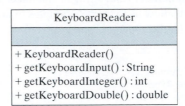

KeyboardReader
+ KeyboardReader() + getKeyboardInput() : String + getKeyboardInteger() : int + getKeyboardDouble() : double

Figure 2.27   A UML class diagram of the KeyboardReader class.

The fact that we can use a Scanner object to write Java code that ignores exceptions does not mean that exceptions will not be generated by keyboard input. If the user enters letters rather than digits for the nextInt() method to process, the program will be terminated with an error message.

It must be stressed that the strategy for handling keyboard input outlined above is a temporary strategy until the topic of exceptions is covered in Chapter 11. Real software applications that use keyboard input should carefully handle the possibility that a user will enter something unexpected. In Java, this can only be done by handling exceptions.

2.6.2   Keyboard Input with the KeyboardReader Class

If you are using an older version of Java that does not have the Scanner class, a user-defined class can be used instead. A KeyboardReader class that uses the BufferedReader class will be developed in Chapter 4. It has methods that read data from the keyboard in a manner very similar to those of the Scanner class. A partial list of its public methods is given in the UML class diagram shown in Figure 2.27. To use the KeyboardReader class for keyboard input, copy the source code KeyboardReader.java from Chapter 4 into the same directory as the source code of your current Java class (and add it to your current project if you are using a integrated development environment).

To use a KeyboardReader object, we need to create an instance of the class with a constructor. Then calling one of the three methods will return an int, double, or String when data is input from the keyboard. Any of the three methods of a KeyboardReader object will attempt to process the entire string input from the keyboard up to the point that the enter key is hit. That is, the character or characters generated by hitting the return or enter key are the delimiters used by KeyboardReader. The TestKeyboardReader class definition in Figure 2.28 reads an integer from the keyboard and squares it just like the TestScanner class. In the remainder of the text, any time the Scanner class is used for keyboard input, the same program can be run using the KeyboardReader class after making the obvious substitutions.

```java
public class TestKeyboardReader
{
  public static void main(String[] args)
  {                                          // Create KeyboardReader object
    KeyboardReader kb = new KeyboardReader();
    System.out.print("Input an integer:");   // Prompt
    int num = kb.getKeyboardInteger();       // Read an integer
    System.out.println(num + " squared = " + num*num);
  } // main()
} // TestKeyboardReader class
```

Figure 2.28   A very brief program with a KeyboardReader object used for keyboard input.

SELF-STUDY EXERCISE

EXERCISE 2.8 Modify the `main()` method of the `TestScanner` class so that it reads a real number from the keyboard rather than an integer.

CHAPTER SUMMARY

Technical Terms

access modifier	method call and return
class-level variable	null pointer
default value	null pointer exception
delimiter	pointer
empty string	reference
flow of control	reference variable
interface	static modifier
local variable	user interface

Summary of Important Points

- Dot notation is used to refer to an object's public elements.
- Designing a class is a matter of deciding what role it will play and what information and actions it will have.
- Writing a Java program is a matter of defining one or more classes. A class definition serves as a template for creating instances of the class.
- Classes typically contain two kinds of elements, variables and methods. An object's state is defined by its instance variables.
- Class elements declared `public` can be accessed by other objects. Elements declared `private` are hidden from other objects.
- A class's instance variables are usually declared `private` and so cannot be accessed directly by other objects.
- An object's public instance methods can be called by other objects. Thus, they make up the object's interface with other objects.
- Object instantiation is the process of creating an object, using the `new` operator in conjunction with a constructor method.
- A class definition consists of a header and a body. The header gives the class a name, and specifies its accessibility (`public`) and its place in the Java class hierarchy (`extends Object`). The class body contains declarations of the class's variables and definitions of its methods.
- By default, a newly defined class is considered a subclass of `Object`.
- Class elements declared `static`, such as the `main()` method, are associated with the class (not with its instances).
- A Java application program must contain a `main()` method, which is where it begins execution.

- Methods used solely for the internal operations of the class should be declared `private`.
- An instance variable declaration reserves memory for the instance variable within the object, associates a name and a type with the location, and specifies its accessibility.
- A method definition consists of two parts: a header, which names the method and provides other general information about it, and a body, which contains its executable statements.
- Declaring a variable creates a name for an object but does not create the object itself. An object is created by using the `new` operator and a constructor method.

SOLUTIONS TO SELF-STUDY EXERCISES

SOLUTION 2.1   The Java code fragment prints out the following:

```
The singing king.
```

SOLUTION 2.2   For the `Riddle` class (Fig. 2.12),

a. The name of the class: `Riddle`
b. The names of two instance variables: `question, answer`
c. The names of three methods: `Riddle(), getQuestion(), getAnswer()`

SOLUTION 2.3   For `RiddleUser` class (Fig. 2.15),

a. The names of two `Riddle` instances: `riddle1, riddle2`
b. All six method calls of the `Riddle` objects in the program:

```
Riddle("What is black and white and red all over?",
                       "An embarrassed zebra.")
Riddle("What is black and white and read all over?",
                       "A newspaper.")
riddle1.getQuestion()
riddle1.getAnswer()
riddle2.getQuestion()
riddle2.getAnswer()
```

c. Qualified names: `riddle1.getQuestion()` and `riddle1.getAnswer()`

SOLUTION 2.4   Definition of new instance variable in the `Riddle` class:

```
private String hint = "This riddle is too easy for a hint";
```

SOLUTION 2.5   The header for a `getHint()` method of the `Riddle` class, which should be a `public` method, is:

```
public String getHint();
```

SOLUTION 2.6   The header for a `setHint()` method of the `Riddle` class is:

```
public void setHint(String aHint);
```

The result type is `void`. Although the identifier used for the parameter is arbitrary, it is a good practice to make it descriptive by referring in some way to the `hint` instance variable.

SOLUTION 2.7   The partial definition of the `Student` class is given below.

```
public class Student
{   private String firstName;
    private String lastName;
    private int studentID;

    public void setStudent(String fName, String lName, int anID);
    public int getStudentID();
    public String getStudentName();
}
```

SOLUTION 2.8   A main method that reads and squares a real number is given below.

```
public static void main(String[] args)
{                                              // Create Scanner object
    Scanner sc = Scanner.create(System.in);
    System.out.print("Input a real number:");  // Prompt
    double realNum= sc.nextDouble();           // Read a double
    System.out.println(num + " squared = " + realNum*realNum);
} // main()
```

EXERCISES

EXERCISE 2.1   Consider the transaction of asking your professor for your grade in your computer science course. Identify the objects in this transaction and the types of messages that would be passed among them.

EXERCISE 2.2   Now suppose that the professor in the preceding exercise decides to automate the transaction of looking up student grades and has asked you to design a program to perform this task. The program should let students type in their names and ID numbers and the program then should display their grades for the semester, with a final average. Suppose there are five quiz grades, three exams, and two programming exercise grades. Identify the objects in this program and the type of messages that would be passed among them. (*Hint*: The grades themselves are just data values, not objects.)

Note: For programming exercises, **first** draw a UML class diagram describing all classes and their inheritance relationships and/or associations.

EXERCISE 2.3   In the `RiddleUser` class (Fig. 2.15), give two examples of object instantiation and explain what is being done.

EXERCISE 2.4   Explain the difference between a method definition and a method call. Give an example of each from the `Riddle` and `RiddleUser` examples discussed in this chapter.

EXERCISE 2.5   In the `RiddleUser` class (Fig. 2.15), identify three examples of method calls and explain what is being done.

EXERCISE 2.6   Describe how the slogan "define, create, use" applies to the `Riddle` example.

EXERCISE 2.7   An identifier is the name for a _____, _____, or a _____.

EXERCISE 2.8   Which of the following would be valid identifiers?

```
int   74ElmStreet   Big_N      L$&%#    boolean   Boolean   _number
Int   public        Private    Joe      j1        2*K       big numb
```

EXERCISE 2.9   Explain the difference between a `class variable` and an `instance variable`.

EXERCISE 2.10   Identify the syntax error (if any) in each declaration. Remember that some parts of an instance variable declaration are optional.

a. `public boolean isEven ;`
b. `Private boolean isEven ;`
c. `private boolean isOdd`
d. `public boolean is Odd ;`
e. `string S ;`
f. `public String boolean ;`
g. `private boolean even = 0 ;`
h. `private String s = helloWorld ;`

EXERCISE 2.11   Write declarations for each of the following instance variables.

a. A `private boolean` variable named `bool` that has an initial value of `true`.
b. A `public String` variable named `str` that has an initial value of "hello."
c. A `private int` variable named `nEmployees` that is not assigned an initial value.

EXERCISE 2.12   Identify the syntax error (if any) in each method header:

a. `public String boolean()`
b. `private void String ()`

c. `private void myMethod`

d. `private myMethod()`

e. `public static void Main (String argv[])`

EXERCISE 2.13   Identify the syntax error (if any) in each assignment statement. Assume that the following variables have been declared:

```
public int m;
public boolean b;
public String s;
```

a. `m = "86" ;`

b. `m = 86 ;`

c. `m = true ;`

d. `s = 1295 ;`

e. `s = "1295" ;`

f. `b = "true" ;`

g. `b = false`

EXERCISE 2.14   Given the following definition of the `NumberAdder` class, add statements to its `main()` method to create two instances of this class, named `adder1` and `adder2`. Then add statements to set `adder1`'s numbers to 10 and 15, and `adder2`'s numbers to 100 and 200. Then add statements to print their respective sums.

```
public class NumberAdder
{
    private int num1;
    private int num2;

    public void setNums(int n1, int n2)
    {
      num1 = n1;
      num2 = n2;
    }
    public int getSum()
    {
      return num1 + num2 ;
    }

    public static void main(String args[])
    {
    }
}
```

EXERCISE 2.15   For the `NumberAdder` class in the preceding exercise, what are the names of its instance variables and instance methods? Identify three expressions that occur in the program and explain what they do. Identify two assignment statements and explain what they do.

EXERCISE 2.16   Explain the difference between each of the following pairs of concepts.

   a. A method definition and a method call.

   b. Declaring a variable of reference type and creating an instance.

   c. A variable of reference type and a variable of primitive type.

EXERCISE 2.17   Define a Java class named NumberCruncher that has a single int variable as its only instance variable. Then define methods that perform the following operations on its number: get, double, triple, square, and cube. Set the initial value of the number with a constructor, as was done with the instance variables in the Riddle class.

EXERCISE 2.18   Write a main() method and add it to the NumberCruncher class defined in the preceding problem. Use it to create a NumberCruncher instance with a certain initial value, and then get it to report its double, triple, square, and cube.

EXERCISE 2.19   Write a Java class definition for a Cube object that has an integer attribute for the length of its side. The object should be capable of reporting its surface area and volume. The surface area of a cube is six times the area of any side. The volume is calculated by cubing the side.

EXERCISE 2.20   Write a Java class definition for a CubeUser object that will use the Cube object defined in the preceding exercise. This class should create three Cube instances, each with a different side, and then report their respective surface areas and volumes.

EXERCISE 2.21   Challenge: Modify your solution to the preceding exercise so that it lets the user input the side of the cube. Follow the example shown in this chapter's "From the Java Library" section.

EXERCISE 2.22   Challenge: Define a Java class that represents an address book entry, Entry, which consists of a name, address, and phone number, all represented as Strings. For the class's interface, define methods to set and get the values of each of its instance variables. Thus, for the name variable, it should have a setName() and a getName() method.

UML Exercises

EXERCISE 2.23   Draw a UML class diagram to represent the following class hierarchy: There are two types of languages, natural languages and programming languages. The natural languages include Chinese, English, French, and German. The programming languages include Java, Smalltalk, and C++, which are object-oriented languages, FORTRAN, COBOL, Pascal, and C, which are imperative languages, Lisp and ML, which are functional languages, and Prolog, which is a logic language.

EXERCISE 2.24   Draw a UML class diagram to represent different kinds of automobiles, including trucks, sedans, wagons, SUVs, and the names and manufacturers of some popular models in each category.

EXERCISE 2.25 Draw a UML object diagram of a triangle with attributes for three sides, containing the values 3, 4, and 5.

EXERCISE 2.26 Suppose you are writing a Java program to implement an electronic address book. Your design is to have two classes, one to represent the user interface and one to represent the address book. Draw a UML diagram to depict this relationship. See Figure 2.14.

EXERCISE 2.27 Draw an UML object diagram to depict the relationship between an applet that serves as a user interface and three `Triangle`s named `t1`, `t2`, and `t3`.

Photograph courtesy of Getty Images - Digital Vision.

3

Methods: Communicating with Objects

OBJECTIVES

After studying this chapter, you will

- Understand the role that methods play in an object-oriented program.
- Know how to use parameters and arguments to pass data to an object.
- Understand how constructor methods are used to instantiate objects.
- Know the difference between passing a value and passing a reference to an object.
- Be able to design your own methods.
- Know how to use the if-else and while control structures.

OUTLINE

3.1   Introduction

In this chapter, we take a look at Java methods and parameters. Methods and parameters are the primary mechanisms for passing information into and out of an object. We will once again focus on the OneRowNim simulation designed in the preceding chapter. That first version was sufficient to introduce us to Java objects and classes, but it had only limited ability to communicate with other objects.

In this chapter, we want to expand OneRowNim to make our simulation more realistic. We begin by learning how to pass information to an object. That will enable us to specify the number of sticks to remove using a single method. We then consider special methods called constructors, which are used to initialize an object's state when it is created. We also learn how to retrieve information from an object. That will enable us to request a OneRowNim object for several different bits of information. Then we consider the if-else and while control structures, which allow us to define more useful methods and write more realistic test programs.

3.2   Passing Information to an Object

One convention of object-oriented programming is to provide public methods to *set* and *get* the values of some of its private instance variables. Methods that set or modify an object's instance variables are called **mutator methods**. Methods that get or retrieve the value of an instance variable are called **accessor methods**.

> **EFFECTIVE DESIGN: Accessor and Mutator Methods.**   An **accessor method** is a public method used to *get* the value of an object's instance variable. Such methods are often named *getVarName()*, where *VarName* is the name of the variable being accessed. A **mutator method** is a public method used to modify the value of one or more instance variables. The special type of mutator method that *sets*, or assigns, a variable a specified value is often called *setVarName()*.

It is up to the designer of the class to determine which private variables require accessor and mutator methods. If you were designing a BankAccount class, you might want a public getAccountNumber() method, so that clients could retrieve information about their bank accounts, but you would probably not want a public getAccountPassword() method or a public setAccountBalance() method.

In the remainder of this section, we will be concerned with mutator methods. We defined three mutator methods named takeOne(), takeTwo(), and takeThree as part of the OneRowNim class in the preceding chapter. All three of these methods change the values of the instance variables nSticks and player. All three methods have very similar bodies. The definition of the takeOne() is:

```java
public void takeOne()
{   nSticks = nSticks - 1;
    player = 3 - player;
}
```

The only difference in the bodies of the other two methods is that they subtract 2 and 3 from nSticks instead of 1. Instead of having three virtually identical methods, it would be a more efficient design to define a single method where the number to be subtracted from nSticks would be supplied as an argument when the method is called. In order to be able to handle such an argument, we must design a new method that uses a *parameter* to handle the argument.

A **formal parameter**, or more simply a **parameter**, is a variable used to pass information into a method when the method is invoked. The *type* and *variable name* of the formal parameter must appear in the *formal parameter list* that follows the method's name in the method header. The formal parameter is used to hold a value that it is passed while the method is executing.

Formal parameter

> **JAVA LANGUAGE RULE** **Formal Parameter.** A **formal parameter** is a variable that serves as a storage location for information passed to a method. To specify a formal parameter, you must provide a type identifier followed by a variable identifier, and you must place this declaration inside the parentheses that follow the method's name.

Consider the following definition for a takeSticks() method:

```java
public void takeSticks(int num)
{   nSticks = nSticks - num;
    player = 3 - player;
}
```

Note that executing the body of takeSticks() when the parameter num stores the value 1 accomplishes precisely the same task as executing takeOne(). If, instead, a value of 2 or 3 is stored in num, then calling the method acts either like takeTwo() or takeThree() respectively. Thus, using parameters enables us to design methods that are more general in what they do, which is an important principle of good program design.

Another example of a mutator method is one that defines a *set method* to allow the starting number of sticks to be set for an instance of OneRowNim. For this, we could define:

```java
public void setSticks(int sticks)
{    nSticks = sticks;
} // setSticks()
```

As we will see in Section 3.3, we can also define a constructor method that can be used when the game is created to set the initial value of nSticks. It is often desirable to have more than one method that can set the values of an object's instance variables.

If a method uses more than one parameter, separate the individual parameter declarations in the method header with commas. For example, if we wanted a method for OneRowNim that specified both the number of sticks for the start of a game and which player takes a turn first, it could be defined as:

```java
public void setGame(int sticks, int starter)
{   nSticks = sticks;
    player = starter;
} // setGame()
```

The Scope of Parameters, Variables, and Methods

Scope

The bodies of the mutator methods in the preceding section make use of both instance variables and parameters. There is an important difference in where these two types of variables can be used. The **scope** of a variable or method refers to where it can be used in a program.

A parameter's scope is limited to the body of the method in which it is declared. Variables declared in the body of a method have scope that extends from the point where they are declared to the end of the block of code in which they are declared. Parameters are local variables declared in the parameter list of a method's header. They have initial values specified by the arguments in a method call. The scope of a parameter is the same as the scope of a variable declared at the very beginning of the body of a method. Once the flow of execution leaves a method, its parameters and other local variables cease to exist. The scope of local variables is referred to as **local scope**.

Local scope

> **JAVA LANGUAGE RULE** **Scope.** Local variables, that is, parameters and variables declared in the body of a method, have **local scope** that extends from the point where they are defined to the end of the block of code in which they are defined. In particular, the scope of a parameter is the entire body of the method in which it is declared.

Class scope

By contrast, instance variables, class variables, and all methods have scope that extends throughout the entire class. This is known as **class scope**. They can be used in the body of any method and in expressions that assign initial values to class-level variables. There are two restrictions to remember. First, instance variables and instance methods cannot be used in the body of a class method, one modified with `static`, unless an instance of the class is created there, and then the dot notation of qualified names must be used to refer to the variable or method. This is because class methods are called without reference to a particular instance of the class. The `main()` method of the `OneRowNim` class defined in Chapter 2 is an example of such a class method. In that case, we tested the instance methods of `OneRowNim` by creating an instance of `OneRowNim` and using it to call its instance methods:

```
OneRowNim game = new OneRowNim();    // Create instance
game.report();                        // Call an instance method
```

The second restriction involved in class scope is that one class-level variable can be used in the expression that initializes a second class-level variable only if the first is declared before the second. There is no similar restriction on methods.

> **JAVA LANGUAGE RULE** **Scope.** Class-level variables, that is, instance variables and class variables, have **class scope**, which extends throughout the class. Methods also have class scope.

Simple vs. qualified names

Except for the restrictions noted above, methods and class-level variables can be referred to within the same class by their simple names, with just the method (or variable) name itself, rather than by their qualified names, with the dot operator. Thus, in `OneRowNim`, we can refer to `nSticks` and `report()` in the bodies of other instance methods. In a class method, such as `main()`, we would have to create an instance of `OneRowNim` with a name like `game` and refer to `game.report()`.

> **JAVA LANGUAGE RULE**   **Qualified Names.** Within the same class, references to class methods or class variables can be made in terms of simple names. Within the bodies of instance methods, references to instance variables and references to other instance methods can also be made in terms of simple names. However, within the bodies of class methods, qualified names, or dot notation, must be used to refer to instance methods or instance variables just as they are referred to in other classes.

> **DEBUGGING TIP: Scope Error.**   It would be a syntax error to refer to a method's parameters or other local variables from outside the method.

3.2.1   Arguments and Parameters

The new class definition for OneRowNim is given in Figure 3.1. Now that we have a single method, takeSticks(), that can be used to take away a variable number of sticks, we have removed the three methods we wrote in Chapter 2, takeOne(), takeTwo(), and takeThree(), from OneRowNim. Using a single method, with a parameter, is clearly a better design. To see this, just imagine what we would have to do if we did not use a parameter and we wanted to take away four sticks, or five, or more. If we did not have parameters, we would have to write a separate method for each case, which is clearly a bad idea. Using parameters in this way leads to a more generally useful method and thus is an example of the generality principle.

Now let's consider how we would create a OneRowNim instance and use the new method in the main() method or in a different class. If we want to have an instance of OneRowNim object to remove three sticks on the first move by using the takeSticks() method, we need to pass the int value 3 to the method. In order to effect this action, we would use the following statements:

```
OneRowNim game = new OneRowNim();
game.takeSticks(3);
```

```
public class OneRowNim
{ private int nSticks = 7;              // Start with 7 sticks
  private int player = 1;              // Player 1 plays first

  public void takeSticks(int num)
  { nSticks = nSticks - num;
    player = 3 - player;
  } // takeSticks()

  public void report()
  { System.out.println("Number of sticks left: " + nSticks);
    System.out.println("Next turn by player " + player);
  } // report()
} // OneRowNim1 class
```

Figure 3.1 The OneRowNim class definition with takeSticks() method.

Because the definition of `takeSticks()` includes a single `int` parameter, we must supply a single `int` value (such as 3) when we invoke it. When the method is invoked, its formal parameter (`num`) will be set to the value we supply (3). The value we supply does not have to be a literal `int` value. We can supply any expression or variable that evaluates to an `int` value. For example:

```
int val = 7 - 5;
game.takeSticks(val);
```

In this case, the value being passed to `takeSticks()` is 2, the value that `val` has at the time the method call is made.

It would be an error to try to pass a value that is not a `int` to `takeSticks()`. For example, each of the following invocations of `takeSticks()` results in a syntax error:

```
game.takeSticks();       // no argument is supplied
game.takeSticks("3");    // "3" is a String, not an int
game.takeSticks(int);    // int not is an int value
```

Parameter vs. argument

As you will recall from Chapter 0, the value passed to a method when it is invoked is called an argument. Even though the terms *argument* and *parameter* are sometimes used interchangeably, it will be useful to observe a distinction. We will use *parameter* to refer to the formal parameter in the method definition—the variable used to pass data to a method. We use *argument* to refer to the actual value supplied when the method is invoked.

> **DEBUGGING TIP: Type Error.** It would be a syntax error to use an argument whose type does not match the type of its corresponding parameter.

Defining vs. calling a method

The distinction between parameter and argument is related to the difference between *defining* a method and *invoking* a method. Defining a method is a matter of writing a method definition, such as

```
public void printStr(String s)
{   System.out.println(s);
}
```

Invoking a method

This definition defines a method that takes a single `String` parameter, `s`, and simply prints the value of its parameter. On the other hand, invoking a method is a matter of writing a method call statement, such as

```
printStr("HelloWorld");
```

This statement calls the `printStr()` method and passes it the string "HelloWorld." This notation assumes that the call to the instance method `printStr()` is made within the body of another instance method of the same class.

```
public static void main (String argv[])
{   OneRowNim game;                     // Declare a OneRowNim object
    game = new OneRowNim();             // Instantiate the references
    game.takeSticks(3);                 // remove 3 sticks
} // main()
```

Figure 3.2   A main() method to test the takeSticks() method.

3.2.2   Passing an int Value to a OneRowNim Method

To get a clearer picture of the interaction that takes place when we invoke takeSticks() and pass it an int value, let's write a main() method to test our new version of OneRowNim.

Our first version of main() is shown in Figure 3.2. We will use it to trace how the parameter of takeSticks() interacts with the instance variables nSticks and player. The statements in the main() program simply create an instance of OneRowNim that is referenced by game and invoke the setSticks() method with an argument of 3.

To get a clearer understanding of how a parameter works, it will be instructive to trace through the code in main(). Figure 3.3 displays how the states of the instance variables of game and the parameter of takeSticks() interact.

Executing the first two statements of main() creates the instance game of OneRowNim. Figure 3.2(a) shows the initial state of game. When the takeSticks(3) method call is made, a parameter (which is a local variable) named num is created and the value 3 is stored in it. The state of the instance variables and the parameter are shown in (b). Then the body of takeSticks() is executed. The new state of game is shown in (c). After the flow of control leaves the body of takeSticks() and returns to main(), the memory location which stored the value of the parameter num is released for other uses. The state of game at this point is shown in (d). Note that the value of nSticks has been reduced to 4.

Figure 3.3   Tracing the state of game (a) Just before calling take-Sticks(3). (b) Just before executing the body of takeSticks(3). (c) Just after executing the body of take-Sticks(3). (d) After flow of control leaves takeSticks().

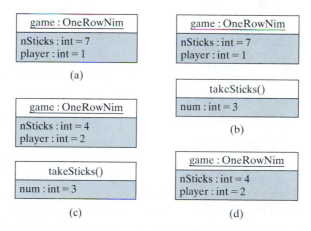

3.2.3   Passing Keyboard Input to takeSticks()

To complete this section, let's modify our main() method in Figure 3.2 so that it prompts the user to input an integer from the keyboard and then uses a Scanner object, introduced in Chapter 2, to read the integer. That integer will then be used as the argument in a call to

```
import java.util.Scanner;

public static void main (String argv[])
{ Scanner sc;                          // Declare a Scanner variable
  sc = Scanner.create(System.in);      // Instantiate it
  OneRowNim game;                      // Declare a OneRowNim variable
  game = new OneRowNim();              // Instantiate it
  game.report();                       // Report state of game
  System.out.println("Input 1, 2, or 3 and hit enter:");
  int num = sc.nextInt();              // Read an int from keyboard
  game.takeSticks(num);                // Use the value read
  game.report();                       // Report state of game
} // main()
```

Figure 3.4   A main() method with keyboard input for OneRowNim.

takeSticks(). These modifications have been incorporated into the revised version of the main() method shown in Figure 3.4. If we now run this program, the following output will be generated in the console window before waiting for keyboard input:

```
Number of sticks left: 7
Next turn by player 1
Input 1, 2, or 3 and hit enter:
```

If the user then inputs a 2 from the keyboard, that input will be read and the takeSticks() method will remove two sticks. The output in the console window will now look like:

```
Number of sticks left: 7
Next turn by player 1
Input 1, 2, or 3 and hit enter:2
Number of sticks left: 5
Next turn by player 2
```

SELF-STUDY EXERCISES

EXERCISE 3.1   Explain the difference between a *method declaration* and a *method invocation*.

EXERCISE 3.2   Explain the difference between a *formal parameter* and an *argument*.

EXERCISE 3.3   Modify the OneRowNim class of Figure 3.4 by adding two instance variables of type String to store the names of the two players. Choose names for the instance variables that would be appropriate for storing names for player 1 and player 2. Write a method named setNames() with two string parameters that assigns the first parameter to the instance variable you created for the name of player 1. The second parameter should be assigned to the other new instance variable.

EXERCISE 3.4   Write a statement that calls the setName() method of the preceding exercise and sets the name of player 1 of game to "Xena" and the name of player 2 to "Yogi."

3.3   Constructor Methods

In the preceding section, we looked at several examples of mutator methods that change the values of private instance variables of an object. It is possible to define mutator methods to set the initial values of instance variables after an object is created, but initial values can also be set by constructors.

As you will recall from Chapter 0, a *constructor* method is used to create an instance (or object) of a class and to assign initial values to instance variables. A constructor declaration looks just like a method definition except that it must have the same name as the class, and it cannot declare a result type. Unlike the class-level variables and methods of a class, constructors are not considered members of the class. Therefore, they are not inherited by a class's subclasses. Access to constructors is governed by the access modifiers `public` and `private`. Here is a simple constructor for our `OneRowNim` class:

Constructor names

```
public OneRowNim()
{   nSticks = 7;
    player = 1;
}
```

This constructor merely sets the initial values of the instance variables, `nSticks` and `player`. In our current version of `OneRowNim`, these variables are given initial values by using initializer statements when they are first declared:

Constructing an object

```
private int nSticks = 7;
private int player = 1;
```

So we now have two ways to initialize a class's instance variables. In the `OneRowNim` class it doesn't really matter which way we do it. However, the constructor provides more flexibility because it allows the state of the object to be initialized at runtime. Of course, it would be somewhat redundant (though permissible) to initialize the same variable twice, once when it is declared and again in the constructor, so we should choose one or the other way to do this. For now, let's stick with initializing the instance variables when they are declared.

Initializing variables

EFFECTIVE DESIGN: Constructors.   Constructors provide a flexible way to initialize an object's instance variables when the object is created.

A constructor cannot return a value, and therefore its declaration cannot include a return type. Because they cannot return values, constructors cannot be invoked by a regular method invocation. Instead, constructors are invoked as part of an *instance creation expression* when instance objects are created. An instance creation expression involves the keyword `new` followed by the constructor invocation:

Constructors can't return a value

```
OneRowNim game1          // Declare
    = new OneRowNim();   // and instantiate game1
OneRowNim game2          // Declare
    = new OneRowNim();   // and instantiate game2
```

Note here that we have combined variable declaration and instantiation into a single statement, whereas in some previous examples we used separate declaration and instantiation statements. Either way is acceptable.

> **JAVA LANGUAGE RULE**   **Constructors.** Constructors cannot return a value. Therefore, no return type should be declared when a constructor is defined.

> **DEBUGGING TIP: When to Use Return.**   All method definitions except constructors must declare a return type.

State initialization

Constructors should be used to perform the necessary initialization operations during object creation. In the case of a `OneRowNim` object, what initializations could be performed? One initialization that would seem appropriate is to initialize the initial number of sticks to a specified number. In order to do this, we would need a constructor with a single `int` parameter:

```
public OneRowNim(int sticks)
{    nSticks = sticks;
}
```

Now that we have this constructor, we can use it when we create instances of `OneRowNim`:

```
OneRowNim game1 = new OneRowNim(21);
OneRowNim game2 = new OneRowNim(13);
```

The effect of these statements is the same as if we had used the `setSticks()` method that was discussed briefly on page 105. The difference is that we can now set the number of sticks when we create the object.

Should we keep the preceding constructor, the `setSticks()` method, or both in our class definition? The constructor can only be invoked as part of a `new` statement when the object is created, but the `setSticks()` method could be called anytime we want. In many cases, having redundant methods for doing the same task in different ways would be an asset, because it allows for more flexibility in how the class can be used. However, for a game like One-Row Nim, a major concern is that the two instance variables get changed only in a manner consistent with the rules for One-Row Nim. The best way to guarantee this is to have `takeSticks()` as the only method that changes the instance variables `nSticks` and `player`. The only time it should be possible to set the number of sticks for a game is when a constructor is used to create a new instance of `OneRowNim`.

SELF-STUDY EXERCISES

EXERCISE 3.5   What's wrong with the following constructor definition?

```
public void OneRowNim(int sticks)
{    nSticks = sticks;
}
```

EXERCISE 3.6   Change the `OneRowNim(int sticks)` constructor so that it sets the number of sticks, and also have it also set player 2 as the player who takes the first turn.

3.3.1   Default Constructors

As we noted in Chapter 2, Java automatically provides a *default constructor* when a class does not contain a constructor.

> **JAVA LANGUAGE RULE**   **Default Constructor.**   If a class contains no constructor declarations, Java will automatically supply a default constructor. The default constructor takes no parameters. If the class is `public`, the default constructor will also be `public` and, thus, accessible to other objects.

The default constructor's role is simply to create an instance (an object) of that class. It takes no parameters. In terms of what it does, the default constructor for OneRowNim would be equivalent to a `public` constructor method with an empty body:

```
public OneRowNim() { }
```

This explains why the following statement was valid when a class definition of OneRowNim contained no explicit definition of a constructor:

```
OneRowNim game = new OneRowNim();
```

3.3.2   Constructor Overloading and Method Signatures

It is often quite useful to have more than one constructor for a given class. For example, consider the following two OneRowNim constructors:

Flexible design

```
public OneRowNim() {} // Constructor #1
public OneRowNim(int sticks)    // Constructor #2
{    nSticks = sticks;
}
```

The first is an explicit representation of the default constructor. The second is the constructor we defined earlier to initialize the number of sticks in a OneRowNim object. Having multiple constructors lends flexibility to the design of a class. In this case, the first constructor merely accepts OneRowNim's default initial state. The second enables the user to initialize the number of sticks to something other than the default value.

In Java, as in some other programming languages, when two different methods have the same name, it is known as **method overloading**. In this case, OneRowNim is used as the name for two different constructor methods. What distinguishes one constructor from another is its *signature*, which consists of its name together with the number and types of formal parameters it takes. Thus, our OneRowNim constructors have the following signatures:

Method overloading

```
OneRowNim()
OneRowNim(int)
```

Both have the same name, but the first takes no parameters, whereas the second takes a single `int` parameter.

Methods are known by their signatures

The same point applies to methods in general. Two methods can have the same name as long as they have distinct signatures. A **method signature** consists of its name, and the number, types, and order of its formal parameters. A class may not contain two methods with the same signature, but it may contain several methods with the same name, provided each has a distinct signature.

JAVA LANGUAGE RULE   Method Signature. A **method signature** consists of the method's name, plus the number, types, and order of its formal parameters. A class may not contain two methods with the same signature.

There is no limit to the amount of overloading that can be done in designing constructors and methods. The only restriction is that each method have a distinct signature. For example, suppose that in addition to the two constructors we have already defined, we want a constructor that would let us set both the number of sticks and the player who starts first. The following constructor will do what we want:

```
public OneRowNim(int sticks, int starter)
{    nSticks = sticks;    // Set the number of sticks
     player = starter;    // Set who starts
}
```

When calling this constructor, we would have to take care to pass the number of sticks as the value of the first argument and either 1 or 2 as the value of the second argument:

```
OneRowNim game3 = new OneRowNim(14, 2);
OneRowNim game4 = new OneRowNim(31, 1);
```

If we mistakenly reversed 14 and 2 in the first of these statements, we would end up with a `OneRowNim` game that starts with two sticks and has player 14 as the player with the first move.

We have now defined three constructor methods for the `OneRowNim` class. Each constructor has the name `OneRowNim`, but each has a distinct signature:

```
OneRowNim()
OneRowNim(int)
OneRowNim(int, int)
```

3.3.3 Constructor Invocation

A constructor method is invoked only as part of a `new` expression when an instance object is first created. Each of these is a valid invocation of a `OneRowNim` constructor:

A constructor is invoked once to create an object

```
OneRowNim game1 = new OneRowNim();       // Default constructor
OneRowNim game2 = new OneRowNim(21);      // Sets number of sticks
OneRowNim game3 = new OneRowNim(19, 2);   // Sets both instance variables
```

The following constructor invocations are invalid because there are no matching constructor definitions:

```
OneRowNim game4 = new OneRowNim("21");      // No matching constructors
OneRowNim game5 = new OneRowNim(12, 2, 5);
```

In the first case, there is no constructor method that takes a `String` parameter, so there is no matching constructor. In the second case, there is no constructor that takes three `int` arguments. In both cases, the Java compiler would complain that there is no constructor method that matches the invocation.

> **DEBUGGING TIP: Method Call.** The signature of the method call—its name and the number, types, and order of its arguments—must exactly match the signature of the method definition.

3.4 Retrieving Information from an Object

The modifications we have made to the `OneRowNim` class allow us to set the instance variables of a `OneRowNim` object with a constructor, but there is no way for us to retrieve their values other than to use the `report()` method to write a message to the console. We will want to be able to ask a `OneRowNim` object to provide us with the number of sticks remaining and who plays next when we develop a graphical user interface for `OneRowNim` in the next chapter. We declared `nSticks` and `player` as `private` variables, so we cannot access them directly. Therefore, we will need accessor methods to *get* the values of each of the instance variables. Consider the following method definitions:

```
public int getSticks()
{   return nSticks;
}
public int getPlayer()
{   return player;
}
```

Recall that a method's *ResultType* is specified just in front of the *MethodName*. We want the two methods to return `int` values that represent `OneRowNim`'s instance variables. Therefore, their result types are both declared `int`.

Before we discuss how the value that is returned by a method is used when the method is called, let's consider one more method definition. Many methods that return a value do a computation rather than simply return the value of an instance variable. For example, suppose that we wish to define a method for the `OneRowNim` class that will inform the user of an instance of the class that the game is over. Thus we want a method that, when called, returns a `true` or `false` depending on whether or not all the sticks have been taken. `gameOver()` is a descriptive name of such a method, and the method should have a `boolean` result type. This method should return `true` when the instance variable `nSticks` no longer contains a positive `int` value. Thus we can define:

```java
public boolean gameOver()
{    return (nSticks <= 0);
}
```

The expression `(nSticks <= 0)` evaluates to a `false` value if `nSticks` stores a positive value, and it evaluates to `true` otherwise. Thus the value returned is precisely what is required.

3.4.1 Invoking a Method that Returns a Value

Retrieving
information

When we invoke a method that returns a value, the invocation expression takes on, or is replaced by, the value that is returned. For example, if we execute the statements

```java
OneRowNim game1 = new OneRowNim(11);
int sticksLeft = game1.getSticks();
```

the expression `game1.getSticks()` will take on the value 11 after the `getSticks()` method is finished executing. At that point, the second statement above can be treated as if expression `game1.getSticks()` is replaced with the value 11, which is assigned to `sticks-Left`. In effect, the second statement is equivalent to the following statement:

```java
int sticksLeft = 11;
```

JAVA LANGUAGE RULE   **Evaluating Method Calls.** A nonvoid method call is an expression that has a value of a particular type. After the method is executed, the method call expression becomes the value returned.

We can use a value returned by a method call the same way we use a literal value of the same type. It can be assigned to variables, be part of a numerical expression, or be an argument of another method. All of the following statements involve valid calls of methods that return values:

```java
int fewerSticks = game1.getSticks() - 1;
boolean done = game1.gameOver();
System.out.println(game1.getPlayer());
game1.getSticks();
```

In each statement, the method call can be replaced with the value it returns. Note that the last statement is valid but does nothing useful. In Java and some other languages like C and C++, methods that return a value can simply be called without making use of the value returned. This may be useful if the method changes the state of instance variables or sends a message to another object or an output device. The method `getSticks()` does nothing but return the value of `nSticks`, so simply calling the method accomplishes nothing.

3.4.2   An Expanded `OneRowNim` Class

Let's add the new methods that return values to our `OneRowNim` class. We might note that the `report()` method from the preceding chapter displays the values of `nSticks` and `player` in the console window, which now could be done by using the methods `getSticks()` and `getPlayer()` with `System.out.println()`. Calling `report()` is an easy way to display the values of both instance variables, but it cannot provide access to either variable as an `int` value. So let's keep all three methods in our class definition. The inconvenience of a small amount of redundancy is outweighed by the added flexibility of being able to call all three methods.

Redundancy and flexibility

> **EFFECTIVE DESIGN: Using Redundancy.**   Incorporating some redundancy into a class, such as providing more than one way to access the value of an instance variable, makes the class more widely usable.

Figure 3.5 provides a UML class diagram of the expanded `OneRowNim` class.

Let's also consider a new `main()` method to test the new methods of the class. A very short list of statements that call each of the three new methods returning values is given in the `main()` method in Figure 3.6. The output to the console when this program is run will be:

```
The game is over is: false
The next turn is by player: 1
Sticks remaining: 11
```

Note that the constructor sets `player` to 2, so `player` stores the value 1 after one turn.

OneRowNim
− nSticks : int
− player : int
+ OneRowNim()
+ OneRowNim(in sticks : int)
+ OneRowNim(in sticks : int, in starter : int)
+ takeSticks(in num : int)
+ getSticks() : int
+ getPlayer() : int
+ gameOver() : boolean
+ report()

Figure 3.5   A UML class diagram for the expanded `OneRowNim`.

```
public static void main(String[] args)
{ OneRowNim game = new OneRowNim(13,2);
  game.takeSticks(2);
  System.out.print("The game is over is: ");
  System.out.println(game.gameOver());
  System.out.print("The next turn is by player: ");
  System.out.println(game.getPlayer());
  System.out.print("Sticks remaining: ");
  System.out.println(game.getSticks());
} // main()
```

Figure 3.6   A main() method that tests the new methods for OneRowNim

SELF-STUDY EXERCISES

EXERCISE 3.7   What would these segments of Java code display on the screen?

```
OneRowNim myGame = new OneRowNim(10,2);
System.out.println(myGame.getPlayer());
System.out.println(2 * myGame.getSticks());
System.out.println(myGame.gameOver());
```

EXERCISE 3.8   Suppose that an int instance variable named nMoves that counts the number of moves taken in a One-Row Nim game is added to the OneRowNim class. Write a Java method for the OneRowNim class to *get* the value stored in nMoves.

EXERCISE 3.9   Write a method for the OneRowNim class called playerOneGoesNext() that returns a boolean value. The value returned should be true if and only if player 1 has the next turn.

3.5   Passing a Value and Passing a Reference

The effect of passing arguments to a method differs depending on whether you are passing a value of primitive type (such as 5 or true) or a value of reference type (such as "Hello" or game1). When an argument of primitive type is passed to a method, a copy of the argument is passed to the formal parameter. For example, consider the PrimitiveCall class shown in Figure 3.7. Note that we have an int variable k, which initially stores the value 5, and a method myMethod(), which takes an int parameter n. In this case, when we invoke myMethod(k), k's value (5) is copied into n and stored there during the method.

Passing a primitive value

One implication of passing a copy of a primitive value to a method is that the original value of k in main() cannot be altered from inside the method. Thus, the output generated by PrimitiveCall would be

```
main: k= 5
myMethod: n= 5
myMethod: n= 100
main: k= 5
```

```
public class PrimitiveCall
{
    public static void myMethod(int n)
    {   System.out.println("myMethod: n= " + n);
        n = 100;
        System.out.println("myMethod: n= " + n);
    } // myMethod()

    public static void main(String argv[])
    {   int k = 5;
        System.out.println("main: k= " + k);
        myMethod(k);
        System.out.println("main: k= " + k);
    } // main()
} // PrimitiveCall class
```

Figure 3.7 Passing a primitive value to a method.

Note that in `main()`, k's value is printed both before and after `myMethod()` is called, but its value is unaffected even though n's value is changed within the method. This is because `myMethod()` contains just a *copy* of k's value, not k itself. Any changes to the copy within `myMethod()` leave k unaltered (see Fig. 3.8).

> **JAVA LANGUAGE RULE** **Passing a Primitive Value.** When a value of a primitive type, like `boolean` or `int`, is passed to a method, a copy of the value is passed. That's why its original value remains unchanged outside the method even if the copy is changed inside the method.

In contrast to this, when an argument of a reference type is passed to a method, a copy of the reference to the object itself is assigned to the parameter. For example, in the case of a `String` parameter or a `OneRowNim` parameter, the method would be given a reference to the object—that is, the address of the object. The object itself is *not* passed, because it would be too inefficient to copy the entire object with all its data and methods. However, because the object's reference gives the object's location in memory, the method will have access to the object and can make changes to the original object from within the method.

For example, consider the `ReferenceCall` class (Fig. 3.9). In this case, `myMethod()` takes a parameter g of type `OneRowNim`. Because a `OneRowNim` instance is an object, g is a

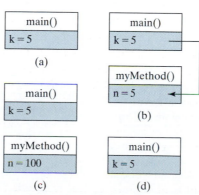

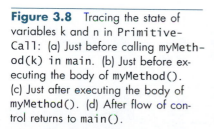

Figure 3.8 Tracing the state of variables k and n in `Primitive-Call`: (a) Just before calling myMethod(k) in main. (b) Just before executing the body of myMethod(). (c) Just after executing the body of myMethod(). (d) After flow of control returns to main().

```java
public class ReferenceCall
{
    public static void myMethod(OneRowNim g)
    {   System.out.print("myMethod: Number of sticks: ");
        System.out.println(g.getSticks());
        g.takeSticks(3);
        System.out.print("myMethod: Number of sticks: ");
        System.out.println(g.getSticks());
    } // myMethod()

    public static void main(String argv[])
    {   OneRowNim game = new OneRowNim(10);
        System.out.print("main: Number of sticks: ");
        System.out.println(game.getSticks());
        myMethod(game);
        System.out.print("main: Number of sticks: ");
        System.out.println(game.getSticks());
    // main()
} // ReferenceCall class
```

Figure 3.9 Passing a reference value to a method.

reference variable. So when myMethod(game) is invoked in main(), a reference to game is passed to myMethod(). Note that in myMethod(), we use takeSticks(3) to change the number of sticks of g from 10 to 7, and this change persists even after the method returns control to main(). The reason is that during the method's execution, both game and g refer to the exact same object (see Fig. 3.10). The output generated by ReferenceCall would be

```
main: Number of sticks: 10
myMethod: Number of sticks: 10
myMethod: Number of sticks: 7
main: Number of sticks: 7
```

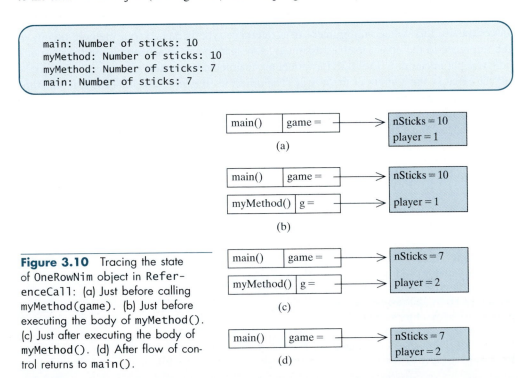

Figure 3.10 Tracing the state of OneRowNim object in ReferenceCall: (a) Just before calling myMethod(game). (b) Just before executing the body of myMethod(). (c) Just after executing the body of myMethod(). (d) After flow of control returns to main().

This illustrates that when passing a reference variable to a method, it is possible for the method to change the state of the object associated with the reference variable. In subsequent chapters we will see ways to make use of this feature of reference parameters.

JAVA LANGUAGE RULE **Passing a Reference.** When a reference to an object is passed to a method, any changes made to the object from within the method will persist when the method is finished executing.

DEBUGGING TIP: Side Effects. An unintended change to an object is called a **side effect**. In designing methods, care should be taken to ensure that the method does not produce unwanted side effects in objects passed as reference parameters.

3.6 Flow of Control: Control Structures

We have been ignoring a couple of problems with the definition of the OneRowNim class. One problem is that we would describe a One-Row Nim game as two players taking turns until there are no more sticks. An object using OneRowNim would need a way to repeatedly execute a group of statements. One command in Java that controls the repetition of a block of statements is called a *while loop*. We will consider it later in this section.

A second problem is with the definition of takeSticks():

```java
public void takeSticks(int num)
{   nSticks - num;
    player = 3 - player;
}
```

It is possible to call this method with an argument greater than 3 or less than 1. The call game.takeSticks(5) will remove five sticks even though the rules of One-Row Nim say that you must remove one, two, or three. While you might assume that the user interface should prevent the user from breaking this rule, it is a far better design to deal with this in OneRowNim. To do so we need a Java structure that executes different statements depending on whether the parameter is greater than 3, less than 1, or between 1 and 3. The Java if-else statement has this capability. A fuller treatment of control structures appears in Chapter 6, but in this section, we will briefly introduce a couple of simple control structures. This will enable us to write programs that take more interesting actions.

3.6.1 The Simple if Statement

A **selection** control structure, allows a program to select between two or more alternative paths of execution. The if statement is the most basic selection control structure in Java. Most programming languages have its equivalent.

Simple if
statement

JAVA LANGUAGE RULE if **Statement.** The if statement has the following syntax:

> *if* (*boolean expression*)
> *containedstatement*;

The statement contained in the `if` statement can be any valid Java statement, including a compound statement. (Recall from Chapter 1 that a compound statement is a set of statements contained within curly braces.) The `boolean expression` is an expression that is either `true` or `false`. We have seen examples of boolean expressions that involve `int` variables, `int` values, and the inequality or equality operators. A method call to a method with a `boolean` result type is another example of a `boolean` expression. Given this description of `if` statement syntax, the following are examples of valid `if` statements:

```java
if (true) System.out.println("Hello");
if (nSticks <= 0) System.out.println("game is over");
```

For readability, we usually write an `if` statement with its contained statement indented on the next line:

```java
if (true)
    System.out.println("Hello");
if (nSticks <= 0)
    System.out.println("game is over");
```

The following are all examples of syntax errors involving the `if` statement:

```java
if true                              // Parentheses are missing
    System.out.println("Hello");
if  (nSticks <= 0) return            // Semicolon missing
if  ("true") return;                 // "true" is not a boolean
if  (true) "Hello";                  // "Hello" is  not a statement
```

Semantically, the `if` statement has the following interpretation: First, the boolean condition is evaluated. If it is true, then the contained statement is executed; if it is false, then the contained statement is not executed. This is shown in Figure 3.11. The flowchart clearly shows that program flow will take one or the other of the alternative paths coming out of the diamond-shaped boolean condition box. The branch through the rectangular statement box will be taken when the boolean condition is true; otherwise the statement will be skipped.

Figure 3.11 Flowchart of the `if` statement. Diamond-shaped symbols at the branch points contain `boolean` expressions. Rectangular symbols can only contain executable statements. Circles act simply as connectors, to connect two or more paths.

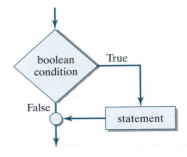

As another example, consider the definition of a `getPlayerString()` method for the `OneRowNim` class:

```java
public String getPlayerString()
{
  if (player == 1)
    return "Player One";    // Exit the method
  if (player == 2)
    return "Player Two";    // Exit the method
  return "Player error";    // Exit the method
}
```

The flowchart in Figure 3.12 shows the program flow of the entire `getPlayerString()` method. It is important to note that when a `return` statement is executed in a method, control is returned immediately to the calling method. Thus, if `player == 1` is true, the string "Player One" is returned to the calling method and the `getPlayerString()` method exits at this point. If it is false, then `player == 2` should be true (if we have a consistent state) and the string "Player Two" should be returned and the method exited. Thus, if we have a consistent state—that is, if `player` has value 1 or 2—then the third `return` statement should never be reached.

The following example shows the more common case where the statement contained in an `if` statement can be a compound statement:

Compound statement

```java
if (player == 1)
{   String s = "Player One";
    System.out.print (s);
    System.out.println (" plays next");
    System.out.println (" The game is not over");
}
```

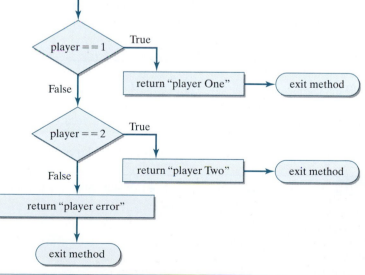

Figure 3.12 Flowchart of the getPlayerString() method.

Local scope

If `player == 1` is true, then all four statements in the contained compound statement will be executed. Note here that we are declaring the local variable, `s`, in this block. Its scope would extend only to the end of the block. Note also that when we use a compound statement, the compound statement itself is not followed by a semicolon because it is already enclosed in braces.

Forgetting the braces around the compound statement is a common programming error. Merely indenting the statements following the `if` clause does not alter the logic of the `if` statement. For example, the following if statement still has only one statement in its `if` clause:

```
if (condition1)
    System.out.println("One");
    System.out.println("Two"); // Not part of if statement
```

This segment will always print "Two" because the second `println()` is not part of the `if` statement. To include it in the `if` statement, you must enclose both `println()` statements within braces:

```
if (condition1)
{   System.out.println("One");
    System.out.println("Two");
}
```

DEBUGGING TIP: Indentation.   Indentation can improve the readability of a program but does not affect its logic. Braces must be used to group statements in the `if` clause.

3.6.2   The `if-else` Statement

A second version of the `if` statement incorporates an `else` clause into the structure. This allows us to execute either of two separate statements (simple or compound) as the result of one boolean expression. For example, the statement

```
if (player == 1)
    System.out.println("Player One");
else
    System.out.println("Player Two");
```

will print "Player One" if `player == 1` is true. Otherwise, it will print "Player Two."

JAVA LANGUAGE RULE   If-else **Statement.** The `if-else` statement has the following syntax:

$$if \quad (boolean expression)$$
$$statement1;$$
$$else$$
$$statement2;$$

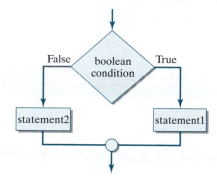

Figure 3.13 Flowchart of the
`if-else` statement.

If-else syntax

As in the case of the simple `if` statement, the keyword `if` is followed by a parenthesized *boolean expression*, which is followed by *statement1*, which may be either simple or compound. If *statement1* is a simple statement, then it is followed by a semicolon. The `else clause` follows immediately after *statement1*. It begins with the keyword `else`, which is followed by *statement2*, which can also be either a simple or compound statement. Note that there is no boolean expression following the `else` keyword. In an `if-else` statement, the boolean expression following the keyword `if` goes with both the `if` and `else` clauses.

Semantically, the `if-else` statement has the following interpretation: If the *boolean expression* is true, execute *statement1*; otherwise execute *statement2*. This interpretation is shown in Figure 3.13.

3.6.3 The Nested `if-else` Multiway Selection Structure

The statements that one inserts in place of *statement1* and *statement2* in the `if-else` statement can be any executable statement, including another `if` statement or `if-else` statement. In other words, it is possible to embed one or more `if-else` statements inside another `if-else` statement, thereby creating a *nested* control structure. As with most things, making a control structure too complex is not a good idea, but there is a standard nested `if-else` control structure that is very useful. It is known as **multiway selection**. As shown in Figure 3.14, the multiway structure is used when you want to select one and only one option from several alternatives.

Suppose we have an `int` variable `num` that will contain one of the values 1, 2, or 3 unless there has been an error assigning a value to it. Suppose that we want to write code that will write out the English word for the value in `num`. In the example shown in Figure 3.14 there are three alternatives plus an error state. Here is the Java code for this example:

```java
if (num == 1)
   System.out.println("One");
else if (num == 2)
   System.out.println("Two");
else if (num == 3)
   System.out.println("Three");
else
   System.out.println("Error: Unknown value");
```

Note that the multiway structure has a single entry point and that only one of the four possible alternatives is executed. The code will print exactly one of the strings.

Multiple alternatives

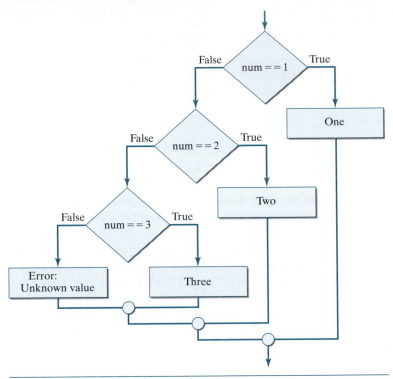

Figure 3.14 Flowchart of a nested if-else statement.

We will have many occasions to use the if-else structure. Although it does not represent a significant change, we could rewrite our takeStick() method to make use of the if-else instead of the somewhat obscure statement

```
player = 3 - player;
```

to change the value of player from 1 to 2, or vice versa:

```
public String takeSticks(int num)
{   nSticks = nSticks - num;
    if (player == 1)
      player = 2;    // From 1 to 2
    else
      player = 1;    // From 2 to 1
}
```

This version of takeSticks() involves four lines of code instead of one but in some respects is simpler to understand. The if-statement tests whether the value of player is 1. If it is, the value is changed to 2. If the value of player is not 1, then the value must be 2 and so the value is changed to 1. Since both versions of the code will give precisely the same result, a programmer could choose to write the code either way.

SELF-STUDY EXERCISES

EXERCISE 3.10   Consider the following method with `boolean` parameter.

```
public String getStatus(boolean isDone)
{   if (isDone)
        return "Done";
    else
        return "Not Done";
}
```

Draw a flowchart for the `if-else` version of the `getStatus()` method, using the figures in
this section as a guide. The `if-else` structure should be drawn exactly as shown in Figure 3.11.
It should have a single entry point that leads directly to the top of a diamond-shaped box that
contains a boolean condition. There should be two branches coming out of the condition box.
The one going to the right is the true case, and the one going to the left is the false case. Each of
these branches should contain one rectangular box, which contains the statements that would
be executed in that case. The left and right branches should be connected by a circular symbol
that is aligned directly under the diamond box whose conditions it connects. There should be
a single exit arrow pointing directly down.

*Flowchart
symbols*

EXERCISE 3.11   Identify the error in the following statements:

```
if (isHeavy == true)
    System.out.println("Heavy");
else ;
    System.out.println("Light");

if (isLong == true)
    System.out.println("Long")
else
    System.out.println("Short");
```

EXERCISE 3.12   Suppose we have an `int` instance variable named `player` in some class describing a three-person game. Write a method named `getPlayerName()` that returns a `String`.
It should return "Ann," "Bill," "Cal," or "Error" when the value of `player` is respectively 1,
2, 3, or any other value.

EXERCISE 3.13   How does a parameter for a primitive type differ from a parameter for a reference
type?

3.6.4   The `while` Structure

A **repetition structure** is a control structure that repeats a statement or sequence of statements
in a controlled way. Repetition structures are also referred to as **loop structures**. Many types
of programming tasks require a repetition structure. Consider some examples.

- You want to add up the squares of the numbers from 1 to 100.
- You want to compute compound interest on an amount of money in a savings account with
  a fixed interest rate if it is kept there for 30 years.
- A computer security employee wants to try every possible password in order to break into
  the account of a suspected spy.

- You want to have players input moves for a turn in a game until the game is over. Our OneRowNim is an example.

We will study several different repetition structures of Java in depth in Chapter 6. We will briefly consider the while statement here so as to be able to define more powerful and more interesting methods. Let us write a method that solves a slight generalization of the first problem above. We will use the while statement to sum the squares of integers from 1 to a number specified as a parameter of the method. Thus, the method call sumSquares(3) should return the value 14, since $1*1 + 2*2 + 3*3 = 1 + 4 + 9 = 14$.

```java
public int sumSquares(int max)
{ int num = 1;
  int sum = 0;
  while (num <=  max) {     // While num <= max
    sum = sum + num*num;    // Add square to sum
    num = num + 1;          // Add 1 to num
  }                         // while
  return sum;               // Return the sum
}
```

In this example, the variable num is assigned an initial value of 1 before the while statement. The boolean expression num <= max in parentheses after while states the condition for which we wish to continue summing squares. Finally, the last statement in the block following the boolean expression adds 1 to num—that is, this variable is updated at the end of the block.

The while **statement** is a loop statement in which the loop entry condition occurs before the loop body. It has the following general form:

JAVA LANGUAGE RULE   While **Statement.** The while statement has the following syntax:

$$while \quad (loop \; entry \; condition)$$
$$loop \; body$$

When the while statement is executed, the loop entry condition is evaluated, and if it evaluates to false, execution continues at the statement immediately after the loop body. If the loop entry condition evaluates to true, the loop body is executed and then the entry condition is evaluated again. The loop body continues to be executed until the loop entry condition evaluates to false.

To have a while statement accomplish a task, the variable or variables in the loop entry condition must be initialized correctly before the while statement, and these variables must be correctly updated at the end of the loop body. We can refer to the initializer statement followed by a while statement as a while **structure**. We can restate the above guidelines as a design principle:

EFFECTIVE DESIGN: Loop Structure.   A properly designed while structure must include an initializer, a loop entry condition, and an updater. The updater should guarantee that the loop entry condition eventually fails, thereby allowing the loop to terminate.

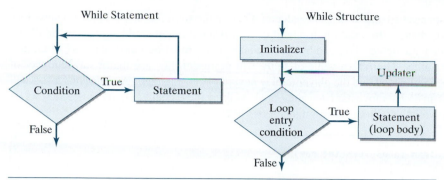

Figure 3.15 Flowchart of the `while` statement and `while` structure.

In pseudocode, the `while` *structure* would take the following form:

```
InitializerStatements;          // Initializer
while (loop entry condition)    // Bound test
{
    Statements;                 // Loop body
    UpdaterStatements;          // Updater
}
```

As its form suggests, the `while` structure is designed so that on some conditions the loop body will never be executed. Because it tests for the loop entry condition before the loop body, it is possible that the loop body may never be executed. We might say that the structure is designed to perform zero or more iterations.

For example, if the method call `sumSquares(-3)` is executed, the loop body will be skipped, because the loop entry condition `num <= max` is false to begin with. No iterations will be performed, and the algorithm will simply return the value 0.

Note also that the bound test in the `while` statement is preceded by initializer statements, and the loop body contains updater statements. The semantics of the `while` structure are shown in Figure 3.15.

SELF-STUDY EXERCISE

EXERCISE 3.14   Modify the definition of the `sumSquares()` method to define a method named `sumCubes()` that sums the cubes of integers from a minimum value up to a maximum value and returns the sum. `sumCubes()` should have two parameters that will store the minimum and maximum values. Thus the method call `sumCubes(2,3)` should return 35, since $2 * 2 * 2 + 3 * 3 * 3 = 8 + 27 = 35$.

3.7   Testing an Improved OneRowNim

Let us use the control structures we have discussed to improve the definition of the `take-Sticks()` method of `OneRowNim`. We noted earlier that our current definition allows four or more sticks to be removed from `nSticks` even though the rules of One-Row Nim indicate that a player must take one, two, or three sticks on a turn. We can use `if-else` statements to make certain that no more than three sticks are removed.

What should happen if the method `takeSticks()` is called with an argument that does not represent a legal number of sticks to remove? In this case, it would probably make sense to remove no sticks at all and to keep the value of `player` the same, so that the player whose turn it is does not change. In addition, it would be nice if the method could signal that an illegal move has been attempted. This can be accomplished if we redefine `takeSticks()` to return a `boolean` value. The return value of `true` will represent the case that a valid number of sticks has been removed and the player to play next has been changed. A return of `false` will indicate that an illegal move has been attempted. Making these changes to the `takeSticks()` method will yield a method definition that looks like:

```java
public boolean takeSticks(int num)
{    if (num < 1) {
        return false;              // Error
    } else if ( num > 3) {
        return false;              // Error
    } else
      {
          nSticks = nSticks - num;
          player = 3 - player;
          return true;
      } // else
} // takeSticks()
```

The new definition of the `takeSticks()` method has a boolean return type. Note that the `if-else` multiway structure is used to handle the three cases of the parameter `num` being less than 1, more than 3, or a valid number.

Let us add one more method to the `OneRowNim` class. We will define a method called `getWinner()` that will return the number of the winning player if the game is over. Recall that the player who takes the last stick loses, so after that last play, the player whose turn it is to play next is the winner. However, we should be concerned about what value to return if the game is not over when the method is called. A common strategy is to have a method return a special value to indicate that it is in a state in which it cannot return the value requested. Returning a 0 value is a good way to indicate that the game is not over and a winner cannot be identified. With this information, the `if-else` statement can be used in the definition of `getWinner()`.

```java
public int getWinner()
{    if (nSticks < 1)
        return player;
    else
        return 0;
} // getWinner()
```

We now have the final version (for this chapter) of the `OneRowNim` class whose implementation is given in Figure 3.16. We have turned a very simple class into one that contains quite a few elements. Compared to our first version (in Chapter 1), the current version of `OneRowNim` presents an interface (to other objects) that is easy and convenient to use. The constructor methods with parameters provide an easy way to create a `OneRowNim` instance with any number of sticks. The use of `private` instance variables and a single, carefully designed mutator method, `takeSticks()`, prevents other objects from tampering with the state of a `OneRowNim` object's state. The other methods provide a flexible way to find out the state of a `OneRowNim` object. The complete implementation of this `OneRowNim` is shown in Figure 3.16.

```java
public class OneRowNim
{    private int nSticks = 7;
     private int player = 1;

     public OneRowNim()
     {
     } // OneRowNim() constructor

     public OneRowNim(int sticks)
     {    nSticks = sticks;
     } // OneRowNim() constructor2

     public OneRowNim(int sticks, int starter)
     {    nSticks = sticks;
          player = starter;
     } // OneRowNim() constructor3

     public boolean takeSticks(int num)
     {    if (num < 1) return false;         // Error
          else if ( num > 3) return false;   // Error
          else                               // this is a valid move
          {    nSticks = nSticks - num;
               player = 3 - player;
               return true;
          } // else
     } // takeSticks()

     public int getSticks()
     {    return nSticks;
     } // getSticks()

     public int getPlayer()
     {    return player;
     } // getPlayer()

     public boolean gameOver()
     {    return (nSticks <= 0);
     } // gameOver()

     public int getWinner()
     {    if (nSticks < 1) return getPlayer();
          else return 0;   // game is not over
     } // getWinner()

     public void report()
     {    System.out.println("Number of sticks left: " + getSticks());
          System.out.println("Next turn by player " + getPlayer());
     } // report()
} // OneRowNim class
```

Figure 3.16 The OneRowNim class with improved methods.

We will now use a `while` statement to test the new methods of the class. A pseudocode description of how a game is played might look like:

```
Choose the initial number of sticks for the game
while the game is not over
{   Report the state of the game
    Process the next move
}
Report the state of the game
Report who the winner is
```

Translating this pseudocode into Java code in a `main()` method in a separate class gives us the class shown in Figure 3.17. We will use the `Scanner` class introduced in Chapter 2 to get moves from the keyboard for both players. Before each move, `game.report()` describes the state of the game before the user is prompted to input a move for one of the players. Readers interested in seeing the lengthy output to the console when the `TestOneRowNim` class is run are encouraged to actually run the program.

The return value of the `takeSticks()` method is ignored in this test program. We will make use of the return value in test programs in the next chapter when better user interfaces are developed for `OneRowNim`. Note, however, that taken together, the public methods for `OneRowNim` provide other objects with an interface that they can use to communicate with individual `OneRowNim` objects.

EFFECTIVE DESIGN: Interfaces.   Well-designed objects provide a useful public interface and protect the object's private elements from other objects.

Intelligent Agents

Wouldn't it be nice if we had a computer program that could schedule appointments for us, remind us of meetings and commitments, find information for us on the World Wide Web, and manage our email messages for us? Wouldn't it be nice to have a computerized personal assistant?

Actually, such programs are called *intelligent agents*, a term indicating that they are capable of acting autonomously to carry out certain tasks. Intelligent agent technology is becoming an important research area in computer science. Most agent programs incorporate some kind of machine-learning capability, so that their performance improves over time.

As a typical agent activity, suppose I was able to tell my intelligent agent to buy me a copy of a certain book. Given a command like "buy me a copy of X," the agent would perform a search of online book sellers and come up with the best deal. Once it found the best buy, the agent would communicate with a computer-based agent representing the book seller. My agent would make the order and pay for it (assuming I gave it authority to do so), and the book seller's agent would process the order.

As far-fetched as the capability may now seem, this is the direction in which research in this area is headed. Researchers are developing agent languages and describing protocols that agents can use to exchange information in a reliable and trustworthy environment. Obviously, you wouldn't want your agent to give your money to a fraudulent book seller, so there are significant problems to solve in this area that go well beyond the problem of simply exchanging information between two agents.

The best way to learn more about this research area is to do a Web search using the search string "Intelligent Agent." There are numerous research groups and companies that provide online descriptions and demos of their products.

```
import java.util.Scanner;

public class TestOneRowNim
{
    public static void main(String argv[])
    { Scanner sc = Scanner.create(System.in);
        OneRowNim game = new OneRowNim(11);
        while(game.gameOver() == false)
        {   game.report();                           // Prompt the user
            System.out.print("Input 1, 2, or 3: ");
            int sticks = sc.nextInt();               // Get move
            game.takeSticks(sticks);                 // Do move
            System.out.println();
        } // while
        game.report();                               // The game is now over
        System.out.print("Game won by player ");
        System.out.println(game.getWinner());
    } // main()
} // TestOneRowNim class
```

Figure 3.17   The TestOneRowNim class with a `while` loop.

To reiterate a point made at the outset, object-oriented programming is a process of constructing objects that will interact with each other. Object-oriented programs must ensure that the objects themselves are well designed in terms of their ability to carry out their designated functions. Good design in this sense requires careful selection of instance variables and careful design of methods to ensure that the object can carry out its assigned tasks. However, equal care must be taken to ensure that the interactions among objects are constrained in ways that make sense for the particular program. This aspect of designing objects comes into play in designing the methods—constructor, accessor, and mutator—that make up the object's interface.

Object-oriented design

3.8 From the Java Library: `java.lang.Object`

The most general class in Java's class hierarchy is the `java.lang.Object` class. This is the superclass of all the classes that occur in Java programs. By default, it is the direct superclass of any class that does not explicitly specify a pedigree in its class definition.

All subclasses of `Object` **inherit** the `public` and `protected` methods contained in `Object`, so all such methods can be thought of as belonging to the subclasses. This means that all classes inherit the methods of the `Object` class, because every class is a subclass of it. In this section, we will look briefly at how we can use an inherited method and also at how we can **override** it—that is, redefine the method—if it doesn't exactly suit our purposes.

One of the most useful methods in the `Object` class is the `toString()` method:

java.sun.com/docs

```
public class Object
{
    public String toString() ;
}
```

The `toString()` method returns a `String` representation of its object. For example, `o1.toString()` will return a `String` that in some sense describes `o1`.

Because `OneRowNim` is a subclass of `Object`, it inherits the `toString()` method. To illustrate the default behavior of `toString()`, let's use it with a `OneRowNim` instance:

```
OneRowNim g1 = new OneRowNim(11);
OneRowNim g2 = new OneRowNim(13);
System.out.println(g1.toString());
System.out.println(g2.toString());
```

This code segment creates two `OneRowNim` instances, one named `g1` and the other named `g2`. The inherited `toString()` method is then invoked on each `OneRowNim` instance, which produces the following output:

```
OneRowNim@1dc6077b
OneRowNim@1dc60776
```

What this experiment shows is that the default definition of `toString()` returns some kind of internal representation of its object. It looks as if it returns the name of the object's class concatenated with its memory address. This may be useful for some applications. But for most objects we will want to override the default definition to make the `toString()` method return a string that is more appropriate for `OneRowNim`.

What `String` should the `g1.toString()` method return? Let's have it return a `String` that reports the `OneRowNim` instances's current state, which are the values stored in the two instance variables. To override a method, you simply define a method with the same signature in the subclass. If you call `toString()` with an instance of the subclass, its version of the method will be used. In this way, the subclass method overrides the superclass version. Thus, `OneRowNim.toString()` will have the following signature:

```
public String toString();
```

Let us describe the state of a `oneRowNim` instance very briefly in the string returned by the `toString()` method:

```
public String toString()
{ return "nSticks = " + nSticks + ", player = " + player;
}
```

If we add the `toString()` method to the `OneRowNim` class and then run the program shown in Figure 3.18, we get the following output:

```
nSticks = 9, player = 2
nSticks = 13, player = 1
```

```
public class TestToString
{
  public static void main(String argv[])
  { OneRowNim g1 = new OneRowNim(11);
    OneRowNim g2 = new OneRowNim(13);
    g1.takeSticks(2);
    System.out.println(g1.toString());
    System.out.println(g2.toString());
  } // main()
} // TestToString class
```

Figure 3.18   An application to test the overridden `toString()` method.

While this new method may not play an important role in the `OneRowNim` class, it does provide a very brief, understandable description of the state of the object. That is why the `toString()` method was included in the `Object` class.

3.9   Object-Oriented Design: Inheritance and Polymorphism

This use of `Object`'s `toString()` method provides our first look at Java's inheritance mechanism and how it promotes the generality and extensibility of the object-oriented approach. As a subclass of `Object`, our `OneRowNim` class automatically inherits `toString()` and any other `public` or `protected` methods defined in `Object`. We can simply use these methods as is, insofar as they are useful to us. As we saw in this case, the default version of `toString()` was not very useful. In that case, we can override the method by defining a method in our class with the exact same method signature. The new version of `toString()` can be customized to do exactly what is most appropriate for the subclass.

Inheritance

One of the great benefits of the object-oriented approach is the ability to define a task, such as `toString()`, at a very high level in the class hierarchy and let the inheritance mechanism spread the task throughout the rest of the hierarchy. Because `toString()` is defined in `Object`, you can invoke this method for any Java object. Moreover, if you override `toString()` in the classes you define, you will be contributing to its usefulness. Two important lessons from this example are

EFFECTIVE DESIGN: Inheritance.   The higher up in the class hierarchy that a method is defined, the more widespread its use can be.

EFFECTIVE DESIGN: Overriding `toString()`.   The `toString()` method can be overridden in any user-defined Java class. It is a useful thing to do in any class where the state of an object can be defined briefly.

Obviously there is much more that needs to be explained about Java's inheritance mechanism. Therefore, we will frequently revisit this topic in subsequent chapters.

Another important concept of object-oriented design is polymorphism. The `toString()` method is an example of a polymorphic method. The term **polymorphism** is from the Greek terms *poly*, which means "many," and *morph*, which means "form." The `toString()` method is polymorphic because it has different behaviors when invoked on different objects.

For example, suppose we design a class, `Student`, as a subclass of `Object` and define its `toString()` method to return the student ID number. Given this design, then `obj.toString()` will return a student ID if `obj` is an instance of `Student`, but if it is an instance of `OneRowNim`, it will return the description of its state that we defined above. The following code segment illustrates the point:

```
Object obj;                             // obj can refer to any Object
obj = new Student("12345");             // obj refers to a Student
System.out.println(obj.toString());     // Prints "12345"
obj = new OneRowNim(11);                // obj refers to a OneRowNim
System.out.println(obj.toString());     // Prints: nSticks = 11, player = 1
```

In this case, the variable `obj` is used to refer to a `Student` and then to a `OneRowNim` instance. This is okay because both classes are subclasses of `Object`. When `toString()` is invoked on `obj`, Java will figure out what subclass of `Object` the instance belongs to and invoke the appropriate `toString()` method.

3.10   Drawing Lines and Defining Graphical Methods (Optional)

We used a `Graphics` object in Chapter 2 to draw rectangles and ovals in an applet window. The `Graphics` class also possesses a method for drawing a line segment. Problems involving drawing pictures in an applet window using a series of line segments can be a source of examples of defining useful methods and also of making good use of loops.

The `Graphics` class has a public instance method with the header:

```
public void drawLine(int x1, int y1, int x2, int y2)
```

The method call `g.drawLine(x1, y1, x2, y2)` draws a line from the point $(x1, y1)$ to $(x2, y2)$, where (x, y) refers to a point that is x pixels from the left edge of the area that `g` is drawing in and y pixels from the top edge. Thus `g.drawLine(10, 10, 10, 60)` draws a vertical line segment that is 50 pixels long and 10 pixels from the left edge of the drawing area, that is, a line segment from the point $(10, 10)$ to the point $(10, 60)$.

Consider the problem of creating an applet program with a method called `drawSticks()` to draw any specified number of vertical line segments. This method might be useful for an applet user interface to the `OneRowNim` game to draw the number of sticks at a given point in a game. Suppose that this method must have an `int` parameter to specify the number of vertical lines to draw and two `int` parameters to specify the location of the top endpoint of the leftmost line segment. The `drawSticks()` method will need to use a `Graphics` object connected to the applet window for drawing the line segment. The only such `Graphics` object available is the parameter in the `paint()` method of an applet. Thus the method must have a `Graphics`

```
/**
 * DrawLineApplet demonstrates some graphics commands.
 * It draws a set of 12 vertical lines and a set of 7 lines.
 */
import java.awt.*;
import java.applet.*;

public class DrawSticksApplet extends Applet
  /**
   * drawSticks(g,x,y,num) will draw num vertical line
   * segments.  The line segments are 10 pixels apart and
   * 50 pixels long.  The top endpoint of the left most
   * line segment is at the point (x,y).
   */
  public void drawSticks(Graphics g, int x, int y, int num)
  { int k = 0;
      while (k < num)
      {   g.drawLine(x, y, x, y + 50);
          x = x + 10;
          k = k + 1;
      } // while
  } // drawSticks()

  public void paint(Graphics g)
  {   drawSticks(g, 25, 25, 12);
      g.setColor(Color.cyan);
      drawSticks(g, 25, 125, 7);
  } // paint()
} // DrawSticksApplet class
```

Figure 3.19 An applet program with a method for drawing a set of sticks.

parameter, and it will be called in the `paint()` method using the `Graphics` object there as an argument. Thus the header of the method should look like:

```
public void drawSticks(Graphics g, int x, int y, int num)
```

The length of the line segments and the distance between them are not specified by parameters, so we need to choose some fixed values for these quantities. Let us assume that the line segments are 10 pixels apart and 50 pixels long. We now have enough information to complete the definition of an applet to solve this problem. Such a class definition is reproduced in Figure 3.19.

Note that the body of `drawSticks()` uses a `while` loop to draw the lines, and declares and initializes a local variable to zero to use for counting the number of lines drawn. The statement `g.drawLine(x, y, x, y + 50);` draws a vertical line 50 pixels long. Increasing the value of x by 10 each time through the loop moves the next line 10 pixels to the right.

The first call to `drawSticks()` in the `paint()` method draws 12 lines with (25,25) the top point of the leftmost line. The second call to `drawSticks()` will draw seven cyan sticks 100 pixels lower. Note that changing the color of `g` before passing it as an argument to `drawSticks()` changes the drawing color.

To run this applet, one needs the following HTML document, which specifies the applet code as `DrawSticksApplet.class`:

```
<HTML>
<HEAD>
<TITLE> Draw Sticks Web Page</TITLE>
</HEAD>
<BODY>
<H2> DrawSticksApplet will appear below.</H2>
<APPLET CODE = "DrawSticksApplet.class"
                WIDTH = 400 HEIGHT = 200>
</APPLET>
</BODY>
</HTML>
```

An image of the `DrawSticksApplet` as it appears in a browser window is shown in Figure 3.20.

As we have seen in this example, defining methods with parameters to draw an object makes the code reusable and makes it possible to draw a complex scene by calling a collection of simpler methods. It is a typical use of the divide-and-conquer principle. The `while` loop can be useful in drawing almost any geometrically symmetric object.

Figure 3.20 The DrawSticksApplet as displayed in a browser window.

CHAPTER SUMMARY

Technical Terms

accessor method	mutator method
class scope	multiway selection
formal parameter	override
`if` statement	polymorphism
`if-else` statement	repetition structure
inherit	scope
local scope	selection
loop structure	side effect
method overloading	`while` statement
method signature	`while` structure

Summary of Important Points

- A *formal parameter* is a variable in a method declaration. It always consists of a type followed by a variable identifier. An *argument* is a value passed to a method via a formal parameter when the method is invoked. A method's *parameters* constrain the type of information that can be passed to a method.

- When an argument of primitive type is passed to a method, it cannot be modified within the method. When an argument of reference type is passed to a method, the object it refers to can be modified within the method.

- Except for `void` methods, a *method invocation* or *method call* is an expression which has a value of a certain type. For example, `nim.getSticks()` returns a `int` value.

- The *signature* of a method consists of its name, and the number, types, and order of its formal parameters. A class may not contain more than one method with the same signature.

- A *constructor* is a method that is invoked when an object is created. If a class does not contain a constructor method, the Java compiler supplies a *default constructor*.

- Restricting access to certain portions of a class is a form of *information hiding*. Generally, instance variables are hidden by declaring them `private`. The class's `public` methods make up its interface.

- The `if` *statement* executes a statement only if its boolean condition is true. The `if-else` *statement* executes one or the other of its statements depending on the value of its boolean condition. *Multiway selection* allows one and only one of several choices to be selected depending on the value of its boolean condition.

- The `while` statement is used for coding loop structures that repeatedly execute a block of code while a boolean condition is satisfied.

SOLUTIONS TO SELF-STUDY EXERCISES

SOLUTION 3.1   A *method declaration* defines the method by specifying its name, qualifiers, return type, formal parameters, and algorithm, thereby associating a name with a segment of executable code. A *method invocation* calls or uses a defined method.

SOLUTION 3.2   A *formal parameter* is a variable in the method declaration. Its purpose is to store a value while the method is running. An *argument* is a value passed to a method in place of a formal parameter.

SOLUTION 3.3   The following code declares two instance variables for names of players and defines a `setName()` method:

```
private String nameOne = "Player One";
private String nameTwo = "Player Two";

public void setNames(String name1, String name2)
{    nameOne = name1;
     nameTwo = name2;
}
```

Of course, there are many other appropriate names for the variables and parameters and other initial assignments.

SOLUTION 3.4   A method call that sets the names of the players of `game1` is:

```
game1.setNames("Xena","Yogi");
```

SOLUTION 3.5   A constructor cannot have a return type, such as void.

SOLUTION 3.6   One definition for the method is:

```
public OneRowNim(int sticks)
{    nSticks = sticks;
     player = 2;
}
```

SOLUTION 3.7   The following would be displayed on the screen:

```
1
20
false
```

SOLUTION 3.8   One definition for the method is:

```
public int getMoves()
{    return nMoves;
}
```

SOLUTION 3.9   One definition for the method is:

```java
public boolean playerOneIsNext()
{    return (player == 1);
}
```

SOLUTION 3.10   See Figure 3.21.

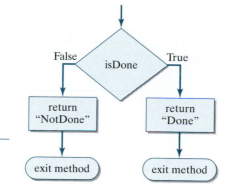

Figure 3.21 Flowchart of the if-else version of the getStatus() method.

SOLUTION 3.11

```java
if (isHeavy == true)
      System.out.println("Heavy") ;
else; // Error (remove this semicolon)
      System.out.println("Light");

if (isLong == true)
      System.out.println("Long")
else                              // Error (end line above with semicolon)
      System.out.println("Short");
```

SOLUTION 3.12

```java
public String getPlayerName()
{    if (player == 1)
         return "Ann";
     else if (player == 2)
         return "Bill";
     else if (player == 3)
         return "Cal";
     else
         return "Error";
}
```

SOLUTION 3.13 When passing an argument for a primitive type, a copy of the argument's value is passed. The actual argument cannot be changed inside the method. When passing a reference to an object, the object can be changed within the method.

SOLUTION 3.14

```java
public int sumCubes(int min, int max)
{
    int num = min;
    int sum = 0;
    while (num <=  max) {            // While num <= max
        sum = sum + num*num*num;     // Add cube of num to sum
        num = num + 1;               // Add 1 to num
    }                                // while
    return sum;                      // Return the sum
}
```

EXERCISES

EXERCISE 3.1 Fill in the blanks in each of the following sentences:

a. When two different methods have the same name, this is an example of _____.

Note: For programming exercises, **first** draw a UML class diagram describing all classes and their inheritance relationships and/or associations.

b. Methods with the same name are distinguished by their _____.

c. A method invoked when an object is created is known as a _____ method.

d. A method whose purpose is to provide access to an object's instance variables is known as an _____ method.

e. A `boolean` value is an example of a _____ type.

f. A `OneRowNim` variable is an example of a _____ type.

g. A method's parameters have _____ scope.

h. A class's instance variables have _____ scope.

i. Generally, a class's instance variables should have _____ access.

j. The methods that make up an object's interface should have _____ access.

k. A method that returns no value should be declared _____.

l. Java's `if` statement and `if-else` statement are both examples of _____ control structures.

m. An expression that evaluates to either `true` or `false` is known as a _____.

n. In an `if-else` statement, an `else` clause matches _____.

o. The ability to use a superclass method in a subclass is due to Java's _____ mechanism.

p. The process of redefining a superclass method in a subclass is known as _____ the method.

EXERCISE 3.2 Explain the difference between the following pairs of concepts:

   a. *Parameter* and *argument.*
   b. *Method definition* and *method invocation.*
   c. *Local scope* and *class scope.*
   d. *Primitive type* and *reference type.*
   e. *Access method* and *constructor method.*

EXERCISE 3.3 Translate each of the following into Java code:

   a. If b1 is true, then print "one"; otherwise, print "two."
   b. If b1 is false and b2 is true, then print "one"; otherwise, print "two."
   c. If b1 is false and b2 is true, then print "one"; otherwise, print "two," or print "three."

EXERCISE 3.4 Identify and fix the syntax errors in each of the following:

   a.

```java
if (isWalking == true) ;
    System.out.println("Walking");
else
    System.out.println("Not walking");
```

   b.

```java
if (isWalking)
    System.out.println("Walking")
else
    System.out.println("Not walking");
```

   c.

```java
if (isWalking)
    System.out.println("Walking");
else
    System.out.println("Not walking")
```

   d.

```java
if (isWalking = false)
    System.out.println("Walking");
else
    System.out.println("Not walking");
```

EXERCISE 3.5   For each of the following, suppose that isWalking is true and isTalking is false (first draw a flowchart for each statement and then determine what would be printed by each statement):

a.

```
if (isWalking == false)
    System.out.println("One");
    System.out.println("Two");
```

b.

```
if (isWalking == true)
    System.out.println("One");
    System.out.println("Two");
```

c.

```
if (isWalking == false)
{
    System.out.println("One");
    System.out.println("Two");
}
```

d.

```
if (isWalking == false)
    if (isTalking == true)
        System.out.println("One");
    else
        System.out.println("Two");
else
    System.out.println("Three");
```

EXERCISE 3.6   Show what the output would be if the following version of main() were executed:

```
public static void main(String argv[])
{
    System.out.println("main() is starting");
    OneRowNim game1;
    game1  = new OneRowNim(21);
    OneRowNim game2;
    game2 = new OneRowNim(8);
    game1.takeSticks(3);
    game2.takeSticks(2);
    game1.takeSticks(1);
    game1.report();
    game2.report();
    System.out.println("main() is finished");
}
```

EXERCISE 3.7   Determine the output of the following program:

```java
public class Mystery
{
    public String myMethod(String s)
    {
        return("Hello" + s);
    }
    public static void main(String argv[])
    {
        Mystery mystery = new Mystery();
        System.out.println( mystery.myMethod(" dolly"));
    }
}
```

EXERCISE 3.8   Write a `boolean` method—a method that returns a `boolean`—that takes an `int` parameter and converts the integers 0 and 1 into `false` and `true`, respectively.

EXERCISE 3.9   Define an `int` method that takes a `boolean` parameter. If the parameter's value is `false`, the method should return 0; otherwise, it should return 1.

EXERCISE 3.10   Define a `void` method named `hello` that takes a single `boolean` parameter. The method should print "Hello" if its parameter is true; otherwise, it should print "Goodbye."

EXERCISE 3.11   Define a method named `hello` that takes a single `boolean` parameter. The method should return "Hello" if its parameter is true; otherwise it should return "Goodbye." Note the difference between this method and the one in the preceding exercise. This one returns a `String`. That one was a `void` method.

EXERCISE 3.12   Write a method named `hello` that takes a single `String` parameter. The method should return a `String` that consists of the word "Hello" concatenated with the value of its parameter. For example, if you call this method with the expression `hello("dolly")`, it should return "hello dolly." If you call it with `hello("young lovers wherever you are")`, it should return "hello young lovers wherever you are."

EXERCISE 3.13   Define a void method named `day1` that prints "a partridge in a pear tree."

EXERCISE 3.14   Write a Java application program called `TwelveDays` that prints the Christmas carol "Twelve Days of Christmas." For this version, write a void method named `intro()` that takes a single `String` parameter that gives the day of the verse and prints the introduction to the song. For example, `intro("first")` should print, "On the first day of Christmas my true love gave to me." Then write methods `day1()`, `day2()`, and so on, each of which prints its version of the verse. Then write a `main()` method that calls the other methods to print the whole song.

EXERCISE 3.15   Define a `void` method named `verse` that takes two `String` parameters and returns a verse of the Christmas carol "Twelve Days of Christmas." For example, if you call this method with `verse("first", "a partridge in a pear tree")`, it should return, "On the first day of Christmas my true love gave to me, a partridge in a pear tree."

EXERCISE 3.16   Define a void method named `permute` that takes three `String` parameters and prints out all possible arrangements of the three strings. For example, if you called `permute("a", "b", "c")`, it would produce the following output: abc, acb, bac, bca, cab, cba, with each permutation on a separate line.

EXERCISE 3.17   Design a method that can produce limericks given a bunch of rhyming words. That is, create a limerick template that will take any five words or phrases and produce a limerick. For example, if you call

```
limerick("Jones","stones","rained","pained","bones");
```

your method might print (something better than)

```
There once a person named Jones
Who had a great liking for stones,
But whenever it rained,
Jones' expression was pained,
Because stones weren't good for the bones.
```

For each of the following exercises, write a complete Java application program:

EXERCISE 3.18   Define a class named `Donor` that has two instance variables, the donor's name and rating, both of which are `String`s. The name can be any string, but the rating should be one of the following values: "high," "medium," or "none." Write the following methods for this class: a constructor, `Donor(String,String)`, that allows you to set both the donor's name and rating; and access methods to set and get both the name and rating of a donor.

EXERCISE 3.19   Challenge.   Define a `CopyMonitor` class that solves the following problem. A company needs a monitor program to keep track of when a particular copy machine needs service. The device has two important (boolean) variables: its toner level (too low or not) and whether it has printed more than 100,000 pages since its last servicing (it either has or has not). The servicing rule that the company uses is that service is needed when either 100,000 pages have been printed or the toner is too low. Your program should contain a method that reports either "service needed" or "service not needed" based on the machine's state. (Pretend that the machine has other methods that keep track of toner level and page count.)

EXERCISE 3.20   Challenge.   Design and write an `OldMacdonald` class that sings several verses of "Old MacDonald Had a Farm." Use methods to generalize the verses. For example, write a method named `eieio()` to "sing" the "E I E I O" part of the verse. Write another method with the signature `hadAnX(String s)`, which sings the "had a duck" part of the verse, and a method `withA(String sound)` to sing the "with a quack quack here" part of the verse. Test your class by writing a `main()` method.

ADDITIONAL EXERCISES

EXERCISE 3.21   Suppose you have an `Object` A, with public methods `a()` and `b()`, and private method `c()`. And suppose you have a subclass of A named B with methods named `b()`, `c()`, and `d()`. Draw a UML diagram showing the relationship between these two classes. Explain the inheritance relationships between them and identify the methods that would be considered polymorphic.

EXERCISE 3.22   Consider the definition of the class C. Define a subclass of C named B that overrides method `m1()` so that it returns the difference between m and n instead of their sum.

```java
public class C {
    private int m;
    private int n;
    public C(int mIn, int nIn) {
        m = mIn;
        n = nIn;
    }
    public int m1() {
        return m+n;
    }
}
```

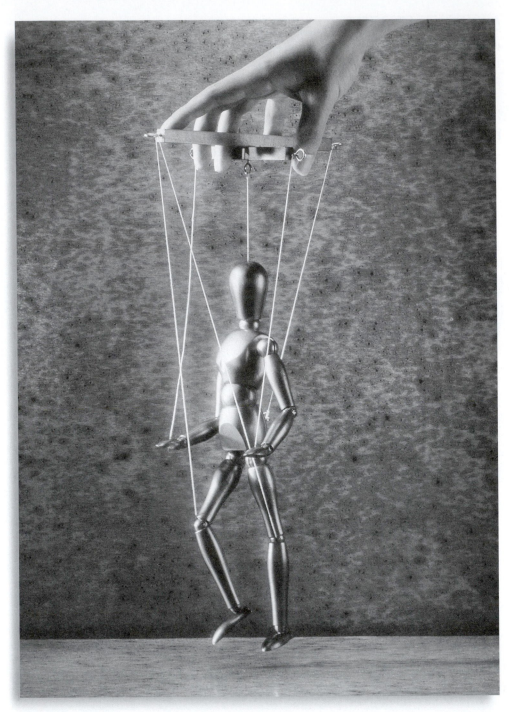

Photograph courtesy of George Logan, Getty Images, Inc. - Taxi.

4

Input/Output: Designing the User Interface

OBJECTIVES

After studying this chapter, you will

- Understand the importance of the user interface.
- Know how to use a simple command-line interface.
- Be able to program and use a simple Graphical User Interface (GUI).
- Understand the concept of event-driven programming.
- Know how to program and use a Java applet.

OUTLINE

4.1   Introduction

One of the most important parts of learning a programming language is learning how to program an application to accept input and produce output (I/O). Computers wouldn't be very useful if we could not give them data to manipulate and compute, and if we were not able to read or understand the results they produce. In general, a computer program's input and output capabilities are known collectively as its **user interface**.

An **input operation** is any action that transfers data from the user to the computer's main memory via one of the computer's input devices. An **output operation** is any action that transfers data from the computer's main memory to one of the computer's output devices.

In this chapter, we will introduce three simple user interfaces: a **command-line interface** and two **graphical user interfaces** (GUIs). These interfaces can be used interchangeably with the material in most of the subsequent chapters. Indeed, one of the most important design principles emphasized in this chapter is that the user interface should be designed to function independently of the computational task. In other words, it should be possible to take an application, such as a computer game, and design it for use with a variety of different user interfaces.

4.2   The User Interface

User interface

The user interface is the part of a program that handles the input and output interactions between the user and the program. As an interface, it limits or constrains the manner in which the user can interact with the program.

Computer programs are just one of the many things that require a user interface. Virtually every device we use has one. For example, consider again the difference between the user interface of a digital versus an analog watch. A digital watch has a display that tells you the time to the exact hour, minute, and second. An analog watch, one with a sweep second hand, can never display the time to the exact second. Similarly, a digital watch has buttons that let you set the time to the exact hour, minute, and second. An analog watch has a small wheel that allows you to set the time only approximately. Thus, the user interface constrains the kinds of interactions that are possible between the user and the device.

Division of labor

With regard to our Java programs, one way to divide up the labor is to distinguish between the user interface and the computational functions. The role of the user interface is to transmit data back and forth between the user and the program. The role of the computational part of the program is to perform some kind of computation, in the broad sense of the term. The computation might be to play a game, or calculate a square root, or monitor a hospital patient. Figure 4.1 provides a generic picture of the relationship between the user interface and the computational object.

In this chapter we focus our attention on the user interface side of the relationship shown in Figure 4.1. In subsequent chapters we will focus more on the computational side of the

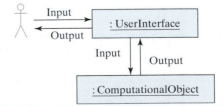

Figure 4.1 The user interface transmits data back and forth between the user and the program's computational objects.

relationship. What we desire is an approach that lets us combine a computational object with any one of the three different kinds of user interfaces.

EFFECTIVE DESIGN: The User Interface Module   Separating the user interface from the computational object is a good way to divide up the labor in programs that perform I/O.

4.3   A Command-Line Interface

A command-line interface is perhaps the simplest, and most old-fashioned, way to design the interaction between a user and a program. According to this approach, user input is taken from the keyboard, and the program's output is displayed on a console (Fig. 4.2).

The command-line approach might also be called *console interface*. In the early days of computers, before we had graphics-based computer monitors capable of displaying multiple windows, the console was the entire computer display. For today's computers the console might be a window provided by your programming environment, as in Figure 4.3.

In Chapter 1 we described how the System.out.print() and System.out.println() methods are used to output strings to the console. That takes care of the output side of command-line interface. The more challenging task is managing the input-side of the interface.

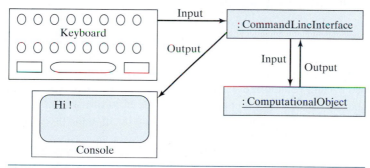

Figure 4.2 A command-line user interface.

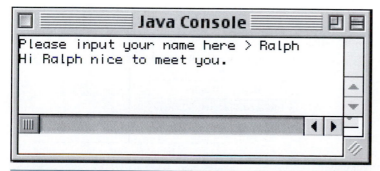

Figure 4.3 The Java console window.

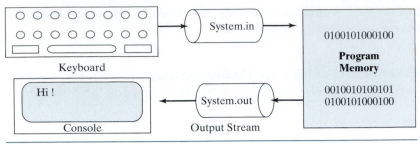

Figure 4.4 Input and output streams.

Streams

In Java, input and output are handled by objects called **streams**. You can think of a stream as a pipe through which data flows (Fig. 4.4). An **input stream** carries data from an input device, such as a keyboard or network connection or a file, to the program's main memory. An **output stream** carries data from the program's memory to an output device, such as a printer or a file.

Every Java program has three standard streams available at startup: `System.in`, `System.out`, and `System.err`. `System.in` is a predefined input stream that is typically associated with the keyboard (Fig. 4.4). That is, it carries data from the keyboard to the program. `System.out` and `System.err` are output streams typically associated with the console. They both carry data from the program to the console. The difference is simply that `System.out` is used for normal program output and `System.err` is used to output error messages.

4.3.1   Using a `BufferedReader` to Input Strings from the Keyboard

We will use a `BufferedReader` object to handle data input from the keyboard. As its name implies, the `BufferedReader` class performs buffered input. A **buffer** is a portion of main memory where input is held until it is needed by the program. Using a buffer between the keyboard and the program allows you to use the Backspace key to delete a character. When you hit the Enter key, any characters you deleted will be ignored when the program retrieves characters from the input buffer. If the user's input were not buffered in this way, it would contain every keystroke, including the Backspaces, and then it would be up to the program to eliminate the characters that were supposed to be deleted.

Buffered input

Figure 4.5 provides a UML diagram of the `BufferedReader` class and shows its relationship to the other classes used for keyboard input. Note that `BufferedReader` along with `InputStreamReader`, is one of several subclasses of the `Reader` class. As the dia-

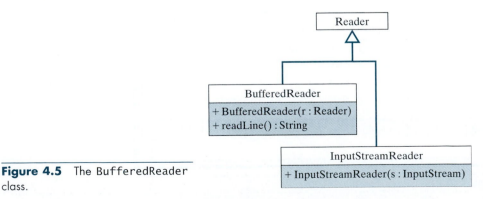

Figure 4.5 The `BufferedReader` class.

gram shows, `BufferedReader` has two important methods. Its constructor method takes a `Reader` parameter, which means that when we create a `BufferedReader` we must provide it with a reference to a `Reader` object. To perform keyboard input, we want to provide a reference to an object that can read `System.in`, the standard input stream. As the figure shows, `InputStreamReader` has a constructor that allows it to read an `InputStream`. Therefore, to construct a `BufferedReader` that will read `System.in` we use the following statement:

```
BufferedReader input = new BufferedReader (new InputStreamReader (System.in));
```

In this statement we are actually creating two objects. We first create an `InputStream-Reader`, giving it a reference to `System.in`. We then pass that object to a `BufferedReader`. The result is a cooperation between two objects that enables us to do buffered reading of the keyboard.

When a `BufferedReader` is created in this way, its `readLine()` method can be used to read a line of characters from the keyboard. For example, a `BufferedReader` named `input` having been created, the following code segment will read one line of input and assign it to the `String` variable named `inputString`.

```
String inputString = input.readLine();
```

When the program encounters the `readLine()` expression, it will wait for the user to hit the Enter key. It will then input into the `String` variable whatever the user typed, minus any characters that were backspaced over.

Keyboard input

JAVA LANGUAGE RULE   **Keyboard Input.** The `BufferedReader.readLine()` method allows the user to backspace over errors during keyboard input.

4.3.2   Inputting Numbers from the Keyboard

As the preceding section showed, we can use a `BufferedReader` object to input `Strings` from the keyboard. In Java, all keyboard input is represented as `Strings`. However, what if we want to input numbers? The answer is that we have to extract numbers from the input strings. To do this, Java provides two special classes, known as wrapper classes: `Integer` and `Double`.

A **wrapper class** contains methods for converting primitive data into objects and for converting data from one type to another. The `Integer` class contains the `parseInt()` method, which extracts an `int` from its `String` argument. For example, in the following usage, the string "55" is converted into the number 55:

Wrapper classes

```
int m = Integer.parseInt("55");
```

Similarly, the `Double` class contains the `parseDouble()` method, which extracts a `double` value from its parameter. In this example, the number 55.2 is extracted from the string "55.2":

```
double num = Double.parseDouble("55.2");
```

If we are writing a program that requires us to input numbers from the keyboard, then, assuming we have created a `BufferedReader` object named `input`, we can use these methods in combination with the `readLine()` method to input and process numbers. For example, this code segment calculates a runner's race pace:

```
String inputString = new String();
System.out.println("How many total miles did you run?  ");
inputString = input.readLine();                            // Input a String
double miles = Double.parseDouble(inputString);            // Convert
System.out.println("How many minutes did it take you?  ");
inputString = input.readLine();                            // Input another String
double minutes = Double.parseDouble(inString);             // Convert
System.out.println("Your average pace was " +
                minutes/miles + " minutes per mile");
```

Note how we included prompts in this example so that the user knows what type of input is expected. Designing appropriate prompts is an important aspect of designing a good user interface.

EFFECTIVE DESIGN: Prompting. In a well-designed user interface, prompts should be used to guide the user through the input process.

4.3.3 Designing a Keyboard Reader Class

Now that we have introduced the library classes and methods that we will use for command-line input, we will design a class to encapsulate these functions. We want a class that will use a `BufferedReader` to read any kind of data—strings, integers, or real numbers—from the keyboard. We also want this class to hide some of the messy details involved in performing keyboard input.

Figure 4.6 presents the design of `KeyboardReader` class. Note that instances of this class will use a `BufferedReader` object to perform the actual keyboard input. That is why we need a private instance variable of type `BufferedReader`. The constructor method will create a `BufferedReader`, which will then be used whenever a read operation is requested. The `KeyboardReader` class has five public methods. The `getKeyboardInput()` method returns a `String`. This is the method we will call when we just want to get the string the user typed from the keyboard. The `getKeyboardInteger()` method returns an `int` value. This is the method we will call when we want an integer from the keyboard. Similarly, the `getKeyboardDouble()` method returns a `double`. This is the method we will call when we want to input a floating-point value from the keyboard. Finally, the `prompt()` and `display()` methods will be used to perform two other important tasks of a user interface: prompting the user and displaying the program's output.

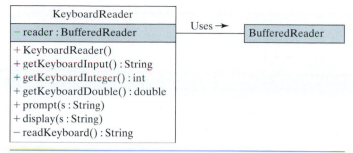

Figure 4.6 Design of the KeyboardReader class.

The following code segment illustrates how we will use a KeyboardReader object to input an integer:

```
KeyboardReader cmdline = new KeyboardReader();
int m = cmdline.getKeyboardInteger();
```

All we need to do is create an instance of the KeyboardReader and ask it to get an integer for us. This greatly simplifies the work we will have to do when we want to perform keyboard input.

Note that Figure 4.6 lists a private method named readKeyboard() in the Keyboard-Reader class. This is the method that does the actual work of reading data from the keyboard. Because it is private, it can only be called by the other methods in KeyboardReader. It cannot be called by other classes. The reason we make it private is to hide it, and the messy details of performing keyboard input, from other classes.

Private helper method

One of those messy details is the fact that it is possible for things to go wrong whenever I/O is performed. The possibility of errors occurring applies to all forms of I/O, not just keyboard I/O. For example, the file a program is trying to read might be missing. Or the Internet connection might malfunction when it is trying to download a Web page.

Because these types of external errors are possible, Java requires that a program performing certain types of I/O must watch out for certain error conditions known as *exceptions*. Exceptions are covered in Chapter 11, so we will not attempt to treat them here. Instead, we will design the readKeyboard() method to take care of this detail for us.

I/O exceptions

JAVA LANGUAGE RULE   **Exceptions.** Java I/O methods require that programs check for certain error conditions during input.

Figure 4.7 gives the full implementation (for now) of the KeyboardReader class. Let's go through it line by line. The first thing to notice is the use of the import statement. Recall that importing a Java package enables us to refer to elements in the package by their short names (BufferedReader) rather than their fully qualified names (java.io.BufferedReader).

```java
import java.io.*;

public class KeyboardReader
{   private BufferedReader reader;

    public KeyboardReader() {
        reader = new BufferedReader (new InputStreamReader(System.in));
    }
    public String getKeyboardInput()
    {   return readKeyboard();
    }
    public int getKeyboardInteger()
    {   return Integer.parseInt(readKeyboard());
    }
    public double getKeyboardDouble()
    {   return Double.parseDouble(readKeyboard());
    }
    public void prompt(String s)
    {   System.out.print(s);
    }
    public void display(String s)
    {   System.out.print(s);
    }
    private String readKeyboard()
    {   String line = "";
        try
        {   line = reader.readLine();
        } catch (IOException e)
        {   e.printStackTrace();
        }
        return line;
    }
}
```

Figure 4.7 Definition of the KeyboardReader class.

Next note how we create a `BufferedReader` object in the `KeyboardReader()` constructor:

```java
reader = new BufferedReader (new InputStreamReader (System.in));
```

The resulting `reader` object will persist as long as our `KeyboardReader` object exists and can be used for all subsequent input operations.

Now consider the definition of the `readKeyboard()` method. It calls the inherited `readLine()` method to input a line from the keyboard and then it returns the line. Note, however, how the call to the `readLine()` method is embedded in a `try...catch` block. This is one way to handle the possibility that an exception might occur during the input operation. Java requires that our program do something to address the possibility of an I/O exception, and as we will learn in Chapter 11, there are other designs that we could have used here. The primary advantage of doing it this way is that we can hide this language detail from the rest of the program. The rest of the program—and any other programs that use the `KeyboardReader` class—will not have to worry about this exception issue. They can just ask the `KeyboardReader` to get them a string or an integer and it will deliver the goods.

We now turn to how the public input methods are defined. The `getKeyboardInput()` method just returns the line that it gets by calling `readKeyboard()`. The `getKeyboard-Integer()` method also calls `readKeyboard()`, but instead of just returning the line, it extracts an integer from it and returns the integer. The `getKeyboardDouble()` method works the same way.

Finally, note how the public output methods are defined. Both the `prompt()` and `display()` methods take a single `String` parameter and do exactly the same thing—they merely print their string. So why do we have two methods when one will suffice? The answer is that these methods encapsulate important and distinct user-interface functions—prompting the user and displaying output—that just happen to be implemented in exactly the same way in this case. When we design our GUI interface, we will use completely different objects to prompt the user and display output. Therefore, despite their similarities, it is important that we distinguish the task of prompting the user from the more general task of displaying output.

4.3.4 Designing a Command-Line Interface

Now that we have defined a special class for performing keyboard input, we now show how it can be used as a user interface in cooperation with the other objects that make up a program. As described in Figure 4.1, the user interface will serve as an intermediary between the user and some type of computational object. Although our command-line interface should work with any application, no matter how complex, we begin with a very simple computational problem. This will allow us to focus on the user interface.

Let us design a program that prompts the user for his or her name and then says hello. The program's I/O should look like this:

```
Hi, please input your name here > Kim
Hi Kim, nice to meet you.
```

There will be two primary objects in the design we use. One will serve as the user interface. This will be our `KeyboardReader`. The second object will serve as the computational object. In this case it will "compute" an appropriate greeting. The computational object will contain the `main()` method and will encapsulate the algorithm for this application. It will use a `KeyboardReader` to handle its I/O needs.

The main advantage of this division of labor is that it enables us to use the `Keyboard-Reader`, as is, with virtually any Java application. Moreover, despite its simplicity, our computational object in this example can serve as a template for future programs.

EFFECTIVE DESIGN: Modularity.   By designing the user interface as a self-contained module, we can use it with just about any application.

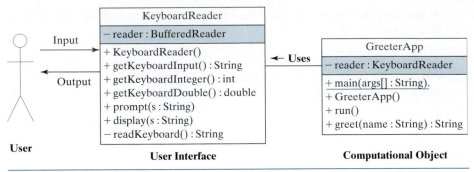

Figure 4.8 Using KeyboardReader as the user interface.

Figure 4.8 provides the details of the design we wish to implement. Note that **Greeter-App** contains an instance variable for a **KeyboardReader**. This will enable it to use the **KeyboardReader** whenever it needs to perform keyboard input. By giving **GreeterApp** a **main()** method, we allow it to be the main class for our application. Its **run()** method will contain the algorithm that controls the application, and its **greet()** method will handle the task of greeting the user.

The full implementation of the **GreeterApp** class is shown in Figure 4.9. It begins by declaring an instance variable for the **KeyboardReader**, which is instantiated in the constructor method. This gives **GreeterApp** a way to refer directly to the user interface whenever it needs keyboard input. The **run()** method encapsulates the application's algorithm. Note how it uses the **KeyboardReader** to prompt the user, to input the user's name, and then to display the greeting. Finally, the **main()** method serves to create an instance of the computational object and calls its **run()** method.

To recap, we have designed a simple command-line interface that can be used, with minor changes, for virtually any programming task in subsequent chapters. Before moving on, it

```java
public class GreeterApp
{    private KeyboardReader reader;

    public GreeterApp()
    {    reader = new KeyboardReader();
    } // GreeterApp()
    public void run()
    {    String name = "";
        reader.prompt("Please input your name here > ");
        name = reader.getKeyboardInput();
        reader.display(greet(name) + "\n");
    } // run()
    public String greet(String name)
    {    return "Hi " + name + " nice to meet you.";
    } // greet()
    public static void main(String args[])
    {    GreeterApp app = new GreeterApp();
        app.run();
    } main()
} // GreaterApp class
```

Figure 4.9 Definition of the GreeterApp class.

may be helpful to touch on some of the important object-oriented principles that went into our design.

- Divide-and-conquer: We see the usefulness of dividing a program into separate objects, one to handle the computations required by the application, and one to handle the user interface.
- Encapsulation: The classes we designed encapsulate only the information and behavior necessary to perform their specific roles.
- Information Hiding: We use a private method to hide certain messy implementation details from other parts of the program.
- Generality and Extensibility: We have developed a design general enough to be extended to other applications.

SELF-STUDY EXERCISE

EXERCISE 4.1   Java's `Math` class has a static method that will generate a random number between 0 and 0.99999999—that is, between 0 and 1, but not including 1. By using simple arithmetic, we can generate random numbers between any two values. For example, the following statement assigns a random integer between 1 and 100 to the variable:

```
secretNumber = 1 + (int)(Math.random() * 100);
```

Given this statement, design and implement an application that will play the following guessing game with the user: The computer generates a random number between 1 and 100 and then lets the user guess the number, telling the user when the guess is too high or too low. Note that for this problem, the user will have to input integers at the keyboard.

4.4   A Graphical User Interface (GUI)

While command-line interfaces are useful, one of the great advantages of the Java language is that its extensive class library makes it relatively easy to develop applications that employ Graphical User Interfaces (GUIs). GUIs have been around now for many years, since the production of the Macintosh in the early 1980s. Today nearly all personal computing applications are GUI-based. Therefore, it is important that beginning programmers be able to design and write programs that resemble, albeit on a simpler scale, the programs they use every day. Among other benefits, developing the ability to write GUI programs like the ones everyone uses today will make it easier for you to show off your work to others, and this may motivate further interest in learning to program.

In this and subsequent sections, we will develop an extensible GUI model that can be used with either a Java application or an applet. By *extensible* we mean a model that can be easily adapted and used in a wide variety of programs. GUI programming involves a computational model known as **event-driven programming**. This means that GUI programs react to events *Event-driven* that are generated mostly by the user's interactions with elements in the GUI. Therefore, we *programming* will have to learn how to use Java's *event model* to handle simple events.

Since this is our first look at some complex topics, we will keep the discussion as simple as possible. We will delay discussion of certain issues that will be taken up in more depth in Chapter 13.

4.4.1 Java's GUI Components

The Java library comes with two separate but interrelated packages of GUI components, the older `java.awt` package and the newer `javax.swing` package. For the most part, the **Swing** classes supersede the **AWT** classes. For example, the `java.awt.Button` class is superseded by the `javax.swing.JButton` class, and the `java.awt.TextField` class is superseded by the `javax.swing.JTextField` class. As these examples show, the newer Swing components add an initial *J* to the names of their corresponding AWT counterparts.

Figure 4.10 illustrates how some of the main components appear in a GUI interface. As can be seen, a `JLabel` is simply a string of text displayed on the GUI, used here as a prompt. A `JTextField` is an input element that can hold a single line of text. In this case, the user has input his name. A `JTextArea` is an output component that can display multiple lines of text. In this example, it displays a simple greeting. A `JButton` is a labeled **control element**, which is an element that allows the user to control the interaction with the program. In this example, the user will be greeted by the name input into the `JTextField` whenever the `JButton` is clicked. As we will learn, clicking on the `JButton` causes an event to occur, which leads the program to take the action of displaying the greeting. Finally, all of these components are contained in a `JFrame`, which is a top-level container. A **container** is a GUI component that can contain other GUI components.

Model-view-controller (MVC) architecture

The Swing classes are generally considered to be superior to their AWT counterparts. For one thing, Swing components use a sophisticated object-oriented design known as the **model-view-controller (MVC) architecture**. This gives them much greater functionality than their AWT counterparts. For example, whereas an AWT `Button` can only have a string as its label, a Swing `JButton` can use an image as a label. (See Chapter 13 for a detailed discussion of the MVC architecture.)

Figure 4.10 Various GUI components from the `javax.swing` package.

Second, Swing components are written entirely in Java, which makes them more portable and enables them to behave the same way regardless of the operating system on which they are run. Because of their portability, Swing components are considered *lightweight*. By contrast, AWT classes use routines that are implemented in the underlying operating system and are therefore not easily portable. Thus, they are considered *heavyweight* components. Whereas a Swing `JButton` should look and act the same regardless of platform, an AWT `Button` would have a different implementation, and hence a different look-and-feel, on a Macintosh and on a Windows system. In this book, we will use the new Swing classes in our programs.

Swing portability

4.4.2 Class Inheritance: Extending a Superclass

As you will recall from Chapter 0, class inheritance is the mechanism by which a class of objects can acquire (*inherit*) the methods and variables of its superclasses. Just as a horse, by virtue of its membership in the class of horses, inherits the attributes and behaviors of a mammal and, more generally, of an animal, a Java subclass inherits the variables and methods of its superclasses. We sometimes lump together an object's attributes and behaviors and refer to them collectively as its *functionality*. So we say that an object of a subclass inherits the functionality of all of its superclasses.

Inheritance

Functionality

By the same token, just as a horse and a cow extend their mammalian attributes and behaviors in their own special ways, a Java subclass extends the functionality of its superclasses in its own special way. Thus, a subclass *specializes* its superclass.

In Chapter 3, we showed how all classes in the Java hierarchy inherit the `toString()` method from the `Object` class. The lesson there was that an object in a subclass can either use or override any `public` method defined in any of its superclasses. In order to implement GUI programs, we need to look at another way to employ inheritance. In particular, we need to learn how to define a new class by *extending* an existing class.

We noted in Chapter 2 that unless a class is explicitly defined as a subclass of some other class, it is implicitly considered to be a direct subclass of `Object`. Thus, the `GreeterApp` class defined earlier in this chapter is a subclass of `Object`. We can make the relationship between `GreeterApp` and `Object` explicit by using the `extends` keyword when we define the `GreeterApp` class:

```
public class GreeterApp extends Object { ... }
```

Thus, the `extends` keyword is used to specify the subclass/superclass relationships that hold in the Java class hierarchy. We sometimes refer to the subclass/superclass relationship as the *is-a* relationship, in the sense that a horse *is a* mammal, and a mammal *is a* animal. Thus, the `extends` keyword is used to define the *is-a* relationship among the objects in the Java class hierarchy.

The is-a relationship

A **top-level container** is a GUI container that cannot be added to another container; it can only have components added to it. Figure 4.11 is a class hierarchy that shows the relationships among some of the top-level Swing and AWT classes. For example, the `javax.swing.JFrame` class, which represents a top-level window, is a subclass of `java.awt.Frame`, and the `javax.swing.JApplet` is a subclass of `java.applet.Applet`. We can see from this figure that a `JApplet` *is-a* `Applet` and an `Applet` *is-a* `Panel` and a `Panel` *is-a* `Container`.

Top-level container

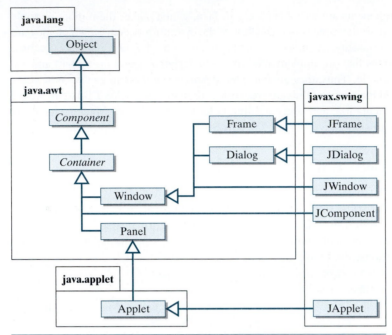

Figure 4.11 Top-level Swing and AWT classes.

These subclass/superclass relationships are created in their respective class definitions by using the `extends` keyword, as follows:

```
public class JApplet extends Applet { ... }
public class Applet extends Panel { ... }
public class Panel extends Container { ... }
```

Specialization

As we will see in the next section, extending a class in this way enables us to create a new class by specializing an existing class.

4.4.3   Top-Level Windows

Referring again to Figure 4.11, note that all of the Swing components are subclasses of the AWT `Container` class. This means that Swing components are `Container`s. They inherit the functionality of the `Container` class. So Swing components can contain other GUI components. That is why a `JButton` can contain an image.

All GUI programs must be contained inside a top-level container of some kind. Swing provides four top-level container classes: `JFrame`, `JWindow`, `JApplet`, and `JDialog`. For our basic GUI, we will use a `JFrame` as the top-level window for standalone applications. We will use a `JApplet` as the top-level window for Java applets.

Content pane

A `JFrame` encapsulates the basic functionality of a top-level window. It has a *content pane* to which other Swing components, such as buttons and text fields, can be added. In addition, it comes with enough built-in functionality to respond to certain basic commands, such as when the user adjusts its size or closes it.

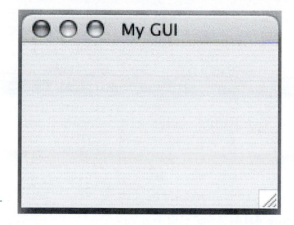

Figure 4.12 A simple window.

Figure 4.12 shows a simple top-level window as it would be displayed on the console. The window has a title ("My GUI"). It is 200 pixels wide, 150 pixels high, and its top-left corner is located at coordinates (100,150) on the console screen. As in other graphical systems, points on the Java console are always given as an ordered pair, (X, Y), with the horizontal coordinate, X, listed first, followed by the vertical coordinate, Y. The horizontal x-axis extends positively from left to right, and the vertical y-axis extends positively from top to bottom.

The class that created and displayed this window is shown in Figure 4.13. Note the use of the `extends` keyword to define `SimpleGUI` as a subclass of `JFrame`. As a subclass, `SimpleGUI` inherits all of the functionality of a `JFrame` (Fig. 4.14). That is, it can contain other GUI components, it knows how to resize and close itself, and so on. The reason we want to define a subclass of `JFrame` rather than just use a `JFrame` instance is because we want eventually to give our subclass additional functionality that is specialized for our application.

EFFECTIVE DESIGN: Specialization. By creating a subclass of `JFrame` we can specialize its functionality for our application.

```java
import javax.swing.*;

public class SimpleGUI extends JFrame
{
    public SimpleGUI(String title)
    {   setSize(200,150);
        setLocation(100, 150);
        setTitle(title);
        setVisible(true);                      // Displays the JFrame
    } // SimpleGUI()

    public static void main(String args[])
    {   new SimpleGUI("My GUI");
    } // main()
} // SimpleGUI class
```

Figure 4.13 A top-level window with a title.

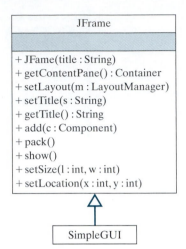

JFrame
+ JFame(title : String)
+ getContentPane() : Container
+ setLayout(m : LayoutManager)
+ setTitle(s : String)
+ getTitle() : String
+ add(c : Component)
+ pack()
+ show()
+ setSize(l : int, w : int)
+ setLocation(x : int, y : int)

Figure 4.14 SimpleGUI is a subclass of JFrame.

Note how SimpleGUI's main() program creates an instance of SimpleGUI by invoking its constructor. There is no need to use a variable here because there are no further references to this object in this class. However, simply constructing a SimpleGUI will not cause it to appear on the Java console. For that to happen, it is necessary to give it a size and to call its setVisible() method. This is done in the constructor method.

The constructor method illustrates how to use some of the methods inherited from JFrame. Figure 4.14 shows some of the methods that SimpleGUI inherits from JFrame. We use the setSize() and setLocation() methods to set SimpleGUI's size and location. We use the setTitle() method to set its title. And we use the setVisible() method to cause it to appear on the console.

4.4.4 GUI Components for Input, Output, and Control

To enable our top-level window to serve as a user interface, it will be necessary to give it some components. Figure 4.15 provides an overview of some of the main Swing components. Generally, there are three types of components, corresponding to the three main functions of a user interface: *input*, *output*, and *control*. A JTextField is an example of an input component. The user can type text into the text field, which can then be transmitted into the program. A JTextArea is an example of an output component. The program can display text in the text area. Control components enable the user to control the actions of the program. A JButton is an example of a control component. It can be associated with an action that can be initiated whenever the user clicks it. We might also consider a JLabel to be an output component, because we can use it to prompt the user as to what type of actions to take.

Let's begin by creating a simple user interface, one that enables us to perform basic input, output, and control operations with a minimum of Swing components. This will allow us to demonstrate the basic principles and techniques of user-interface design and will result in a GUI that can be extended for more sophisticated applications. For this example, we will limit our application to simply greeting the user, just as we did in designing our command-line interface. In other words, the user will be prompted to input his or her name, and the program will respond by displaying a greeting (Fig. 4.10). We will call our GUI GreeterGUI, to suggest its interdependence with the Greeter computational object we used with the command-line interface.

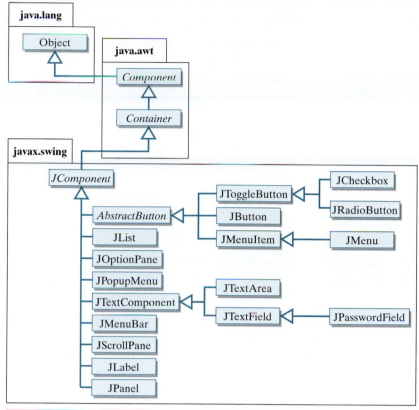

Figure 4.15 Swing components.

For this simple application, our GUI will make use of the following components:

- A JTextField will accept user input.
- A JTextArea will display the program's output.
- A JButton will allow the user to request the greeting.
- A JLabel will serve as a prompt for the JTextField.

Figure 4.16 shows some of the constructors and public methods for the JTextArea, JTextField, JButton, and JLabel components. The following code segments illustrate how to use these constructors to create instances of these components:

```
                                     // Declare instance variables for the components
private JLabel prompt;
private JTextField inField;
private JTextArea display;
private JButton goButton;

                                     // Instantiate the components
prompt = new JLabel("Please type your name here: ");
inField = new JTextField(10);                    // 10 chars wide
display = new JTextArea(10, 30);                 // 10 rows x 30 columns
goButton = new JButton("Click here for a greeting!");
```

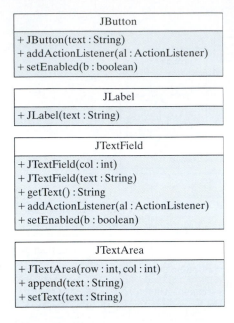

JButton
+ JButton(text : String) + addActionListener(al : ActionListener) + setEnabled(b : boolean)

JLabel
+ JLabel(text : String)

JTextField
+ JTextField(col : int) + JTextField(text : String) + getText() : String + addActionListener(al : ActionListener) + setEnabled(b : boolean)

JTextArea
+ JTextArea(row : int, col : int) + append(text : String) + setText(text : String)

Figure 4.16 Public methods and constructors for basic Swing components.

For this example, we use some of the simpler constructors. Thus, we create a `JTextField` with a size of 10. This means that it can display 10 characters of input. We create a `JTextArea` with 10 rows of text, each 30 characters wide. We create a `JButton` with a simple text prompt meant to inform the user of how to use the button.

4.4.5 Adding GUI Components to a Top-Level Window

Now that we know how to create GUI components, the next task is to add them to the top-level window. A `JFrame` is a top-level `Container` (Fig. 4.11), but instead of adding the components directly to the `JFrame`, we have to add them to the `JFrame`'s content pane, which is also a `Container`.

> **JAVA LANGUAGE RULE**   **Content Pane.** GUI Components cannot be added directly to a `JFrame`. They must be added to its content pane.

Java's `Container` class has several `add()` methods that can be used to insert components into the container:

```
add(Component comp)                       // add comp to end of container
add(Component comp, int index)            // add comp at index
add(String region, Component comp) add comp at region
```

The particular `add()` method to use depends on how we want to arrange the components in the container. The layout of a container is controlled by its default **layout manager**, an object associated with the container that determines the sizing and arrangement of its contained components. For a content pane, the default layout manager is a `BorderLayout`. This is an arrangement whereby components may be placed in the center of the pane and along its north, south, east, and west borders (Fig. 4.17).

Layout manager

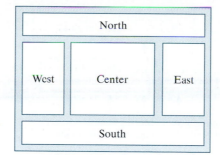

Figure 4.17 Arrangement of components in a border layout.

Components are added to a border layout by using the `add(String region, Component comp)` method, where the `String` parameter specifies either "North", "South", "East", "West", or "Center". For example, to add the `JTextArea` to the center of the `JFrame` we first create a reference to its content pane and then we add the component at its center:

```
Container contentPane = getContentPane();   // Get pane
contentPane.add("Center",display);          // Add JTextArea
```

One limitation of the border layout is that only one component can be added to each area. This is a problem for our example because we want our prompt `JLabel` to be located right before the `JTextField`. To get around this problem, we will create another container, a `JPanel`, and add the prompt, the text field, and the `goButton` to it. That way, all of the components involved in getting the user's input will be organized into one panel. We then add the entire panel to one of the areas on the content pane.

```
JPanel inputPanel = new JPanel();
inputPanel.add(prompt);                     // Add JLabel to panel
inputPanel.add(inField);                    // Add JTextField to panel
inputPanel.add(goButton);                   // Add JButton to  panel
contentPane.add("South", inputPanel);       // Add to JFrame
```

The default layout for a `JPanel` is `FlowLayout`, which means that components are added left to right with the last addition going at the end of the sequence. This is an appropriate layout for this JPanel because it will place the prompt just to the left of the input `JTextField`.

EFFECTIVE DESIGN: Encapsulation.   `JPanel`s can be used to group related components in a GUI.

4.4.6   Controlling the GUI's Action

Now that we know how to place all the components on the GUI, we need to design the GUI's controls. As mentioned earlier, GUIs use a form of event-driven programming. Anything that happens when you are using a computer—every keystroke and mouse movement—is classified as an event. As Figure 4.18 illustrates, events are generated by the computer's hardware and filtered up through the operating system and the application programs. Events are handled by

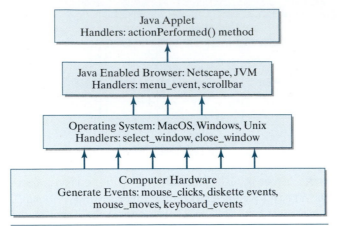

Figure 4.18 Java's event model.

Event listener

special objects called listeners. A **listener** is a specialist that monitors constantly for a certain type of event. Some events, such as inserting a CD in the CD-ROM drive, are handled by listeners in the operating system. Others, such as typing input into a Web page or a Word document, are handled by listeners in a piece of application software, such as a browser or a word processor.

In an event-driven programming model, the program is controlled by an **event loop**. That is, the program repeatedly listens for events, taking some kind of action whenever an event is generated. In effect, we might portray this event loop as follows:

```
Repeat forever or until the program is stopped
    Listen for events
    if event-A occurs, handle it with event-A-handler
    if event-B occurs, handle it with event-B-handler
    ...
```

The event loop listens constantly for the occurrence of events and then calls the appropriate object to handle each event.

Figure 4.19 shows some of the main types of events in the `java.awt.event` package. In most cases, the names of the event classes are suggestive of their roles. Thus, a `MouseEvent` occurs when the mouse is moved. A `KeyEvent` occurs when the keyboard is used. The only event that our program needs to listen for is an `ActionEvent`, the type of event that occurs when the user clicks the `JButton`.

When the user clicks the `JButton`, Java will create an `ActionEvent` object. This object contains important information about the event, such as the time the event occurred and the object, such as a `JButton`, that was the locus of the event. For our application, when the user clicks the `JButton`, the program should input the user's name from the `JTextField` and display a greeting, such as "Hi John nice to meet you" in the `JTextArea`. That is, we want the program to execute the following code segment:

```
String name = inField.getText();
display.append(greeter.greet(name) + "\n");
```

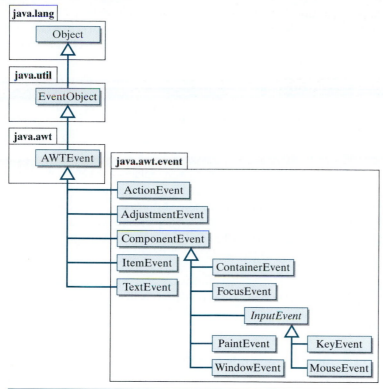

Figure 4.19 Java's event hierarchy.

The first line uses the `JTextField.getText()` method to get the text the user typed into the `JTextField` and stores it in a local variable, `name`. The second line passes the `name` to the `greeter.greet()` method and passes the result it gets back to the `JTextArea.append()` method. This will have the effect of displaying the text at the end of the `JTextArea`.

In this example, we have used a couple of the standard public methods of the `JTextField` and `JTextArea` classes. For our simple GUI, the methods described in Figure 4.16 will be sufficient for our needs. However, if you would like to see the other methods available for these and other Swing components, you should check Java's online API documentation.

java.sun.com/docs

4.4.7 The ActionListener Interface

Given that the code segment just described will do the task of greeting the user, where should we put it in our program? We want the code segment to be invoked whenever the user clicks on the `goButton`. You know enough Java to understand that we have to put the code in a Java method. However, we need a special method in this case, one that will be called automatically by Java whenever the user clicks the button. In other words, we need a special method that the button's listener knows how to call whenever the button is clicked.

Java solves this problem by letting us define a preselected method that can be associated with the `goButton`. The name of the method is `actionPerformed()`, and it is part of the `ActionListener` interface. In this case, an **interface** is a special Java class that contains

Java interface

only methods and constants (final variables). It cannot contain instance variables. (Be careful to distinguish this kind of interface, a specific type of Java class, from the more general kind of interface, whereby we say that a class's public methods make up its interface to other objects.) Here is the definition of the `ActionListener` interface:

```
public abstract interface ActionListener extends EventListener
{    public abstract void actionPerformed(ActionEvent e);
}
```

This resembles a class definition, but the keyword `interface` replaces the keyword `class` in the definition. Note that we are declaring this interface to be `abstract`. An **abstract interface** or **abstract class** is one that contains one or more abstract methods. An **abstract method** is one that consists entirely of its signature; it lacks an implementation—that is, it does not have a method body. Note that the `actionPerformed()` method in `ActionListener` places a semicolon where its body is supposed to be.

> **JAVA LANGUAGE RULE** **Java Interface.** A Java interface is like a Java class except that it cannot contain instance variables.

> **JAVA LANGUAGE RULE** **Abstract Methods and Classes.** An abstract method is a method that lacks an implementation. It has no method body.

Abstract method

Declaring a method `abstract` means that we are leaving its implementation up to the class that implements it. This way, its implementation can be tailored to a particular context, with its signature specifying generally what the method does. Thus, `actionPerformed()` takes an `ActionEvent` object as a parameter and performs some kind of action.

What this means, in effect, is that any class that implements the `actionPerformed()` method can serve as a listener for `ActionEvent`s. Thus, to create a listener for our `JButton`, all we need to do is give an implementation of the `actionPerformed()` method. For our program, the action we want to take when the `goButton` is clicked is to greet the user by name. We want to set things up so that the following `actionPerformed()` method is called whenever the `goButton` is clicked:

```
public void actionPerformed(ActionEvent e)
{   if (e.getSource() == goButton)
    {   String name = inField.getText();
        display.append(greeter.greet(name) + "\n");
    }
}
```

In other words, we place the code that we want executed when the button is clicked in the body of the `actionPerformed()` method. Note that in the `if` statement we get the source of the action from the `ActionEvent` object and check that it was the `goButton`.

This explains what is done when the button is clicked—namely, the code in `action-Performed()` will be executed. But it doesn't explain how Java knows that it should call this method in the first place. To set that up we must do two further things. We must place the `actionPerformed()` method in our `GreeterGUI` class, and we must tell Java that `GreeterGUI` will be the `ActionListener` for the `goButton`.

The following stripped-down version of the `GreeterGUI` class illustrates how we put it all together:

```java
public class GreeterGUI extends Frame implements ActionListener
{ ...
  public void buildGUI()
  {  ...
    goButton = new JButton("Click here for a greeting!");
    goButton.addActionListener(this);
    ...
  }
  ...
  public void actionPerformed(ActionEvent e)
  {   if (e.getSource() == goButton)
    {   String name = inField.getText();
        display.append(greeter.greet(name) + "\n");
    }
  }
  ...
}
```

First, we declare that `GreeterGUI` implements the `ActionListener` interface in the class header. This means that the class must provide a definition of the `actionPerformed()` method, which it does. It also means that `GreeterGUI` is an `ActionListener`. So SimpleGUI is both a `JFrame` and an `ActionListener`.

Second, note how we use the `addActionListener()` method to associate the listener with the `goButton`:

```java
goButton.addActionListener(this)
```

The `this` keyword is a self-reference—that is, it always refers to the object in which it is used. It's the same as when we refer to ourselves by saying "I." When used here, the `this` keyword refers to the `GreeterGUI`. In other words, we are setting things up so that the `GreeterGUI` will serve as the listener for action events on the `goButton`.

> **JAVA LANGUAGE RULE**   **This Object.** The `this` keyword always refers to the object that uses it. It is like saying "I" or "me."

4.4.8   Connecting the GUI to the Computational Object

Figure 4.20 gives the complete source code for our `GreeterGUI` interface. Because there is a lot going on here, it might be helpful to go through the program carefully even though we have introduced most of its elements already. That will help us put together the various concepts we have introduced.

```java
import javax.swing.*;
import java.awt.*;
import java.awt.event.*;

public class GreeterGUI extends JFrame implements ActionListener
{ private JTextArea display;
  private JTextField inField;
  private JButton goButton;
  private Greeter greeter;

  public GreeterGUI(String title)
  { greeter = new Greeter();
    buildGUI();
    setTitle(title);
    pack();
    setVisible(true);
  } // GreeterGUI()
  private void buildGUI()
  { Container contentPane = getContentPane();
    contentPane.setLayout(new BorderLayout());
    display = new JTextArea(10,30);
    inField = new JTextField(10);
    goButton = new JButton("Click here for a greeting!");
    goButton.addActionListener(this);
    JPanel inputPanel = new JPanel();
    inputPanel.add(new JLabel("Input your name here: "));
    inputPanel.add(inField);
    inputPanel.add(goButton);
    contentPane.add("Center", display);
    contentPane.add("South", inputPanel);
  } // buildGUI()
  public void actionPerformed(ActionEvent e)
  { if (e.getSource() == goButton)
    { String name = inField.getText();
      display.append(greeter.greet(name) + "\n");
    }
  } // actionPerformed()
} // GreeterGUI class
```

Figure 4.20 Definition of the GreeterGUI class.

To begin with, note the several Java packages that must be included in this program. The `javax.swing` package includes definitions for all of the Swing components. The `java.awt.event` package includes the `ActionEvent` class and the `ActionListener` interface, and the `java.awt` packages contain the `Container` class.

Extending a class

Next note how the `GreeterGUI` class is defined as a subclass of `JFrame` and as implementing the `ActionListener` interface. `GreeterGUI` thereby inherits all of the functionality of a `JFrame`. Plus, we are giving it additional functionality. One of its functions is to serve as an `ActionListener` for its `goButton`. The `ActionListener` interface consists entirely of the `actionPerformed()` method, which is defined in the program. This method encapsulates the actions that will be taken whenever the user clicks the `goButton`.

Implementing an interface

The next elements of the program are its four instance variables, the most important of which is the `Greeter` variable. This is the variable that sets up the relationship between the GUI and the computational object. In this case, because the variable is declared in the GUI, we say that the GUI *uses* the computational object, as illustrated in Figure 4.8. This is slightly different from the relationship we set up in the command-line interface, in which the computational object uses the interface (Fig. 4.2).

The computational object

The other instance variables are for GUI components that must be referred to throughout the class. For example, note that the goButton, inField, and display are instantiated in the buildGUI() method and referenced again in the actionPerformed() method.

The next element in the program is its constructor. It begins by creating an instance of the Greeter computational object. It is important to do this first in case we need information from the computational object in order to build the GUI. In this case we don't need anything from Greeter, but we will need such information in other programs.

We've already discussed the fact that the constructor's role is to coordinate the initialization of the GreeterGUI object. Thus, it invokes the buildGUI() method, which takes care of the details of laying out the GUI components. And, finally, it displays itself by calling the pack() and setVisible() methods, which are inherited from JFrame. The pack() method sizes the frame according to the sizes and layout of the components it contains. The setVisible() method is what actually causes the GUI to appear on the Java console.

Finally, note the details of the buildGUI() method. We have discussed each of the individual statements already. Here we see the order in which they are combined. Note that we can declare the contentPane and inputPanel variables locally, because they are not used elsewhere in the class.

SELF-STUDY EXERCISE

EXERCISE 4.2   There is a simple modification that we can make to GreeterGUI. The JText-Field can serve as both an input element and a control element for action events. An Action-Event is generated whenever the user presses the Return or Enter key in a JTextField so that the JButton can be removed. Of course, it will be necessary to designate the inField as an ActionListener in order to take advantage of this feature. Make the appropriate changes to the buildGUI() and actionPerformed() methods so that the inField can function as both a control and input element. Call the new class GreeterGUI2.

4.4.9   Using the GUI in a Java Application

As you know, a Java application is a standalone program, one that can be run on its own. We have designed our GUI so that it can easily be used with a Java application. We saw in the preceding section that the GUI has a reference to the Greeter object, which is the computational object. Therefore, all we need to get the program to run as an application is a main() method.

One way to use the GUI in an application is simply to create an instance in a main() method. The main() method can be placed in the GreeterGUI class itself or in a separate class. Here is an example with main() in a separate class:

```
public class GreeterApplication
{  public static void main(String args[])
    {
       new GreeterGUI("Greeter");
    }
}
```

The `main()` method creates an instance of `GreeterGUI`, passing it a string to use as its title. If you prefer, this same `main()` method can be incorporated directly into the `GreeterGUI` class.

4.4.10 Using the GUI in a Java Applet

Using our GUI with a Java applet is just as easy as using it with an application. The only difference is that we instantiate `GreeterGUI` in the applet's `init()` method rather than in a `main()` method:

```java
import javax.swing.*;

public class GreeterApplet extends JApplet
{
    public void init()
    {
        new GreeterGUI("Greeter");
    }
}
```

When this applet is run from a browser, it will open a separate top-level window that is identical to the window opened by the application. Unlike the other applets we have seen, the GUI will not be embedded directly in the Web page, because it is not possible to add a `JFrame`, which our `GreeterGUI` is, to a `JApplet`. The rule is that you cannot add one top-level window to another top-level window.

JAVA LANGUAGE RULE **Top-level Windows.** Top-level Java windows cannot contain other top-level windows as components.

It is a relatively simple matter to modify `GreeterGUI` so that it can be embedded directly in the applet window. The main change we have to make is to define the GUI as a subclass of `JPanel` rather than as a subclass of `JFrame`. Figure 4.21 presents a full implementation of the revised class, which we name `GreeterGUIPanel`.

The revised `GreeterGUIPanel` class requires the following two changes:

- Unlike `JFrame`s, `JPanel`s do not have titles and do not have a `pack()` method. Therefore we modify the constructor method to the simpler form shown here.
- Unlike `JFrame`s, `JPanel`s do not use a content pane. Swing components are added directly to the `JPanel`. This simplifies the `buildGUI()` method.

Given these changes, we would then change the applet's `init()` method to the following:

```java
import javax.swing.*;

public class GreeterPanelApplet extends JApplet
{   public void init()
    {   getContentPane().add(new GreeterGUIPanel());
    }
}
```

```
import javax.swing.*;
import java.awt.*;
import java.awt.event.*;

public class GreeterGUIPanel extends JPanel implements ActionListener
{ private JTextArea display;
  private JTextField inField;
  private JButton goButton;
  private Greeter greeter;

  public GreeterGUIPanel()
  {   greeter = new Greeter();
      buildGUI();
  } // GUIPanel()
  private void buildGUI()
  { display = new JTextArea(10,30);
    inField = new JTextField(10);
    goButton = new JButton("Click here for a greeting!");
    goButton.addActionListener(this);
    JPanel inputPanel = new JPanel();
    inputPanel.add(new JLabel("Input your name here: "));
    inputPanel.add(inField);
    inputPanel.add(goButton);
    add("Center", display);
    add("South", inputPanel);
  } // buildGUI()
  public void actionPerformed(ActionEvent e)
  {   if (e.getSource() == goButton)
      {   String name = inField.getText();
          display.append(greeter.greet(name) + "\n");
      } // if
  } // actionPeformed()
} // GreeterGUIPanel class
```

Figure 4.21   Definition of the GreeterGUIPanel class.

Since a JApplet has a content pane, we add the GreeterGUIPanel to the content pane
rather than to the applet itself. The result would be the applet shown in Figure 4.22.

4.5   CASE STUDY: The One-Row Nim Game

In this section, we show how to develop alternative interfaces for our case study game of One-
Row Nim that was developed in Chapters 2 and 3. As you will recall, the One-Row Nim game
starts with, say, 21 sticks on a table. Players take turns picking up one, two, or three sticks,
and the player to pick up the last stick loses. We wish to develop an application program that
the will enable the user of the program to play this game against the computer, that is, against
the program.

As in our other examples in this chapter, our design will divide this problem into two
primary objects: a computational object, in this case OneRowNim, and a user interface object,
for which we will use either a KeyboardReader or a OneRowNimGUI. One goal of our design
was to develop the OneRowNim class so that it can be used, without changes, with either a
command-line interface or a GUI.

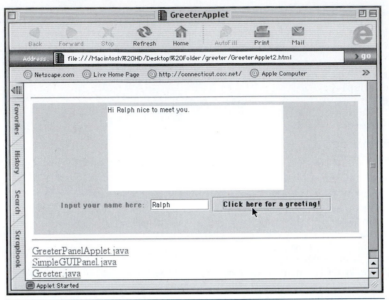

Figure 4.22 The Greeter applet. This version is embedded directly in the Web page.

Recall that we designed the OneRowNim class to maintain the state of the game and to provide methods that enforce the rules of the game. Thus, we know that after each legal move, the number of sticks will decline, until it is zero or less, which indicates that the game is over. Also, an instance of OneRowNim keeps track of whose turn it is and can determine whether the game is over and who the winner is when the game is over. Finally, the game ensures that players cannot cheat either by taking too few or too many sticks on one turn. Figure 4.23 shows the UML diagram of the OneRowNim class as described at the end of the Chapter 3.

4.5.1 A Command-Line Interface to OneRowNim

We will now focus on connecting a OneRowNim instance with a KeyboardReader instance, the command-line interface we developed at the beginning of this chapter. To do so requires no changes to KeyboardReader (Fig. 4.6). Unlike in the greeter example, we will use a third object to serve as the main program. The OneRowNimApp class will contain the run() method

Figure 4.23 A UML diagram of the OneRowNim class.

OneRowNim
− nSticks : int = 21 − player : int = 1
+ OneRowNim(() + OneRowNim(sticks : int) + OneRowNim(st : int, pl : int) + takeSticks(num : int) + getSticks() : int + getPlayer() : int + gameOver() : boolean + getWinner() : int + report()

that controls the game's progress. OneRowNimApp will use the KeyboardReader object to prompt the user, to display the program's output, and to perform input from the keyboard. It will use the OneRowNim object to keep track of the game.

In fact, the main challenge for this part of our problem is designing the run() method, which will use a loop algorithm to play the game. The user and the computer will repeatedly take turns picking up sticks until the game is over. The game ends when there are no more sticks to pick up. Thus, we can use the game's state—the number of sticks left—as our loop's entry condition. We will repeat the loop while there are more than zero sticks remaining.

Loop algorithm

The following pseudocode describes the remaining details of our algorithm. We refer to the OneRowNim instance as the game object, and to the KeyboardReader instance as the reader object. We use the notation game:get the number of sticks left to indicate that we are sending a message to the game object.

```
Create a game object with 21 sticks
Create a reader object
sticksLeft = game:get the number of sticks left
reader:display the rules of the game
while (game: the game is not over)
    whoseMove = game: find out whose turn it is
    if (whoseMove == user)
        game: user chooses number of sticks to take
    else
        game: computer chooses number of sticks to take
    sticksLeft = game: get the number of sticks left
    reader: report the number of sticks left
                                    // At this point the game is over.
if game: the user is the winner
        reader: report that the user wins
else
        reader: report that the computer wins
```

In this algorithm, the initializations we perform consist of creating the game and reader objects and initializing sticksLeft. We use a while loop structure to control the game. The loop's entry condition is that the "the game is not over." This is a piece of information that comes directly from the game object. As long as "the game is not over," the body of the loop will be executed. Note that either the player or the computer makes a move in the loop's body. Again, it is up to the game object to determine whose move it is. Following the move we ask the game how many sticks are left, and we use the reader object to report this.

The loop structure has the three necessary elements. The initializer in this case is the creation of a OneRowNim object. We know that this will cause the game to have 21 sticks and it will be the user's move. The loop-entry condition is that the game is not over, based on the fact that there are still sticks remaining to be picked up. But again, this knowledge is kept by the game object. Finally, we have an updater that consists of either the computer or the user picking up some sticks. This in turn changes the value of sticksLeft on each iteration, moving us ever closer to the condition that there are no sticks left, at which point the game will be over.

Loop structure: Initializer, entry condition, updater

Left out of this algorithm are the details of the user's moves and the computer's moves. These are the kinds of actions that are good to put into separate methods, where we can worry about checking whether the user made a legal move and other such details.

Figure 4.24 provides the implementation of the OneRowNimApp application. It uses a KeyboardReader as a command-line interface and a OneRowNim instance as its computational object. Thus, it has private instance variables for each of these objects, which are instantiated in the constructor method. The algorithm we just described has been placed in the run() method, which is called from main() after the application is instantiated. The use of the boolean method gameOver() to control the loop makes this code segment easier to understand. Also, it leaves it up to the game object to determine when the game is over. From an object-oriented design perspective, this is an appropriate division of responsibility. If you doubt this, imagine what could go wrong if this determination was left up to the user interface.

Division of labor

```java
public class OneRowNimApp
{ private KeyboardReader reader;
  private OneRowNim game;

  public OneRowNimApp()
  { reader = new KeyboardReader();
    game = new OneRowNim(21);
  } // OneRowNim()

  public void run()
  { int sticksLeft = game.getSticks();
    reader.display("Let's play One-Row Nim. You go first.\n");
    reader.display("There are " + sticksLeft + " sticks left.\n");
    reader.display("You can pick up 1, 2, or 3 at a time\n.");
    while (game.gameOver() == false)
    { if (game.getPlayer() == 1)  userMove();
      else computerMove();
      sticksLeft = game.getSticks();
      reader.display("There are " + sticksLeft + " sticks left.\n");
    } // while
    if (game.getWinner() == 1)
      reader.display("Game over. You win. Nice game.\n");
    else  reader.display("Game over. I win. Nice game.\n");
  } // run()

  private void userMove()
  { reader.prompt("Do you take 1, 2, or 3 sticks?: ");
    int userTakes = reader.getKeyboardInteger();
    if (game.takeSticks(userTakes))
    { reader.display("You take " + userTakes + ".\n");
    } else
    { reader.display("You can't take " + userTakes + ". Try again\n");
    } // else
  } // userMove()

  private void computerMove()
  { game.takeAway(1);                          // Temporary strategy.
    reader.display("I take 1 stick. ");
  } // computerMove()

  public static void main(String args[])
  { OneRowNimApp app = new OneRowNimApp();
    app.run();
  } // main()
} // OneRowNimApp class
```

Figure 4.24 Definition of OneRowNimApp, a command-line interface to the OneRowNim.

A user-interface programmer might end up mistakenly implementing the wrong rule for the game being over. A similar point applies to the `getWinner()` method. This determination rests with the game, not the user interface. If left up to the user interface, it is possible that a programming mistake could lead to the loss of the game's integrity.

The `run()` method calls `userMove()` and `computerMove()` to perform the specific set of actions associated with each type of move. The `userMove()` method uses the `Keyboard-Reader()` to prompt the user and input his or her move. It then passes the user's choice to `game.takeSticks()`. Note how it checks the return value to determine whether the move was legal or not and provides an appropriate response through the interface.

Finally, note how we use private methods to implement the actions associated with the user's and computer's moves. These private methods are not part of the object's interface and can only be used within the object. Thus they are, in a sense, secondary to the object's public instance methods. We sometimes refer to them as **helper methods**. This division of labor allows us to organize all of the details associated with the moves into a single module. The `computerMove()` method uses a temporary strategy of taking a single stick and passes the number 1 to `game.takeSticks()`. Finally, `computerMove()` reports its choice through the interface. After we have covered operators of the `int` data type in the next chapter, we will be able to describe better strategies for the computer to make a move.

This example shows how simple and straightforward it is to use our `KeyboardReader` user interface. In fact, for this problem, our interface didn't require any changes. Although there might be occasions where we will want to extend the functionality of `KeyboardReader`, it can be used without changes for a wide variety of problems in subsequent chapters.

> **EFFECTIVE DESIGN: Code Reuse.**   A well-designed user interface can be used with many computational objects.

4.5.2   A GUI for `OneRowNim`

The first task in designing a GUI for `OneRowNim` is to decide how to use input, output, and control components to interact with the user. Following the design we used in the GUI for our greeter application, we can use a `JTextField` for the user's input and a `JTextArea` for the game's output. Thus, we will use the `JTextArea` to report on the progress of the game and to display any error messages that arise. As in the greeter example, we can use both the `JTextField` and `JButton` as control elements and a `JLabel` as a prompt for the input text field. For the most part, then, the use of GUI components will remain the same as in our previous example. This is as we would expect. The relationship between the user and the interface are pretty similar in both this and the previous application.

In contrast, the relationship between the interface and the game are quite different from what we saw in the greeter application. As in that application, the GUI will still need a reference to its associated computational object, in this case the game:

```
private OneRowNim game;
...
game = new OneRowNim();
```

The biggest difference between this GUI and the one we used with the greeter application occurs in the details of the interaction between the GUI and the game. These details are the responsibility of the `actionPerformed()` method, whose actions depend on the actual progress of the individual game.

Unlike in the command-line version, there is no need to use a loop construct in the `actionPerformed()` method. Instead, because we are using event-driven programming here, we will rely on Java's event loop to move the game from one turn to another.

As in the greeter example, the `actionPerformed()` method will be called automatically whenever the `JButton` is clicked. It is the responsibility of the GUI to ensure that it is the user's turn whenever this action occurs. Therefore, we design `actionPerformed()` so that each time it is called, it first performs the user's move and then, assuming the game is not over and an error did not occur on the user's move, it performs the computer's move. Thus, the basic algorithm is as follows:

```
Let the user move.
If game:game is not over and computer turn
    let the computer move.
Game: how many sticks are left.
display: report how many sticks are left
If game:game is over
     Stop accepting moves.
     Report the winner.
```

If the user picks up the last stick, the game is over. In that case, the computer does not get a move. Or perhaps the user makes an error. In that case it would still be the user's move. These possibilities have to be considered in the algorithm before the computer gets to move. As the pseudocode shows, it is the `OneRowNim` object's responsibility to keep track of whether the game is over and whose turn it is.

Figure 4.25 shows the complete implementation of the `OneRowNimGUI` class. In terms of its instance variables, constructor, and `buildGUI()` method, there are only a few minor differences between this GUI and the `GreeterGUI` (Fig. 4.20). This GUI has instance variables for its `JTextField`, `JTextArea`, and `JButton`, as well as one for the `OneRowNim` instance, its computational object. It needs to be able to refer to these objects throughout the class. Hence we give them class scope.

The constructor method plays the same role here as in the previous GUI: it creates an instance of the computational object, builds the GUI's layout, and then displays the interface on the console.

```java
import javax.swing.*;
import java.awt.*;
import java.awt.event.*;

public class OneRowNimGUI extends JFrame implements ActionListener
{ private JTextArea display;
  private JTextField inField;
  private JButton goButton;
  private OneRowNim game;
```

Figure 4.25 The OneRowNimGUI class. (*Continued on next page*)

```java
  public OneRowNimGUI(String title)
  { game = new OneRowNim(21);
    buildGUI();
    setTitle(title);
    pack();
    setVisible(true);
  } // OneRowNimGUI()
  private void buildGUI()
  { Container contentPane = getContentPane();
    contentPane.setLayout(new BorderLayout());
    display = new JTextArea(20,30);
    display.setText("Let's play Take Away. There are " + game.getSticks() +
      " sticks.\n" + "Pick up 1,2, or 3 at a time.\n" + "You go first.\n");
    inField = new JTextField(10);
    goButton = new JButton("Take Sticks");
    goButton.addActionListener(this);
    JPanel inputPanel = new JPanel();
    inputPanel.add(new JLabel("How many sticks do you take: "));
    inputPanel.add(inField);
    inputPanel.add(goButton);
    contentPane.add("Center", display);
    contentPane.add("South", inputPanel);
  } // buildGUI
  private void userMove()
  { int userTakes = Integer.parseInt(inField.getText());
    if (game.takeSticks(userTakes))
      display.append("You take " + userTakes + ".\n");
    else display.append("You can't take " + userTakes + ". Try again\n");
  } // userMove()
  private void computerMove()
  { if (game.gameOver()) return;
    if (game.getPlayer() == 2)
    {   game.takeSticks(1); // Temporary strategy
      display.append("I take one stick. ");
    } // if
  } // computerMove()
  private void endGame()
  { goButton.setEnabled(false);  // Disable button and textfield
    inField.setEnabled(false);
    if (game.getWinner() == 1)
      display.append("Game over. You win. Nice game.\n");
    else  display.append("Game over. I win. Nice game.\n");
  } // endGame()
  public void actionPerformed(ActionEvent e)
  { if (e.getSource() == goButton)
    { userMove();
      computerMove();
      int sticksLeft = game.getSticks();
      display.append("There are " + sticksLeft + " sticks left.\n");
      if (game.gameOver()) endGame();
    } // if
  } // actionPerformed()
} // OneRowNimGUI class
```

Figure 4.25   The OneRowNimGUI class. (*Continued from previous page*)

All of the changes in the buildGUI() method have to do with application-specific details, such as the text we use as the prompt and the goButton's label. One new method we use here is the setText() method. Unlike the append() method, which is used to add text to the existing text in a JTextArea, the setText() method replaces the text in a JTextArea or a JTextField.

Next we will consider the private userMove() and computerMove() methods. Their roles are very similar to the corresponding methods in the command-line interface: They encapsulate the details involved in performing the players' moves. The primary difference here is that for the user move we input the user's choice from a JTextField rather than from the keyboard. We use getText() to retrieve the user's input from the JTextField, and we use Integer.parseInt() to convert it to an int value:

```
int userTakes = Integer.parseInt(inField.getText());
```

Another difference is that we use a JTextField to display the program's messages to the user.

As we have noted, the main differences between this and the GreeterGUI occur in the actionPerformed() method. Note how we use OneRowNim's public methods, get-Player(), gameOver(), and getWinner(), to control the interaction with the user.

One issue that differs substantially from the command-line interface is: How do we handle the end of the game? Because we are using Java's built-in event loop, the GUI will continue to respond to user events unless we stop it from doing so. One way to do this is to disable the JButton and the JTextField. By disabling a control element, we render it unable to respond to events. To do this we use the setEnabled() method, passing it the value false to, in effect, "turn off" that component:

```
if (game.gameOver())
{  goButton.setEnabled(false);   // End the game
   inField.setEnabled(false);
   ...
}
```

Although it doesn't apply in this situation, the setEnabled() method can be used repeatedly in a GUI to turn components on and off as the context of the interaction dictates.

GUI input, output, and control

This example shows how simple and straightforward it can be to build a GUI for just about any application. One main design issue is deciding what kinds of input, output, and control elements to use. For most applications, we can use JTextField, JTextArea, JLabel, and JButton as the GUI's basic elements. A second design issue concerns the development of the actionPerformed() method, which must be designed in an application-specific way. Here we apply what we have learned about Java's event-programming model: we designate one or more of our elements to serve as an ActionListener, and we design algorithms to handle the action events that occur on that element.

Of course, for some applications we may need two JTextFields to handle input. At some point, we also might want to introduce JMenus and other advanced GUI elements. Some of these options will be introduced in upcoming chapters. Others will be covered in Chapter 13, which provides a more comprehensive view of Java's GUI capabilities.

EFFECTIVE DESIGN: GUI Design A well-designed GUI makes appropriate use of input, output, and control elements.

4.6 From the Java Library: `java.io.File` and File Input (Optional)

java.sun.com/docs

In addition to command-line and GUI user interfaces, there is one more standard user interface, files. In this section we show how the `Scanner` class, used in Chapter 2 for keyboard input, can also read input from files. Reading input from a file is relevant to only certain types of programming problems. It is hard to imagine how a file would be used in playing the One-Row Nim game, but a file might very well be useful to store a collection of riddles that could be read and displayed by a Java program. We will develop such a program later in this section.

Java has two types of files, *text files* and *binary files*. A **text file** stores a sequence of characters and is the type of file created by standard text editors like *NotePad* and *WordPad* on a Windows computer or *SimpleText* on a Macintosh. A **binary file** has a more general format that can store numbers and other data the way they are stored in the computer. In this section we will only consider text files. Binary files are considered in Chapter 11.

4.6.1 File Input with the `File` and `Scanner` Classes

An instance of the `java.io.File` class stores information that a `Scanner` object needs to create an input stream connected to the sequence of characters in a text file. A partial list of the public methods of the `File` class is given in the UML class diagram in Figure 4.26. We will only need to use the `File()` constructor in this section. The `File` instance created with the statement

```
File theFile = new File("riddles.txt");
```

will obtain and store information about the "riddles.txt" file in the same directory as the java code being executed, if such a file exists. If no such file exists, the `File` object stores information needed to create such a file but does not create it. In Chapter 11, we will describe how other objects can use a file object to create a file in which to write data. If we wish to create a `File` object that describes a file in a directory other than the one containing the Java program, we must call the constructor with a string argument that specifies the file's complete path name—that is, one that lists the sequence of directories containing the file. In any case, while we will not use it at this time, the `exists()` method of a `File` instance can be used to determine whether or not a file has been found with the specified name.

Figure 4.26 A UML class diagram of the `File` class with a partial list of public methods.

File
+ File(in String : path)
+ exists() : boolean
+ delete() : boolean
+ mkdir() : boolean

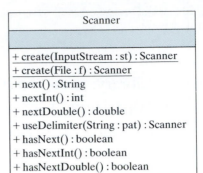

Scanner
+ create(InputStream : st) : Scanner
+ create(File : f) : Scanner
+ next() : String
+ nextInt() : int
+ nextDouble() : double
+ useDelimiter(String : pat) : Scanner
+ hasNext() : boolean
+ hasNextInt() : boolean
+ hasNextDouble() : boolean

Figure 4.27 A UML class diagram of the Scanner class with an expanded list of public methods.

In order to read data from a file with a Scanner object, we will need to use methods that were not discussed in Chapter 2. An expanded list of methods of the Scanner class is given in Figure 4.27. Note that there is a Scanner() constructor with a File object as an argument. Unlike the create() method used in Chapter 2, this create() throws an exception that must be handled. The following code will create a Scanner object that will be connected to an input stream that can read from a file:

```
try
{   File theFile = new File("riddles.txt");
    fileScan = new Scanner(theFile);
    fileScan = fileScan.useDelimiter("\r\n");
} catch (IOException e)
{    e.printStackTrace();
} // catch()
```

We will discuss the try-catch commands when exceptions are covered in Chapter 10. Until then, the try-catch structures can be copied exactly as above if you wish to use a Scanner object for file input. In the code above, the useDelimiter() method is used to set the Scanner object so that spaces can occur in strings that are read by the Scanner object. For the definition of a class to read riddles from a file, the above code belongs in a constructor method.

After we create a Scanner object connected to a file, we can make a call to nextInt(), nextDouble(), or next() method to read, respectively, an integer, real number, or string from the file. Unlike the strategy for using a Scanner object to get keyboard input, it is suggested that you test to see if there is more data in a file before reading it. This can be done with the hasNext(), hasNextInt(), and hasNextDouble() methods. These methods return the value true if there is more data in the file.

The program in Figure 4.28 is the complete listing of a class that reads riddles from a file and displays them. In the body of the method readRiddles(), the statements

```
String ques = null;
String ans = null;
Riddle theRiddle = null;
```

make explicit the fact that variables that refer to objects are assigned `null` as a value when they are declared. The statements:

```java
if (fileScan.hasNext())
    ques = fileScan.next();
if (fileScan.hasNext())
{   ans = fileScan.next();
    theRiddle = new Riddle(ques, ans);
}
```

```java
import java.io.*;
import java.util.Scanner;
public class RiddleFileReader
{   private Scanner fileScan; // For file input
    private Scanner kbScan;   // For keyboard input

    public RiddleFileReader(String fName)
    {   kbScan = new Scanner(System.in);
        try
        {   File theFile = new File(fName);
            fileScan = new Scanner(theFile);
            fileScan = fileScan.useDelimiter("\r\n");
        } catch (IOException e)
        {   e.printStackTrace();
        } // catch()
    } // RiddleFileReader() constructor
    public Riddle readRiddle()
    {   String ques = null;
        String ans = null;
        Riddle theRiddle = null;
        if (fileScan.hasNext())
            ques = fileScan.next();
        if (fileScan.hasNext())
        {   ans =  fileScan.next();
            theRiddle = new Riddle(ques, ans);
        } // if
        return theRiddle;
    } // readRiddle()
    public void displayRiddle(Riddle aRiddle)
    {   System.out.println(aRiddle.getQuestion());
        System.out.print("Input any letter to see answer:");
        String str = kbScan .next();   // Ignore KB input
        System.out.println(aRiddle.getAnswer());
        System.out.println();
    } // displayRiddle()
    public static void main(String[] args)
    {   RiddleFileReader rfr =
            new RiddleFileReader("riddles.txt");
        Riddle riddle = rfr.readRiddle();
        while (riddle != null)
        {   rfr.displayRiddle(riddle);
            riddle = rfr.readRiddle();
        } // while
    } // main()
} // RiddleFileReader class
```

Figure 4.28 A program that reads riddles from a file and displays them.

will read Strings into the variables ques and ans only if the file contains lines of data for them. Otherwise the readRiddle() method will return a null value. The main() method uses this fact to terminate a while loop when it runs out of string data to assign to Riddle questions and answers. There is a separate method, displayRiddle(), using a separate instance of Scanner attached to the keyboard to display the question of a riddle before the answer.

The contents of the "riddles.txt" file should be a list of riddles with each question and answer on a separate line. The following three riddles saved in a text file would comprise a good example to test the RiddleFileReader class.

```
What is black and white and red all over?
An embarrassed zebra
What is black and white and read all over?
A newspaper
What other word can be made with the letters of ALGORITHM?
LOGARITHM
```

When the main() method is executed, the user will see output in the console window that looks like:

```
What is black and white and red all over?
Input any letter to see answer: X
An embarrassed zebra

What is black and white and read all over?
Input any letter to see answer:
```

Files are covered in depth in Chapter 11. Information on writing data to a file and reading data from a file without using the Scanner class can be found there.

SELF-STUDY EXERCISE

EXERCISE 4.3 Modify the RiddleFileReader class to create a program NumberFileReader that opens a file named "numbers.txt" and reports the sum of the squares of the integers in the file. Assume that the file "numbers.txt" contains a list of integers in which each integer is on a separate line. The program should print the sum of the squares in the System.out console window. In this case, there is no need to have a method to display the data being read or a Scanner object connected to the keyboard. You will want a constructor method and a method that reads the numbers and computes the sum of squares.

CHAPTER SUMMARY

Technical Terms

abstract class	AWT
abstract interface	binary file
abstract method	buffer

command-line interface	layout manager
container	listener
control element	model-view-controller (MVC) architecture
event-driven programming	output operation
event loop	output stream
graphical user interface (GUI)	stream
helper method	Swing
inheritance	text file
input operation	top-level container
input stream	user interface
interface	wrapper class

Summary of Important Points

- An input operation is any action that transfers data from the user to the computer's main memory via one of the computer's input devices. An output operation is any action that transfers data from the computer's main memory to one of the computer's output devices.
- The user interface is the part of the program that handles the input and output interactions between the user and the program. As an interface, it limits or constrains the manner in which the user can interact with the program.
- In a command-line interface, user input is taken from the keyboard, and the program's output is displayed on a console.
- A buffer is a portion of main memory where input is held until it is needed by the program. Using a buffer between the keyboard and the program allows you to use the Backspace key to delete a character.
- A wrapper class contains methods for converting primitive data into objects and for converting data from one type to another.
- Designing appropriate prompts is an important aspect of designing a good user interface.
- I/O operations must watch out for certain types of I/O exceptions.
- GUI programming involves a computational model known as event-driven programming. This means that GUI programs react to events that are generated mostly by the user's interactions with elements in the GUI.
- Java has two packages of GUIs, the older `java.awt` and the newer `javax.swing`.
- Swing components are based on the object-oriented model-view-controller (MVC) architecture.
- The `extends` keyword is used to specify subclass/superclass relationships in the Java class hierarchy.
- A top-level container is a GUI container that cannot be added to another container; it can only have components added to it. All GUI programs must be contained in a top-level container.
- There are generally three kinds of GUI components, corresponding to the three main functions of a user interface: input, output, and control.
- Events are handled by special objects called listeners. A listener is a specialist that listens constantly for a certain type of event.
- An interface is a special Java class that contains only methods and constants (final variables).

SOLUTIONS TO SELF-STUDY EXERCISES

SOLUTION 4.1   The following modification of the `GreeterApp` class is an implementation of the High-Low Game:

```java
public class HighLowApp
{ private KeyboardReader reader;
  private int secretNumber;

  public HighLowApp()
  { reader = new KeyboardReader();
    secretNumber = 1 + (int)(Math.random() * 100);
  } // HighLowApp() constructor
  public void run()
  { int userGuess = -1;
    reader.display("Guess my secret number between 1 and 100.");
    while (userGuess != secretNumber)
    {   reader.prompt("Please input your guess here > ");
      userGuess = reader.getKeyboardInteger();
      if (userGuess > secretNumber)
        reader.display("Your guess was too high.");
      if (userGuess < secretNumber)
        reader.display("Your guess was too low.");
    } // while
    reader.display("Congratulations. Your guess was correct.");
  } // run()

  public static void main(String args[])
  { HighLowApp app = new HighLowApp();
    app.run();
  } // main()
} // HighLowApp class
```

SOLUTION 4.2   The following modification of `GreeterGUI` eliminates the `JButton`.

```java
import javax.swing.*;
import java.awt.*;
import java.awt.event.*;

public class GreeterGUI2 extends JFrame implements ActionListener
{ private JTextArea display;
  private JTextField inField;
  private Greeter greeter;
  public GreeterGUI2(String title)
  {   greeter = new Greeter();
      buildGUI();
      setTitle(title);
      pack();
      setVisible(true);
  } // GreeterGUI2()
```

```
    private void buildGUI()
    {   Container contentPane = getContentPane();
        contentPane.setLayout(new BorderLayout());
        display = new JTextArea(10,30);
        inField = new JTextField(10);
        inField.addActionListener(this);
        JPanel inputPanel = new JPanel();
        inputPanel.add(new
                JLabel("Input your name and type enter: "));
        inputPanel.add(inField);
        contentPane.add("Center", display);
        contentPane.add("South", inputPanel);
    } // buildGUI()
    public void actionPerformed(ActionEvent e)
    {   if (e.getSource() == inField)
        {   String name = inField.getText();
            display.append(greeter.greet(name) + "\n");
        }
    } // actionPerformed()
} // GreeterGUI2 class
```

SOLUTION 4.3   Java code that prints out the sum of the squares of a set of integers read from a file named "numbers.txt":

```
import java.io.*;
import java.util.Scanner;

public class NumberFileReader
{   private Scanner fileScan;                        // For file input

    public NumberFileReader(String fName)
    {   try
        {   File theFile = new File(fName);
            fileScan = new Scanner(theFile);
        } catch (IOException e)
        {   e.printStackTrace();
        } // catch()
    } // NumberFileReader()

    public void readNumbers()
    {   int num = 0;                                 // To store integers read
        int sum = 0:                                 // To store sum of squares
        while (fileScan.hasNextInt())
        {   num = fileScan.nextInt();
            sum = sum + num * num;
        } // while
        System.out.println("The sum of squares = " + sum);
    } // readNumbers()
    public static void main(String[] args)
    {   NumberFileReader nfr =
            new NumberFileReader("numbers.txt");
        nfr.readNumbers()
    } // main()
} // NumberFileReader
```

EXERCISES

Note: For programming exercises, **first** draw a UML class diagram describing all classes and their inheritance relationships and/or associations.

EXERCISE 4.1 Fill in the blanks in each of the following sentences:

a. An _____ is a Java program that can be embedded in a Web page.
b. A method that lacks a body is an _____ method.
c. An _____ is like a class except that it contains only instance methods, no instance variables.
d. In a Java class definition a class can _____ a class and _____ an interface.
e. Classes and methods not defined in a program must be _____ from the Java class library.
f. A subclass of a class inherits the class's _____ instance variables and instance methods.
g. An object can refer to itself by using the _____ keyword.
h. The `JButton`, `JTextField`, and `JComponent` classes are defined in the _____ package.
i. Java applets utilize a form of control known as _____ programming.
j. When the user clicks on an applet's `JButton`, an _____ will automatically be generated.
k. Two kinds of objects that generate `ActionEvent`s are _____ and _____.
l. `JButton`s, `JTextField`s, and `JLabel`s are all subclasses of _____.
m. The `JApplet` class is a subclass of _____.
n. If an applet intends to handle `ActionEvent`s, it must implement the _____ interface.
o. When an applet is started, its _____ method is called automatically.

EXERCISE 4.2 Explain the difference between the following pairs of concepts:

a. *Class* and *interface*.
b. *Extending a class* and *instantiating an object*.
c. *Defining a method* and *implementing a method*.
d. A `protected` method and a `public` method.
e. A `protected` method and a `private` method.
f. An `ActionEvent` and an `ActionListener()` method.

EXERCISE 4.3 Draw a hierarchy chart to represent the following situation. There are lots of languages in the world. English, French, Chinese, and Korean are examples of natural languages. Java, C, and C++ are examples of formal languages. French and Italian are considered romance languages, while Greek and Latin are considered classical languages.

EXERCISE 4.4 Arrange the Java library classes mentioned in the Chapter Summary into their proper hierarchy, using the `Object` class as the root of the hierarchy.

EXERCISE 4.5 Look up the documentation for the `JButton` class on Sun's Web site:

```
http://java.sun.com/j2se/1.5.0/docs/api/
```

List the signatures of all its constructors.

EXERCISE 4.6   Suppose we want to set the text in our applet's JTextField. What method should we use, and where is it defined? (*Hint*: Look up the documentation for JTextField. If no appropriate method is defined there, see if it is inherited from a superclass.)

EXERCISE 4.7   Does a JApplet have an init() method? Explain.

EXERCISE 4.8   Does a JApplet have an add() method? Explain.

EXERCISE 4.9   Does a JButton have an init() method? Explain.

EXERCISE 4.10   Does a JButton have an add() method? Explain.

EXERCISE 4.11   Suppose you type the URL for a "Hello World" applet into your browser. Describe what happens—that is, describe the processing that takes place in order for the applet to display "Hello World" in your browser.

EXERCISE 4.12   Suppose you have an applet containing a JButton named button. Describe what happens, in terms of Java's event-handling model, when the user clicks the button.

EXERCISE 4.13   Java's Object class contains a public method, toString(), which returns a string that represents this object. Because every class is a subclass of Object, the toString() method can be used by any object. Show how you would invoke this method for a JButton object named button.

EXERCISE 4.14   The applet that follows contains a semantic error in its init() method. The error will cause the actionPerformed() method never to display "Clicked" even though the user clicks the button in the applet. Why? (*Hint*: Think scope!)

```
public class SomeApplet extends JApplet
                        implements ActionListener
{
                                        // Declare instance variables
    private JButton button;
    public void init()
    {
                                        // Instantiate the instance variable
        JButton button = new JButton("Click me");
        add(button);
        button.addActionListener(this);
    } // init()
    public void actionPerformed(ActionEvent e)
    {
        if (e.getSource() == button)
            System.out.println("Clicked");
    } // actionPerformed()
} // SomeApplet class
```

EXERCISE 4.15   What would be output by the following applet?

```java
public class SomeApplet extends JApplet
{
                                             // Declare instance variables
  private JButton button;
  private JTextField field;

  public void init()
  {
                                             // Instantiate instance variables
    button = new JButton("Click me");
    add(button);
    field = new JTextField("Field me");
    add(field);
    System.out.println(field.getText() + button.getText());
  } // init()
} // SomeApplet class
```

EXERCISE 4.16   Design and implement a GUI that has a `JButton`, a `JTextField`, and a `JLabel` and then uses the `toString()` method to display each object's string representation.

EXERCISE 4.17   The `JButton` class inherits a `setText(String s)` from its `AbstractButton()` superclass. Using that method, design and implement a GUI that has a single button labeled initially "The Doctor is out." Each time the button is clicked, it should toggle its label to "The Doctor is in" and vice versa.

EXERCISE 4.18   Design and implement a GUI that contains two `JButton`s, initially labeled "Me first!" and "Me next!" Each time the user clicks either button, the labels on both buttons should be exchanged. (*Hint*: You don't need an `if-else` statement for this problem.)

EXERCISE 4.19   Modify the GUI in the preceding exercise so that it contains three `JButton`s, initially labeled "First," "Second," and "Third." Each time the user clicks one of the buttons, the labels on the buttons should be rotated. Second should get First's label, Third should get Second's, and First should get Third's.

EXERCISE 4.20   Design and implement a GUI that contains a `JTextField` and two `JButton`s, initially labeled "Left" and "Right." Each time the user clicks a button, display its label in the `JTextField`. A `JButton()`'s label can be gotten with the `getText()` method.

EXERCISE 4.21   You can change the size of a `JFrame` by using the `setSize(int h, int v)` method, where *h* and *v* give its horizontal and vertical dimensions in pixels. Write a GUI application that contains two `JButton`s labeled "Big" and "Small." Whenever the user clicks on Small, set the `JFrame`'s dimensions to 200 × 100, and whenever the user clicks on Big, set the dimensions to 300 × 200.

EXERCISE 4.22   Rewrite your solution to the preceding exercise so that it uses a single button whose label is toggled appropriately each time it is clicked. Obviously, when the `JButton` is labeled "Big," clicking it should give the `JFrame` its big dimensions.

EXERCISE 4.23   Challenge: Design and write a Java GUI application that allows the user to change the JFrame's background color to one of three choices, indicated by buttons. Like all other Java Components, JFrames have an associated background color that can be set by the following commands:

```
setBackground(Color.red);
setBackground(Color.yellow);
```

The setBackground() method is defined in the Component class, and 13 primary colors—black, blue, cyan, darkGray, gray, green, lightGray, magenta, orange, pink, red, white, yellow—are defined in the java.awt.Color class.

ADDITIONAL EXERCISES

EXERCISE 4.24   Given the classes with the following headers

```
public class Animal ...
public class DomesticAnimal extends Animal ...
public class FarmAnimal extends DomesticAnimal...
public class HousePet extends DomesticAnimal...
public class Cow extends FarmAnimal ...
public class Goat extends FarmAnimal ...
public class DairyCow extends Cow ...
```

draw a UML class diagram representing the hierarchy created by these declarations.

EXERCISE 4.25   Given the preceding hierarchy of classes, which of the following are legal assignment statements?

```
DairyCow dc = new FarmAnimal();
FarmAnimal fa = new Goat();
Cow c1 = new DomesticAnimal();
Cow c2 = new DairyCow();
DomesticAnimal dom = new HousePet();
```

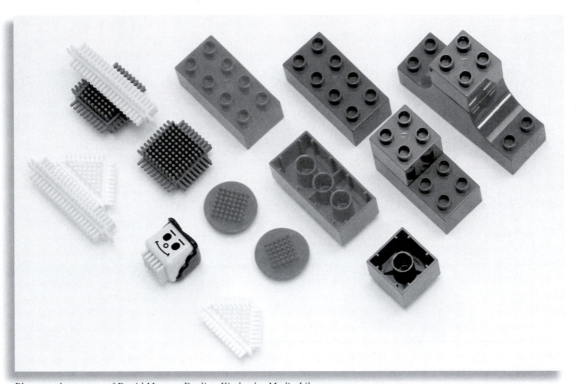

Photograph courtesy of David Murray, Dorling Kindersley Media Library

5

Java Data and Operators

OBJECTIVES

After studying this chapter, you will

- Understand the role that data play in effective program design.
- Be able to use all of Java's primitive types and their operators.
- Appreciate the importance of information hiding.
- Be able to use class constants and class methods.
- Know how to use Java's `Math` and `NumberFormat` classes.
- Be able to perform various kinds of data conversions.

OUTLINE

5.1 Introduction

This chapter has two primary goals. One is to elaborate on Java's *primitive data types*, which were first introduced in Chapter 1. We will cover boolean, integer, character, and real number data types, including the various operations that you can perform on these types. We will provide examples, including several modifications of the `OneRowNim` class, to show typical uses of the various data types.

Our second goal is to illustrate the idea that programming is a matter of choosing an appropriate way to represent a problem as well as an appropriate sequence of actions to solve the problem. Programming is a form of problem solving that can be viewed as a two-part process: *representation* and *action*.

Representation means finding a way to look at the problem. This might involve seeing the problem as closely related to a known problem or seeing that parts of the problem can be broken up into smaller problems that you already know how to solve. In terms of programming problems, representation often means choosing the right kinds of objects and structures.

Action is the process of taking well-defined steps to solve a problem. Given a particular way of representing the problem, what steps must we take to arrive at its solution?

Choosing an appropriate representation is often the key to solving a problem. For example, consider this problem: Can a chess board, with its top-left and bottom-right squares removed, be completely tiled by dominoes that cover two squares at a time?

One way to solve this problem might be to represent the chess board and dominoes as shown in Figure 5.1. If we represent the board in this way, then the actions needed to arrive at a solution involve searching for a tiling that completely covers the board. In other words, we can try one way of placing the dominoes on the board. If that doesn't work, we try another way. And so on. This process will be very time consuming, because there are millions of different ways of trying to tile the board.

An alternative way to represent this problem comes from seeing that the top-left and bottom-right squares of the board are both white. If you remove them, you'll have a board with 62 squares, 32 black and 30 white. Because each domino must cover one white and one black square, it is impossible to tile a board with an unequal number of black and white squares.

Thus, by representing the problem as the total number of black and white squares, the actions required to solve it involve a very simple reasoning process. This representation makes it almost trivial to find the solution. On the other hand, the *brute force* representation presented first—trying all possible combinations—made it almost impossible to solve the problem.

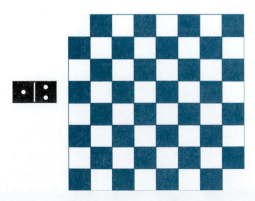

Figure 5.1 Can the chess board be tiled with dominoes?

5.2   Boolean Data and Operators

As we learned in Chapter 1, the `boolean` type is one of Java's primitive types. For this type, there are only two possible values, `true` and `false`. The `boolean` type is derived from the work of British mathematician George Boole, who in the 1850s developed an algebra to process logical expressions such as *p and q*. Such *boolean expressions* produce a value that is either *true* or *false*. Every modern programming language provides some means of representing boolean expressions.

George Boole

The `boolean` type has several important uses. As we saw in Chapter 1, expressions of the form `num == 7` and `5 < 7` have `boolean` values. Similarly, as we saw in Chapter 3, the `boolean` type is also used to represent the condition in the `if` statement:

Conditional statement

> `if` (*boolean expression*)
>   *statement*;

For this reason, boolean expressions are also called *conditions*. Along the same lines, a `boolean` variable can be used as a *flag* or *signal* to "remember" whether or not a certain condition holds. For example, in the following code fragment, we use `isDone` to mark when a particular process is completed:

Boolean flag

```
boolean isDone = false; // Initialize the flag
...                     // Do some processing task
isDone = true;          // Set flag when the task done
...                     // Do some other stuff
if (isDone)             // Check if finished the task
...                     //  If so, do something
else
...                     //  Or, do something else
```

5.2.1   Boolean (or Logical) Operations

Like all the other simple data types, the `boolean` type consists of certain data—the values `true` and `false`—and certain actions or operations that can be performed on the data. For the boolean type there are four basic operations: AND (signified by &&), OR (signified by ||), EXCLUSIVE-OR (signified by ∧), and NOT (signified by !). These are defined in the *truth table* shown in Table 5.1. A truth table defines boolean operators by giving their values in all possible situations. The first two columns of the table give possible boolean values for two *operands*, *o1* and *o2*. An **operand** is a value used in an operation. Note that each row gives a different value assignment to the two operands, so that all possible assignments are represented. The remaining columns give the values that result for the various operators given the assignment of values to *o1* and *o2*.

Data and operations

To see how to read this table, let's look at the AND operation, which is defined in column 3. The AND operator is a **binary operator**—that is, it requires two operands, *o1* and *o2*. If both *o1* and *o2* are true, then (*o1* && *o2*) is true (row 1). If either *o1* or *o2* or both *o1* and *o2* are false, then the expression (*o1* && *o2*) is false (rows 2–4).

Binary operator

Table 5.1. Truth-table definitions of the boolean operators: AND (&&), OR (||), EXCLUSIVE-OR (∧), and NOT (!)

o1	o2	o1 && o2	o1 || o2	o1 ∧ o2	!o1
true	true	true	true	false	false
true	false	false	true	true	false
false	true	false	true	true	true
false	false	false	false	false	true

The boolean OR operation (column 4 of Table 5.1) is also a binary operation. If both *o1* and *o2* are false, then (*o1* || *o2*) is false (row 4). If either *o1* or *o2* or both *o1* and *o2* are true, then the expression (*o1* || *o2*) is true (rows 1–3). Thus, the only case in which (*o1* || *o2*) is false is when both *o1* and *o2* are false.

The boolean EXCLUSIVE-OR operation (column 5 of Table 5.1) is a binary operation, which differs from the OR operator in that it is true when either *o1* or *o2* is true (rows 2 and 3), but it is false when both *o1* and *o2* are true (row 1).

Unary operator

The NOT operation (the last column of Table 5.1) is a **unary operator**—it takes only one operand—and it simply reverses the truth value of its operand. Thus, if *o1* is true, !*o1* is false, and vice versa.

5.2.2   Precedence and Associativity

In order to evaluate complex boolean expressions, it is necessary to understand the order in which boolean operations are carried out by the computer. For example, what is the value of the following expression?

```
true || true && false
```

The value of this expression depends on whether we evaluate the || first or the && first. If we evaluate the || first, the expression's value will be false; if we evaluate the && first, the expression's value will be true. In the following example, we use parentheses to force one operation to be done before the other:

```
EXPRESSION                      EVALUATION
----------                      ----------
( true || true ) && false ==> true && false ==> false
true || ( true && false ) ==> true || false ==> true
```

Parentheses
supersede

As these evaluations show, we can use parentheses to force one operator or the other to be evaluated first. However, in Java, the && operator has higher precedence than the || operator. Therefore, the second alternative corresponds to the default interpretation that Java would apply to the expression that has no parentheses. In other words, given the expression *true || true && false*, the AND operation would be evaluated before the OR operation even though the OR operator occurs first (i.e., to the left) in the unparenthesized expression.

Table 5.2. Precedence order of the boolean operators

Precedence Order	Operator	Operation
1	( )	Parentheses
2	!	NOT
3	∧	EXCLUSIVE-OR
4	&&	AND
5	||	OR

As this example illustrates, the boolean operators have a built-in **precedence order** which is used to determine how boolean expressions are to be evaluated (Table 5.2). A simple method for evaluating an expression is to parenthesize the expression and then evaluate it. For example, to evaluate the complex expression

```
true || !false ∧ false && true
```

we would first parenthesize it according to the precedence rules set out in Table 5.2, which gives the following expression:

```
true || (((!false) ∧ false) && true)
```

We can then evaluate the fully parenthesized expression step by step, starting at the innermost parentheses:

```
Step 1. true || ((true ∧ false) && true)
Step 2. true || (true && true)
Step 3. true || true
Step 4. true
```

JAVA PROGRAMMING TIP: Parentheses.   Parentheses can (and should) be used to clarify any expression that seems ambiguous or to override Java's default precedence rules.

In addition to operator precedence, it is necessary to know about an operator's *associativity* in order to evaluate boolean expressions of the form *(op1 || op2 || op3)*. Should this expression be evaluated as *((op1 || op2) || op3)* or as *(op1 || (op2 || op3))*? The binary boolean operators all associate from left to right. Thus, the expressions

```
true ∧ true ∧ true    // Same as: (true ∧ true) ∧ true
true && true && true  // Same as: (true && true) && true
true || true || true  // Same as: (true || true) || true
```

would be evaluated as follows:

```
EXPRESSION                EVALUATION
----------------          ------------------
(true ∧ true)  ∧ true     ==> false ∧ true  ==> true
(true && true) && true    ==> true  && true ==> true
(true || true) || true    ==> true  || true ==> true
```

5.2.3   Short-Circuit Evaluation

Another important feature of the boolean operators is that they utilize a form of evaluation known as *short-circuit evaluation*. In **short-circuit evaluation**, a boolean expression is evaluated from left to right, and the evaluation is discontinued as soon as the expression's value can be determined, regardless of whether it contains additional operators and operands. For example, in the expression

```
expr1 && expr2
```

if `expr1` is false, then the AND expression must be false, so `expr2` need not be evaluated. Similarly, in the expression

```
expr1 || expr2
```

if `expr1` is true, then the OR expression must be true, so `expr2` need not be evaluated.

In addition to being a more efficient way of evaluating boolean expressions, short-circuit evaluation has some practical uses. For example, we can use short-circuit evaluation to guard against null pointer exceptions. Recall from Chapter 2 that a null pointer exception results when you try to use an uninstantiated reference variable—that is, a reference variable that has not been assigned an object. For example, if we declare a `OneRowNim` variable without instantiating it and then try to use it, a null pointer exception will result:

```
OneRowNim game;            // Uninstantiated Reference
if (!game.gameOver())      // Null pointer exception
    game.takeSticks(num);
```

In this code, a null pointer exception results when we use `game` in the method call `game.gameOver()`. We can use short-circuit evaluation to prevent the exception from occurring:

```
if ((game != null) && (!game.gameOver()))
    game.takeSticks(num);
```

In this case, because `game != null` is false, neither method call involving `game` is made, thus avoiding the exception.

SELF-STUDY EXERCISE

EXERCISE 5.1   Suppose the following variable declarations are made:

```
boolean A = true, B = true, C = true;
boolean X = false, Y = false, Z = false;
```

Given these declarations, evaluate each of the following expressions (don't forget to take operator precedence and associativity into account):

a. A || B && Z

b. A ^ X && Z

c. A ^ X || C

d. !A && !B

e. A && B && X && Y

f. (!X ^ A) && (B ^ !Y)

Are We Computers?

George Boole published his seminal work, *An Investigation of the Laws of Thought*, in 1854. His achievement was in developing an algebra for logic—that is, a purely abstract and symbolic system for representing the laws of logic. Boole's was not the first attempt to explore the relationship between the human mind and an abstract system of computation. Back in 1655, Thomas Hobbes had already claimed that all thought was computation.

It is estimated that the human brain contains ($10^{12} = 10,000,000,000,000$) *neurons*, and that each neuron contains something like 10,000 *dendrites*, the fibers that connect one neuron to another. Together, the neurons and dendrites make up a web of enormous complexity. Since the 1840s it has been known that the brain is primarily electrical, and by the 1940s scientists had developed a pretty good model of the electrical interactions among neurons. According to this model, neurons emit short bursts of electricity along their *axons*, which function like output wires. The bursts leap over the gap separating axons and dendrites, which function like the neurons' input wires.

In 1943, just before the first digital computers were developed, Warren McCulloch, a neurophysiologist, and Walter Pitts, a mathematician, published a paper titled "A Logical Calculus of the Ideas Imminent in Nervous Activity." In this paper, they showed that McCulloch & all of the boolean operators—AND, OR, NOT, and EXCLUSIVE-OR—could be represented by the behavior of small sets of neurons. For example, they showed that three neurons could be connected together in such a way that the third neuron fired if and only if both of the other two neurons fired. This is exactly analogous to the definition of the boolean AND operator.

A few years later, when the first computers were built, many scientists and philosophers were struck by the similarity between the logic elements that made up the computer's circuits and the neuronal models that McCulloch and Pitts had developed.

The area of neural networks is a branch of artificial intelligence (one of the applied areas of computer science) and is based on this insight by McCulloch and Pitts. Researchers in this exciting and rapidly advancing field develop neural network models of various kinds of human thinking and perception.

5.2.4   Using Booleans in OneRowNim

Now that we have introduced the `boolean` data type, let's use it to improve the `OneRowNim` class, the latest version of which, from Chapter 3, is given in Figure 3.16. Previously we used an `int` variable, `player`, to represent whose turn it is. For a two-person game, such as One-Row Nim, a `boolean` variable is well suited for this purpose, because it can toggle between true and false. For example, let's declare a variable, `onePlaysNext`, and initialize it to true, to represent the fact that player 1 will play first:

```
private boolean onePlaysNext = true;
```

When `onePlaysNext` is true, it will be player 1's turn. When it is false, it will be player 2's turn. Note that we are deliberately remaining uncommitted as to whether one or the other player is the computer.

Given this new variable, it is necessary to redefine the methods that previously used the `player` variable. The first method that needs revision is the constructor:

```
public OneRowNim(int sticks, int starter)
{   nSticks = sticks;
    onePlaysNext = (starter == 1);
} // OneRowNim() constructor3
```

In the constructor, the `starter` parameter is used with a value of 1 or 2 to set which player goes first. Note how we use an assignment statement to set `onePlaysNext` to true if `starter` equals 1; otherwise it is set to false. The assignment statement first evaluates the expression on its right-hand side (`starter == 1`). Because this is a boolean expression, it will have a value of true or false, which will be assigned to `onePlaysNext`. Thus, the assignment statement is equivalent to the following `if/else` statement:

```
if (player == 1)
    onePlaysNext = true;
else
    onePlaysNext = false;
```

The remaining changes are shown in Figure 5.2. There are only two instance methods that need revision to accommodate the use of `boolean` variables. The `takeSticks()` method contains two revisions. The first uses the boolean OR operator to test whether a move is valid:

```
public boolean takeSticks(int num)
{   if (num < 1 || num > 3 || num > nSticks)
        return false;                    // Error
    else                                 // Valid move
    {   nSticks = nSticks - num;
        onePlaysNext = !onePlaysNext;
        return true;
    } // else
} // takeSticks()
```

```java
public class OneRowNim
{    private int nSticks = 7;
     private boolean onePlaysNext = true;

     public OneRowNim()
     {
     } // OneRowNim() constructor1
     public OneRowNim(int sticks)
     {   nSticks = sticks;
     } // OneRowNim() constructor2
     public OneRowNim(int sticks, int starter)
     {   nSticks = sticks;
         onePlaysNext = (starter == 1);
     } // OneRowNim() constructor3
     public boolean takeSticks(int num)
     {   if (num < 1 || num > 3 || num > nSticks)
             return false;                       // Error
         else                                    // Valid move
         {   nSticks = nSticks - num;
             onePlaysNext = !onePlaysNext;
             return true;
         } // else
     } // takeSticks()
     public int getSticks()
     {   return nSticks;
     } // getSticks()
     public int getPlayer()
     {   if (onePlaysNext) return 1;
         else return 2;
     } // getPlayer()
     public boolean gameOver()
     {   return (nSticks <= 0);
     } // gameOver()
     public int getWinner()
     {   if (nSticks < 1) return getPlayer();
         else return 0;   // game is not over
     } // getWinner()
     public void report()
     {   System.out.println("Number of sticks left: " + getSticks());
         System.out.println("Next turn by player " + getPlayer());
     } // report()
} // OneRowNim class
```

Figure 5.2   The revised OneRowNim uses a boolean variable to keep track of whose turn it is.

It also uses the boolean NOT operator to toggle the value of **onePlaysNext**, to switch to the other player's turn:

```java
onePlaysNext = !onePlaysNext;
```

Finally, the `getPlayer()` method now uses an `if/else` statement to return either 1 or 2 depending on whose turn it is:

```java
public int getPlayer()
{   if (onePlaysNext)
        return 1;
    else return 2;
} // getPlayer()
```

5.3 Numeric Data and Operators

Java has two kinds of numeric data: integers, which have no fractional part, and real numbers, or *floating-point numbers*, which contain a fractional component. Java recognizes four different kinds of integers: `byte`, `short`, `int`, and `long`. They are distinguished by the number of *bits* used to represent them. A **binary digit**, or **bit**, is a 0 or a 1. (Recall that computers read instructions as series of 0s and 1s.) Java has two different kinds of real numbers, `float` and `double`. These are also distinguished by the number of bits used to represent them. See Table 5.3.

The more bits a data type has, the more values it can represent. One bit can represent two possible values, 1 and 0, which can be used to stand for true and false, respectively. Two bits can represent four possible values: 00, 01, 10, and 11; three bits can represent eight possible values: 000, 001, 010, 100, 101, 110, 011, 111. And, in general, an *n*-bit quantity can represent 2^n different values.

Integer data types

As illustrated in Table 5.3, the various integer types represent positive or negative whole numbers. Perhaps the most commonly used integer type in Java is the `int` type, which is represented in 32 bits. This means that Java can represent 2^{32} different `int` values, which range from $-2,147,483,648$ to $2,147,483,647$, that is, from -2^{31} to $(2^{31} - 1)$. Similarly, an 8-bit integer, a `byte`, can represent 2^8 or 256 different values, ranging from -128 to $+127$. A 16-bit integer, a `short`, can represent 2^{16} different values, which range from -32768 to 32767. And a 64-bit integer, a `long`, can represent whole-number values ranging from -2^{63} to $2^{63} - 1$.

For floating-point numbers, a 32-bit `float` type can represent 2^{32} different real numbers and a 64-bit `double` value can represent 2^{64} different real numbers.

EFFECTIVE DESIGN: Platform Independence. In Java, a data type's size (number of bits) is part of its definition and, therefore, remains consistent across all platforms. In C and C++, the size of a data type is dependent on the compiler.

Table 5.3. Java's numeric types

Type	Bits	Range of Values
byte	.8	-128 to $+127$
short	16	-32768 to 32767
int	32	-2147483648 to 2147483647
long	64	-2^{63} to $2^{63} - 1$
float	32	$-3.40292347E + 38$ to $+3.40292347E + 38$
double	64	$-1.79769313486231570E + 308$ to $+1.79769313486231570E + 308$

It is worth noting that just as model airplanes are representations of real airplanes, Java's numeric types are representations, or models, of the numbers we deal with in mathematics. In designing Java's data types, various trade-offs have been made in order to come up with practical implementations.

Data types are abstractions

One trade-off is that the set of integers is infinite, but Java's int type can only represent a finite number of values. Similarly, Java cannot represent the infinite number of values that occur between, say, 1.111 and 1.112. So certain real numbers cannot be represented at all. For example, because Java uses binary numbers to represent its numeric types, one number that cannot be represented exactly is $\frac{1}{10}$. This inability to exactly represent a value is known as **round-off error**. Being unable to represent certain values can cause problems in some programs. For example, it might be difficult to represent dollars and cents accurately.

Representation trade-offs

Round-off error

Another source of problems in dealing with numeric data is due to limits in their *precision*. For example, a decimal number represented as a double value can have a maximum of 17 *significant digits*, and a float can have a maximum of 8. A significant digit is one that contributes to the number's value. If you tried to store values such as 12345.6789 or 0.123456789 in a float variable, they would be rounded off to 12345.679 and 0.12345679, respectively, causing a possible error.

> **DEBUGGING TIP: Significant Digits.**   In using numeric data, be sure the data type you choose has enough precision to represent the values your program needs.

SELF-STUDY EXERCISES

EXERCISE 5.2   List all of the binary values that can be represented in 4 bits—that is, all the values in the range 0000 to 1111.

EXERCISE 5.3   If a 6-bit representation were used for an integer type, how many different integers could be represented?

EXERCISE 5.4   If you were writing a program to process scientific data that had to be accurate to at least 12 significant (decimal) digits, what type of data would you use?

5.3.1   Numeric Operations

The operations that can be done on numeric data include the standard algebraic operations: *addition* (+), *subtraction* (−), *multiplication* (*), *division* (/), as well as the *modulus* (%) operator. Note that in Java, the multiplication symbol is * and not ×. The arithmetic operators are binary operators, meaning that they each take two operands. Table 5.4 compares expressions involving the Java operators with their standard algebraic counterparts.

Numeric operators

Table 5.4. The standard arithmetic operators in Java

Operation	Operator	Java	Algebra
Addition	+	$x + 2$	$x + 2$
Subtraction	−	$m - 2$	$m - 2$
Multiplication	*	$m * 2$	$2m$ or $2 \times m$
Division	/	x/y	$x \div y$ or $\frac{x}{y}$
Modulus	%	$x \% y$	x modulo y (for integers x and y)

Although these operations should seem familiar, there are some important differences between their use in algebra and their use in a Java program. Consider the following list of expressions:

```
3 / 2      ==>  value 1     An integer result
3.0 / 2.0 ==>  value 1.5   A floating-point result
3 / 2.0   ==>  value 1.5   A floating-point result
3.0 / 2   ==>  value 1.5   A floating-point result
```

In each of these cases we are dividing the quantity 3 by the quantity 2. However, different results are obtained depending on the *type* of the operands involved. When both operands are integers, as in (3/2), the result must also be an integer. Hence, (3/2) has the value 1, an integer. Because integers cannot have a fractional part, the 0.5 is simply discarded. Integer division (/) always gives an integer result. Thus, the value of (6/2) is 3 and the value of (7/2) is also 3. Because 3.5 is not an integer, the result of dividing 7 by 2 cannot be 3.5.

Integer division gives an integer result

DEBUGGING TIP: Integer Division.   A common source of error among beginning programmers is forgetting that integer division always gives an integer result.

On the other hand, when either operand is a real number, as in the last three cases, the result is a real number. Thus, while the same symbol (/) is used for dividing integers and real numbers, there are really two different operations involved here: *integer division* and *floating-point division*. Using the same symbol (/) for different operations (integer division and real division) is known as **operator overloading**. It is similar to method overloading, which was discussed in Chapter 3.

Modular arithmetic

What if you want to keep the remainder of an integer division? Java provides the modulus operator (%), which takes two operands. The expression (7 % 5) gives the remainder after dividing 7 by 5—2 in this case. In general, the expression (*m* % *n*) (read *m* mod *n*) gives the remainder after *m* is divided by *n*. Here are several examples:

```
7 % 5    ==>  7 mod 5 equals 2
5 % 7    ==>  5 mod 7 equals 5
-7 % 5   ==>  -7 mod 5 equals -2
7 % -5   ==>  7 mod -5 equals 2
```

The best way to interpret these examples is to perform long division on the operands, keeping both the quotient and the remainder. For example, when you do long division on $-7 \div 5$, you get a quotient of -1 and a remainder of -2. The quotient is the value of $-7/5$, and the remainder is the value of $-7\%5$. When you do long division on $7 \div -5$, you get a quotient of -1 and a remainder of 2. The quotient is the value of $7/-5$, and the remainder is the value of $7\%-5$.

We will encounter many practical uses for the modulus operator in our programs. For a simple example, we use it when we want to determine whether an integer is even or odd. Numbers that leave a 0 remainder when divided by 2 are even:

```
if (N % 2 == 0)
    System.out.println(N + " is even");
```

More generally, we could use the mod operator to define divisibility by 3, 4, 10, or by any number.

Numeric Promotion Rules

Java is considered a *strongly typed* language because all expressions in Java, such as (3/2), have a type associated with them. In cases where one arithmetic operand is an integer and one is a floating-point number, Java *promotes* the integer into a floating-point value and performs a floating-point operation.

Expressions have a type

Promotion is a matter of converting one type to another type. For example, in the expression (5 + 4.0), the value 5 must be promoted to 5.0 before floating-point addition can be performed on (5.0 + 4.0). Generally speaking, automatic promotions such as these are allowed in Java whenever it is possible to perform the promotion *without loss of information*. Because an integer (5) does not have a fractional component, no information will be lost in promoting it to a real number (5.0). On the other hand, you cannot automatically convert a real number (5.4) to an integer (5) because that might result in a loss of information. This leads to the following rule:

> **JAVA LANGUAGE RULE** **Integer Promotion.** In an operation that contains an integer and a floating-point operand, the integer is *promoted* to a floating-point value *before* the operation is performed.

This rule is actually an instance of a more general rule, for whenever an expression involves operands of different types, some operands must be converted before the expression can be evaluated. Consider the following example:

```
byte n = 125;
short m = 32000;
n * m;
```

In this case, *(n * m)* involves two different integer types, `byte` and `short`. Before evaluating this expression Java must first promote the `byte` to a `short` and carry out the operation as the multiplication of two `short`s. Conversion of `short` to `byte` would not be possible because there is no way to represent the value 32000 as a `byte`.

Bear in mind that this conversion rule applies regardless of the actual values of the operands. In applying the rule, Java looks at the operand's type, not its value. So even if *m* were assigned a value that could be represented as a byte (for example, 100), the promotion would still go from smaller to larger type. This leads to the following general rule:

Promotion is automatic

> **JAVA LANGUAGE RULE** **Type Promotion.** In general, when two different types are involved in an operation, the smaller type—the one with fewer bits—is converted to the larger type before the operation is performed. To do otherwise would risk losing information.

Table 5.5. Java promotion rules for mixed arithmetic operators. If two rules apply, choose the one that occurs first in this table.

If either operand is	The other is promoted to
double	double
float	float
long	long
byte *or* short	int

Table 5.5 summarizes the actual promotion rules used by Java in evaluating expressions involving mixed operands. Note that the last rule implies that integer expressions involving byte or short or int are performed as int. This explains why integer literals—such as 56 or −108—are represented as int types in Java.

SELF-STUDY EXERCISES

EXERCISE 5.5 Evaluate each of the following integer expressions:

a. 8 / 2
b. 9 / 2
c. 6 / 8

d. 9 % 2
e. 8 % 6
f. 6 % 8

g. 8 % 4
h. 4 % 8

EXERCISE 5.6 Evaluate each of the following expressions, paying special attention to the *type* of the result in each case:

a. 8 / 2.0
b. 9 / 2.0

c. 6 / 8
d. 0.0 / 2

e. 8.0 / 6.0

EXERCISE 5.7 Suppose that the following variable declarations are made:

```
byte m = 3;  short n = 4;  int p = 5;
long q = 6;  double r = 7.0;
```

Use type promotion rules to determine the type of expression and then evaluate each of the following expressions:

a. m + n
b. p * q

c. m + n + r
d. p * q * m

e. r − m

5.3.2 Operator Precedence

Arithmetic precedence order

The built-in precedence order for arithmetic operators is shown in Table 5.6. Parenthesized expressions have highest precedence and are evaluated first. Next come the multiplication, division, and modulus operators, followed by addition and subtraction. When we have an unparenthesized expression that involves both multiplication and addition, the multiplication would be done first, even if it occurs to the right of the plus sign. Operators at the same level in the precedence hierarchy are evaluated from left to right. For example, consider the following expression:

Table 5.6. Precedence order of the arithmetic operators

Precedence Order	Operator	Operation
1	( )	*Parentheses*
2	* / %	*Multiplication, Division, Modulus*
3	+ −	*Addition, Subtraction*

```
9 + 6 - 3 * 6 / 2
```

In this case, the first operation to be applied will be the multiplication (*), followed by division (/), followed by addition (+), and then finally the subtraction (−). We can use parentheses to clarify the order of evaluation. A parenthesized expression is evaluated outward from the innermost set of parentheses:

```
Step 1.  ( (9 + 6) - ((3 * 6) / 2 ) )
Step 2.  ( (9 + 6) - (18 / 2 ) )
Step 3.  ( (9 + 6) - 9 )
Step 4.  ( 15 - 9 )
Step 5.  6
```

Parentheses can (and should) always be used to clarify the order of operations in an expression. For example, addition will be performed before multiplication in the following expression:

```
(a + b) * c
```

Another reason to use parentheses is that Java's precedence and promotion rules will sometimes lead to expressions that look fine but contain subtle errors. For example, consider the following expressions:

```
System.out.println(5/3/2.0);   // 0.5
System.out.println(5/(3/2.0)); // 3.33
```

The first gives a result of 0.5, but the use of parentheses in the second gives a result of 3.33. If the second is the expected interpretation, then the parentheses here helped avoid a subtle semantic error.

JAVA PROGRAMMING TIP: Parenthesize!   To avoid subtle bugs caused by Java's precedence and promotion rules, use parentheses to specify the order of evaluation in an expression.

SELF-STUDY EXERCISE

EXERCISE 5.8 Parenthesize and then evaluate each of the expressions that follow, taking care to observe operator precedence rules. Watch for subtle syntax errors.

a. 4 + 5.0 * 6   d. (4 + 5) / 6   g. 9 % 2 * 7 / 3
b. (4 + 5) * 6   e. 4 + 5 % 3   h. 5.0 / 2 * 3
c. 4 + 5 / 6   f. (4 + 5) % 3

5.3.3 Increment and Decrement Operators

Java provides a number of unary operators that are used to increment or decrement an integer variable. For example, the expression $k++$ uses the *increment operator* ++ to increment the value of the integer variable k. The expression $k++$ is equivalent to the following Java statements:

```
int k;
k = k + 1;// Add 1 to k and assign the result back to k
```

The unary ++ operator applies to a single-integer operand, in this case to the variable k. It increments k's value by 1 and assigns the result back to k. It may be used either as a *preincrement*

Preincrement and postincrement

or a *postincrement* operator. In the expression $k++$, the operator *follows* the operand, indicating that it is being used as a *postincrement* operator. This means that the increment operation is done *after* the operand's value is used.

Contrast that with the expression $++k$ in which the ++ operator *precedes* its operand. In this case, it is used as a *preincrement* operator, which means that the increment operation is done *before* the operand's value is used.

When they are used in isolation, there is no practical difference between $k++$ and $++k$. Both are equivalent to $k = k + 1$. However, when used in conjunction with other operators, there is a significant difference between preincrement and postincrement. For example, in the following code segment,

```
int j = 0, k = 0;    // Initially both j and k are 0
j = ++k;             // Final values of both j and k are 1
```

Precedence order

the variable k is incremented *before* its value is assigned to j. After execution of the assignment statement, j will equal 1 and k will equal 1. The sequence is equivalent to

```
int j = 0, k = 0;    // Initially both j and k are 0
k = k + 1;
j = k;               // Final values of both j and k are 1
```

However, in the following example,

```
int i = 0, k = 0; // Initially both i and k are 0
i = k++;          // Final value of i is 0 and k is 1
```

Table 5.7. Java's increment and decrement operators

Expression	Operation	Interpretation
$j = ++k$	*Preincrement*	$k = k + 1; j = k;$
$j = k++$	*Postincrement*	$j = k; k = k + 1;$
$j = --k$	*Predecrement*	$k = k - 1; j = k;$
$j = k--$	*Postdecrement*	$j = k; k = k - 1;$

the variable k is incremented *after* its value is assigned to i. After execution of the assignment statement, i will have the value 0 and k will have the value 1. The preceding sequence is equivalent to

```
int i = 0, k = 0;    // Initially both i and k are 0
i = k;
k = k + 1;           // Final value of i is 0 and k is 1
```

In addition to the increment operator, Java also supplies the *decrement* operator $--$, which can also be used in the predecrement and postdecrement forms. The expression $--k$ will first decrement k's value by 1 and then use k in any expression in which it is embedded. The expression $k--$ will use the current value of k in the expression in which k is contained and then it will decrement k's value by 1. Table 5.7 summarizes the increment and decrement operators. The unary increment and decrement operators have higher precedence than any of the binary arithmetic operators.

Predecrement and postdecrement

JAVA LANGUAGE RULE **Pre- and Postincrement/Decrement.** If an expression like $++k$ or $--k$ occurs in an expression, k is incremented or decremented *before* its value is used in the rest of the expression. If an expression like $k++$ or $k--$ occurs in an expression, k is incremented or decremented *after* its value is used in the rest of the expression.

JAVA PROGRAMMING TIP: Increment and Decrement Operators. Because of their subtle behavior, be careful how you use the unary increment and decrement operators. They are most appropriate and useful for incrementing and decrementing loop variables, as we will see later.

SELF-STUDY EXERCISE

EXERCISE 5.9 What value will j and k have after each of the calculations that follow? Assume that k has the value 0 and j has the value 5 before each operation is performed.

a. k = j;

b. k = j++;

c. k = ++j;

d. k = j--;

e. k = --j;

Table 5.8. Java's assignment operators

Operator	Operation	Example	Interpretation
$=$	*Simple assignment*	$m = n;$	$m = n;$
$+=$	*Addition then assignment*	$m += 3;$	$m = m + 3;$
$-=$	*Subtraction then assignment*	$m -= 3;$	$m = m - 3;$
$*=$	*Multiplication then assignment*	$m *= 3;$	$m = m * 3;$
$/=$	*Division then assignment*	$m /= 3;$	$m = m/3;$
$\%=$	*Remainder then assignment*	$m \%= 3;$	$m = m\%3;$

5.3.4 Assignment Operators

In addition to the simple assignment operator (=), Java supplies a number of shortcut assignment operators that allow you to combine an arithmetic operation and an assignment in one operation. These operations can be used with either integer or floating-point operands. For example, the += operator allows you to combine addition and assignment into one expression. The statement

```
k += 3;
```

is equivalent to the statement

```
k = k + 3;
```

Similarly, the statement

```
r += 3.5 + 2.0 * 9.3 ;
```

is equivalent to

```
r = r + (3.5 + 2.0 * 9.3);  // i.e., r = r + 22.1;
```

As these examples illustrate, when using the += operator, the expression on its right-hand side is first evaluated and then *added* to the current value of the variable on its left-hand side.

Table 5.8 lists the other assignment operators that can be used in combination with the arithmetic operators. For each of these operations, the interpretation is the same: evaluate the expression on the right-hand side of the operator and then perform the arithmetic operation (such as addition or multiplication) to the current value of the variable on the left of the operator.

SELF-STUDY EXERCISES

EXERCISE 5.10 What value will j and k have after each of the calculations that follow? Assume that k has the value 10 and that j has the value 5 before each operation is performed.

a. `k += j;`
b. `k -= j++;`

c. `k *= ++j * 2;`
d. `k /= 25 * j--;`

e. `k %= j - 3;`

EXERCISE 5.11 Write four different statements that add 1 to the `int` k.

5.3.5   Relational Operators

There are several *relational* operations that can be performed on integers: <, >, <=, >=, ==, and !=. These correspond to the algebraic operators <, >, ≤, ≥, =, and ≠. Each of these operators takes two operands (integer or real) and returns a boolean result. They are defined in Table 5.9.

Note that several of these relational operators require two symbols in Java. Thus, the familiar equals sign (=) is replaced in Java by ==. This ensures that the equality operator can be distinguished from the assignment operator. Less than or equal to (<=), greater than or equal to (>=), and not equal to (!=) also require two symbols instead of the familiar ≤, ≥, and ≠ from algebra. In each case, the two symbols should be consecutive. It is an error in Java for a space to appear between the < and = in <=.

Equals vs. assigns

> **DEBUGGING TIP: Equality and Assignment.**   A common semantic error of beginning programmers is to use the assignment operator (=) when the equality operator (==) is intended.

Among the relational operators, the inequalities (<, >, <=, and >=) have higher precedence than the equality operators (== and !=). In an expression that involves both kinds of operators, the inequalities would be evaluated first. Otherwise, the expression is evaluated from left to right.

Taken as a group the relational operators have lower precedence than the arithmetic operators. Therefore, in evaluating an expression that involves both arithmetic and relational operators, the arithmetic operations are done first. Table 5.10 includes all of the numeric operators introduced so far.

To take an example, let us evaluate the following complex expression:

```
9 + 6 <= 25 * 4 + 2
```

To clarify the implicit operator precedence, we first parenthesize the expression

```
( 9 + 6 ) <= ( (25 * 4 ) + 2 )
```

Table 5.9. Relational operators

Operator	Operation	Java Expression
<	*Less than*	5 < 10
>	*Greater than*	10 > 5
<=	*Less than or equal to*	5 <= 10
>=	*Greater than or equal to*	10 >= 5
==	*Equal to*	5 == 5
!=	*Not equal to*	5 != 4

Table 5.10. Numeric operator precedence including relations

Precedence Order	Operator	Operation
1	( )	*Parentheses*
2	++ --	*Increment, decrement*
3	* / %	*Multiplication, division, modulus*
4	+ -	*Addition, subtraction*
5	< > <= >=	*Relational operators*
6	== !=	*Equality operators*

and then evaluate it step by step:

```
Step 1. ( 9 + 6 ) <= ( (25 * 4 ) + 2 )
Step 2. ( 9 + 6 ) <= ( 100 + 2 )
Step 3. 15 <= 102
Step 4. true
```

The following expression is an example of an ill-formed expression:

```
9 + 6 <= 25 * 4 == 2
```

That the expression is ill-formed becomes obvious if we parenthesize it and then attempt to evaluate it:

```
Step 1. ( ( 9 + 6 )  <= ( 25 * 4 ) ) == 2
Step 2. ( 15  <= 100 ) == 2
Step 3. true == 2        // Syntax error results here
```

The problem here is that the expression `true == 2` is an attempt to compare an `int` and a `boolean` value, which can't be done. As with any other binary operator, the `==` operator

Strong typing

requires that both of its operands be of the same type. This is another example of Java's strong type checking.

SELF-STUDY EXERCISES

EXERCISE 5.12   For each of these questions, what is the value of *m*? Assume that *k* equals 2, *j* equals 3, and *m* equals 10 before each question. Don't forget about precedence.

a. m = j++ + k ;
b. m = ++j + k;

c. m += j + k;
d. m *= j++ + k++;

e. m *= ++j + ++k;

EXERCISE 5.13   Evaluate each of the following expressions, taking care to observe operator precedence rules. If an expression is illegal, mark it illegal and explain why.

a. 4 + 5 ==   6 * 2
b. (4 + 5) <= 6 / 3
c. 4 + 5 / 6 >= 10 % 2
d. (4 = 5) / 6

e. 4 + 5 % 3 != 7 - 2
f. (4 + 5) % 3 = 10 -4
g. 9 % 2 * 7 / 3 > 17

5.4 From the Java Library: `java.lang.Math`

java.sun.com/docs

The `java.lang.Math` class provides many common mathematical functions that will prove useful in performing numerical computations. As an element of the `java.lang` package, it is included implicitly in all Java programs. Table 5.11 lists some of the most commonly used `Math` class methods.

All `Math` methods are `static` *class methods* and are, therefore, invoked through the class name. For example, we would calculate 2^4 as `Math.pow(2,4)`, which evaluates to 16. Similarly, we compute the square root of 225.0 as `Math.sqrt(225.0)`, which evaluates to 15.0.

Indeed, Java's `Math` class cannot be instantiated and cannot be subclassed. Its basic definition is

```
public final class Math      // Final, can't subclass
{    private Math() {}        // Private, can't invoke
     ...
     public static native double sqrt(double a)
           throws ArithmeticException;
}
```

By declaring the `Math` class `public final`, we indicate that it can be accessed (`public`) but cannot be extended or subclassed (`final`). By declaring its default constructor to be

Table 5.11. A selection of `Math` class methods

Method	Description	Examples
int abs(int x) *long abs(long x)* *float abs(float x)*	*Absolute value of x*	*if x >= 0 abs(x) is x* *if x < 0 abs(x) is −x*
int ceil(double x)	*Rounds x to the smallest integer not less than x*	*ceil(8.3) is 9* *ceil(−8.3) is −8*
int floor(double x)	*Rounds x to the largest integer not greater than x*	*floor (8.9) is 8* *floor(−8.9) is −9*
double log(double x)	*Natural logarithm of x*	*log (2.718282) is 1.0*
double pow(double x, double y)	*x raised to the y power (x^y)*	*pow(3, 4) is 81.0* *pow(16.0, 0.5) is 4.0*
double random()	*Generates a random number in the interval [0,1)*	*random() is 0.5551* *random() is 0.8712*
long round(double x)	*Rounds x to an integer*	*round(26.51) is 27* *round (26.499) is 26*
double sqrt(double x)	*Square root of x*	*sqrt(4.0) is 2.0*

`private`, we prevent this class from being instantiated. The idea of a class that cannot be subclassed and cannot be instantiated may seem a little strange at first. The justification here is that it provides a convenient and efficient way to introduce helpful math functions into the Java language.

Defining the `Math` class in this way makes it easy to use its methods, because you don't have to create an instance of it. It is also a very efficient design because its methods are static elements of the `java.lang` package. This means that they are loaded into memory at the beginning of your program's execution, and they persist in memory throughout your program's lifetime. Because `Math` class methods do not have to be loaded into memory each time they are invoked, their execution time will improve dramatically.

> **EFFECTIVE DESIGN: Static Methods.**   A method should be declared `static` if it is intended to be used whether or not there is an instance of its class.

5.5   Numeric Processing Examples

In this section we consider several numeric programming examples. They have been carefully chosen to illustrate different issues and concepts associated with processing numeric data.

5.5.1   Example: Rounding to Two Decimal Places

As an example of how to use `Math` class methods, we begin with the problem of rounding numbers. When dealing with applications that involve monetary values—dollars and cents—it is often necessary to round a calculated result to two decimal places. For example, suppose a program computes the value of a certificate of deposit (CD) to be 75.19999. Before we output *Algorithm design* this result, we would want to round it to two decimal places—75.20. The following algorithm can be used to accomplish this:

```
1. Multiply the number by 100, giving 7519.9999.
2. Add 0.5 to the number giving 7520.4999.
3. Drop the fractional part giving 7520
4. Divide the result by 100, giving 75.20
```

Step 3 of this algorithm can be done using the `Math.floor(R)` method, which rounds its real argument, *R*, to the largest integer not less than *R* (from Table 5.11). If the number to be rounded is stored in the `double` variable *R*, then the following expression will round R to two decimal places:

```
R = Math.floor(R * 100.0 + 0.5) / 100.0;
```

Alternatively, we could use the `Math.round()` method (Table 5.11). This method rounds a floating-point value to the nearest integer. For example, `Math.round(65.3333)` rounds to 65 and `Math.round(65.6666)` rounds to 66. The following expression uses it to round to two decimal places:

```
R = Math.round(100.0 * R) / 100.0;
```

Note that it is important here to divide by 100.0 and not by 100. Otherwise, the division will give an integer result and we will lose the two decimal places.

DEBUGGING TIP: Division. Using the correct type of literal in division operations is necessary to ensure that you get the correct type of result.

5.5.2 Example: Converting Fahrenheit to Celsius

To illustrate some of the issues that arise in using numeric data, we will now design a program that performs temperature conversions from Fahrenheit to Celsius, and vice versa.

Problem Decomposition

This problem requires two classes, a `Temperature` class and a `TemperatureUI` class. The `Temperature` class will perform the temperature conversions, and `TemperatureUI` will serve as the user interface (Fig. 5.3).

What objects do we need?

Class Design: `Temperature`

The purpose of the `Temperature` class is to perform the temperature conversions. To convert a Celsius temperature to Fahrenheit, or vice versa, it is not necessary to store the temperature value. Rather, a conversion method could take the Celsius (or Fahrenheit) temperature as a parameter, perform the conversion, and return the result. Therefore, the `Temperature` class does not need any instance variables. In this respect the `Temperature` class resembles the `Math` class. Unlike `OneRowNim`, which stores the game's state—the number of sticks remaining and whose turn it is—the `Math` and `Temperature` classes are stateless.

What data do we need?

Thus, following the design of the `Math` class, the `Temperature` class will have two public static methods: one to convert from Fahrenheit to Celsius, and one to convert from Celsius to Fahrenheit. Recall that static methods are associated with the class rather than with its instances. Therefore, we need not instantiate a `Temperature` object to use these methods. Instead, we can invoke the methods through the class itself.

What methods do we need?

The methods will use the standard conversion formulas: $F = \frac{9}{5}C + 32$ and $C = \frac{5}{9}(F - 32)$. Each of these methods should have a single parameter to store the temperature value that is being converted.

Because we want to be able to handle temperatures such as 98.6, we will use real-number data for the methods' parameters. Generally speaking, the `double` type is more widely used than `float` because Java represents real literals such as 98.6 as `double`s. Because `double`s are more widely used in Java, using `double` wherever a floating-point value is needed will cut down on the number of implicit data conversions that a program would have to perform. Therefore, each of our conversion methods should take a `double` parameter and return a `double` result. These considerations lead to the design shown in Figure 5.4.

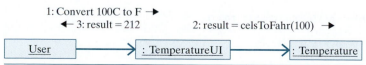

Figure 5.3 Interacting objects: The user interacts with the user interface (TemperatureUI), which interacts with the Temperature object.

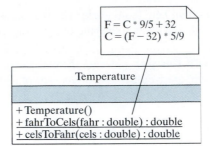

Figure 5.4 The Temperature class. Note that static elements are underlined in UML.

$$F = C * 9/5 + 32$$
$$C = (F - 32) * 5/9$$

Temperature
+ Temperature()
+ fahrToCels(fahr : double) : double
+ celsToFahr(cels : double) : double

> **JAVA PROGRAMMING TIP: Numeric Types.** Java uses the `int` type for integer literals and `double` for real-number literals. When possible, using `int` and `double` for numeric variables and parameters reduces the number of implicit conversions a program would have to perform.

Implementation: `Temperature`

The implementation of the `Temperature` class is shown in Figure 5.5. Note that because `celsToFahr()` uses the `double` value `temp` in its calculation, it uses floating-point literals (9.0, 5.0, and 32.0) in its conversion expression. This helps to reduce the reliance on Java's built-in promotion rules, which can lead to subtle errors. For example, suppose we had written what looks like an equivalent calculation using integer literals:

```
return(9 / 5 * temp + 32); // Error: equals (temp + 32)
```

Semantic error

Because 9 divided by 5 gives the integer result 1, this expression is always equivalent to `temp + 32`, which is not the correct conversion formula. This kind of subtle semantic error can be avoided if you avoid mixing types wherever possible.

```java
public class Temperature
{
    public Temperature() {}
    public static double fahrToCels(double temp)
    {
        return (5.0 * (temp - 32.0) / 9.0);
    }
    public static double celsToFahr(double temp)
    {
        return (9.0 * temp / 5.0 + 32.0);
    }
} // Temperature class
```

Figure 5.5 The Temperature class.

JAVA PROGRAMMING TIP: Don't Mix Types.   You can reduce the incidence of semantic errors caused by implicit type conversions if, whenever possible, you explicitly change all the literals in an expression to the same type.

Testing and Debugging

The next question to be addressed concerns the way to test this program. As always, the program should be tested in a stepwise fashion. As each method is coded, you should test it both in isolation and in combination with the other methods, if possible.

Testing strategy

In addition, you should develop appropriate *test data*. It is not enough to just plug in any values. The values you use should test for certain potential problems. For this program, the following tests are appropriate:

Designing test data

- Test converting 0 degrees C to 32 degrees F.
- Test converting 100 degrees C to 212 degrees F.
- Test converting 212 degrees F to 100 degrees C.
- Test converting 32 degrees F to 0 degrees C.

The first two tests use the `celsToFahr()` method to test the freezing-point and boiling-point temperatures, two boundary values for this problem. A **boundary value** is a value at the beginning or end of the range of values that a variable or calculation is meant to represent. The second pair of tests performs similar checks with the `fahrToCels()` method. One advantage of using these values is that we know what results the methods should return.

EFFECTIVE DESIGN: Test Data.   Developing appropriate test data is an important part of program design. One type of test data should check the boundaries of the calculations you are making.

DEBUGGING TIP: Test, Test, Test!   The fact that your program runs correctly on some data is no guarantee of its correctness. The more testing, and the more careful the testing, the better.

The `TemperatureUI` Class

The purpose of the `TemperatureUI` class is to serve as a user interface—that is, as an interface between the user and a `Temperature` object. It will accept a Fahrenheit or Celsius temperature from the user, pass it to one of the public methods of the `Temperature` object for conversion, and display the result that is returned.

As we discussed in Chapter 4, the user interface can take various forms, ranging from a command-line interface to a graphical interface. Figure 5.6 shows a design for the user interface based on the command-line interface developed in Chapter 4. The `TemperatureUI` uses a `KeyboardReader` to handle interaction with the user and uses `static` methods in the `Temperature` class to perform the temperature conversions.

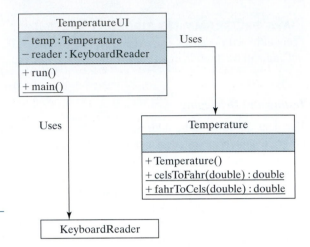

Figure 5.6   A command-line user interface.

SELF-STUDY EXERCISES

EXERCISE 5.14   Following the design in Figure 5.6, implement the `TemperatureUI` class and use it to test the methods in `Temperature` class. The `run()` method should use an **input-process-output** algorithm: Prompt the user for input, perform the necessary processing, and output the result. Since `Temperature`'s conversion methods are class methods, you do not need to instantiate a `Temperature` object in this project. You can invoke the conversion methods directly through the `Temperature` class:

```
double fahr = Temperature.celsToFahr(98.6);
```

EXERCISE 5.15   Following the design for the GUI developed in Chapter 4, implement a GUI to use for testing the `Temperature` class. The GUI should have the layout shown in Figure 5.7.

5.5.3   Example: Using Class Constants

As we noted in Chapter 0, in addition to instance variables, which are associated with instances (objects) of a class, Java also allows class variables, which are associated with the class itself. One of the most common uses of such variables is to define named constants to replace literal

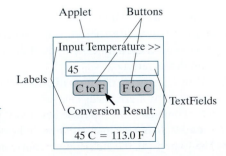

Figure 5.7   Layout design of a GUI that performs temperature conversions.

values. A **named constant** is a variable that cannot be changed once it has been given an initial value. In this section, we use our running example, OneRowNim, to illustrate using class constants.

Recall that methods and variables associated with a class must be declared with the static modifier. If a variable is declared static, there will be exactly one copy of that variable created no matter how many times its class is instantiated. To turn a variable into a constant, it must be declared with the final modifier. Thus, the following are examples of **class constants**—constant values associated with the class rather than with its instances:

```
public static final int PLAYER_ONE = 1;
public static final int PLAYER_TWO = 2;
public static final int MAX_PICKUP = 3;
public static final int MAX_STICKS = 7;
```

The final modifier indicates that the value of a variable cannot be changed. When final is used in a variable declaration, the variable must be assigned an initial value. After a final variable is properly declared, it is a syntax error to attempt to try to change its value. For example, given the preceding declarations, the following assignment statement would cause a compiler error:

```
PLAYER_ONE = 5; // Syntax error; PLAYER_ONE is a constant
```

Note how we use uppercase letters and underscore characters (_) in the names of constants. This is a convention that professional Java programmers follow, and its purpose is to make it easy to distinguish the constants from the variables in a program. This makes the program easier to read and understand.

JAVA PROGRAMMING TIP: Readability. To make your programs more readable, use uppercase font for constant identifiers.

Another way that named constants improve the readability of a program is by replacing the reliance on literal values. For example, for the OneRowNim class, compare the following two if conditions:

```
if (num < 1 || num > 3 || num > nSticks) ...
if (num < 1 || num > MAX_PICKUP || num > nSticks) ...
```

Clearly, the second condition is easier to read and understand. In the first condition, we have no good idea what the literal value 3 represents. In the second, we know that MAX_PICKUP represents the most sticks a player can pick up.

Thus, to make `OneRowNim` more readable, we should replace all occurrences of the literal value 3 with the constant MAX_PICKUP. The same principle would apply to some of the other literal values in the program. Thus, instead of using 1 and 2 to represent the two players, we could use PLAYER_ONE and PLAYER_TWO to make methods such as the following easier to read and understand:

Readability

```java
public int getPlayer()
{   if (onePlaysNext)
        return PLAYER_ONE;
    else return PLAYER_TWO;
} // getPlayer()
```

JAVA PROGRAMMING TIP: Readability.   To make your programs more readable use named constants instead of literal values.

Another advantage of named constants (over literals) is that their use makes the program easier to modify and maintain. For example, suppose that we decide to change `OneRowNim` so that the maximum number of sticks that can be picked up is four instead of three. If we used literal values, we would have to change all occurrences of 4 that were used to represent the maximum pick-up. If we use a named constant, we need only change its declaration to:

Maintainability

```java
public static final int MAX_PICKUP = 4;
```

EFFECTIVE DESIGN: Maintainability.   Constants should be used instead of literal values in a program. This will make the program easier to modify and maintain.

All of the examples we have presented so far show why named constants (but not necessarily class constants) are useful. Not all constants are class constants. That is, not all constants are declared `static`. However, the idea of associating constants with a class makes good sense. Creating just a single copy of the constant saves memory resources, and in addition constants such as MAX_STICKS and PLAYER_ONE make more conceptual sense when associated with the class itself rather than with any particular `OneRowNim` instance.

Class constants are used extensively in the Java class library. For example, as we saw in Chapter 2, Java's various built-in colors are represented as constants of the `java.awt.Color` class—`Color.blue` and `Color.red`. Similarly, `java.awt.Label` uses `int` constants to specify how a label's text should be aligned: `Label.CENTER`.

Another advantage of class constants is that they can be used *before* instances of the class exist. For example, a class constant (as opposed to an instance constant) may be used during object instantiation:

```java
OneRowNim game = new OneRowNim(OneRowNim.MAX_STICKS);
```

Note how we use the name of the class to refer to the class constant. Of course, MAX_STICKS has to be a public variable in order to be accessible outside the class. MAX_STICKS has to

```java
public class OneRowNim
{   public static final int PLAYER_ONE = 1;
    public static final int PLAYER_TWO = 2;
    public static final int MAX_PICKUP = 3;
    public static final int MAX_STICKS = 11;
    public static final boolean GAME_OVER = false;

    private int nSticks = MAX_STICKS;
    private boolean onePlaysNext = true;

    public OneRowNim()
    {
    } // OneRowNim() constructor1
    public OneRowNim(int sticks)
    {   nSticks = sticks;
    } // OneRowNim() constructor2
    public OneRowNim(int sticks, int starter)
    {   nSticks = sticks;
        onePlaysNext = (starter == PLAYER_ONE);
    } // OneRowNim() constructor3
    public boolean takeSticks(int num)
    {   if (num < 1 || num > MAX_PICKUP || num > nSticks)
            return false;                        // Error
        else                                     // Valid move
        {   nSticks = nSticks - num;
            onePlaysNext = !onePlaysNext;
            return true;
        } // else
    } // takeSticks()
    public int getSticks()
    {   return nSticks;
    } // getSticks()
    public int getPlayer()
    {   if (onePlaysNext)
            return PLAYER_ONE;
        else return PLAYER_TWO;
    } // getPlayer()
    public boolean gameOver()
    {   return (nSticks <= 0);
    } // gameOver()
    public int getWinner()
    {   if (nSticks < 1)
            return getPlayer();
        else return 0;                           // Game is not over
    } // getWinner()
    public String report()
    {   return ("Number of sticks left: " + getSticks()
        + "\nNext turn by player " + getPlayer() + "\n");
    } // report()
} // OneRowNim class
```

Figure 5.8 This version of OneRowNim uses named constants.

be a class constant if it is to be used as a constructor argument, because at this point in the program there are no instances of OneRowNim. A new version of OneRowNim that uses class constants is shown in Figure 5.8.

It is important to note that Java also allows class constants to be referenced through an instance of the class. Thus, once we have instantiated game, we can refer to MAX_STICKS with either OneRowNim.MAX_STICKS or game.MAX_STICKS.

SELF-STUDY EXERCISE

EXERCISE 5.16 Implement a command-line interface class named KBTestOneRowNim that uses our new version of OneRowNim. Make use of MAX_STICKS and MAX_PICKUP in the user interface.

5.5.4   Object-Oriented Design: Information Hiding

Preserving the public interface

The fact that the two new versions of OneRowNim developed in this chapter are *backward compatible* with the earlier version is due in large part to the way we have divided up its public and private elements. Because the new versions still present the same public interface, programs that use the OneRowNim class, such as the OneRowNimApp from Chapter 4 (Fig. 4.24), can continue to use the class without changing a single line of their code. To confirm this, see the Self-Study Exercise at the end of this section.

Information hiding

Although we have made significant changes to the underlying representation of OneRowNim, the implementation details—its data and algorithms—are hidden from other objects. As long as OneRowNim's public interface remains compatible with the old version, changes to its private elements won't cause any inconvenience to objects dependent on the old version. This ability to change the underlying implementation without affecting the outward functionality of a class is one of the great benefits of the information-hiding principle.

EFFECTIVE DESIGN: Information Hiding.   In designing a class, other objects should be given access only to the information they need and nothing more.

The lesson to be learned here is that the public parts of a class should be restricted to whatever must be accessible to other objects. Everything else should be private. Things work better, in Java programming and in the real world, when objects are designed with the principle of information hiding in mind.

SELF-STUDY EXERCISE

EXERCISE 5.17   To confirm that our new version of OneRowNim still works correctly with the user interfaces we developed in Chapter 4, compile and run it with OneRowNimApp (Fig. 4.24).

5.5.5   Example: A Winning Algorithm for One-Row Nim

Now that we have access to numeric data types and operators, we will develop an algorithm that can win the One-Row Nim game. Recall that in Chapter 4 we left things such that when the computer moves, it always takes one stick. Let's replace that strategy with a more sophisticated approach.

If you have played One-Row Nim, you have probably noticed that in a game with 21 sticks, you can always win the game if you leave your opponent with 1, 5, 9, 13, 17, or 21 sticks. This is obvious for the case of one stick. For the case where you leave your opponent five sticks, you can make a move that leaves the other player with one stick no matter what the other player does. For example, if your opponent takes one stick, you can take three; if your opponent takes two, you can take two; and if your opponent takes three, you can take one. In any case, you can win the game by making the right move if you have left your opponent with five sticks. The same arguments apply for the other values: 9, 13, 17, and 21.

What relationship is common to the numbers in this set? Note that you always get 1 if you take the remainder after dividing each of these numbers by 4:

```
 1 % 4  == 1
 5 % 4  == 1
 9 % 4  == 1
13 % 4  == 1
17 % 4  == 1
21 % 4  == 1
```

Thus, we can base our winning strategy on the goal of leaving the opponent with a number of sticks, N, such that N % 4 equals 1.

To determine how many sticks to take in order to leave the opponent with N, we need to use a little algebra. Let's suppose that `sticksLeft` represents the number of sticks left before our turn. The first thing we have to acknowledge is that if *sticksLeft %4 == 1*, then we have been left with 1, 5, 9, 13, and so on, sticks, so we cannot force a win. In that case, it doesn't matter how many sticks we pick up. Our opponent should win the game.

Now let's suppose that *sticksLeft % 4 != 1*, and let M be the number of sticks to pick up in order to leave our opponent with N, such that *N % 4 == 1*. Then we have the following two equations:

```
sticksLeft - M == N
N % 4 == 1
```

We can combine these into a single equation, which can be simplified as follows:

```
(sticksLeft - M)  % 4 == 1
```

If *sticksLeft - M* leaves a remainder of 1 when divided by 4, that means that *sticksLeft - M* is equal to some integer quotient, *Q* times 4 plus 1:

```
(sticksLeft - M)   ==   (Q * 4) + 1
```

By adding M to both sides and subtracting 1 from both sides of this equation, we get:

```
 (sticksLeft - 1)   ==   (Q * 4) + M
```

The equation is saying that *(sticksLeft - 1) % 4 == M*. That is, when you divide *sticksLeft-1* by 4, you will get a remainder of M, which is the number of sticks you should pick up. Thus, to decide how many sticks to take, we want to compute:

```
M == (sticksLeft -1) % 4
```

To verify this, let's look at some examples:

```
sticksLeft        (sticksLeft -1) % 4       sticksLeft
  Before                                     After
-------------------------------------------------------
    9              (9-1) % 4 == 0           Illegal Move
    8              (8-1) % 4 == 3           5
    7              (7-1) % 4 == 2           5
    6              (6-1) % 4 == 1           5
    5              (5-1) % 4 == 0           Illegal Move
```

The examples in this table show that when we use *(sticksLeft-1) % 4* to calculate our move, we always leave our opponent with a losing situation. Note that when `sticksLeft` equals 9 or 5, we can't apply this strategy because it would lead to an illegal move.

Let us now convert this algorithm into Java code. In addition to incorporating our winning strategy, this `move()` method makes use of two important `Math` class methods:

```java
public int move()
{ int sticksLeft = nim.getSticks();                          // Get number of sticks
  if (sticksLeft % (nim.MAX_PICKUP + 1) != 1)                // If winnable
    return (sticksLeft - 1) % (nim.MAX_PICKUP +1);
  else {                                                     // Else pick random
    int maxPickup = Math.min(nim.MAX_PICKUP, sticksLeft);
    return 1 + (int)(Math.random() * maxPickup);
  }
}
```

The `move()` method will return an `int` representing the best move possible. It begins by getting the number of sticks left from the `OneRowNim` object, which is referred to as `nim` in this case. It then checks whether it can win by computing *(sticksLeft-1) % 4*. Rather than use the literal value 4, however, we use the named constant `MAX_PICKUP`, which is accessible through the `nim` object. This is an especially good use for the class constant because it makes our algorithm completely general—that is, our winning strategy will continue to work even if the game is changed so that the maximum pickup is five or six. The `then` clause computes and returns *(sticksLeft-1) % (nim.MAX_PICKUP+1)*, but here again it uses the class constant.

The `else` clause would be used when it is not possible to make a winning move. In this case we want to choose a random number of sticks between one and some maximum number. The maximum number depends on how many sticks are left. If there are more than three sticks left, then the most we can pick up is three, so we want a random number between 1 and 3. However, if there are two sticks left, then the most we can pick up is two and we want a random number between 1 and 2. Note how we use the `Math.min()` method to decide the maximum number of sticks that can be picked up:

```java
int maxPickup = Math.min(nim.MAX_PICKUP, sticksLeft);
```

The `min()` method returns the minimum value between its two arguments.

Finally, note how we use the `Math.random()` method to calculate a random number between 1 and the maximum:

```
1 + (int)(Math.random() * maxPickup);
```

The `random()` method returns a real number between 0 and 0.999999—that is, a real number between 0 and 1 but not including 1:

```
0 <= Math.random() < 1.0
```

If we multiply `Math.random()` times 2, the result would be a value between 0 and 1.9999999. Similarly, if we multiplied it by 3, the result would be a value between 0 and 2.9999999. In order to use the random value, we have to convert it into an integer. We do this by using the `(int)` cast operator:

```
(int)(Math.random() * maxPickup);
```

Recall that when a `double` is cast into an `int`, Java just throws away the fractional part. Therefore, this expression will give us a value between 0 and `maxPickup-1`. If `maxPickup` is 3, this will give a value between 0 and 2, whereas we want a random value between 1 and 3. To achieve this desired value, we merely add 1 to the result. Thus, using the expression

```
1 + (int)(Math.random() * maxPickup)
```

gives us a random number between 1 and `maxPickup`, where `maxPickup` is either 1, 2, or 3, depending on the situation of the game at that point.

SELF-STUDY EXERCISES

EXERCISE 5.18   Implement a class named `NimPlayer` that incorporates the `move()` method designed in this section. The class should implement the design shown in Figure 5.9. That is, in addition to the `move()` method, it should have an instance variable, `nim`, which will serve as a reference to the `OneRowNim` game. Its constructor method should take a `OneRowNim` parameter, allowing the `NimPlayer` to be given a reference when it is instantiated.

EXERCISE 5.19   Modify `OneRowNim`'s command-line interface to play One-Row Nim between the user and the computer, where the `NimPlayer` implemented in the preceding exercise represents the computer.

NimPlayer
− nim : OneRowNim
+ NimPlayer(g : OneRowNim) + move() : int

Figure 5.9 The `NimPlayer` class.

5.6   From the Java Library: `java.text.NumberFormat`

Although the `Math.round()` method is useful for rounding numbers, it is not suitable for business applications. Even for rounded values, Java will drop trailing zeroes. So a value such as $10,000.00 would be output as $10000.0. This wouldn't be acceptable for a business report.

Fortunately, Java supplies the `java.text.NumberFormat` class precisely for the task of representing numbers as dollar amounts, percentages, and other formats (Fig. 5.10).

The `NumberFormat` class is an **abstract** class, which means that it cannot be directly instantiated. Instead, you would use its static `getInstance()` methods to create an instance that can then be used for the desired formatting tasks.

Once a `NumberFormat` instance has been created, its `format()` method can be used to put a number into a particular format. The `setMaximumFractionDigits()` and `setMaximumIntegerDigits()` methods can be used to control the number of digits before and after the decimal point.

For example, the following statements can be used to format a decimal number as a currency string in dollars and cents:

```
NumberFormat dollars = NumberFormat.getCurrencyInstance();
System.out.println(dollars.format(10962.555));
```

These statements would cause the value 10962.555 to be shown as $10,962.56. Similarly, the statements,

```
NumberFormat percent = NumberFormat.getPercentInstance();
percent.setMaximumFractionDigits(2);
System.out.println(percent.format(0.0655));
```

would display the value 0.0655 as 6.55%. The utility of the `Math` and `NumberFormat` classes illustrates the following principle:

EFFECTIVE DESIGN: Code Reuse.   Often the best way to solve a programming task is to find the appropriate methods in the Java class library.

NumberFormat
+ getInstance() : NumberFormat
+ getCurrencyInstance() : NumberFormat
+ getPercentInstance() : NumberFormat
+ format(in n : double) : String
+ format(in n : long) : String
+ getMaximumFractionDigits() : int
+ getMaximumIntegerDigits() : int
+ setMaximumFractionDigits(in n : int)
+ setMaximumIntegerDigits(in n : int)

Figure 5.10
The `java.text.NumberFormat` class.

BankCD
− principal : double
− rate : double
− years : double
+ BankCD(p : double, r : double, y : double)
+ calcYearly() : double
+ calcDaily() : double

Figure 5.11 The BankCD class.

SELF-STUDY EXERCISE

EXERCISE 5.20 A Certificate of Deposit (CD) is an investment instrument that accumulates interest at a given rate for an initial principal over a fixed number of years. The formula for compounding interest is shown in Table 5.12. It assumes that interest is compounded annually. For daily compounding, the annual rate must be divided by 365, and the compounding period must be multiplied by 365, giving: $a = p(1 + r/365)^{365n}$. Implement a **BankCD** class that calculates the maturity value of a CD. Figure 5.11 gives the design of the class. It should have three instance variables for the CD's principal, rate, and years. Its constructor method sets the initial values of these variables when a **BankCD** is instantiated. Its two public methods calculate the maturity value using yearly and daily compounding interest, respectively. Use the **Math.pow()** method to calculate maturity values. For example, the following expression calculates maturity value with annual compounding:

```
principal * Math.pow(1 + rate, years)
```

Table 5.12. Formula for calculating compound interest

$a = p(1 + r)^n$ where
- a is the CD's value at the end of the nth year
- p is the principal, or original investment amount
- r is the annual interest rate
- n is the number of years, or the compounding period

EXERCISE 5.21 Design a command-line user interface to the **BankCD** class that lets the user input principal, interest rate, and years, and reports the CD's maturity value with both yearly and daily compounding. Use **NumberFormat** objects to display percentages and dollar figures in an appropriate format. The program's output should look something like the following (user's inputs are in green):

```
*********************** OUTPUT ********************
Compare daily and annual compounding for a Bank CD.
 Input CD initial principal, e.g.   1000.55 > 2500
 Input CD interest rate, e.g.   6.5 > 7.8
 Input the number of years to maturity, e.g., 10.5 > 5
For Principal = $2,500.00 Rate= 7.8% Years= 5.0
 The maturity value compounded yearly is $3,639.43
 The maturity value compounded daily is: $3,692.30
*********************** OUTPUT ********************
```

5.7 Character Data and Operators

Unicode

Another primitive data type in Java is the character type, char. A character in Java is represented by a 16-bit unsigned integer. This means that a total of 2^{16} or 65536 different Unicode characters can be represented, corresponding to the integer values 0 to 65535. The **Unicode** character set is an international standard that has been developed to enable computer languages to represent characters in a wide variety of languages, not just English. Detailed information about this encoding can be obtained at

```
http://www.unicode.org/
```

It is customary in programming languages to use unsigned integers to represent characters. This means that all the digits (0, . . . , 9), alphabetic letters (a, . . . , z, A, . . . , Z), punctuation symbols (such as . ; , " " ! _ -), and nonprinting control characters (LINE_FEED, ESCAPE, CARRIAGE_RETURN, . . .) that make up the computer's character set are represented in the computer's memory by integers. A more traditional set of characters is the *ASCII* (American Standard Code for Information Interchange) character set. ASCII is based on a 7-bit code and, therefore, defines 2^7 or 128 different characters, corresponding to the integer values 0 to 127. In order to make Unicode backward compatible with ASCII systems, the first 128 Unicode characters are identical to the ASCII characters. Thus, in both the ASCII and Unicode encoding, the printable characters have the integer values shown in Table 5.13.

ASCII code

5.7.1 Character to Integer Conversions

Is 'A' a character or an integer? The fact that character data are stored as integers in the computer's memory can cause some confusion about whether a given piece of data is a character or an integer. In other words, when is a character, for example 'A', treated as the integer (65) instead of as the character 'A'? The rule in Java is that a character literal—'a' or 'A' or '0'

Table 5.13. ASCII codes for selected characters

Code	32	33	34	35	36	37	38	39	40	41	42	43	44	45	46	47
Char	SP	!	"	#	$	%	&	'	(	)	*	+	,	-	.	/

Code	48	49	50	51	52	53	54	55	56	57
Char	0	1	2	3	4	5	6	7	8	9

Code	58	59	60	61	62	63	64
Char	:	;	<	=	>	?	@

Code	65	66	67	68	69	70	71	72	73	74	75	76	77
Char	A	B	C	D	E	F	G	H	I	J	K	L	M

Code	78	79	80	81	82	83	84	85	86	87	88	89	90
Char	N	O	P	Q	R	S	T	U	V	W	X	Y	Z

Code	91	92	93	94	95	96
Char	[	\	]	^	_	'

Code	97	98	99	100	101	102	103	104	105	106	107	108	109
Char	a	b	c	d	e	f	g	h	i	j	k	l	m

Code	110	111	112	113	114	115	116	117	118	119	120	121	122
Char	n	o	p	q	r	s	t	u	v	w	x	y	z

Code	123	124	125	126
Char	{	|	}	~

or `'?'`—is always treated as a character, unless we explicitly tell Java to treat it as an integer. So if we display a literal's value

```
System.out.println('a');
```

the letter `'a'` will be displayed. Similarly, if we assign `'a'` to a `char` variable and then display the variable's value,

```
char ch = 'a';
System.out.println(ch);        // Displays 'a'
```

the letter `'a'` will be shown. If, on the other hand, we wish to output a character's integer value, we must use an explicit cast operator as follows:

```
System.out.println((int)'a') ;   // Displays 97
```

A **cast operation**, such as (`int`), converts one type of data (`'a'`) into another (97). This is known as a **type conversion**. Similarly, if we wish to store a character's integer value in a variable, we can *cast* the `char` into an `int` as follows:

```
int k = (int)'a';      // Converts 'a' to 97
System.out.println(k);  // Displays 97
```

As these examples show, a *cast* is a type conversion operator. Java allows a wide variety of both explicit and implicit type conversions. Certain conversions (for example, promotions) take place when methods are invoked, when assignment statements are executed, when expressions are evaluated, and so on.

The cast operator

Type conversion in Java is governed by several rules and exceptions. In some cases Java allows the programmer to make implicit cast conversions. For example, in the following assignment a `char` is converted to an `int` even though no explicit cast operator is used:

```
char ch;
int k;
k = ch; // convert a char into an int
```

Java permits this conversion because no information will be lost. A character `char` is represented in 16 bits, whereas an `int` is represented in 32 bits. This is like trying to put a small object into a large box. Space will be left over, but the object will fit inside without being damaged. Similarly, storing a 16-bit `char` in a 32-bit `int` will leave the extra 16 bits unused. This *widening primitive conversion* changes one primitive type (`char`) into a wider one (`int`), where a type's *width* is the number of bits used in its representation.

Implicit type conversion

Widening conversion

On the other hand, trying to assign an `int` value to a `char` variable leads to a syntax error:

```
char ch;
int k;
ch = k;    // Syntax error: can't assign int to char
```

Trying to assign a 32-bit int to 16-bit char is like trying to fit a big object into an undersized box. The object won't fit unless we shrink it in some way. Java will allow us to assign an int value to a char variable, but only if we perform an explicit cast on it:

```
ch = (char)k; // Explicit cast of int k into char ch
```

Narrowing
conversion

The (char) cast operation performs a careful "shrinking" of the int by lopping off the last 16 bits of the int. This can be done without loss of information provided that k's value is in the range 0 to 65535—that is, in the range of values that fit into a char variable. This *narrowing primitive conversion* changes a wider type (32-bit int) to a narrower type (16-bit char). Because of the potential here for information loss, it is up to the programmer to determine whether the cast can be performed safely.

> **JAVA LANGUAGE RULE**   **Type Conversion.** Java permits *implicit* type conversions from a narrower type to a wider type. A *cast* operator must be used when converting a wider type into a narrower type.

The cast operator can be used with any primitive type. It applies to the variable or expression that immediately follows it. Thus, parentheses must be used to cast the expression $m + n$ into a char:

```
char ch = (char)(m + n);
```

The following statement would cause a syntax error because the cast operator would only be applied to m:

```
char ch = (char)m + n; // Error: right side is an int
```

In the expression on the right-hand side, the character produced by (char)m will be promoted to an int because it is part of an integer operation whose result will still be an int. Therefore, it cannot be assigned to a char without an explicit cast.

SELF-STUDY EXERCISE

EXERCISE 5.22   Suppose that m and n are integer variables of type int and that $ch1$ and $ch2$ are character variables of type char. Determine in each of the cases that follow whether the assignment statements are valid. If not, modify the statement to make it valid.

a. m = n;   c. ch2 = n;   e. ch1 = m - n;
b. m = ch1;   d. ch1 = ch2;

Table 5.14. Relational operations on characters

Operation	Operator	Java	True Expression
Precedes	<	$ch1 < ch2$	$'a' < 'b'$
Follows	>	$ch1 > ch2$	$'c' > 'a'$
Precedes or equals	<=	$ch1 <= ch2$	$'a' <= 'a'$
Follows or equals	>=	$ch2 >= ch1$	$'a' >= 'a'$
Equal to	==	$ch1 == ch2$	$'a' == 'a'$
Not equal to	!=	$ch1 != ch2$	$'a' != 'b'$

5.7.2   Lexical Ordering

The order in which the characters of a character set are arranged, their **lexical order**, is an important feature of the character set. It especially comes into play for such tasks as arranging strings in alphabetical order.

Although the actual integer values assigned to the individual characters by ASCII and UNI-CODE encoding seem somewhat arbitrary, the characters are, in fact, arranged in a systematic order. For example, note that various sequences of digits, `'0'...'9'`, and letters, `'a'...'z'` and `'A'...'Z'`, are represented by sequences of integers (Table 5.11). This makes it possible to represent the lexical order of the characters in terms of the *less than* relationship among integers. The fact that `'a'` comes before `'f'` in alphabetical order is represented by the fact that 97 (the integer code for `'a'`) is less than 102 (the integer code for `'f'`). Similarly, the digit `'5'` comes before the digit `'9'` in an alphabetical sequence because 53 (the integer code for `'5'`) is less than 57 (the integer code for `'9'`).

This ordering relationship extends throughout the character set. Thus, it is also the case that `'A'` comes before `'a'` in the lexical ordering because 65 (the integer code for `'A'`) is less than 97 (the integer code for `'a'`). Similarly, the character `'['` comes before `'}'` because its integer code (91) is less than 125, the integer code for `'}'`.

5.7.3   Relational Operators

Given the lexical ordering of the `char` type, the following relational operators can be defined: `<, >, <=, >=, ==, !=`. Given any two characters, *ch1* and *ch2*, the expression *ch1 < ch2* is true if and only if the integer value of *ch1* is less than the integer value of *ch2*. In this case we say that *ch1 precedes ch2* in lexical order. Similarly, the expression *ch1 > ch2* is true if and only if the integer value of *ch1* is greater than the integer value of *ch2*. In this case we say that *ch1 follows ch2*. And so on for the other relational operators. This means that we can perform comparison operations on any two character operands (Table 5.14).

char relations

5.8   Example: Character Conversions

Another interesting implication of representing the characters as integers is that we can represent various character operations in terms of integer operations. For example, suppose we want to capitalize a lowercase letter. Table 5.13 shows that the entire sequence of lowercase letters (`'a' ... 'z'`) is displaced by 32 from the sequence of uppercase letters (`'A' ... 'Z'`), so we can convert any lowercase letter into its corresponding uppercase letter by subtracting 32 from its integer value, provided we perform an explicit cast on the result. When we perform the cast `(char) ('a' - 32 )`, the resulting value is `'A'`, as the following example shows:

Lowercase to uppercase

```
(char)('a' - 32)                    ==>   'A'
```

Recall that in evaluating `'a'` - 32 Java will promote `'a'` to an `int` and then perform the subtraction. Thus, a step-by-step evaluation of the expression would go as follows:

```
Step 1. (char)((int)'a' - 32) // Promote 'a' to int
Step 2. (char)(97 - 32)       // Subtract
Step 3. (char) (65)           // Cast result to a char
Step 4. 'A'                   // Results in 'A'
```

Uppercase to lowercase

Similarly, we can convert an uppercase letter into the corresponding lowercase letter by simply adding 32 to its integer code and casting the result back to a char:

```
(char)('J' + 32)                    ==>   'j'
```

We can group these ideas into a method that performs conversion from lowercase to uppercase:

```
char toUpperCase(char ch) {
  if ((ch >= 'a') && (ch <= 'z'))
    return ch - 32 ;  // Error: can't return an int
  return ch;
}
```

This method takes a single `char` parameter and returns a `char` value. It begins by checking whether *ch* is a lowercase letter—that is, whether *ch* falls between `'a'` and `'z'` inclusive. If so, it returns the result of subtracting 32 from *ch*. If not, it returns *ch* unchanged. However, **Type error** the method contains a syntax error that becomes apparent if we trace through its steps. If we invoke it with the expression `toUpperCase('b')`, then, since `'b'` is between `'a'` and `'z'`, the method will return `'b'` − 32. Because the integer value of `'b'` is 98, it will return *98* − *32*, or 66, which is the integer code for the character `'B'`. However, the method is supposed to return a `char`, so this last statement will generate the following syntax error:

```
Incompatible type for return. An explicit cast needed
to convert int to char.
>>      return ch - 32 ;
>>      ^
```

In order to avoid this error, the result must be converted back to `char` before it can be returned:

```
char toUpperCase (char ch) {
  if ((ch >= 'a') && (ch <= 'z'))
    return (char)(ch - 32);  // Explicit cast
  return ch;
}
```

Another common type of conversion is to convert a digit to its corresponding integer value. For example, we convert the character '9' to the integer 9 by making use of the fact that the digit '9' is nine characters beyond the digit '0' in the lexical order. Therefore, subtracting '0' from '9' gives integer 9 as a result:

Digit to integer

```
('9' - '0')  ==> (57 - 48) ==>   9
```

More generally, the expression $ch - '0'$ will convert any digit, *ch*, to its integer value. We can encapsulate these ideas into a method that converts any digit into its corresponding integer value:

```
int digitToInteger(char ch) {
  if ((ch >= '0') && (ch <= '9'))
    return ch - '0';
  return -1 ;
}
```

This method takes a single `char` parameter and returns an `int`. It first checks that *ch* is a valid digit, and if so, it subtracts the character '0' from it. If not, the method just returns −1, which indicates that the method received an invalid input parameter. Obviously, when an object invokes this method, it should first make sure that the value it passes is in fact a digit.

The Java application program shown in Figure 5.12 illustrates several of the ideas discussed in this section. Note that both the `digitToInteger()` and `toUpperCase()` are declared

```
public class Test {
    public static void main(String argv[]) {
        char ch = 'a';                          // Local variables
        int k = (int)'b';
        System.out.println(ch);
        System.out.println(k);
        ch = (char)k;                           // Cast needed here
        System.out.println(ch);
        System.out.println(toUpperCase('a'));
        System.out.println(toUpperCase(ch));
        System.out.println(digitToInteger('7'));
    }
    public static char toUpperCase(char ch) {
        if ((ch >= 'a') && (ch <= 'z'))
            return (char)(ch - 32);
        return ch;
    }
    public static int digitToInteger(char ch) {
        if ((ch >= '0') && (ch <= '9'))
            return ch - '0';
        return -1 ;
    }
} // Test class
```

Figure 5.12   A Java program illustrating character conversions. When run, the program will generate the following outputs, one per line: a, 98, b, A, B, 7.

static. This allows us to call them directly from the (static) `main()` method, a useful and justifiable shortcut if, as in this case, we are just testing the methods.

5.9   Problem Solving = Representation + Action

As you have seen in this chapter, designing classes involves a careful interplay between representation (data) and action (methods). Our several modifications to the `OneRowNim` class illustrate that the data used to represent an object's state can either complicate or simplify the design of the methods needed to solve a problem.

We hope that it is becoming clear to you that in writing object-oriented programs, choosing an appropriate data representation is just as important as choosing the correct algorithm. The concept of an object allows us to encapsulate representation and action into a single entity. It is a very natural way to approach problem solving.

If you look closely enough at any problem, you will find a close relationship between representation and action. For example, compare the task of performing multiplication using Arabic numerals (65 * 12 = 380) and the same task using Roman numerals (LXV * XII = DCCLXXX). It's doubtful that science and technology would be where they are today if our civilization had to rely forever on the Roman way of representing numbers!

EFFECTIVE DESIGN: Representation and Action.   Representation (data) and action (methods) are equally important parts of the problem-solving process.

CHAPTER SUMMARY

Technical Terms

action	operator overloading
binary digit (bit)	precedence order
binary operator	promotion
boundary value	representation
cast operation	round-off error
class constant	short-circuit evaluation
input-process-output	type conversion
lexical-order	unary operator
named constant	Unicode
operand	

Summary of Important Points

- The way we approach a problem can often help or hinder our ability to solve it. Choosing an appropriate *representation* for a problem is often the key to solving it.
- In order to evaluate complex expressions, it is necessary to understand the *precedence order* and *associativity* of the operators involved. Parentheses can always be used to override an operator's built-in precedence.

- Java provides several types of integer data, including the 8-bit `byte`, 16-bit `short`, 32-bit `int`, and 64-bit `long` types. Unless otherwise specified, integer literals are represented as `int` data in a Java program.

- Java provides two types of floating-point data, the 32-bit `float` type and the 64-bit `double` type. Unless otherwise specified, floating-point literals are represented as `double` data.

- In general, if a data type uses n bits in its representation, then it can represent 2^n different values.

- Defining primitive types in terms of a specific number of bits is one way that Java promotes *platform independence*.

- It is necessary to distinguish integer operations from floating-point operations even though the same symbols are used. For example, (7/2) is 3, while (7.0/2) is 3.0.

- In revising a class used by other classes, it is important to preserve as much of the class's *interface* as possible.

- In Java, character data are based on the Unicode character set, which provides $2^{16} = 65,536$ different character codes. To provide backward compatibility with the ASCII code, the first 128 characters are the ASCII coded characters.

- Java operators are evaluated according to the precedence hierarchy shown in Table 5.15. The lower the precedence number, the earlier an operator is evaluated. So the operators at the top of the table are evaluated before operators that occur below them in the table. Operators at the same precedence level are evaluated according to their *association*, either left to right (L to R) or right to left (R to L).

Table 5.15. Java operator precedence and associativity table

Order	Operator	Operation	Association
0	( )	*Parentheses*	
1	++ -- .	*Postincrement, postdecrement, dotOperator*	*L to R*
2	++ -- + - !	*Preincrement, predecrement Unary plus, unary minus, boolean NOT*	*R to L*
3	(*type*) *new*	*Type cast, object instantiation*	*R to L*
4	* / %	*Multiplication, division, modulus*	*L to R*
5	+ - +	*Addition, subtraction, string concatenation*	*L to R*
6	< > <= >=	*Relational operators*	*L to R*
7	== !=	*Equality operators*	*L to R*
8	^	*Boolean XOR*	*L to R*
9	&&	*Boolean AND*	*L to R*
10	||	*Boolean OR*	*L to R*
11	= += -= *= /= %=	*Assignment operators*	*R to L*

SOLUTIONS TO SELF-STUDY EXERCISES

SOLUTION 5.1 a. true b. false c. true d. false e. false f. false

SOLUTION 5.2

```
0000, 0001, 0010, 0011, 0100, 0101, 0110, 0111,
1000, 1001, 1010, 1011, 1100, 1101, 1110, 1111
```

SOLUTION 5.3 In 6 bits, you can represent $2^6 = 64$ different values.

SOLUTION 5.4 If you have to represent up to 12 significant digits, you should use `double`, which goes up to 17 digits.

SOLUTION 5.5 a. 4 b. 4 c. 0 d. 1 e. 2 f. 6 g. 0 h. 4

SOLUTION 5.6 a. 4.0 b. 4.5 c. 0 d. 0.0 e. 1.33

SOLUTION 5.7 a. 7 `int` b. 30 `long` c. 14.0 `double` d. 90 `long` e. 4.0 `double`

SOLUTION 5.8 a. 34.0 b. 54 c. 4 d. 1 e. 6 f. 0 g. 2 h. 7.5

SOLUTION 5.9 a. k==5, j==5 b. k==5, j==6 c. k==6, j==6 d. k==5, j==4 e. k==4, j==4

SOLUTION 5.10 a. k==15, j==5 b. k==5, j==6 c. k==120, j==6 d. k==0, j==4 e. k==0, j==5

SOLUTION 5.11 k = k + 1;   k += 1;   k++;   ++k;

SOLUTION 5.12 a. m = 5 b. m = 6 c. m = 15 d. m = 50 e. m = 70

SOLUTION 5.13 a. false b. false c. true d. illegal e. true f. illegal g. false

SOLUTION 5.14

```java
public class TemperatureUI
{ private KeyboardReader reader;                    // Handles command line I/O
  public TemperatureUI()
    { reader = new KeyboardReader();                // Create reader object
    }
    // Input-process-output algorithm to convert temperatures.
  public void run()
    { reader.prompt("Converts Fahrenheit and Celsius.\n");
      reader.prompt("Input a temperature in Fahrenheit > ");
      double tempIn = reader.getKeyboardDouble();
      double tempResult = Temperature.fahrToCels(tempIn);
      reader.display(tempIn + " F = " + tempResult + " C\n");
      reader.prompt("Input a temperature in Celsius > ");
      tempIn = reader.getKeyboardDouble();
      tempResult = Temperature.celsToFahr(tempIn);
      reader.display(tempIn + " C = " + tempResult + " F\n ");
    } // run()
  public static void main(String args[])
    { TemperatureUI ui = new TemperatureUI();        // Create and
      ui.run();                                      // run the user interface.
    } // main()
} // TemperatureUI class
```

SOLUTION 5.15

```java
import javax.swing.*;
import java.awt.*;
import java.awt.event.*;
 // Use this panel with a JApplet top-level window (as per Chapter 4)
public class TemperatureJPanel extends JPanel implements ActionListener
{ private JTextField inField = new JTextField(15);    // GUI components
  private JTextField resultField = new JTextField(15);
  private JLabel prompt1 = new JLabel("Input Temperature >>");
  private JLabel prompt2 = new JLabel("Conversion Result:");
  private JButton celsToFahr = new JButton("C to F");
  private JButton fahrToCels = new JButton("F to C");
  private JPanel panelN = new JPanel();                // Panels
  private JPanel panelC = new JPanel();
  private JPanel panelS = new JPanel();
  private Temperature temperature = new Temperature();// Temperature object

  public TemperatureJPanel()                           // Set up  user interface
  { setLayout(new BorderLayout());                     // Use BorderLayout
    panelN.setLayout(new BorderLayout());
    panelC.setLayout(new BorderLayout());
    panelS.setLayout(new BorderLayout());
    panelN.add("North", prompt1);                      // Input elements
    panelN.add("South", inField);
    panelC.add("West", celsToFahr);                    // Control buttons
    panelC.add("East", fahrToCels);
    panelS.add("North", prompt2);                      // Output elements
    panelS.add("South", resultField);
    add("North", panelN);                              // Input at the top
    add("Center", panelC);                             // Buttons in the center
    add("South", panelS);                              // Result at the bottom
    celsToFahr.addActionListener(this);                // Register with listeners
    fahrToCels.addActionListener(this);
    setSize(175,200);
  } // TemperatureJPanel()

  public void actionPerformed(ActionEvent e)
  { String inputStr = inField.getText();               // User's input
    double userInput = double.parseDouble(inputStr);   // Convert to double
    double result = 0;
    if (e.getSource() == celsToFahr) {                 // Process and report
      result = temperature.celsToFahr(userInput);
      resultField.setText(inputStr + " C = " + result  + " F");
    } else {
      result = temperature.fahrToCels(userInput);
      resultField.setText(inputStr + " F = " + result  + " C");
    }
  } // actionPerformed()
} // TemperatureJPanel class
```

SOLUTION 5.16

```java
public class KBTestOneRowNim
{  public static void main(String argv[])
   {  KeyboardReader kb = new KeyboardReader();
      OneRowNim game = new OneRowNim(11);
      while(game.gameOver() == false)
      {  game.report();                              // Prompt the user
         System.out.print("Input 1, 2, or 3: ");
         int sticks = kb.getKeyboardInteger();       // Get move
         game.takeSticks(sticks);                     // Do move
         System.out.println();
      } // while
      game.report();                                  // The game is now over
      System.out.print("Game won by player ");
      System.out.println(game.getWinner());
   } // main()
} // KBTestOneRowNim class
```

SOLUTION 5.17 The new version of OneRowNim should run properly with the user interface from Chapter 4. This shows that our new definition for OneRowNim is backward compatible with the old user interface. This is a good thing.

SOLUTION 5.18

```java
public class NimPlayer
{  private OneRowNim nim;
   public NimPlayer (OneRowNim game)
   {  nim = game;
   } // NimPlayer()
   public int move()
   {  int sticksLeft = nim.getSticks();
      if (sticksLeft % (nim.MAX_PICKUP + 1) != 1)
         return (sticksLeft - 1) % (nim.MAX_PICKUP +1);
      else
      {  int maxPickup = Math.min(nim.MAX_PICKUP, sticksLeft);
         return 1 + (int)(Math.random() * maxPickup);
      } // else
   } // move()
} // NimPlayer class
```

SOLUTION 5.19

```java
public class KBComputerNim
{ public static void main(String argv[])
    {    KeyboardReader kb = new KeyboardReader();
      OneRowNim game = new OneRowNim(OneRowNim.MAX_STICKS);
      NimPlayer computer = new NimPlayer(game);
      System.out.println("Let's play One Row Nim");
      while(game.gameOver() == false)  {
        if (game.getPlayer() == game.PLAYER_ONE)
        { kb.prompt("Sticks left = " + game.getSticks() + "Your move.");// Prompt
          kb.prompt("You can pick up between 1 and " +
            Math.min(game.MAX_PICKUP,game.getSticks()) +" :");
          int sticks = kb.getKeyboardInteger();          // Get move
          game.takeSticks(sticks);                        // Do move
        } else
        { kb.prompt("Sticks left = " + game.getSticks() + " My move. ");
          int sticks = computer.move();
          game.takeSticks(sticks);
          System.out.println("I take " + sticks);
        } // else
      } // while

                                                   // The game is now over
      kb.display("Sticks left = " + game.getSticks());
      if (game.getWinner() == game.PLAYER_ONE)
        System.out.println(" You win. Nice game!");
      else
        System.out.println(" I win. Nice game!");
    } // main()
} // KBComputerNim class
```

SOLUTION 5.20

```java
public class BankCD
{ private double principal;              // The CD's initial principal
  private double rate;                   // CD's interest rate
  private double years;                  // Number of years to maturity
  public BankCD(double p, double r, double y)
  {    principal = p;
    rate = r;
    years = y;
  } // BandCD()
  public double calcYearly()
  {    return principal * Math.pow(1 + rate, years);
  } // calcYearly()
  public double calcDaily()
  {    return principal * Math.pow(1 + rate/365, years*365);
  } // calcDaily()
} // BankCD class
```

SOLUTION 5.21

```java
import java.text.NumberFormat;   // For formatting $nn.dd or n%

public class TestBankCD
{ private KeyboardReader reader = new KeyboardReader();
  private NumberFormat dollars = NumberFormat.getCurrencyInstance();
  private NumberFormat percent = NumberFormat.getPercentInstance();
  private BankCD cd;
  public void run()
  { reader.display("Compares daily and annual compounding for a CD.\n");
    reader.prompt("Input the CD's initial principal, e.g.  1000.55 > ");
    double principal = reader.getKeyboardDouble();
    reader.prompt("Input the CD's interest rate, e.g.  6.5 > ");
    double rate = reader.getKeyboardDouble() / 100.0;
    reader.prompt("Input the number of years to maturity, e.g., 10.5 > ");
    double years = reader.getKeyboardDouble();
    cd = new BankCD(principal, rate, years);
    percent.setMaximumFractionDigits(2);
    System.out.println(" For Principal = " + dollars.format(principal) +
                       " Rate = " + percent.format(rate) +
                       " Years = " + years);
    double cdAnnual = cd.calcYearly();          // Compounded yearly
    double cdDaily =  cd.calcDaily();           // Compounded annually
    System.out.println(" The maturity value compounded yearly is " +
                  dollars.format(cdAnnual));
    System.out.println(" The maturity value compounded daily is: " +
                  dollars.format(cdDaily));
  } // run()
  public static void main( String args[] )
  { TestBankCD cd = new TestBankCD();
    cd.run();
  } // main()
} // TestBankCD class
```

SOLUTION 5.22

a. valid

b. valid

c. ch2 = (char)n;

d. valid

e. ch1 = (char)(m-n);

EXERCISES

Note: For programming exercises, **first** draw a UML class diagram describing all classes and their inheritance relationships and/or associations.

EXERCISE 5.1   Explain the difference between the following pairs of terms:

a. *Representation* and *action*.

b. *Binary operator* and *unary operation*.

c. *Class constant* and *class variable*.

d. *Helper method* and *class method*.

e. *Operator overloading* and *method overloading*.

f. *Method call* and *method composition*.

g. *Type conversion* and *type promotion*.

EXERCISE 5.2   For each of the following data types, list how many bits are used in its representation and how many values can be represented:

   a. `int`
   b. `char`
   c. `byte`
   d. `long`
   e. `double`

EXERCISE 5.3   Fill in the blanks.

   a. Methods and variables that are associated with a class rather than with its instances must be declared _____ .
   b. When an operation involves values of two different types, one value must be _____ before the expression can be evaluated.
   c. Constants should be declared _____ .
   d. Variables that take `true` and `false` as their possible values are known as _____ .

EXERCISE 5.4   Arrange the following data types into a *promotion* hierarchy: `double`, `float`, `int`, `short`, `long`.

EXERCISE 5.5   Assuming that *o1* is true, *o2* is false, and *o3* is false, evaluate each of the following expressions:

   a. `o1 || o2 && o3`
   b. `o1 ^ o2`
   c. `!o1 && !o2`

EXERCISE 5.6   Arrange the following operators in precedence order:

```
+ - () * / % < ==
```

EXERCISE 5.7   Arrange the following operators into a precedence hierarchy:

```
*,++, %, ==
```

EXERCISE 5.8   Parenthesize and evaluate each of the following expressions (if an expression is invalid, mark it as such):

   a. `11 / 3 % 2 == 1`
   b. `11 / 2 % 2 > 0`
   c. `15 % 3 >= 21 %`
   d. `12.0 / 4.0 >= 12 / 3`
   e. `15 / 3 == true`

EXERCISE 5.9 What value would *m* have after each of the statements that follow is executed? Assume that *m, k, j* are reinitialized before each statement.

```
int m = 5, k = 0, j = 1;
```

a. `m = ++k + j;`
b. `m += ++k * j;`
c. `m %= ++k + ++j;`
d. `m = m - k - j;`
e. `m = ++m;`

EXERCISE 5.10 What value would *b* have after each of the statements that follow is executed? Assume that *m, k, j* are reinitialized before each statement. It may help to parenthesize the right-hand side of the statements before evaluating them.

```
boolean b;
int m = 5, k = 0, j = 1;
```

a. `b = m > k + j;`
b. `b = m * m != m * j;`
c. `b = m <= 5 && m % 2 == 1;`
d. `b = m < k  || k < j;`
e. `b = --m == 2 * ++j;`

EXERCISE 5.11 For each of the following expressions, if it is valid, determine the value of the variable on the left-hand side (if not, change it to a valid expression):

```
char c = 'a' ;
int  m = 95;
```

a. `c = c + 5;`
b. `c = 'A' + 'B';`
c. `m = c + 5;`
d. `c = (char) m + 1;`
e. `m = 'a' - 32;`

EXERCISE 5.12 Translate each of the following expressions into Java:

a. Area equals *pi* times the radius squared.
b. Area is assigned *pi* times the radius squared.
c. Volume is assigned *pi* times radius cubed divided by *h*.
d. If *m* and *n* are equal, then *m* is incremented by one; otherwise *n* is incremented.
e. If *m* is greater than *n* times 5, then square *m* and double *n*; otherwise square *n* and double *m*.

EXERCISE 5.13   What would be output by the following code segment?

```
int m - 0, n - 0, j - 0, k - 0;
m = 2 * n++;
System.out.println("m= " + m + " n= " + n);
j += ( --k * 2 );
System.out.println("j= " + j + " k= " + k);
```

Each of the problems that follow asks you to write a method. Test the method as you develop it in a stepwise fashion. Here's a simple application program that you can use for this purpose:

```
public class MethodTester {
    public static int square(int n) {
        return n * n;
    }

    public static void main(String args[]) {
        System.out.println("5 squared = " + square(5));
    }
}
```

Replace the `square()` method with your method. Note that you must declare your method `static` if you want to call it directly from `main()` as we do here.

EXERCISE 5.14   Write a method to calculate the sales tax for a sale item. The method should take two `double` parameters, one for the sales price and the other for the tax rate. It should return a `double`. For example, `calcTax(20.0, 0.05)` should return 1.0.

EXERCISE 5.15   **Challenge:** Suppose you're writing a program that tells what day of the week someone's birthday falls on this year. Write a method that takes an `int` parameter representing what day of the year it is and returns a `String` like "Monday". For example, for 2004, a leap year, the first day of the year was on Thursday. The thirty-second day of the year (February 1, 2004) was a Sunday, so `getDayOfWeek(1)` should return "Thursday", and `getDayOfWeek(32)` should return "Sunday". (*Hint*: If you divide the day of the year by 7, the remainder will always be a number between 0 and 6, which can be made to correspond to days of the week.)

EXERCISE 5.16   **Challenge:** As part of the birthday program, you'll want a method that takes the month and the day as parameters and returns what day of the year it is. For example, `getDay(1,1)` should return 1; `getDay(2,1)` should return 32; and `getDay(12,31)` should return 365. (*Hint*: If the month is 3, and the day is 5, you have to add the number of days in January plus the number of days in February to 5 to get the result: 31 + 28 + 5 = 64.)

EXERCISE 5.17   Write a Java method that converts a `char` to lowercase. For example, `toLowerCase('A')` should return `'a'`. Make sure you guard against method calls like `toLowerCase('a')`.

EXERCISE 5.18   Challenge: Write a Java method that shifts a char by *n* places in the alphabet, wrapping around to the start of the alphabet, if necessary. For example, shift('a',2) should return 'c'; shift('y',2) should return 'a'. This method can be used to create a Caesar cipher, in which every letter in a message is shifted by *n* places—hfuju? (Refer to the Chapter 1 exercises for a refresher on Caesar cipher.)

EXERCISE 5.19   Write a method that converts its boolean parameter to a String. For example, boolToString(true) should return "true".

EXERCISE 5.20   Write a Java application that first prompts the user for three numbers that represent the sides of a rectangular cube, and then computes and outputs the volume and the surface area of the cube.

EXERCISE 5.21   Write a Java application that prompts the user for three numbers and then outputs them in increasing order.

EXERCISE 5.22   Write a Java application that inputs two integers and then determines whether the first is divisible by the second. (*Hint*: Use the modulus operator.)

EXERCISE 5.23   Write a Java application that prints the following table:

```
N    SQUARE    CUBE
1    1         1
2    4         8
3    9         27
4    16        64
5    25        125
```

EXERCISE 5.24   Design and write a Java GUI that converts kilometers to miles, and vice versa. Use a JTextField for I/O and JButtons for the various conversion actions.

EXERCISE 5.25   Design and write a GUI that allows a user to calculate the maturity value of a CD. The user should enter the principal, interest rate, and years, and the applet should then display the maturity value. Make use of the BankCD class covered in this chapter. Use separate JTextFields for the user's inputs and a separate JTextField for the result.

EXERCISE 5.26   Design and write a GUI that lets the user input a birth date (month and day) and reports what day of the week it falls on. Use the getDayOfWeek() and getDay() methods that you developed in previous exercises.

EXERCISE 5.27   Design and write a GUI that allows users to input their exam grades for a course and computes their averages and probable letter grades. The applet should contain a single JTextField for inputting a grade and a single JTextField for displaying the average and letter grade. The program should keep track internally of how many grades each student has entered. Whenever a new grade is entered, it should display the current average and probable letter grade.

EXERCISE 5.28   One of the reviewers of this text has suggested an alternative design for the Temperature class (Fig. 5.5). According to this design, the class would contain an instance variable, say, temperature, and access methods that operate on it. The access methods would be: setFahrenheit(double), getFahrenheit():double, setCelsius(double), and getCelsius(): double. One way to implement this design is to store the temperature in the Kelvin scale and then convert from and to Kelvin in the access methods. The formula for converting Kelvin to Celsius is

```
K = C + 273.15
```

Draw a UML class diagram representing this design of the Temperature class. Which design is more object oriented, this one or the one used in Figure 5.5?

EXERCISE 5.29   Write an implementation of the Temperature class using the design described in the preceding exercise.

Photograph courtesy of John Matchett / ACE Photo Agency, Picture Perfect USA, Inc.

Control Structures

6

OBJECTIVES

After studying this chapter, you will

- Be able to solve problems involving repetition.
- Understand the differences between various loop structures.
- Know the principles used to design effective loops.
- Improve your algorithm design skills.
- Understand the goals and principles of structured programming.

OUTLINE

6.1 Introduction

As we learned in Chapter 3, a control structure is a language element that changes the flow of control of a program. Thus far, we have used the `if` and `if/else` statements to select between two or more alternative paths in a program. We have used the `while`-loop structure to repeat statements. And we have used method-call-and-return to invoke methods that carry out certain well-defined tasks in a program.

In this chapter we will extend our repertoire of control structures. We will introduce the *for* and *do-while* statements, both of which are used in programs that require calculations to be repeated. We will also introduce the `switch` statement, which will give us another way, in addition to `if/else`, to select from among several alternative paths in a program.

We begin by introducing the idea of a *counting loop*, which is used for repetitive tasks when you know beforehand exactly how many repetitions are necessary. This type of loop is most often implemented using a `for` statement.

We then distinguish two kinds of *conditional loops*, which are used for performing repetitive tasks where the number of repetitions depends on a noncounting condition. These kinds of loops are usually implemented using Java's `while` and `do-while` statements. We give examples of several kinds of *loop bounds* and use them to identify several useful principles of loop design. Finally, we introduce some of the key principles of the *structured programming* approach, a disciplined design approach that preceded the object-oriented approach.

6.2 Flow of Control: Repetition Structures

As we saw in Chapter 3, a **repetition structure** is a control structure that repeats a statement or sequence of statements. Many programming tasks require a repetition structure. Consider some examples.

- You're working for the National Security Agency trying to decipher secret messages intercepted from foreign spies, and you want to count the number of times a certain letter, "a," occurs in a document containing *N* characters. In this case, you would employ something like the following (pseudocode) algorithm:

```
initialize totalAs to 0
for each character in the document
    if the character is an 'a'
        add 1 to totalAs
return totalAs as the result
```

- You're working for a caterer who wants to number the invitations to a client's wedding, so you need to print the numbers between 1 and 5000 on the invitation cards (it's a big wedding)! In this case, you want to go through each number, 1 to 5000, and simply print it out:

```
for each number, N, from 1 to 5000
    print N on the invitation card
```

- You are helping the forest service in Alaska to track the number of black bear sightings, and you want to compute the average number of sightings per month. Suppose the user enters each month's count at the keyboard, and uses a special number, say, 9999, to signify the end of the sequence. However, 9999 should not be figured into the average. This example differs a bit from the preceding ones, because here you don't know exactly how many numbers the user will input:

```
initialize sumOfBears to 0
initialize numOfMonths to 0
repeat the following steps
    read a number from the keyboard
    if the number is NOT 9999
        add it to the sumOfBears
        add 1 to numOfMonths
until the number read is 9999
divide sumOfBears by numOfMonths giving average
return average as the result
```

We repeat the process of reading numbers and adding them to a running total "until the number read is 9999."

- Student records are stored in a file and you want to calculate Erika Wilson's current GPA. Here we need to perform a repetitive process—searching through the file for Erika Wilson's record—but again we don't know exactly how many times to repeat the process:

```
repeat the following steps
    read a record from the file
until Erika Wilson's record is read
compute Erika Wilson's GPA
return gpa as the result
```

As these examples suggest, two types of loops are used: counting loops and noncounting loops. Counting loops are used whenever you know in advance exactly how many times an action must be performed. Noncounting loops are used when the number of repetitions depends on some condition—for example, the number of data items input from the keyboard or the input of a particular record from a file.

6.3   Counting Loops

A **counting loop**, or *counter-controlled loop*, is a loop in which you know beforehand how many times it will be repeated. Among the preceding examples, the first two are counting loops.

Because you know the exact number of times the loop repeats beforehand, a counting loop can be made dependent on the value of a counter. For example, if you want to print the word "Hello" 100 times, you can use the following `while` structure:

```
int k = 0;
while (k < 100) {
    System.out.println("Hello");
    k++;
}
```

In this case, the counter is the variable k, which counts from 0 through 99—that is, it counts 100
times. Note that we start counting from 0 instead of 1. Counting from 0 is known as **zero
indexing**, and it is a common programming convention for counting loops. Although it doesn't
really make any practical difference in this case, later on we will use loops to process structures,
such as strings and arrays, which use zero indexing. It will be easier to process these structures
if our loop counter also starts at 0.

Zero indexing

The variable k in this example is called a *counter variable* or *loop counter*. Although it is
certainly possible to name the counter variable anything we like, it is customary to use single
letters like i, j, and k as loop counters. The fundamental feature of a counting loop is that we
must know beforehand exactly how many iterations the loop will take.

Loop counter

EFFECTIVE DESIGN: Loop Design.   A *counting loop* can be used whenever you know
exactly how many times a process must be repeated.

Although we can use a `while`-structure to code a counting loop, Java's `for` statement is ideally
suited for this purpose. For example, the following `for` statement will also print the word
"Hello" 100 times:

```
for (int k = 0; k < 100; k++)
    System.out.println("Hello");
```

In fact, this `for` statement is equivalent to the preceding `while` structure.

The `for` statement has the following syntax:

JAVA LANGUAGE RULE   For **Statement.** The `for` statement has the following syntax:

for   (*initializer; loop entry condition; updater*)
                  for loop body

The `for` statement begins with the keyword `for`, which is followed by a parenthesized list
of three expressions separated by semicolons: an **initializer**, a **loop-entry condition**, and
an **updater**. Following the parenthesized list is the **for loop body**, which is either a single
statement or a sequence of statements contained in curly brackets, {...}.

6.3.1   The `for` Structure

Figure 6.1 shows how the `for` statement works. It might be useful to compare this flowchart
with the flowchart for the `while` structure (Fig. 6.2), which was introduced in Chapter 3. As
you can see, it has exactly the same structure. The initializer is evaluated first. Thus, the
initializer sets the integer variable k to 0. Then the loop-entry condition, which must be a

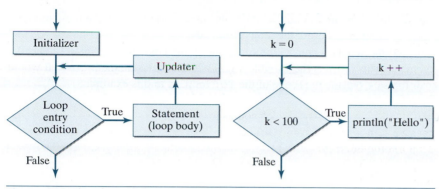

Figure 6.1 Flowchart of the `for` statement.

boolean expression, is evaluated. If it is true, the body of the loop is executed; if it is false, the body of the loop is skipped and control passes to the next statement following the `for` statement. The updater is evaluated after the loop body is executed. After completion of the updater, the loop-entry condition is reevaluated and the loop body is either executed again or not, depending on the truth value of the loop-entry condition. This process is repeated until the loop-entry condition becomes false.

Tracing the order in which the `for` loop components are evaluated gives this sequence:

```
evaluate initializer
evaluate loop entry condition ==> True
execute for loop body;
evaluate updater
evaluate loop entry condition ==> True
execute for loop body;
evaluate updater
evaluate loop entry condition ==> True
execute for loop body;
evaluate updater
 .
 .
 .
evaluate loop entry condition ==> False
```

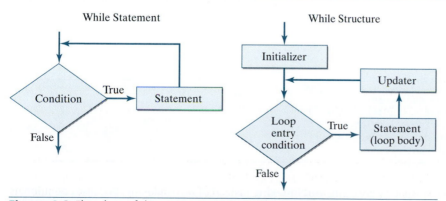

Figure 6.2 Flowchart of the `while` statement and `while` structure.

As this trace shows, the loop-entry condition controls entry to the body of the loop and will, therefore, be the last thing done before the loop terminates.

Loop variable scope

We have followed the standard convention of declaring the counter variable in the header of the `for` statement. This restricts the variable's *scope* to the `for` statement itself. It would be a syntax error to use *k* outside the scope of the `for` loop, as in this example:

```java
for (int k = 0; k < 100; k++)
  System.out.println("Hello");
                                  // Syntax error, k undeclared
System.out.println("k = " + k);
```

For some problems, it might be necessary to use the loop variable outside the scope of the `for` statement, in which case the variable should be declared before the `for` statement. For example, if we want to print the value of the loop variable, k, after the loop completes, we have to declare it before the loop:

```java
int k = 0;                       // Declare the loop variable here
for (k = 0; k < 100; k++)
    System.out.println("Hello");
System.out.println("k = " + k);  // To use it here
```

In this example, the loop will exit when k becomes 100, so "k = 100" will be printed.

6.3.2   Loop Bounds

Loop bound

A counting loop starts at some initial value and counts zero or more iterations. A **loop bound** is a value that controls how many times a loop is repeated. A loop will repeat until its loop bound is reached. In a counting loop, the *loop-entry condition* should be a boolean expression that tests whether the loop's bound has been reached. Similarly, in a counting loop, the *updater* should modify the loop counter so that it makes progress toward reaching its bound. Counting loops often increment or decrement their counter by 1, depending on whether the loop is counting forward or backward. The following method contains a countdown loop, which prints 10 9 8 7 6 5 4 3 2 1 BLASTOFF. In this case, progress toward the loop bound is made by decrementing the loop counter:

```java
public void countdown() {
    for (int k = 10; k > 0; k--)
        System.out.print(k + " ");
    System.out.println("BLASTOFF");
} // countdown()
```

Unit indexing

Note in this case that we are using **unit indexing** instead of zero indexing, because countdowns repeat, or *iterate*, from 10 down to 1, not from 10 down to 0.

6.3.3   Infinite Loops

If the loop bound is never reached, the loop-entry condition will never become false and the loop will repeat forever. This is known as an **infinite loop**. Can you see why each of the following `for` statements will result in an infinite loop?

Infinite loop

```java
for (int k = 0; k < 100; k--)        // Infinite loop
    System.out.println("Hello");
for (int k = 1; k != 100; k+=2)      // Infinite loop
    System.out.println("Hello");
for (int k = 98; k < 100; k = k / 2) // Infinite loop
    System.out.println("Hello");
```

In the first example, k starts out at 0 and is decremented on each iteration, taking on values $-1, -2, -3$, and so on, so k will never reach its loop bound.

In the second example, k starts out at 1 and is incremented by 2 on each iteration, taking on the values 3, 5, 7, and so on. Because all these values are odd, k will never equal 100. A much safer loop bound in this case would be $k <= 100$.

In the third example, k starts out at 98 and is halved on each iteration, taking on the values 49, 24, 12, 6, 3, 1, 0, 0, and so on, forever. Thus, it too will be stuck in an infinite loop.

Encountering an unintended infinite loop when developing a program can be very frustrating. If the program is stuck in a loop that generates output, it will be obvious that it is looping, but if no output is being generated, the computer will appear to "freeze," no longer responding to your keyboard or mouse commands. Some programming environments allow you to break out of a looping program by typing a special keyboard command such as CONTROL-C or CTRL-ALT-DELETE or CONTROL-APPLE-ESCAPE, but if that doesn't work you will have to reboot the computer, possibly causing a loss of data. The best way to avoid infinite loops is to determine that the loop's updater expression will cause the loop to eventually reach its bound.

Stuck in a loop

> **EFFECTIVE DESIGN: Loop Design.**   To guard against infinite loops, make sure that the loop bound will eventually be reached.

6.3.4   Loop Indentation

Note how indentation is used to distinguish the loop body both from the heading and from the statement that follows the loop:

```java
for (int k = 10; k > 0; k--)       // Loop heading
    System.out.print (k + " ");    // Indent the body
System.out.println( "BLASTOFF" )   // After the loop
```

Indenting the loop body is a stylistic convention intended to make the code more readable. However, the indentation itself has no effect on how the code is interpreted by Java. Each of the following code segments would still produce the same countdown:

```
for (int k = 10; k > 0; k--)
System.out.print (k + " ");
System.out.println("BLASTOFF");

for (int k = 10; k > 0; k--) System.out.print(k +" ");
System.out.println("BLASTOFF");

for
(int k = 10; k > 0; k--)
System.out.print (k + " ");
System.out.println("BLASTOFF");
```

In each case the statement, `System.out.println("BLASTOFF")`, is not part of the `for` loop body and is executed only once when the loop terminates.

JAVA PROGRAMMING TIP: Loop Indentation.   To make loops more readable, indent the loop body to set it off from the heading and to highlight which statement(s) will be repeated.

DEBUGGING TIP: Loop Indentation.   Loop indentation has no effect on how Java interprets the loop. The loop body is determined entirely by the syntax of the `for` statement.

Up to this point the loop body has consisted of a single statement, such as a `println()` statement. But the loop body may consist of any Java statement, including an `if` or `if-else` statement or a compound statement, which contains a sequence of statements enclosed within braces. Consider the following examples. The first example prints the sequence 0, 5, 10, 15, ... 95. Its loop body consists of a single `if` statement:

```
for (int k = 0; k < 100; k++) // Print 0 5 10... 95
   if (k % 5 == 0)             // Loop body: single if statement
      System.out.println("k= " + k);
```

The next example prints the lowercase letters of the alphabet. In this case, the loop counter is of type `char`, and it counts the letters of the alphabet. The loop body consists of a single `print()` statement:

```
for (char k = 'a'; k <= 'z'; k++) // Print 'a' 'b'... 'z'
   System.out.print (k + " ");    // Loop body: single print()
```

The next example prints the sequence 5, 10, 15, ... 50, but it uses several statements within the loop body:

```
for (int k = 1; k <= 10; k++) {    // Print 5 10 15... 50
   int m = k * 5;                  // Begin body
   System.out.print (m + " ");
}                                  // End body
```

In this example, the scope of the local variable *m*, declared within the loop body, is limited to the loop body and cannot be used outside of that scope.

> **JAVA LANGUAGE RULE** **Loop Body.** The body of a `for` statement consists of the statement that immediately follows the `for` loop heading. This statement can be either a simple statement or a compound statement—a sequence of statements enclosed within braces, {...}.

Although braces are not required when the body of a `for` loop consists of a single statement, some coding styles recommend that braces should always be used for the body of a loop statement. For example, it is always correct to code a `for` loop as

```
for (int k = 1; k <= 10; k++) {  // Print 1 2 ...  10
    System.out.print (k + " ");   // Begin body
}                                 // End body
```

Another advantage of this coding style is that you can easily place additional statements in the loop body by placing them within the braces.

> **DEBUGGING TIP: Missing Braces.**   A common programming error for novices is to forget to use braces to group the statements they intend to put in the loop body. When braces are not used, only the first statement after the loop heading will be iterated.

SELF-STUDY EXERCISES

EXERCISE 6.1   Identify the syntax error in the following `for` loop statements.

a.

```
for (int k = 5, k < 100, k++)
    System.out.println(k);
```

b.

```
for (int k = 0; k < 12 ; k--;)
    System.out.println(k);
```

EXERCISE 6.2   Identify statements that result in infinite loops.

a.

```
for (int k = 0; k < 100; k = k )
    System.out.println(k);
```

b.

```
for (int k = 1; k == 100; k = k + 2 )
    System.out.println(k);
```

c.

```
for (int k = 1; k >= 100; k = k - 2 )
    System.out.println(k);
```

EXERCISE 6.3 Suppose you're helping your little sister learn to count by fours. Write a `for` loop that prints the following sequence of numbers: 1, 5, 9, 13, 17, 21, 25.

EXERCISE 6.4 What value will j have when the following loop terminates?

```
for (int i = 0; i < 10; i++) {
    int j;
    j = j + 1;
}
```

6.3.5 Nested Loops

A **nested loop** is a structure in which one loop is contained inside the body of another loop, as when a `for` loop body contains a `for` loop. For example, suppose you are working for Giant Auto Industries, and your boss wants you to print a table for buyers to figure the cost of buying multiple quantities of a certain part. The cost of individual parts ranges from $1 to $9. The cost of N items is simply the unit price times the quantity. Thus, you'll want to print something like the following table of numbers, where the prices per unit are listed in the top row, and the prices for two, three, and four units are listed in subsequent rows:

```
1  2   3   4   5   6   7   8   9
2  4   6   8   10  12  14  16  18
3  6   9   12  15  18  21  24  27
4  8   12  16  20  24  28  32  36
```

To produce this multiplication table, we could use the following nested `for` loops:

```
1. for (int row = 1; row <= 4 ; row++) {      // For each of 4 rows
2.     for (int col = 1; col <= 9; col++)      // For each of 9 columns
3.         System.out.print(col * row + "\t" ); // Print number
4.     System.out.println();                    // Start a new row
5. } // for row
```

Inner and outer loop

Note how indenting is used here to distinguish the levels of nesting and to make the code more readable. In this example, the *outer loop* controls the number of rows in the table, hence our

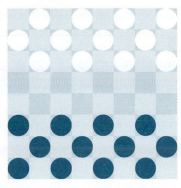

Figure 6.4 A checkerboard with checkers.

6.5 Graphics Example: Drawing a Checkerboard

In this section we will combine some of the graphics methods we have learned with the nested for-loop structure to draw a checkerboard with checkers on it (Fig. 6.4). For this example, we will concentrate on drawing the checkerboard. We will not worry about providing a full checkerboard representation of the sort we would need if we were writing a program to play the game of checkers. Thus, our design will not involve instance variables for whose turn it is, how many checkers each player has, where the checkers are located on the board, and other elements of the game's state. Still, our visible representation of the board should be designed to be useful in case we eventually want to develop a checkers game.

Problem Description and Specification

The specification for this problem is to develop a program that will draw a checkerboard and place the checkers on it in their appropriate starting positions. As with many of our programs, the design will involve two classes, one which defines the user interface and the other which represents the computational object. For this problem, the computational object will be defined in the CheckerBoard class. The details of its design are described in the next section.

Because the purpose of this example is to focus on how to use loops and drawing methods, we will employ a very simple applet interface, whose implementation is given in Figure 6.5.

```
import java.awt.*;
import java.applet.*;
import javax.swing.*;

public class CheckerBoardApplet extends JApplet {
    private CheckerBoard theBoard;

    public void init() {
        theBoard = new CheckerBoard();
    } // init()
    public void paint(Graphics g) {
        theBoard.draw(g);
    } // paint()
} // CheckerBoardApplet class
```

Figure 6.5 The CheckerBoardApplet class.

---

choice of row as its loop counter. The println() statement is executed after the *inner loop* is done iterating, which allows us to print a new row on each iteration of the outer loop. The inner loop prints the nine values in each row by printing the expression *col * row*. Obviously, the value of this expression depends on both loop variables.

Let's dissect this example a bit. How many times is the for statement in line 2 executed? The inner loop is executed once for each iteration of the outer loop. Thus, it is executed four times, which is the same number of times that line 4 is executed. How many times is the statement on line 3 executed? The body of the inner loop is executed 36 times—nine times for each execution of line 2.

Sometimes it is useful to use the loop variable of the outer loop as the bound for the inner loop. For example, consider the following pattern:

Algorithm design

```
# # # # #
# # # #
# # #
# #
#
```

The number of # symbols in each row varies inversely with the row number. In row 1, we have five symbols; in row 2 we have four; and so on down to row 5, where we have one #.

To produce this kind of two-dimensional pattern, we need two counters: one to count the row number, and one to count the number of # symbols in each row. Because we have to print each row's symbols before moving on to the next row, the outer loop will count row numbers, and the inner loop will count the symbols in each row. But note that the inner loop's bound will depend on the row number. Thus, in row 1 we want five symbols; in row 2 we want four symbols; and so on. If we let row be the row number, then in each row we want to print 6−*row* symbols. The following table shows the relationship we want:

Row	Bound (6−row)	Number of Symbols
1	6−1	5
2	6−2	4
3	6−3	3
4	6−4	2
5	6−5	1

If we let j be the counter for the inner loop, then j will be bound by the expression 6−*row*. This leads to the following nested loop structure:

```
for (int row = 1; row <= 5; row++) {   // For each row
  for (int j = 1; j <= 6 - row; j++)   // Print the row
    System.out.print('#');
  System.out.println();                // Start a new line
} // for row
```

Note that the bound of the inner loop varies according to the value of *row*, the loop counter for the outer loop.

SELF-STUDY EXERCISE

EXERCISE 6.5 As the engineer hired to design ski jumps, write a nested `for` loop to print the following pattern:

```
#
# #
# # #
# # # #
# # # # #
```

6.4 Example: Car Loan

Recall the self-study exercise from Chapter 5 that calculated the value of a bank CD (a) given its initial principal (p), interest rate (r), and number of years (n), using the formula $a = p(1 + r)^n$. This section explains how to use the same formula to calculate the cost of a car loan for different interest rates over various time periods.

Problem Description

Suppose you are planning on buying a car that costs $20,000. You find that you can get a car loan ranging anywhere from 8 to 11 percent, and you can have the loan for periods as short as two years and as long as eight years. Let's use our loop constructs to create a table to show what the car will actually cost you, including financing. In this case, a will represent the total cost of the car, including the financing, and p will represent the price tag on the car ($20,000):

```
           8%          9%          10%         11%
Year 2  $23,469.81  $23,943.82  $24,427.39  $24,920.71
Year 3  $25,424.31  $26,198.42  $26,996.07  $27,817.98
Year 4  $27,541.59  $28,665.32  $29,834.86  $31,052.09
Year 5  $29,835.19  $31,364.50  $32,972.17  $34,662.19
Year 6  $32,319.79  $34,317.85  $36,439.38  $38,692.00
Year 7  $35,011.30  $37,549.30  $40,271.19  $43,190.31
Year 8  $37,926.96  $41,085.02  $44,505.94  $48,211.60
```

Algorithm Design

Nested loop design

The key element in this program is the nested `for` loop that generates the table. Because the table contains seven rows, the outer loop should iterate seven times, through the values 2, 3, . . . 8:

```java
for (int years = 2; years <= 8; years++)
```

The inner loop should iterate through each of the interest rates, 8 through 11:

```java
for (int years = 2; years <= 8; years++) {
    for (int rate = 8; rate <= 11; rate++) {
    } // for rate
} // for years
```

The financing calculation should be placed in the body of the inner loop together with a statement to print one cell (not row) of the table. Suppose the variable we use for a in the formula is `carPriceWithLoan`, and the variable we use for the actual price of the car is `carPrice`. Then our inner loop body is

```java
carPriceWithLoan = carPrice * Math.pow(1 + rate/100.0/365.0, years * 365.0);
System.out.print(dollars.format(carPriceWithLoan) +"\t");
```

Note that the rate is divided by both 100.0 (to make it a percentage) and 365.0 (for daily compounding), and the year is multiplied by 365.0 before these values are passed to the `Math.pow()` method. It is important here to use 100.0 and not 100 so that the resulting value is a `double` and not the `int` 0.

Implementation

The program must also contain statements to print the row and column headings. The row headings should be printed within the outer loop, because each row must be printed. The column headings should be printed before the outer loop is entered. Finally, our program should contain code to format the dollar and cents values properly. For this we use the `java.text.NumberFormat` class described in Chapter 5. The complete program is shown in Figure 6.3.

Formatting output

```java
import java.text.NumberFormat;    // For formatting $nn.dd or n%

public class CarLoan {
  public static void main(String args[]) {
    double carPrice = 20000;               // Car's actual price
    double carPriceWithLoan;               // Total cost of the car plus financing
                                           // Number formatting code
    NumberFormat dollars = NumberFormat.getCurrencyInstance();
    NumberFormat percent = NumberFormat.getPercentInstance();
    percent.setMaximumFractionDigits(2);
                                  Print the table
    for (int rate = 8; rate <= 11; rate++) // Print the column heading
      System.out.print("\t" + percent.format(rate/100.0) + "\t" );
    System.out.println();

    for (int years = 2; years <= 8; years++) {  // For years 2 through 8
      System.out.print("Year " + years + "\t"); // Print row heading
      for (int rate = 8; rate <= 11; rate++) {  // Calc and print CD value
        carPriceWithLoan = carPrice *
              Math.pow(1 + rate / 100.0 / 365.0, years *  365.0);
        System.out.print( dollars.format(carPriceWithLoan)  + "\t");
      } // for rate
      System.out.println();                 // Start a new row
    } // for years
  } // main()
} // CarLoan class
```

Figure 6.3 The CarLoan application.

As shown there, the applet simply creates a `CheckerBoard` instance in its `init()` method, and then invokes the `CheckerBoard`'s `draw` method in its `paint()` method. The reason we invoke the `draw()` method in `paint()` is because we need to have access to the applet's `Graphics` context, which is passed as an argument to the `draw()` method. Recall that the `init()` method and then the `paint()` method are invoked automatically by the browser or appletviewer when an applet is started. Thus, the action taken by this applet is simply to draw a visual representation of the checkerboard.

Class Design: `CheckerBoard`

Because the applet will invoke its `draw()` method, this method must be part of the `Checker-Board`'s interface. Hence, it must be declared `public`. The task of drawing a checkerboard involves two distinct subtasks: (1) drawing the board itself, which will involve drawing a square with smaller squares of alternating colors; and (2) drawing the checkers on the checkerboard. A good design for the `draw()` method would be simply to invoke helper methods that encapsulate these two subtasks. This is good method design because it results in relatively small methods, each of which performs a very well-defined task. Let's call these methods `draw-Board()` and `drawCheckers()`, respectively. Their signatures are shown in Figure 6.6, which summarizes the design of the `CheckerBoard` class.

Before getting into the details of the `drawBoard` and `drawCheckers()` methods, we must first discuss `CheckerBoard`'s several instance variables. The first two variables, LEFT_X and UPPER_Y, give the absolute position of the upper-left corner of the checkerboard on the applet's drawing panel. The SQ_SIDE variable gives the size of the checkerboard's individual squares. N_ROWS and N_COLS give the number of rows and columns in the checkerboard (typically, 8 by 8). All of these variables are integers. The final four variables, SQ_COLOR1, SQ_COLOR2, CHECKER_COLOR1, and CHECKER_COLOR2, specify the colors of the checkerboard and the checkers.

The names of all the instance variables are written in uppercase letters. This is to identify them as symbolic constants—that is, as final variables whose values do not change once they are initialized. Because their actual values are not important, we do not show them in the UML diagram and we won't discuss them here. Recall that the advantage of defining class constants, rather than sprinkling literal values throughout the program, is that they make it easy to modify the program if we decide to change the size, location, or color of the checkerboard.

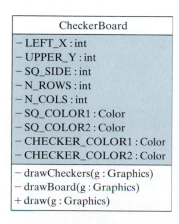

Figure 6.6 Design of the Checker-Board class.

Method Design

Returning now to the design of `CheckerBoard`'s instance methods, the complete definition of the `CheckerBoard` class is given in Figure 6.7. Note how simple its `draw()` method is. As we noted earlier, in order to use Java's drawing commands, it is necessary to have a reference to a `Graphics` object. This is passed to the `draw()` method when the `draw()` method is invoked

```java
import java.awt.*;

public class CheckerBoard {
                                        // Default values for a standard checkerboard
  private final int LEFT_X = 10;                    // Position of left
  private final int UPPER_Y = 10;                   // upper corner
  private final int SQ_SIDE = 40;                   // Size of each square
  private final int N_ROWS = 8;                     // Checkerboard rows
  private final int N_COLS = 8;                     // Checkerboard columns
  private final Color SQ_COLOR1 = Color.lightGray;  // Colors
  private final Color SQ_COLOR2 = Color.gray;       // of squares
  private final Color CHECKER_COLOR1 = Color.white; // and
  private final Color CHECKER_COLOR2 = Color.black; // checkers

  private void drawBoard(Graphics g) {
    for(int row = 0; row < N_ROWS; row++)           // For each row
      for(int col = 0; col < N_COLS; col++) {       // For each square
        if ((row + col) % 2 == 0)                   // Alternate colors
          g.setColor(SQ_COLOR1);                    // Light
        else
          g.setColor(SQ_COLOR2);                    // or dark
        g.fillRect(LEFT_X+col*SQ_SIDE,
                   UPPER_Y+row*SQ_SIDE,SQ_SIDE,SQ_SIDE);
    } // for
  } // drawBoard()

  private void drawCheckers(Graphics g) {           // Place checkers
    for(int row = 0; row < N_ROWS; row++)           // For each row
      for(int col = 0; col < N_COLS; col++)         // For each square
        if ((row + col)%2 == 1) {                   // One player has top 3 rows
          if (row < 3) {
            g.setColor(CHECKER_COLOR1);
            g.fillOval(LEFT_X+col*SQ_SIDE,
                       UPPER_Y+row*SQ_SIDE,SQ_SIDE-2,SQ_SIDE-2);
          } // if
          if (row >= N_ROWS - 3) {                  // Other has bottom 3 rows
            g.setColor(CHECKER_COLOR2);
            g.fillOval(LEFT_X+col*SQ_SIDE,
                       UPPER_Y+row*SQ_SIDE,SQ_SIDE-2,SQ_SIDE-2);
          } // if
        } // if
  } // drawCheckers()

  public void draw(Graphics g) {                    // Draw board and checkers
    drawBoard(g);
    drawCheckers(g);
  } // draw()
} // CheckerBoard class
```

Figure 6.7   The CheckerBoard class.

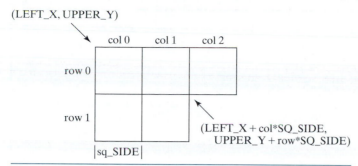

(LEFT_X, UPPER_Y)

col 0   col 1   col 2

row 0

row 1

(LEFT_X + col*SQ_SIDE,
UPPER_Y + row*SQ_SIDE)

|sq_SIDE|

Figure 6.8 Calculating the locations of the checkerboard squares.

in the applet. Because the `draw()` method delegates the details of the drawing algorithm to its helper methods, `drawBoard()` and `drawCheckers()`, it has to pass them a reference to the `Graphics` object.

The `drawBoard()` method uses a nested `for` loop to draw an 8×8 array of rectangles of alternating colors. The loop variables, `row` and `col`, both range from 0 to 7. The expression used to determine alternating colors tests whether the sum of the row and column subscripts is even: $((row + col)\%2 == 0)$. If their sum is even, we use one color; if odd, we use the other color.

As the table in the margin shows for a 4×4 board, the sum of a board's row and column subscripts alternates between even and odd values. Thus, in row 2 column 3, the sum of the subscripts is 5.

To switch from one color to the other, we use the `Graphics setColor()` method to alternate between the two colors designated for the checkerboard, `SQ_COLOR1` and `SQ_COLOR2`. We then use the following method call to draw the colored squares:

	0	1	2	3
0	0	1	2	3
1	1	2	3	4
2	2	3	4	5
3	3	4	5	6

```
g.fillRect(LEFT_X+col*SQ_SIDE,UPPER_Y+row*SQ_SIDE,SQ_SIDE,SQ_SIDE);
```

Note how we use the loop variables, `row col`, together with the constants specifying the top-left corner of the board (`UPPER_Y` and `LEFT_X`) and the size of the squares (`SQ_SIDE`) to calculate the location and size of each square. The calculation here is illustrated in Figure 6.8. The first two parameters in `fillRect(left,top,width,height)` specify the coordinates for the rectangle's top-left corner. These are calculated as a function of the rectangle's row and column position within the checkerboard and the rectangle's width and height, which are equal for the squares of a checkerboard.

The `drawCheckers()` method also uses a nested `for` loop to trace through the checkerboard's rows and columns. In this case, however, we draw checkers only on the dark-colored squares—that is, those that satisfy the expression $(row + col)\%2 == 1)$—on the first three rows of each player's side of the board. So each player's checkers are initially located in the first three rows and last three rows of the checkerboard:

```
if ((row + col)%2 == 1) {                          // One player has top 3 rows
    if (row < 3){
        g.setColor(CHECKER_COLOR1);
        g.fillOval(LEFT_X+col*SQ_SIDE,
            UPPER_Y+row*SQ_SIDE,SQ_SIDE-2,SQ_SIDE-2);
    } // if
    if (row >= N_ROWS - 3) {                        // Other has bottom 3 rows
        g.setColor(CHECKER_COLOR2);
        g.fillOval(LEFT_X+col*SQ_SIDE,
            UPPER_Y+row*SQ_SIDE,SQ_SIDE-2,SQ_SIDE-2);
    } // if
} // if
```

Because the checkers are circles, we use the `fillOval()` method to draw them. Note that the parameters for `fillOval(left, top, width, height)` are identical to those for `fillRect()`. The parameters specify an enclosing rectangle in which the oval is inscribed. In this case, of course, the enclosing rectangle is a square, which causes `fillOval()` to draw a circle.

Our design of the `CheckerBoard` class illustrates an important principle of method design. First, rather than place all of the commands for drawing the checkerboard and the checkers into one method, we broke up this larger task into distinct subtasks. This resulted in small methods, each of which has a well-defined purpose.

EFFECTIVE DESIGN: Method Decomposition. Methods should be designed to have a clear focus. If you find a method becoming too long, you should break its algorithm into subtasks and define a separate method for each subtask.

6.6 Conditional Loops

Unlike the problems in the preceding sections, not all loops can be coded as counting loops. Here is a problem that can't be solved by a counting loop.

Mathematicians, especially number theorists, have found that certain operations on numbers lead to interesting sequences. For example, the $3N + 1$ *problem* is a conjecture in number theory which says that if N is any positive integer, then the sequence generated by the following rules will always terminate at 1.

```
Case            Operation
----            ---------
N is odd        N = 3 * N + 1
N is even       N = N / 2
```

In other words, start with any positive integer N. If N is odd, multiply it by 3 and add 1. If N is even, divide it by 2. In either case, assign the result back to N. The conjecture states that N will eventually equal 1. For example, if N is initially 26, then the sequence generated is 26, 13, 40, 20, 10, 5, 16, 8, 4, 2, 1.

The $3N + 1$ problem is an example of a noncounting loop. Because we don't know how long the $3N + 1$ sequence will be for any given N, we need a loop that terminates when the loop variable reaches a certain value, called a *sentinel* value—when N equals 1. This is an example of a loop that is terminated by a **sentinel bound**. With the exception of infinite loops, all loops are bounded by some condition, which is why they are sometimes referred to as **conditional loop** structures. The count and sentinel bounds are just special cases of the conditional loop structure.

Sentinel bound

6.6.1 The `while` Structure Revisited

Consider the following pseudocode algorithm for the $3N + 1$ problem:

```
Algorithm for computing the 3N+1 sequence
    While N is not equal to 1, do: {
        Print N.
        If N is even, divide it by 2.
        If N is odd, multiply N by 3 and add 1.
    }
    Print N
```

In this structure, the body of the loop prints N and then updates N's value, using the $3N + 1$ rules. Suppose N equals 5 when this code segment begins. It will print the following sequence: 5, 16, 8, 4, 2, 1. Note that the loop body is entered as long as N is not equal to 1. So the loop-entry condition in this case is $N \mathrel{!=} 1$. Conversely, the loop will terminate when N equals 1. Also note that in this code segment the loop bound is tested *before* the body of the loop is executed.

We can implement this algorithm using Java's `while` statement, whose flowchart is shown in Figure 6.2:

```java
while (N != 1) {                     // While N not equal to 1
    System.out.print(N + " ");   // Print N
    if (N % 2 == 0)                  // If N is even
        N = N / 2;                   //    divide it by 2
    else                             // If N is odd
        N = 3 * N + 1;               //    multiply by 3 and add 1
}
System.out.println(N);               // Print N
```

Recall that unlike the `for` statement, the `while` statement does not contain syntax for the initializer and the updater. These must be coded separately. As we pointed out in Chapter 3, the `while` structure (as opposed to the `while` statement) is a segment of code built by the programmer that satisfies the following design principle:

EFFECTIVE DESIGN: Loop Structure. A properly designed *loop structure* must include an *initializer* a *loop-entry condition*, and an *updater*. The updater should guarantee that the loop-entry condition will eventually become false, thereby causing the loop to terminate.

The `while` structure has the following form:

```
InitializerStatements;          // Initializer
while (loop-entry condition) {  // Bound test
    Statements;                 // Loop body
    UpdaterStatements;          // Updater
}
```

As its form suggests, the `while` structure is designed so that on some conditions the loop body will never be executed. Because it tests for the loop bound *before* the loop body, the loop body may never be executed. We might say that the `while` structure is designed to perform zero or more iterations.

For example, going back to the $3N + 1$ problem, what if N equals 1 initially? In that case, the loop body will be skipped, because the loop-entry condition is false to begin with. No iterations will be performed, and the algorithm will simply print the value 1.

The `while` structure would be an appropriate control structure for the following type of problem:

```
write the problems on the assignment sheet // Initializer
while there are problems on the sheet       // Bound test
    do a problem                            // Loop body
    cross it off the assignment sheet       // Updater
```

It is possible that the assignment sheet contains no homework problems to begin with. In that case, there's no work for the body of the loop to do, and it should be skipped.

SELF-STUDY EXERCISES

EXERCISE 6.6 Identify the syntax error in the following `while` structures:

a.

```
int k = 5;
while (k < 100) {
    System.out.println(k);
    k++
}
```

b.

```
int k = 0;
while (k < 12 ;) {
    System.out.println(k);
    k++;
}
```

EXERCISE 6.7   Determine the output and/or identify the error in each of the following `while` structures:

a.

```
int k = 0;
while (k < 100)
    System.out.println(k);
```

b.

```
while (k < 100) {
    System.out.println(k);
    k++;
}
```

EXERCISE 6.8   Your younger sister is now learning how to count by sixes. Write a `while` loop that prints the following sequence of numbers: 0, 6, 12, 18, 24, 30, 36.

EXERCISE 6.9   Here's another number theory problem. Start with any positive integer N. If N is even, divide it by 2. If N is odd, subtract 1 and then divide it by 2. This will generate a sequence that is guaranteed to terminate at 0. For example, if N is initially 15, then you get the sequence: 15, 7, 3, 1, 0. Write a method that implements this sequence using a `while` statement.

6.6.2   The `do-while` Structure

Here's another problem that can't be solved with a counting loop. Your father has been fretting about the bare spots on the front lawn and is considering hiring the ChemSure Lawn Service to fertilize. However, your scientifically minded younger sister wants to reassure him that at the rate the grass is dying, there will be enough to last through the summer. Using techniques she learned in biology, your sister estimates that the grass is dying at the rate of 2 percent per day. How many weeks will it take for half the lawn to disappear? *Problem description*

One way to solve this problem would be to keep subtracting 2 percent from the current amount of grass until the amount dips below 50 percent, all the while counting the number of iterations required. Consider the following pseudocode algorithm: *Algorithm design*

```
Algorithm for calculating grass loss
    Initialize amtGrass to 100.0
    Initialize nDays to 0
    Repeat the following statements
        amtGrass -= amtGrass * 0.02;
        ++nDays;
    As long as amtGrass > 50.0
    Print nDays / 7
```

We begin by initializing `amtGrass` to 100.0, representing 100 percent. And we initialize our counter, nDays to 0. Then we repeatedly subtract 2 percent of the amount and increment the counter until the amount drops below 50 percent. In other words, in this case, we repeat the loop body as long as the amount of grass remains above 50 percent of the original. When the loop finishes, we report the number of weeks it took by dividing the number of days by 7.

Limit bound   The loop bound in this case is known as a **limit bound**. The loop will terminate when a certain limit has been reached—in this case, when the amount of grass dips below 50 percent of the original amount. Note that in this case the loop bound is tested *after* the loop body. This is appropriate for this problem, because we know in advance that the loop will iterate at least once. We can implement this algorithm using Java's *do-while statement*:

```java
public int losingGrass(double perCentGrass) {
    double amtGrass = 100.0;             // Initialize amount grass
    int nDays = 0;                       // Initialize day counter
    do {                                 // Repeat
      amtGrass -= amtGrass * LOSSRATE;   // Update amount
      ++nDays;                           // Increment the counter
    } while (amtGrass > perCentGrass);
                                         // As long as enough grass remains
    return nDays / 7;                    // Return the number of weeks
} // losingGrass()
```

The **do-while statement** is a loop statement in which the loop-entry condition occurs after the loop body. It has the following general form:

> **JAVA LANGUAGE RULE** Do-While **Statement.** The `do-while` statement has the following syntax:
>
> > do   *loop body*
> > while   (*loop entry condition*);

Note, again, that unlike the `for` statement, the `do-while` statement does not contain syntax for the initializer and the updater. These must be coded separately.

To further highlight the difference between a loop statement and a loop structure, the `do-while` structure takes the following form:

```java
InitializerStatements1;              // Initializer
do {                                 // Beginning of loop body
  InitializerStatements2;            //   Another initializer
  Statements;                        //   Loop body
  UpdaterStatements                  //   Updater
} while (loop-entry condition);      // Bound test
```

Initializer statements may be placed before the loop body, at the beginning of the loop body, or in both places, depending on the problem. Like the other loop structures, updater statements occur within the body of the loop. A flowchart of the `do-while` structure is shown in Figure 6.9.

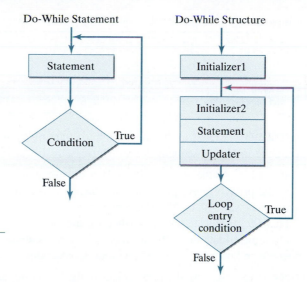

Figure 6.9 Flowchart of the do-while statement and do-while structure.

The `do-while` structure would be an appropriate control structure for the following type of problem:

```
do
  dial the desired telephone number   // Initializer
  if you get a busy signal
    hang up                           // Updater
while there is a busy signal          // Bound test
```

In this case, you want to perform the actions in the body of the loop at least once and possibly more than once (if you continue to receive a busy signal).

EFFECTIVE DESIGN: Do-While Loop.   The `do-while` loop is designed for solving problems in which at least one iteration must occur.

EFFECTIVE DESIGN: While versus Do-While Structures.   For problems where a non-counting loop is required, the `while` loop structure is more general and, therefore, preferable to the `do-while` structure. Use `do-while` only when at least one iteration must occur.

SELF-STUDY EXERCISES

EXERCISE 6.10   Identify the syntax error in the following `do-while` structures:

a.

```
int k = 0;
do while (k < 100)
{   System.out.println(k);
    k++
}
```

b.

```java
int k = 0;
do {
    System.out.println(k);
    k++;
} while (k < 12)
```

EXERCISE 6.11 Your sister has moved on to counting by sevens. Write a do-while loop that prints the following sequence of numbers: 1, 8, 15, 22, 29, 36, 43.

EXERCISE 6.12 As the owner of Pizza Heaven, every night at the close of business you quickly enter the price of every pizza ordered that day. You take the data from the servers' receipts. Pizzas cost $8, $10, or (the Heavenly Special) $15. You enter the data without dollar signs, and use 99 to indicate you're finished for the day. Write a Java method to input and validate a single pizza-data item. If an incorrect price is entered, the program should print an error message and prompt for corrected input. Correct input is used to compute a daily total.

EXERCISE 6.13 Because the pizza prices in the preceding exercise are fixed, you can save time on keyboarding by changing the method. Instead of entering the price, you'll enter codes of 1, 2, or 3 (corresponding to the $8, $10, and $15 pizzas), and 0 to indicate that you're finished. Validate that the data value entered is correct and then convert it to the corresponding price before returning it.

6.7   Example: Computing Averages

Algorithm design: what kind of loop?

Suppose you want to compute the average of your exam grades in a course. Grades, represented as real numbers, will be input from the keyboard using our KeyboardReader class. To signify the end of the list, we will use a sentinel value—9999 or −1 or some other value that won't be confused with a legitimate grade. Because we do not know exactly how many grades will be entered, we will use a noncounting loop in this algorithm. Because there could be no grades to average, we will use a while structure so that it will be possible to skip the loop entirely in the case that there are no grades to average.

Algorithm design

The algorithm should add each grade to a running total, keeping track of the number of grades entered. Thus, this algorithm requires two variables: one to keep track of the running total and the other to keep track of the count. Both should be initialized to 0. After the last grade has been entered, the total should be divided by the count to give the average. In pseudocode, the algorithm for this problem is as follows:

```
initialize runningTotal to 0            // Initialize
initialize count to 0
prompt and read the first grade         // Priming read
while the grade entered is not 9999 {   // Sentinel test
    add it to the runningTotal
    add 1 to the count
    prompt and read the next grade      // Update
}
if (count > 0)                          // Guard against divide by 0
    divide runningTotal by count
output the average as the result
```

Note that in this problem our loop variable, grade, is read before the loop test is made. This Priming read is known as a **priming read.** It is necessary in this case because the loop test depends on the value that is read. Within the loop's body, the updater reads the next value for grade. This is a standard convention for coding while structures that involve input, as this problem does. Note also that we must make sure that count is not 0 before we attempt to compute the average, because dividing by 0 would cause a divide-by-zero error.

Translating the pseudocode algorithm into Java raises several issues. Suppose we store each grade that is input in a double variable named grade. The loop will terminate when grade equals 9999, so its entry condition will be (grade != 9999). Because this condition uses grade, it is crucial that the grade variable be initialized before the bound test is made. This requires a priming read. Reading the first value of grade before the loop-entry condition is tested ensures that the loop will be skipped if the user happens to enter the sentinel (9999) on the very first prompt. In addition to reading the first exam score, we must initialize the variables used for the running total and the counter. Thus, for our initialization step, we get Initialization step the following code:

```java
double runningTotal = 0;
int count = 0;
reader.prompt("Input a grade (e.g., 85.3) " +
     "or 9999 to indicate the end of the list >> ");
double grade = reader.getKeyboardDouble();         // Priming input
```

Within the body of the loop we must add the grade to the running total and increment the counter. Since these variables are not tested in the loop-entry condition, they will not affect the loop control. Our loop updater in this case must read the next grade. Placing the updater statement at the end of the loop body will ensure that the loop terminates immediately after Updater step the user enters the sentinel value:

```java
while (grade != 9999) {                            // Loop test: sentinel
  runningTotal += grade;
  count++;
  reader.prompt("Input a grade (e.g., 85.3) " +
     "or 9999 to indicate the end of the list >> ");
  grade = reader.getKeyboardDouble();              // Update:input
} // while
```

You can see that it is somewhat redundant to repeat the same statements needed to do the initializating and the updating of the grade variable. A better design would be to encapsulate these into a method and then call the method both before and within the loop. The method Modularity should take care of prompting the user, reading the input, converting it to double, and returning the input value. The method doesn't require a parameter:

```java
private double promptAndRead() {
  reader.prompt("Input a grade (e.g., 85.3) " +
    "or 9999 to indicate the end of the list >> ");
  double grade = reader.getKeyboardDouble();       // Confirm input
  System.out.println("You input " + grade + "\n");
  return grade;
}
```

Note that we have declared this as a `private` method. It will be used to help us perform our task but won't be available to other objects. Such private methods are frequently called *helper methods*.

This is a much more modular design. In addition to cutting down on redundancy in our code, it makes the program easier to maintain. For example, there is only one statement to change if we decide to change the prompt message. It also makes the program easier to debug. Input errors are now localized to the `promptAndRead()` method.

EFFECTIVE DESIGN: Modularity.   Encapsulating code in a method is a good way to avoid redundancy in a program.

DEBUGGING TIP: Localization.   Encapsulating code in a method removes the need to have the same code at several locations in a program. By localizing the code in this way, you make it easier to modify and debug.

Another advantage of encapsulating the input task in a separate method is that it simplifies the task of calculating the average. This task should also be organized into a separate method:

```
public double inputAndAverageGrades() {
  double runningTotal = 0;
  int count = 0;
  double grade = promptAndRead();   // Priming initializer
  while (grade != 9999) {           // Loop test: sentinel
    runningTotal += grade;
    count++;
    grade = promptAndRead();        // Update: get next grade
  } // while
  if (count > 0)                    // Guard against divide-by-zero
    return runningTotal / count;    // Return the average
  else
    return 0;                       // Special (error) return value
}
```

Note that we have declared this as a `public` method. This will be the method you call to calculate your course average.

Method decomposition

Because we have decomposed the problem into its subtasks, each subtask is short and simple, making it easier to read and understand. As we saw in the checkerboard example, the use of small, clearly focused methods is a desirable aspect of designing a program.

The complete `Average.java` application is shown in Figure 6.10. Its overall design is similar to the application programs we designed in previous chapters. The only instance variable it uses is the `KeyboardReader` variable. The other variables are declared locally, within the methods. In this case, declaring them locally makes the algorithms easier to read.

```java
import java.io.*;
public class Average {                              // Console I/O
  private KeyboardReader reader = new KeyboardReader();

  private double promptAndRead() {
    reader.prompt("Input a grade (e.g., 85.3) " +
            "or 9999 to indicate the end of the list >> ");
    double grade = reader.getKeyboardDouble();
    System.out.println("You input " + grade + "\n"); // Confirm input
    return grade;
  }
  public double inputAndAverageGrades() {
    double runningTotal = 0;
    int count = 0;
    double grade = promptAndRead();              // Initialize:  priming input
    while (grade != 9999) {                       // Loop test:  sentinel
      runningTotal += grade;
      count++;
      grade = promptAndRead();                    // Update:  get next grade
    } // while

    if (count > 0)                                // Guard against divide-by-zero
      return runningTotal / count;                // Return the average
    else
      return 0;                                   // Special (error) return value
  }
  public static void main(String argv[]) {
    System.out.println("This program calculates average grade.");
    Average avg = new Average();
    double average = avg.inputAndAverageGrades();
    if (average == 0)                             // Error check
      System.out.println("You didn't enter any grades.");
    else
      System.out.println("Your average is " + average);
  } // main()
} // Average class
```

Figure 6.10 A program to compute average grade using a `while` structure.

One final point about this program: note the care taken in the design of the user interface to explain the program to the user, prompt the user before a value is input, and confirm the user's input after the program has read it.

EFFECTIVE DESIGN: User Interface.   Whenever you ask a user for input, the user should know *why* you are asking and *what* you are asking for. Prompts should be used for this purpose. It is also a good idea to confirm that the program has received the correct input.

6.8   Example: Data Validation

A frequent programming task is *data validation*. This task can take different forms depending on the nature of the program. One use for data validation occurs when accepting input from the user.

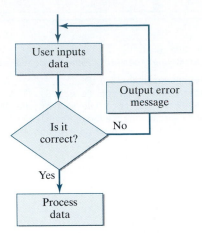

Figure 6.11 Do-while is a good structure for the data-validation algorithm.

In the program in the preceding section, suppose the user types −10 by mistake when asked to input an exam grade. Obviously this is not a valid exam grade and should not be added to the running total. How should a program handle this task?

Algorithm design

Because it is possible that the user may make one or more attempts to correct an input problem, we should use a `do-while` structure for this problem. The program should first input a number from the user. The number should then be checked for validity. If it is valid, the loop should exit and the program should continue computing the average grade. If it is not valid, the program should print an error message and input the number again. A flowchart for this algorithm is shown in Figure 6.11.

For example, suppose only numbers between 0 and 100 are considered valid. The data-validation algorithm would be as follows:

```
do
  Get the next grade                                  // Initialize: priming input
  if the grade < 0 or grade > 100 and grade != 9999
    print an error message                            // Error case
while the grade < 0 or grade > 100 and grade != 9999  // Sentinel test
```

Note here that initialization and updating of the loop variable are performed by the same statement. This is acceptable because we must update the value of `grade` on each iteration *before* checking its validity. Note also that for this problem the loop-entry condition is also used in the `if` statement to check for an error. This allows us to print an appropriate error message if the user makes an input error.

Let's incorporate this data-validation algorithm into the `promptAndRead()` method that we designed in the preceding section (Fig. 6.10). The revised method will handle and validate all input and return a number between 0 and 100 to the calling method. To reflect its expanded purpose, we will change the method's name to `getAndValidateGrade()`, and incorporate it into a revised application, which we name `Validate` (Fig. 6.12).

```java
import java.io.*;
public class Validate {                                    // Console input
  private KeyboardReader reader = new KeyboardReader();

  private double getAndValidateGrade() {
    double grade = 0;
    do {
      reader.prompt("Input a grade (e.g., 85.3) " +
                    "or 9999 to indicate the end of the list >> ");
      grade = reader.getKeyboardDouble();
      if ((grade != 9999) && ((grade < 0) || (grade > 100))) // If error
        System.out.println("Error: grade must be between 0 and 100 \n");
      else
        System.out.println("You input " + grade + "\n");  // Confirm input
    } while ((grade != 9999) && ((grade < 0) || (grade > 100)));
    return grade;
  }
  public double inputAndAverageGrades() {
    double runningTotal = 0;
    int count = 0;
    double grade = getAndValidateGrade();      // Initialize:  priming input
    while (grade != 9999) {                     // Loop test:  sentinel
      runningTotal += grade;
      count++;
      grade = getAndValidateGrade();            // Update:  get next grade
    }                                           // while

    if (count > 0)                              // Guard against divide-by-zero
      return runningTotal / count;              // Return the average
    else
      return 0;                                 // Special (error) return value
  }
  public static void main(String argv[]) {
    System.out.println("This program calculates average grade."); // Explain
    Average avg = new Average();
    double average = avg.inputAndAverageGrades();
    if (average == 0)                           // Error check
      System.out.println("You didn't enter any grades.");
    else
      System.out.println("Your average is " + average);
  } // main()
} // Validate class
```

Figure 6.12   A program to compute average grade using a `while` structure. This version validates the user's input.

6.9 Principles of Loop Design

Before moving on, it will be useful to summarize the main principles involved in correctly constructing a loop.

- A *counting loop* can be used whenever you know in advance exactly how many iterations are needed. Java's *for statement* is an appropriate structure for coding a counting loop.
- A *while structure* should be used when the problem suggests that the loop body may be skipped entirely. Java's *while statement* is specially designed for the `while` structure.
- A *do-while structure* should be used only when a loop requires one or more iterations. Java's *do-while statement* is specially designed for the `do-while` structure.

Table 6.1. Design decisions required when coding a loop

Use	If	Java Statement
Counting loop	*Number of iterations known in advance*	`for`
`While` *structure*	*Number of iterations not known* *Loop may not be entered at all*	`while`
`Do-while` *structure*	*Number of iterations not known* *Loop must be entered at least once*	`do-while`

- The *loop variable* is used to specify the *loop-entry condition*. It must be initialized to an appropriate initial value, and it must be updated on each iteration of the loop.
- A loop's *bound* may be a *count*, a *sentinel*, or, more generally, a *conditional bound*. It must be correctly specified in the loop-entry expression, and progress toward the bound must be made in the *updater*.
- An *infinite loop* may result if the initializer, loop-entry expression, or updater expression is not correctly specified.

The loop types are summarized in Table 6.1.

SELF-STUDY EXERCISE

EXERCISE 6.14   For each of the following problems, decide whether a counting loop structure, a `while` structure, or a `do-while` structure should be used, and write a pseudocode algorithm.

- Print the names of all visitors to your Web site.
- Validate that a number input by the user is positive.
- Change all the backslashes (\) in a Windows Web page address to the slashes (/) used in a Unix Web page address.
- Find the car with the best miles-per-gallon ratio among the cars in the *Consumer Reports* database.

6.10   The `switch` Multiway Selection Structure

Another selection structure to add to our repertoire is the **switch/break structure**. It is meant to provide a shorthand way of coding the following type of multiway selection structure:

```
  if (integralVar == integralValue1)
                                        // some statements
else if (integralVar == integralValue2)
                                        // some statements
else if (integralVar == integralValue3)
                                        // some statements
  else                                  // some statements
```

Note that each of the conditions in this case involves the equality of an integral variable and an integral value. This type of structure occurs so frequently in programs that most languages contain statements specially designed to handle it. In Java, we use a combination of the `switch` and `break` statements to implement multiway selection.

The `switch` is designed to select one of several actions depending on the value of some integral expression:

```
switch (integralExpression)
{   case integralValue1:
                        // some statements
    case integralValue2:
                        // some statements
    case integralValue3:
                        // some statements
    default:
                        // some statements
}
```

The *integralExpression* must evaluate to a primitive integral value of type `byte`, `short`, `int`, `char`, or `boolean`. It may not be a `long`, `float`, `double`, or a class type. The *integralValues* must be literals or `final` variables. They serve as labels in the one or more case clauses that make up the `switch` statement body. The `default` clause is optional, but it is a good idea to include it.

Integral expression

A `switch` statement is executed according to the following rules:

Rule 1.   The *integralExpression* is evaluated.

Rule 2.   Control passes to the statements following the `case` label whose value equals the *integralExpression* or, if no cases apply, to the `default` clause.

Rule 3.   Beginning at the selected label or at the default, all of the statements up to the end of the `switch` are executed.

Consider the following example:

```
int m = 2;
switch (m)
{   case 1:
        System.out.print(" m = 1");
    case 2:
        System.out.print(" m = 2");
    case 3:
        System.out.print(" m = 3");
    default:
        System.out.print(" default case");
}
```

In this case, because *m* equals 2, the following output would be produced:

```
m = 2 m = 3 default case
```

Obviously, this output does not match the following `if-else` multiway selection structure, which would output, simply, m = 2:

```
int m = 2;
if (m == 1)
    System.out.print(" m = 1");
else if (m == 2)
    System.out.print(" m = 2");
else if (m == 3)
    System.out.print(" m = 3");
else
    System.out.print(" default case");
```

The reason for this disparity is that the `switch` executes *all* statements following the label that matches the value of the *integralExpression* (see again Rule 3 on the preceding page).

In order to use the switch as a multiway selection, you must force it to `break` out of the case clause after executing that clause's statements:

```
int m = 2;
switch (m)
{   case 1:
        System.out.print(" m = 1");
        break;
    case 2:
        System.out.print(" m = 2");
        break;
    case 3:
        System.out.print(" m = 3");
        break;
    default:
        System.out.print(" default case");
}
```

In this example, the `break` statement causes control to pass to the end of the `switch`, with the effect being that one and only one case will be executed within the `switch`. Thus, the output of this code segment will be simply m = 2, matching exactly the behavior of the multiway `if-else` selection structure (Fig. 6.13).

JAVA PROGRAMMING TIP: Multiway Selection. A `switch` statement is typically used together with `break` to code a multiway selection structure.

JAVA LANGUAGE RULE break. The `break` statement transfers control out of its enclosing *block*, where a block is any sequence of statements contained within curly brackets { and }.

DEBUGGING TIP: Switch without break. A common error in coding `switch`-based multiway selection is forgetting to put a `break` statement at the end of each clause. This may cause more than one case to be executed.

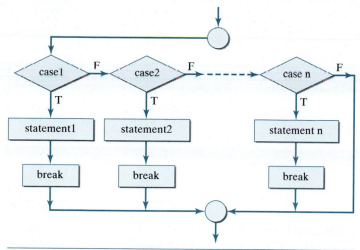

Figure 6.13 Flowchart of the multiway switch structure. Note that because of the break statement, one and only one case is executed.

SELF-STUDY EXERCISES

EXERCISE 6.15   Identify any errors in the following switch structures (if there is no error, specify the output):

a.

```java
int k = 0;
switch (k)
case 0:
    System.out.println("zero");
    break;
case 1:
    System.out.println("one");
    break;
default:
    System.out.println("default");
    break;
```

b.

```java
int k = 0;
switch (k + 1)
{   case 0:
        System.out.println("zero");
        break;
    case 1:
        System.out.println("one");
        break;
    default:
        System.out.println("default");
        break;
}
```

c.

```java
int k = 6;
switch (k / 3.0)
{    case 2:
         System.out.println("zero");
         break;
     case 3:
         System.out.println("one");
         break;
     default:
         System.out.println("default");
         break;
}
```

EXERCISE 6.16   Flavors of ice cream are represented as integers where 0 is vanilla, 1 is chocolate, and 2 is strawberry. Write a `switch` statement that checks an integer variable `flavor` and prints out the name of the ice cream flavor or prints "Error" in the default case.

EXERCISE 6.17   Modify your solution to the previous exercise to use constants (final variables) to represent the ice cream flavors.

6.11   Object-Oriented Design: Structured Programming

Structured programming is the practice of writing programs that are built up from a small set of predefined control structures. As an overall approach to programming, structured programming has largely been superseded by the object-oriented approach. Nevertheless, its design principles are still relevant to the design of the algorithms and methods that make up a program's objects.

The principles of structured programming seem so obvious today that it may be difficult to appreciate their importance. In the 1960s and 1970s, one of the main controls used in programs was the infamous *go-to* statement, which could be used to transfer control of a program to any arbitrary location within it, and from there to any other arbitrary location, and so on. This led to incredibly complex and ill-formed programs—so-called "spaghetti code"—that were almost impossible to understand and modify.

Spaghetti code

Structured programming evolved in reaction to the unstructured software-development practices of the 1960s, which were fraught with budget overruns, costly delays, and failed products. One of the classic research results of that era was a 1966 paper by Boehm and Jacopini that showed that any program using `go-to`'s could be represented by an equivalent program that used a sequence of two types of controls: `if-else` and `while` structures. Another influential paper, by Edgar Dikjstra ("GoTo Statement Considered Harmful"), pointed out the various ways in which the `go-to` statement could lead to impossibly complex programs.

The Pascal language, introduced by Nicklaus Wirth in 1971, was designed to promote structured programming techniques and became the language of choice in academic institutions because of its suitability as a teaching language. In Pascal, the `go-to` was replaced with the four structures that control the flow of execution in a program (Fig. 6.14):

- *Sequence*: The statements in a program are executed in sequential order unless their flow is interrupted by one of the following control structures.

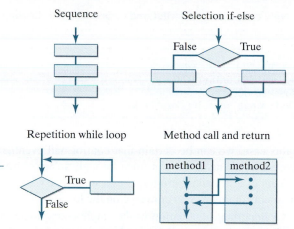

Figure 6.14 Flowcharts of the four types of control structures. Each small rectangle represents a single executable statement.

- *Selection*: The `if`, `if-else`, and `switch` statements are *branching* statements that allow choice through the forking of the control path into two or more alternatives.
- *Repetition*: The `for`, `while`, and `do-while` statements are *looping* statements that allow the program to repeat a sequence of statements.
- *Method Call*: Invoking a method transfers control temporarily to a named method. Control returns to the point of invocation when the method is completed.

No matter how large or small a program you write, its flow of control can be constructed as a combination of these four basic types of structures.

Preconditions and Postconditions

The Java language supplies us with a good collection of control structures, and Java's syntax constrains the way we can use them. One of the features of the four control structures is that each has a single entry point and exit (Fig. 6.14). This is an extremely important property. To grasp its importance, consider the following debugging problem:

```
k = 0;                              // 1. Unstructured code
System.out.println("k= " + k);      // 2. k should equal 0 here
goto label1;                        // 3.
label2:
System.out.println("k= " + k);      // 4. k should equal 1 here
```

In this example a `go-to` statement is used to jump to `label1`, a label that marks a section of code somewhere else in the program. Suppose we're trying to determine how *k* has acquired an erroneous value and that its value is correct in line 2 of this sequence. Given the `go-to` statement on line 3, there's no guarantee that control will ever return to the `println()` statement on line 4. Thus, in unstructured code it is very difficult to narrow the scope of an error to a fixed segment of code. Because the `go-to` statement can transfer control anywhere in the program, with no guarantee of return, any segment of code can have multiple entry points and multiple exits.

Now contrast the unstructured code with the following well-structured code:

```
k = 0;                              // 1. Structured code
System.out.println("k= " + k);      // 2. k should equal 0 here
someMethod();                       // 3.
System.out.println("k= " + k);      // 4. k should equal 1 here
```

Debugging with
println()

In this case, we can be certain that control will eventually return to line 4. If *k*'s value is erroneous on line 4, we can trace through someMethod() to find the error. Because any segment of a structured program has a single entry and exit, we can use a pair of println() statements in this way to converge on the location of the program bug.

An important implication of the single-entry/single-exit property is that we can use **preconditions** and **postconditions** to help us design and debug our code. The preceding example provided a simple example: The precondition is that *k* should equal 0 on line 2, and the postcondition is that *k* should equal 1 on line 4. Figure 6.15 shows some additional examples.

```
int k = 0;                          // Precondition: k == 0
k = 5;                              // Assignment to k
                                    // Postcondition: k == 5
```

```
int k = 0;                          // Precondition: k == 0
while (k < 100) {                   // While loop
    k = 2 * k + 2;
}
                                    // Postcondition: k >= 100
```

```
/*
 * factorial(n):
 *    factorial(n) is 1 if n is 0
 *    factorial(n) is n * n-1 * n-2 * ...  * 1 if n > 0
 * Precondition:   n >= 0
 * Postcondition:
 *   factorial(n) = 1 if n = 0
 *                = n * n-1 * n-2 * ...  * 1 if n > 0
 */
public int factorial(int n) {
    if (n == 0)
        return 1;
    else {
        int f = 1;                  // Init a temporary variable
        for (int k = n; k >= 1; k--) // For n down to 1
            f = f * k;              // Accumulate the product
        return f;                   // Return the factorial
    } // else
} // factorial()
```

Figure 6.15 Using pre- and postconditions to document code.

In the first example, we use pre- and postconditions to define the semantics of an assignment statement. No matter what value k has before the assignment, the execution of the assignment (k = 5) will make the postcondition (k == 5) true.

In the second example, the postcondition follows from the semantics of the `while` loop. The loop-entry condition is k < 100, so when the loop exits the postcondition, (k >= 100) must be true.

The third example shows how pre- and postconditions can be used to design and document methods. The *factorial(n)* is defined for $n \geq 0$ as follows:

```
factorial(n) is 1, if n == 0
factorial(n) is n * n-1 * n-2 * ... * 1, if n > 0
```

In other words, the factorial of N is defined as the cumulative product of multiplying 1 times 2, times 3, and so on up to N. For example, if N is 5, then `factorial(5)` is 1 * 2 * 3 * 4 * 5 = 120.

Note how the factorial computation is done in the method. The variable f, which is used to accumulate the product, is initialized to 1. Then on each iteration of the `for` loop, f is multiplied by k and the product is assigned back to f. This is similar to the way we accumulate a sum, except that in this case we are accumulating a product.

The precondition on the `factorial()` method represents the condition that must be true in order for the method to work correctly. Factorial is undefined for $n < 0$, so it is important that n be greater than or equal to 0 whenever this method is called. Given that the precondition holds, the postcondition gives a precise specification of what must be true when the method is finished.

Design: Defensive Programming

The pre- and postconditions for a method can be used to design defensive code—that is, code that guards against errors. For example, what action should `factorial()` take if its precondition fails to hold? In Java, the best way to handle this situation is to *throw* an `IllegalArgumentException`, as the following example illustrates:

```java
public int factorial(int n) {
    if (n < 0)                          // Precondition failure
        throw new IllegalArgumentException("Factorial:"+ n);
    if (n == 0)
        return 1;
    else {
        int f = 1;                      // Init a temporary variable
        for (int k = n; k >= 1; k--)    // For n down to 1
            f = f * k;                  // Accumulate the product
        return f;                       // Return the factorial
    }
} // factorial()
```

An *exception* is an erroneous condition (an error) that arises during the running of a program. An `Exception` is an object that encapsulates information about the erroneous condition. A program can *throw* an `Exception`, thereby stopping the program, when an erroneous condition is detected. In this example, we create a new `IllegalArgumentException` that would report the illegal value of *n* with something like the following error message:

```
Exception in thread "main" java.lang.IllegalArgumentException:
        Factorial: -1
  at Test.factorial(Param.java:5)
  at Test.main(Param.java:18)
```

You have undoubtedly already encountered thrown exceptions during program development. Java has an extensive hierarchy of `Exceptions`, which we will cover in some depth in Chapter 11. For now, however, we just note how to use the `IllegalArgumentException`. As its name implies, an `IllegalArgumentException` is used when an argument in a method call is not legal.

Rather than continuing the program with an erroneous data value, throwing an exception causes the program to stop and print an error message. Determining whether an argument is legal or illegal is an important use of the method's preconditions. The failure of the precondition in `factorial()` points to a problem elsewhere in the program, because it is doubtful that the program deliberately passed a negative value to `factorial()`. The discovery of this error should lead to modifications in the part of the program where `factorial()` was invoked— perhaps to some validation of the user's input:

```java
int num = Integer.parseInt(textIn.getText());
if (num >= 0)                           // If factorial() precondition valid
    factNum = factorial(num);           // Compute factorial
else
    System.out.println("Error");  // Report input error
```

That would be the traditional way to handle this kind of error.

Using Pre- and Postconditions

The use of preconditions and postconditions in the ways we have described can help improve a program's design at several distinct stages of its development:

- *Design stage*: Using pre- and postconditions helps to clarify the design and provides a precise measure of correctness.
- *Implementation and testing stage*: Test data can be designed to demonstrate that the preconditions and postconditions hold for any method or code segment.
- *Documentation stage*: Using pre- and postconditions to document the program makes the program more readable and easier to modify and maintain.

- *Debugging stage*: Using pre- and postconditions provides precise criteria that can be used to isolate and locate bugs. A method is incorrect if its precondition is true and its postcondition is false. A method is improperly invoked if its precondition is false.

Like other programming skills and techniques, learning how to use pre- and postconditions effectively requires practice. One way to develop these skills is to incorporate pre- and post-conditions into the documentation of the methods you write for laboratories and programming exercises. Appendix A provides guidelines on how to incorporate pre- and postconditions into your program's documentation. However, it would be a mistake to get in the habit of leaving the identification of pre- and postconditions to the documentation stage. The method's documentation, including its pre- and postconditions, should be developed during the design stage and should play a role in all aspects of program development.

Effective Program Design

What we are really saying here is that using pre- and postconditions forces you to analyze your program's logic. It is not enough to know that a single isolated statement within a program works correctly at the present time. You have to ask yourself whether it will continue to work if you change some other part of the program, and whether other parts of the program will continue to work if you revise it. No matter how clever you are, you cannot possibly keep an entire model of a good-sized program in your head at one time. It is always necessary to focus on a few essential details and leave aside certain others. Ideally, what you hope is that the details you've left aside for the moment are not the cause of the bug you're trying to fix. Using pre- and postconditions can help you determine the correctness of the details you choose to set aside.

EFFECTIVE DESIGN: Pre- and Postconditions. Pre- and postconditions are an effective way of analyzing the logic of your program's loops and methods. They should be identified at the earliest stages of design and development. They should play a role in the testing and debugging of the program. Finally, they should be included, in a systematic way, in the program's documentation.

JAVA PROGRAMMING TIP: Develop your program's documentation at the same time that you develop its code, and include the pre- and postconditions in the documentation.

As the programs you write become longer and more complex, the chances that they contain serious errors increase dramatically. There's no real way to avoid this complexity. The only hope is to try to manage it. In addition to analyzing your program's structure, another important aspect of program design is the attempt to reduce its complexity.

EFFECTIVE DESIGN: Reducing Complexity. Design your programs with an aim toward reducing their complexity.

Perhaps the best way to reduce complexity is to build your programs using a small collection of standard structures and techniques. The basic control structures (Fig. 6.14) help reduce the complexity of a program by constraining the kinds of branching and looping structures that can be built. The control structures help to manage the complexity of your program's algorithms. In the same way, the following practices can help reduce and manage the complexity in a program.

JAVA PROGRAMMING TIP: Standard Techniques.   Acquire and use standard programming techniques for standard programming problems. For example, using a temporary variable to swap the values of two variables is a standard technique.

JAVA PROGRAMMING TIP: Encapsulation.   Use methods wherever appropriate in your own code to encapsulate important sections of code and thereby reduce complexity.

JAVA PROGRAMMING TIP: Code Reuse.   Instead of reinventing the wheel, use library classes and methods whenever possible. These have been carefully designed by experienced programmers. Library code has been subjected to extensive testing.

SELF-STUDY EXERCISES

EXERCISE 6.18   Identify the pre- and postconditions on j and k where indicated in the following code segment:

```java
int j = 0; k = 5;
do {
    if (k % 5 == 0)  {
                      // Precondition
        j += k;
        k--;
    }
    else k *= k;
} while (j <= k);
                      // Postcondition
```

EXERCISE 6.19   Identify the pre- and postconditions for the following method, which computes x^n for $n \geq 0$:

```java
public double power(double x, int n) {
    double pow = 1;
    for (int k = 1; k <= n; k++)
        pow = pow * x;
    return pow;
} // power()
```

Special Topic: What Can Be Computed?

Did you ever wonder whether there are problems that cannot be solved by a computer, no matter what kind of control structures are used? Well, back in 1939, in his seminal paper titled "On Computable Numbers," Alan Turing proved that indeed there are an infinite number of unsolvable problems. Prior to this, mathematicians and logicians thought that all problems could be solved. So Turing's proof was quite a blow!

To help prove this point, Turing defined an abstract computer that has come to be known as a Turing machine. A Turing machine has an alphabet of symbols; a read/write head; an infinitely long tape on which the read/write head can write symbols, and from which it can read symbols; and a control unit, that controls the movement and action of the read/write head. Note that the Turing machine elements correspond to key components of a computer, although Turing invented this concept a decade before the first computers were developed. The read/write head corresponds to a computer's central processing unit (CPU). The tape corresponds to the computer's memory. And the control unit corresponds to the computer program.

A Turing machine represents a purely abstract concept of computation. It represents the pure idea of an algorithmic solution to a problem. Equipped with this concept, Turing was able to prove that there are unsolvable problems—that is, problems for which no algorithm can arrive at a solution.

One such problem is the *halting problem*. This problem asks whether an algorithm can be devised to determine whether an arbitrary program will eventually halt. If there were such an algorithm, it could be used to detect programs that contain infinite loops, a service that might be really helpful in an introductory computing lab, among other places! But, alas, there can be no such algorithm.

Here's an outline of a proof that shows that the halting problem is unsolvable. (This particular version of the proof was suggested by J. Glenn Brookshear in *Computer Science: An Overview*, Benjamin-Cummings, 1985.)

Suppose you had a program, P, that solves the halting problem. That is, whenever P is given a self-halting program, it sets a variable *isTerminating* to true, and otherwise it sets *isTerminating* to false. Now let's create a new version of P, named P', which is identical to P except that right after where P sets *isTerminating* to true or false, P' contains the following loop:

```
while (isTerminating == true);   // Infinite if isTerminating true
```

In other words, if the input to P' is a self-terminating program, then P' will enter an infinite loop and will not terminate. Otherwise, if a non-self-terminating program is input to P', P' will skip the loop and will terminate.

Now what if we give a representation of P' to itself? Will it halt? The answer generates a contradiction: If P' is a self-terminating program, then when it is input to itself, it will not terminate. And if P' is not self-terminating, then when it is input to itself, it will terminate. Because our assumption that P solves the halting problem has led to a contradiction, we have to conclude that it wasn't a very good assumption in the first place. Therefore, there is no program that can solve the halting problem.

The topic of computability is a fundamental part of the computer science curriculum, usually taught in a sophomore- or junior-level theory of computation course.

CHAPTER SUMMARY

Technical Terms

conditional loop	postcondition
counting loop	pre-condition
do-while statement	priming read
for ststement	repetition structure
infinite loop	sentinel bound
initializer	switch/break structure
limit bound	unit indexing
loop body	updater
loop bound	while statement
loop-entry condition	zero indexing
nested loop	

Summary of Important Points

- A *repetition structure* is a control structure that allows a statement or sequence of statements to be repeated.
- All loop structures involve three elements—an *initializer*, a *loop-entry condition* or a *loop-boundary condition*, and an *updater*.
- When designing a loop, it is important to analyze the loop structure to make sure that the loop bound will eventually be satisfied.
- The for statement has the following syntax:

$$\text{for} \quad (\textit{ initializer}; \; \textit{loop-entry condition}; \; \textit{updater})$$
$$\textit{loop body}$$

- The while statement takes the following form:

$$\text{while} \; (\; \textit{loop-entry condition} \;)$$
$$\textit{loop body}$$

- The do-while statement has the following general form:

$$\text{do} \; \textit{loop body}$$
$$\text{while} \; (\; \textit{loop-entry condition} \;);$$

- When designing a loop, it is important to analyze the loop structure to make sure that the loop bound will eventually be satisfied. Table 6.2 summarizes the types of loop bounds that we have identified.
- *Structured programming* is the practice of writing programs that are built up from a small set of predefined control structures—the *sequence*, *selection*, *repetition*, and *method-call* structures. An important feature of these structures is that each has a single entry and exit.

Table 6.2. Summary of loop bounds

Bound	Example
Counting	$k < 100$
Sentinel	$input \mathrel{!=} 9999$
Flag	$done \mathrel{!=} true$
Limit	$amount < 0.5$

- A *pre-condition* is a condition that must be true before a certain code segment executes. A *postcondition* is a condition that must be true when a certain code segment is finished. Pre-conditions and postconditions should be used in the design, coding, documentation, and debugging of algorithms and methods.

SOLUTIONS TO SELF-STUDY EXERCISES

SOLUTION 6.1   Identify the syntax error in the following `for` loop statements:

a. Commas are used instead of semicolons in the header.

```
for (int k = 5; k < 100; k++)
    System.out.println(k);
```

b. There should not be three semicolons in the header

```
for (int k = 0; k < 12 ; k--)
    System.out.println(k);
```

SOLUTION 6.2   Identify the statements that result in infinite loops:

a. Infinite loop because k is never incremented.
b. Infinite loop because k is always odd and thus never equal to 100.

SOLUTION 6.3   Your sister is learning to count by fours. Write a `for` loop that prints the following sequence of numbers: 1, 5, 9, 13, 17, 21, 25.

```
for (int k = 1; k <= 25; k = k+4)
    System.out.print(k + " ");
```

SOLUTION 6.4   What value will *j* have when the following loop terminates? *Answer*: *j* will be undefined when the loop terminates. It is a local variable whose scope is limited to the loop body.

```
for (int i = 0; i < 10; i++)
{
    int j;
    j = j + 1;
}
```

SOLUTION 6.5   Write a nested `for` loop to print the following geometric pattern:

```
#
# #
# # #
# # # #
# # # # #

for (int row = 1; row <= 5; row++)  {     // For each row
  for (int col = 1; col <= row; col++)    // Columns per row
    System.out.print('#');
  System.out.println();                   // New line
}                                         // row
```

SOLUTION 6.6   Identify the syntax error in the following `while` structures:

a.

```
int k = 5;
while (k < 100) {
    System.out.println(k);
    k++                      ≪ Missing semicolon
}
```

b.

```
int k = 0;
while (k < 12;) {            ≪ Extra semicolon
    System.out.println(k);
    k++;
}
```

SOLUTION 6.7   Determine the output and/or identify the error in each of the following `while` structures.

a.

```
int k = 0;
while (k < 100)
  System.out.println(k);   ≪ Missing updater in loop body
```

Output: infinite loop prints 0 0 0 0 0. . .

b.

```
while (k < 100) {              ≪ Missing initializer
  System.out.println(k);
  k++;
}
```

Output: unpredictable since k's initial value is not known

SOLUTION 6.8   Your younger sister is now learning how to count by sixes. Write a `while` loop that prints the following sequence of numbers: 0, 6, 12, 18, 24, 30, 36.

```
int k = 0;                    // Initializer
while (k <= 36) {             // Loop-entry condition
    System.out.println(k);
    k += 6;                   // Updater
}
```

SOLUTION 6.9   If N is even, divide it by 2. If N is odd, subtract 1 and then divide it by 2. This will generate a sequence that is guaranteed to terminate at 0. For example, if N is initially 15, then you get the sequence 15, 7, 3, 1, 0. Write a method that implements this sequence using a `while` statement.

```
public static void sub1Div2(int N) {
    while(N != 0) {
        System.out.print(N + " ");
        if (N % 2 == 0)
            N = N / 2;
        else
            N = (N - 1) / 2;
    }
    System.out.println( N );
} // sub1Div2()
```

SOLUTION 6.10   Identify the syntax error in the following `do-while` structures:

a.

```
int k = 0;
do while (k < 100)  « Misplaced condition
{
    System.out.println(k);
    k++;
}                         « Belongs here
```

b.

```
int k = 0;
do {
    System.out.println(k);
    k++;
} while (k < 12)  « Missing semicolon
```

SOLUTION 6.11 Your sister has moved on to counting by sevens. Write a do-while loop that prints the following sequence of numbers: 1, 8, 15, 22, 29, 36, 43.

```
n = 1;                               // Initializer
do {
    System.out.print(n + " ");
    n += 7;                          // Updater
} while (n <= 43);                   // Loop entry condition
```

SOLUTION 6.12 Write a method to input and validate pizza sales.

```
public int getAndValidatePizzaPrice() {  // Uses KeyboardReader
  int pizza = 0;
  do {
    reader.prompt("Input a pizza price (8, 10, or 15) ");
    reader.prompt("or 99 to end the list >> ");
    pizza = reader.getKeyboardInteger();
    if ((pizza != 99) && (pizza != 8) && (pizza != 10) && (pizza != 15))
      System.out.println("Error: you've entered an "
        + "invalid pizza price\n");        // Error input
    else                                    // OK input
        System.out.println("You input " + pizza + "\n");
  } while ((pizza != 99) && (pizza != 8) && (pizza != 10) && (pizza != 15));
  return pizza;
} // getAndValidatePizzaPrice()
```

SOLUTION 6.13 Write a method to input and validate pizza sales using the numbers 1, 2, and 3 to represent pizzas at different price levels.

```
public int getAndValidatePizzaPrice() {  // Uses KeyboardReader
  int pizza = 0;
  do {
    reader.prompt("Input a 1,2 or 3 to indicate pizza"
            + "price ( 1($8), 2($10), or 3($15) ) ");
    reader.prompt("or 0 to end the list >> ");
    pizza = reader.getKeyboardInteger();
    if ((pizza < 0) || (pizza > 3))        // Error check
        System.out.println("Error: you've entered an " + "invalid value\n");
    else                                    // OK input
        System.out.println("You input " + pizza + "\n");
  } while ( (pizza < 0) || (pizza > 3) );
  if (pizza == 1)
    return 8;
  else if (pizza == 2)
    return 10;
  else if (pizza == 3)
    return 15;
  else
    return 0;
} // getAndValidatePizzaPrice()
```

SOLUTION 6.14 For each of the following problems, decide whether a counting loop structure, a while structure, or a do-while structure should be used, and write a pseudocode algorithm.

• Printing the names of all the visitors to a Web site could use a counting loop because the exact number of visitors is known.

```
for each name in the visitor's log
    print the name
```

• Validating that a user has entered a positive number requires a do-while structure in which you repeatedly read a number and validate it.

```
do
    read a number
    if number is invalid, print error message
while number is invalid
```

• Changing all the backslashes (\) in a Windows Web page address to the slashes (/) used in a Unix Web page address.

```
for each character in the Web page address
    if it is a backslash replace it with slash
```

• Finding the largest in a list of numbers requires a while loop to guard against an empty list.

```
initialize maxMPG to smallest possible number
while there are more cars in the database
    if current car's MPG is greater than maxMPG
        replace maxMPG with it
```

SOLUTION 6.15 Identify any errors in the following switch structures (if there is no error, specify the output):

a.

```
int k = 0;
switch (k)   // Syntax error: missing braces
case 0:
    System.out.println("zero");
    break;
case 1:
    System.out.println("one");
    break;
default:
    System.out.println("default");
    break;
```

b.

```java
int k = 0;
switch (k + 1)
{
    case 0:
        System.out.println("zero");
        break;
    case 1:
        System.out.println("one"); // Output "one"
        break;
    default:
        System.out.println("default");
        break;
}
```

c.

```java
int k = 6;
switch (k / 3.0) // Syntax error: not an integral value
{
    case 2:
        System.out.println("zero");
        break;
    case 3:
        System.out.println("one");
        break;
    default:
        System.out.println("default");
        break;
}
```

SOLUTION 6.16   A `switch` statement to print ice cream flavors:

```java
switch (flavor)
{
    case 1:
        System.out.println("Vanilla");
        break;
    case 2:
        System.out.println("Chocolate");
        break;
    case 3:
        System.out.println("Strawberry");
        break;
    default:
        System.out.println("Error");
}
```

SOLUTION 6.17

```
public final int VANILLA = 0,
               CHOCOLATE = 1,
               STRAWBERRY = 2;
switch (flavor)
{
    case VANILLA:
        System.out.println("Vanilla");
        break;
    case CHOCOLATE:
        System.out.println("Chocolate");
        break;
    case STRAWBERRY:
        System.out.println("Strawberry");
        break;
    default:
        System.out.println("Error");
}
```

SOLUTION 6.18   Identify the pre- and postconditions on j and k where indicated in the following code segment:

```
int j = 0; k = 5;
do {
    if (k % 5 == 0) {
                        // Precondition: j <= k

        j += k;
        k--;
    }
    else k *= k;
} while (j <= k);
                        // Postcondition: j > k
```

SOLUTION 6.19   Identify the pre- and postconditions for the following method, which computes x^n for $n >= 0$.

```
                              // Precondition: N >= 0
                              // Postcondition: power(x,n) == x to the n
public double power(double x, int n ) {
    double pow = 1;
    for (int k = 1; k <= n; k++)
        pow = pow * x;
    return pow;
} // power()
```

EXERCISES

Note: For programming exercises, **first** draw a UML class diagram describing all classes and their inheritance relationships and/or associations.

EXERCISE 6.1 Explain the difference between the following pairs of terms:

a. *Counting loop* and *conditional loop*.

b. *For statement* and *while statement*.

c. *While statement* and *do-while statement*.

d. *Zero indexing* and *unit indexing*.

e. *Sentinel bound* and *limit bound*.

f. *Counting bound* and *flag bound*.

g. *Loop initializer* and *updater*.

h. *Named constant* and *literal*.

i. *Compound statement* and *null statement*.

EXERCISE 6.2 Fill in the blank.

a. The process of reading a data item before entering a loop is known as a _____.

b. A loop that does nothing except iterate is an example of _____.

c. A loop that contains no body is an example of a _____ statement.

d. A loop whose entry condition is stated as ($k < 100 \mathbin{||} k >= 0$) would be an example of an _____ loop.

e. A loop that should iterate until the user types in a special value should use a _____ bound.

f. A loop that should iterate until its variable goes from 5 to 100 should use a _____ bound.

g. A loop that should iterate until the difference between two values is less than 0.005 is an example of a _____ bound.

EXERCISE 6.3 Identify the syntax errors in each of the following:

```
a. for (int k = 0; k < 100; k++) System.out.println(k)
b. for (int k = 0; k < 100; k++); System.out.println(k);
c. int k = 0 while  k < 100 {System.out.println(k);  k++;}
d. int k = 0; do {System.out.println(k); k++;} while k < 100 ;
```

EXERCISE 6.4 Determine the output and/or identify the error in each of the following code segments:

```
a. for (int k = 1; k == 100; k += 2) System.out.println(k);
b. int k = 0; while (k < 100) System.out.println(k); k++;
c. for (int k = 0; k < 100; k++) ; System.out.println(k);
```

EXERCISE 6.5   Write pseudocode algorithms for the following activities, paying particular attention to the *initializer*, *updater*, and *boundary condition* in each case.

a. a softball game

b. a five-question quiz

c. looking up a name in the phone book

EXERCISE 6.6   Identify the pre- and postconditions for each of the statements that follow. Assume that all variables are `int` and have been properly declared.

a. `int result = x / y;`

b. `int result = x % y;`

c. `int x = 95; do x /= 2; while(x >= 0);`

EXERCISE 6.7   Write three different loops—a `for` loop, a `while` loop, and a `do-while` loop—to print all the multiples of 10, including 0, up to and including 1,000.

EXERCISE 6.8   Write three different loops—a `for` loop, a `while` loop, and a `do-while` loop—to print the following sequence of numbers: 45, 36, 27, 18, 9, 0, −9, −18, −27, −36, −45.

EXERCISE 6.9   Write three different loops—a `for` loop, a `while` loop, and a `do-while` loop—to print the following ski-jump design:

```
#
# #
# # #
# # # #
# # # # #
# # # # # #
# # # # # # #
```

EXERCISE 6.10   The Straight Downhill Ski Lodge in Gravel Crest, Vermont, gets lots of college students on breaks. The lodge likes to keep track of repeat visitors. Straight Downhill's database includes an integer variable, *visit*, which gives the number of times a guest has stayed at the lodge (one or more). Write the pseudocode to catch those visitors who have stayed at the lodge at least twice and send them a special promotional package (pseudocode = send promo). (*Note:* The largest number of stays recorded is eight. The number nine is used as an end-of-data flag.)

EXERCISE 6.11   Modify your pseudocode in the preceding exercise. In addition to every guest who has stayed at least twice at the lodge receiving a promotional package, any guest with three or more stays should also get a $40 coupon good for lodging, lifts, or food.

EXERCISE 6.12   Write a method that is passed a single parameter, N, and displays all the even numbers from 1 to N.

EXERCISE 6.13   Write a method that is passed a single parameter, N, that prints all the odd numbers from 1 to N.

EXERCISE 6.14   Write a method that is passed a single parameter, N, that prints all the numbers divisible by 10 from N down to 1.

EXERCISE 6.15   Write a method that is passed two parameters—a char Ch and an int N—and prints a string of N Chs.

EXERCISE 6.16   Write a method that uses a nested for loop to print the following multiplication table:

```
   1  2  3  4  5  6  7  8  9
1  1
2  2  4
3  3  6  9
4  4  8 12 16
5  5 10 15 20 25
6  6 12 18 24 30 36
7  7 14 21 28 35 42 49
8  8 16 24 32 40 48 56 64
9  9 18 27 36 45 54 63 72 81
```

EXERCISE 6.17   Write a method that uses nested for loops to print the patterns that follow. Your method should use the following statement to print the patterns: System.out.print('#').

```
# # # # # # #     # # # # # # #     # # # # # # #     # # # # # # #
  # # # # # #     # # # # # # #     #           #               #
    # # # # #     # # # # #         #       #             #
      # # # #     # # # # #           # #             #
        # # #     # # # #             # #           #
          # #     # # #             #       #     #
            #     # #             #           #   #
                  #             # # # # # # #     # # # # # # #
```

EXERCISE 6.18   Write a program that asks the user for the number of rows and the number of columns in a box of asterisks. Then use nested loops to generate the box.

EXERCISE 6.19 Write a Java application that lets the user input a sequence of consecutive numbers. In other words, the program should let the user keep entering numbers as long as the current number is one greater than the previous number.

EXERCISE 6.20 Write a Java application that lets the user input a sequence of integers terminated by any negative value. The program should then report the largest and smallest values that were entered.

EXERCISE 6.21 How many guesses does it take to guess a secret number between 1 and N? For example, I'm thinking of a number between 1 and 100. I'll tell you whether your guess is too high or too low. Obviously, an intelligent first guess would be 50. If that's too low, an intelligent second guess would be 75. And so on. If we continue to divide the range in half, we'll eventually get down to one number. Because you can divide 100 seven times (50, 25, 12, 6, 3, 1, 0), it will take at most seven guesses to guess a number between 1 and 100. Write a Java applet that lets the user input a positive integer, N, and then reports how many guesses it would take to guess a number between 1 and N.

EXERCISE 6.22 Suppose you determine that the fire extinguisher in your kitchen loses X percent of its foam every day. How long before it drops below a certain threshold (Y percent), at which point it is no longer serviceable? Write a Java applet that lets the user input the values X and Y and then reports how many weeks the fire extinguisher will last.

EXERCISE 6.23 Leibnitz's method for computing π is based on the following convergent series:

$$\frac{\pi}{4} = 1 - \frac{1}{3} + \frac{1}{5} - \frac{1}{7} + \cdots$$

How many iterations does it take to compute π to a value between 3.141 and 3.142 using this series? Write a Java program to find out.

EXERCISE 6.24 Newton's method for calculating the square root of N starts by making a (nonzero) guess at the square root. It then uses the original guess to calculate a new guess, according to the following formula:

```
guess = (( N / guess) + guess) / 2;
```

No matter how wild the original guess is, if we repeat this calculation, the algorithm will eventually find the square root. Write a square root method based on this algorithm. Then write a program to determine how many guesses are required to find the square roots of different numbers. Uses `Math.sqrt()` to determine when to terminate the guessing.

EXERCISE 6.25   Your employer is developing encryption software and wants you to develop a Java applet that will display all of the primes less than N, where N is a number to be entered by the user. In addition to displaying the primes themselves, provide a count of how many there are.

EXERCISE 6.26   Your little sister asks you to help her with her multiplication, and you decide to write a Java application that tests her skills. The program will let her input a starting number, such as 5. It will generate multiplication problems ranging from 5×1 to 5×12. For each problem she will be prompted to enter the correct answer. The program should check her answer and should not let her advance to the next question until the correct answer is given to the current question.

EXERCISE 6.27   Write an application that prompts the user for four values and draws corresponding bar graphs using an ASCII character. For example, if the user entered 15, 12, 9, and 4, the program would draw

```
*****************
************
*********
****
```

EXERCISE 6.28   Revise the application in the preceding problem so that the bar charts are displayed vertically. For example, if the user inputs 5, 2, 3, and 4, the program should display

```
**
**          **
**       ** **
** ** ** **
** ** ** **
------------
```

EXERCISE 6.29   The Fibonacci sequence (named after the Italian mathematician Leonardo of Pisa, ca. 1200) consists of the numbers 0, 1, 1, 2, 3, 5, 8, 13, . . . in which each number (except for the first two) is the sum of the two preceding numbers. Write a method `fibonacci(N)` that prints the first N Fibonacci numbers.

EXERCISE 6.30   The Nuclear Regulatory Agency wants you to write a program that will help determine how long certain radioactive substances will take to decay. The program should let the user input two values: a string giving the substance's name and its half-life in years. (A substance's half-life is the number of years required for the disintegration of half of its atoms.) The program should report how many years it will take before there is less than 2 percent of the original number of atoms remaining.

EXERCISE 6.31   Modify the `CarLoan` program so that it calculates a user's car payments for loans of different interest rates and different loan periods. Let the user input the amount of the loan. Have the program output a table of monthly payment schedules.

The next chapter also contains a number of loop exercises.

Photograph courtesy of John Chase, Dorling Kindersley Media Library

7

Strings and String Processing

OBJECTIVES

After studying this chapter, you will

- Be more familiar with Java `String`s.
- Know how to solve problems that involve manipulating strings.
- Be able to use loops in designing string-processing algorithms.

OUTLINE

7.1 Introduction

You have already had an introduction to Strings in the early chapters of this text. In Chapter 2, we introduced the String data type and showed how to create String objects and use String methods, such as length(), concat(), and equals().

We have seen Strings used for GUI I/O operations where they were used as the contents of JTextFields and other text components, as the values of JLabels, as the labels for JButtons, and so on. Strings are also used extensively in command-line interfaces.

Another important task that Strings are used for are as a standard way of presenting or displaying information about objects. As we saw in Chapter 2, it is a key convention of the Java class hierarchy that every class inherits the Object.toString() method, which can be used to provide a string representation of any object. For example, Integer.toString() converts an int to a String, so that it can be used in JTextFields or JLabels.

Programmers often have to work with strings. Think of some of the tasks performed by a typical word processor, such as cut, paste, copy, and insert. When you cut and paste text from one part of a document to another, the program has to move one string of text, the cut, from one location in the document and insert it in another.

Strings are also important because they are our first look at a *data structure*. A **data structure** is a collection of data that is organized (structured) in some way. A **string** is a collection of character (char) data. Strings are important data structures in a programming language, and they are used to represent a wide variety of data.

The main purpose of this chapter is to provide a detailed discussion of Java's string-related classes, including the String, StringBuffer, and StringTokenizer classes. These are the important classes for writing string-processing applications. Our goal is to introduce the important String methods and illustrate common string-processing algorithms. We will review how to create strings from scratch and from other data types. We will learn how to find characters and substrings inside bigger strings. We will learn how to take strings apart and how to rearrange their parts. Finally, we will learn how to apply these string-processing skills in a program that plays the game of Hang Man.

7.2 String Basics

Before we cover the new material on Strings, let's first review what we know about this topic. In Java, Strings are considered full-fledged objects. A String object is a sequence of the characters that make up the string, plus the methods used to manipulate the string. The java.lang.String class (Fig. 7.1) is a direct subclass of Object, and it contains many public methods that can be used to perform useful operations on strings (such as concatenation). We will discuss a selection of the more commonly used methods, but for a full listing and description of the String methods see

Are strings objects?

http://java.sun.com/j2se/docs/

Like other object variables, String variables serve as *references* to their respective objects. However, unlike other Java objects, Strings have certain characteristics in common with the primitive data types. For example, as we have already seen, Java allows for literal strings. A **string literal** is a sequence of zero or more characters contained in double quotes, such as "Socrates" and "" (the **empty string**). Java allows us to perform operations on literal strings, such as concatenation. As we have already seen, the expression "Hello" + "world" results

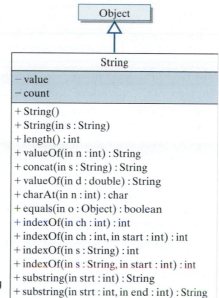

Figure 7.1 The `java.lang.String` class.

in the string `"Helloworld"`. Java also allows us to use string literals to initialize `String` variables with an assignment statement. These exceptional features greatly simplify the use of `String`s in our programs. Given how much we use `String`s, incorporating these features into Java seems like a good design decision.

7.2.1 Constructing Strings

To create `String` objects, the `String` class provides many constructors, including the following:

```
public String();                    // Creates an empty string
public String(String initial_value);// Copy constructor: Creates copy of a string
```

When we create an object using the first constructor, as in

```
String name = new String();
```

Java will create a `String` object and make `name` the reference to it. Figure 7.2 shows a hypothetical representation of a `String` object. In addition to storing the sequence of characters that make up the string, Java also stores an integer value representing the number of characters in the string. We have chosen to represent these two elements as the private instance variables `value`, for the sequence of characters, and `count`, for the number of characters. In fact, we

Figure 7.2 An empty string is a `String` object with value `""` and count 0.

name : String
value = " "
count = 0

Figure 7.3 The literal String "Socrates".

```
"Socrates" : String
value = "Socrates"
count = 8
```

don't know exactly how Java stores the sequence of characters. That information is hidden. As Figure 7.2 illustrates, when we use the default constructor, the value of the String is the empty string and its count is 0.

The second constructor is the *copy constructor* for the String class. A **copy constructor** is a constructor that makes a duplicate, sometimes called a clone, of an object. Many Java classes have copy constructors. Consider the following statements:

```
String s1 = new String("Hello");
String s2 = new String(s1);
```

These two statements would result in two distinct String objects, both storing the word "Hello".

Note that in the first of the preceding statements, we used the literal string "Hello" in the constructor. When Java encounters a new literal string in a program, it constructs an object for it. For example, if your program contained the literal "Socrates", Java would create an object for it and treat the literal itself as a reference to the object (Fig. 7.3).

We often use a string literal to assign a value to a String variable:

```
String s;          // The value of s is initially null
s = "Socrates";    // s now refers to "Socrates" object
```

In this case, the reference variable *s* is initially null—that is, it has no referent, no object, to refer to. However, after the assignment statement, *s* would refer to the literal object "Socrates", which is depicted in Figure 7.3. Given these two statements, we still have only one object, the String object containing the word "Socrates". But now we have two references to it: the literal string "Socrates" and the reference variable *s*.

Assignment statements can also be used as initializers when declaring a String variable:

```
String name1 = "";            // Reference to the empty string
String name2 = "Socrates";    // References to "Socrates"
String name3 = "Socrates";
```

In this example, Java does not construct new String objects. Instead, as Figure 7.4 shows, it simply makes the variables name1, name2, and name3 serve as references to the same objects

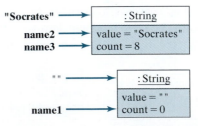

Figure 7.4 The variables name1, name2, and name3 serve as references to the literal String objects "Socrates" and "".

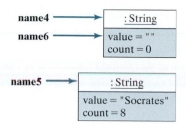

Figure 7.5 Together with the objects in Figure 7.4, there are now four different `String` objects with eight different references to them, including the literals "Socrates" and "".

that are referred to by the literal strings "" and "Socrates". This is a direct consequence of Java's policy of creating only one object to serve as the referent of a literal string, no matter how many occurrences there are of that literal in the program. Thus, these declarations result in no new objects, just new references to existing objects. The justification for this policy is that it saves lots of memory in our programs. Instead of creating a `String` object for each occurrence of the literal "Socrates", Java creates one object and lets all occurrences of "Socrates" refer to that object.

Finally, consider the following declarations, which do invoke the `String` constructors:

```
String name4 = new String();           // Creates an object
String name5 = new String("Socrates");
String name6 = name4;
```

In this case, as shown in Figure 7.5, Java creates two new objects and sets `name4` to refer to the first and `name5` to refer to the second. It gives `name4` the empty string as its value, and it gives `name5` "Socrates" as its value. But these two objects must be distinguished from the objects corresponding to the literals ("" and "Socrates") themselves. The declaration of `name6` just creates a second reference to the object referred to by `name4`.

> **JAVA LANGUAGE RULE** **Strings.** Java `Strings` are full-fledged objects, but they have some properties in common with primitive types. They can have literal values and they can be used in assignment statements.

dftgdsgh

> **JAVA LANGUAGE RULE** **String Declaration and Instantiation.** Unless a `String()` constructor is called explicitly, no new `String` object is created when declaring a `String` variable and assigning it an initial value.

7.2.2 Concatenating Strings

Another way to build a `String` object is to concatenate two other strings. Recall from Chapter 2 that there are two ways to perform string concatenation in Java: the `concat()` method and the concatenation operator, +.

```
String lastName = "Onassis";
String jackie = new String("Jacqueline " + "Kennedy " + lastName);
System.out.println("Jacqueline".concat(lastName));
```

String
concatenation

The second of these statements uses the *concatenation operator*, +, to create the String "Jacqueline Kennedy Onassis". The third statement uses the String method, concat(), to print "JacquelineOnassis".

Operator
overloading

Using the + symbol as the string concatenation operator is another example of *operator overloading*—using the same operator for two or more different operations—which we encountered in Chapter 5.

> **JAVA LANGUAGE RULE** **String Concatenation.** When surrounded on either side by a String, the + symbol is used as a binary **concatenation** operator. It has the effect of joining two strings together to form a single string.

Note that primitive types are automatically promoted to Strings when they are mixed with concatenation operators. Thus, the statement

```
System.out.println("The sum of 5 and 5 = "+ (5 + 5));
```

will print the string "The sum of 5 and 5 = 10". Note that the integer addition—(5 + 5)—is performed first, before the integer result is converted into a String. If we had left off the parentheses around the addition operation, the second plus sign would also be interpreted as a concatenation operator. Thus,

```
System.out.println("The concatenation of 5 and 5 = " + 5 + 5);
```

would print "The concatenation of 5 and 5 = 55".

SELF-STUDY EXERCISES

EXERCISE 7.1 What will be printed by each of the following segments of code?

    a. String s1 = "silly"; System.out.println(s1);
    b. String s2 = s1; System.out.println(s2);
    c. String s3 = new String (s1 + " stuff"); System.out.println(s3);

EXERCISE 7.2 Write a String declaration that satisfies each of the following descriptions:

    a. Initialize a String variable, *str1*, to the empty string.
    b. Instantiate a String object, *str2*, and initialize it to the word *stop*.
    c. Initialize a String variable, *str*, to the concatenation of *str1* and *str2*.

EXERCISE 7.3   Evaluate the following expressions:

```
int M = 5, N = 10;
String s1 = "51", s2 = "75";
```

a. M + N
b. M + s1
c. s1 + s2

EXERCISE 7.4   Draw a picture, similar to Figure 7.5, showing the objects and references created by the following declarations:

```
String s1, s2 = "Hello", s3 = "Hello";
String s4 = "hello";
String s5 = new String("Hello");
String s6 = s5;
String s7 = s3;
```

7.2.3   Indexing `Strings`

Programmers often need to take strings apart or put them together or rearrange them. Just think of the many word-processing tasks, such as cut and paste, that involve such operations. To help simplify such operations, it is useful to know how many characters a string contains and to number, or *index*, the characters that make up the string.

The number of characters in a string is called its *length*. The `String` instance method, `length()`, returns an integer that gives a `String`'s length. For example, consider the following `String` declarations and the corresponding values of the `length()` method for each case:

String length

```
String string1 = "";              string1.length()  ==> 0
String string2 = "Hello";         string2.length()  ==> 5
String string3 = "World";         string3.length()  ==> 5
String string4 = string2 + " " + string3;  string4.length()  ==> 11
```

The position of any given character in a string is called its **string index**. All `Strings` in Java are **zero indexed**—that is, the index of the first character is zero. (Remember, zero indexing is contrasted with **unit indexing**, in which we start counting at 1.) For example, in "Socrates", the letter *S* occurs at index 0, the letter *o* occurs at index 1, *r* occurs at index 3, and so on. Thus, the `String` "Socrates" contains eight characters indexed from 0 to 7 (Fig. 7.6). Zero indexing is customary in programming languages. We will see other examples of this when we talk about arrays and vectors.

Figure 7.6 The string "Socrates" has eight characters, indexed from 0 to 7. This is an example of *zero indexing*.

Indexes
0 1 2 3 4 5 6 7

S o c r a t e s

> **JAVA LANGUAGE RULE** **String Indexing.** Strings are indexed starting at 0. The first character in a string is at position 0.

> **DEBUGGING TIP: Zero versus Unit Indexing.**   Syntax and semantic errors will result if you forget that strings are zero indexed. In a string of N characters, the first character occurs at index 0 and the last at index $N - 1$. This is different from the `String.length()` method, which gives the number of characters in the string, counting from 1.

7.2.4   Converting Data to Strings

The `String.valueOf()` method is a *class method* used to convert a value of some primitive type into a `String` object. For example, the expression `String.valueOf(128)` converts its `int` argument to the `String` "128".

There are different versions of `valueOf()`, each of which has the following type of signature:

```
public static String valueOf(Type);
```

where `Type` stands for any primitive data type, including `boolean`, `char`, `int`, `double`, and so on.

The `valueOf()` method is most useful for initializing `Strings`. Because `valueOf()` is a class method, it can be used as follows to instantiate new `String` objects:

```
String number = String.valueOf(128);     // Creates "128"
String truth = String.valueOf(true);     // Creates "true"
String bee = String.valueOf('B');        // Creates "B"
String pi = String.valueOf(Math.PI);     // Creates "3.14159"
```

We have already seen that Java automatically promotes primitive type values to `String` where necessary, so why do we need the `valueOf()` methods? For example, we can initialize a `String` to "3.14159" as follows:

```
String pi = new String(""+Math.PI);      // Creates "3.14"
```

In this case, because it is part of a concatenation expression, the value of `Math.PI` will automatically be promoted to a `String` value. The point of the `valueOf()` method is twofold. First, it may be the method that the Java compiler relies on to perform string promotions like this one. Second, using it in a program—even when it is not completely necessary—makes the promotion operation explicit rather than leaving it implicit. This helps to make the code more readable. (Also, see Exercise 7.9.)

Readability

SELF-STUDY EXERCISES

EXERCISE 7.5   Evaluate each of the following expressions:

a. `String.valueOf (45)`
b. `String.valueOf (128 - 7)`
c. `String.valueOf ('X')`

EXERCISE 7.6   Write an expression to satisfy each of the following descriptions:

a. Convert the integer value 100 to the string "100."
b. Convert the character 'V' to the string "V."
c. Initialize a new String object to X times Y.

7.3   Finding Things within a String

Programmers often have to find the location of a particular character or substring in a string. For example, user names and passwords are sometimes stored in a single string in which the name and password are separated from each other by a special character, such as a colon (`username:password`). In order to get the name or password from such a string, it is convenient to have methods that will search the string and report the index of the colon character.

The `indexOf()` and `lastIndexOf()` methods are instance methods that can be used to find the index position of a character or a substring within a `String`. There are several versions of each:

```java
public int indexOf(int character);
public int indexOf(int character, int startingIndex);
public int indexOf(String string);
public int indexOf(String string, int startingIndex);

public int lastIndexOf(int character);
public int lastIndexOf(int character, int startingIndex);
public int lastIndexOf(String string);
public int lastIndexOf(String string, int startingIndex);
```

The `indexOf()` method searches from left to right within a `String` for either a character or a substring. The `lastIndexOf()` method searches from right to left for a character or a substring. To illustrate, suppose we have declared the following `String`s:

```java
String string1 = "";
String string2 = "Hello";
String string3 = "World";
String string4 = string2 + " " + string3;
```

Recalling that `String`s are indexed starting at 0, searching for *o* in the various strings gives the following results:

```java
string1.indexOf('o') ==> -1        string1.lastIndexOf('o') ==> -1
string2.indexOf('o') ==>  4        string2.lastIndexOf('o') ==>  4
string3.indexOf('o') ==>  1        string3.lastIndexOf('o') ==>  1
string4.indexOf('o') ==>  4        string4.lastIndexOf('o') ==>  7
```

Figure 7.7 The indexing of the "Hello World" string.

Sentinel return value

Because `string1` is the empty string, `""`, it does not contain the letter o. Therefore, `indexOf()` returns -1, a value that cannot be a valid index for a `String`. This convention is followed in `indexOf()` and `lastIndexOf()`. Because `string2` and `string3` each contain only one occurrence of the letter o, both `indexOf()` and `lastIndexOf()` return the same value when used on these `String`s. Because `string4` contains two occurrences of o, `indexOf()` and `lastIndexOf()` return different values in this case. As Figure 7.7 shows, the first o in "Hello World" occurs at index 4, the value returned by `indexOf()`. The second o occurs at index 7, which is the value returned by `lastIndexOf()`.

By default, the single-parameter versions of `indexOf()` and `lastIndexOf()` start their searches at their respective (left or right) ends of the string. The two-parameter versions of these methods allow you to specify both the direction and starting point of the search. The second parameter specifies the starting index. Consider these examples:

```
string4.indexOf('o', 5)     ==> 7
string4.lastIndexOf('o', 5) ==> 4
```

If we start searching in both cases at index 5, then `indexOf()` will miss the o that occurs at index 4. The first o it finds will be the one at index 7. Similarly, `lastIndexOf()` will miss the o that occurs at index 7 and will find the o that occurs at index 4.

The `indexOf()` and `lastIndexOf()` methods can also be used to find substrings:

```
string1.indexOf("or") ==> -1      string1.lastIndexOf("or") ==> -1
string2.indexOf("or") ==> -1      string2.lastIndexOf("or") ==> -1
string3.indexOf("or") ==>  1      string3.lastIndexOf("or") ==>  1
string4.indexOf("or") ==>  7      string4.lastIndexOf("or") ==>  7
```

The substring "or" does not occur in either `string1` or `string2`. It does occur beginning at location 1 in `string3` and beginning at location 7 in `string4`. For this collection of examples, it doesn't matter whether we search from left to right or right to left.

SELF-STUDY EXERCISES

EXERCISE 7.7 Suppose the `String` variable s has been initialized to "mom". Evaluate each of the following expressions:

   a. `s.indexOf("m");`
   b. `s.indexOf("o");`
   c. `s.indexOf("M");`

EXERCISE 7.8   Evaluate the expressions given the `String` declaration

$$\texttt{String s1 = "Java, Java, Java";}$$

a. `s1.length()`
b. `String.valueOf(s1.length())`
c. `s1.indexOf('a')`
d. `s1.lastIndexOf('a')`
e. `s1.indexOf("av")`
f. `s1.lastIndexOf("av")`
g. `s1.indexOf('a', 5)`
h. `s1.lastIndexOf('a', 5)`
i. `s1.indexOf("av", s1.length() - 10)`
j. `s1.lastIndexOf("av", s1.length() - 4)`
k. `s1.indexOf("a", s1.indexOf("va"))`

EXERCISE 7.9   Evaluate the following expression:

```
String tricky = "abcdefg01234567";
tricky.indexOf(String.valueOf( tricky.indexOf("c")));
```

7.4   Example: Keyword Search

One of the most widely used Web browser functions is the search utility. You probably know how it works. You type in a keyword and click on a button, and it returns with a list of Web pages that contain the keyword.

Suppose you were writing a browser in Java. How would you implement this function? Of course, we don't know yet how to read files or Web pages, and we won't cover that until Chapter 11. But for now, we can write a method that will search a string for all occurrences of a given keyword. That's at least part of the task that the browser's search engine would have to do.

So we want a method, `keywordSearch()`, that takes two `String` parameters, one for the string that's being searched, and the other representing the keyword. Let's have the method return a `String` that lists the number of keyword occurrences, followed by the index of each occurrence. For example, if we asked this method to find all occurrences of *is* in "This is a test", it should return the string "2: 2 5" because there are two occurrences of *is* in the string, one starting at index 2 and the other at index 5.

Method design

The algorithm for this method will require a loop, because we want to know the location of every occurrence of the keyword in the string. One way to do this would be to use the `indexOf()` method to search for the location of substrings in the string. If it finds the keyword

Algorithm design

at index N, it should record the location and then continue searching for more occurrences starting at index $N + 1$ in the string. It should continue in this way until there are no more occurrences.

> Suppose S is our string and K is the keyword.
> Initialize a counter variable and result string.
> Set Ptr to the indexOf() the first occurrence of K in S.
> While (Ptr != -1)
>   Increment the counter
>   Insert Ptr into the result string
>   Set Ptr to the next location of the keyword in S
> Insert the count into the result string
> Return the result string as a String

Implementation

As this pseudocode shows, the algorithm uses a `while` loop with a *sentinel bound*. The algorithm terminates when the `indexOf()` method returns a -1, indicating that there are no more occurrences of the keyword in the string.

Translating the pseudocode into Java gives us the method shown in Figure 7.8. Note how string concatenation is used to build the `resultStr`. Each time an occurrence is found, its location (`ptr`) is concatenated to the right-hand side of the `resultStr`. When the loop terminates, the number of occurrences (`count`) is concatenated to the left-hand side of the `resultStr`.

Testing and Debugging

What test data do we need?

What test data should we use for the `keywordSearch()` method? One important consideration in this case is to test whether the method works for all possible locations of the keyword within the string. Thus, the method should be tested on strings that contain keyword occur-

```java
/**
 * Pre:  s and keyword are any Strings
 * Post: keywordSearch() returns a String containing the
 *   number of occurrences of keyword in s, followed
 *   by the starting location of each occurrence
 */
public String keywordSearch(String s, String keyword) {
    String resultStr = "";
    int count = 0;
    int ptr = s.indexOf(keyword);
    while (ptr != -1) {
        ++count;
        resultStr = resultStr + ptr + " ";
        ptr = s.indexOf(keyword, ptr + 1);   // Next occurrence
    }
    resultStr = count + ": " + resultStr;   // Insert the count
    return resultStr;                        // Return as a String
} // keywordSearch()
```

Figure 7.8 The `keywordSearch()` method.

Table 7.1. Testing the `keywordSearch()` method

Test Performed	Expected Result
`keywordSearch("this is a test","is")`	2: 2 5
`keywordSearch("able was i ere i saw elba","a")`	4: 0 6 18 24
`keywordSearch("this is a test","taste")`	0:

rences at the beginning, middle, and end of the string. We should also test the method with a string that doesn't contain the keyword. Such tests will help verify that the loop will terminate properly in all cases. Given these considerations, Table 7.1 shows the tests that were made. As you can see from these results, the method did produce the expected outcomes. While these tests do not guarantee its correctness, they provide considerable evidence that the algorithm works correctly.

> **EFFECTIVE DESIGN: Test Data.**   In designing test data to check the correctness of a string-searching algorithm, it's important to use data that test all possible outcomes.

7.5   From the Java Library: `java.lang.StringBuffer`

java.sun.com/docs

One problem with the `keywordSearch()` method is that it is not very efficient because a `String` in Java is a **read-only** object. This means that a `String` cannot be changed once it has been instantiated. You cannot insert new characters or delete existing characters.

> **JAVA LANGUAGE RULE**   **Strings Are Immutable.** Once instantiated, a Java `String` cannot be altered in any way.

Given this fact, how is it possible that the `resultStr` in the `keywordSearch()` ends up with the correct value? The answer is that every time we assign a new value to `resultStr`, Java has to create a new `String` object. Figure 7.9 illustrates the process. Thus, given the statement

```
resultStr = resultStr + ptr + " ";
```

Java will evaluate the right-hand side, which creates a new `String` object whose value would be the concatenation of the right-hand-side elements, `resultStr + ptr + " "` (Fig. 7.9a). It would then assign the new object as the new referent of `resultStr` (Fig. 7.9b). This turns the previous referent of `resultStr` into an **orphan object**—that is, an object that no longer has any references to it. Java will eventually dispose of these orphaned objects, removing them from memory in a process known as **garbage collection**. However, creating and disposing of objects is a task that consumes the computer's time.

The fact that this assignment statement occurs within a loop means that several new objects are created and later garbage collected. Because object creation is a relatively time-consuming and memory-consuming operation, this algorithm is somewhat wasteful of Java's resources.

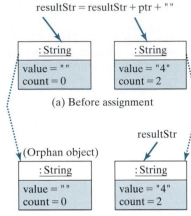

resultStr = resultStr + ptr + " "

Figure 7.9 Evaluating result-Str = resultStr + ptr + " " creates an orphan object that must be garbage collected.

Of course, except for the inefficiency of doing it this way, no real harm is done by using this algorithm in the `keywordSearch()` method. Java's garbage collector will automatically reclaim the memory used by the orphaned object. However, this algorithm does consume more of Java's resources than other algorithms we might use.

JAVA LANGUAGE RULE **Automatic Garbage Collection.** An object that has no reference to it can no longer be used in a program. Therefore, Java will automatically get rid of it. This is known as *garbage collection*.

Choosing the appropriate data structure

A more efficient way to write the `keywordSearch()` method would make use of a `StringBuffer` to store and construct the `resultStr`. Like the `String` class, the `java.lang.StringBuffer` class also represents a string of characters. However, unlike the `String` class, a `StringBuffer` can be modified, and it can grow and shrink in length as necessary. As Figure 7.10 shows, the `StringBuffer` class contains several of the same kinds of methods as the `String` class—for example, `charAt()` and `length()`. But it also contains methods that allow characters and other types of data to be inserted into a string, such as `append()`, `insert()`, and `setCharAt()`. Most string-processing algorithms use `StringBuffer`s instead of `String`s as their preferred data structure.

JAVA PROGRAMMING TIP: StringBuffer. A `StringBuffer` should be used instead of a `String` for any task that involves modifying a string.

The `StringBuffer` class provides several methods that are useful for string processing. The constructor method, `StringBuffer(String)`, makes it easy to convert a `String` into a `StringBuffer`. Similarly, once you are done processing the buffer, the `toString()` method makes it easy to convert a `StringBuffer` back into a `String`.

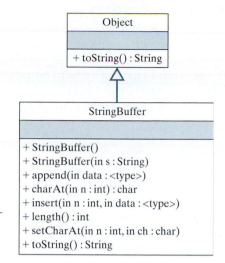

Figure 7.10
The `java.lang.StringBuffer` class.

The typical way to use a `StringBuffer` is shown in the following revised version of the `keywordSearch()` method:

```
public String keywordSearch(String s, String keyword) { // Create StringBuffer
    StringBuffer resultStr = new StringBuffer();
    int count = 0;
    int ptr = s.indexOf(keyword);
    while (ptr != -1) {
        ++count;
        resultStr.append(ptr + " ");                        // Append to buffer
        ptr = s.indexOf(keyword, ptr + 1);
    }
    resultStr.insert(0, count + ": ");
    return resultStr.toString();                            // Convert buffer to String
} // keywordSearch()
```

We declare `resultStr` as a `StringBuffer` instead of a `String`. Then, instead of concatenating the `ptr` and reassigning the `resultStr`, we `append()` the `ptr` to the `resultStr` for each occurrence of a keyword. Similarly, after the loop exits, we `insert()` the `count` at the front (index 0) of the `resultStr`. Finally, we convert `resultStr` into a `String` by using the `toString()` method before returning the method's result.

One advantage of the `StringBuffer` class is that there are several versions of its `insert()` and `append()` methods. These make it possible to insert any type of data—`int`, `double`, `Object`, and so on—into a `StringBuffer`. The method itself takes care of converting the data into a string for us.

To summarize, `String` objects in Java are *immutable*. So when a `String` is "modified," this really means that a new `String` object is created and the old `String` object must be garbage collected. This is somewhat inefficient, especially if done repeatedly within a loop. To avoid these inefficiencies, use a `StringBuffer` instead of a `String` in such contexts.

Strings are immutable

7.6   Retrieving Parts of Strings

Programmers often need to retrieve an individual character or a part of a string from a string, as, for example, in a word-processing program when a part of a string is copied or deleted. In this section we look at methods that help us with these kinds of tasks.

The charAt(int index) method is a String instance method that can be used to retrieve the character stored at a certain index. The several varieties of the substring() method can be used to retrieve a substring of characters from a String. These methods are defined as follows:

```java
public char charAt(int index)
public String substring(int startIndex)
public String substring(int startIndex, int endIndex)
```

The charAt() method returns the character located at the index supplied as its parameter. Thus, str.charAt(0) retrieves the first character in str, while str.charAt(str.length()-1) retrieves the last character.

The substring() methods work in a similar way, except that you need to specify both the starting and the ending index of the substring you wish to retrieve. The first version of substring(int startIndex) takes a single parameter and returns a String consisting of all the characters beginning with startIndex and continuing up to the end of the String. For example, if the str is "HelloWorld", then str.substring(5) would return "World" and str.substring(3) would return "loWorld":

```java
String str = "HelloWorld";
str.substring(5)            ==> "World"
str.substring(3)            ==> "loWorld"
```

The substring(int, int) version requires that you specify both the starting and ending index of the substring. The second index always points to the character that is one beyond the last character in the String you want to retrieve. For example,

```java
//   INDEX:    0123456789
String str = "HelloWorld";
str.substring(5,7)              ==> "Wo"
str.substring(0,5)              ==> "Hello"
str.substring(5, str.length()) ==> "World"
```

Note here that when we want to retrieve "Wo" from str, we specify its substring as indexes 5 and 7; the 7 points to the character just beyond "Wo". Similarly, substring(0,5) picks out the first five characters ("Hello"). In the third example, the length() method specifies the substring beginning at index 5 and extending to the end of the string. This is equivalent to str.substring(5):

```java
//   INDEX:    0123456789
String str = "HelloWorld";
str.substring(5, str.length()) ==> "World"
str.substring(5)               ==> "World"
```

The fact that the second parameter in `substring()` refers to the character one beyond the desired substring may seem a bit confusing at first, but it is actually a very useful way to designate a substring. For example, many string-processing problems have to do with retrieving substrings from a **delimited string**, which is a string that contains special characters that separate the string into certain substrings. For example, consider the string `"substring1:substring2"`,   Delimited strings
in which the *delimiter* is the colon, `':'`. The following code retrieves the substring preceding the delimiter:

```
String str = "substring1:substring2";
int n = str.indexOf(':');
str.substring(0,n)                   ==> "substring1"
```

Thus, by making the second index of `substring()` refer to the character one beyond the last character in the desired substring, we can use `indexOf()` and `substring()` together to process delimited strings. Note that it is not necessary to use a temporary variable *n* to store the index of the delimiter, because the two method calls can be nested:

```
String str = "substring1:substring2";
str.substring(0,str.indexOf(':'))  ==> "substring1"
```

DEBUGGING TIP: substring(int p1, int p2). Don't forget that the second parameter in the `substring()` methods refers to the character just past the last character in the substring.

SELF-STUDY EXERCISES

EXERCISE 7.10   Given the `String` declaration

```
String s = "abcdefghijklmnopqrstuvwxyz";
```

evaluate each of the following expressions:

  a. `s.substring(20)`
  b. `s.substring(1, 5)`
  c. `s.substring(23)`
  d. `s.substring(23, 25)`
  e. `s.substring(s.indexOf('x'))`

EXERCISE 7.11   Given the preceding declaration of s, evaluate each of the following expressions:

  a. `s.substring(20, s.length())`
  b. `s.substring(s.indexOf('b'), s.indexOf('f'))`
  c. `s.substring(s.indexOf("xy"))`
  d. `s.substring(s.indexOf(s.charAt(23)))`
  e. `s.substring(s.length() - 3)`

7.7 Example: Processing Names and Passwords

Many computer systems store user names and passwords as delimited strings, such as

```
smith:bg1s5xxx
mccarthy:2ffo900ssi
cho:biff4534ddee4w
```

Obviously, if the system is going to process passwords, it needs some way to take apart these name-password pairs.

Let's write methods to help perform this task. The first method will be passed a name–password pair and will return the name. The second method will be passed a name–password pair and will return the password. In both cases, the method takes a single `String` parameter and returns a `String` result:

Algorithm design

```
String getName(String str);
String getPassword(String str);
```

To solve this problem we can make use of two `String` methods. We use the `indexOf()` method to find the location of the *delimiter*—that is, the colon, `":"`—in the name–password pair, and then we use `substring()` to take the substring occurring before or after the delimiter. It may be easier to see this if we take an example:

```
INDEX:               1           2
INDEX: 012345678901234567890
       jones:b34rdffg12      // (1)
       cho:rtf546            // (2)
```

In the first case, the delimiter occurs at index position 5 in the string. Therefore, to take the name substring, we would use `substring(0,5)`. To take the password substring, we would use `substring(6)`. Of course, in the general case, we would use variables to indicate the position of the delimiter, as in the following methods:

```java
public static String getName(String str) {
  int posColon = str.indexOf(':');             // Find the delimiter
  String result = str.substring(0, posColon);  // Get name
  return result;
}
public static String getPassword(String str) {
  int posColon = str.indexOf(':');             // Find the delimiter
  String result = str.substring(posColon + 1); // Get passwd
  return result;
}
```

Note that in both of these cases we have used local variables, `posColon` and `result`, to store the intermediate results of the computation—that is, the index of the `":"` and the name or password substring.

An alternative way to code these operations would be to use nested method calls to reduce the code to a single line:

```
return str.substring(0, str.indexOf(':'));
```

In this line, the result of `str.indexOf(':')` is passed immediately as the second argument to `str.substring()`. This version dispenses with the need for additional variables. And the result in this case is not unreasonably complicated. But whenever you are faced with a trade-off of this sort—nesting versus additional variables—you should opt for the style that will be easier to read and understand.

> **EFFECTIVE DESIGN: Nested Method Calls.**   Nested method calls are fine as long as there are not too many levels of nesting. The goal should be to produce code that is easy to read and understand.

7.8   Processing Each Character in a `String`

Many string-processing applications require you to process every character in a string. For example, to encrypt the string "hello" into "jgnnq", we have to go through every letter of the string and change each character to its substitute.

Algorithms of these types usually involve a counting loop bounded by the length of the string. Recall that the `length()` method determines the number of characters in a `String` and that strings are zero indexed. This means that the first character is at index 0, and the last character is at index `length()-1`. For example, to print each character in a string on a separate line, we would step through the string from its first to its last character and print each character:

Counting-loop algorithm

```
// Precondition:   str is not null
// Postcondition: the letters in str will have been printed
public void printLetters(String str) {
  for (int k = 0; k < str.length(); k++)// For each char
    System.out.println(str.charAt(k));  // Print it
}
```

Our loop bound is `k < str.length()`, since the index of the last character of any `String` is `length()-1`. Note the use of `str.charAt(k)` to retrieve the *k*th character in `str` on each iteration of the loop.

Counting bound

As you will have observed, pre- and postconditions are used in the method's comment block. The precondition states that `str` has been properly initialized—that is, it is not `null`. The postcondition merely states the expected behavior of the method.

7.8.1   Off-by-One Error

A frequent error in coding counter-controlled loops is known as the **off-by-one error**. Such errors can occur in many different ways. For example, if we had coded the loop boundary

```
// Precondition: Neither str nor ch are null
// Postcondition: countchar() == the number of ch in str
public int countChar(String str, char ch) {
  int counter = 0;                        // Initialize a counter
  for (int k = 0; k < str.length(); k++)  // For each char
    if (str.charAt(k) == ch)              //  If it's a ch
      counter++;                          //   count it
  return counter;                         // Return the result
}
```

Figure 7.11   A method to count the occurrences of a particular character in a string.

Off-by-one error condition as k <= str.length(), this would cause an off-by-one error because the last character in str is at location length()-1. This would lead to a Java IndexOutOfBounds-Exception, which would be reported as soon as the program executed this statement.

The only way to avoid off-by-one errors is to check your loop bounds whenever you code a loop. Always make sure you have the loop counter's initial and final values right.

DEBUGGING TIP: Off-by-One Errors.   Loops should be carefully checked to make sure they don't commit an off-by-one error. During program testing, develop data that tests the loop variable's initial and final values.

7.8.2   Example: Counting Characters

As another example of an algorithm that processes every character in a string, consider the problem of computing the frequency of the letters in a given document. Certain text-analysis programs, such as programs that analyze encrypted data and spam filters, perform this type of function.

Method design The countChar() method will count the number of occurrences of any particular character in a String (Fig. 7.11). This method takes two parameters: a String parameter that stores the string being searched, and a char parameter that stores the character being counted.

Algorithm design Begin by initializing the local variable, counter, to 0. As in the preceding example, the for loop here will iterate through each character of the String—from 0 to length()-1. On each iteration a check is made to see if the character in the kth position (str.charAt(k)) is the character being counted. If so, counter is incremented. The method ends by returning counter, which, when the method completes, will store an integer representing the number of ch's in str.

7.8.3   Example: Reversing a String

Another interesting method that processes every character in a string is the reverse() method. This method reverses the letters in a string. For example, the reverse of "java" is "avaj".

Algorithm design The algorithm for the reverse() method should use a simple counting loop to reverse the letters in its String parameter. In this case, however, we can process the string from right to left, beginning at its last character and ending with its first character. That way we can just append each character, left to right, in the result string:

```
/**
 * Pre:  s is any non null string
 * Post: s is returned in reverse order
 */
public String reverse(String s) {
    StringBuffer result = new StringBuffer();
    for (int k = s.length()-1; k >= 0; k--) {
        result.append(s.charAt(k));
    } // for
    return result.toString();
} // reverse()
```

As in the other string-manipulation algorithms—for example, keywordSearch()—we should use a StringBuffer to store the method's result. Thus we declare the result String-Buffer at the beginning of the method and convert it back into a String at the end of the method.

> **JAVA PROGRAMMING TIP: Changing Each Character in a String.** Algorithms that require you to alter a string should use a StringBuffer to store the result.

7.8.4 Example: Capitalizing the First Letter

Another string-manipulation method is the capitalize() method, which returns a String whose initial letter is capitalized but whose other letters are lowercase—for example, "Hello". *Algorithm design* We use the static toUpperCase() and toLowerCase() methods from the Character class to convert individual letters. We could also have used the methods of the same name that we wrote in Section 5.7. The algorithm converts the first letter to uppercase and then loops through the remaining letters converting each to lowercase:

```
/*
 * Pre:  s is any non null string
 * Post: s is returned with only its first letter capitalized
 */
public String capitalize(String s) {
    if (s.length() == 0)                              // Special case: empty string
        return s;
    StringBuffer result = new StringBuffer();
    result.append(Character.toUpperCase(s.charAt(0)));// Convert the first letter
    for (int k = 1; k < s.length(); k++) {            // And the rest
        result.append(Character.toLowerCase(s.charAt(k)));
    } // for
    return result.toString();
} // capitalize()
```

SELF-STUDY EXERCISES

EXERCISE 7.12   Write a Java program to test the methods described in this section. Organize the methods into a single class, named StringProcessor, and design a second class to serve as the user interface. Because these methods are similar to the utility methods of the Math class, it would be useful to declare them static. The user interface should prompt the user to input a string and should then print out the result of passing that string to each of the methods we developed.

EXERCISE 7.13   Add a method to the `StringProcessor` class that will remove all blanks from a string. It should take a `String` parameter and return a `String` result.

7.8.5   Miscellaneous `String` Methods

In addition to the several `String` class methods we have discussed—`valueOf()`, `equals()`, `indexOf()`, `lastIndexOf()`, `charAt()`, `substring()`—Table 7.2 shows some of the other useful methods in the `String` class. Because of the read-only nature of `String`s, methods such as `toUpperCase()`, `toLowerCase()`, and `trim()` do not change their strings. Instead they produce new strings. If you want to use one of these methods to convert a string, you must reassign its result back to the original string:

```
String s = new String("hello world");
s = s.toUpperCase(); // s now equals "HELLO WORLD"
```

7.9   Comparing Strings

Comparing strings is another important task. For example, when a word processor performs a search and replace operation, it needs to identify strings in the text that match the target string.

Strings are compared according to their *lexicographic order*—that is, the order of their characters. For the letters of the alphabet, lexicographic order just means alphabetical order. Thus, *a* comes before *b*, and *d* comes after *c*. The string "hello" comes before "jello" because *h* comes before *j* in the alphabet.

For Java and other programming languages, the definition of lexicographic order is extended to cover all the characters that make up the character set. We know, for example, that in Java's Unicode character set, the uppercase letters come before the lowercase letters (Table 5.13). So the letter *H* comes before the letter *h*, and the letter *Z* comes before the letter *a*.

H precedes h

Lexicographic order can be extended to include strings of characters. Thus, "Hello" precedes "hello" in lexicographic order because its first letter, *H*, precedes the first letter, *h*, in "hello". Similarly, the string "Zero" comes before "aardvark", because *Z* comes before *a*. To determine lexicographic order for strings, we must perform a character-by-character

Table 7.2. Some useful `String` methods applied to the literal string "Perfection."

Method Signature	Example
`boolean endsWith(String suffix)`	`"Perfection".endsWith("tion")` ⇒ true
`boolean startsWith(String prefix)`	`"Perfection".startsWith("Per")` ⇒ true
`boolean startsWith(String prefix, int offset)`	`"Perfection".startsWith("fect",3)` ⇒ true
`String toUpperCase()`	`"Perfection".toUpperCase()` ⇒ "PERFECTION"
`String toLowerCase()`	`"Perfection".toLowerCase()` ⇒ "perfection"
`String trim()`	`" Perfection ".trim()` ⇒ "Perfection"

comparison, starting at the first character and proceeding left to right. As an example, the following strings are arranged in lexicographic order:

```
"" "!" "0" "A" "Andy" "Z" "Zero" "a" "an" "and" "andy" "candy" "zero"
```

We can define **lexicographic order** for strings as follows:

> **JAVA LANGUAGE RULE** **Lexicographic Order.** For strings $s1$ and $s2$, $s1$ precedes $s2$ in lexicographic order if its first character precedes the first character of $s2$. If their first characters are equal, then $s1$ precedes $s2$ if its second character precedes the second character of $s2$; and so on. An empty string is handled as a special case, preceding all other strings.

Perhaps a more precise way to define lexicographic order is to define a Java method:

```java
public boolean precedes(String s1, String s2)   {
                                    // Pick shorter length
  int minlen = Math.min(s1.length(), s2.length());

  for (int k=0; k < minlen; k++) {       // For each char in shorter string
    if (s1.charAt(k) != s2.charAt(k))    // If chars unequal
      return s1.charAt(k) < s2.charAt(k);// return true if s1's char precedes s2's
  }
  return s1.length() < s2.length();      // If all characters so far are equal
                                    // then s1 < s2 if it is shorter than s2
} // precedes()
```

This method does a character-by-character comparison of the two strings, proceeding left to right, starting at the first character in both strings. Its `for` loop uses a counting bound, which starts at k equal to zero and counts up to the length of the shorter string. This is an important point in designing this algorithm. If you don't stop iterating when you get past the last character in a string, your program will generate a `StringIndexOutOfBounds` exception. To prevent this error, we need to use the shorter length as the loop bound.

Algorithm: Loop bound

   Note that the loop will terminate early if it finds that the respective characters from $s1$ and $s2$ are unequal. In that case, $s1$ precedes $s2$ if $s1$'s kth character precedes $s2$'s. If the loop terminates normally, that means that all the characters compared were equal. In that case, the shorter string precedes the longer. For example, if the two strings were "alpha" and "alphabet", then the method would return true, because "alpha" is shorter than "alphabet".

SELF-STUDY EXERCISES

EXERCISE 7.14   Arrange the following strings in lexicographic order:

```
zero bath bin alpha Alpha Zero Zeroes a A z Z
```

EXERCISE 7.15   Modify the `precedes()` method so that it will also return true when $s1$ and $s2$ are equal—for example, when $s1$ and $s2$ are both "hello".

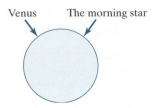

Figure 7.12 Venus is the morning star, so "Venus" and "the morning star" are two references to the same object.

7.9.1 Object Identity versus Object Equality

Java provides several methods for comparing `String`s:

```
public boolean equals(Object anObject); // Overrides Object.equals()
public boolean equalsIgnoreCase(String  anotherString);
public int compareTo(String  anotherString);
```

The first comparison method, `equals()`, overrides the `Object.equals()` method. Two `String`s are equal if they have the exact same letters in the exact same order. Thus, for the following declarations,

Equality vs. identity

```
String s1 = "hello";
String s2 = "Hello";
```

`s1.equals(s2)` is `false`, but `s1.equals("hello")` is `true`.

You have to be careful when using Java's `equals()` method. According to the default definition of `equals()`, defined in the `Object` class, "equals" means "identical." Two `Object`s are equal only if their names are references to the same object.

This is like the old story of the morning star and the evening star, which were thought to be different objects before it was discovered that both were just the planet Venus. After the discovery, it was clear that "the morning star" and "the evening star" and "Venus" were just three different references to one and the same object (Fig. 7.12).

We can create an analogous situation in Java by using the following `JButton` definitions:

```
JButton b1 = new Button("a");
JButton b2 = new Button("a");
JButton b3 = b2;
```

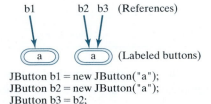

b1   b2 b3 (References)

a   a   (Labeled buttons)

JButton b1 = new JButton("a");
JButton b2 = new JButton("a");
JButton b3 = b2;

Figure 7.13 For most objects, equality means identity. JButtons b2 and b3 are identical (and hence equal), but JButtons b1 and b2 are not identical (and hence unequal).

```
import java.awt.*;

public class TestEquals {
  static Button b1 = new Button ("a");
  static Button b2 = new Button ("b");
  static Button b3 = b2;
  private static void isEqual(Object o1, Object o2) {
    if (o1.equals(o2))
      System.out.println(o1.toString() + " equals " + o2.toString());
    else
      System.out.println(o1.toString() + " does NOT equal " + o2.toString());
  } // isEqual()
  private static void isIdentical(Object o1, Object o2) {
    if (o1 == o2)
      System.out.println(o1.toString() + " is identical to " + o2.toString());
    else
      System.out.println(o1.toString() + " is NOT identical to " + o2.toString());
  } // isIdentical()
  public static void main(String argv[]) {
    isEqual(b1, b2);        // not equal
    isEqual(b1, b3);        // not equal
    isEqual(b2, b3);        // equal

    isIdentical(b1, b2);    // not identical
    isIdentical(b1, b3);    // not identical
    isIdentical(b2, b3);    // identical
  } // main()
} // TestEquals class
```

Figure 7.14 The `TestEquals` program tests Java's default `equals()` method, which is defined in the `Object` class.

Given these three declarations, `b1.equals(b2)` and `b1.equals(b3)` would be `false`, but `b2.equals(b3)` would be `true` because b2 and b3 are just two names for the same object (Fig. 7.13). So in this case "equals" really means "identical."

Moreover, in Java, when it is used to compare two objects, the equality operator (==) is interpreted in the same way as the default `Object.equals()` method. So it really means object identity. Thus, `b1 == b2` would be `false` because b1 and b2 are different objects, but `b2 == b3` would be `true` because b2 and b3 refer to the same object.

```
java.awt.Button[button0,0,0,0x0,invalid,label=a]
   does NOT equal java.awt.Button[button1,0,0,0x0,invalid,label=b]
java.awt.Button[button0,0,0,0x0,invalid,label=a]
   does NOT equal java.awt.Button[button1,0,0,0x0,invalid,label=b]
java.awt.Button[button1,0,0,0x0,invalid,label=b]
   equals java.awt.Button[button1,0,0,0x0,invalid,label=b]
java.awt.Button[button0,0,0,0x0,invalid,label=a]
   is NOT identical to java.awt.Button[button1,0,0,0x0,invalid,label=b]
java.awt.Button[button0,0,0,0x0,invalid,label=a]
   is NOT identical to java.awt.Button[button1,0,0,0x0,invalid,label=b]
java.awt.Button[button1,0,0,0x0,invalid,label=b]
   is identical to java.awt.Button[button1,0,0,0x0,invalid,label=b]
```

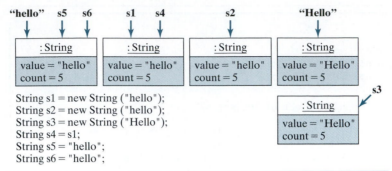

Figure 7.15 For String objects, equality and identity are different. Two distinct (nonidentical) String objects are equal if they store the same string value. So s1, s2, s4, s5, and s6 are equal. Strings s1 and s4 are identical, and so are strings s5 and s6.

These points are illustrated in the program shown in Figure 7.14. This program uses methods isEquals() and isIdentical() to perform the comparisons and print the results. This program will produce the following output:

7.9.2 String Identity versus String Equality

In comparing Java Strings, we must be careful to distinguish between object identity and string equality. Thus, consider the following declarations, which create the situation shown in Figure 7.15.

```
String s1 = new String("hello");
String s2 = new String("hello");
String s3 = new String("Hello");
String s4 = s1;              // s1 and s4 are now identical
String s5 = "hello";
String s6 = "hello";
```

Equality vs. identity

Given these declarations, we would get the following results if we compare the equality of the Strings:

```
s1.equals(s2) ==> true          s1.equalsIgnoreCase(s3)  ==> true
s1.equals(s3) ==> false         s1.equals(s5)            ==> true
s1.equals(s4) ==> true          s1.equals(s6)            ==> true
```

and the following results if we compare their identity:

```
s1 == s2  ==> false       s1 == s3  ==> false
s1 == s4  ==> true        s1 == s5  ==> false
s5 == s6  ==> true
```

```
import java.awt.*;

public class TestStringEquals {
  static String s1 = new String("hello");  // s1 and s2 are equal, not identical
  static String s2 = new String("hello");
  static String s3 = new String("Hello");  // s1 and s3 are not equal
  static String s4 = s1;                    // s1 and s4 are identical
  static String s5 = "hello";               // s1 and s5 are not identical
  static String s6 = "hello";               // s5 and s6 are identical

  private static void testEqual(String str1, String str2) {
    if (str1.equals(str2))
      System.out.println(str1 + " equals " + str2);
    else
      System.out.println(str1 + " does not equal " + str2);
  } // testEqual()

  private static void testIdentical(String str1, String str2) {
    if (str1 == str2)
      System.out.println(str1 + " is identical to " + str2);
    else
      System.out.println(str1 + " is not identical to " + str2);
  } // testIdentical()

  public static void main(String argv[]) {
    testEqual(s1, s2);              // equal
    testEqual(s1, s3);              // not equal
    testEqual(s1, s4);              // equal
    testEqual(s1, s5);              // equal
    testEqual(s5, s6);              // equal

    testIdentical(s1, s2);         // not identical
    testIdentical(s1, s3);         // not identical
    testIdentical(s1, s4);         // identical
    testIdentical(s1, s5);         // not identical
    testIdentical(s5, s6);         // identical
  } // main()
} // TestStringEquals class

            ------Program Output-----
            hello equals hello
            hello does not equal Hello
            hello equals hello
            hello equals hello
            hello equals hello
            hello is not identical to hello
            hello is not identical to Hello
            hello is identical to hello
            hello is not identical to hello
            hello is identical to hello
```

Figure 7.16   Program illustrating the difference between string equality and string identity.

The only true identities among these Strings are *s1* and *s4*, and *s5* and *s6*. In the case of *s5* and *s6*, both are just references to the literal string "hello", as we described in Section 7.2. The program in Figure 7.16 illustrates these points.

SELF-STUDY EXERCISES

EXERCISE 7.16   Given the `String` declarations,

```
String s1 = "java", s2 = "java", s3 = "Java";
String s4 = new String(s2);
String s5 = new String("java");
```

evaluate the following expressions:

   a. `s1 == s2`
   b. `s1.equals(s2)`
   c. `s1 == s3`
   d. `s1.equals(s3)`
   e. `s2 == s3`
   f. `s2.equals(s4)`
   g. `s2 == s4`
   h. `s1 == s5`
   i. `s4 == s5`

EXERCISE 7.17   Why are the variables in `TestStringEquals` declared `static`?

EXERCISE 7.18   Given the following declarations,

```
String s1 = "abcdefghijklmnopqrstuvwxyz";
String s2 = "hello world";
```

write Java expressions to carry out each of the following operations:

   a. Swap the front and back halves of `s1` giving a new string.
   b. Swap "world" and "hello" in `s2` giving a new string.
   c. Combine parts of `s1` and `s2` to create a new string "hello abc."

java.sun.com/docs

7.10 From the Java Library: `java.util.StringTokenizer`

One of the most widespread string-processing tasks is that of breaking up a string into its components, or **tokens**. For example, when processing a sentence, you may need to break the sentence into its constituent words, which are considered the sentence tokens. When processing a name–password string, such as "boyd:14irXp", you may need to break it into a name and a password. Tokens are separated from each other by one or more characters which is known as **delimiters**. For a sentence, *white space*, including blank spaces, tabs, and line feeds, serve as the delimiters. For the password example, the colon character serves as a delimiter.

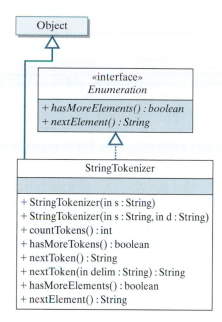

Figure 7.17
The `java.util.StringTokenizer`
class.

Java's `java.util.StringTokenizer` class is specially designed for breaking strings into their tokens (Fig. 7.17). When instantiated with a `String` parameter, a `String-  Tokenizer` breaks the string into tokens, using white space as delimiters. For example, if we instantiated a `StringTokenizer` as in the code

```
StringTokenizer sTokenizer
    = new StringTokenizer("This is an English sentence.");
```

it would break the string into the following tokens, which would be stored internally in the `StringTokenizer` in the order shown:

```
This
is
an
English
sentence.
```

Note that the period is part of the last token ("sentence."). This is because punctuation marks are not considered delimiters by default.

If you wanted to include punctuation symbols as delimiters, you could use the second `StringTokenizer()` constructor, which takes a second `String` parameter (Fig. 7.17). The second parameter specifies a string of characters that should be used as delimiters. For example, in the instantiation,

```
StringTokenizer sTokenizer
    = new StringTokenizer("This is an English sentence.", "\b\t\n,;.!");
```

punctuation symbols (periods, commas, and so on) are included among the delimiters. Note that escape sequences (\b\t\n) are used to specify backspaces, tabs, and new lines.

The hasMoreTokens() and nextToken() methods can be used to process a delimited string one token at a time. The first method returns true as long as more tokens remain; the second gets the next token in the list. For example, here is a code segment that will break a standard URL string into its constituent parts:

```
String url = "http://java.trincoll.edu/~jjj/index.html";
StringTokenizer sTokenizer = new StringTokenizer(url,":/");
while (sTokenizer.hasMoreTokens()) {
    System.out.println(sTokenizer.nextToken());
}
```

This code segment will produce the following output:

```
http
java.trincoll.edu
~jjj
index.html
```

The only delimiters used in this case were the ":" and "/" symbols. And note that next-Token() does not return the empty string between ":" and "/" as a token.

7.11 Handling Text in a Graphics Context (Optional)

In order to create attractive GUIs, it is often necessary to be able to select and control the font that is used. Even a simple drawing task, such as being able to center a message in a panel, requires that we know the font's dimensions and be able to manipulate them. In this section, we learn how to work with Java's fonts and font-control methods.

Every graphics context has an associated Font and FontMetrics object, and the Graphics class (Fig. 7.18) provides several methods to access them. A FontMetrics is an object that encapsulates important data about a font, such as its height and width. Java assigns a default font to each Graphics object. For example, this is the font used by the drawString()

Graphics
+ getFont() : Font
+ getFontMetrics() : FontMetrics
+ setFont(in f : Font)
+ setFontMetrics(in f : FontMetrics)

Figure 7.18 Methods to access the Font and FontMetrics objects associated with every Graphics context.

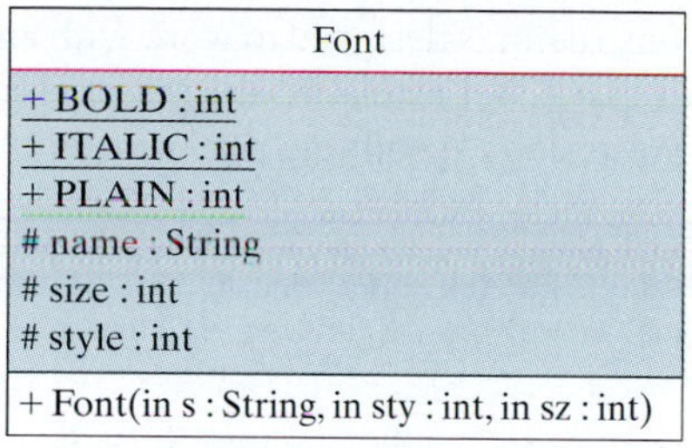

Font
+ BOLD : int
+ ITALIC : int
+ PLAIN : int
# name : String
# size : int
# style : int
+ Font(in s : String, in sty : int, in sz : int)

Figure 7.19 The Font class.

method, which we used in our very first Java programs back in Chapter 1. The particular font used is system dependent, but to override the default one can simply invoke the `setFont()` method:

```
g.setFont(new Font("TimesRoman", Font.ITALIC, 12));
```

In this case, the `Font()` constructor is used to specify a 12-point, italicized, *TimesRoman* font. Once the font is set, it will be used in all subsequent drawings.

7.11.1 The `Font` and `FontMetrics` Classes

The `Font` class (Fig. 7.19) provides a platform-independent representation of an individual font. A font is distinguished by its name, size, and style, and the `Font` class includes `protected` instance variables for these properties, as well as a constructor method that allows these three characteristics to be specified.

In order to understand how fonts work, it is necessary to distinguish between a *character*, which is a symbol that represents a certain letter or digit, and a **glyph**, which is a shape used to display the character. When you display a string, such as "Hello", Java maps each individual character into a corresponding shape, as defined by the font that is selected.

Java distinguishes between *physical* and *logical* fonts. A **physical font** is an actual font library that contains the data and tables needed to associate the correct glyph with a given character. Generally speaking, a given platform (host computer plus operating system) will have a collection of fonts available on it.

A **logical font** is one of the five font families supported by the Java runtime environment. These include Serif, SansSerif, Monospaced, Dialog, and DialogInput. Java also supports the following font styles: PLAIN, BOLD, ITALIC, and BOLD+ITALIC. Whereas the physical fonts are platform dependent, the logical fonts and styles are platform independent. When used in a program, they are mapped to real fonts available on the host system. If the host system does not have an exact match for the specified font, it will supply a substitute. For example, if you specify a 48-point, italic, Monospaced font,

```
Font myFont = new Font("Monospaced", Font.ITALIC, 48);
```

the system may map this to a 24-point, italic, Courier font, if that is the largest fixed-space font available.

The Font() constructor is designed to work with any set of arguments. Thus, if you supply the name of a font that is not available, the system will supply a default font as a substitute. For example, on my system, specifying a nonexistent font named Random,

```
g.setFont(new Font("Random", Font.ITALIC, 12) );
g.drawString("Hello World!  (random, italic, 12)", 30, 45);
```

produces the same font used as the mapping for a font named *Dialog*.

EFFECTIVE DESIGN: Font Portability.   The fact that Font() will produce a font for virtually any set of arguments is important in ensuring that a Java program can run on any platform. This is another example of how Java has been designed for portability.

The Component.setFont() method can be used to assign a specific font to a button or window or other graphics component. All AWT and JFC components have an associated font, which can be accessed using the Component.setFont() and Component.getFont() methods. For example, the following code could be used to override a Button's font:

```
Button b = new Button("Label");
b.setFont(new Font("Times", Font.ITALIC, 14));
```

If 14-point, italic, Times font is not available on the host system, a substitute will be supplied.

7.11.2   Font Metrics

Problem
statement

To illustrate how to use the FontMetrics class, let's write a "Hello World" application that centers its message both horizontally and vertically in its window. The message should be centered regardless of the size of the application window. Thus, we will have to position the text relative to the window size, which is something we learned in positioning geometric shapes. The message should also be centered no matter what font is used. This will require us to know certain characteristics of the font, such as the height and width of its characters, whether the characters have a fixed or variable width, and so on. In order to get access to these properties, we will use the FontMetrics class.

Figure 7.20 illustrates the various properties associated with a font. The **baseline** of a font refers to the line on which the bottom of most characters occurs. When drawing a string, the *x*- and *y*-coordinates determine the baseline of the string's first character. Thus, in

```
g.drawString("Hello World", 10, 40);
```

the bottom left of the *H* in "Hello World" would be located at (10, 40).

Figure 7.20   Illustration of font measurements.

```
                    FontMetrics
   # font : Font
   # FontMetrics(in font : Font)
   + charWidth(in ch : int) : int
   + charWidth(in ch : char) : int
   + getAscent() : int
   + getDescent() : int
   + getFont() : Font
   + getHeight() : int
   + getLeading() : int
   + getMaxAdvance() : int
   + getMaxDescent() : int
   + stringWidth() : int
```

Figure 7.21   The FontMetrics class.

All characters ascend some distance above the baseline. This is known as the character's **ascent**.   Some characters, such as *y*, may extend below the baseline, into what is known as the *descent*. Each font has a *maximum descent*. Similarly, some characters, such as accent characters, may extend above the *maximum ascent* into a space known as the *leading*.

The *height* of a font is defined as the sum (in pixels) of the ascent, descent, and leading values. The height is a property of the font itself rather than of any individual character. Except for fixed-width fonts, in which the width of all the characters is the same, the characters that make up a font have varying widths. The width of an individual character is known as its *advance*.

The FontMetrics class (Fig. 7.21) provides methods for accessing a font's properties. These can be useful to control the layout of text on a GUI. For example, when drawing multiple lines of text, the getHeight() method is useful for determining how much space should be left between lines. When drawing character by character, the charWidth() method can be used to determine how much space must be left between characters. Alternatively, the stringWidth() method can be used to determine the number of pixels required to draw the entire string.

7.11.3   Example: Centering a Line of Text

Given this background, let's take on the task of centering a message in an application window. In order for this application to work for any font, we must take care not to base its design on characteristics of the particular font we happen to be using. To underscore this point, let's design it to work for a font named Random, which, as we noted earlier, will be mapped to some font by the system on which the application is run. In other words, we will let the system pick a font for this application's message. An interesting experiment would be to run the application on different platforms to see what fonts are chosen.

Algorithm design: Generality

The only method we need for this application is the paint() method. We begin by setting the font used by the graphics context to a random font. To get the characteristics of this font, we create a FontMetrics object and get the font metrics for the font we just created:

```
g.setFont(new Font("Random", Font.BOLD, 24));
FontMetrics metrics = g.getFontMetrics();
```

Dimension
+ height : int
+ width : int
+ Dimension()
+ Dimension(in d : Dimension)
+ Dimension(in width : int, in height : int)
+ equals(in o : Object) : boolean
+ getSize() : Dimension
+ setSize(in d : Dimension)
+ setSize(in width : int, in height : int)
+ toString() : String

Figure 7.22 The Dimension class.

The next step is to determine the JFrame's dimensions using the getSize() method. This method returns an object of type Dimension. The java.awt.Dimension class (Fig. 7.22) represents the size (width and height) of a GUI component. A Dimension makes it possible to manipulate an object's width and height as a single entity. Note that the height and width variables are defined as public, which is an exception from the usual convention of defining instance variables as private or protected. The justification for this exception is probably to simplify the syntax of referring to an object's width and height. For example, the following syntax can be used to refer to a component's dimensions:

```
Dimension d = new Dimension(100, 50);
System.out.println("width = " + d.width + " height = " + d.height);
```

Note the redundancy built into the Dimension class. For example, in addition to being able to set a Dimension's instance variables directly, public access methods are provided. Also, by defining more than one version of some access methods, the class achieves a higher level of flexibility. The same can be said for its providing of several different constructors, including a copy constructor. Finally, note how the class overrides the equals() and toString() methods. These are all examples of good object-oriented design.

EFFECTIVE DESIGN: Redundancy. Redundancy is often a desirable characteristic of object design. It makes the object easier to use and more widely applicable.

Centering text

The Dimension object is used to calculate the x- and y-coordinates for the string. In order to center the string horizontally, we need to know its width, which is supplied by the metrics object. If the JFrame is d.width pixels wide, then the following expression subtracts the width of the string from the width of the JFrame and then divides the leftover space in half:

```
int x = (d.width - metrics.stringWidth(str)) / 2;  // Calculate coordinates
```

```java
import java.awt.*;
import javax.swing.*;

public class CenterText extends JFrame {

    public void paint(Graphics g) {        // Print hello world!  in center of frame
        String str = "Hello World!";
        g.setFont(new Font("Random", Font.PLAIN, 24));    // Random font
        FontMetrics metrics = g.getFontMetrics();         // And its metrics

        Dimension d = getSize();                          // Get the frame's size
                                                          // Clear the frame
        g.setColor(getBackground());
        g.fillRect(0,0,d.width,d.height);
        g.setColor(Color.black);
                                                          // Calculate coordinates
        int x = (d.width - metrics.stringWidth(str)) / 2;
        int y = (d.height + metrics.getHeight()) / 2;

        g.drawString( str, x, y );                        // Draw the string
    } // paint()

    public static void main(String args[]) {
        CenterText ct = new CenterText();
        ct.setSize(400,400);
        ct.setVisible(true);
    } // main()
} // CenterText class
```

Figure 7.23 The CenterText application.

Similarly, the following expression adds the height of the string to the height of the JFrame and divides the leftover space in half:

```java
int y = (d.height + metrics.getHeight()) / 2;
```

Taken together, these calculations give the coordinates for the lower-left pixel of the first character in "Hello World!" The only remaining task is to draw the string (Fig. 7.23). Because the paint() method is called automatically whenever the JFrame is resized, this application, whose output is shown in Figure 7.24, will recenter its message whenever it is resized by the user.

JAVA PROGRAMMING TIP: Generality.   By using a component's size and font as the determining factors, you can center text on virtually any component. These values are available via the component's getFont() and getSize() methods.

Figure 7.24 The CenterText application keeps its message centered no matter how its window is resized.

CHAPTER SUMMARY

Technical Terms

baseline

concatenation

copy constructor

data structure

delimited string

delimiter

empty string

garbage collection

glyph

lexicographic order

logical font

off-by-one error

orphan object

physical font

read only

string

string index

string literal

token

unit indexed

zero indexed

Summary of Important Points

- A `String` literal is a sequence of zero or more characters enclosed within double quotation marks. A `String` object is a sequence of zero or more characters, plus a variety of class and instance methods and variables.

- A `String` object is created automatically by Java the first time it encounters a *literal string*, such as "Socrates", in a program. Subsequent occurrences of the literal do not cause additional objects to be instantiated. Instead, every occurrence of the literal "Socrates" refers to the initial object.

- A `String` object is created whenever the `new` operator is used in conjunction with a `String()` constructor—for example, `new String("hello")`.

- The `String` concatenation operator is the overloaded `+` symbol; it is used to combine two `String`s into a single `String`: "hello" + "world" ==> "helloworld".

- `String`s are indexed starting at 0. The `indexOf()` and `lastIndexOf()` methods are used for finding the first or last occurrence of a character or substring within a `String`. The `valueOf()` methods convert a nonstring into a `String`. The `length()` method determines the number of characters in a `String`. The `charAt()` method returns the single character at a particular index position. The various `substring()` methods return the substring at particular index positions in a `String`.

- The overloaded `equals()` method returns `true` if two `String`s contain the same exact sequence of characters. The `==` operator, when used on `String`s, returns true if two references designate the same `String` object.

- `String` objects are *immutable*. They cannot be modified.
- A `StringBuffer` is a string object that can be modified using methods such as `insert()` and `append()`.
- A `StringTokenizer` is an object that can be used to break a `String` into a collection of *tokens* separated by *delimiters*. The whitespace characters—tabs, blanks, and new lines—are the default delimiters.
- The `FontMetrics` class is used to obtain the specific dimensions of the various `Font`s. It is useful when you wish to center text. `Font`s are inherently platform dependent. For maximum portability, it is best to use default fonts.

SOLUTIONS TO SELF-STUDY EXERCISES

SOLUTION 7.1

a. silly
b. silly
c. silly stuff

SOLUTION 7.2

a. `String str1 = "";`
b. `String str2 = new String("stop");`
c. `String str3 = str1 + str2;`

SOLUTION 7.3

a. 15
b. `"551"`
c. `"5175"`

SOLUTION 7.4   See Figure 7.25.

SOLUTION 7.5

a. `"45"`
b. `"121"`
c. `"X"`

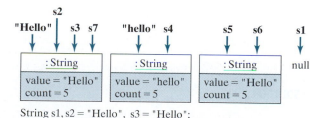

Figure 7.25 Answer to Exercise 7.4. Note that **s1** is `null` because it has not been instantiated and has not been assigned a literal value.

String s1, s2 = "Hello", s3 = "Hello";
String s4 = "hello";
String s5 = new String ("Hello");
String s6 = s5;
String s7 = s3;

SOLUTION 7.6

a. `String.valueOf(100)`

b. `String.valueOf('V');`

c. `String s = new String(String.valueOf(X * Y));`

SOLUTION 7.7

a. 0

b. 1

c. −1

SOLUTION 7.8

a. 16

b. "16"

c. 1

d. 15

e. 1

f. 13

g. 7

h. 3

i. 7

j. 7

k. 3

SOLUTION 7.9 Evaluate the following expression:

```
String tricky = "abcdefg01234567";
tricky.indexOf(String.valueOf(tricky.indexOf("c")));
tricky.indexOf(String.valueOf(2));
tricky.indexOf("2");
Answer: 9
```

SOLUTION 7.10

a. "uvwxyz"

b. "bcde"

c. "xyz"

d. "xy"

e. "xyz"

SOLUTION 7.11

a. "uvwxyz"

b. "bcde"

c. "xyz"

d. "xyz"

e. "xyz"

SOLUTION 7.12   A class to test the string methods.

```java
public class StringProcessorTest {
  public static void main(String[] args) {
    KeyboardReader kb = new KeyboardReader();
    kb.prompt("Input a String or - stop - to quit: ");
    String str = kb.getKeyboardInput();
    while (!str.equals("stop")){
      kb.display("Testing printLetters()\n");
      StringProcessor.printLetters(str);
      kb.display("testing countChars()\n");
      kb.display("Total occurences of e = ");
      kb.display(StringProcessor.countChar(str,'e') + "\n");
      kb.display("Testing reverse()\n");
      kb.display(StringProcessor.reverse(str)+ "\n");
      kb.display("Testing capitalize()\n");
      kb.display(StringProcessor.capitalize(str) + "\n\n");
      kb.prompt("Input a String or - stop - to quit: ");
      str = kb.getKeyboardInput();
    } // while
  } // main()
} // StringProcessorTest class
```

SOLUTION 7.13   Method to remove all blanks from a string:

```java
// Pre: s is a non null string
// Post: s is returned with all its blanks removed
public String removeBlanks(String s) {
  StringBuffer result = new StringBuffer();
  for (int k = 0; k < s.length();  k++)
    if (s.charAt(k) != ' ')          // If this is not a blank
      result.append(s.charAt(k));  // append it to result
  return result.toString();
}
```

SOLUTION 7.14   `A Alpha Z Zero Zeroes a alpha bath bin z zero`

SOLUTION 7.15   To modify `precedes` so that it also returns true when its two string arguments are equal, just change the operator in the final return statement to <=:

```java
if (s1.charAt(k) <= s2.charAt(k) )
  return true;
```

SOLUTION 7.16

a. true
b. true
c. false

d. false
e. false
f. true

g. false
h. false
i. false

SOLUTION 7.17   The variables in `TestStringEquals` are declared `static` because they are used in `static` methods. Whenever you call a method directly from `main()`, it must be `static` because `main()` is static. Remember that `static` elements are associated with the class, not with its instances. So `main()` can only use static elements because they don't depend on the existence of instances.

SOLUTION 7.18

a. `String s3 = s1.substring(s1.indexOf('n'))`
   `+ s1.substring(0,s1.indexOf('n'));`

b. `String s4 = s2.substring(6) + " " + s2.substring(0,5);`

c. `String s5 = s2.substring(0,6) + s1.substring(0,3);`

EXERCISES

Note: For programming exercises, **first** draw a UML class diagram describing all classes and their inheritance relationships and/or associations.

EXERCISE 7.1   Explain the difference between the following pairs of terms:

a. *Unit indexing* and *zero indexing*.

b. *Data structure* and *data type*.

c. `StringBuffer` and `String`.

d. `String` and `StringTokenizer`.

e. *Declaring a variable* and *instantiating a* `String`.

f. A `Font` and a `FontMetrics` object.

EXERCISE 7.2   Fill in the blanks.

a. When the first character in a string has index 0, this is known as _____.

b. A sequence of characters enclosed within quotes is known as a _____.

EXERCISE 7.3   Given the `String` *str* with the value "to be or not to be that is the question," write Java expressions to extract each of the substrings shown below. For each substring, provide two sets of answers: one that uses the actual index numbers of the substrings—for example, the first "to" goes from 0 to 2—and a second, more general solution that will also retrieve the substring from the following string "it is easy to become what you want to become." (*Hint*: In the second case, use `length()` and `indexOf()` along with `substring()` in your expressions. If necessary, you may use local variables to store intermediate results. The answer to (a) is provided as an example.)

a. the first "to" in the string

```
str.substring(0, 2)                                    // Answer 1
str.substring(str.indexOf("to"), str.indexOf("to") + 2)  // Answer 2
```

b. the last "to" in the string
c. the first "be" in the string
d. the last "be" in the string

e. the first four characters in the string
f. the last four characters in the string

EXERCISE 7.4 Identify the syntax errors in each of the following, assuming that s is the literal string "exercise":

a. `s.charAt("hello")`
b. `s.indexOf(10)`
c. `s.substring("er")`

d. `s.lastIndexOf(er)`
e. `s.length`

EXERCISE 7.5 Evaluate each of the following expressions, assuming that s is the literal string "exercise":

a. `s.charAt(5)`
b. `s.indexOf("er")`
c. `s.substring(5)`

d. `s.lastIndexOf('e')`
e. `s.length()`

EXERCISE 7.6 Write your own `equalsIgnoreCase()` method using only other `String` methods.

EXERCISE 7.7 Write your own `String` equality method without using the `String` class's `equals()` method. (*Hint*: Modify the `precedes()` method.)

EXERCISE 7.8 Even though Java's `String` class has a built-in `toLowerCase()` method, write your own implementation of this method. It should take a `String` parameter and return a `String` with all its letters written in lowercase.

EXERCISE 7.9 Write a method that converts its `String` parameter so that letters are written in blocks five characters long. For example, consider the following two versions of the same sentence:

```
Plain :   This is how we would ordinarily write a sentence.
Blocked : Thisi showw ewoul dordi naril ywrit easen tence
```

EXERCISE 7.10 Design and implement an applet that lets the user type a document into a `TextArea` and then provides the following analysis of the document: the number of words in the document, the number of characters in the document, and the percentage of words that have more than six letters.

EXERCISE 7.11 Design and write an applet that searches for single-digit numbers in a text and changes them to their corresponding words. For example, the string "4 score and 7 years ago" would be converted into "four score and seven years ago".

EXERCISE 7.12 A palindrome is a string that is spelled the same way backward and forward. For example, *mom, dad, radar, 727* and *able was i ere i saw elba* are all examples of palindromes. Write a Java applet that lets the user type in a word or phrase and then determines whether the string is a palindrome.

EXERCISE 7.13   Write a maze program that uses a string to store a representation of the maze. Write a method that accepts a `String` parameter and prints a two-dimensional representation of a maze. For example, the maze shown here, where O marks the entrance and exit, can be generated from the following string:

```
String: XX_XXXXXXXX_XXX_XXXX_XX___XXX_XX_XX_XXX___X___XXXXXXXX_X
  O
XX XXXXXXX
X  XXX XXX
X XX    XX
X XX XX XX
X    X     O
XXXXXXXX X
```

Sam Penn
14 Bridge St.
Hoboken, NJ 01881

EXERCISE 7.14   Write a method that takes a delimited string to store a name and address from which you can print a mailing label. For example, if the string contains "Sam Penn:14 Bridge St.:Hoboken, NJ 01881", the method should print the label shown in the margin.

EXERCISE 7.15   Design and implement an applet that plays Time Bomb with the user. Here's how the game works. The computer picks a secret word and then prints one asterisk for each letter in the word: * * * * *. The user guesses at the letters in the word. For every correct guess, an asterisk is replaced by a letter: * e * * *. For every incorrect guess, the time bomb's fuse grows shorter. When the fuse disappears, after, say, six incorrect guesses, the bomb explodes. Store the secret words in a delimited string and invent your own representation for the time bomb.

EXERCISE 7.16   **Challenge:** The global replace function is a string-processing algorithm found in every word processor. Write a method that takes three `String` arguments: a document, a target string, and a replacement string. The method should replace every occurrence of the target string in the document with the replacement string. For example, if the document is "To be or not to be, that is the question", and the target string is "be", and the replacement string is "see", the result should be, "To see or not to see, that is the question".

EXERCISE 7.17   **Challenge:**   Design and implement an applet that plays the following game with the user. Let the user pick a letter between *A* and *Z*. Then let the computer guess the secret letter. For every guess the player has to tell the computer whether it's too high or too low. The computer should be able to guess the letter within five guesses. Do you see why?

EXERCISE 7.18   **Challenge:** A *list* is a sequential data structure. Design a `List` class that uses a comma-delimited `String`—such as, "a,b,c,d,12,dog"—to implement a list. Implement the following methods for this class:

```
void addItem( Object o );      // Use Object.toString()
String getItem(int position);
String toString();
void deleteItem(int position);
void deleteItem(String item);
int getPosition(String item);
String getHead();              // First element
List getTail();                // All but the first element
int length();                  // Number of items
```

EXERCISE 7.19   Challenge: Use a delimited string to create a `PhoneList` class with an instance method to insert names and phone numbers, and a method to look up a phone number when a user provides a person's name. Since your class will take care of looking things up, you don't have to worry about keeping the list in alphabetical order. For example, the following string could be used as such a directory:

```
mom:860-192-9876::bill g:654-0987-1234::mary lancelot:123-842-1100
```

EXERCISE 7.20   Design and implement an applet or application that displays a multiline message in various fonts and sizes input by the user. Let the user choose from among a fixed selection of fonts, sizes, and styles.

Photograph courtesy of Gary Gay, Creative Eye/MIRA.com.

8

Inheritance and Polymorphism

OBJECTIVES

After studying this chapter, you will

- Understand the concepts of inheritance and polymorphism.
- Know how Java's dynamic binding mechanism works.
- Be able to design and use abstract methods and classes.
- Be able to design and use polymorphic methods.
- Gain a better understanding of object-oriented design.

OUTLINE

8.1 Introduction

Among the most important concepts in object-oriented programming are the concepts of inheritance and polymorphism. We first introduced the idea of inheritance in Chapter 0. There we compared inheritance to the natural form of inheritance, in which horses and cows share certain inherited characteristics, such as being warm-blooded, by virtue of their being mammals. We also gave the example of a hierarchy of chess pieces and showed how different kinds of chess pieces, such as `Pawn` and `Bishop`, inherited certain shared characteristics from their `ChessPiece` superclass.

We took a more technical look at inheritance in Chapter 3, where we talked about the `toString()` method and how it is inherited from the `Object` class. We illustrated there how subclasses of `Object` could override the inherited `toString()` method in order to customize it for their purposes. We also introduced the idea of polymorphism, in which a method call, such as `obj.toString()`, can have different behaviors depending on the type of object, `obj`, on which it is called.

In Chapter 4, we continued introducing inheritance and polymorphism, when we learned about Java's Abstract Windowing Toolkit (AWT) and Swing hierarchies, the class hierarchies that are used to create Graphical User Interfaces (GUIs). We also learned how to extend a class to create our own subclass, and we made limited use of inheritance in the design of the `SimpleGUI` class. We were also introduced to the concept of a Java interface, and we learned how to use the `ActionListener` interface to enable a `SimpleGUI` to handle action events while the GUI is running.

In this chapter we will take a much closer look at these important object-oriented concepts. We will learn how Java's *dynamic binding* mechanism works and how it makes polymorphism possible. Most important, we will see why inheritance and polymorphism are essential elements of object-oriented design, and we will learn how to use these important tools to design several different programs. In keeping with our running games example, we will develop a `TwoPlayerGame` hierarchy and show how it can simplify the implementation of `OneRowNim` and other two-player games.

8.2 Java's Inheritance Mechanism

As we described in Chapter 0, **class inheritance** is the mechanism whereby a class acquires (*inherits*) the methods and variables of its superclasses. To remind you of the basic concept, let's repeat an earlier example: Just as horses inherit the attributes and behaviors associated with mammals and vertebrates, a Java subclass inherits the attributes and behaviors of its superclasses.

Figure 8.1 uses a UML diagram to illustrate the relationships among horses, mammals, vertebrates, and animals. As the root of the hierarchy, which is always shown at the top, the Animal class contains the most general attributes, such as being alive and being able to move. All animals share these attributes. The class of vertebrates is a somewhat more specialized type of animal, in that vertebrates have backbones. Similarly, the class of mammals is a further specialization over the vertebrates in that mammals are warm-blooded and nurse their young. Finally, the class of horses is a further specialization over the class of mammals, in that all horses have four legs. Some mammals, such as humans, do not have four legs. Thus, by virtue of its class's position in this hierarchy, we can infer that a horse is a living, moving, four-legged vertebrate, which is warm blooded and nurses its young.

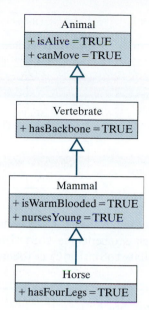

Figure 8.1 A class hierarchy for horses.

We have deliberately used an example from the natural world to show that the concept of inheritance in Java is inspired by its counterpart in the natural world. But how exactly does the concept of inheritance apply to Java (and to other object-oriented languages)? And, more important, how do we use the inheritance mechanism in object-oriented design?

8.2.1   Using an Inherited Method

In Java, the public and protected instance methods and instance variables of a superclass are inherited by all of its subclasses. This means that objects belonging to the subclasses can use the inherited variables and methods as their own.

We have already seen some examples of this in earlier chapters. For example, recall that by default all Java classes are subclasses of the `Object` class, which is the most general class in Java's class hierarchy. One public method that is defined in the `Object` class is the `toString()` method. Because every class in the Java hierarchy is a subclass of `Object`, every class inherits the `toString()` method. Therefore, `toString()` can be used with any Java object.

To illustrate this, suppose we define a `Student` class as follows:

```java
public class Student {
    protected String name;
    public Student(String s) {
        name = s;
    }
    public String getName() {
        return name;
    }
}
```

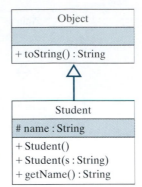

Figure 8.2   The Student class hierarchy.

Figure 8.2 shows the relationship between this class and the `Object` class. As a subclass of `Object`, the `Student` class inherits the `toString()` method. Therefore, for a given `Student` object, we can call its `toString()` as follows:

```
Student stu = new Student("Stu");
System.out.println(stu.toString());
```

How does this work? That is, how does Java know where to find the `toString()` method, which, after all, is not defined in the `Student` class? The answer to this question is crucial to understanding how Java's inheritance mechanism works.

Note in this example that the variable `stu` is declared to be of type `Student` and is assigned an instance of the `Student` class. When the expression `stu.toString()` is executed, Java will first look in the `Student` class for a definition of the `toString()` method. Not finding one there, it will then search up the `Student` class hierarchy (Fig. 8.2) until it finds a public or protected definition of the `toString()` method. In this case, it finds a `toString()` method in the `Object` class and executes that implementation of `toString()`. As you know from Chapter 3, this would result in the expression `stu.toString()` returning something like:

```
Student@cde100
```

The default implementation of `toString()` returns the name of the object's class and the address (`cde100`) where the object is stored in memory. However, this type of result is much too general and not particularly useful.

8.2.2   Overriding an Inherited Method

In Chapter 3 we pointed out that the `toString()` method is designed to be *overridden*—that is, to be redefined in subclasses of `Object`. Overriding `toString()` in a subclass provides a customized string representation of the objects in that subclass. By redefining `toString()` in our `OneRowNim` class, we were able to customize its actions so that it returned useful information about the current state of a `OneRowNim` game.

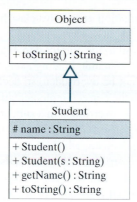

Figure 8.3 The revised Student class hierarchy.

To override `toString()` for the `Student` class, let's add the following method definition to the `Student` class:

```java
public String toString() {
  return "My name is " + name +  " and I am a Student.";
}
```

Given this change, the revised `Student` class hierarchy is shown in Figure 8.3. Note that both `Object` and `Student` contain implementations of `toString()`. Now, when the expression `stu.toString()` is invoked, the following, more informative, output is generated:

```
My name is Stu and I am a Student.
```

In this case, when Java encounters the method call `stu.toString()`, it invokes the `toString()` method that it finds in the `Student` class (Fig. 8.3).

These examples illustrate two important object-oriented concepts: inheritance and method overriding.

EFFECTIVE DESIGN: Inheritance.   The public and protected instance methods (and variables) in a class can be used by objects that belong to the class's subclasses.

EFFECTIVE DESIGN: Overriding a Method.   Overriding an inherited method is an effective way to customize that method for a particular subclass.

8.2.3   Static Binding, Dynamic Binding, and Polymorphism

The mechanism that Java uses in these examples is known as **dynamic binding**. In dynamic binding, a method call is bound to the correct implementation of the method at runtime by the Java Virtual Machine (JVM).

Dynamic binding is contrasted with **static binding**, the mechanism by which the Java compiler *resolves* the association between a method call and the correct method implementation when the program is compiled. In order for dynamic binding to work, the JVM needs to maintain some kind of representation of the Java class hierarchy, including classes defined by the programmer. When the JVM encounters a method call, it uses information about the class hierarchy to *bind* the method call to the correct implementation of that method.

Dynamic binding

In Java, all method calls use dynamic binding except methods that are declared `final` or `private`. Final methods cannot be overridden, so declaring a method as `final` means that the Java compiler can bind it to the correct implementation. Similarly, private methods are not inherited and therefore cannot be overridden in a subclass. In effect, private methods are final methods and the compiler can perform the binding at compile time.

Polymorphism

Java's dynamic-binding mechanism, which is also called *late* binding or *runtime* binding, leads to what is know as *polymorphism*. **Polymorphism** is a feature of object-oriented languages whereby the same method call can lead to different behaviors depending on the type of object on which the method call is made. The term *polymorphism* means, literally, having many (poly) shapes (morphs). Here's a simple example:

```
Object obj;                                // Static type: Object
obj = new Student("Stu");                  // Actual type: Student
System.out.println(obj.toString());        // Prints "My name is Stu..."
obj = new OneRowNim(11);                    // Actual type: OneRowNim
System.out.println(obj.toString());        // Prints "nSticks = 11, player = 1"
```

The variable `obj` is declared to be of type `Object`. This is its **static**, or *declared*, type. A variable's static type never changes. However, a variable also has an **actual**, or *dynamic*, type. This is the actual type of the object that has been assigned to the variable. As you know, an `Object` variable can be assigned objects from any `Object` subclass. In the second statement, `obj` is assigned a `Student` object. Thus, at this point in the program, the actual type of the variable `obj` is `Student`. When `obj.toString()` is invoked in the third line, Java begins its search for the `toString()` method at the `Student` class, because that is the variable's actual type.

In the fourth line, we assign a `OneRowNim` object to `obj`, thereby changing its actual type to `OneRowNim`. Thus, when `obj.toString()` is invoked in the last line, the `toString()` method is bound to the implementation found in the `OneRowNim` class.

Thus, we see that the same expression, `obj.toString()`, is bound alternatively to two different `toString()` implementations, based on the actual type of the object, `obj`, on which

Polymorphic method

it is invoked. This is polymorphism, and we will sometimes say that the `toString()` method is a *polymorphic* method. A **polymorphic method** is a method that behaves differently when it is invoked on different objects. An overridden method, such as the `toString()` method, is an example of a polymorphic method because its use can lead to different behaviors depending upon the object on which it is invoked.

The example given above is admittedly somewhat contrived. In some object-oriented languages, a code segment such as the one in the example would use static binding rather than dynamic binding. In other words, the compiler would be able to figure out the bindings. So let's take an example where static binding, also called *early* binding, is not possible. Consider the following method definition:

```
public void polyMethod(Object obj) {
    System.out.println(obj.toString()); // Polymorphic
}
```

The method call in this method, `obj.toString()`, cannot be bound to the correct implementation of `toString()` until the method is actually invoked—that is, at runtime. For example, suppose we make the following method calls in a program:

```
Student stu = new Student("Stu");
polyMethod(stu);
OneRowNim nim = new OneRowNim();
polyMethod(nim);
```

The first time `polyMethod()` is called, the `obj.toString()` is invoked on a `Student` object. Java will use its dynamic-binding mechanism to associate this method call with the `toString()` implementation in `Student` and output "My name is Stu and I am a Student". The second time `polyMethod()` is called, the `obj.toString()` expression is invoked on a `OneRowNim` object. In this case, Java will bind the method call to the implementation in the `OneRowNim` class. The output generated in this case will report how many sticks are left in the game.

The important point here is that polymorphism occurs when an overridden method is called on a superclass variable, `obj`. In such a case, the actual method implementation that is invoked is determined at runtime. The determination depends on the type of object assigned to the variable. Thus, we say that the method call `obj.toString()` is polymorphic because it is bound to different implementations of `toString()` depending on the actual type of the object bound to `obj`.

8.2.4 Polymorphism and Object-Oriented Design

Now that we understand how inheritance and polymorphism work in Java, it will be useful to consider an example that illustrates how these mechanisms can be useful in designing classes and methods. We have been using the various `System.out.print()` and `System.out.println()` methods since Chapter 1. The `print()` and `println()` methods are examples of **overloaded** methods—that is, methods that have the same name but different parameter lists. Remember that a method's signature involves its name, plus the type, number, and order of its parameters. Methods that have the same name but different parameters are said to be overloaded.

Overloaded methods

Here are the signatures of some of the different `print()` and `println()` methods:

```
print(char c);          println(char c);
print(int i);           println(int i);
print(double d);        println(double d);
print(float f);         println(float f);
print(String s);        println(String s);
print(Object o);        println(Object o);
```

Basically, there are `print()` and `println()` methods for every type of primitive data, plus methods for printing any type of object. When Java encounters an expression involving `print()` or `println()`, it chooses which particular `print()` or `println()` method to call. To determine the correct method, Java relies on the differences in the signatures of the various `print()` methods. For example, the argument of the expression `print(5)` is an `int`, so it is associated with the method whose signature is `print(int i)` because its parameter is an `int`.

Note that there is only one set of print() and println() methods for printing Objects. The reason is that the print(Object o) and println(Object o) methods use polymorphism to print any type of object. While we do not have access to the source code for these methods, we can make an educated guess that their implementations utilize the polymorphic toString() method, as follows:

```java
public void print(Object o) {
    System.out.print(o.toString());
}

public void println(Object o) {
    System.out.println(o.toString());
}
```

Here again we have a case where an expression, o.toString(), is bound dynamically to the correct implementation of toString() based on the type of Object that the variable o is bound to. If we call System.out.print(stu), where stu is a Student, then the toString() method in the Student class is invoked. On the other hand, if we call System.out.print(game), where game is a OneRowNim, then the toString() method in the OneRowNim class is invoked.

Extensibility   The beauty of using polymorphism in this way is the flexibility and extensibility it allows. The print() and println() methods can print any type of object, even new types of objects that did not exist when these library methods were written.

SELF-STUDY EXERCISES

EXERCISE 8.1   To confirm that the print() and println() methods are implemented along the lines that we suggest here, compile and run the TestPrint program shown below. Describe how it confirms our claim.

```java
public class TestPrint {
    public static void main(String args[]) {
        System.out.println(new Double(56));
        System.out.println(new TestPrint());
    }
}
```

EXERCISE 8.2   Override the toString() method in the TestPrint class and rerun the experiment. Describe how this adds further confirmation to our claim.

8.2.5   Using super to Refer to the Superclass

One question that might occur to you is: Once you override the default toString() method, is it then impossible to invoke the default method on a Student object? The default toString() method (and any method from an object's superclass) can be invoked using the super keyword. For example, suppose that within the Student class, you wanted to concatenate the results of the default and new toString() methods. The following expression would accomplish that:

```java
super.toString() + toString()
```

The `super` keyword specifies that the first `toString()` is the one implemented in the super-class. The second `toString()` refers simply to the version implemented within the `Student` class. We will see additional examples of using the `super` keyword in the following sections.

Keyword `super`

SELF-STUDY EXERCISES

EXERCISE 8.3   Consider the following class definitions and determine the output that would be generated by the code segment.

```java
public class A {
    public void method() { System.out.println("A"); }
}
public class B extends A {
    public void method() { System.out.println("B"); }
}

                          // Determine the output from this code segment
A a = new A();
a.method();
a = new B();
a.method();
B b = new B();
b.method();
```

EXERCISE 8.4   For the class B defined in the preceding exercise, modify its `method()` so that it invokes A's version of `method()` before printing out *B*.

EXERCISE 8.5   Given the definitions of the classes A and B, which of the following statements are valid? Explain.

```java
A a = new B();
a = new A();
B b = new A();
b = new B();
```

8.2.6   Inheritance and Constructors

Java's inheritance mechanism applies to a class's public and protected instance variables and methods. It does not apply to a class's constructors. To illustrate some of the implications of this language feature, let's define a subclass of `Student` called `CollegeStudent`:

```java
public class CollegeStudent extends Student {
    public CollegeStudent() { }
    public CollegeStudent(String s) {
        super(s);
    }
    public String toString() {
        return "My name is " + name +
                " and I am a CollegeStudent.";
    }
}
```

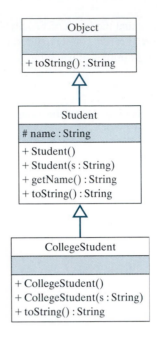

Figure 8.4   The class hierarchy for CollegeStudent.

Because CollegeStudent is a subclass of Student, it inherits the public and protected instance methods and variables from Student. So a CollegeStudent has an instance variable for name, and it has a public getName() method. Recall that a protected element, such as the name variable in the Student class, is accessible only within the class and its subclasses. Unlike public elements, it is not accessible to other classes.

Note that CollegeStudent overrides the toString() method, giving it a more customized implementation. The hierarchical relationship between CollegeStudent and Student is shown in Figure 8.4. A CollegeStudent is a Student, and both are Objects.

Note how we have implemented the CollegeStudent(String s) constructor. Because the superclass's constructors are not inherited, we have to implement this constructor in the subclass if we want to be able to assign a CollegeStudent's name during object construction. The method call, super(s), is used to invoke the superclass constructor and pass it s, the student's name. The superclass constructor will then assign s to the name variable.

Constructor chaining

As we have noted, a subclass does not inherit constructors from its superclasses. However, if the subclass constructor does not explicitly invoke a superclass constructor, Java will automatically invoke the default superclass constructor—in this case, super(). By "default superclass constructor" we mean the constructor that has no parameters. For a subclass that is several layers down in the hierarchy, this automatic invoking of the super() constructor will be repeated upward through the entire class hierarchy. Thus when a CollegeStudent is constructed, Java will automatically call Student() and Object(). If one of the superclasses does not contain a default constructor, this will result in a syntax error.

If you think about this, it makes good sense. How else will the inherited elements of the object be created? For example, in order for a CollegeStudent to have a name variable, a Student object, where name is declared, must be created. The CollegeStudent constructor then extends the definition of the Student class. Similarly, in order for a Student object to have the attributes common to all objects, an Object instance must be created and then extended into a Student.

Thus, unless a constructor explicitly calls a superclass constructor, Java will automatically invoke the default superclass constructors. It does this *before* executing the code in its own constructor. For example, if you had two classes, A and B, where B is a subclass of A, then whenever you create an instance of B, Java will first invoke A's constructor before executing the code in B's constructor. Thus, Java's default behavior during construction of B is equivalent to the following implementation of B's constructor:

```java
public B() {
    A();   // Call the superconstructor
           // Now continue with this constructor's code
}
```

Calls to the default constructors are made all the way up the class hierarchy, and the superclass constructor is always called before the code in the class's constructor is executed.

SELF-STUDY EXERCISES

EXERCISE 8.6 Consider the following class definitions and describe what would be output by the code segment.

```java
public class A {
    public A() { System.out.println("A"); }
}
public class B extends A {
    public B() { System.out.println("B"); }
}
public class C extends B {
    public C() { System.out.println("C"); }
}

            // Determine the output.
A a = new A();
B b = new B();
C c = new C();
```

8.3 Abstract Classes, Interfaces, and Polymorphism

In Java, there are three kinds of polymorphism:

- Overriding an inherited method.
- Implementing an abstract method.
- Implementing a Java interface.

In the preceding section we saw examples of the first type of polymorphism. All forms of polymorphism are based on Java's dynamic-binding mechanism. In this section we will develop an example that illustrates the other two types of polymorphism and discuss some of the design implications involved in choosing one or the other approach.

8.3.1 Implementing an Abstract Method

An important feature of polymorphism is the ability to invoke a polymorphic method that has been defined only abstractly in the superclass. To illustrate this feature, we will develop a hierarchy of simulated animals that make characteristic animal sounds, an example that is widely used to illustrate polymorphism.

Extensibility   As we all know from our childhood, animals have distinctive ways of speaking. A cow goes "moo"; a pig goes "oink"; and so on. Let's design a hierarchy of animals that simulates this characteristic by printing the characteristic sounds these animals make. We want to design our classes so that any given animal will return something like "I am a cow and I go moo" when we invoke the `toString()` method. Moreover, we want to design this collection of classes so that it is extensible—that is, so that we can continue to add new animals to our menagerie without having to change any of the code in the other classes.

Figure 8.5 provides a summary of the design we will implement. The `Animal` class is an `abstract` class. That is why its name is italicized in the UML diagram. This class is abstract because its `speak()` method is an **abstract method**, namely, a method definition that does not contain an implementation. That is, the method definition contains just the method's signature, not its body. Any class that contains an abstract method must itself be declared abstract. Here is the definition of the `Animal` class:

```
public abstract class Animal {
    protected String kind;                              // Cow, pig, cat, etc.

    public Animal()  {  }
    public String toString() {
        return "I am a " + kind + " and I go " + speak();
    }
    public abstract String speak();                     // Abstract method
}
```

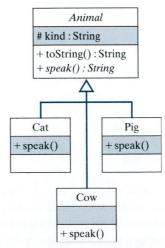

Figure 8.5 The `Animal` class hierarchy.

Note how we declare the abstract method (`speak()`) and the abstract class. Because one or more of its methods is not implemented, an abstract class cannot be instantiated. That is, you cannot say:

```
Animal animal = new Animal(); // Error: Animal is abstract
```

Even though it is not necessary, we give the `Animal` class a constructor. If we had left this off, Java would have supplied a default constructor that would be invoked when `Animal` subclasses are created.

Java has the following rules on using abstract methods and classes.

Rules for abstract classes

- Any class containing an `abstract` method must be declared an `abstract` class.
- An `abstract` class cannot be instantiated. It must be subclassed.
- A subclass of an `abstract` class may be instantiated only if it implements *all* of the superclass's `abstract` methods. A subclass that implements only some of the `abstract` methods must itself be declared `abstract`.
- A class may be declared `abstract` even it contains no `abstract` methods. It could, for example, contain instance variables that are common to all its subclasses.

Even though an abstract method is not implemented in the superclass, it can be called in the superclass. Indeed, note how the `toString()` method calls the abstract `speak()` method. The dynamic binding mechanism is the reason this works in Java. The polymorphic `speak()` method will be defined in the various `Animal` subclasses. When the `Animal.toString()` method is called, Java will decide which actual `speak()` method to call based on what subclass of `Animal` is involved.

Definitions for two such subclasses are shown in Figure 8.6. In each case the subclass extends the `Animal` class and provides its own constructor and its own implementation of the `speak()` method. Note that in their respective constructors, we can refer to the `kind` instance

```java
public class Cat extends Animal {
    public Cat() {
        kind = "cat";
    }
    public String speak() {
        return "meow";
    }
}
public class Cow extends Animal {
    public Cow() {
        kind = "cow";
    }
    public String speak() {
        return "moo";
    }
}
```

Figure 8.6 Two `Animal` subclasses.

variable, which is inherited from the `Animal` class. By declaring `kind` as a `protected` variable, it is inherited by all `Animal` subclasses but hidden from all other classes. On the other hand, if `kind` had been declared `public`, it would be inherited by `Animal` subclasses, but it would also be accessible to every other class, which would violate the information-hiding principle.

Given these definitions, we can now demonstrate the power and flexibility of inheritance and polymorphism. Consider the following code segment:

```
Animal animal = new Cow();
System.out.println(animal.toString()); // A cow goes moo
animal = new Cat();
System.out.println(animal.toString()); // A cat goes meow
```

We first create a `Cow` object and then invoke its (inherited) `toString()` method. It returns "I am a cow and I go moo." We then create a `Cat` object and invoke its (inherited) `toString()` method, which returns "I am a cat and I go meow." In other words, Java is able to determine the appropriate implementation of `speak()` at runtime in each case. The invocation of the abstract `speak()` method in the `Animal`'s `toString()` method is a second form of polymorphism.

Advantage of polymorphism

What is the advantage of polymorphism here? The main advantage is the extensibility it affords our `Animal` hierarchy. We can define and use completely new `Animal` subclasses without redefining or recompiling the rest of the classes in the hierarchy. Note that the `toString()` method in the `Animal` class does not need to know what type of `Animal` subclass will be executing its `speak()` method. The `toString()` method will work correctly for any subclass of `Animal` because every nonabstract subclass of `Animal` must implement the `speak()` method.

To get a better appreciation of the flexibility and extensibility of this design, it might be helpful to consider an alternative design that does not use polymorphism. One such alternative would be to define each `Animal` subclass with its own speaking method. A `Cow` would have a `moo()` method; a `Cat` would have a `meow()` method; and so forth. Given this design, we could use a `switch` statement to select the appropriate method call. For example, consider the following method definition:

```
public String talk(Animal a) {
  if (a instanceof Cow)
    return "I am a " + kind + " and I go " + a.moo();
  else if (a instanceof Cat)
    return "I am a " + kind + " and I go " + a.meow();
  else
    return "I don't know what I am";
}
```

In this example, we introduce the `instanceof` operator, which is a built-in boolean operator. It returns true if the object on its left-hand side is an instance of the class on its right-hand side.

The `talk()` method would produce more or less the same result. If you call `talk(new Cow())`, it will return "I am a cow and I go moo". However, with this design, it is not possible to extend the `Animal` hierarchy without rewriting and recompiling the `talk()` method.

Extensibility

Thus, one of the chief advantages of using polymorphism is the great flexibility and extensibility it affords. We can define new `Animal` subclasses and define their `speak()` methods.

These will all work with the `toString()` method in the `Animal` class without any need to revise that method.

Another advantage of using abstract methods is the control that it gives the designer of the `Animal` hierarchy. By making it an abstract class with an abstract `speak()` method, any nonabstract `Animal` subclass must implement the `speak()` method. This lends a great degree of predictability to the subclasses in the hierarchy, making it easier to use them in applications.

SELF-STUDY EXERCISES

EXERCISE 8.7   Following the examples in this section, define an `Animal` subclass named `Pig` that goes "oink."

EXERCISE 8.8   Show how you would have to modify the `talk()` method defined above to incorporate the `Pig` class.

8.3.2   Implementing a Java Interface

A third form of polymorphism results through the implementation of Java **interfaces**, which are like classes but contain only abstract method definitions and constant (`final`) variables. An interface cannot contain instance variables. We have already seen interfaces, as when we encountered the `ActionListener` interface in Chapter 4.

Java interface

The designer of an interface specifies what methods will be implemented by classes that *implement* the interface. This is similar to what we did when we implemented the abstract `speak()` method in the animal example. The difference between implementing a method from an interface and from an abstract superclass is that a subclass *extends* an abstract superclass but *implements* an interface.

Java's interface mechanism gives us another way to design polymorphic methods. To see how this works, we will provide an alternative design for our animal hierarchy. Rather than defining `speak()` as an abstract method within the `Animal` superclass, we will define it as an abstract method in the `Speakable` interface (Fig. 8.7).

Note the differences between this definition of `Animal` and the previous definition. This version no longer contains the abstract `speak()` method. Therefore, the class itself is not an abstract class. However, because the `speak()` method is not declared in this class, we cannot call the `speak()` method in the `toString()` method unless we cast this object into a `Speakable` object.

```java
public interface Speakable {
    public String speak();
}

public class Animal {
    protected String kind;                         // Cow, pig, cat, etc.
    public Animal()  {  }
    public String toString() {
        return "I am a " + kind + " and I go " + ((Speakable)this).speak();
    }
}
```

Figure 8.7   Defining and using the `Speakable` interface.

Cast operation

We encountered the cast operation in Chapter 5, where we used it with primitive types such as (int) and (char). Here we use it to specify the actual type of some object. In this toString() example, this object is some type of Animal subclass, such as a Cat. The cast operation, (Speakable), changes the object's actual type to Speakable, which syntactically allows its speak() method to be called.

Given these definitions, Animal subclasses will now extend the Animal class and implement the Speakable interface:

```java
public class Cat extends Animal implements Speakable {
    public Cat() { kind = "cat"; }
    public String speak() { return "meow";  }
}
public class Cow extends Animal implements Speakable {
    public Cow() { kind = "cow";  }
    public String speak() { return "moo";  }
}
```

To implement a Java interface, one must provide a method implementation for each of the abstract methods in the interface. In this case there is only one abstract method, the speak() method.

Note, again, the expression from the toString() method in the Animal class

```java
((Speakable)this).speak();
```

which casts this object into a Speakable object. This cast is required because an Animal does not necessarily have a speak() method. A speak() method is not defined in the Animal class. However, the Cat subclass of Animal does implement a sleep() method as part of its Speakable interface. Therefore, in order to invoke speak() on an object from one of the Animal subclasses, the object must actually be a Speakable and we must perform the cast as shown here.

Interface inheritance

This illustrates, by the way, that a Cat, by virtue of extending the Animal class and implementing the Speakable interface, is both an Animal and a Speakable. In general, a class that implements an interface has that interface as one of its types. Interface implementation is itself a form of inheritance. A Java class can be a direct subclass of only one superclass. But it can implement any number of interfaces.

Given these definitions of the Cow and Cat subclasses, the following code segment will produce the same results as in the preceding section.

```java
Animal animal = new Cow();
System.out.println(animal.toString());  // A cow goes moo
animal = new Cat();
System.out.println(animal.toString());  // A cat goes meow
```

Although the design is different, both approaches produce the same result. We will put off, for now, the question of how one decides whether to use an abstract method or a Java interface. We will get to this question when we design the TwoPlayerGame class hierarchy later in this chapter.

8.4 Example: A Toggle Button

The ability to extend an existing class is one of the most powerful features of object-oriented programming. It allows objects to reuse code defined in the superclasses without having to redefine or recompile the code. As we saw in Chapter 4, a programmer-defined applet, such as `GreeterApplet`, uses the `public` methods defined for `JApplets`, `JPanels`, `Containers`, `Components`, and `Objects` simply because it is a subclass of `JApplet` (Fig. 4.11). By the same token, it can use all of the `public` and `protected` instance variables and constants defined in these classes by simply referring to them in its own code.

Reusing code

In this section, we present an example of how inheritance can be used to extend and customize the functionality of a Java library class. As we saw in Chapter 4, a `JButton` is a GUI component that can be associated with a particular action by implementing the `ActionListener` interface. For example, we used a `JButton` in the `GreeterApplet` to generate a greeting to the user.

In this section, we will design a more sophisticated button. We will call it a `ToggleButton` and define it as a `JButton` subclass that toggles its label whenever it is clicked, in addition to carrying out some kind of associated action.

Problem decomposition

A light switch behaves similarly to a `ToggleButton` in this sense. Whenever you flick a light switch, it changes its label from "on" to "off," but it also turns the lights on or off. Although different switches are associated with different lights, every light switch toggles its label each time it is clicked. So let's design a `ToggleButton` that behaves like a light switch.

The main idea in our design is that a `ToggleButton` is a `JButton` that has two labels. By default, a `JButton` has just a single label. Thus, because of the type of behavior we want to elicit, we need to define `ToggleButton` as a subclass of `JButton` with two `String` variables that will serve as its alternative labels (Fig. 8.8). Note that we give it a constructor method that will allow us to provide the initial value of its two label strings. Another important feature of a `ToggleButton` is that it should act as its own `ActionListener` so that it can toggle its label whenever it is clicked. Therefore, it must also implement the `ActionListener` interface.

The complete definition of `ToggleButton` is given in Figure 8.9. Note how we have defined its constructor. Recall that the `JButton` class has a constructor method with the signature `JButton(String)`, which allows us to set a `JButton`'s label during instantiation. We need to do the same thing with one of `ToggleButton`'s two labels. That is, when we create a `Toggle-Button`, we want to initialize its label to one of its two alternative labels (here, "On" or "Off").

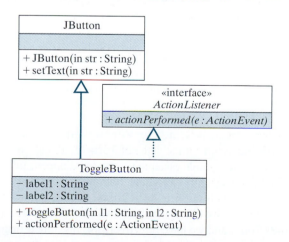

Figure 8.8 A `ToggleButton` is a `JButton` with two labels.

```java
import java.awt.*;
import java.awt.event.*;
import javax.swing.*;
public class ToggleButton extends JButton implements ActionListener {
    private String label1;                          // Toggle between two labels
    private String label2;

    public ToggleButton(String l1, String l2) {     // Constructor
        super(l1);                                  // Use l1 as the default label
        label1 = l1;
        label2 = l2;
        addActionListener(this);
    }
    public void actionPerformed(ActionEvent e) {
        String tempS = label1;                      // Swap the labels
        label1 = label2;
        label2 = tempS;
        setText(label1);
    } // actionPerformed()
} // ToggleButton class
```

Figure 8.9 Definition of the ToggleButton class.

Because constructor methods are *not* inherited by the subclass, we want to invoke the superclass's constructor in the ToggleButton() constructor using the super keyword. This must be done as the first statement in the ToggleButton() constructor. By passing l1 to the superconstructor, we are making the first string that the user gives us the default label for our ToggleButton. This will be the label that appears on the button when it is first displayed in the applet.

Swapping algorithm

Note also in the ToggleButton() constructor that the ToggleButton is designated as its own ActionListener, so whenever it is clicked, its actionPerformed() method will be invoked. The actionPerformed() method exchanges the button's current label for its other label. Swapping two values in memory is a standard programming practice used in many different algorithms. In order to do it properly, you must use a third variable to temporarily store one of the two values you are swapping. The comments in actionPerformed() provide a step-by-step trace of the values of the three variables involved.

JAVA PROGRAMMING TIP: Swapping Values. It is necessary to use a temporary variable whenever you are swapping two values of any type in memory. The temporary variable holds the first value while you overwrite it with the second value.

Swapping values requires a temporary variable

The first statement in actionPerformed() creates a temporary String variable named tempS and assigns it the value of label1. Recall that label1 was the button's initial label. To make this example easier to follow, let's suppose that initially label1 is "off" and label2 is "on". After line 1 is executed, both tempS and label1 contain "off" as their value. Line 2 then assigns label2's value to label1. Now both label1 and label2 store "on" as their value. In line 3 we assign tempS's value to label2. Now label2 stores "off" and label1 stores "on", and we have effectively swapped their original values.

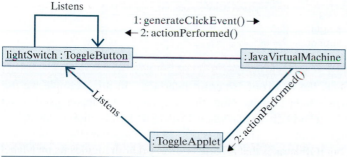

Figure 8.10 The `ToggleButton` has two `ActionListeners`. When the button is clicked, the JVM will call each listener's `actionPerformed()` method, and each listener will take its own independent action.

The next time we invoke `actionPerformed()`, `label1` and `label2` will have their opposite values initially. Swapping them a second time will assign them their initial values again. We can continue toggling their values in this way indefinitely. To complete the method, the last statement in `actionPerformed()` assigns `label1`'s current value as the new `ToggleButton`'s label.

Now that we have seen that a `ToggleButton` toggles its label between two values, what about performing an associated action? To do this, we need a design involving multiple event handlers, one to handle the toggling of the button's label and the other to handle its associated action (Fig 8.10). In this design, `lightSwitch` has two listeners that respond to its events: the `lightSwitch` itself, as a result of the `actionPerformed()` method in its class, and the `ToggleApplet`, as a result of the `actionPerformed()` method in this class.

The implementation of this design is given by `ToggleApplet`, an applet that uses a `ToggleButton` (Fig. 8.11). Like the applet we designed in Chapter 4, this applet extends the

Multiple event handlers

```
import java.applet.*;
import java.awt.*;
import java.awt.event.*;
import javax.swing.*;

public class ToggleApplet extends JApplet implements ActionListener {
  private ToggleButton lightSwitch;

  public void init() {
    lightSwitch = new ToggleButton ("off","on");
    getContentPane().add(lightSwitch);
    lightSwitch.addActionListener(this);
  } // init()

  public void actionPerformed(ActionEvent e)  {
    showStatus("The light is " + lightSwitch.getText());
  } // actionPerformed()
} // ToggleApplet class
```

Figure 8.11   Definition of the `ToggleApplet` class.

Figure 8.12 When clicked, ToggleApplet button causes "The light is on" or "The light is off" to appear in the applet's status bar.

JApplet class and implements the ActionListener interface. In this example we use a ToggleButton to simulate a light switch. Note that we assign the applet itself as an ActionListener for the lightSwitch, so that when lightSwitch is clicked, the applet displays the message "The light is on" or "The light is off" in its status bar (Fig. 8.12). This is a somewhat trivial action, but it illustrates that a ToggleButton both toggles its own label *and* carries out some associated action.

The ToggleButton design satisfies several key design principles of object-oriented programming. First and foremost, it uses inheritance to extend the functionality of the predefined JButton class—the extensibility principle. Second, it encapsulates a ToggleButton's essential behavior within the ToggleButton class itself—the modularity principle. Finally, it hides the mechanism by which a ToggleButton manages its labels—the information-hiding principle.

Object-oriented design principles

EFFECTIVE DESIGN: Inheritance. Inheritance enables you to specialize an object's behavior. A ToggleButton does everything a JButton does, plus it can toggle its own label.

SELF-STUDY EXERCISES

EXERCISE 8.9 Write a code segment (not a whole method) to swap two boolean variables, b1 and b2.

EXERCISE 8.10 Suppose you are designing an applet that plays a card game, and you want a single button that can be used both to deal the cards and to collect the cards. Write a code segment that creates this type of button, adds it to the applet, and designates the applet as its ActionListener.

8.5 Example: The Cipher Class Hierarchy

Problem decomposition

Suppose we wish to design a collection of cipher classes, including a Caesar cipher and a transposition cipher. Because the basic operations used in all forms of encryption are the same, both the Caesar class and the Transpose class will have methods to encrypt() and decrypt() messages, where each message is assumed to be a string of words separated by spaces. These methods will take a String of words and translate each word using the encoding method appropriate for that cipher. Therefore, in addition to encrypt() and decrypt(), each cipher class will need polymorphic encode() and decode() methods, which take a single word and encode or decode it according to the rules of the particular cipher.

From a design perspective, the encrypt() and decrypt() methods will be the same for every class: They simply break the message into words and encode or decode each word. However, the encode() and decode() methods will be different for each different cipher. The Caesar.encode() method should replace each letter of a word with its substitute, whereas the Transpose.encode() method should rearrange the letters of the word. Given these considerations, how should we design this set of classes?

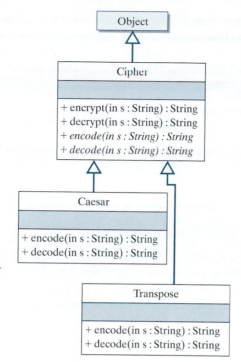

Figure 8.13 A hierarchy of cipher classes. The Cipher class implements operations common to all ciphers. The Caesar and Transpose classes implement functions unique to those kinds of ciphers.

Because all of the various ciphers will have the same methods, it will be helpful to define a common Cipher superclass (Fig. 8.13). Cipher will encapsulate the features that the individual cipher classes have in common—the encrypt(), decrypt(), encode(), and decode() methods.

Some of these methods can be implemented in the Cipher class itself. For example, the encrypt() method should take a message in a String parameter, encode each word in the message, and return a String result. The following method definition will work for any cipher:

```
public String encrypt(String s) {
  StringBuffer result = new StringBuffer("");
  StringTokenizer words = new StringTokenizer(s);     // Tokenize
  while (words.hasMoreTokens()) {                      // Encode each word
    result.append(encode(words.nextToken()) + " ");
  }
  return result.toString();                            // Return result
} // encrypt()
```

This method creates a local StringBuffer variable, result, and uses StringTokenizer to break the original String into its component words. It uses the encode() method to encode the word, appending the result into result. The result is converted back into a String and returned as the encrypted translation of s, the original message.

Inheritance   If we define `encrypt()` in the superclass, it will be inherited by all of `Cipher`'s subclasses. Thus, if we define `Caesar` and `Transpose` as

```
public class Caesar extends Cipher { ... }
public class Transpose extends Cipher { ... }
```

instances of these classes will be able to use the `encrypt()` method.

Historical Cryptography

Cryptography, the study of secret writing, has had a long and interesting history. Modern-day cryptographic techniques employ sophisticated mathematics to *encrypt* and *decrypt* messages. Today's most secure encryption schemes are safe from attack by even the most powerful computers. Given our widespread dependence on computers and the Internet, secure encryption has become an important application area in computer science. While the cryptographic techniques used up through World War II are too simple to serve as the basis for modern-day encryption schemes, they can provide an interesting and accessible introduction to this important area of computer science.

One of the earliest and simplest *ciphers* is the Caesar cipher, used by Julius Caesar during the Gallic wars. According to this scheme, letters of the alphabet are *shifted* by three letters, wrapping around at the end of the alphabet:

```
PlainText:     abcdefghijklmnopqrstuvwxyz
CaesarShifted: defghijklmnopqrstuvwxyzabc
```

When encrypting a message, you take each letter of the message and replace it with its corresponding letter from the shifted alphabet. To decrypt a secret message, you perform the operation in reverse—that is, you take the letter from the shifted alphabet and replace it with the corresponding letter from the **plaintext** alphabet. Thus, "hello" would be Caesar encrypted as "khoor."

The Caesar cipher is a **substitution cipher**, because each letter in the plaintext message is replaced with a substitute letter from the **ciphertext** alphabet. A more general form of substitution cipher uses a *keyword* to create a ciphertext alphabet:

```
PlainText:  abcdefghijklmnopqrstuvwxyz
Ciphertext: xylophneabcdfgijkmqrstuvwz
```

In this example, the keyword "xylophone", (with the second *o* removed) is used to set up a substitution alphabet. According to this cipher, the word "hello" would be encrypted as "epddi". Substitution ciphers of this form are found frequently in cryptogram puzzles in the newspapers.

Another type of cipher is known as a **transposition cipher**. In this type of cipher, the letters in the original message are rearranged in some methodical way. A simple example would be if we reversed the letters in each word so that "hello" became "olleh".

On the other hand, the polymorphic `encode()` method cannot be implemented within `Cipher`. This is because, unlike the `encrypt()` method, which is the same for every `Cipher` subclass, the `encode()` method will be different for every subclass. However, by declaring the `encode()` method as `abstract`, we can leave its implementation up to the `Cipher` subclasses. Thus, within the `Cipher` class, we would define `encode()` and `decode()` as follows:

```
                                                // Abstract methods
public abstract String encode(String word);
public abstract String decode(String word);
```

These declarations within the `Cipher` class tell the compiler that these methods will be implemented in `Cipher`'s subclasses. By defining it as `abstract`, `encode()` can be used in the `Cipher` class, as it is within the `encrypt()` method.

8.5.1 Class Design: `Caesar`

Figure 8.14 provides the full definition of the `Cipher` class. The `encode()` and `decode()` methods are declared abstract. They are intended to be implemented by `Cipher`'s subclasses.

Note again that `encrypt()` and `decrypt()`, which are implemented in `Cipher`, invoke `encode()` and `decode()`, respectively, which are declared in `Cipher` but implemented in `Cipher`'s subclasses. Java's dynamic-binding mechanism will take care of invoking the appropriate implementation of `encode()` or `decode()`, depending on what type of object is involved. For example, if `caesar` and `transpose` are `Caesar` and `Transpose` objects,

encode() and decode() are polymorphic

```java
import java.util.*;

public abstract class Cipher {
  public String encrypt(String s) {
    StringBuffer result = new StringBuffer("");      // Use a StringBuffer
    StringTokenizer words = new StringTokenizer(s);  // Break s into its words
    while (words.hasMoreTokens()) {                  // For each word in s
      result.append(encode(words.nextToken()) + " "); // Encode it
    }
    return result.toString();                        // Return the result
  } // encrypt()

  public String decrypt(String s) {
    StringBuffer result = new StringBuffer("");      // Use a StringBuffer
    StringTokenizer words = new StringTokenizer(s);  // Break s into words
    while (words.hasMoreTokens()) {                  // For each word in s
      result.append(decode(words.nextToken()) + " "); //  Decode it
    }
    return result.toString();                        // Return the decryption
  } // decrypt()

  public abstract String encode(String word);        // Abstract methods
  public abstract String decode(String word);
} // Cipher class
```

Figure 8.14 The abstract `Cipher` class.

respectively, then the following calls to encrypt() will cause their respective encode() methods to be invoked:

```
caesar.encrypt("hello world");       // Invokes caesar.encode()
transpose.encrypt("hello world");    // Invokes transpose.encode()
```

When caesar.encrypt() is called, it will in turn invoke caesar.encode()—that is, it will call the encode() method implemented in the Caesar class. When transpose.encrypt() is invoked, it will in turn invoke transpose.encode(). In this way, each object can perform the encoding algorithm appropriate for its type of cipher.

Method polymorphism

8.5.2   Algorithm Design: Shifting Characters

The Caesar class is defined as an extension of Cipher (Fig. 8.15). The only methods implemented in Caesar are encode() and decode(). The encode() method takes a String parameter and returns a String result. It takes each character of its parameter (word.charAt(k)) and performs a Caesar shift on the character. Note how the shift is done:

```
ch = (char)('a' + (ch -'a'+ 3) % 26); // Caesar shift
```

Recall from Chapter 5 that char data in Java are represented as 16-bit integers. This enables us to manipulate characters as numbers. Thus, to shift a character by 3, we simply add 3 to its integer representation.

```java
public class Caesar extends Cipher {
  public String encode(String word) {
    StringBuffer result = new StringBuffer();        // Initialize a string buffer
    for (int k = 0; k < word.length(); k++) {        // For each character in word
      char ch = word.charAt(k);                      //  Get the character
      ch = (char)('a' + (ch -'a'+ 3) % 26);          //  Perform caesar shift
      result.append(ch);                             //  Append it to new string
    }
    return result.toString();                        // Return the result as a string
  } // encode()
  public String decode(String word) {
    StringBuffer result = new StringBuffer();        // Initialize a string buffer
    for (int k = 0; k < word.length(); k++) {        // For each character in word
    char ch = word.charAt(k);                        //  Get the character
      ch = (char)('a' + (ch - 'a' + 23) % 26);       //  Perform reverse shift
      result.append(ch);                             //  Append it to new string
    }
    return result.toString();                        // Return the result as a string
  } // decode()
} // Caesar class
```

Figure 8.15 The Caesar class.

For example, suppose that the character (`ch`) is *h*, which has an ASCII code of 104 (see *Character* Table 5.13). We want to shift it by 3, giving *k*, which has a code of 107. In this case, we could *conversions* simply add 3 to 104 to get the desired result. However, suppose that `ch` was the character *y*, which has an ASCII code of 121. If we simply add 3 in this case, we get 124, a code that corresponds to the symbol "|" which is not our desired result. Instead, we want the shift in this case to "wrap around" to the beginning of the alphabet, so that *y* gets shifted into *b*. In order to accomplish this we need to do some modular arithmetic.

Let us suppose that the 26 characters *a* to *z* were numbered 0 through 25, so that *a* corresponds to 0, *b* to 1, and so on up to *z* as 25. If we take any number *N* and divide it (modulo 26), we would get a number between 0 and 25. Suppose, for example, *y* were numbered 24. Shifting it by 3 would give us 27, and 27 % 26 would give us 1, which corresponds to *b*. So if the *a* to *z* were numbered 0 through 25, then we can shift any character within that range by using the following formula:

```
(ch + 3) % 26          // Shift by 3 with wraparound
```

To map a character in the range *a* to *z* onto the integers 0 to 25, we can simply subtract *a* from it:

```
'a' - 'a' = 0
'b' - 'a' = 1
'c' - 'a' = 2
...
'z' - 'a' = 25
```

Finally, we simply map the numbers 0 through 25 back to the characters *a* to *z* to complete the shift operation:

```
(char)('a' + 0) = 'a'
(char)('a' + 1) = 'b'
(char)('a' + 2) = 'c'
...
(char)('a' + 25) = 'z'
```

Note the use here of the cast operator (`char`) to convert an integer into a `char`.

To summarize, we can shift any character by 3 if we map it into the range 0 to 25, then add 3 to it modulo 26, then map the result back into the range *a* to *z*. Thus, shifting *y* would *Modular* go as follows: *arithmetic*

```
(char)('a' + (ch -'a'+ 3) % 26)      // Perform Caesar shift
(char)('a' + ('y' - 'a' +3) % 26)    // on 'y'
(char)(97 + (121 - 97 + 3) % 26)     // Map 'y' to 0..25
(char)(97 + (27 % 26))               // Shift by 3, wrapping around
(char)(97 + 1)                       // Map result back to 'a' to 'z'
(char)(98)                           // Convert from int to char
'b'
```

```
public class Transpose extends Cipher {
                                    // encode() reverses and returns a word
  public String encode(String word) {
    StringBuffer result = new StringBuffer(word);
    return result.reverse().toString();
  } // encode()
  public String decode(String word) {
    return encode(word);              // Just call encode
  } // decode()
} // Transpose class
```

Figure 8.16   The Transpose class.

Note that in `decode()` a reverse Caesar shift is done by shifting by 23, which is $26 - 3$. If the original shift is 3, we can reverse it by shifting an additional 23. Together this gives a shift of 26, which will give us back our original string.

8.5.3   Class Design: `Transpose`

The `Transpose` class (Fig. 8.16) is structured the same as the `Caesar` class. It implements both the `encode()` and `decode()` methods. The key element here is the transpose operation, which in this case is a simple reversal of the letters in the word. Thus, "hello" becomes "olleh". This is very easy to do when using the `reverse()` method from the `StringBuffer` class. The `decode()` method is even simpler, because all you need to do in this case is call `encode()`. Reversing the reverse of a string gives you back the original string.

8.5.4   Testing and Debugging

Figure 8.17 provides a simple test program for testing `Cipher` and its subclasses. It creates a `Caesar` cipher and a `Transpose` cipher and then encrypts and decrypts the same sentence using each cipher. If you run this program, it will produce the following output:

```
********* Caesar Cipher Encryption *********
PlainText: this is the secret message
Encrypted: wklv lv wkh vhfuhw phvvdjh
Decrypted: this is the secret message
********* Transpose Cipher Encryption *********
PlainText: this is the secret message
Encrypted: siht si eht terces egassem
Decrypted: this is the secret message
```

SELF-STUDY EXERCISES

EXERCISE 8.11   Modify the `Caesar` class so that it will allow various-sized shifts to be used. (*Hint*: Use an instance variable to represent the shift.)

EXERCISE 8.12   Modify `Transpose.encode()` so that it uses a rotation instead of a reversal. That is, a word like "hello" should be encoded as "ohell" with a rotation of one character.

```
public class TestEncrypt {
  public static void main(String argv[]) {
    Caesar caesar = new Caesar();
    String plain = "this is the secret message";      // Here's the message
    String secret = caesar.encrypt(plain);             // Encrypt the message
    System.out.println(" ********* Caesar Cipher Encryption *********");
    System.out.println("PlainText: " + plain);         // Display the results
    System.out.println("Encrypted: " + secret);
    System.out.println("Decrypted: " + caesar.decrypt(secret)); // Decrypt

    Transpose transpose = new Transpose();
    secret = transpose.encrypt(plain);
    System.out.println("\n ********* Transpose Cipher Encryption *********");
    System.out.println("PlainText: " + plain);         // Display the results
    System.out.println("Encrypted: " + secret);
    System.out.println("Decrypted: " + transpose.decrypt(secret)); // Decrypt
  } // main()
} // TestEncrypt class
```

Figure 8.17 The TestEncrypt class.

8.6 CASE STUDY: A Two-Player Game Hierarchy

In this section we will redesign our OneRowNim game to fit within a hierarchy of classes of two-player games. There are many games that characteristically involve two players: checkers, chess, tic-tac-toe, guessing games, and so forth. However, there are also many games that involve just one player: blackjack, solitaire, and others. There are also games that involve two or more players, such as many card games. Thus, our redesign of OneRowNim as part of a two-player game hierarchy will not be our last effort to design a hierarchy of game-playing classes. We will certainly redesign things as we learn new Java language constructs and as we try to extend our game library to other kinds of games.

This case study will illustrate how we can apply inheritance and polymorphism, as well as other object-oriented design principles. The justification for revising OneRowNim at this point is to make it easier to design and develop other two-player games. As we have seen, one characteristic of class hierarchies is that more general attributes and methods are defined in top-level classes. As one proceeds down the hierarchy, the methods and attributes become more specialized. Creating a subclass is a matter of specializing a given class.

8.6.1 Design Goals

One of our design goals is to revise the OneRowNim game so that it fits into a hierarchy of two-player games. One way to do this is to generalize the OneRowNim game by creating a superclass that contains those attributes and methods that are common to all two-player games. The superclass will define the most general and generic elements of two-player games. All two-player games, including OneRowNim, will be defined as subclasses of this top-level superclass and will inherit and possibly override its public and protected variables and methods. Also, our top-level class will contain certain abstract methods, whose implementations will be given in OneRowNim and other subclasses.

Generic superclass

A second goal is to design a class hierarchy that makes it possible for computers to play the game, as well as human users. Thus, for a given two-player game, it should be possible for two humans to play each other, or for two computers to play each other, or for a human to play against a computer. This design goal will require that our design exhibit a certain amount of flexibility. As we shall see, this is a situation in which Java interfaces will come in handy.

Another important goal is to design a two-player game hierarchy that can easily be used with a variety of different user interfaces, including command-line interfaces and GUIs. To handle this feature, we will develop Java interfaces to serve as interfaces between our two-player games and various user interfaces.

8.6.2   Designing the TwoPlayerGame Class

To begin revising the design of the OneRowNim game, we first need to design a top-level class, which we will call the TwoPlayerGame class. What variables and methods belong in this class? One way to answer this question is to generalize our current version of OneRowNim by moving any variables and methods that apply to all two-player games up to the TwoPlay-erGame class. All subclasses of TwoPlayerGame—which includes the OneRowNim class— would inherit these elements. Figure 8.18 shows the current design of OneRowNim.

What variables and methods should we move up to the TwoPlayerGame class? Clearly, the class constants, PLAYER_ONE and PLAYER_TWO, apply to all two-player games. These should be moved up. On the other hand, the MAX_PICKUP and MAX_STICKS constants apply just to the OneRowNim game. They should remain in the OneRowNim class.

The nSticks instance variable is a variable that only applies to the OneRowNim game but not to other two-player games. It should stay in the OneRowNim class. On the other hand, the onePlaysNext variable applies to all two-player games, so we will move it up to the TwoPlayerGame class.

Constructors are not inherited

Because constructors are not inherited, all of the constructor methods will remain in the OneRowNim class. The instance methods, takeSticks() and getSticks(), are specific to OneRowNim, so they should remain there. However, the other methods, getPlayer(), gameOver(), getWinner(), and reportGameState(), are methods that would be useful to all two-player games. Therefore these methods should be moved up to the superclass. Of course, while these methods can be defined in the superclass, some of them can only be im-

OneRowNim
+ **PLAYER_ONE** : int = 1
+ **PLAYER_TWO** : int = 2
+ **MAX_PICKUP** : int = 3
+ **MAX_STICKS** : int = 11
− nSticks : int
− onePlaysNext : boolean
+ OneRowNim()
+ OneRowNim(nsticks : int)
+ OneRowNim(nsticks : int, starter : int)
+ takeSticks(n : int) : boolean
+ getSticks() : int
+ getPlayer() : int
+ gameOver() : boolean
+ getWinner() : int
+ reportGameState() : String

Figure 8.18 The current OneRowNim class.

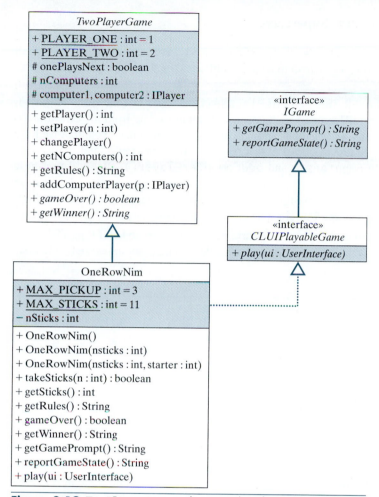

Figure 8.19 TwoPlayerGame is the superclass for OneRowNim and other two-player games.

plemented in subclasses. For example, the `reportGameState()` method reports the current state of the game, so it has to be implemented in `OneRowNim`. Similarly, the `getWinner()` method defines how the winner of the game is determined, a definition that can only occur in the subclass. Every two-player game needs methods such as these. Therefore, we will define these methods as abstract methods in the superclass. The intention is that `TwoPlayerGame` subclasses will provide game-specific implementations for these methods.

Given these considerations, we come up with the design shown in Figure 8.19. The design shown in this figure is much more complex than the designs used in earlier chapters. However, the complexity comes from combining ideas already discussed in previous sections of this chapter, so don't be put off by it.

To begin with, note that we have introduced two Java interfaces into our design in addition to the `TwoPlayerGame` superclass. As we will show, these interfaces lead to a more flexible design and one that can easily be extended to incorporate new two-player games. Let's take each element of this design separately.

8.6.3   The TwoPlayerGame Superclass

As we have stated, the purpose of the TwoPlayerGame class is to serve as the superclass for all two-player games. Therefore, it should define the variables and methods shared by two-player games.

The PLAYER_ONE, PLAYER_TWO, and onePlaysNext variables and the getPlayer(), setPlayer(), and changePlayer() methods have been moved up from the OneRowNim class. Clearly, these variables and methods apply to all two-player games. Note that we have also added three new variables, nComputers, computer1, computer2, and their corresponding methods, getNComputers() and addComputerPlayer(). We will use these elements to give our games the capability to be played by computer programs. Because we want all of our two-player games to have this capability, we define these variables and methods in the superclass rather than in OneRowNim and subclasses of TwoPlayerGame.

Note that the computer1 and computer2 variables are declared to be of type IPlayer. IPlayer is an interface containing a single method declaration, the makeAMove() method:

```
public interface IPlayer {
    public String makeAMove(String prompt);
}
```

Why do we use an interface here rather than some type of game-playing object? This is a good design question. Using an interface here makes our design more flexible and extensible because it frees us from having to know the names of the classes that implement the makeAMove() method. The variables computer1 and computer2 will be assigned objects that implement IPlayer via the addComputerPlayer() method.

Game-dependent algorithms

The algorithms used in the various implementations of makeAMove() are *game-dependent*—they depend on the particular game being played. It would be impossible to define a game-playing object that would suffice for all two-player games. Instead, if we want an object that plays OneRowNim, we would define a OneRowNimPlayer and have it implement the IPlayer interface. Similarly, if we want an object that plays checkers, we would define a CheckersPlayer and have it implement the IPlayer interface. By using an interface here,

The IPlayer interface

our TwoPlayerGame hierarchy can deal with a wide range of differently named objects that play games, as long as they implement the IPlayer interface. Using the IPlayer interface adds flexibility to our game hierarchy and makes it easier to extend it to new, yet undefined, classes. We will discuss the details of how to design a game player in Section 8.6.7.

Turning now to the methods defined in TwoPlayerGame, we have already seen implementations of getPlayer(), setPlayer(), and changePlayer() in the OneRowNim class. We will just move those implementations up to the superclass. The getNComputers() method is the assessor method for the nComputers variable, and its implementation is routine. The addComputerPlayer() method adds a computer player to the game. Its implementation is as follows:

```
public void addComputerPlayer(IPlayer player) {
   if (nComputers == 0)
      computer2 = player;
   else if (nComputers == 1)
      computer1 = player;
   else
      return;                              // No more than 2 players
   ++nComputers;
}
```

As we noted earlier, the classes that play the various TwoPlayerGames must implement the IPlayer interface. The parameter for this method is of type IPlayer. The algorithm we use checks the current value of nComputers. If it is 0, which means that this is the first IPlayer added to the game, the player is assigned to computer2. This allows the human user to be associated with PLAYERONE if this is a game between a computer and a human user.

If nComputers equals 1, which means that we are adding a second IPlayer to the game, we assign that player to computer1. In either of these cases, we increment nComputers. Note what happens if nComputers is neither 1 nor 2. In that case, we simply return without adding the IPlayer to the game and without incrementing nComputers. This, in effect, limits the number of IPlayers to two. (A more sophisticated design would throw an exception to report an error, but we will leave that for a subsequent chapter.)

The addComputerPlayer() method is used to initialize a game after it is first created. If this method is not called, the default assumption is that nComputers equals zero and that computer1 and computer2 are both null. Here's an example of how it could be used:

```
OneRowNim nim = new OneRowNim(11);   // 11 sticks
nim.add(new NimPlayer(nim));         // 2 computer players
nim.add(new NimPlayerBad(nim));
```

Note that the NimPlayer() constructor takes a reference to the game as its argument. Clearly, our design should not assume that the names of the IPlayer objects would be known to the TwoPlayerGame superclass. This method allows the objects to be passed in at runtime. We will discuss the details of NimPlayerBad in Section 8.6.7.

The getRules() method is a new method whose purpose is to return a string that describes the rules of the particular game. This method is implemented in the TwoPlayerGame class with the intention that it will be overridden in the various subclasses. For example, its implementation in TwoPlayerGame is:

Overriding a method

```
public String getRules() {
   return "The rules of this game are: ";
}
```

and its redefinition in `OneRowNim` is:

```java
public String getRules() {
  return "\n*** The Rules of One Row Nim ***\n" +
  "(1) A number of sticks between 7 and " + MAX_STICKS +
        " is chosen.\n" +
  "(2) Two players alternate making moves.\n" +
  "(3) A move consists of subtracting between 1 and\n\t" +
  MAX_PICKUP +
  " sticks from the current number of sticks.\n" +
  "(4) A player who cannot leave a positive\n\t" +
  " number of sticks for the other player loses.\n";
}
```

The idea is that each `TwoPlayerGame` subclass will take responsibility for specifying its own set of rules in a form that can be displayed to the user.

You might recognize that defining `getRules()` in the superclass and allowing it to be overridden in the subclasses is a form of polymorphism. It follows the design of the `toString()` method, which we discussed earlier. This design will allow us to use code that takes the following form:

Polymorphism

```java
TwoPlayerGame game = new OneRowNim();
System.out.println(game.getRules());
```

In this example the call to `getRules()` is polymorphic. The dynamic-binding mechanism is used to invoke the `getRules()` method defined in the `OneRowNim` class.

The remaining methods in `TwoPlayerGame` are defined abstractly. The `gameOver()` and `getWinner()` methods are both *game-dependent* methods. That is, the details of their implementations depend on the particular `TwoPlayerGame` subclass in which they are implemented.

This is good example of how abstract methods should be used in designing a class hierarchy. We give abstract definitions in the superclass and leave the detailed implementations up to the individual subclasses. This allows the different subclasses to tailor the implementations to their particular needs, while allowing all subclasses to share a common signature for these tasks. This enables us to use polymorphism to create flexible, extensible class hierarchies.

Figure 8.20 shows the complete implementation of the abstract `TwoPlayerGame` class. We have already discussed the most important details of its implementation.

EFFECTIVE DESIGN: Abstract Methods.   Abstract methods allow you to give general definitions in the superclass and leave the implementation details to the different subclasses.

```
public abstract class TwoPlayerGame {
  public static final int PLAYER_ONE = 1;
  public static final int PLAYER_TWO = 2;

  protected boolean onePlaysNext = true;
  protected int nComputers = 0;              // How many computers
                                             // Computers are IPlayers

  protected IPlayer computer1, computer2;
  public void setPlayer(int starter) {
    if (starter == PLAYER_TWO)
      onePlaysNext = false;
    else onePlaysNext = true;
  } // setPlayer()
  public int getPlayer() {
    if (onePlaysNext)
      return PLAYER_ONE;
    else return PLAYER_TWO;
  } // getPlayer()
  public void changePlayer() {
    onePlaysNext = !onePlaysNext;
  } // changePlayer()
  public int getNComputers() {
    return nComputers;
  } // getNComputers()
  public String getRules() {
    return "The rules of this game are: ";
  } // getRules()
  public void addComputerPlayer(IPlayer player) {
    if (nComputers == 0)
      computer2 = player;
    else if (nComputers == 1)
      computer1 = player;
    else
      return;                                // No more than 2 players
    ++nComputers;
  } // addComputerPlayer()
  public abstract boolean gameOver();        // Abstract Methods
  public abstract String getWinner();
} // TwoPlayerGame class
```

Figure 8.20 The TwoPlayerGame class

8.6.4   The `CLUIPlayableGame` Interface

We turn now to the two interfaces shown in Figure 8.19. Taken together, the purpose of these interfaces is to create a connection between any two-player game and a command-line user interface (CLUI). The interfaces provide method signatures for the methods that will implement the details of the interaction between a `TwoPlayerGame` and a `UserInterface`. Because the details of this interaction vary from game to game, it is best to leave the implementation of these methods to the games themselves.

Note that `CLUIPlayableGame` extends the `IGame` interface. The `IGame` interface contains two methods that are used to define a standard form of communication between the CLUI and the game. The `getGamePrompt()` method defines the prompt used to signal the user for a move of some kind—for example, `"How many sticks do you take (1, 2, or 3)?"` And

Extending an interface

the `reportGameState()` method defines how the game will report its current state—for example, "There are 11 sticks remaining." `CLUIPlayableGame` adds the `play()` method to these two methods. As we will see shortly, the `play()` method contains the code that will control the playing of the game.

The source code for these interfaces is very simple:

```java
public interface CLUIPlayableGame extends IGame {
    public abstract void play(UserInterface ui);
}
public interface IGame {
    public String getGamePrompt();
    public String reportGameState();
} // IGame
```

Note that the `CLUIPlayableGame` interface extends the `IGame` interface. A `CLUIPlayableGame` is a game that can be played through a CLUI. The purpose of its `play()` method is to contain the *game-dependent* control loop that determines how the game is played via a user interface (UI). In pseudocode, a typical control loop for a game would look something like the following:

```
Initialize the game.
While the game is not over
  Report the current state of the game via the UI.
  Prompt the user (or the computer) to make a move via the UI.
  Get the user's move via the UI.
  Make the move.
  Change to the other player.
```

The play loop sets up an interaction between the game and the UI. The `UserInterface` parameter allows the game to connect directly to a particular UI. To allow us to play our games through a variety of UIs, we define `UserInterface` as the following Java interface:

```java
public interface UserInterface {
    public String getUserInput();
    public void report(String s);
    public void prompt(String s);
}
```

Any object that implements these three methods can serve as a UI for one of our `TwoPlayerGames`. This is another example of the flexibility of using interfaces in object-oriented design.

To illustrate how we use `UserInterface`, let's attach it to our `KeyboardReader` class, thereby letting a `KeyboardReader` serve as a CLUI for `TwoPlayerGames`. We do this simply by implementing this interface in the `KeyboardReader` class, as follows:

```java
public class KeyboardReader implements UserInterface
```

As it turns out, the three methods listed in `UserInterface` match three of the methods in the current version of `KeyboardReader`. This is no accident. The design of `UserInterface` was arrived at by identifying the minimal number of methods in `KeyboardReader` that were needed to interact with a `TwoPlayerGame`.

> **EFFECTIVE DESIGN: Flexibility of Java Interfaces.**   A Java interface provides a means of associating useful methods with a variety of different types of objects, leading to a more flexible object-oriented design.

The benefit of defining the parameter more generally as a `UserInterface` instead of as a `KeyboardReader` is that we will eventually want to allow our games to be played via other kinds of command-line interfaces. For example, we might later define an Internet-based CLUI that could be used to play `OneRowNim` among users on the Internet. This kind of extensibility—the ability to create new kinds of UIs and use them with `TwoPlayerGames`—is another important design feature of Java interfaces.

Generality principle

> **EFFECTIVE DESIGN: Extensibility and Java Interfaces.**   Using interfaces to define useful method signatures increases the extensibility of a class hierarchy.

As Figure 8.19 shows, `OneRowNim` implements the `CLUIPlayableGame` interface, which means it must supply implementations of all three abstract methods: `play()`, `getGame-Prompt()`, and `reportGameState()`.

8.6.5 Object-Oriented Design: Interfaces or Abstract Classes?

Why are these methods defined in interfaces? Couldn't we just as easily define them in the `TwoPlayerGame` class and use inheritance to extend them to the various game subclasses? After all, isn't the net result the same, namely, that `OneRowNim` must implement all three methods.

These are very good design questions, exactly the kinds of questions one should ask when designing a class hierarchy of any sort. As we pointed out in the `Animal` example earlier in the chapter, you can get the same functionality from an abstract interface and an abstract superclass method. When should we put the abstract method in the superclass, and when does it belong in an interface? A very good discussion of these and related object-oriented design issues is available in *Java Design, 2nd Edition*, by Peter Coad and Mark Mayfield (Yourdan Press, 1999). Our discussion of these issues follows many of the guidelines suggested by Coad and Mayfield.

Interfaces vs. abstract methods

We have already seen that using Java interfaces increases the flexibility and extensibility of a design. Methods defined in an interface exist independently of a particular class hierarchy. By their very nature, interfaces can be attached to any class, and this makes them very flexible to use.

Flexibility of interfaces

Another useful guideline for answering this question is that the superclass should contain the basic common attributes and methods that define a certain type of object. It should not necessarily contain methods that define certain *roles* that the object plays. For example, the `gameOver()` and `getWinner()` methods are fundamental parts of the definition of a `TwoPlayerGame`. One cannot define a game without defining these methods. By contrast, methods such as `play()`, `getGamePrompt()`, and `reportGameState()` are important for playing the game but they do not contribute in the same way to the game's definition. Thus these methods are best put into an interface. Therefore, one important design guideline is:

EFFECTIVE DESIGN: Abstract Methods. Methods defined abstractly in a superclass should contribute in a fundamental way to the basic definition of that type of object, not merely to one of its roles or its functionality.

8.6.6 The Revised `OneRowNim` Class

Figure 8.21 provides a listing of the revised `OneRowNim` class, one that fits into the `TwoPlayerGame` class hierarchy. Our discussion in this section will focus on the features of the game that are new or revised.

The `gameOver()` and `getWinner()` methods, which are now inherited from the `TwoPlayerGame` superclass, are virtually the same as in the previous version. One small change is that `getWinner()` now returns a `String` instead of an `int`. This makes the method more generally useful as a way of identifying the winner for all `TwoPlayerGames`.

Similarly, the `getGamePrompt()` and `reportGameState()` methods merely encapsulate functionality that was present in the earlier version of the game. In our earlier version the prompts to the user were generated directly by the main program. By encapsulating this information in an inherited method, we make it more generally useful to all `TwoPlayerGames`.

Inheritance and generality

The major change to `OneRowNim` comes in the `play()` method, which controls the playing of `OneRowNim` (Fig. 8.22). Because this version of the game incorporates computer players, the play loop is a bit more complex than in earlier versions of the game. The basic idea is still the same: The method loops until the game is over. On each iteration of the loop, one or the other of the two players, PLAYER_ONE or PLAYER_TWO, takes a turn making a move—that is, deciding how many sticks to pick up. If the move is a legal move, then it becomes the other player's turn.

Let's look now at how the code decides whether it is a computer's turn to move or a human player's turn. Note that at the beginning of the `while` loop, it sets the `computer` variable to null. It then assigns `computer` a value of either `computer1` or `computer2`, depending on whose turn it is. But recall that one or both of these variables may be `null`, depending on how many computers are playing the game. If there are no computers playing the game, then both variables will be null. If only one computer is playing, then `computer1` will be null. This is determined during initialization of the game, when the `addComputerPlayer()` is called. (See above.)

In the code following the `switch` statement, if `computer` is not `null`, then we call `computer.makeAMove()`. As we know, the `makeAMove()` method is part of the `IPlayer` interface. The `makeAMove()` method takes a `String` parameter that is meant to serve as a prompt, and returns a `String` that is meant to represent the `IPlayer`'s move:

```
public interface IPlayer {
    public String makeAMove(String prompt);
}
```

```java
public class OneRowNim extends TwoPlayerGame implements CLUIPlayableGame {
  public static final int MAX_PICKUP = 3;
  public static final int MAX_STICKS = 11;
  private int nSticks = MAX_STICKS;

  public OneRowNim() { }                                       // Constructors
  public OneRowNim(int sticks) {
    nSticks = sticks;
  } // OneRowNim()
  public OneRowNim(int sticks, int starter) {
    nSticks = sticks;
    setPlayer(starter);
  } // OneRowNim()
  public boolean takeSticks(int num) {
    if (num < 1 || num > MAX_PICKUP || num > nSticks)
      return false;                                            // Error
    else                                                       // Valid move
    {   nSticks = nSticks - num;
        return true;
    } // else
  } // takeSticks()
  public int getSticks() {
    return nSticks;
  } // getSticks()
  public String getRules() {
    return "\n*** The Rules of One Row Nim ***\n" +
    "(1) A number of sticks between 7 and " + MAX_STICKS +
        " is chosen.\n" +
    "(2) Two players alternate making moves.\n" +
    "(3) A move consists of subtracting between 1 and\n\t" +
        MAX_PICKUP + " sticks from the current number of sticks.\n" +
    "(4) A player who cannot leave a positive\n\t" +
    " number of sticks for the other player loses.\n";
  } // getRules()
  public boolean gameOver() {    /*** From TwoPlayerGame */
    return (nSticks <= 0);
  } // gameOver()
  public String getWinner()  {        /*** From TwoPlayerGame */
    if (gameOver()) //{
      return "" + getPlayer() + " Nice game.";
    return "The game is not over yet.";    // Game is not over
  } // getWinner()
```

Figure 8.21   The revised OneRowNim class, Part I.

In OneRowNim the "move" is an integer, representing the number of sticks the player picks. Therefore, in play() OneRowNim has to convert the String into an int, which represents the number of sticks the IPlayer picks up.

On the other hand, if computer is null, this means that it is a human user's turn to play. In this case, play() calls ui.getUserInput(), employing the user interface to input a value from the keyboard. The user's input must also be converted from String to int. Once the value of sticks is set, either from the user or from the IPlayer, the play() method calls takeSticks(). If the move is legal, then it changes whose turn it is, and the loop repeats.

```
/** From CLUIPlayableGame */
public String getGamePrompt() {
  return "\nYou can pick up between 1 and " +
               Math.min(MAX_PICKUP,nSticks) + " : ";
} // getGamePrompt()
public String reportGameState() {
  if (!gameOver())
     return ("\nSticks left: " + getSticks() +
        " Who's turn: Player " + getPlayer());
  else
     return ("\nSticks left: " + getSticks() +
      " Game over!  Winner is Player "  + getWinner() +"\n");
}   // reportGameState()
public void play(UserInterface ui) { // From CLUIPlayableGame interface
  int sticks = 0;
  ui.report(getRules());
  if (computer1 != null)
    ui.report("\nPlayer 1 is a " + computer1.toString());
  if (computer2 != null)
    ui.report("\nPlayer 2 is a " + computer2.toString());
  while(!gameOver()) {
    IPlayer computer = null;                          // Assume no computers
    ui.report(reportGameState());
    switch(getPlayer()) {
    case PLAYER_ONE:                                  // Player 1's turn
      computer = computer1;
      break;
    case PLAYER_TWO:                                  // Player 2's turn
      computer = computer2;
      break;
    } // cases
    if (computer != null) {                           // If computer's turn
      sticks = Integer.parseInt(computer.makeAMove(""));
      ui.report(computer.toString() + " takes " + sticks + " sticks.\n");
    } else {                                          // otherwise, user's turn
      ui.prompt(getGamePrompt());
      sticks =
         Integer.parseInt(ui.getUserInput());         // Get user's move
    }
    if (takeSticks(sticks))                           // If a legal move
      changePlayer();
  } // while
  ui.report(reportGameState());                       // The game is now over
} // play()
} // OneRowNim class
```

Figure 8.22   The revised OneRowNim class, Part II.

Encapsulation of game-dependent knowledge

There are a couple of important points about the design of the play() method. First, the play() method has to know what to do with the input it receives from the user or the IPlayer. This is game-dependent knowledge. The user is inputting the number of sticks to take in OneRowNim. For a tic-tac-toe game, the "move" might represent a square on the tic-tac-toe board. This suggests that play() is a method that should be implemented in OneRowNim, as it is here, because OneRowNim encapsulates the knowledge of how to play the One-Row Nim game.

The second point is that the method call `computer.makeAMove()` is another example of polymorphism at work. The `play()` method does not know what type of object the `computer` is, other than that it is an `IPlayer`—that is, an object that implements the `IPlayer` interface. As we will show in the next section, the `OneRowNim` game can be played by two different `IPlayers`: one named `NimPlayer` and another named `NimPlayerBad`. Each has its own game-playing strategy, as implemented by its own version of the `makeAMove()` method. Java uses dynamic binding to decide which version of `makeAMove()` to invoke depending on the type of `IPlayer` whose turn it is. Thus, by defining different `IPlayers` with different `makeAMove()` methods, this use of polymorphism makes it possible to test different game-playing strategies against each other.

Polymorphism

8.6.7   The `IPlayer` Interface

The last element of our design is the `IPlayer` interface, which, as we just saw, consists of the `makeAMove()` method. To see how we use this interface, let's design a class to play the game of `OneRowNim`. We will call the class `NimPlayerBad` and give it a very weak playing strategy. For each move it will pick a random number between 1 and 3, or between 1 and the total number of sticks left, if there are fewer than three sticks. (We will leave the task of defining `NimPlayer`, a good player, as an exercise.)

As an implementer of the `IPlayer` interface, `NimPlayerBad` will implement the `makeAMove()` method. This method will contain `NimPlayerBad`'s strategy (algorithm) for playing the game. The result of this strategy will be the number of sticks the player will pick up.

What other elements (variables and methods) will a `NimPlayerBad` need? Clearly, in order to play `OneRowNim`, the player must know the rules and the current state of the game. The best way to achieve this is to give the Nim player a reference to the `OneRowNim` game. Then it can call `getSticks()` to determine how many sticks are left, and it can use other public elements of the `OneRowNim` game. Thus, we will have a variable of type `OneRowNim`, and we will assign it a value in a constructor method.

Figure 8.23 shows the design of `NimPlayerBad`. Note that we have added an implementation of the `toString()` method. This will be used to give a string representation of `NimPlayerBad`. Also note that we have added a private helper method named `randomMove()`, which will generate an appropriate random number of sticks as the player's move.

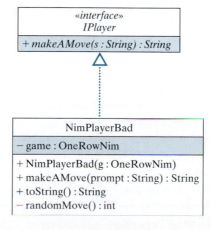

Figure 8.23 Design of the Nim-PlayerBad class.

```java
public class NimPlayerBad implements IPlayer {
  private OneRowNim game;

  public NimPlayerBad (OneRowNim game) {
    this.game = game;
  } // NimPlayerBad()

  public String makeAMove(String prompt) {
    return "" + randomMove();
  } // makeAMove()

  private int randomMove() {
    int sticksLeft = game.getSticks();
    return 1 + (int)(Math.random() * Math.min(sticksLeft, game.MAX_PICKUP));
  } // randomMove()

  public String toString() {
    String className =
        this.getClass().toString();            // Gets 'class NimPlayerBad'
    return className.substring(5);             // Cut off the word 'class'
  } // toString()
} // NimPlayerBad class
```

Figure 8.24   The `NimPlayerBad` class.

The implementation of `NimPlayerBad` is shown in Figure 8.24. The `makeAMove()` method converts `randomMove()` to a `String` and returns it, leaving it up to `OneRowNim`, the calling object, to convert that move back into an `int`. Recall the statement in `OneRowNim` where `makeAMove()` is invoked:

```java
sticks = Integer.parseInt(computer.makeAMove(""));
```

In this context, the **computer** variable, which is of type `IPlayer`, is bound to a `NimPlayer-Bad` object. In order for this interaction between the game and a player to work, the `OneRowNim` object must know what type of data is being returned by `NimPlayerBad`. This is a perfect use for a Java interface that specifies the signature of `makeAMove()` without committing to any particular implementation of the method. Thus, the association between `OneRowNim` and `IPlayer` provides a flexible and effective model for this type of interaction.

 EFFECTIVE DESIGN: Interface Associations.   Java interfaces provide a flexible way to set up associations between two different types of objects.

Finally, note the details of the `randomMove()` and `toString()` methods. The only new thing here is the use of the `getClass()` method in `toString()`. This is a method that is defined in the `Object` class and inherited by all Java objects. It returns a `String` of the form "class X" where *X* is the name of the object's class. Note here that we are removing the word "class" from the string before returning the class name. This allows our `IPlayer` objects to report what type of players they are, as in the following statement from `OneRowNim`:

```java
ui.report("\nPlayer 1 is a " + computer1.toString());
```

If `computer1` is a `NimPlayerBad`, it would report "Player1 is a NimPlayerBad".

EXERCISE 8.13   Define a class `NimPlayer` that plays the optimal strategy for `OneRowNim`. This strategy was described in Chapter 5.

8.6.8   Playing `OneRowNim`

Let's now write a `main()` method to play `OneRowNim`:

```java
public static void main(String args[]) {
  KeyboardReader kb = new KeyboardReader();
  OneRowNim game = new OneRowNim();
  kb.prompt("How many computers are playing, 0, 1, or 2?  ");
  int m = kb.getKeyboardInteger();
  for (int k = 0; k < m; k++) {
    kb.prompt("What type of player, " +
              "NimPlayerBad = 1, or NimPlayer = 2 ?  ");
    int choice = kb.getKeyboardInteger();
    if (choice == 1) {
      IPlayer computer = new NimPlayerBad(game);
      game.addComputerPlayer(computer);
    } else {
      IPlayer computer = new NimPlayer(game);
      game.addComputerPlayer(computer);
    }
  }
  game.play(kb);
} // main()
```

After creating a `KeyboardReader` and then creating an instance of `OneRowNim`, we prompt the user to determine how many computers are playing. We then repeatedly prompt the user to identify the names of the `IPlayer` and use the `addComputerPlayer()` method to initialize the game. Finally, we get the game started by invoking the `play()` method, passing it a reference to the `KeyboardReader`, our `UserInterface`.

In this example we have declared a `OneRowNim` variable to represent the game. This is not the only way to do things. For example, suppose we wanted to write a `main()` method that could be used to play a variety of different `TwoPlayerGame`s. Can we make this code more general? That is, can we rewrite it to work with any `TwoPlayerGame`?   *Generality*

A `OneRowNim` object is a `TwoPlayerGame` by virtue of inheritance, and it is also a `CLUIPlayableGame` by virtue of implementing that interface. Therefore, we can use either of these types to represent the game. Thus, one alternative way of coding this is as follows:

```java
TwoPlayerGame game = new OneRowNim();
...
IPlayer computer = new NimPlayer((OneRowNim)game);
...
((CLUIPlayableGame)game).play(kb);
```

Here we use a `TwoPlayerGame` variable to represent the game. However, note that we now have to use a cast expression, `(CLUIPlayableGame)`, in order to call the `play()` method. If we don't cast `game` in this way, Java will generate the following syntax error:

```
OneRowNim.java:126: cannot resolve symbol
symbol   : method play (KeyboardReader)
location: class TwoPlayerGame
       game.play(kb);
          ^
```

The reason for this error is that `play()` is not a method in the `TwoPlayerGame` class, so the compiler cannot find the `play()` method. By using the cast expression, we are telling the compiler to consider `game` to be a `CLUIPlayableGame`. That way it will find the `play()` method. Of course, the object assigned to `nim` must actually implement the `CLUIPlayableGame` interface in order for this to work at runtime. We also need a cast operation in the `NimPlayer()` constructor in order to make the argument (`computer`) compatible with that method's parameter.

Another alternative for the `main()` method would be the following:

```
CLUIPlayableGame game = new OneRowNim();
...
IPlayer computer = new NimPlayer((OneRowNim)game);
((TwoPlayerGame)game).addComputerPlayer(computer);
...
game.play(kb);
```

By representing the game as a `CLUIPlayableGame` variable, we don't need the cast expression to call `play()`, but we do need a different cast expression, `(TwoPlayerGame)`, to invoke `addComputerPlayer()`. Again, the reason is that the compiler cannot find the `addComputerPlayer()` method in the `CLUIPlayableGame` interface, so we must tell it to consider `game` as a `TwoPlayerGame`, which of course it is. We still need the cast operation for the call to the `NimPlayer()` constructor.

All three of the code options that we have considered will generate something like the interactive session shown in Figure 8.25 for a game in which two `IPlayer`s play each other.

Given our object-oriented design for the `TwoPlayerGame` hierarchy, we can now write generalized code that can play any `TwoPlayerGame` that implements the `CLUIPlayableGame` interface. We will give a specific example of this in the next section.

8.6.9   Extending the `TwoPlayerGame` Hierarchy

Now that we have described the design and the details of the `TwoPlayerGame` class hierarchy, let's use it to develop a new game. If we've gotten the design right, developing new two-player games and adding them to the hierarchy should be much simpler than developing them from scratch.

The new game is a guessing game in which the two players take turns guessing a secret word. The secret word will be generated randomly from a collection of words maintained by the game object. The letters of the word will be hidden with question marks, as in "????????". On each turn a player guesses a letter. If the letter is in the secret word, it replaces one or more question marks, as in "??????E?". A player continues to guess until an incorrect guess is made and then it becomes the other player's turn. Of course, we want to develop a version of this game that can be played either by two humans, or by one human against a computer—that is, against an `IPlayer`, or by two different `IPlayer`s.

```
How many computers are playing, 0, 1, or 2? 2
*** The Rules of One Row Nim ***
(1) A number of sticks between 7 and 11 is chosen.
(2) Two players alternate making moves.
(3) A move consists of subtracting between 1 and
        3 sticks from the current number of sticks.
(4) A player who cannot leave a positive
        number of sticks for the other player loses.
Player 1 is a  NimPlayerBad
Player 2 is a  NimPlayer
Sticks left: 11 Who's turn: Player 1 NimPlayerBad takes 2 sticks.
Sticks left: 9 Who's turn: Player 2 NimPlayer takes 1 sticks.
Sticks left: 8 Who's turn: Player 1 NimPlayerBad takes 2 sticks.
Sticks left: 6 Who's turn: Player 2 NimPlayer takes 1 sticks.
Sticks left: 5 Who's turn: Player 1 NimPlayerBad takes 3 sticks.
Sticks left: 2 Who's turn: Player 2 NimPlayer takes 1 sticks.
Sticks left: 1 Who's turn: Player 1 NimPlayerBad takes 1 sticks.
Sticks left: 0 Game over! Winner is Player 2 Nice game.
```

Figure 8.25   A typical run of `OneRowNim` using a command-line user interface.

Let's call the game class `WordGuess`. Following the design of `OneRowNim`, we get the design shown in Figure 8.26. The `WordGuess` class extends the `TwoPlayerGame` class and

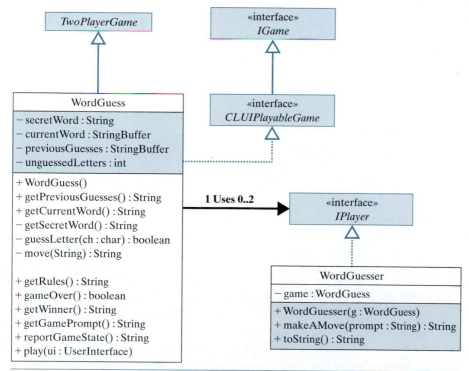

Figure 8.26 Design of the `WordGuess` class as part of `TwoPlayerGame` hierarchy.

implements the CLUIPlayableGame interface. We don't show the details of the interfaces and the TwoPlayerGame class, as these have not changed. Also, following the design of Nim-PlayerBad, the WordGuesser class implements the IPlayer interface. Note how we show the association between WordGuess and zero or more IPlayers. A WordGuess uses between zero and two instances of IPlayers, which in this game are implemented as WordGuessers.

Let's turn now to the details of the WordGuess class, whose source code is shown in Figures 8.27 and 8.28. The game needs to have a supply of words from which it can choose a secret word to present to the players. The getSecretWord() method will take care of this task. It calculates a random number and then uses that number, together with a switch statement, to select from among several words that are coded right into the switch statement. The secret word is stored in the secretWord variable. The currentWord variable stores the partially guessed word. Initially, currentWord consists entirely of question marks. As the players make correct guesses, currentWord is updated to show the locations of the guessed letters. Because currentWord will change as the game progresses, it is stored in a StringBuffer rather than in a String. Recall that Strings are immutable in Java, whereas a StringBuffer contains methods to insert letters and remove letters.

```java
public class WordGuess extends TwoPlayerGame implements CLUIPlayableGame {
    private String secretWord;
    private StringBuffer currentWord;
    private StringBuffer previousGuesses;
    private int unguessedLetters;

    public WordGuess() {
        secretWord = getSecretWord();
        currentWord = new StringBuffer(secretWord);
        previousGuesses = new StringBuffer();
        for (int k = 0; k < secretWord.length(); k++)
            currentWord.setCharAt(k,'?');
        unguessedLetters = secretWord.length();
    } // WordGuess()
    public String getPreviousGuesses() {
        return previousGuesses.toString();
    } // getPreviousGuesses()
    public String getCurrentWord() {
        return currentWord.toString();
    } // getCurrentWord()
    private String getSecretWord() {
        int num = (int)(Math.random()*10);
        switch (num)
        {   case 0:   return "SOFTWARE";
            case 1:   return "SOLUTION";
            case 2:   return "CONSTANT";
            case 3:   return "COMPILER";
            case 4:   return "ABSTRACT";
            case 5:   return "ABNORMAL";
            case 6:   return "ARGUMENT";
            case 7:   return "QUESTION";
            case 8:   return "UTILIZES";
            case 9:   return "VARIABLE";
```

Figure 8.27   The WordGuess class, Part I. (***Continued on next page***)

```
            default: return "MISTAKES";
        } // switch
    } // getSecretWord()
    private boolean guessLetter(char letter) {
        previousGuesses.append(letter);
        if (secretWord.indexOf(letter) == -1)
            return false;                        // letter is not in secretWord
        else // find positions of letter in secretWord
        {   for (int k = 0; k < secretWord.length(); k++)
            {   if (secretWord.charAt(k) == letter)
                {   if (currentWord.charAt(k) == letter)
                        return false;            // already guessed
                    currentWord.setCharAt(k,letter);
                    unguessedLetters--;          // one less to find
                } // if
            } // for
            return true;
        } // else
    } // guessLetter()

    public String getRules() { // Overridden from TwoPlayerGame
        return "\n*** The Rules of Word Guess ***\n" +
        "(1) The game generates a secret word.\n" +
        "(2) Two players alternate taking moves.\n" +
        "(3) A move consists of guessing a letter in the word.\n" +
        "(4) A player continues guessing until a letter is wrong.\n" +
        "(5) The game is over when all letters of the word are guessed\n" +
        "(6) The player guessing the last letter of the word wins.\n";
    } // getRules()
```

Figure 8.27   The WordGuess class, Part I. (*Continued from previous page*)

```
    public boolean gameOver() {                  // From TwoPlayerGame
        return (unguessedLetters <= 0);
    } // gameOver()
    public String getWinner() {                  // From TwoPlayerGame
        if (gameOver())
            return "Player " + getPlayer();
        else return "The game is not over.";
    } // getWinner()
    public String reportGameState() {
        if (!gameOver())
            return "\nCurrent word " + currentWord.toString()
                + " Previous guesses " + previousGuesses
                + "\nPlayer " + getPlayer() + " guesses next.";
        else
            return "\nThe game is now over!  The secret word is " + secretWord
                + "\n" + getWinner() + " has won!\n";
    } // reportGameState()
```

Figure 8.28   The WordGuess class, Part II. (*Continued on next page*)

```
    public String getGamePrompt() {                          // From CLUIPlayableGame
        return "\nGuess a letter that you think is in the secret word: ";
    } // getGamePrompt()
    public String move(String s) {
        char letter = s.toUpperCase().charAt(0);
        if (guessLetter(letter)) {                           // if correct
            return "Yes, the letter " + letter +
                    " IS in the secret word\n";
        } else {
            changePlayer();
            return "Sorry, " + letter + " is NOT a " +
                    "new letter in the secret word\n";
        }
    } // move()
    public void play(UserInterface ui) {                     // From CLUIPlayableGame
        ui.report(getRules());
        if (computer1 != null)
            ui.report("\nPlayer 1 is a " + computer1.toString());
        if (computer2 != null)
            ui.report("\nPlayer 2 is a " + computer2.toString());

        while(!gameOver()) {
            IPlayer computer = null; // Assume no computers playing
            ui.report(reportGameState());
            switch(getPlayer()) {
            case PLAYER_ONE:                                 // Player 1's turn
                computer = computer1;
                break;
            case PLAYER_TWO:                                 // Player 2's turn
                computer = computer2;
                break;
            } // cases

            if (computer != null) {                          // If computer's turn
                ui.report(move(computer.makeAMove("")));
            } else {                                         // otherwise, user's turn
                ui.prompt(getGamePrompt());
                ui.report(move(ui.getUserInput()));
            }
        } // while
        ui.report(reportGameState());                        // The game is now over
    } // play()
} // WordGuess class
```

Figure 8.28   The WordGuess class, Part II. (*Continued from previous page*)

The unguessedLetters variable stores the number of letters remaining to be guessed. When unguessedLetters equals 0, the game is over. This condition defines the gameOver() method, which is inherited from TwoPlayerGame. The winner of the game is the player who guessed the last letter in the secret word. This condition defines the getWinner() method, which is also inherited from TwoPlayerGame. The other methods that are inherited from TwoPlayerGame or implemented from the CLUIPlayableGame are also implemented in a straightforward manner.

```
public class WordGuesser implements IPlayer {
  private WordGuess game;
  public WordGuesser (WordGuess game) {
    this.game = game;
  }
  public String makeAMove(String prompt)  {
    String usedLetters = game.getPreviousGuesses();
    char letter;
    do {                                            // Pick one of 26 letters
      letter = (char)('A' + (int)(Math.random() * 26));
    } while (usedLetters.indexOf(letter) != -1);
    return "" + letter;
  }
  public String toString() {                        // returns 'NimPlayerBad'
    String className = this.getClass().toString();
    return className.substring(5);
  }
} // WordGuesser class
```

Figure 8.29 The WordGuesser class.

A move in the WordGuess game consists of trying to guess a letter that occurs in the secret word. The move() method processes the player's guesses. It passes the guessed letter to the guessLetter() method, which checks whether the letter is a new, secret letter. If so, guessLetter() takes care of the various housekeeping tasks. It adds the letter to previousGuesses, which keeps track of all the players' guesses. It decrements the number of unguessedLetters, which will become 0 when all the letters have been guessed. And it updates currentWord to show where all the occurrences of the secret letter are located. Note how guessLetter() uses a for loop to cycle through the letters in the secret word. As it does so, it replaces the question marks in currentWord with the correctly guessed secret letter. The guessLetter() method returns false if the guess is incorrect. In that case, the move() method changes the player's turn. When correct guesses are made, the current player keeps the turn.

The WordGuess game is a good example of a string-processing problem. It makes use of several of the String and StringBuffer methods that we learned in Chapter 7. The implementation of WordGuess as an extension of TwoPlayerGame is quite straightforward. One advantage of the TwoPlayerGame class hierarchy is that it decides many of the important design issues in advance. Developing a new game is largely a matter of implementing methods whose definitions have already been determined in the superclass or in the interfaces. This greatly simplifies the development process.

Reusing code

Let's now discuss the details of the WordGuesser class (Fig. 8.29). Note that the constructor takes a WordGuess parameter. This allows WordGuesser to be passed a reference to the game, which accesses the game's public methods, such as getPreviousGuesses(). The toString() method is identical to the toString() method in the NimPlayerBad example. The makeAMove() method, which is part of the IPlayer interface, is responsible for specifying the algorithm that the player uses to make a move. The strategy in this case is to repeatedly pick a random letter from *A* to *Z* until a letter is found that is not contained in `previousGuesses`. That way, the player will not guess letters that have already been guessed.

8.7   Principles of Object-Oriented Design

To conclude this chapter, it will be helpful to focus briefly on how the examples we have seen address the various object-oriented design (OOD) principles we set out at the beginning of the book.

- **Divide-and-Conquer Principle.** All of the problems tackled in this chapter have been solved by dividing them into several classes, with each of the classes divided into separate methods. The very idea of a class hierarchy is an application of this principle.

- **Encapsulation Principle.** The superclasses in our designs, `Cipher` and `TwoPlayerGame`, encapsulate the features of the class hierarchy that are shared by all objects in the hierarchy. The subclasses `CaesarCipher` and `OneRowNim` encapsulate features that make them distinctive with the class hierarchy.

- **Interface Principle.** The Java interfaces we have designed, `IPlayer`, `CLUIPlayableGame`, and `UserInterface`, specify clearly how various types of related objects will interact with each other through the methods contained in the interfaces. Clean interfaces make for clear communication among objects.

- **Information-Hiding Principle.** We have continued to make consistent use of the `private` and `public` qualifiers, and have now introduced the `protected` qualifier to extend this concept. The inheritance mechanism gives subclasses access to protected and public elements of their superclasses.

- **Generality Principle.** As you move down a well-designed class hierarchy, you go from the more general to the more specific features of the objects involved. The abstract *encode()* method specifies the general form that encoding will take, while the various implementations of this method in the subclasses provide the specializations necessary to distinguish, say, `Caesar` encoding from `Transpose` encoding. Similarly, the abstract `makeAMove()` method in the `IPlayer` interface provides a general format for a move in a two-player game, while its various implementations provide the specializations that distinguish one game from another.

- **Extensibility Principle.** Overriding inherited methods and implementing abstract methods from either an abstract superclass or a Java interface provide several well-designed ways to extend the functionality in an existing class hierarchy. Extending a class is a form of specialization of the features inherited from the superclass.

- **Abstraction Principle.** Designing a class hierarchy is an exercise in abstraction, as the more general features of the objects involved are moved into the superclasses. Similarly, designing a Java interface or an abstract superclass method is a form of abstraction, whereby the signature of the method is distinguished from its various implementations.

These, then, are some of the ways that the several examples we have considered and this chapter's discussion have contributed to a deepening understanding of object-oriented design.

CHAPTER SUMMARY

Technical Terms

abstract method

actual type (dynamic type)

ciphertext

class inheritance

cryptography

dynamic binding (late binding)

interface

overloaded method

plaintext

polymorphic method

polymorphism

static binding (early binding)

static type (declared type)

substitution cipher

transposition cipher

Summary of Important Points

- Inheritance is an object-oriented mechanism whereby subclasses inherit the public and protected instance variables and methods from their superclasses.

- Dynamic binding (or late binding) is the mechanism by which a method call is bound to (associated with) the correct implementation of the method at runtime. In Java, all method calls except for `final` or `private` methods are resolved using dynamic binding.

- Static binding (or early binding) is the association of a method call with its corresponding implementation at compile time.

- Polymorphism is an object-oriented language feature in which a method call can lead to different actions depending on the object on which it is invoked. A polymorphic method is a method signature that is given different implementations by different classes in a class hierarchy.

- A static type is a variable's declared type. A dynamic type, or actual type, is the type of object assigned to that variable at a given point in a running program.

- An `abstract` method is a method definition that lacks an implementation. An `abstract` class is one that contains one or more `abstract` methods. An `abstract` class can be subclassed but not instantiated.

- A Java interface is a class that contains only method signatures and (possibly) constant declarations, but no variables. An interface can be implemented by a class by providing implementations for all of its abstract methods.

SOLUTIONS TO SELF-STUDY EXERCISES

SOLUTION 8.1   Running the TestPrint program will produce the output shown here. It is clear that the inherited toString() method is used by println() when printing a TestPrint object.

```
56.0
TestPrint@be2d65
```

SOLUTION 8.2   If you override the toString() method in TestPrint, you should get something like the output shown here, depending on how you code toString(). It is clear that the toString() method is used polymorphously by println().

```
56.0
Hello from TestPrint
```

SOLUTION 8.3   The output produced when constructing objects of type A and B in the order shown in the exercise would be as follows, with each letter occurring on a separate line:

```
A B B
```

SOLUTION 8.4   The new implementation of B's method() will invoke A's version of the method before printing B. This will print A A B A B.

```
void method () {
    super.method();
    System.out.println("B");
}
```

SOLUTION 8.5   Given the definitions of classes A and B in the exercise, the marked statements would be invalid:

```
A a = new B();    // Valid a B is an A
a = new A();      // Ok
B b = new A();    // Invalid. An A is not necessarily a B
b = new B();      // OK
```

SOLUTION 8.6   Given the class definitions and code segment in this exercise, the output would be A A B A B C, with each letter printing on a separate line.

SOLUTION 8.7   Definition of an `Pig` subclass of `Animal`:

```java
public class Pig extends Animal {
    public Pig() {
        kind = "pig";
    }
    public String speak() {
        return "oink";
    }
}
```

SOLUTION 8.8   If polymorphism was not used in our design, the `talk()` method would have to be modified to the following in order to accommodate a `Pig` subclass:

```java
public String talk(Animal a) {
  if (a instanceof Cow)
     return "I am a " + kind + " and I go " + a.moo();
  else if (a instanceof Cat)
     return "I am a " + kind + " and I go " + a.meow();
  else if (a instanceof Pig)
     return "I am a " + kind + " and I go " + a.oink();
  else
     return "I don't know what I am";
}
```

SOLUTION 8.9   Code to swap two `boolean` variables:

```java
boolean temp = b1;     // Save b1's value
b1 = b2;               // Change b1 to b2
b2 = temp;             // Change b2 to b1's original value
```

SOLUTION 8.10   Creating a `ToggleButton` that can be used to deal or collect cards:

```java
private ToggleButton dealer = new ToggleButton("deal","collect");
add(dealer);
dealer.addActionListener(this);
```

SOLUTION 8.11   Modify the `Caesar` class so that it will allow various-sized shifts to be used.

```java
private int shift;
public void setShift(int n) { shift = n;    }
public int getShift()       { return shift; }
                                         // Modification to encode():
ch = (char)('a' + (ch -'a'+ shift) % 26);      // Shift
                                         // Modification to decode():
ch = (char)('a' + (ch -'a'+ (26-shift)) % 26); // Shift
```

SOLUTION 8.12 Modify `Transpose.encode()` so that it uses a rotation instead of a reversal. The operation here is very similar to the shift operation in the Caesar cipher. It uses modular arithmetic to rearrange the letters in the word. For example, suppose the word is "hello". Its letters are indexed from 0 to 4. The following table shows how the expression `((k+2) % 5)` will rearrange the letters as k varies from 0 to 4:

```
k  charAt(k)  (k+2) % 5   charAt((k+2) % 5)
------------------------------------------
0   'h'          2            'l'
1   'e'          3            'l'
2   'l'          4            'o'
3   'l'          0            'h'
4   'o'          1            'e'
```

```java
// Modification to encode():
public String encode(String word) {
    StringBuffer result = new StringBuffer();
    for (int k=0; k < word.length(); k++)
        result.append(word.charAt((k+2) % word.length()));
    return result.toString();
}
```

SOLUTION 8.13 A `NimPlayer` class that plays the optimal `OneRowNim` game would be identical to the `NimPlayerBad` class except that the `move():int` method would be replaced with the following implementation:

```java
public int move() {
    int sticksLeft = game.getSticks();
    if (sticksLeft % (game.MAX_PICKUP + 1) != 1)
        return (sticksLeft - 1) % (game.MAX_PICKUP +1);
    else {
        int maxPickup = Math.min(game.MAX_PICKUP, sticksLeft);
        return 1 + (int)(Math.random() * maxPickup);
    }
}
```

EXERCISES

Note: For programming exercises, **first** draw a UML class diagram describing all classes and their inheritance relationships and/or associations.

EXERCISE 8.1 Fill in the blanks in each of the following sentences:

a. A method that lacks a body is an _____ method.

b. An _____ is like a class except that it contains only instance methods, no instance variables.

c. Two ways for a class to inherit something in Java are to _____ a class and _____ an interface.

d. Instance variables and instance methods that are declared _____ or _____ are inherited by the subclasses.

e. An object can refer to itself by using the _____ keyword.

f. If an applet intends to handle `ActionEvents`, it must implement the _____ interface.

g. A _____ method is one that does different things depending upon the object that invokes it.

EXERCISE 8.2   Explain the difference between the following pairs of concepts:

a. *Class* and *interface*.

b. *Stub method* and *abstract method*.

c. *Extending a class* and *instantiating an object*.

d. *Defining a method* and *implementing a method*.

e. A `protected` method and a `public` method.

f. A `protected` method and a `private` method.

EXERCISE 8.3   Draw a hierarchy to represent the following situation. There are lots of languages in the world. English, French, Chinese, and Korean are examples of natural languages. Java, C, and C++ are examples of formal languages. French and Italian are considered romance languages, while Greek and Latin are considered classical languages.

EXERCISE 8.4   Look up the documentation for the `JButton` class on Sun's Web site:

```
http://java.sun.com/j2se/docs/
```

List the names of all the methods that would be inherited by the `ToggleButton` subclass that we defined in this chapter.

EXERCISE 8.5   Design and write a `toString()` method for the `ToggleButton` class defined in this chapter. The `toString()` method should return the `ToggleButton`'s current label.

EXERCISE 8.6   Design a class hierarchy rooted in the class `Employee` that includes subclasses for `HourlyEmployee` and `SalaryEmployee`. The attributes shared in common by these classes include the name and job title of the employee, plus the assessor and mutator methods needed by the attributes. The salaried employees need an attribute for weekly salary, and the corresponding methods for accessing and changing this variable. The hourly employees should have a pay rate and an hours-worked variable. There should be an abstract method called `calculateWeeklyPay()`, defined abstractly in the superclass and implemented in the subclasses. The salaried worker's pay is just the weekly salary. Pay for an hourly employee is simply hours worked times pay rate.

EXERCISE 8.7   Design and write a subclass of `JTextField` called `IntegerField` that is used for inputting integers but behaves in all other respects like a `JTextField`. Give the subclass a public method called `getInteger()`.

EXERCISE 8.8 Implement a method that uses the following variation of the Caesar cipher. The method should take two parameters, a `String` and an `int` N. The result should be a `String` in which the first letter is shifted by N, the second by $N + 1$, the third by $N + 2$, and so on. For example, given the string "Hello", and an initial shift of 1, your method should return "Igopt". Write a method that converts its `String` parameter so that letters are written in blocks five characters long.

EXERCISE 8.9 Design and implement an applet that lets the user type a document into a `TextArea` and then provides the following analysis of the document: the number of words in the document, the number of characters in the document, and the percentage of words that have more than six letters.

EXERCISE 8.10 Design and implement a `Cipher` subclass to implement the following substitution cipher: Each letter in the alphabet is replaced with a letter from the opposite end of the alphabet: *a* is replaced with *z*, *b* with *y*, and so forth.

EXERCISE 8.11 One way to design a substitution alphabet for a cipher is to use a keyword to construct the alphabet. For example, suppose the keyword is "zebra". You place the keyword at the beginning of the alphabet, and then fill out the other 21 slots with the remaining letters, giving the following alphabet:

```
Cipher alphabet:   zebracdfghijklmnopqstuvwxy
Plain alphabet:    abcdefghijklmnopqrstuvwxyz
```

Design and implement an `Alphabet` class for constructing substitution alphabets. It should have a single public method that takes a keyword `String` as an argument and returns an alphabet string. Note that an alphabet cannot contain duplicate letters, so repeated letters in a keyword like "xylophone" would have to be removed.

EXERCISE 8.12 Design and write a `Cipher` subclass for a substitution cipher that uses an alphabet from the `Alphabet` class created in the preceding exercise.

EXERCISE 8.13 **Challenge:** Find a partner and concoct your own encryption scheme. Then work separately, with one partner writing `encode()` and the other writing `decode()`. Test to see that a message can be encoded and then decoded to yield the original message.

EXERCISE 8.14 Design a `TwoPlayerGame` subclass called `MultiplicationGame`. The rules of this game are that the game generates a random multiplication problem using numbers between 1 and 10, and the players, taking turns, try to provide the answer to the problem. The game ends when a wrong answer is given. The winner is the player who did not give the wrong answer.

EXERCISE 8.15 Design a class called `MultiplicationPlayer` that plays the multiplication game described in the preceding exercise. This class should implement the `IPlayer` interface.

EXERCISE 8.16   Design a TwoPlayerGame subclass called RockPaperScissors. The rules of this game are that both players simultaneously make a pick: either a rock, a paper, or a scissors. For each round, the rock beats the scissors, the scissors beats the paper, and the paper beats the rock. Ties are allowed. The game is won in a best out of three fashion when one of the players wins two rounds.

EXERCISE 8.17   Design a class called RockPaperScissorsPlayer that plays the game described in the preceding exercise. This class should implement the IPlayer interface.

Photograph courtesy of Michael Kelley, Getty Images, Inc. - Stone Allstock.

9

Arrays and Array Processing

OBJECTIVES

After studying this chapter, you will

- Know how to use array data structures.
- Be able to solve problems that require collections of data.
- Know how to sort an array of data.
- Be familiar with sequential and binary search algorithms.
- Gain a better understanding of inheritance and polymorphism.

OUTLINE

9.1   Introduction

In this chapter we will learn about arrays. An **array** is a named collection of contiguous storage locations—storage locations that are next to each other—that contain data items of the same type.

Arrays offer a more streamlined way to store data than using individual data items for each variable. Arrays also allow you to work with their data more efficiently than with data stored in individual variables.

Let's see why. Suppose you want to create a GUI that has 26 buttons on it, one for each letter of the alphabet. Given our present knowledge of Java, our only alternative would be to declare a separate JButton variable for each letter of the alphabet:

```
JButton button1;
JButton button2;
...
JButton button26;
```

Obviously, requiring 26 separate variables for this problem is tedious and inconvenient. Similarly, to instantiate and assign a label to each button would require 26 statements:

```
button1 = new JButton("A");
button2 = new JButton("B");
...
button26 = new JButton("Z");
```

This approach is also tedious. What we need is some way to use a loop to process each button, using a loop counter, k, to refer to the kth button on each iteration of the loop. An array lets us do that. For example, the following code will declare an array for storing 26 JButtons and then instantiate and label each button:

```
JButton letter[]  = new JButton[26];
for (int k = 0; k < 26; k++)
    letter[k] = new JButton("A" + k);
```

You don't yet understand the code in this segment, but you can see how economical it is. It uses just three lines of code to do what would have required 50 or 60 lines of code without arrays.

Our discussion of arrays will show how to store and retrieve data from one-, two-, and three-dimensional arrays. We also study sorting and searching algorithms to process arrays. Finally, we illustrate how arrays can be used in a variety of applications, including an animation problem, a sorting class, and a card-playing program.

9.2   One-Dimensional Arrays

An array is a *data structure*. A **data structure** is an organized collection of data. In an array, data are arranged in a linear or sequential structure, with one element following another. When referencing elements in an array, we refer to the positions of the particular elements

The array data structure

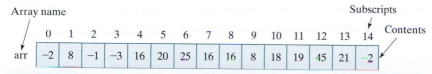

Figure 9.1 An array of 15 integers named arr.

within the array. For example, if the array is named `arr`, then the elements are named `arr[0]`, `arr[1]`, `arr[2]`, ... `arr[n-1]`, where *n* gives the number of elements in the array. This naming also reflects the fact that the array's data are contained in storage locations that are next to each other. In Java, as in C, C++, and some other programming languages, the first element of an array has index 0. (This is the same convention we used for `Strings`.) Zero indexing

Figure 9.1 shows an array named `arr` that contains 15 `int` elements. The syntax for referring to elements of an array is

> *arrayname* [*subscript*]

where *arrayname* is the name of the array—any valid identifier will do—and *subscript* is the position of the element within the array. As Figure 9.1 shows, the first element in the array has subscript 0, the second has subscript 1, and so on.

A **subscript** is an integer quantity contained in square brackets that is used to identify an array element. An subscript must be either an integer value or an integer expression. Using Figure 9.1 to illustrate an example, suppose that *j* and *k* are integer variables equaling 5 and 7, respectively. Each of the following would then be a valid reference to elements of the array *arr*: Subscript expressions

```
arr[4]    // Refers to 16
arr[j]    // Is arr[5] which refers to 20
arr[j + k] // Is arr[5+7] which is arr[12] which refers to 45
arr[k % j] // Is arr[7%5] which is arr[2] which refers to -1
```

These examples show that when an expression, such as `j + k`, is used as a subscript, it is evaluated (to 12 in this case) before the reference is made.

It is a syntax error to use a noninteger type as an array subscript. Both of the following expressions would be invalid:

```
arr[5.0]  // 5.0 is a float and can't be an array subscript
arr["5"]  // "5" is a string not an integer
```

For a given array, a valid array subscript must be in the range 0 ... N-1, where N is the number of elements in the array, and if not it, is considered out-of-bounds. An out-of-bounds subscript creates a runtime error—that is, an error that occurs when the program is running—rather than a syntax error, which can be detected when the program is compiled. For the array `arr`, all of the following expressions contain out-of-bounds subscripts:

```
arr[-1]      // Arrays cannot have negative subscripts
arr['5']     // Char '5' promoted to its Unicode value, 53
arr[15]      // The last element of arr has subscript 14
arr[j*k]     // Since j*k equals 35
```

Each of these references would lead to an `IndexOutOfBoundsException`. (Exceptions are covered in detail in Chapter 10.)

> **JAVA LANGUAGE RULE**   **Array Subscripts.** Array subscripts must be integer values in the range $0 \ldots (N-1)$, where N is the number of elements in the array.

DEBUGGING TIP: Array Subscripts.   In developing array algorithms, it is important to design test data that show that array subscripts do not cause runtime errors.

9.2.1   Declaring and Creating Arrays

Are arrays objects?

For the most part, arrays in Java are treated as objects. Like objects, they are instantiated with the `new` operator and they have instance variables (for example, `length`). Like variables for objects, array variables are considered *reference* variables. When arrays are used as parameters, a reference to the array is passed rather than a copy of the entire array. The primary difference between arrays and full-fledged objects is that arrays are not defined in terms of an `Array` class. Thus, arrays do not fit into Java's `Object` hierarchy. They do not inherit any properties from `Object`, and they cannot be subclassed.

You can think of an array as a container that contains a number of variables. As we have seen, the variables contained in an array object are not referenced by name but by their relative positions in the array. The variables are called *components*. If an array object has N components, then we say that the **array length** is N. Each of the components of the array has the same type, which is called the array's *component type*. An *empty* array is one that contains zero variables.

Components and elements

A **one-dimensional** array has components that are called the array's **elements**. Their type is the array's **element type**. An array's elements may be of any type, including primitive and reference types. This means you can have arrays of `int`, `char`, `boolean`, `String`, `Object`, `Image`, `TextField`, `TwoPlayerGame`, and so on.

When declaring a one-dimensional array, you have to indicate both the array's element type and its length. Just as in declaring and creating other kinds of objects, creating an array object requires that we create both a name for the array and then the array itself. The following statements create the array shown in Figure 9.1:

```
int arr[];          // Declare a name for the array
arr = new int[15];  // Create the array itself
```

These two steps can be combined into a single statement, as follows:

```
int arr[] = new int[15];
```

In this example, the array's element type is `int` and its `length` is 15, which is fixed and cannot be changed. This means that the array contains 15 variables of type `int`, which will be referred to as `arr[0]`, `arr[1]`, ...`arr[14]`.

9.2.2 Array Allocation

Creating the array in Figure 9.1 means allocating 15 storage locations that can store integers. One difference between declaring an array and declaring some other kind of object is that square brackets (`[]`) are used to declare an array type. The brackets can be attached either to the array's name or to its type, as in the following examples:

Allocating memory

```
int arr[];       // The brackets may follow the array's name
int[] arr;       // The brackets may follow the array's type
```

The next example creates an array of five `String`s and then uses a `for` loop to assign the strings `"hello1"`, `"hello2"`, `"hello3"`, `"hello4"`, and `"hello5"` to the five array locations:

```
String strarr[];                         // Declare a name for the array
strarr = new String[5];                  // Create the array itself
                                         // Assign strings to the array
for (int k = 0; k < strarr.length; k++)  // For each element
  strarr[k] = new String("hello" + (k + 1));  // Assign a string
```

The expression `k < strarr.length` specifies the loop bound. Every array has a `length` instance variable, which refers to the number of elements contained in the array. As we mentioned, arrays, like `String`s, are zero indexed, so the last element of the array is always given by its `length-1`. However, `length` is an instance variable for arrays, whereas `length()` is an instance method for `String`s. Therefore, it would be a syntax error in this example to refer to `strarr.length()`.

length vs. length()

> **DEBUGGING TIP: Array Length.** A common syntax error involves forgetting that for arrays `length` is an instance variable, not an instance method, as it is for `String`s.

In the example, we first use the **new** operator to create `strarr`, an array of type `String` of length 5. We then use a `String` constructor to create the five `String`s that are stored in the array. It is important to realize that creating an array to store five `Object`s (as opposed to five primitive data elements) does not also create the `Object`s that will be stored in the array.

When an `array` of objects is created, the array's elements are references to those objects (Fig. 9.2). Their initial values, like all reference variables, are `null`. So to create and *initialize* the array `strarr`, we need to create *six* objects—the array itself, which will contain five `String`s, and then the five `String`s that will be stored in `strarr`.

Arrays of objects

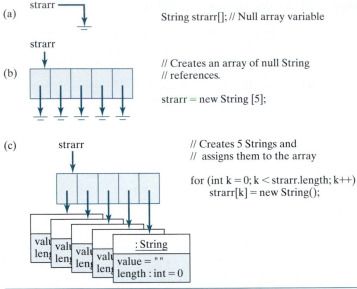

(a) strarr   String strarr[]; // Null array variable

(b) strarr   // Creates an array of null String
// references.

strarr = new String [5];

(c) strarr   // Creates 5 Strings and
// assigns them to the array

for (int k = 0; k < strarr.length; k++)
    strarr[k] = new String();

: String
value = " "
length : int = 0

Figure 9.2 Creating an array of five Strings involves six objects, because the array itself is a separate object. In (a), the array variable is declared. In (b), the array is instantiated, creating an array of five null references. In (c), the five Strings are created and assigned to the array.

One more example will underscore this point. The following statements create four *new* Objects, an array to store three Students plus the three Students themselves:

```
Student school[] = new Student[3];      // A 3 Student array
school[0] = new Student("Socrates");    // The first Student
school[1] = new Student("Plato");       // The second Student
school[2] = new Student("Aristotle");   // The third Student
```

The first statement creates an array named school to store three Students, and the next three statements create the individual Students and assign them to the array (Fig. 9.3). Thus, creating the array and initializing its elements require four new statements. The following sequence of statements would lead to a null pointer exception because the array's elements have not been instantiated:

```
Student students[] = new Student[3];        // A 3 Student array
System.out.println(students[0].getName());
```

In this case, students[0] is a null reference, thus causing the exception.

DEBUGGING TIP: Array Instantiation. Creating a new array does not also create the objects stored in the array. They must be instantiated separately. It is a semantic error to refer to an uninstantiated (null) array element.

school

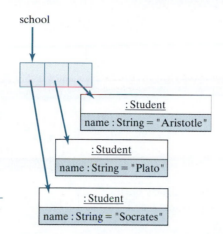

Figure 9.3 An array of Students.

Now that we have assigned the three `Student`s to the array, we can refer to them by means of subscripted references. A reference to the `Student` named "Socrates" is now `school[0]`, and a reference to the `Student` named "Plato" is `school[1]`. In other words, to refer to the three individual students, we must refer to their locations within `school`. Of course, we can also use variables, such as loop counters, to refer to a `Student`'s location within `school`. The following `for` loop invokes each `Student`'s `getState()` method to print out its current state:

```
for (int k = 0; k < school.length; k++)
    System.out.println(school[k].getState());
```

What if the three `Student`s already existed before the array was created? In that case, we could just assign their references to the array elements, as in the following example:

```
Student student1 = new Student("Socrates");
Student student2 = new Student("Plato");
Student student3 = new Student("Aristotle");
Student school = new Student[3];              // A 3 Student array
school[0] = student1;
school[1] = student2;
school[2] = student3;
```

In this case, each of the three `Student` objects can be referenced by two different references—its variable identifier (such as `student1`) and its array location (such as `school[0]`). For arrays of objects, Java stores just the reference to the object in the array rather than the entire object. This conserves memory, since references require only 4 bytes each, whereas each object may require hundreds of bytes (Fig. 9.4).

When an array of *N* elements is created, the compiler *allocates* storage for *N* variables of the element's type. In the case of `arr` that we discussed earlier, the compiler would allocate storage for 15 `int`s—60 contiguous bytes of storage, because each `int` requires 4 bytes (32 bits) of storage. If we declare an array of 20 `double`s,

```
double arr[] = new double[20];
```

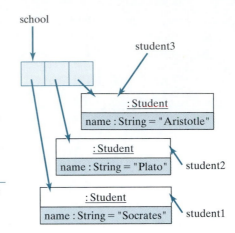

Figure 9.4 Arrays of objects store references to the objects, not the objects themselves.

the compiler will allocate 160 bytes of storage—20 variables of 8 bytes (64 bits) each. In the case of the `Student` examples and the `String` examples, because these are objects (not primitive types), the compiler will allocate space for N addresses, where N is the length of the array and each address requires 4 bytes.

How much memory?

SELF-STUDY EXERCISE

EXERCISE 9.1   How much space (in bytes) would be allocated for each of the following?

    a. `int a[] = new int[5];`
    b. `double b[] = new double[10];`
    c. `char c[] = new char[30];`
    d. `String s[] = new String[10];`
    e. `Student p[] = new Student[5];`

9.2.3   Initializing Arrays

Array elements are automatically initialized to default values that depend on the element type. Boolean elements are initialized to `false`, and integer and real types are initialized to 0. Reference types—that is, arrays of objects—are initialized to `null`.

Default initialization

Arrays can also be assigned initial values when they are created, although this is feasible only for relatively small arrays. An **array initializer** is written as a list of expressions separated by commas and enclosed by braces. For example, we can declare and initialize the array shown in Figure 9.1 with the following statement:

Array initializer

```
int arr[] = {-2,8,-1,-3,16,20,25,16,16,8,18,19,45,21,-2};
```

Similarly, to create and initialize an array of `String`s, we can use the following statement:

```
String strings[] = {"hello", "world", "goodbye", "love"};
```

This example creates and stores four `String`s in the array. Subsequently, to refer to `"hello"`, we would use the reference `strings[0]`, and to refer to `"love"`, we would use the reference `strings[3]`. Note in these examples that when an array declaration contains an initializer, it is not necessary to use `new` and it is not necessary to specify the number of elements in the array. The number of elements is determined from the number of values in the initializer list.

9.2.4 Assigning and Using Array Values

Array elements can be used in the same way as other variables. The only difference, of course, is that references to elements are subscripted. For example, the following assignment statements assign values to the elements of two arrays, named `arr` and `strings`:

Array assignment

```
arr[0] = 5;
arr[5] = 10;
arr[2] = 3;
strings[0] = "who";
strings[1] = "what";
strings[2] = strings[3] = "where";
```

The following loop assigns the first 15 squares—1, 4, 9 ...—to the array `arr`:

```
for (int k = 0; k < arr.length; k++)
    arr[k] = (k+1) * (k+1);
```

The following loop prints the values of the array `arr`:

```
for (int k = 0; k < arr.length; k++)
    System.out.println(arr[k]);
```

SELF-STUDY EXERCISES

EXERCISE 9.2   Declare an array named `farr` that contains ten `float`s initialized to the values 1.0, 2.0, ..., 10.0.

EXERCISE 9.3   Write an expression that prints the first element of `farr`.

EXERCISE 9.4   Write an assignment statement that assigns 100.0 to the last element in `farr`.

EXERCISE 9.5   Write a loop to print all of the elements of `farr`.

9.3   Simple Array Examples

The program in Figure 9.5 creates two arrays of ten elements each and displays their values on the Java console. In this example, the elements of `intArr` have not been given initial values, whereas the elements of `realArr` have been initialized. Note the use of the integer constant `ARRSIZE` to store the arrays' size. By using the constant in this way, we do not have to use the literal value `10` anywhere in the program, thereby making it easier to read and modify the program. If we want to change the size of the array the program handles, we can just change the value of `ARRSIZE`. This is an example of the maintainability principle.

Maintainability principle

```
public class PrintArrays {
  static final int ARRSIZE = 10;                         // The array's size
  static int intArr[] = new int[ARRSIZE];                // Create int array
  static double realArr[] = { 1.1, 2.2, 3.3, 4.4,
    5.5, 6.6, 7.7, 8.8, 9.9, 10.10 };                    // And a double array

  public static void main(String args[]) {
    System.out.println("Ints \t Reals");                 // Print a heading
                      // For each int and double element
    for (int k = 0; k < intArr.length; k++)
      System.out.println( intArr[k] + " \t " + realArr[k]);// Print them
    } // main()
} // PrintArrays class
```

Figure 9.5 A program that displays two arrays. Its output is shown in Figure 9.6.

EFFECTIVE DESIGN: Symbolic Constants. Using symbolic constants (final variables) instead of literal values makes the program easier to read and to maintain.

Note the use of the `static` qualifier throughout the `PrintArrays` class. This enables us to refer to the array and the other variables from within the `main()` method. If `intArr` were not declared `static`, we would get the compiler error `attempt to make static use of a non-static variable`. This use of `static` is justified mainly as a coding convenience rather than as a principle of object-oriented design. The only examples we have seen so far in which static elements were a necessary design element were the use of static elements in the `Math` class—`Math.PI` and `Math.sqrt()`—and the use of static final variables in `TwoPlayerGame`—`TwoPlayerGame.PLAYER_ONE`.

It is not always feasible to initialize large arrays in an initializer statement. Consider the problem of initializing an array with the squares of the first 100 integers. Not only would setting these values in an initializer statement be tedious, it would also be error prone, since it is relatively easy to type in the wrong value for one or more of the squares.

DEBUGGING TIP: Array Initialization. Initializer statements should be used only for relatively small arrays.

Ints	Reals
0	1.1
0	2.2
0	3.3
0	4.4
0	5.5
0	6.6
0	7.7
0	8.8
0	9.9
0	10.1

Figure 9.6 Output of the `PrintArrays` program.

```
public class Squares {
    static final int ARRSIZE = 50;                    // The array's size
    static int intArr[] = new int[ARRSIZE];           // Instantiate
    public static void main(String args[]) {
        for (int k = 0; k < intArr.length; k++)        // Initialize
            intArr[k] = (k+1) * (k+1);
        System.out.print("The first 50 squares are");
        for (int k = 0; k < intArr.length; k++) {      // Print
            if (k % 5 == 0)                            // For each 5th square
                System.out.println(" ");              // print a new line
            System.out.print( intArr[k] + " ");
        } // for
    } // main()
} // Squares class
```

Figure 9.7   A program with an array that stores the squares of the first 50 integers. Its output is shown in Figure 9.8.

The example in Figure 9.7 creates an array of 50 integers and then fills the elements with the values 1, 4, 9, 16, and so on. It then prints the entire array.

This example illustrates some important points about the use of array variables. The array's elements are individual storage locations. In this example, intArr has 50 storage locations. Storing a value in one of these variables is done by an assignment statement:

```
intArr[k] = (k+1) * (k+1);
```

The use of the variable k in this assignment statement allows us to vary the location that is assigned on each iteration of the for loop. Note that in this example, k occurs as the array index on the left-hand side of the expression, while $k + 1$ occurs on the right-hand side as the value to be squared. The reason for this is that arrays are indexed starting at 0 but we want our table of squares to begin with the square of 1. So the square of some number $n + 1$ will always be stored in the array whose index is 1 less than the number itself—that is, n.

Zero vs. unit indexing

```
1  4  9  16  25
36  49  64  81  100
121  144  169  196  225
256  289  324  361  400
441  484  529  576  625
676  729  784  841  900
961  1024  1089  1156  1225
1296  1369  1444  1521  1600
1681  1764  1849  1936  2025
2116  2209  2304  2401  2500
```

Figure 9.8   Output of the Squares program.

An array's `length` variable can always be used as a loop bound when iterating through all elements of the array:

```
for (int k = 0; k < intArr.length; k++)
    intArr[k] = (k+1) * (k+1);
```

Off-by-one error

However, it is important to note that the last element in the array is always at location `length-1`. Attempting to refer to `intArr[length]` would cause an `IndexOutOfBounds-Exception` because no such element exists.

DEBUGGING TIP: Off-by-One Error.   Because of zero indexing, the last element in an array is always *length* − 1. Forgetting this fact can cause an off-by-one error.

SELF-STUDY EXERCISE

EXERCISE 9.6   Declare an array of 100 `double`s and write a loop to assign the first 100 square roots to its elements. Use `Math.sqrt(double)`.

9.4   Example: Counting Frequencies of Letters

Suppose you wish to write a program to break a text message encrypted with one of the historical ciphers discussed in the two preceding chapters. It is well known that historical ciphers often can be broken. Put differently, the plaintext can be found from the ciphertext, by examining the frequencies of letters and comparing them to the average frequencies of typical samples of plaintext. For example, E and T are the two most frequently used letters in the English language. So, in a ciphertext encrypted with a Caesar cipher, E and T are good guesses as the plaintext letter corresponding to the most frequent letter in the ciphertext message.

Let's write a program that will count how many times each of the 26 letters of the English language appears in a given string. There are a number of ways to design such a program, depending on how flexible you wish it to be. Let us keep this example simple by assuming that we will only be interested in counting occurrences of the letters A through Z and not occurrences of spaces or punctuation marks. Assume further that we will change lowercase letters in our string sample to uppercase before counting letters and that we will want to print out the frequencies of letters to the console window. Finally, assume that, later in the chapter after we discuss sorting arrays, we will want to enhance our program so that it can print out the letter frequencies in order of increasing frequency.

9.4.1   A Class to Store the Frequency of One Letter

It is clear that an array should be used for storing the frequencies, but a decision must also be made as to what to store as the array elements. If we store letter frequencies as `int` values, with the frequency of A stored at index 0, and the frequency of B at index 1, and so forth, we will not be able to rearrange the frequencies into increasing order without losing track of which letter corresponds to which frequency. One way of solving this problem is to create an array of objects, where each object stores both a letter and its frequency.

```
                        LetterFreq
                 − letter : char
                 − freq : int
                 + LetterFreq(in I : char, in f : int)
                 + getLetter() : char
                 + getFreq() : int
                 + incrFreq()
```

Figure 9.9 UML for `LetterFreq`.

So let us design a `LetterFreq` class that stores a letter in an instance variable of type `char` and its frequency in an instance variable of type `int`. These instance variables can be declared as:

```java
private char letter;     // A character being counted
private int freq;        // The frequency of letter
```

We will want a constructor that can initialize these two values and two accessor methods to return these values. Since we are familiar enough with these kinds of methods, it will not be necessary to discuss them any further. We need one additional method to increment `freq` whenever we encounter the letter while processing the string:

```java
public void incrFreq() {
    freq++;
} // setFreq()
```

A UML diagram for the `LetterFreq` class is given in Figure 9.9, and the class definition is given in Figure 9.10. We will have to make a minor modification to this class later in the chapter to enable us to sort an array of objects from the class.

```java
public class LetterFreq {
    private char letter;     // A character being counted
    private int freq;        // The frequency of letter

    public LetterFreq(char ch, int fre) {
        letter = ch;
        freq = fre;
    }
    public char getLetter() {
        return letter;
    }
    public int getFreq() {
        return freq;
    }
    public void incrFreq() {
        freq++;
    }
} // LetterFreq class
```

Figure 9.10 The `LetterFreq` class definition.

AnalyzeFreq
− freqArr : LetterFreq[]
+ AnalyzeFreq() + countLetters(str : String) + printArray()

Figure 9.11   UML for Analyze-
Freq.

9.4.2   A Class to Count Letter Frequencies

Now let us turn to designing a class named `AnalyzeFreq` that will use an array of objects of
type `LetterFreq` to count the frequencies of the letters A through Z in a given string. The
array—let's call it `freqArr`—will be the only instance variable of the class. The class needs
a constructor to instantiate the array and to create the 26 array elements, each with a different
letter and an initial frequency of 0. This class should also have two methods: one to count the
frequencies of the 26 letters in a given string and, the other to print out the frequency of each
letter to the console window. The UML diagram for the class is given in Figure 9.11.

The array instance variable can be declared by:

```
private LetterFreq[] freqArr; // An array of frequencies
```

The constructor creates an array of 26 elements to store references to `LetterFreq` objects
with the statement

```
freqArr = new LetterFreq[26];
```

The indices of the array range from 0 to 25, and the elements at these locations should store the
letters A to Z. Recall that in Java, `char` data are a form of `int` data and can be used in arithmetic.
If we let k be an integer that ranges between 0 and 25, then the expression `(char)('A' + k)`
will correspond to the letters A to Z. Thus, the following loop will initialize the array correctly.

```
for (int k = 0; k < 26; k++) {
    freqArr[k] = new LetterFreq((char)('A' + k), 0);
} // for
```

The `countLetters()` method must identify the array index for `LetterFreq` object that
stores a letter between A and Z. If `let` is a `char` variable that stores such a letter, then the
expression `(let - 'A')` will give the index of the array element corresponding to `let`. Thus
the following code will calculate the frequencies of the letters in the string parameter `str`:

```
public void countLetters(String str) {
    char let;                              // For use in the loop.
    str = str.toUpperCase();
    for (int k = 0; k < str.length(); k++) {
        let = str.charAt(k);
        if ((let >= 'A') && (let <= 'Z')) {
            freqArr[let - 'A'].incrFreq();
        } // if
    } // for
} // countLetters()
```

```java
public class AnalyzeFreq {
  private LetterFreq[] freqArr;                  // An array of frequencies

  public AnalyzeFreq() {
    freqArr = new LetterFreq[26];
    for (int k = 0; k < 26; k++) {
      freqArr[k] = new LetterFreq((char)('A' + k), 0);
    } // for
  }
  public void countLetters(String str) {
    char let;                                    // For use in the loop.
    str = str.toUpperCase();
    for (int k = 0; k < str.length(); k++) {
      let = str.charAt(k);
      if ((let >= 'A') && (let <= 'Z')) {
        freqArr[let - 'A'].incrFreq();
      } // if
    } // for
  }
  public void printArray() {
    for (int k = 0; k < 26; k++) {
      System.out.print("letter: " + freqArr[k].getLetter());
      System.out.println(" freq: " + freqArr[k].getFreq());
    } // for
  }
} // AnalyzeFreq class
```

Figure 9.12   The AnalyzeFreq class definition.

The definition of the `printArray()` method is completely straightforward:

```java
public void printArray() {
  for (int k = 0; k < 26; k++) {
    System.out.print("letter: " + freqArr[k].getLetter());
    System.out.println("    freq: " + freqArr[k].getFreq());
  } // for
} // printArray()
```

The entire definition of `AnalyzeFreq` is given in Figure 9.12. We will modify this class later in the chapter to be able to sort the array after counting. The following `main()` method, either in this class or in its own class, will demonstrate how the class methods are used.

```java
public static void main(String[] argv) {
  AnalyzeFreq af = new AnalyzeFreq();
  af.countLetters("Now is the time for all good students" +
    " to study computer related topics.");
  af.printArray();
} // main()
```

SELF-STUDY EXERCISE

EXERCISE 9.7   Rewrite the `main()` of the `AnalyzeFreq` class so that it opens a file named `freqtest.txt` and counts the frequencies of the letters of the text stored in the file. You will need to use the `Scanner` class to read from the file, as was done in Chapter 4. Create a file named `freqtest.txt` that contains several hundred characters of typical English text to test the new `main()` method.

9.5   Array Algorithms: Sorting

Sorting an array is the process of arranging its elements in ascending or descending order. Sorting algorithms are among the most widely used algorithms. Any time large amounts of data are maintained, there is some need to arrange them in a particular order. For example, the telephone company needs to arrange its accounts by the last name of the account holder as well as by phone number.

9.5.1   Insertion Sort

The first sorting algorithm we will look at is known as **insertion sort**, so named because, as it traverses through the array from the first to the last element, it inserts each element into its correct position in the partially sorted array.

For an array of N elements, let's think of the array as divided into two parts. The *sorted* part will be the left-hand side of the array. And the *unsorted* part will be the right-hand side of the array. Initially, the sorted part consists of the first element in the array—the element at index 0.

Insertion sort moves through the unsorted portion of the array—that is its loop variable, k, ranges from 1 through $N - 1$. On each iteration it inserts the kth element into its correct position in the sorted part of the array. To insert an element into the sorted part of the array, it may be necessary to move elements greater than the one being inserted out of the way.

In pseudocode, insertion sort can be represented as follows:

```
Insertion Sort of an array, arr, of N elements into ascending order
1. For k assigned 1 through N-1
2.    Remove the element arr[k] and store it in x.
3.    For i starting at k-1 and for all preceding elements greater than x
4.       Move arr[i] one position to the right in the array.
5.    Insert x at its correct location.
```

As is apparent from the pseudocode, we have a nested `for` loop. The outer (k) loop, iterates through the array from 1 to $N - 1$. The inner loop iterates as many times as necessary, starting with the element just to the left of the kth element in order to insert the kth element into its correct position in the sorted portion. Note that the kth element is always removed from the array (and stored in the variable x), to make room for elements that have to be moved to the right.

To see how this works, consider an integer array containing the ages of five friends:

```
21 |  20  27  24  19       x = 20
      k
```

For this five-element array, insertion sort initially will assume that the element at index 0 is in the correct position. The vertical line marks the boundary between the sorted and unsorted portions of the array. The outer loop will look at each of the remaining elements, one at a time, inserting it into its proper position in the sorted portion of the array. To insert 20, the number at index 1, the inner loop will move 21 to the right by one position. To do this, the algorithm will copy 20 from its location and store it in x. It will then move 21 one space to the right. Finally, it will insert 20, which is stored in x, at index 0, where it belongs relative to the other elements in the sorted part of the array. At this point, the sorted portion of the array consists of the first two elements, which are in the correct order relative to each other.

```
20  21 |  27  24  19      x = 27
            k
```

For the next element, 27, none of the elements in the sorted portion need to be moved, so the inner for loop will iterate zero times. This gives us:

```
20  21  27 |  24  19      x = 24
              k
```

For the fourth element, 24, only the previous element, 27, needs to be moved to the right, giving:

```
20  21  24  27 | 19      x = 19
                 k
```

At this point, the sorted part of the array consists of the first four elements, which are in the correct order relative to each other. Finally, for the last element, 19, all of the elements in the sorted part of the array need to be moved one space to the right. This will require four iterations of the inner loop. We show the state of the array after each iteration of the inner for loop:

```
                 k
20 21 24 27 | 19     Remove 19 and store it x = 19
20 21 24 27 | 27     Move 27 to the right
20 21 24 24 | 27     Move 24 to the right
20 21 21 24 | 27     Move 21 to the right
20 20 21 24 | 27     Move 20 to the right
19 20 21 24 27 |     Insert x=19 at index 0
```

The fact that so many elements may have to move on each iteration of the outer loop shows that insertion sort is not a very efficient algorithm.

The Sort class (Fig. 9.13) provides an implementation of the insertionSort() method. There are several points worth noting about this code. First, because it takes an int array as a parameter, the insertionSort() method will sort any array of integers, regardless of the array's length.

Second, note how empty brackets ([]) are used to declare an array parameter. If the brackets were omitted, then arr would be indistinguishable from an ordinary int parameter. Using the brackets indicates that this method takes an array of integers as its parameter.

Array parameters

```
public class Sort {
  public void insertionSort(int arr[]) {
    int temp;                                // Temporary variable for insertion
    for (int k = 1; k < arr.length; k++)  {
      temp = arr[k];                         // Remove element from array
      int i;                                 // For larger preceding elements
      for (i = k-1; i >= 0 && arr[i] > temp; i--)
        arr[i+1] = arr[i];                   // Move it right by one
      arr[i+1] = temp;                       // Insert the element
    }
  } // insertionSort()
  public void print(int arr[]) {
    for (int k = 0; k < arr.length; k++)     // For each integer
      System.out.print( arr[k] + " \t ");    // Print it
    System.out.println();
  } // print()
  public static void main(String args[]) {
    int intArr[] = { 21, 20, 27, 24, 19 };
    Sort sorter = new Sort();
    sorter.print(intArr);
    sorter.insertionSort(intArr);            // Passing an array
    sorter.print(intArr);
  } // main()
} // Sort class
```

Figure 9.13   Source code for the `insertionSort()` method. Note in `main()` how an integer array is passed to the method.

DEBUGGING TIP: Array Parameter.   When declaring an array parameter, empty brackets must be used either after the array name or after the type name to distinguish it from a nonarray parameter.

Third, note how an array of integers is passed to the `insertionSort()` method in the `main()` method:

```
sorter.insertionSort(intArr);    // Pass intArr to the method
```

That is, when passing an array to a method, you use just the name of the array, without brackets. Both of the following statements would cause syntax errors:

```
sorter.insertionSort(intArr[]);    // Err: Can't have brackets
sorter.insertionSort(intArr[5]);   // Err: passing an integer
```

In the first case, empty brackets are only used when you declare an array variable, not when you are passing the array to a method. In the second case, `intArr[5]` is an `int`, not an array, and cannot legally be passed to `insertionSort()`.

DEBUGGING TIP: Passing an Array Argument.   It is a syntax error to use empty brackets when passing an array argument to a method, where only the array's name should be used. Empty brackets are only used when declaring an array variable.

Finally, within the `insertionSort()` method itself, note that we declare the index for the inner `for` loop outside of the `for` statement. This is so that it can be used outside the scope of the `for` loop to insert `temp` at location `arr[i+1]`, its correct location. Note also that the index of its correct location is `i+1`, rather than just `i`. This is because the inner loop might iterate past location 0, which would give `i` a value of -1 at that point.

9.5.2   Selection Sort

There are a large variety of array-sorting algorithms. Selection sort is different from, but comparable to, insertion sort in its overall performance. To illustrate the **selection sort** algorithm, suppose you want to sort a deck of 25 index cards, numbered from 1 to 25. Lay the 25 cards out on a table, one card next to the other. Starting with the first card, look through the deck and find the smallest card, the number 1 card, and exchange it with the card in the first location. Then go through the deck again starting at the second card, find the next-smallest card, the number 2 card, and exchange it with the card in the second location. Repeat this process 24 times.

Selection sort algorithm

Translating this strategy into pseudocode gives the following algorithm:

```
Selection sort of a 25-card deck from small to large
1. For count assigned 1 to 24                    // Outer loop
2.    smallestCard = count
3.    For currentCard assigned count+1 to 25     // Inner loop
4.       If deck[currentCard] < deck[smallestCard]
5.          smallestCard = currentCard
6.       If smallestCard != count                // You need to swap
7.          Swap deck[count] and deck[smallestCard]
```

For a deck of 25 cards, you need to repeat the outer loop 24 times. In other words, you must select the smallest card and insert it in its proper location 24 times. The inner loop takes care of finding the smallest remaining card.

On each iteration of this outer loop, the algorithm assumes that the card specified by the outer loop variable, `count`, is the smallest card (line 2). It usually won't be, of course, but we have to start somewhere.

The inner loop then iterates through the remaining cards (from `count+1` to 25) and compares each one with the card that is currently the smallest (lines 4 and 5). Whenever it finds a card that is smaller than the smallest card, it designates it as the smallest card (line 5). At the end of the loop, the `smallestCard` variable will remember where the smallest card is in the deck.

Finally, when the inner loop is finished, the algorithm swaps the smallest card with the card in the location designated by `count`.

9.5.3   Algorithm: Swapping Memory Elements

An important feature of the selection sort algorithm is its need to swap two array elements, or cards, to continue our example. Swapping two memory elements, whether they are array elements or not, requires the use of a temporary variable. For example, to swap the jth and kth elements in an `int` array named `arr`, you would use the following algorithm:

Swapping algorithm

```
int temp = arr[j];    // Store the jth element in temp
arr[j] = arr[k];      // Move the kth element into j
arr[k] = temp;        // Move the jth element into k
```

The `temp` variable temporarily stores the jth element so that its value is not lost when its location is overwritten by the kth element. The need for this variable is a subtlety that beginning programmers frequently overlook. But consider what would happen if we used the following erroneous algorithm:

Swapping blunder

```
arr[j] = arr[k];    // Erroneous swap code
arr[k] = arr[j];
```

If `arr[j]` refers to 4 and `arr[k]` refers to 2 in the array 1 4 2 8, then the erroneous algorithm would produce 1 2 2 8, the wrong result.

JAVA PROGRAMMING TIP: Swapping Variables. When swapping two memory elements, a temporary variable must be used to store one of the elements while its memory location is being overwritten.

The following method implements the swap algorithm for two elements, *el1* and *el2* of an `int` array:

```
void swap(int arr[], int el1, int el2) {
    int temp = arr[el1];     // Assign first element to temp
    arr[el1] = arr[el2];     // Overwrite first with second
    arr[el2] = temp;         // Overwrite second with first
}                            // swap()
```

SELF-STUDY EXERCISES

EXERCISE 9.8   Sort the array 24 18 90 1 0 85 34 18 using the insertion sort algorithm. Show the order of the elements after each iteration of the outer loop.

EXERCISE 9.9   Sort the array 24 18 90 1 0 85 34 18 using the selection sort algorithm. Show the order of the elements after each iteration of the outer loop.

EXERCISE 9.10   Write a Java code segment to swap two `Student` objects, `student1` and `student2`.

EXERCISE 9.11   Write a Java implementation of the `selectionSort()` method to sort an array of `int`.

9.5.4   Passing a Value and Passing a Reference

Recall from Chapter 3 that when an `Object` is passed to a method, a copy of the reference to the `Object` is passed. Because an array is an object, a reference to the array is passed to `insertionSort()` rather than the whole array itself. This is in contrast to how a value of a primitive type is passed. In that case, a copy of the actual value is passed.

JAVA LANGUAGE RULE   Primitive vs. Object Parameters. When a value of a primitive data type—`int`, `double`, `char`, `boolean`—is passed as an argument to a method, a copy of the value is passed; when a reference to an `Object` is passed, a copy of the reference is passed.

One implication of this distinction is that for arguments of primitive type, the original argument cannot be changed from within the method because the method has only a copy of its value.

For example, the following method takes an `int` parameter *n*, which is incremented within the method:

```
public void add1(int n) {
    System.out.print("n = " + n);
    n = n + 1;
    System.out.println(",    n = " + n);
}
```

But because *n* is a parameter of primitive type, incrementing it within the method has no effect on its associated argument. Thus, in the following segment, the value of *Num*—*n*'s associated argument—will not be affected by what goes on inside the `add()` method. The output produced by the code segment is shown in the comments:

Passing a primitive value

```
int Num = 5;
System.out.println("Num = " + Num);     // Prints Num = 5
add1(Num);                              // Prints n = 5,   n = 6
System.out.println("Num = " + Num);     // Prints Num = 5
```

Note that while *n*'s value has changed inside the method, *Num*'s value remains unaffected.

The case is much different when we pass a reference to an object. In that case, the object itself can be manipulated from within the method. The `insertionSort()` method is a good illustration. In the following code segment, the array `anArr` is printed, then sorted, and then printed again:

Passing an object

```
Sort sorter = new Sorter();
int anArr[] = { 5, 10, 16, -2, 4, 6, 1 };
sorter.print(anArr);                 // Prints 5 10 16 -2 4 6 1
sorter.insertionSort(anArr);         // Sorts anArr
sorter.print(anArr);                 // Prints -2 1 4 5 6 10 16
```

As you can see, the object itself (the array) has been changed from within the method. This shows that changes within `insertionSort` to the array referenced by `arr` are actually being made to `anArr` itself. If fact, because `insertionSort()` is passed a copy of the reference variable `anArr`, both `arr` and `anArr` are references to the very same object—that is, to the same array (Fig. 9.14).

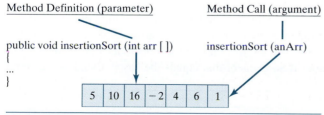

Method Definition (parameter)   Method Call (argument)

public void insertionSort (int arr [ ])   insertionSort (anArr)

Figure 9.14 When an array is passed to a method, both the parameter and the corresponding argument refer to the same object.

The justification for passing a reference to an object rather than the entire object itself is a matter of efficiency. A reference uses just 4 bytes of data, whereas an object may use thousands of bytes. It would just be too inefficient to copy hundreds of bytes each time an object is passed to a method. Instead, the method is passed a reference to the object, thereby giving it access to the object without incurring the expense of copying large amounts of data. Indeed, Java provides no way to pass a copy of an object to a method.

SELF-STUDY EXERCISE

EXERCISE 9.12   Give the values that will be stored in `myArr` and k after you invoke `mystery(myArr, k)`, where `myArr`, k and `mystery()` are declared as follows:

```
int myArr[] = {1,2,3,4,5};     int k = 3;
void mystery(int a[], int m) {
    ++a[m];
    --m;
}
```

9.6   Array Algorithms: Searching

Suppose we have a large array and we need to find one of its elements. We need an algorithm to search the array for a particular value, usually called the *key*. If the elements of the array are not arranged in any particular order, the only way we can be sure to find the key, assuming it is in the array, is to search every element, beginning at the first element, until we find it.

9.6.1   Sequential Search

This approach is known as a **sequential search**, because each element of the array will be examined in sequence until the key is found (or the end of the array is reached). A pseudocode description of this algorithm is as follows:

```
1. For each element of the array
2.     If the element equals the key
3.         Return its index
4. If the key is not found in the array
5.     Return -1 (to indicate failure)
```

This algorithm can easily be implemented in a method that searches an integer array, which is passed as the method's parameter. If the key is found in the array, its location is returned. If it is not found, then -1 is returned to indicate failure.

The `Search` class (Figs. 9.15 and 9.16) provides the Java implementation of the `sequentialSearch()` method. The method takes two parameters: the array to be searched and the key to be searched for. It uses a `for` statement to examine each element of the array, checking whether it equals the key or not. If an element that equals the key is found, the method

Search
+ sequentialSearch(in arr : int[], in key : int)
+ binarySearch(in arr : int[], in key : int)

Figure 9.15   The Search class.

```java
public class Search {

    public int sequentialSearch(int arr[], int key) {
        for (int k = 0; k < arr.length; k++)
            if (arr[k] == key)
                return k;
        return -1;                             // Failure if this is reached
    } // sequentialSearch()

    public int binarySearch(int arr[], int key) {
        int low = 0;                           // Initialize bounds
        int high = arr.length - 1;
        while (low <= high) {                  // While not done
            int mid = (low + high) / 2;
            if (arr[mid] == key)
                return mid;                    // Success
            else if (arr[mid] < key)
                low = mid + 1;                 // Search top half
            else
                high = mid - 1;                // Search bottom half
        } // while
        return -1;   // Post:  if low > high search failed
    } // binarySearch()
} // Search class
```

Figure 9.16   The Search class contains both a `sequentialSearch()` and a `binarySearch()`.

immediately returns that element's index. The last statement in the method will only be reached if no element matching the key is found.

> **EFFECTIVE DESIGN: Sentinel Return Value.**   Like Java's `indexOf()` method, the `sequentialSearch()` returns a sentinel value (-1) to indicate that the key was not found. This is a common design for search methods.

9.6.2   Binary Search

If the elements of an array have been sorted into ascending or descending order, it is not necessary to search sequentially through each element of the array in order to find the key. Instead, the search algorithm can make use of the knowledge that the array is ordered and perform a **binary search**—a divide-and-conquer algorithm that divides the array in half on each iteration and limits its search to just the half that could contain the key.

To illustrate a binary search, recall the familiar guessing game in which you try to guess a secret number between 1 and 100, being told "too high" or "too low" or "just right" on each guess. A good first guess should be 50. If this is too high, the next guess should be 25, because if 50 is too high the number must be between 1 and 49. If 50 was too low, the next guess should be 75, and so on. After each wrong guess, a good guesser should pick the midpoint of the sublist that would contain the secret number.

Proceeding in this way, the correct number can be guessed in at most $log_2 N$ guesses, because the base-2 logarithm of N is the number of times you can divide N in half. For a list of 100 items, the search should take no more than seven guesses ($2^7 = 128 > 100$). For a list of 1,000 items, a binary search would take at most 10 guesses ($2^{10} = 1,024 > 1,000$). How many guesses?

So a binary search is a much more efficient way to search, provided the array's elements are in order. Note that "order" here needn't be numeric order. We could use binary search to look up a word in a dictionary or a name in a phone book.

A pseudocode representation of the binary search is given as follows:

```
TO SEARCH AN ARRAY OF N ELEMENTS IN ASCENDING ORDER
1. Assign 0 low and assign N-1 to high initially
2. As long as low is not greater than high
3.     Assign (low + high) / 2 to mid
4.     If the element at mid equals the key
5.          then return its index
6.     Else if the element at mid is less than the key
7.          then assign mid + 1 to low
8.     Else assign mid - 1 to high
9. If this is reached return -1 to indicate failure
```

Just as with the sequential search algorithm, this algorithm can easily be implemented in a method that searches an integer array that is passed as the method's parameter (Fig. 9.16). If the key is found in the array, its location is returned. If it is not found, then −1 is returned to indicate failure. The binarySearch() method takes the same type of parameters as sequentialSearch(). Its local variables, low and high, are used as pointers, or references, to the current low and high ends of the array, respectively. Note the loop-entry condition: low <= high. If low ever becomes greater than high, this indicates that key is not contained in the array. In that case, the algorithm returns −1.

As a binary search progresses, the array is repeatedly cut in half, and low and high will be used to point to the low and high index values in the portion of the array still being searched. The local variable mid is used to point to the approximate midpoint of the unsearched portion of the array. If the key is determined to be past the midpoint, then low is adjusted to mid+1; if the key occurs before the midpoint, then high is set to mid-1. The updated values of low and high limit the search to the unsearched portion of the original array.

Unlike sequential search, binary search does not have to examine every location in the array to determine that the key is not in the array. It searches only the part of the array that could contain the key. For example, suppose we are searching for −5 in the following array:

```
int sortArr[] = { 1,2,3,4,5,6,7,8,9,10,11,12,13,14,15,16,17,18,19,20 };
```

The −5 is smaller than the smallest array element. Therefore, the algorithm will repeatedly divide the low end of the array in half until the condition low > high becomes true. We can see this by tracing the values that low, mid, and high will take during the search:

Key	Iteration	Low	High	Mid
-5	0	0	19	9
-5	1	0	8	4
-5	2	0	3	1
-5	3	0	0	0
-5	4	0	-1	Failure

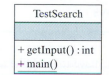

Figure 9.17 The TestSearch class.

As this trace shows, the algorithm examines only four locations to determine that −5 is not in the array. After checking location 0, the new value for high will become −1, which makes the condition low <= high false. So the search will terminate.

The TestSearch class (Figs. 9.17 and 9.18) provides a program that can be used to test two search methods. It creates an integer array whose values are in ascending order. It then uses the getInput() method to input an integer from the keyboard and performs both a sequentialSearch() and a binarySearch() for the number.

SELF-STUDY EXERCISE

EXERCISE 9.13 For an array containing the elements 2, 4, 6, and so on up to 28 in that order, draw a trace showing which elements are examined if you search for 21 using a binary search.

```java
import java.io.*;
public class TestSearch {
  public static int getInput() {
    KeyboardReader kb = new KeyboardReader();
    kb.prompt("This program searches for values in an array.");
    kb.prompt(
    "Input any positive integer (or any negative to quit) : ");
    return kb.getKeyboardInteger();
  } // getInput()

  public static void main(String args[]) throws IOException {
    int intArr[] = { 2,4,6,8,10,12,14,16,18,20,22,24,26,28};
    Search searcher = new Search();
    int key = 0, keyAt = 0;
    key = getInput();
    while (key >= 0) {
      keyAt = searcher.sequentialSearch( intArr, key );
      if (keyAt != -1)
        System.out.println("   Sequential: " + key +
                            " is at intArr[" + keyAt + "]");
      else
        System.out.println("   Sequential: " + key +
                            " is not contained in intArr[]");
      keyAt = searcher.binarySearch(intArr, key);
      if (keyAt != -1)
        System.out.println("   Binary: " + key +
                            " is at intArr[" + keyAt + "]");
      else
        System.out.println("   Binary: " + key +
                            " is not contained in intArr[]");
      key = getInput();
    } // while
  } // main()
} // TestSearch class
```

Figure 9.18 The TestSearch class.

9.7 Two-Dimensional Arrays

A **two-dimensional array**, an array whose components are themselves arrays, is necessary or useful for certain kinds of problems. For example, you would use this type of array if you are doing a scientific study in which you have to track the amount of precipitation for every day of the year.

One way to organize this information would be to create a one-dimensional array consisting of 365 elements:

```
double rainfall[] = new double[365];
```

However, this representation would make it very difficult to calculate the average rainfall within a given month, which might be an important part of your study.

What data do we need?

A better representation for this problem would be to use a two-dimensional array, one dimension for the months and one for the days. The following statement declares the array variable `rainfall` and creates a 12 × 31 array object as its reference:

```
double rainfall[][] = new double[12][31];
```

Thus, `rainfall` is an *array of arrays*. You can think of the first array as the 12 months required for the problem. And you can think of each month as an array of 31 days. The months will be indexed from 0 to 11, and the days will be indexed from 0 to 30.

Choosing an appropriate representation

The problem with this representation is that when we want to refer to the rainfall for January 5, we would have to use `rainfall[0][4]`. This is awkward and misleading. The problem is that dates—1/5/1999—are unit indexed, while arrays are zero indexed. Because it will be difficult to remember this fact, our representation of the rainfall data may cause us to make errors when we start writing our algorithms.

We can easily remedy this problem by just defining our array to have an extra month and an extra day each month:

```
double rainfall[][] = new double[13][32];
```

This representation creates an array with 13 months, indexed from 0 to 12, with 32 days per month, indexed from 0 to 31. However, we can simply ignore the 0 month and 0 day by using unit indexing in all of the algorithms that process the array. In other words, if we view this array as a two-dimensional table consisting of 13 rows and 32 columns, we can leave row 0 and column 0 unused (Fig. 9.19).

As Figure 9.19 shows, the very first element of this 416-element array has subscripts (0,0), while the last location has subscripts (12,31). The main advantages of this representation are that the program as a whole will be much easier to read and understand and much less prone to error.

EFFECTIVE DESIGN: Readability. To improve a program's robustness and readability, it may be preferable to use unit array indexing by declaring extra array elements and ignoring those with index 0.

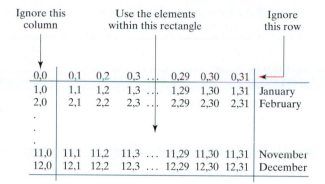

Figure 9.19 A two-dimensional array with 13 rows and 32 columns. To represent 12 months of the year, we can simply ignore row 0 and column 0.

In order to refer to an element in a two-dimensional array, you need to use two subscripts. For the `rainfall` array, the first subscript will specify the *month* and the second will specify the *day* within the month. Thus, the following statements assign 1.15 to the `rainfall` element representing January 5, and then print its value:

Referencing two-dimensional arrays

```
rainfall[1][5] = 1.15;    // Rainfall for January 5
System.out.println( rainfall[1][5] );
```

Just as in the case of one-dimensional arrays, it is an error to attempt to reference an element that is not in the array. Each of the following examples would cause Java to raise an `IndexOutOfBoundsException`:

```
rainfall[13][32] = 0.15 ;   // No such element
rainfall[11][33] = 1.3;     // No such column
rainfall[14][30] = 0.74;    // No such row
```

If the initial values of an array's elements are supposed to be zero, there is no need to initialize the elements. Java will do it automatically when you create the array with `new`. However, for many array problems it is necessary to initialize the array elements to some other value. For a two-dimensional array, this would require a nested loop. To illustrate this algorithm, let's use a nested `for` loop to initialize each element of the `rainfall` array to 0:

Initializing two-dimensional arrays

```
// Note that both loops are unit indexed.
for (int month = 1; month < rainfall.length; month++)
  for (int day = 1; day < rainfall[month].length; day++)
    rainfall[month][day] = 0.0;
```

Note that both `for` loops use unit indexing. This is in keeping with our decision to leave month 0 and day 0 unused.

Remember that when you have a nested `for` loop, the inner loop iterates faster than the outer loop. Thus, for each month, the inner loop will iterate over 31 days. This is equivalent to processing the array as if you were going across each row and then down to the next row in the representation shown in Figure 9.19.

Nested `for` loops

Table 9.1. Initialized `rainfall` array.   Unused array elements are shown as dashes.

	0	1	2	3	. . .	30	31
0	–	–	–	–	. . .	–	–
1	–	0.0	0.0	0.0	. . .	0.0	0.0
2	–	0.0	0.0	0.0	. . .	0.0	0.0
⋮	⋮	⋮	⋮	⋮	⋮	⋮	⋮
10	–	0.0	0.0	0.0	. . .	0.0	0.0
11	–	0.0	0.0	0.0	. . .	0.0	0.0
12	–	0.0	0.0	0.0	. . .	0.0	0.0

Note that for a two-dimensional array, both dimensions have an associated `length` variable, which is used in this example to specify the upper bound of each `for` loop. For the `rainfall` array, the first dimension (months) has a length of 13, and the second dimension (days) has a length of 32.

Another way to view the `rainfall` array is to remember that it is an array of arrays. The length of the first array, which corresponds to the number of months (13), is given by `rainfall.length`. The length of each month's array, which corresponds to the number of days in a month (32), is given by `rainfall[month].length`.

Array of arrays

The outer loop of the nested `for` loop iterates through months 1 through 12, and the inner `for` loop iterates through days 1 through 31. In this way, $372 = 12 \times 31$ elements of the array are set to 0.0. In Table 9.1, the boldface numbers along the top represent the day subscripts, while the boldface numbers along the left represent the month subscripts.

SELF-STUDY EXERCISES

EXERCISE 9.14   Declare a two-dimensional array of `int`, named `int2d`, that contains five rows, each of which contains 10 integers.

EXERCISE 9.15   Write a statement that prints the last integer in the third row of the array that you created in the preceding exercise. Then write an assignment statement that assigns 100 to the last element in the `int2d` array.

EXERCISE 9.16   Write a loop to print all of the elements of `int2d`, declared in the preceding exercise. Print one row per line with a space between each element on a line.

9.7.1   Two-Dimensional Array Methods

Now that we have figured out how to represent the data for our scientific experiment, let's develop methods to calculate some results. First, we want a method to initialize the array. This method will simply incorporate the nested loop algorithm we developed previously:

```
public void initRain(double rain[][]) {
    for (int month = 1; month < rain.length; month++)
        for (int day = 1; day < rain[month].length; day++)
            rain[month][day] = 0.0;
} // initRain()
```

Note how we declare the parameter for a multidimensional array. In addition to the element type (`double`) and the name of the parameter (`rain`), we must also include a set of brackets for *each* dimension of the array.

Array parameters

Note also that we use the parameter name within the method to refer to the array. As with one-dimensional arrays, the parameter is a reference to the array, which means that any changes made to the array within the method will persist when the method is exited.

The `avgDailyRain()` Method

One result that we need from our experiment is the average daily rainfall. To calculate this result, we would add up all of the rainfalls stored in the 12 × 31 array and divide by 365. Of course, the array itself contains more than 365 elements. It contains 416 elements, but we're not using the first month of the array, and in some months—those with fewer than 31 days—we're not using some of the day elements. For example, there's no such day as `rainfall[2][30]`, which would represent February 30. However, because we initialized all of the array's elements to 0, the rainfall recorded for the nondays will be 0, which won't affect our overall average.

Algorithm design

The method for calculating average daily rainfall should take our two-dimensional array of `double` as a parameter, and it should return a `double`. Its algorithm will use a nested `for` loop to iterate through the elements of the array, adding each element to a running total. When the loops exits, the total will be divided by 365 and returned:

Method design

```
public double avgDailyRain(double rain[][]) {
    double total = 0;
    for (int month = 1; month < rain.length; month++)
        for (int day = 1; day < rain[month].length; day++)
            total += rain[month][day];
    return total/365;
} // avgDailyRain()
```

The `avgRainForMonth()` Method

One reason we used a two-dimensional array for this problem is so we could calculate the average daily rainfall for a given month. Let's write a method to solve this problem. The algorithm for this method will not require a nested `for` loop. We will just iterate through the 31 elements of a given month, so the month subscript will not vary. For example, suppose we are calculating the average for January, which is represented in our array as month 1:

Algorithm design

```
double total = 0;
for (int day = 1; day < rainfall[1].length; day++)
    total = total + rainfall[1][day];
```

Thus, the month subscript is held constant (at 1) while the day subscript iterates from 1 to 31. Of course, in our method we would use a parameter to represent the month, thereby allowing us to calculate the average daily rainfall for any given month.

Method design

Another problem that our method has to deal with is that months don't all have 31 days, so we can't always divide by 31 to compute the monthly average. There are various ways to solve this problem, but perhaps the easiest is to let the number of days for the month be specified as a

Method design: What data do we need?

third parameter. That way, the month itself and the number of days for the month are supplied by the user of the method:

```
public double avgRainForMonth(double rain[][], int month, int nDays) {
    double total = 0;
    for (int day = 1; day < rain[month].length; day++)
        total = total + rain[month][day];
    return total/nDays;
} // avgRainForMonth()
```

Given this definition, we can call this method to calculate and print the average daily rainfall for March, as in the following statement:

```
System.out.println("March: " + avgRainForMonth(rainfall,3,31));
```

Note that when passing the entire two-dimensional array to the method, we just use the name of the array. We do not have to follow the name with subscripts.

9.7.2   Passing Part of an Array to a Method

Instead of passing the entire rainfall array to the `avgRainForMonth()` method, we could redesign this method so that it is only passed the particular month that is being averaged. Remember that a two-dimensional array is an array of arrays, so if we pass the month of January, we are passing an array of 32 days. If we use this approach, we need only two parameters: the month, which is an array of days, and the number of days in the month:

Method design: What data?

```
public double avgRainForMonth(double monthRain[], int nDays) {
    double total = 0;
    for (int day = 1; day < monthRain.length; day++)
        total = total + monthRain[day];
    return total/nDays;
} // avgRainForMonth()
```

Given this definition, we can call it to calculate and print the average daily rainfall for March, as in the following statement:

```
System.out.println("March: " + avgRainForMonth(rainfall[3],31));
```

In this case, we are passing an array of `double` to the method, but in order to reference it, we have to pull it out of the two-dimensional array by giving its *row* subscript as well. Thus, `rainfall[3]` refers to one month of data in the two-dimensional array, the month of March. But `rainfall[3]` is itself a one-dimensional array. Figure 9.20 helps to clarify this point.

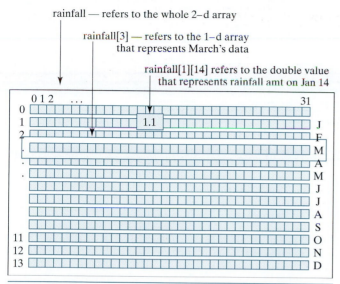

rainfall — refers to the whole 2–d array

rainfall[3] — refers to the 1–d array
that represents March's data

rainfall[1][14] refers to the double value
that represents rainfall amt on Jan 14

Figure 9.20 Referencing individual elements and array elements in a two-dimensional array.

Deciding whether to use brackets when passing data to a method is not just a matter of whether you are passing an array. It is a matter of what type of data the method parameter specifies. Whenever you call a method that involves a parameter, you have to look at the method definition to see what kind of data that parameter specifies. Then you must supply an argument that refers to that type of data.

Specifying an argument

For our two-dimensional `rainfall` array, we can refer to the entire array as `rainfall`. We can refer to one of its months as `rainfall[j]`, where *j* is any integer between 1 and 12. And we can refer to any of its elements as `rainfall[j][k]`, where *j* is any integer between 1 and 12, and *k* is any integer between 1 and 31.

JAVA LANGUAGE RULE **Arguments and Parameters.** The argument in a method call must match the data type in the method definition. This applies to all parameters, including array parameters.

The `Rainfall` class (Figs. 9.21 and 9.22) shows how we can test our array algorithms. It creates the `rainfall` array in the `main()` method. It then initializes the array and prints out average daily rainfall and average daily rainfall for the month of March. However, note that we have made a slight modification to the `initRain()` method. Instead of just assigning 0 to each element, we assign a random value between 0 and 2.0:

```
rain[month][day] = Math.random() * 2.0;
```

Using the `Math.random()` method in this way enables us to generate some realistic test data. In this case, we have scaled the data so that the daily rainfall is between 0 and 2 inches. (Rainfall like this would probably be appropriate for an Amazonian rain forest!) Testing our algorithms with these data provides some indication that our methods are in fact working properly.

Generating test data

Rainfall
+ initRain(in rain : double[][])
+ avgDailyRain(in rain : double[][]) : double
+ avgDailyRainForMonth(in monthRain : double[], in nDays : int) : double
+ main()

Figure 9.21 The Rainfall class.

```java
public class Rainfall {
  /**
   * Initializes the rainfall array
   * @ param rain is a 2D-array of rainfalls
   * Pre:  rain is non null
   * Post: rain[x][y] == 0 for all x,y in the array
   * Note that the loops use unit indexing.
   */
  public void initRain(double rain[][]) {
    for (int month = 1; month < rain.length; month++)
      for (int day = 1; day < rain[month].length; day++)
        rain[month][day] = Math.random() * 2.0;     // Random rainfall
  } // initRain()
  /**
   * Computes average daily rainfall for a year of rainfall data
   * @ param rain is a 2D-array of rainfalls
   * @ return The sum of rain[x][y] / 356
   * Pre:  rain is non null
   * Post: The sum of rain / 365 is calculated
   * Note that the loops are unit indexed
   */
  public double avgDailyRain(double rain[][]) {
    double total = 0;
    for (int month = 1; month < rain.length; month++)
      for (int day = 1; day < rain[month].length; day++)
        total += rain[month][day];
    return total/365;
  } // avgDailyRain()
  /**
   * Computes average daily rainfall for a given month containing nDays
   * @ param monthRain is a 1D-array of rainfalls
   * @ param nDays is the number of days in monthRain
   * @ return The sum of monthRain / nDays
   * Pre:  1 <= nDays <= 31
   * Post: The sum of monthRain / nDays is calculated
   */
  public double avgRainForMonth(double monthRain[], int nDays) {
    double total = 0;
    for (int day = 1; day < monthRain.length; day++)
      total = total + monthRain[day];
    return total/nDays;
  } // avgRainForMonth()
```

Figure 9.22   Definition of the Rainfall class. (***Continued on next page***)

```
public static void main(String args[]) {
    double rainfall[][] = new double[13][32];
    Rainfall data = new Rainfall();
    data.initRain(rainfall);
    System.out.println("The average daily rainfall = "
                        + data.avgDailyRain(rainfall));
    System.out.println("The average daily rainfall for March = "
                        + data.avgRainForMonth(rainfall[3],31));
} // main()
} // Rainfall class
```

Figure 9.22   Definition of the Rainfall class. (***Continued from previous page***)

EFFECTIVE DESIGN: Generating Test Data.   The Math.random() method can be used to generate numeric test data when large amounts of data are required. The data can be scaled to fit within the expected range of the actual data.

SELF-STUDY EXERCISES

EXERCISE 9.17   Suppose you're going to keep track of the daily newspaper sales at the local kiosk. Declare a 52 × 7 two-dimensional array of int and initialize each of its elements to 0.

EXERCISE 9.18   Write a method to calculate the average number of newspapers sold per week, using the array you declared in the preceding exercise.

EXERCISE 9.19   Write a method to calculate the average number of newspapers sold on Sundays, using the array you declared in the preceding exercise. Assume that Sunday is the last day of the week.

9.8   Multidimensional Arrays (Optional)

Java does not limit arrays to just two dimensions. For example, suppose we decide to extend our rainfall survey to cover a 10-year period. For each year we now need a two-dimensional array. This results in a three-dimensional array consisting of an array of years, each of which contains an array of months, each of which contains an array of days:

```
final int NYEARS = 10;
final int NMONTHS = 13;
final int NDAYS = 32;
double rainfall[][][] = new double[NYEARS][NMONTHS][NDAYS];
```

Following the design convention of not using the 0 month and 0 days, we end up with a 10 × 13 × 32 array. Note the use of final variables to represent the size of each dimension of the array. This helps to make the program more readable.

In Figure 9.23, each year of the rainfall data is represented as a separate page. On each page, there is a two-dimensional table that consists of 12 rows (1 per month) and 31 columns (1 per day).

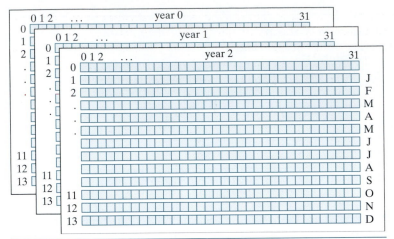

Figure 9.23 Three-dimensional data can be viewed as a collection of pages, each of which contains a two-dimensional table.

If our study could be extended to cover rainfall data from a number of different cities, that would result in a four-dimensional array, with the first dimension now being the city. Of course, for this to work, cities would have to be represented by integers, because array subscripts must be integers.

As you might expect, the algorithms for processing each element in a three-dimensional table would require a three-level nested loop. For example, the following algorithm would be used to initialize all the elements of our three-dimensional rainfall array:

```
for (int year = 0; year < rainfall.length; year++)
  for (int month = 0; month < rainfall[year].length; month++)
    for (int day = 0; day < rainfall[year][month].length; day++)
      rainfall[year][month][day] = 0.0;
```

Note again the proper use of the `length` attribute for each of the three dimensions of the array. In the outer loop, `rainfall.length`, we're referring to the number of years. In the middle loop, `rainfall[year].length`, we're referring to number of months within a given year. In the inner loop, `rainfall[year][month].length`, we're referring to the number of days within a month.

If we added a fourth dimension to our array and wanted to extend the algorithm to initialize it, we would simply embed the three-level loop within another `for` loop that would iterate over each city.

9.8.1 Array Initializers

It is possible to use an initializer with a **multidimensional array**. For instance, the following examples create several small arrays and initialize their elements:

```
int a[][] = {{1,2,3}, {4,5,6}};
char c[][] = {{'a','b'}, {'c','d'}};
double d[][] = {{1.0,2.0,3.0}, {4.0,5.0}, {6.0,7.0,8.0,9.0}};
```

The first of these declarations creates a 2×3 array of integers. The second example creates a 2×2 array of characters, and the third example creates an array of **double** consisting of three rows, each of which has a different number of elements. The first row contains three elements, the second contains two elements, and the last row contains four elements. As this last example shows, the rows in a multidimensional array don't all have to have the same length.

Using initializers, as in these examples, is feasible only for relatively small arrays. To see why, just imagine what the initializer expression would be for our three-dimensional **rainfall** array. It would require $4,160 = 10 \times 13 \times 32$ zeroes, separated by commas!

JAVA PROGRAMMING TIP: Array Initializers.   Initializer (assignment) expressions can be used to assign initial values to relatively small arrays. For larger arrays, an initializer method should be designed.

9.9   Object-Oriented Design: Polymorphic Sorting (Optional)

One limitation of the sort routines developed so far is that they only work on one particular type of data. If you've written an insertion sort to sort **int**s, you can't use it to sort **double**s. What would be far more desirable is a **polymorphic sort method**—one method that could sort any kind of data. This is easily done by making use of Java wrapper classes, such as **Integer** and **Double**, together with the **java.lang.Comparable** interface, which is specially designed for this purpose.

The **java.lang.Comparable** interface consists of the **compareTo()** method:

```
public abstract interface Comparable {
  public int compareTo(Object o);   // Abstract method
}
```

By implementing **compareTo()**, a class can impose an order on its objects. The **Comparable** interface is implemented by all of Java's wrapper classes—that is, by **Integer**, **Double**, **Float**, **Long**, and so on (Fig. 9.24).

As we saw in Chapter 8, Java interfaces allow us to create a form of *multiple inheritance*. For example, as Figure 9.24 shows, an **Integer** is both an **Object** and a **Comparable**. One implication of this is that an **Integer** can be used in any method that takes either an **Object** parameter or a **Comparable** parameter.

The **compareTo()** method takes an **Object** parameter and returns an **int**. It is meant to be invoked as **o1.compareTo(o2)**, where **o1** and **o2** are objects of the same type. Classes that implement **compareTo()** must abide by the following rules for its return value:

```
if (o1 < o2)        then o1.compareTo(o2) < 0
if (o1.equals(o2)) then o1.compareTo(o2) == 0
if (o1 > o2)        then o1.compareTo(o2) > 0
```

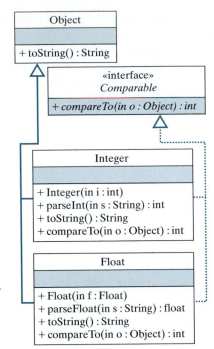

Figure 9.24 Java wrapper classes, such as `Integer` and `Double`, implement the `Comparable` interface.

In other words, if `o1 < o2`, then `o1.compareTo(o2)` will return a negative integer. If `o1 > o2`, then `o1.compareTo(o2)` will return a positive integer. And if `o1` and `o2` are equal, then `o1.compareTo(o2)` will return 0.

For a class that implements `Comparable`, we can use the `compareTo()` method to help sort its elements. For example, the following revised version of the `insertionSort()` method can be used to sort any array of `Comparable` objects—that is, any array of objects whose class implements `Comparable`:

```java
public void sort(Comparable[] arr) {
  Comparable temp;                             // Temporary variable for insertion
  for (int k = 1; k < arr.length; k++)  {
    temp = arr[k];                             // Remove it from array
    int i;
    for (i = k-1; i >= 0 && arr[i].compareTo(temp) > 0; i--)
      arr[i+1] = arr[i];                       // Move it right by one
    arr[i+1] = temp;                           // Insert the element
  }
} // sort()
```

In this version, the parameter is an array of `Comparable`. Thus, we can pass it any array whose elements implement `Comparable`, including an array of `Integer` or `Float`, and so on. Then, to compare elements of a `Comparable` array, we use the `compareTo()` method:

```java
for (i = k-1; i >= 0 && arr[i].compareTo(temp) > 0; i--)
```

TestSort
+ MAXSIZE : int
+ sort(in arr : Comparable[])
+ print(in arr : Comparable[])
+ main()

Figure 9.25 The TestSort() class.

Note that our algorithm no longer refers to `int`s, as in the original insertion sort. Indeed, it doesn't mention the specific type—`Integer`, `Float`, or whatever—of the objects it is sorting. It refers only to `Comparable`s. Therefore, we can use this method to sort any type of object, as long as the object's class implements the `Comparable` interface. Thus, by using `Comparable`, we have a more general `insertionSort()` method, one that can sort any one-dimensional array of `Comparable`s.

The `TestSort` class (Figs. 9.25 and 9.26) provides an example of how to use the polymorphic `sort()` method. It contains three methods: The `sort()` method that we just described;

```java
public class TestSort {
  public static int MAXSIZE = 25;

  public void sort(Comparable[] arr) {
    Comparable temp;                           // Temporary variable for insertion
    for (int k = 1; k < arr.length; k++) {  // For each element
      temp = arr[k];                          // Remove it
      int i;
      for (i = k-1; i >= 0 && arr[i].compareTo(temp) > 0; i--)
        arr[i+1] = arr[i];                    // Move larger to the right
      arr[i+1] = temp;                        // Insert the element
    }
  } // sort()
  public void print(Comparable arr[]) {
    for (int k = 0; k < arr.length; k++) {
      if (k % 5 == 0)  System.out.println();  // New row
        System.out.print(arr[k].toString() + "\t");
    }
    System.out.println();
  }
  // Sorts two different types of array with the same method.
  public static void main(String args[]) {
    Integer iArr[] = new Integer[TestSort.MAXSIZE];
    Float fArr[] = new  Float[TestSort.MAXSIZE];
    for (int k = 0; k < TestSort.MAXSIZE; k++) { // Create data
      iArr[k] = new Integer((int) (Math.random() * 10000));
      fArr[k] = new  Float(Math.random() * 10000);
    }
    TestSort test = new TestSort();
    test.sort(iArr);                            // Sort and print Integers
    test.print(iArr);
    test.sort(fArr);                            // Sort and print Floats
    test.print(fArr);
  } // main()
} // TestSort class
```

Figure 9.26 TestSort uses the polymorphic `sort()` method to sort either `Integer`s or `Float`s.

a polymorphic `print()` method, which can be used to print the values of any array of `Comparable`; and a `main()` method. The `main()` method creates arrays of `Integer` and `Float` and then uses the polymorphic `sort()` method to sort them. Note how the `print()` method uses the polymorphic `toString()` method to print the elements of a `Comparable` array.

This example of polymorphic sorting illustrates once again the great power of inheritance and polymorphism in object-oriented programming. The `Integer` and `Float` classes use class inheritance to inherit features from the `Object` class, and they use interface implementation to inherit the `compareTo()` method from the `Comparable` class. By implementing versions of the `toString()` and `compareTo()` methods that are appropriate for these wrapper classes, Java makes it easier to use `Integer` and `Float` objects in a variety of contexts. Taken together, inheritance and polymorphism enable us to design very general and extensible algorithms. In this example, we have defined a `sort()` method that can sort an array containing any kind of object as long as the object implements the `Comparable` interface.

9.9.1 The `java.util.Arrays.sort()` Method

While sorting algorithms provide a good way to introduce the concepts of array processing, real-world programmers never write their own sort algorithms. Instead they use library methods written and optimized by programming experts. Library sort routines use sort algorithms that are much more efficient than the ones we have discussed.

The `java.util.Arrays` class contains a polymorphic sort method that is very simple to use. For example, here is how we would use it to sort the two arrays declared in the `TestSort` program:

```
java.util.Arrays.sort(iArr);
java.util.Arrays.sort(fArr);
```

That's all there is to it! Obviously, learning how to use Java's class and method library saves real-world programmers lots of effort.

SELF-STUDY EXERCISES

EXERCISE 9.20   Add a definition of a `compareTo()` method to the `LetterFreq` class so that it implements the `Comparable` interface. The method should define one object to be less than another object if its `freq` instance variable is less.

EXERCISE 9.21   Add a definition of a `sort()` method that can be added to the definition of the `AnalyzeFreq` class. Make it so that the array in the class can be sorted into ascending order using the ordering of `LetterFreq` defined in the preceding exercise. Use the `java.util.Arrays.sort()` method.

EXERCISE 9.22   Rewrite the `main()` of the `AnalyzeFreq` class to make use of the `sort()` method from the preceding exercise.

9.10   From the Java Library: `java.lang.Vector`

java.sun.com/docs

The `java.util.Vector` class implements an array of objects that can grow in size as needed. One limitation of regular arrays is that their lengths remain fixed. Once the array is full—once every element is used—you can't allocate additional elements.

The `Vector` class contains methods for storing and retrieving objects, and for accessing objects by their index positions within the `Vector` (Fig. 9.27).

One use for a `Vector` would be when a program needs to store input from the user or a file without knowing in advance how many items there are. Using a `Vector` is less efficient than an array in terms of processing speed, but it gives you the flexibility of growing the data structure to meet the storage requirements.

As an illustration of this idea, the program in Figure 9.28 creates a random number of integers and then stores them in a `Vector`. The `Vector`, which is declared and instantiated in `main()`, is initially empty. Integers from 0 to the random **bound** are then inserted into the `Vector`. In this case, insertions are done with the `addElement()` method, which causes the `Vector` object to insert the element at the next available location, increasing its size, if necessary.

Vector
+ Vector()
+ Vector(in size : int)
+ addElement(in o : Object)
+ elementAt(in index : int) : Object
+ insertElementAt(in o : Object, in x : int)
+ indexOf(in o : Object) : int
+ lastIndexOf(in o : Object) : int
+ removeElementAt(in index : int)
+ size() : int

Figure 9.27   The `java.util.Ve-ctor` class.

```java
import java.util.Vector;

public class VectorDemo {

  public static void printVector(Vector v) {
    for (int k=0; k < v.size(); k++)
      System.out.println(v.elementAt(k).toString());
  } // printVector()

  public static void main(String args[]) {
    Vector vector = new Vector();           // An empty vector

    int bound = (int)(Math.random() * 20);
    for (int k = 0; k < bound; k++ )        // Insert a random
      vector.addElement(new Integer(k));    // number of Integers
    printVector(vector);                    // Print the elements
  } // main()
} // VectorDemo class
```

Figure 9.28   Demonstration of the Vector class.

Once all the integers have been inserted, the `printVector()` method is called. It uses the `size()` method to determine how many elements the `Vector` contains. This is similar to using the `length()` method to determine the number of characters in a `String`.

Finally, note that a `Vector` stores objects. It cannot be used to store primitive data values. You cannot store an `int` in a `Vector`. Therefore, we need to use the `Integer` wrapper class to convert `int`s into `Integer`s before they can be inserted into the `Vector`. Because you can't just print an `Integer`, or any other `Object`, the `toString()` method is used to print the string representation of the object.

Vectors store objects

By defining `Vector` to store `Object`s, Java's designers have made it as general as possible and, therefore, as widely useful as possible.

EFFECTIVE DESIGN: Generality.   Defining a data collection, such as an array or a `Vector`, in terms of the `Object` class makes it capable of storing and processing any type of value, including values of primitive data types. This is because the `Object` class is the root of the Java class hierarchy.

9.11   CASE STUDY: An *N*-Player Computer Game

In this section we will make use of arrays to extend our game-playing library by developing a design that can support games that involve more than two players. We will use an array to store a variable number of players. Following the object-oriented design principles described in Chapter 8, we will make use of inheritance and polymorphism to develop a flexible and extensible design that can be used to implement a wide variety of computer games. As in our `TwoPlayer` game example from Chapter 8, our design will allow both humans and computers to play the games. To help simplify the example, we will modify the `WordGuess` game that we developed in Chapter 8. As you will see, few modifications are needed to convert it from a subclass of `TwoPlayerGame` to a subclass of `ComputerGame`, the superclass for our *N*-Player game hierarchy.

9.11.1   The `ComputerGame` Hierarchy

Figure 9.29 provides a summary overview of the `ComputerGame` hierarchy. This figure shows the relationships among the many classes and interfaces involved. The two classes whose symbols are bold, `WordGuess` and `WordGuesser`, are the classes that define the specific game we will be playing. The rest of the classes and interfaces are designed to be used with any *N*-player game.

At the root of this hierarchy is the abstract `ComputerGame` class. Note that it uses from 1 to *N* `Player`s. These objects will be stored in a one-dimensional array in `ComputerGame`. Recall from Chapter 8 that an *IPlayer* was any class that implements the `makeAMove()` method. In this design, we have put the abstract `makeAMove()` method into the `Player` class, a class that defines a generic player of computer games. For the `WordGuess` game, the `WordGuesser` class extends `Player`. In order to play Word Guess, we will create a `WordGuess` instance, plus one or more instances of `WordGuesser`s. This is similar to the `OneRowNim` example from Chapter 8,

Note where the `TwoPlayerGame` and `OneRowNim` classes occur in the hierarchy. `TwoPlayerGame` will now be an extension of `ComputerGame`. This is in keeping with the fact that a two-player game is a special kind of *N*-player computer game. As we will see when we look at the details of these classes, `TwoPlayerGame` will override some of the methods inherited from `ComputerGame`.

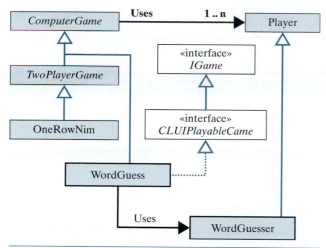

Figure 9.29 Overview of the `ComputerGame` class hierarchy.

Because it contains the abstract `makeAMove()` method, the `Player` class is an abstract class. Its purpose is to define and store certain data and methods that can be used by any computer game. For example, one important piece of information defined in `Player` is whether the player is a computer or a person. `Player`'s data and methods will be inherited by `WordGuesser` and by other classes that extend `Player`. Given its position in the hierarchy, we will be able to define polymorphic methods for `WordGuesser`s that treat them as `Player`s. As we will see, this will give our design great flexibility and extensibility.

9.11.2   The `ComputerGame` Class

Figure 9.30 shows the design details of the `ComputerGame` class. One of the key tasks of the `ComputerGame` class is to manage the one or more computer game players. Because this is a task that is common to all computer games, it makes sense to manage it here in the superclass. Toward this end, `ComputerGame` declares four instance variables and several methods. Three `int` variables define the total number of players (`nPlayers`), the number of players that have been added to the game (`addedPlayers`), and the player whose turn it is (`whoseTurn`).

Figure 9.30   The `ComputerGame` class.

An array named `player` stores the `Player`s. In keeping with the zero-indexing convention of arrays, we number the players from 0 to *nPlayers-1*. These variables are all declared `protected` so that they can be referenced directly by `ComputerGame` subclasses, but as `protected` variables they remain hidden from all other classes.

The `ComputerGame(int)` constructor allows the number of players to be set when the game is constructed. The default constructor sets the number of players to 1. The constructors create an array of length `nPlayers`:

```java
public ComputerGame(int n) {
  nPlayers = n;
  player = new Player[n]; // Create the array
}
```

The `setPlayer()` and `getPlayer()` methods are the mutator and accessor methods for the `whoseTurn` variable. This variable allows a user to determine and set whose turn it is, a useful feature for initializing a game. The `changePlayer()` method uses the default expression,

```java
whoseTurn = (whoseTurn + 1) % nPlayers
```

for changing whose turn it is. Assuming that players are numbered from 0 to `nPlayers-1`, this code gives the turn to the next player, wrapping around to player 0 if necessary. Of course, a subclass of `ComputerGame` can override this method if the game requires some other order of play.

The `addPlayer(Player)` method is used to add a new `Player` to the game, including any subclass of `Player`. The method assumes that `addedPlayers` is initialized to 0. It increments this variable by 1 each time a new player is added to the array. For the game `WordGuess`, we would be adding `Player`s of type `WordGuesser` to the game.

The complete source code for `ComputerGame` is shown in Figure 9.31. There are several points worth noting about this implementation. First, just as in the case of the abstract `TwoPlayerGame` class from Chapter 8, the methods `gameOver()` and `getWinner()` are defined as `abstract`, and the `getRules()` method is given a generic implementation. The intent here is that the subclass will override `getRules()` and provide game-specific implementations for the abstract methods.

Second, note how the `addPlayer()` method is coded. It uses the `addedPlayers` variable as the index into the `player` array, which always has length `nPlayers`. An attempt to call this method when the array is already full will lead to the following exception being thrown by Java:

```
Exception in thread "main"
    java.lang.ArrayIndexOutOfBoundsException: 2
    at ComputerGame.addPlayer(ComputerGame.java:22)
    at TwentyOne.main(TwentyOne.java:121)
```

In other words, it is an error to try to add more players than will fit in the `player` array. In Chapter 10, we will learn how to design our code to guard against such problems.

```java
public abstract class ComputerGame {
  protected int nPlayers;
  protected int addedPlayers = 0;
  protected int whoseTurn;
  protected Player player[];                      // An array of players

  public ComputerGame() {
    nPlayers = 1;                                 // Default:  1 player game
    player = new Player[1];
  }
  public ComputerGame(int n) {
    nPlayers = n;
    player = new Player[n];                        // N-Player game
  }
  public void setPlayer(int starter) {
    whoseTurn = starter;
  }
  public int getPlayer() {
    return whoseTurn;
  }
  public void addPlayer(Player p) {
    player[addedPlayers] = p;
    ++addedPlayers;
  }
  public void changePlayer() {
    whoseTurn = (whoseTurn + 1) % nPlayers;
  }
  public String getRules() {
    return "The rules of this game are: ";
  }
  public String listPlayers() {
    StringBuffer result = new StringBuffer("\nThe players are:\n");
    for (int k = 0; k < nPlayers; k++)
      result.append("Player" + k + " " + player[k].toString() + "\n");
      result.append("\n");
      return result.toString();
  }
  public abstract boolean gameOver();             // Abstract
  public abstract String getWinner();             // methods
} // ComputerGame class
```

Figure 9.31 Implementation of the ComputerGame class.

Finally, note the implementation of the `listPlayers()` method (Fig. 9.31). Here is a good example of polymorphism at work. The elements of the `player` array have a declared type of `Player`. Their dynamic type is `WordGuesser`. So when the expression `player[k].toString()` is invoked, dynamic binding is used to bind this method call to the implementation of `toString()` defined in the `WordGuesser` class. Thus, by allowing `toString()` to be bound at runtime, we are able to define a method here that does not know the exact types of the objects it will be listing.

The power of polymorphism is the flexibility and extensibility it lends to our class hierarchy. Without this feature, we would not be able to define `listPlayers()` here in the superclass, and would instead have to define it in each subclass.

Polymorphism

EFFECTIVE DESIGN: Extensibility. Polymorphic methods allow us to implement methods that can be applied to yet-to-be-defined subclasses.

9.11.3 The WordGuess and WordGuesser Classes

We will assume here that you are familiar with the WordGuess example from Chapter 8. If not, you will need to review that section before proceeding. Word Guess is a game in which players take turns trying to guess a secret word by guessing its letters. Players keep guessing as long as they correctly guess a letter in the word. If they guess wrong, it becomes the next player's turn. The winner of the game is the person who guesses the last secret letter, thereby completely identifying the word.

Figure 9.32 provides an overview of the WordGuess class. If you compare it with the design we used in Chapter 8, the only change in the instance methods and instance variables is the addition of a new constructor, WordGuess(int), and an init() method. This constructor takes an integer parameter representing the number of players. The default constructor assumes that there is one player. Of course, this version of WordGuess extends the ComputerGame class rather than the TwoPlayerGame class. Both constructors call the init() method to initialize the game:

```java
public WordGuess() { super(1); init(); }
public WordGuess(int m) { super(m); init(); }
public void init() {
    secretWord = getSecretWord();
    currentWord = new StringBuffer(secretWord);
    previousGuesses = new StringBuffer();
    for (int k = 0; k < secretWord.length(); k++)
        currentWord.setCharAt(k,'?');
    unguessedLetters = secretWord.length();
}
```

WordGuess
− secretWord : String
− currentWord : StringBuffer
− previousGuesses : StringBuffer
− unguessedLetters : int
+ WordGuess()
+ WordGuess(nplayers : int)
+ init()
− guessLetter(ch : char) : boolean
+ getPreviousGuesses() : String
+ getCurrentWord() : String
+ play(ui : UserInterface)
+ gameOver() : boolean
+ getWinner() : String
+ getGamePrompt() : String
+ reportGameState() : String
+ submitUserMove(s : String) : String

Figure 9.32 The WordGuess class.

The only other change required to convert WordGuess to an *N*-player game is to rewrite its play() method. Because the new play() method makes use of functionality inherited from the ComputerGame() class, it is actually much simpler than the play() method in the Chapter 8 version:

```java
public void play(UserInterface ui) {
  ui.report(getRules());
  ui.report(listPlayers());
  ui.report(reportGameState());

  while(!gameOver()) {
    WordGuesser p = (WordGuesser)player[whoseTurn];
    if (p.isComputer())
      ui.report(submitUserMove(p.makeAMove(getGamePrompt())));
    else {
      ui.prompt(getGamePrompt());
      ui.report(submitUserMove(ui.getUserInput()));
    }
    ui.report(reportGameState());
  } // while
} // play()
```

The method begins by displaying the game's rules and listing its players. The listPlayers() method is inherited from the ComputerGame class. After displaying the game's current state, the method enters the play loop. On each iteration of the loop, a player is selected from the array:

```java
WordGuesser p = (WordGuesser)player[whoseTurn];
```

The use of the WordGuesser variable, p, just makes the code somewhat more readable. Note that we have to use a cast operator, (WordGuesser), to convert the array element, a Player, into a WordGuesser. Because p is a WordGuesser, we can refer directly to its isComputer() method.

If the player is a computer, we prompt it to make a move, submit the move to the submit-UserMove() method, and then report the result. This is all done in a single statement:

```java
ui.report(submitUserMove(p.makeAMove(getGamePrompt())));
```

If the player is a human, we prompt the player and use the KeyboardReader's getUserInput() method to read the user's move. We then submit the move to the submitUserMove() method and report the result. At the end of the loop, we report the game's updated state. The following code segment illustrates a small portion of the interaction generated by this play() method:

```
Current word ???????? Previous guesses GLE
Player 0 guesses next.Sorry, Y is NOT a new letter in the secret word
Current word ???????? Previous guesses GLEY
Player 1 guesses next.Sorry, H is NOT a new letter in the secret word
Current word ???????? Previous guesses GLEYH
Player 2 guesses next.
Guess a letter that you think is in the secret word: a
Yes, the letter A is in the secret word
```

In this example, players 0 and 1 are computers and player 2 is a human.

In our new design, the WordGuesser class is a subclass of Player (Figure 9.33). The WordGuesser class itself requires no changes other than its declaration:

```
public class WordGuesser extends Player
```

As we saw when we were discussing the WordGuess class, the play() method invokes WordGuesser's isComputer() method. But this method is inherited from the Player class. The only other method used by play() is the makeAMove() method. This method is coded exactly the same as it was in the previous version of WordGuesser.

Figure 9.34 shows the implementation of the Player class. Most of its code is very simple. Note that the default value for the kind variable is HUMAN and the default id is −1, indicating the lack of an assigned identification.

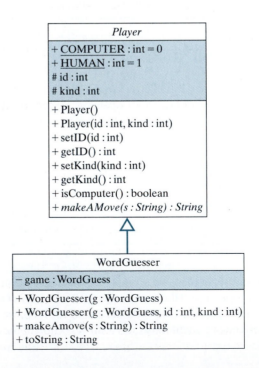

Figure 9.33 The WordGuesser class extends Player.

```
public abstract class Player {
  public static final int COMPUTER=0;
  public static final int HUMAN=1;
  protected int id = -1;              // Stores a valve between 0 and nPlayers-1
  protected int kind = HUMAN;         // Default is HUMAN

  public Player() { }
  public Player(int id, int kind) {
    this.id = id;
    this.kind = kind;
  }
  public void setID(int k) { id = k; }
  public int getID() { return id; }
  public void setKind(int k) { kind = k; }
  public int getKind() { return kind; }
  public boolean isComputer() { return kind == COMPUTER; }
  public abstract String makeAMove(String prompt);
} // Player class
```

Figure 9.34   Implementation of the Player class.

What gives Player its utility is the fact that it encapsulates attributes and actions that are common to all computer game players. Defining these elements in the superclass allows them to be used throughout the Player hierarchy. It also makes it possible to establish an association between a Player and a ComputerGame.

Given the ComputerGame and Player hierarchies and the many interfaces they contain, the task of designing and implementing a new *N*-player game is made much simpler. This too is due to the power of object-oriented programming. By learning to use a library of classes such as these, even inexperienced programmers can create relatively sophisticated and complex computer games.

EFFECTIVE DESIGN: Code Reuse.   Reusing library code by extending classes and implementing interfaces makes it much simpler to create sophisticated applications.

Finally, the following main() method instantiates and runs an instance of the WordGuess game in a command-line user interface (CLUI):

```
public static void main(String args[])
{ KeyboardReader kb = new KeyboardReader();
  ComputerGame game = new WordGuess(3);
  game.addPlayer(new WordGuesser((WordGuess)game, 0, Player.HUMAN));
  game.addPlayer(new WordGuesser((WordGuess)game, 1, Player.COMPUTER);
  game.addPlayer(new WordGuesser((WordGuess)game, 2, Player.COMPUTER);
  ((CLUIPlayableGame)game).play(kb);
} // main()
```

In this example, we create a three-player game in which two of the players are computers. Note how we create a new WordGuesser, passing it a reference to the game itself, as well as its individual identification number and its type (HUMAN or COMPUTER). To run the game, we simply invoke its play() method. You know enough now about object-oriented design principles to recognize that the use of play() in this context is an example of polymorphism.

Figure 9.35 The Sliding Tile Puzzle.

9.12   A GUI-Based Game (Optional Graphics)

Most modern computer games do not use a command-line interface. We now address this shortcoming by expanding our `ComputerGame` hierarchy so that it works with Graphical User Interfaces (GUIs) as well as Command-Line User Interfaces (CLUIs).

The Sliding Tile Puzzle is a puzzle game. It is played by one player, a human. The puzzle consists of six tiles arranged on a board containing seven spaces. Three of the tiles are labeled L and three are labeled R. Initially the tiles are arranged as RRR_LLL. In other words, the R tiles are arranged to the left of the L tiles, with a blank space in the middle. The object of the puzzle is to rearrange the tiles into LLL_RRR. The rules are that tiles labeled R can only move right. Tiles labeled L can only move left. Tiles may move directly into the blank space or they can jump over one tile into the blank space.

Our purpose in this section is to develop a GUI that plays this game. An appropriate GUI is shown Figure 9.35. Here the tiles and the blank space are represented by an array of buttons. To make a move the user clicks on the "tile" he or she wishes to move. The GUI will assume that the user wants to move that tile into the blank space. If the proposed move is legal, the GUI will carry out the move. Otherwise it will just ignore it. For example, if the user were to click on the third R button from the left, a legal move, the GUI would rearrange the labels on the buttons so that their new configuration would be RR_RLLL. On the other hand, if the user were to click on the rightmost L button, the GUI would ignore that move because it is illegal.

9.12.1   The `GUIPlayableGame` Interface

How should we extend our game-playing hierarchy to accommodate GUI-based games? As we learned in Chapter 4, one difference between GUI-based applications and CLUI-based applications is the locus of control. In a CLUI-based application, control resides in the computational object. For games, this is the game object. That is why the `play()` method in our CLUI-based games contains the game's control loop. By contrast, control resides in the GUI's event loop in GUI-based applications. That is why we learned how to manage Java's event hierarchy in Chapter 4. Thus, in the GUI shown in Figure 9.35, the GUI will *listen* and take *action* when the user clicks one of its buttons.

However, given that control will reside in the GUI, there is still a need for communication between the GUI and the game object. In the CLUI-based games, we have used the `CLUIPlayableGame` interface to manage the communication between the game and the user interface. We will follow the same design strategy in this case. Thus, we will design a `GUIPlayableGame` interface that can be implemented by any game that wishes to use a GUI (Fig. 9.36).

What method(s) should this interface contain? One way to answer this question is to think about the type of interaction that must take place when the user clicks one of the tiles. If the user clicks the third R button, the GUI should pass this information to the game. The game should then decide whether or not it is a legal move and communicate this back to the GUI. Assuming it is a legal move, the game should also update its representation of the game's

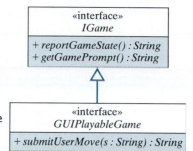

Figure 9.36 The GUIPlayableGame interface extends the IGame interface.

state to reflect that the tile array has changed. And it should somehow communicate the game's state to the GUI.

Because it is impossible to know in advance just what form of data a game's moves might take, we will use Java `String`s to communicate between the user interface and the game object. Thus, a method with the following signature will enable us to submit a `String` representing the user's move to the game and receive in return a `String` representing the game object's response to the move:

```
submitUserMove(String move): String;
```

In addition to this method, a GUI interface could use the `reportGameState()` and `get-GamePrompt()` methods that are part of the `IGame` interface. The design shown in Figure 9.36 leads to the following definition for the `GUIPlayableGame` interface:

```java
public interface GUIPlayableGame extends IGame {
    public String submitUserMove(String theMove);
}
```

Because it extends `IGame`, this interface inherits the `getGamePrompt()` and `reportGame-State()` from the `IGame` interface. The GUI should be able to communicate with any game that implements this interface.

9.12.2 The SlidingTilePuzzle

We will now discuss the design and details of the `SlidingTilePuzzle` itself. Its design is summarized in Figure 9.37. Most of the methods should be familiar to you, because the design closely follows the design we employed in the `WordGuess` example. It has implementations of inherited methods from the `ComputerGame` class and the `GUIPlayableGame` interface.

We will represent the sliding tile puzzle in a one-dimensional array of `char`. We will store the puzzle's solution in a Java `String` and use an `int` variable to keep track of where the blank space is in the array. This leads to the following class-level declarations:

```java
private char puzzle[] = {'R','R','R',' ','L','L','L'};
private String solution = "LLL RRR";
private int blankAt = 3;
```

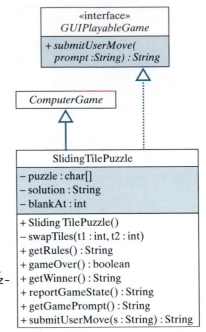

Figure 9.37 The SlidingTilePuzzle is a ComputerGame that implements the GUIPlayableGame interface.

Note how we initialize the `puzzle` array with the initial configuration of seven characters. Taken together, these statements initialize the puzzle's state.

Because a puzzle is a one-person game and our sliding tile puzzle will be played by a human, this leads to a very simple constructor definition:

```
public SlidingTilePuzzle() {
    super(1);
}
```

We call the `super()` constructor (`ComputerGame()`) to create a one-person game.

The puzzle's state needs to be communicated to the GUI as a `String`. This is the purpose of the `reportGameState()` method:

```
public String reportGameState() {
    StringBuffer sb = new StringBuffer();
    sb.append(puzzle);
    return sb.toString();
}
```

We use a `StringBuffer()` to convert the puzzle, a `char` array, into a `String`.

The most important method for communicating with the GUI is the `submitUserMove()` method:

```java
public String submitUserMove(String usermove) {
  int tile = Integer.parseInt(usermove);
  char ch = puzzle[tile];
  if (ch == 'L' && (blankAt == tile-1 || blankAt == tile-2))
    swapTiles(tile,blankAt);
  else if (ch == 'R' && (blankAt == tile+1 || blankAt == tile+2))
    swapTiles(tile,blankAt);
  else
    return "That's an illegal move.\n";
  return "That move is legal.\n";
}
```

This is the method that processes the user's move, which is communicated through the GUI. As we saw, the puzzle's "tiles" are represented by an array of buttons in the GUI. The buttons are indexed 0 through 6 in the array. When the user clicks a button, the GUI should pass its index, represented as a `String`, to the `submitUserMove()` method. Given the index number of the tile that was selected by the user, this method determines whether the move is legal.

The `Integer.parseInt()` method is used to extract the tile's index from the method's parameter. This index is used to get a "tile" from the `puzzle` array. The logic in this method reflects the rules of the game. If the tile is an *L*, then it can only move into a blank space that is either one or two spaces to its left. Similarly, an *R* tile can only move into a blank space that is one or two spaces to its right. All other moves are illegal. For legal moves, we simply swap the tile and the blank space in the array, a task handled by the `swap()` method. In either case, the method returns a string reporting whether the move was legal or illegal.

Figure 9.38 shows the full implementation for the `SlidingTilePuzzle`, the remaining details of which are straightforward.

```java
public class SlidingTilePuzzle extends ComputerGame implements GUIPlayableGame{
  private char puzzle[] = {'R','R','R',' ','L','L','L'};
  private String solution = "LLL RRR";
  private int blankAt = 3;
  public SlidingTilePuzzle() { super(1); }

  public boolean gameOver() {                              // True if puzzle solved
    StringBuffer sb = new StringBuffer();
    sb.append(puzzle);
    return sb.toString().equals(solution);
  }
  public String getWinner() {
    if (gameOver())
      return "\nYou did it! Very Nice!\n";
    else return "\nGood try. Try again!\n";
  }
}
```

Figure 9.38   Implementation of the `SlidingTilePuzzle` class. (***Continued on next page***)

```
public String reportGameState() {
  StringBuffer sb = new StringBuffer();
  sb.append(puzzle);
  return sb.toString();
}
public String getGamePrompt() {
  return "To move a tile, click on it.";
}
public String submitUserMove(String usermove) {
  int tile = Integer.parseInt(usermove);
  char ch = puzzle[tile];
  if (ch=='L' && (blankAt==tile-1 || blankAt==tile-2))
    swapTiles(tile,blankAt);
  else if (ch=='R' && (blankAt==tile+1 || blankAt==tile+2))
    swapTiles(tile,blankAt);
  else
    return "That's an illegal move.\n";
  return "That move is legal.\n";
}
private void swapTiles(int ti, int bl) {
  char ch = puzzle[ti];
  puzzle[ti] = puzzle[bl];
  puzzle[bl] = ch;
  blankAt = ti;                                        // Reset the blank
}
} // SlidingTilePuzzle class
```

Figure 9.38 Implementation of the `SlidingTilePuzzle` class. (*Continued from previous page*)

9.12.3 The `SlidingGUI` Class

Let's now implement a GUI that can be used to play the sliding tile puzzle. We will model the GUI after those we designed in Chapter 4.

Figure 9.39 provides a summary of the design. As an implementor of the `ActionListener` interface, `SlidingGUI` implements the `actionPerformed()` method, which is where the code that controls the puzzle is located. The main data structure is an array of seven `JButton`s, representing the seven tiles in the puzzles. The buttons' labels will reflect the state of the puzzle. They will be rearranged after every legal move by the user. The `reset` button is used to reinitialize the game. This allows users to play again or to start over if they get stuck.

The `puzzleState` is a `String` variable that stores the puzzle's current state, which is updated repeatedly from the `SlidingTilePuzzle` by calling its `reportGameState()` method. The private `labelButtons()` method will read the `puzzleState` and use its letters to set the labels of the GUI's buttons.

The implementation of `SlidingGUI` is shown in Figure 9.40. Its constructor and `build-GUI()` methods are responsible for setting up the GUI. We use a `for` loop in `buildGUI()` to create the `JButton`s, associate an `ActionListener` with them, and add them to the GUI. Except for the fact that we have an array of buttons, this is very similar to the GUI created in Chapter 4. Recall that associating an `ActionListener` with the buttons allows the program to respond to button clicks in its `actionPerformed()` method.

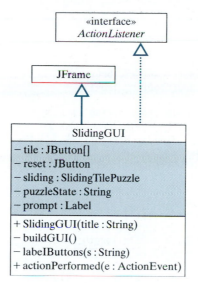

Figure 9.39 The `SlidingGUI` class.

```java
import javax.swing.*;
import java.awt.*;
import java.awt.event.*;
public class SlidingGUI extends JFrame implements ActionListener {
  private JButton tile[] = new JButton[7];
  private JButton reset = new JButton("Reset");
  private SlidingTilePuzzle sliding;
  private String puzzleState;
  private Label label;
  private String prompt = "Goal: [LLL RRR]. " +
    " Click on the tile you want to move." +
    " Illegal moves are ignored.";
  public SlidingGUI(String title) {
    sliding = new SlidingTilePuzzle();
    buildGUI();
    setTitle(title);
    pack();
    setVisible(true);
  } // SlidingGUI()
  private void buildGUI() {
    Container contentPane = getContentPane();
    contentPane.setLayout(new BorderLayout());
    JPanel buttons = new JPanel();
    puzzleState = sliding.reportGameState();
    for (int k = 0; k < tile.length; k++) {
      tile[k] = new JButton(""+puzzleState.charAt(k));
      tile[k].addActionListener(this);
      buttons.add(tile[k]);
    }
```

Figure 9.40 Implementation of the `SlidingGUI` class. (*Continued on next page*)

```
      reset.addActionListener(this);
      label = new Label(prompt);
      buttons.add(reset);
      contentPane.add("Center", buttons);
      contentPane.add("South", label);
   } // buildGUI()
   private void labelButtons(String s) {
      for (int k = 0; k < tile.length; k++)
         tile[k].setText(""+ s.charAt(k));
   } // labelButtons()
   public void actionPerformed(ActionEvent e) {
      String result = "";
      if (e.getSource() == reset) {                        // Reset clicked?
         sliding = new SlidingTilePuzzle();
         label.setText(prompt);
      }
      for (int k = 0; k < tile.length; k++)                // Tile clicked?
         if (e.getSource() == tile[k])
            result = ((GUIPlayableGame)sliding).submitUserMove(""+ k);
      if (result.indexOf("illegal") != -1)
         java.awt.Toolkit.getDefaultToolkit().beep();
      puzzleState = sliding.reportGameState();
      labelButtons(puzzleState);
      if (sliding.gameOver())
         label.setText("You did it!  Very nice!");
   } // actionPerformed()
   public static void main(String args[]) {
      new SlidingGUI("Sliding Tile Puzzle");
   } // main()
} // SlidingGUI class
```

Figure 9.40   Implementation of the `SlidingGUI` class. (*Continued from previous page*)

Note how an instance of the `SlidingTilePuzzle` is created in the constructor, and how its state is retrieved and stored in the `puzzleState` variable:

```
puzzleState = sliding.reportGameState();
```

The `labelButtons()` method transfers the letters in `puzzleState` onto the buttons.

The most important method in the GUI is the `actionPerformed()` method. This method controls the GUI's actions and is called automatically whenever one of the GUI's buttons is clicked. First, we check whether the `reset` button has been clicked. If so, we reset the puzzle by creating a new instance of `SlidingTilePuzzle` and reinitializing the prompt label.

Next we use a `for` loop to check whether one of the tile buttons has been clicked. If so, we use the loop index, k, as the tile's identification and submit this to the puzzle as the user's move:

```
if (e.getSource() == tile[k])
   result = ((GUIPlayableGame)sliding).submitUserMove(""+ k);
```

The cast operation is necessary here because we declared `sliding` as a `SlidingTilePuzzle` rather than as a `GUIPlayableGame`. Note also that we have to convert k to a `String` when passing it to `submitUserMove()`.

As a result of this method call, the puzzle returns a `result`, which is checked to see if the user's move was illegal. If `result` contains the word "illegal", the computer beeps to signal an error:

```
if (result.indexOf("illegal") != -1)
    java.awt.Toolkit.getDefaultToolkit().beep();
```

The `java.awt.Toolkit` is a class that contains lots of useful methods, including the `beep()` method. Note that no matter what action is performed, a reset or a tile click, we update `puzzleState` by calling `reportGameState()` and use it to relabel the tile buttons. The last task in the `actionPerformed()` method is to invoke the puzzle's `gameOver()` method to check whether the user has successfully completed the puzzle. If so, we display a congratulatory message in the GUI's window.

Finally, the `main()` for a GUI is very simple, consisting of a single line of code:

```
new SlidingGUI("Sliding Tile Puzzle");
```

Once a `SlidingGUI` is created, with the title "Sliding Tile Puzzle", it will open a window and manage the control of the puzzle.

CHAPTER SUMMARY

Technical Terms

array	multidimensional array
array initializer	one-dimensional array
array length	polymorphic sort method
binary search	selection sort
data structure	sequential search
element	sorting
element type	subscript
insertion sort	two-dimensional array

Summary of Important Points

- An **array** is a named collection of contiguous storage locations, each of which stores a data item of the same data type. Each element of an array is referred to by a *subscript*—that is, by its position in the array. If the array contains N elements, then its length is N and its indexes are 0, 1, ...N-1.

- Array elements are referred to using the following subscript notation *arrayname[subscript]*, where *arrayname* is any valid identifier, and *subscript* is an integer value in the range 0 to `arrayname.length - 1`. The array's `length` instance variable can be used as a bound for loops that process the array.
- An *array declaration* provides the name and type of the array. An array instantiation uses the keyword `new` and causes the compiler to allocate memory for the array's elements:

```
int arr[];          // Declare a one-dimensional array variable
arr = new int[15];  // Allocate 15 int locations for it
```

- Multidimensional arrays have arrays as their components:

```
int twoDarr[][];               // Declare a two-dimensional array variable
twoDarr = new int[10][15];     // Allocate 150 int locations
```

- An array's values must be initialized by assigning values to each array location. An *initializer* expression may be included as part of the array declaration.
- Insertion sort and selection sort are examples of array-sorting algorithms. Both algorithms require several passes over the array.
- When an array is passed as an argument to a method, a reference to the array is passed rather than the entire array.
- Swapping two elements of an array, or any two locations in memory, requires the use of a temporary variable.
- Sequential search and binary search are examples of array-searching algorithms. Binary search requires that the array be sorted.
- For multidimensional arrays, each dimension of the array has its own `length` variable.
- Inheritance and polymorphism are useful design features for developing a hierarchy of computer games.

SOLUTIONS TO SELF-STUDY EXERCISES

SOLUTION 9.1   Space (in bytes) allocated for each of the following?

```
a. int a[] = new int[5];           // 5 * 4 = 20 bytes
b. double b[] = new double[10];    // 10 * 8 = 80 bytes
c. char c[] = new char[30];        // 30 * 2 = 60 bytes
d. String s[] = new String[10];    // 10 * 4 (reference) = 40 bytes
e. Student s[] = new Student[5];    // 5 * 4 (reference) = 20 bytes
```

SOLUTION 9.2   An array containing 10 `float`s, 1.0 to 10.0.

```
float farr[] = {1.0,2.0,3.0,4.0,5.0,6.0,7.0,8.0,9.0,10.0};
```

SOLUTION 9.3   Prints the first element of `farr`.

```
System.out.println(farr[0]);
```

SOLUTION 9.4   Assigns 100.0 to the last element in `farr`.

```
farr[farr.length-1] = 100.0;
```

SOLUTION 9.5   A loop to print all of the elements of `farr`.

```
for (int j = 0; j < farr.length; j++)
    System.out.println(farr[j]);
```

SOLUTION 9.6   An array containing the first 100 square roots.

```
double doubarr[] = new double[100];
for (int k = 0; k < doubarr.length; k++)
    doubarr[k] = Math.sqrt(k+1);
```

SOLUTION 9.7   Analyzing the letter frequencies in a file.

```
import java.io.*;
import java.util.Scanner;
public static void main(String[] argv) {
  Scanner fileScan;                        // To read lines of text from the file
  String str;                              // To store the line of text
  AnalyzeFreq af = new AnalyzeFreq();
  try {                                    // Create a Scanner
    File theFile = new File("freqtest.txt");
    fileScan = Scanner.create(theFile);
    fileScan = fileScan.useDelimiter("\r\n"); // For Windows
    while (fileScan.hasNext()) { // Read and count
      str = fileScan.next();
      af.countLetters(str);
    } // while
    af.printArray();                       // Print frequencies
  } catch (Exception e) {
    e.printStackTrace();
  } // catch()
} // main()
```

SOLUTION 9.8   Sort 24 18 90 1 0 85 34 18 with insertion sort.

```
24 18 90 1  0  85 34 18 // Initial
18 24 90 1  0  85 34 18 // Pass 1
18 24 90 1  0  85 34 18 // Pass 2
1  18 24 90 0  85 34 18 // Pass 3
0  1  18 24 90 85 34 18 // Pass 4
0  1  18 24 85 90 34 18 // Pass 5
0  1  18 24 34 85 90 18 // Pass 6
0  1  18 18 24 34 85 90 // Pass 7
```

SOLUTION 9.9   Sort 24 18 90 1 0 85 34 18 with selection sort.

```
24 18 90 1   0   85 34 18 // Initial
0  18 90 1   24  85 34 18 // Pass 1
0  1  90 18  24  85 34 18 // Pass 2
0  1  18 90  24  85 34 18 // Pass 3
0  1  18 18  24  85 34 90 // Pass 4
0  1  18 18  24  85 34 90 // Pass 5
0  1  18 18  24  34 85 90 // Pass 6
0  1  18 18  24  34 85 90 // Pass 7
```

SOLUTION 9.10   Code to swap two Students.

```
Student tempStud = student1;
student1 = student2;
student2 = tempStud;
```

SOLUTION 9.11   Implementation of the selectionSort().

```java
public void selectionSort(int arr[]) {
    int smallest;                                // Location of smallest element
    for (int k = 0; k < arr.length-1; k++) {
        smallest = k;
        for (int j = k+1; j < arr.length; j++)
            if (arr[j] < arr[smallest])
                smallest = j;
        if (smallest != k) {                     // Swap smallest and kth
            int temp = arr[smallest];
            arr[smallest] = arr[k];
            arr[k] = temp;
        } // if
    } // outer for
} // selectionSort()
```

SOLUTION 9.12   After `mystery(myArr,k)`, `myArr` will store 1,2,3,5,5 and *k* will store 3.

SOLUTION 9.13   Binary search trace for 21 in 2, 4, 6, 8, 10, 12, 14, 16, 18, 20, 22, 24, 26, 28:

```
key   iteration  low   high    mid
-------------------------------------
21    0          0     13      6
21    1          7     13      10
21    2          7     9       8
21    3          9     9       9
21    4          10    9       failure
```

SOLUTION 9.14   A two-dimensional array with five rows of 10 integers.

```
int int2d[][] = new int[5][10];
```

SOLUTION 9.15   Prints the last integer in the third row `int2d` and assigns 100 to its last element.

```
System.out.println(int2d[2][9]);
int2d[4][9] = 100;
```

SOLUTION 9.16   Prints all of the elements of `int2d`.

```
for (int k = 0; k < int2d.length; k++) {
    for (int j = 0; j < int2d[k].length; j++)
        System.out.print( int2d[k][j] + " ");
    System.out.println();     // new line
}
```

SOLUTION 9.17   A 52 × 7 two-dimensional array of `int`.

```
int sales[][] = new int[52][7];
for (int k = 0; k < sales.length; k++)
    for (int j= 0; j < sales[k].length; j++)
        sales[k][j] = 0;
```

SOLUTION 9.18   A method to calculate average number of newspapers per week.

```
double avgWeeklySales(int arr[][]) {
    double total = 0;
    for (int k = 0; k < arr.length; k++)
        for (int j = 0; j < arr[k].length; j++)
            total += arr[k][j];
    return total/52;
}
```

SOLUTION 9.19   A method to calculate average number of Sunday newspapers.

```
double avgSundaySales(int arr[][]) {
    double total = 0;
    for (int k = 0; k < arr.length; k++)
        total += arr[k][6];
    return total/52;
}
```

SOLUTION 9.20   A compareTo() for LetterFreq.

```
public int compareTo(Object lf) {
    LetterFreq  letFreq = (LetterFreq)lf;
    if (freq < letFreq.getFreq())
        return -1;
    else if (freq > letFreq.getFreq())
        return +1;
    else return 0; // The frequencies must be equal.
} // compareTo()
```

SOLUTION 9.21   A sort() for AnalyzeFreq.

```
public void sort() {
    java.util.Arrays.sort(freqArr);
} // sort()
```

SOLUTION 9.22   A new AnalyzeFreq.main() that uses sort().

```
public static void main(String[] argv) {
    AnalyzeFreq af = new AnalyzeFreq();
    af.countLetters("Now is the time for all good students" +
        " to study computer-related topics.");
    af.sort();
    af.printArray();
} // main()
```

EXERCISES

EXERCISE 9.1   Explain the difference between the following pairs of terms:

a. An *element* and an element *type*.
b. A *subscript* and an *array element*.
c. A *one-dimensional* array and *two-dimensional* array.
d. An *array* and a *vector*.
e. A *insertion sort* and a *selection sort*.
f. A *binary search* and a *sequential search*.

Note: For programming exercises, **first** draw a UML class diagram describing all classes and their inheritance relationships and/or associations.

EXERCISE 9.2   Fill in the blanks.

a. The process of arranging an array's elements into a particular order is known as _____.
b. One of the preconditions of the binary search method is that the array has to be _____.
c. An _____ is an object that can store a collection of elements of the same type.
d. An _____ is like an array except that it can grow.
e. For an array, its _____ is represented by an instance variable.
f. An expression that can be used during array instantiation to assign values to the array is known as an _____.
g. A _____ is an array of arrays.
h. A sort method that can be used to sort different types of data is known as a _____ method.
i. To instantiate an array you have to use the _____ operator.
j. An array of objects stores _____ to the objects.

EXERCISE 9.3   Make each of the following array declarations:

a. A 4 × 4 array of `double`s.
b. A 20 × 5 array of `String`s.
c. A 3 × 4 array of `char` initialized to `'*'`;
d. A 2 × 3 × 2 array of `boolean` initialized to true.
e. A 3 × 3 array of `Student`s.
f. A 2 × 3 array of `String`s initialized to "one", "two", and so on.

EXERCISE 9.4   Identify and correct the syntax error in each of the following expressions:

```
a. int arr = new int[15];
b. int arr[] = new int(15);
c. float arr[] = new [3];
d. float arr[] = new float {1.0,2.0,3.0};
e. int arr[] = {1.1,2.2,3.3};
f. int arr[][] = new double[5][4];
g. int arr[][] = { {1.1,2.2}, {3.3, 1} };
```

EXERCISE 9.5   Evaluate each of the following expressions, some of which may be erroneous:

```
int arr[] = { 2,4,6,8,10 };
```

a. `arr[4]`
b. `arr[ arr.length ]`
c. `arr[ arr[0] ]`
d. `arr[ arr.length / 2 ]`
e. `arr[ arr[1] ]`
f. `arr[ 5 % 2 ]`
g. `arr[ arr[ arr[0] ] ]`
h. `arr[ 5 / 2.0 ]`
i. `arr[ 1 + (int) Math.random() ]`
j. `arr[ arr[3] / 2 ]`

EXERCISE 9.6   What would be printed by the following code segment?

```
int arr[] = { 24, 0, 19, 21, 6, -5, 10, 16};
for (int k = 0; k < arr.length; k += 2)
  System.out.println( arr[k] );
```

EXERCISE 9.7   What would be printed by the following code segment?

```
int arr[][] = { {24, 0, 19}, {21, 6, -5}, {10, 16, 3}, {1, -1, 0} };
for (int j = 0; j < arr.length; j++)
  for (int k = 0; k < arr[j].length; k++)
    System.out.println( arr[j][k] );
```

EXERCISE 9.8   What would be printed by the following code segment?

```
int arr[][] = { {24, 0, 19}, {21, 6, -5}, {10, 16, 3}, {1, -1, 0} };
for (int j = 0; j < arr[0].length; j++)
    for (int k = 0; k < arr.length; k++)
        System.out.println(arr[k][j]);
```

EXERCISE 9.9   What's wrong with the following code segment, which is supposed to swap the values of the int variables, n1 and n2?

```
int temp = n1;
n2 = n1;
n1 = temp;
```

EXERCISE 9.10   Explain why the following method does not successfully swap the values of its two parameters? Hint: Think about the difference between value and reference parameters.

```
public void swapEm(int n1, int n2) {
    int temp = n1;
    n1 = n2;
    n2 = temp;
}
```

EXERCISE 9.11   Declare and initialize an array to store the following two-dimensional table of values:

```
1    2    3    4
5    6    7    8
9   10   11   12
```

EXERCISE 9.12   For the two-dimensional array you created in the preceding exercise, write a nested for loop to print the values in the following order: 1 5 9 2 6 10 3 7 11 4 8 12. That is, print the values going down the columns instead of going across the rows.

EXERCISE 9.13   Define an array that would be suitable for storing the following values:

a. The GPAs of 2,000 students.
b. The lengths and widths of 100 rectangles.
c. A week's worth of hourly temperature measurements, stored so that it is easy to calculate the average daily temperature.
d. A board for a tic-tac-toe game.
e. The names and capitals of the 50 states.

EXERCISE 9.14   Write a code segment that will compute the sum of all the elements of an array of int.

EXERCISE 9.15   Write a code segment that will compute the sum of the elements in a two-dimensional array of int.

EXERCISE 9.16   Write a method that will compute the average of all the elements of a two-dimensional array of float.

EXERCISE 9.17   Write a method that takes two parameters, an int array and an integer, and returns the location of the last element of the array that is greater than or equal to the second parameter.

EXERCISE 9.18   Write a program that tests whether a 3 × 3 array, input by the user, is a *magic square*. A magic square is an $N \times N$ matrix of numbers in which every number from 1 to N^2 must appear just once, and every row, column, and diagonal must add up to the same total. For example,

```
6 7 2
1 5 9
8 3 4
```

EXERCISE 9.19 Revise the program in the preceding exercise so that it allows the user to input the dimensions of the array up to 4 × 4.

EXERCISE 9.20 Modify the `AnalyzeFreq` program so that it can display the relative frequencies of the 10 most frequent and 10 least frequent letters.

EXERCISE 9.21 The *merge sort* algorithm takes two collections of data that have been sorted and merges them together. Write a program that takes two 25-element `int` arrays, sorts them, and then merges them, in order, into one 50-element array.

EXERCISE 9.22 **Challenge:** Design and implement a `BigInteger` class that can add and subtract integers with up to 25 digits. Your class should also include methods for input and output of the numbers. If you're really ambitious, include methods for multiplication and division.

EXERCISE 9.23 **Challenge:** Design a data structure for this problem: As manager of Computer Warehouse, you want to track the dollar amount of purchases made by clients who have regular accounts. The accounts are numbered from 0, 1, ..., *N*. The problem is that you don't know in advance how many purchases each account will have. Some may have one or two purchases. Others may have 50 purchases.

EXERCISE 9.24 An *anagram* is a word made by rearranging the letters of another word. For example, *act* is an anagram of *cat*, and *aegllry* is an anagram of *allergy*. Write a Java program that accepts two words as input and determines whether they are anagrams.

EXERCISE 9.25 **Challenge:** An *anagram dictionary* is a dictionary that organizes words together with their anagrams. Write a program that lets the user enter up to 100 words (in a `TextField`, say). After each word is entered, the program should display (in a `TextArea` perhaps) the complete anagram dictionary for the words entered. Use the following sample format for the dictionary. Here the words entered by the user were: *felt, left, cat, act, opt, pot, top*.

```
act:    act cat
eflt:   felt left
opt:    opt pot top
```

EXERCISE 9.26 Acme Trucking Company has hired you to write software to help dispatch its trucks. One important element of this software is knowing the distance between any two cities that it services. Design and implement a `Distance` class that stores the distances between cities in a two-dimensional array. This class will need some way to map a city name, *Boise*, into an integer that can be used as an array subscript. The class should also contain methods that would make it useful for looking up the distance between two cities. Another useful method would tell the user the closest city to a given city.

EXERCISE 9.27 Rewrite the `main()` method for the `WordGuess` example so that it allows the user to input the number of players and whether each player is a computer or a human. Use a `KeyboardReader`.

EXERCISE 9.28   Write a smarter version of the WordGuesser class that "knows" which letters of the English language are most frequent. *Hint:* Rather than use random guesses, store the player's guesses in a string in order of decreasing frequency: "ETAONRISHLGCMFBDG-PUKJVWQXYZ".

EXERCISE 9.29   Write a CLUI version of the SlidingTilePuzzle. You will need to make modifications to the SlidingTilePuzzle class.

Photograph courtesy of Hussey, Vonda, Getty Images, Inc. - Image Bank.

10

Exceptions: When Things Go Wrong

OBJECTIVES

After studying this chapter, you will

- Understand Java's exception-handling mechanisms.
- Be able to use the Java `try/catch` statement.
- Know how to design effective exception handlers.
- Appreciate the importance of exception handling in program design.
- Be able to design your own `Exception` subclasses.

10.1   Introduction

Mistakes happen. Making mistakes is the norm rather than the exception. This is not to say that we make mistakes more often than we get it right. It is to say that (almost) nothing we do or build is ever perfectly correct, least of all computer software. No matter how well-designed a program is, there is always the chance that some kind of error will arise during its execution.

Exceptions

An **exception** is an erroneous or anomalous condition that arises while a program is running. Examples of such conditions that we have discussed in this text include attempting to divide by zero (arithmetic exception), reading a decimal value when an integer is expected (number format exception), attempting to write to a file that doesn't exist (I/O exception), or referring to a nonexistent character in a string (index out of bounds exception). The list of potential errors and anomalies is endless.

A well-designed program should include code to guard against errors and other exceptional conditions when they arise. This code should be incorporated into the program from the very first stages of its development. That way it can help identify problems during development.

Exception
handling

In Java, the preferred way of handling such conditions is to use **exception handling** a, divide-and-conquer approach that separates a program's normal code from its error-handling code.

This chapter describes Java's exception-handling features. We begin by contrasting the traditional way of handling errors within a program with Java's default exception-handling mechanism. We show how exceptions are raised (thrown) and handled (caught) within a program and identify the rules that apply to different kinds of exceptions. We then focus on some of the key design issues that govern when, where, and how to use exceptions in your programs. Finally, we show how to design and implement one's own `Exception` subclass.

10.2   Handling Exceptional Conditions

To introduce you to handling exceptional conditions, Figure 10.1 shows a method that computes the average of the first N integers, an admittedly contrived example. We use it mainly to illustrate the basic concepts involved in exception handling. As its precondition suggests, the `avgFirstN()` method expects that N will be greater than 0. If N happens to be 0, an error will occur in the expression `sum/N`, because you cannot divide an integer by 0.

10.2.1   Traditional Error Handling

Divide-by-zero
error

Obviously, the method in Figure 10.1 should not simply ignore the possibility that N might be 0. Figure 10.2 shows a revised version of the method, which includes code that takes

```
/**
 * Precondition:  N > 0
 * Postcondition: avgFirstN() = (1+2+... +N)/N
 */
public double avgFirstN(int N) {
    int sum = 0;
    for (int k = 1; k <= N; k++)
        sum += k;
    return sum/N;            // What if N is 0?
} // avgFirstN()
```

Figure 10.1   Poor design. No attempt is made to guard against a divide-by-zero error.

```
/**
 * Precondition:  N > 0
 * Postcondition: avgFirstN() equals (1+2+... +N) divided by N
 */
public double avgFirstN(int N) {
    int sum = 0;
    if (N <= 0) {
        System.out.println("ERROR avgFirstN: N <= 0. Program terminating.");
        System.exit(0);
    }
    for (int k = 1; k <= N; k++)
        sum += k;
    return sum/N;             // What if N is 0?
} // avgFirstN()
```

Figure 10.2   One way to handle a divide-by-zero error might be to terminate the program if there is an attempt to divide by 0, assuming that it is the kind of program that can be safely aborted. This version does not use exception handling.

action if the method's precondition fails. Because there is no way to compute an average of 0 elements, the revised method decides to abort the program. Aborting the program appears to be a better alternative than returning 0 or some other default value (like -1) as the method's result and thereby allowing an erroneous value to spread throughout the program. That would just compound the error.

EFFECTIVE DESIGN: Unfixable Error.   If an unfixable error is detected, it is far better to terminate the program abnormally than to allow the error to propagate throughout the program.

The revised avgFirstN() method takes the traditional approach to error handling. The error-handling code is built right into the algorithm. If N happens to be 0 when avgFirstN() is called, the following output will be generated:

```
ERROR avgFirstN: N <= 0. Program terminating.
```

10.2.2   Java's Default Exception Handling

To help detect and handle common runtime errors, Java's creators incorporated an exception-handling model into the language. In the case of our divide-by-zero error, the Java Virtual Machine (JVM) would detect the error and abort the program. To see this, consider the program in Figure 10.3. Note that the avgFirstN() method is passed an argument of 0 in the CalcAvgTest.main(). When the JVM detects the error, it will abort the program and print the following message:

```
Exception in thread "main"
    java.lang.ArithmeticException:  / by zero
        at CalcAverage.avgFirstN(Compiled Code)
        at CalcAvgTest.main(CalcAvgTest.java:5)
```

```
public class CalcAverage {

    public double avgFirstN(int N) {
        int sum = 0;
        for (int k = 1; k <= N; k++)
            sum += k;
        return sum/N;                           // What if N is 0?
    } // avgFirstN()
} // CalcAverage class
public class CalcAvgTest {
    public static void main(String args[]) {
        CalcAverage ca = new CalcAverage();
        System.out.println( "AVG + " + ca.avgFirstN(0) );
    } // main()
} // CalcAvgTest class
```

Figure 10.3   The two public classes defined in this figure would be saved in separate Java files.

The error message describes the error and provides a trace of the method calls, from last to first, that led to the error. The trace shows that the error occurred in the `CalcAverage.avgFirstN()` method, which was called by the `CalcAvgTest.main()` method.

As this example suggests, Java's default exception handling is able to detect and handle certain kinds of errors and exceptional conditions. In the next section, we will identify what kinds of conditions can be handled by the JVM.

10.3   Java's Exception Hierarchy

The Java class library contains a number of predefined exceptions, some of which are shown in Figure 10.4. The most general type of exception, `java.lang.Exception`, is located in the `java.lang` package, but most of its subclasses are contained in other packages. Some of the various `IOException` classes are contained in the `java.io` package, while others are contained in the `java.net` package. In general, exception classes are placed in the package that contains the methods that throw those exceptions.

Exception hierarchy

Each of the classes in Figure 10.4 identifies a particular type of exception, and each is a subclass of the `Exception` class. Obviously a subclass defines a more specific exception than its superclass. Thus, both `ArrayIndexOutOfBoundsException` and `StringIndexOutOfBoundsException` are more specific than `IndexOutOfBoundsException`.

Table 10.1 gives a brief summary of some of the most important exceptions. You've undoubtedly encountered some of these exceptions, because they are thrown by methods we have used repeatedly in programming examples. Table 10.2 summarizes the exceptions raised by some of the methods we have used most frequently.

SELF-STUDY EXERCISE

EXERCISE 10.1   What type of exception would be thrown for the following statements?

a. `Integer.parseInt("26.2");`
b. `String s; s.indexOf('a');`
c. `String s = "hello"; s.charAt(5);`

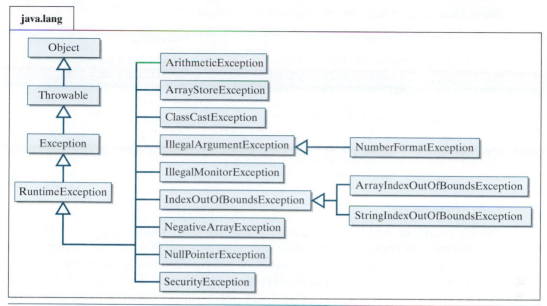

Figure 10.4 Part of Java's exception hierarchy. All subclasses of RuntimeException are known as *unchecked* exceptions. Java programs are not required to catch these exceptions.

10.3.1   Checked and Unchecked Exceptions

Java's exception hierarchy is divided into two types of exceptions. A **checked exception** is one that can be analyzed by the Java compiler. Checked exceptions are thrown by methods such as the BufferedReader.readLine() method, in which there is a substantial likelihood that something might go wrong. When the compiler encounters one of these method calls, it checks whether the program either handles or declares the exception. Compile-time checking for these exceptions is designed to reduce the number of exceptions that are not properly handled within a program. This improves the security of Java programs.

Checked exceptions

> **JAVA LANGUAGE RULE**   **Checked Exceptions.** A checked exception, such as an IOException, must either be handled or declared within the program.

Table 10.1. Some of Java's important exceptions.

Class	Description
ArithmeticException	Division by zero or some other arithmetic problem
ArrayIndexOutOfBoundsException	An array index is less than zero or greater than or equal to the array's length
FileNotFoundException	Reference to a file that cannot be found
IllegalArgumentException	Calling a method with an improper argument
IndexOutOfBoundsException	An array or string index is out of bounds
NullPointerException	Reference to an object that has not been instantiated
NumberFormatException	Use of an illegal number format, as when calling a method
StringIndexOutOfBoundsException	A String index is less than zero or greater than or equal to the String's length

Table 10.2. Some of Java's important exceptions by method

Class	Method	Exception Raised	Description
Double	valueOf(String)	NumberFormatException	The String is not a double
Integer	parseInt(String)	NumberFormatException	The String is not a int
String	String(String)	NullPointerException	The String is null
	indexOf(String)	NullPointerException	The String is null
	lastIndexOf(String)	NullPointerException	The String is null
	charAt(int)	StringIndexOutOfBoundsException	The int is not a valid index
	substring(int)	StringIndexOutOfBoundsException	The int is not a valid index
	substring(int,int)	StringIndexOutOfBoundsException	An int is not a valid index

The throws *Clause*

The IOException, which we encountered in Chapter 4, is a checked exception. The Java compiler knows that readLine() is a method that can throw an IOException. A method that contains an expression that might throw a checked exception must either handle the exception or declare it. Otherwise the compiler would generate a syntax error. The simplest way to avoid such a syntax error is to *declare the exception*; in our case that means qualifying the method header with the expression throws IOException.

Declaring an exception

In general, any method that contains an expression that might throw a checked expression must declare the exception. However, because one method can call another method, declaring exceptions can get a little tricky. If a method calls another method that contains an expression that might throw an unchecked exception, then both methods must have a throws clause. For example, consider the following program:

```java
import java.io.*;
public class Example {
    BufferedReader input = new BufferedReader (new InputStreamReader(System.in));
    public void doRead() throws IOException {
        // May throw IOException
        String inputString = input.readLine();
    }
    public static void main(String argv[]) throws IOException {
        Example ex = new Example();
        ex.doRead();
    }
}
```

In this case, the doRead() method contains a readLine() expression that might throw an IOException. Therefore, the doRead() method must declare that it throws IOException. However, because doRead() is called by main(), the main() method must also declare the IOException.

JAVA LANGUAGE RULE   **Where to Use** throws. Unless a checked exception, such as an IOException, is caught and handled by a method, it must be declared with a throws clause within the method and within any method that calls that method.

The alternative approach would be to *catch* the `IOException` within the body of the method. We will discuss this approach in the next section.

Unchecked Exceptions

An **unchecked exception** is any exception belonging to a subclass of `RuntimeException` (Fig. 10.4). Unchecked exceptions are not checked by the compiler. The possibility that some statement or expression will lead to an `ArithmeticException` or `NullPointerException` is extremely difficult to detect at compile time. The designers of Java decided that forcing programmers to declare such exceptions would not significantly improve the correctness of Java programs.

Therefore, unchecked exceptions do not have to be handled within a program. And they do not have to be declared in a `throws` clause. As shown in the chapter's early divide-by-zero exception example, unchecked exceptions are handled by Java's default exception handlers, unless your program takes specific steps to handle them directly. In many cases leaving the handling of such exceptions up to Java may be the best course of action, as we will see Section 10.5.

Runtime (unchecked) exceptions

> **JAVA LANGUAGE RULE** **Unchecked Exceptions.** An unchecked exception—one belonging to some subclass of `RunTimeException`—does not have to be caught within your program.

10.3.2 The `Exception` Class

The `java.lang.Exception` class itself is very simple, consisting of just two constructor methods (Fig. 10.5). The `Throwable` class, from which `Exception` is derived, is the root class of Java's exception and error hierarchy. It contains definitions for the `getMessage()` and `printStackTrace()` methods, which are two methods that we will use frequently in our error-handling routines.

SELF-STUDY EXERCISE

EXERCISE 10.2   Which of the following are examples of unchecked exceptions?

a. IOException

b. IndexOutOfBoundsException

c. NullPointerException

d. ClassNotFoundException

e. NumberFormatException

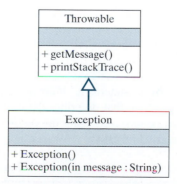

Figure 10.5 The `java.lang.Exception` class.

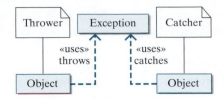

Figure 10.6 Exception handling. When an exception occurs, an object will throw an Exception. The exception handler, possibly the same object, will catch it.

10.4   Handling Exceptions within a Program

This section will describe how to handle exceptions within the program rather than leaving them to be handled by the JVM.

10.4.1   Trying, Throwing, and Catching an Exception

Pulling the program's fire alarm

In Java, errors and other abnormal conditions are handled by throwing and catching exceptions. When an error or an exceptional condition is detected, you can *throw an exception* as a way of signaling the abnormal condition. This is like pulling a fire alarm. When an exception is thrown, an exception handler will catch the exception and deal with it (Fig. 10.6). We will discuss try blocks, which typically are associated with catching exceptions, later in the section.

If we go back to our avgFirstN() example, the typical way of handling this error in Java would be to throw an exception in the avgFirstN() method and catch it in the calling method. Of course, the calling method could be in the same object or it could belong to some other object. In the latter case, the detection of the error is separated from its handling. This division of labor opens up a wide range of possibilities. For example, a program could dedicate a single object to serve as the handler for all its exceptions. The object could be described as the program's "fire department."

To illustrate Java's try/throw/catch mechanism, let's revisit the CalcAvgTest program. The version shown in Figure 10.7 mimics the way Java's default exception handler works. If the avgFirstN() method is called with an argument that is zero or negative, an IllegalArgumentException is thrown. The exception is caught by the catch clause in the CalcAvgTest.main() method.

Let's go through this example step by step. The first thing to notice is that if the CalcAverage.avgFirstN() method has a zero or negative argument, it will throw an exception:

```
if (N <= 0)
  throw new IllegalArgumentException("ERROR: Illegal argument");
```

Note the syntax of the throw statement. It creates a new IllegalArgumentException object and passes it a message that describes the error. This message becomes part of the exception object. It can be retrieved using the getMessage() method, which is inherited from the Throwable class (Fig. 10.4).

```
public class CalcAverage {
  /**
   * Precondition:  N > 0
   * Postcondition: avgFirstN() equals the average of (1+2+... +N)
   */
  public double avgFirstN(int N) {
    int sum = 0;
    if (N <= 0)
      throw new IllegalArgumentException("ERROR: Illegal argument");
    for (int k = 1; k <= N; k++)
      sum += k;
    return sum/N;                              // What if N is 0?
  } // avgFirstN()
} // CalcAverage class
public class CalcAvgTest {
  public static void main(String args[]) {
    try {
      CalcAverage ca = new CalcAverage();
      System.out.println( "AVG + " + ca.avgFirstN(0));
    }
    catch (IllegalArgumentException e) {       // Exception Handler
      System.out.println(e.getMessage());
      e.printStackTrace();
      System.exit(0);
    }
  } // main()
} // CalcAvgTest class
```

Figure 10.7 In this version of the calcAvgTest program, an IllegalArgumentException thrown in CalcAverage.avgFirstN(), would be handled by the catch clause in CalcAvgTest.main().

When a **throw** statement is executed, the JVM interrupts the normal execution of the program and searches for an exception handler. We will describe the details of this search shortly. In this case, the exception handler is the **catch** clause contained in the CalcAvgTest.main() method:

```
catch (IllegalArgumentException e) {// Exception Handler
    System.out.println(e.getMessage());
    e.printStackTrace();
    System.exit(0);
}
```

When an **IllegalArgumentException** is thrown, the statements within this **catch** clause are executed. The first statement uses the **getMessage()** method to print a copy of the error message. The second statement uses the **printStackTrace()** method, which is defined in **Throwable** and inherited by all **Exceptions**, to print a trace of the method calls leading up to the exception. The last statement causes the program to terminate.

When we run this program, the following output will be generated as a result of the illegal argument error:

```
ERROR: Can't average 0 elements
java.lang.IllegalArgumentException: ERROR: Illegal argument
    at java.lang.Throwable.fillInStackTrace(Native Method)
    at java.lang.Throwable.<init>(Throwable.java:94)
    at java.lang.Exception.<init>(Exception.java:42)
    at java.lang.RuntimeException.<init>(RuntimeException.java:47)
    at java.lang.IllegalArgumentException.<init>(IllegalArgumentException.java:43)
    at CalcAverage.avgFirstN(Compiled Code)
    at CalcAvgTest.main(CalcAvgTest.java:5)
```

Thus, as in the previous example of Java's default exception handler, our exception handler also prints out a description of the error and a trace of the method calls that led up to the error. However, in this example, we are directly handling the exception rather than leaving it up to Java's default exception handler. Of course, this example is intended mainly for illustrative purposes. It would make little sense to write our own exception handler if it does nothing more than mimic Java's default handler.

EFFECTIVE DESIGN: Using an Exception.   Unless your program's handling of an exception is significantly different from Java's default handling of it, the program should just rely on the default.

Finally, note that the `catch` clause is associated with a `try` block. The handling of exceptions in Java takes place in two parts: First, we *try* to execute some statements, which may or may not lead to an exception. These are the statements contained within the `try` clause:

```
try {
    CalcAverage ca = new CalcAverage();
    System.out.println( "AVG + " + ca.avgFirstN(0));
}
```

Second, we provide one or more `catch` clauses to handle particular types of exceptions. In this case, we are only handling `IllegalArgumentException`s.

As we said earlier, throwing an exception is like pulling a fire alarm. The throw occurs somewhere within the scope of the `try` block. The "fire department" in this case is the code contained in the `catch` clause that immediately follows the `try` block. This is the exception handler for this particular exception. There's something like a game of catch going on here: a method within the `try` block throws an `Exception` object, which is caught and handled by the `catch` block located in another object (Fig. 10.8).

Responding to the fire alarm

10.4.2   Separating Error Checking from Error Handling

Divide and conquer

As we see in the `CalcAvgTest` example, an important difference between Java's exception handling and more traditional approaches is that error handling can be separated from the normal flow of execution within a program. The `CalcAverage.avgFirstN()` method still checks for the error and still `throws IllegalArgumentException` if *N* does not satisfy

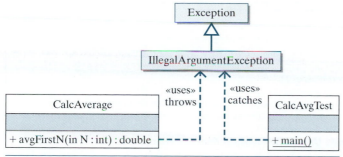

Figure 10.8 Playing catch: In this design, the `IllegalArgument-Exception` is thrown by the `CalcAverage.avgFirstN()` method and caught by the `catch` clause within the `CalcAvgTest.main()` method.

the method's precondition. But it does not contain code for handling the exception. The exception-handling code is located in the `CalcAvgTest` class.

Thus, the `CalcAvgTest` program creates a clear separation between the normal algorithm and the exception-handling code. One advantage of this design is that the normal algorithm is uncluttered by error-handling code and, therefore, easier to read.

Another advantage is that the program's response to errors has been organized into one central location. By locating the exception handler in `CalcAvgTest.main()`, one exception handler can be used to handle other errors of that type. For example, this catch clause could handle *all* `IllegalArgumentException`s that get thrown in the program. Its use of `printStackTrace()` will identify exactly where the exception occurred. In fact, because a Java application starts in the `main()` method, encapsulating all of a program's executable statements within a single `try` block in the `main()` method will effectively handle all the exceptions that occur within a program.

> **EFFECTIVE DESIGN: Normal versus Exceptional Code.** A key element of Java's exception-handling mechanism is that the exception handler—the `catch` block—is distinct from the code that throws the exception—the `try` block. The `try` block contains the normal algorithm. The `catch` block contains code for handling exceptional conditions.

10.4.3 Syntax and Semantics of `Try/Throw/Catch`

A `try` **block** begins with the keyword `try` followed by a block of code enclosed within curly braces. A `catch` *clause*, or `catch` **block**, consists of the keyword `catch`, followed by a parameter declaration that identifies the type of `Exception` being caught, followed by a collection of statements enclosed within curly braces. These are the statements that handle the exception by taking appropriate action.

Try block

Catch block

Once an exception is thrown, control is transferred out of the `try` block to an appropriate `catch` block. Control does not return to the `try` block.

> **JAVA LANGUAGE RULE** **Try Block Control.** If an exception is thrown, the `try` block is exited and control does not return to it.

```
try {
                                // Block of statements
                                // At least one of which may throw an exception
        if ( /* Some condition obtains */ )
              throw new ExceptionName();
} catch (ExceptionName ParameterName) {
                                // Block of statements to be executed
                                // If the ExceptionName exception is thrown in try
}   catch (ExceptionName2 ParameterName) {
                                // Block of statements to be executed
                                // If the ExceptionName2 exception is thrown in try
...                             // Possibly other catch clauses
} finally {

                                // Optional block of statements that is executed
                                // Whether an exception is thrown or not

}
```

Figure 10.9 Java's try/catch statement.

The complete syntax of the **try/catch** statement is summarized in Figure 10.9. The **try** block is meant to include a statement or statements that might throw an exception. The **catch** blocks—there can be one or more—are meant to handle exceptions thrown in the **try** block. A **catch** block will handle any exception that matches its parameter class, including subclasses of the class. The **finally block** clause is an optional clause that is always executed whether an exception is thrown or not.

Normal flow of execution

The statements in the **try** block are part of the program's normal flow of execution. By encapsulating a group of statements within a **try** block, you indicate that they may throw one or more exceptions, and that you intend to catch them. In effect, you are *trying* a block of code with the possibility that something might go wrong.

Exceptional flow of execution

If an exception is thrown within a **try** block, Java exits the block and transfers control to the first **catch** block that matches the particular kind of exception thrown. Exceptions are thrown by using the **throw** statement, which takes the following general form:

```
throw new ExceptionClassName(OptionalMessageString);
```

The keyword **throw** is followed by the instantiation of an object of the **ExceptionClassName** class. This is done the same way we instantiate any object in Java: by using the **new** operator and invoking one of the exception's constructor methods. Some of the constructors take an **OptionalMessageString**, which is the message returned by the exception's **getMessage()** method.

A **catch** block has the following general form:

```
catch (ExceptionClassName ParameterName) {
    // Exception handling statements
}
```

A catch block is very much like a method definition. It contains a parameter, which specifies the class of exception handled by the block. The *ParameterName* can be any valid identifier, but it is customary to use e as the catch block parameter. The parameter's scope is limited to the catch block and is used to refer to the caught exception.

The *ExceptionClassName* must be one of the classes in Java's exception hierarchy (see Fig. 10.4). A thrown exception will match any parameter of its own class or any of its superclasses. Thus, if an ArithmeticException is thrown, it will match both an ArithmeticException parameter and an Exception parameter, because ArithmeticException is a subclass of Exception.

Exceptions are objects

Note that there can be multiple catch clauses associated with a given try block, and the order in which they are arranged is important. A thrown exception will be caught by the first catch clause it matches. Therefore, catch clauses should be arranged in order from most specific to most general (see the exception hierarchy in Figure 10.4). If a more general catch clause precedes a more specific one, it will prevent the more specific one from executing. In effect, the more specific clause will be hidden by the more general one. You might as well just not have the more specific clause at all.

Arranging catch clauses

To illustrate how to arrange catch clauses, suppose an ArithmeticException is thrown in the following try/catch statement:

```java
try {
    // Suppose an ArithmeticException is thrown here
} catch (ArithmeticException e) {
    System.out.println("ERROR: " + e.getMessage() );
    e.printStackTrace();
    System.exit(1);
} catch (Exception e) {
    System.out.println("ERROR: " + e.getMessage() );
}
```

In this case, the exception would be handled by the more specific ArithmeticException block. On the other hand, if some other kind of exception is raised, it will be caught by the second catch clause. The Exception class will match any exception thrown. Therefore, it should always occur last in a sequence of catch clauses.

Which handler to use?

> **JAVA PROGRAMMING TIP: Arranging** Catch **Clauses.** Catch clauses should be arranged from most specific to most general. The Exception clause should always be the last in the sequence.

10.4.4   Restrictions on the try/catch/finally Statement

There are several important restrictions that apply to Java's exception-handling mechanism. We will describe these in more detail later in the chapter.

- A try block must be immediately followed by one or more catch clauses and a catch clause may only follow a try block.

- A `throw` statement is used to throw both checked exceptions and unchecked exceptions, where unchecked exceptions are those belonging to `RuntimeException` or its subclasses. Unchecked exceptions need not be caught by the program.
- A `throw` statement must be contained within the dynamic scope of a `try` block, and the type of `Exception` thrown must match at least one of the `try` block's catch clauses. Or the `throw` statement must be contained within a method or constructor that has a `throws` clause for the type of thrown `Exception`.

> **JAVA LANGUAGE RULE**   Try/Catch **Syntax.** A `try` block must be followed immediately—with no intervening code—by one or more `catch` blocks. A `catch` block can only be preceded by a `try` block or by another `catch` block. You may not place intervening code between `catch` blocks.

10.4.5   Dynamic versus Static Scoping

How does Java know that it should execute the `catch` clause in `CalcAvgTest.main()` when an exception is thrown in `avgFirstN()`? Also, doesn't the latest version of `avgFirstN()` (Fig. 10.7) violate the restriction that a `throw` statement must occur within a `try` block?

An exception can only be thrown within a *dynamically enclosing* `try` block. This means that the `throw` statement must fall within the **dynamic scope** of an enclosing try block. Let's see what this means.

Dynamic scope

Dynamic scoping refers to the way a program is executed. For example, in `CalcAverage` (Fig. 10.7), the `avgFirstN()` method is called from within the `try` block located in `CalcAvgTest.main()`. Thus, it falls within the dynamic scope of that `try` block.

Static scope

Contrast dynamic scoping with what you have learned about **static scope**, which we have used previously to define the scope of parameters and local variables (Fig. 10.10). Static

```
class MyClass{

    public void method1 () {
        int X = 1;
        System.out.println("Hello" + X);
    }

    public void method2 () {
        int Y = 2;
        System.out.println("Hello" + Y);
    }

    public static void main(String argv[]) {
        MyClass myclass = new MyClass();
        if(Math.random() > 0.5)
            myclass.method2 () ;
        else
            myclass.method1 () ;
    }

}
```

Static Scope: Follow the definitions. Neither method1() nor method2() is in the static scope of main().

```
              MyClass
      ┌──────────┼──────────┐
  method1()  method2()    main()
      │          │
      X          Y
```

Dynamic Scope: Follow the execution. If Math.random() > 0.5, method2() is in the dynamic scope of main().

```
      main()
        │
        ▼
    method2()
```

Figure 10.10 Dynamic versus static scoping. Static scoping refers to how the program is written. Look at its definitions. Dynamic scoping refers to how the program executes. Look at what it actually does.

```
public class MyClass {
    public void method1() {
        int X = 1;
        System.out.println("Hello" + X);
    }
    public void method2() {
        int Y = 2;
        System.out.println("Hello" + Y);
    }
    public static void main( String argv[] ) {
        MyClass myclass = new MyClass();
        if (Math.random() > 0.5)
            myclass.method2();
        else
            myclass.method1();
    }
} // MyClass class
```

Figure 10.11   An example of dynamic versus static scoping.

scoping refers to the way a program is written. A statement or variable occurs within the scope of a block if its text is actually written within that block. For example, consider the definition of MyClass (Fig. 10.11). The variable X occurs within the (static) scope of method1(), and the variable Y occurs within the (static) scope of method2().

A method's parameters and local variables occur within its static scope. Also, in the MyClass definition, the System.out.println() statements occur within the static scope of method1() and method2(), respectively. In general, static scoping refers to where a variable is declared or where a statement is located. Static scoping can be completely determined by just reading the program.

Dynamic scoping can only be determined by running the program. For example, in My-Class the order in which its statements are executed depends on the result of Math.random(). Suppose that when random() is executed it returns the value 0.99. In that case, main() will call method2(), which will call System.out.println(), which will print "Hello2". In that case, the statement System.out.println("Hello" + Y) has the following dynamic scope:

```
main()
    method2()
        System.out.println("Hello" + Y);
```

It occurs within the (dynamic) scope of method2(), which is within the (dynamic) scope of main(). On the other hand, if the result of random() had been 0.10, that particular println() statement would not have been executed at all. Thus, to determine the dynamic scope of a statement, you must trace the program's execution. In fact, this is what the printStackTrace() method does. It prints a trace of a statement's dynamic scope.

10.4.6   Exception Propagation: Searching for a Catch Block

When an exception is thrown, Java uses both static and dynamic scoping to find a catch clause to handle it. Java knows how the program is defined—after all, it compiled it. Thus, the

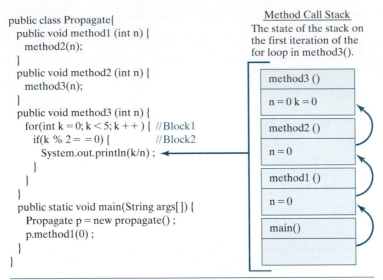

```
public class Propagate{
  public void method1 (int n) {
    method2(n);
  }
  public void method2 (int n) {
    method3(n);
  }
  public void method3 (int n) {
    for(int k = 0; k < 5; k + +) { //Block1
      if(k % 2 = = 0) {            //Block2
        System.out.println(k/n) ;
      }
    }
  }
  public static void main(String args[ ]) {
    Propagate p = new propagate() ;
    p.method1(0) ;
  }
}
```

Method Call Stack
The state of the stack on
the first iteration of the
for loop in method3().

method3 ()

n = 0 k = 0

method2 ()

n = 0

method1 ()

n = 0

main()

Figure 10.12 The method call stack for the `Propagate` program. The curved arrows give a trace of the method calls leading to the program's present state.

static scope of a program's methods is determined by the compiler. Java also places a record
Method call stack   of every method call the program makes on a method call stack. A **method call stack** is a data structure that behaves like a stack of dishes in a cafeteria. For each method call, a *method call block* is placed on top of the stack (like a dish), and when a particular method call returns, its block is removed from the top of the stack (Fig. 10.12).

An important feature of the method call stack is that the current executing method is always represented by the top block on the method call stack. If an exception happens during a method call, you can trace backward through the method calls, if necessary, to find an exception handler for that exception. In Figure 10.12, you can visualize this back trace as a matter of reversing the direction of the curved arrows.

In order to find a matching `catch` block for an exception, Java uses its knowledge of the program's static and dynamic scope to perform a **method stack trace**. The basic idea is that
Method stack   Java traces backward through the program until it finds an appropriate `catch` clause. The
trace   trace begins within the block that threw the exception. Of course, one block can be nested (statically) within another block. If the exception is not caught by the block in which it is thrown, Java searches the enclosing block. This is static scoping. If it is not caught within the enclosing block, Java searches the next-higher enclosing block, and so on. This is still static scoping.

If the exception is not caught at all within the method in which it was thrown, Java uses the method call stack (Fig. 10.12) to search backward through the method calls that were made leading up to the exception. This is dynamic scoping. In the case of our `CalcAvgTest()` example (Fig. 10.7), Java would search backward to the `CalcAvgTest.main()` method, which is where `avgFirstN()` was called, and it would find the `catch` clause there for handling `IllegalArgumentException`s. It would, therefore, execute that `catch` clause.

SELF-STUDY EXERCISES

EXERCISE 10.3   Suppose a program throws an `ArrayIndexOutOfBoundsException`. Using the exception hierarchy in Figure 10.4, determine which of the following `catch` clauses could handle that exception.

   a. `catch (RunTimeException e)`

   b. `catch (StringIndexOutOfBoundsException e)`

   c. `catch (IndexOutOfBoundsException e)`

   d. `catch (Exception e)`

   e. `catch (ArrayStoreException e)`

EXERCISE 10.4   In the program that follows, suppose that the first time `random()` is called it returns 0.98, and the second time it is called it returns 0.44. What output would be printed by the program?

```java
class MyClass2 {
    public void method1(double X) {
        if (X > 0.95)
            throw new ArithmeticException(X + " is out of range");
        System.out.println("Hello " + X);
    }
    public void method2(double Y) {
        if (Y > 0.5)
            throw new ArithmeticException(Y + " is out of range");
        System.out.println("Hello " + Y);
    }
    public static void main(String argv[]) {
        MyClass2 myclass = new MyClass2();
        try {
            myclass.method1(Math.random());
            myclass.method2(Math.random());
        } catch (ArithmeticException e) {
            System.out.println(e.getMessage());
        }
    } // main()
} // MyClass2 class
```

EXERCISE 10.5   For the values returned by `random()` in the preceding exercise, show what would be output if `printStackTrace()` were called in addition to printing an error message.

EXERCISE 10.6   In the `MyClass2` program, suppose that the first time `random()` is called it returns 0.44, and the second time it is called it returns 0.98. What output would be printed by the program?

EXERCISE 10.7   For the values returned by `random()` in the preceding exercise, show what would be output if `printStackTrace()` were called instead of printing an error message.

EXERCISE 10.8   Find the divide-by-zero error in the following program, and then show what stack trace would be printed by the program:

```java
public class BadDivide {
    public void method1 (int n) {
        method2(100, n);
    }
    public void method2 (int n, int d) {
        System.out.println(n / d);
    }
    public static void main(String args[]) {
        BadDivide bd = new BadDivide();
        for (int k = 0; k < 5; k++)
            bd.method1(k);
    }
}
```

EXERCISE 10.9   Modify `method2()` so that it handles the divide-by-zero exception itself instead of letting Java handle it. Have it print an error message and a stack trace.

EXERCISE 10.10   What would be printed by the following code segment if `someValue` equals 1000?

```java
int M = someValue;
try {
    System.out.println("Entering try block");
    if (M > 100)
        throw new Exception(M + " is too large");
    System.out.println("Exiting try block");
} catch (Exception e) {
    System.out.println("ERROR: " + e.getMessage());
}
```

EXERCISE 10.11   What would be printed by the code segment in the preceding question if `someValue` equals 50?

EXERCISE 10.12   Write a `try/catch` block that throws an `Exception` if the value of variable X is less than zero. The exception should be an instance of `Exception`, and, when it is caught, the message returned by `getMessage()` should be "ERROR: Negative value in X coordinate".

10.5   Error Handling and Robust Program Design

An important element of program design is to develop appropriate ways of handling erroneous and exceptional conditions. As we have seen, the JVM will catch any unchecked exceptions that are not caught by the program itself. For your own (practice) programs, the best design may simply be to use Java's default exception handling. The program will terminate when an exception is thrown, and then you can debug the error and recompile the program.

Let Java do it?

Table 10.3. Exception-handling strategies

Kind of Exception	Kind of Program	Action to Be Taken
Caught by Java		Let Java handle it
Fixable condition		Fix the error and resume execution
Unfixable condition	Stoppable	Report the error and terminate the program
Unfixable condition	Not stoppable	Report the error and resume processing

On the other hand, this strategy would be inappropriate for commercial software, which cannot be fixed by its users. A well-designed commercial program should contain exception handlers for those truly exceptional conditions that may arise.

In general there are three ways to handle an exceptional condition that is not already handled by Java (Table 10.3). If the exceptional condition cannot be fixed, the program should be terminated with an appropriate error message. If the exceptional condition can be fixed without invalidating the program, then it should be remedied and the program's normal execution should be resumed. Finally, if the exception cannot be fixed, but the program cannot be terminated, the exceptional condition should be reported or logged in some way, and the program should be resumed.

What action should we take?

EFFECTIVE DESIGN: Handling Exceptions.   There are three general ways to handle exceptions: (1) report the exception and terminate the program; (2) fix the exceptional condition and resume normal execution; and (3) report the exception to a log and resume execution.

10.5.1   Print a Message and Terminate

Our illegal-argument example is a clear case of an exception that is best handled by terminating the program. The particular error is best left to Java's default exception handling, which will terminate the program when the exception is thrown. There is simply no way to satisfy the postcondition of the avgFirstN() method when *N* is less than or equal to 0. This type of error often calls attention to a design flaw in the program's logic that should be caught during program development. The throwing of the exception helps identify the design flaw.

Program development

EFFECTIVE DESIGN: Exceptions and Program Development.   Java's built-in exception handling helps identify design flaws during program development. Your own use of exceptions should follow this approach.

Similar problems can (and often do) arise in connection with errors that are not caught by Java. For example, suppose that your program receives an erroneous input value whose use would invalidate the calculation it is making. This won't be caught by Java. But it should be caught by your program, and an appropriate alternative here is to report the error and terminate the program. Fixing this type of error may involve adding routines to validate the input data before they are used in the calculation.

Don't spread bad data!

In short, rather than allow an erroneous result to propagate throughout the program, it is best to terminate the program.

> **EFFECTIVE DESIGN: Report and Terminate.** If an unfixable exception arises in a program that can be terminated, it is better to report the error and terminate the program. That is better than allowing it to run with an erroneous value.

10.5.2 Log the Error and Resume

Of course, the advice to stop the program assumes that the program *can* be terminated reasonably. Some programs—such as programs that monitor the space shuttle or programs that control a nuclear magnetic resonance (NMR) machine—cannot (and should not) be terminated because of such an error.

Failsafe programs

Such programs are called *failsafe* because they are designed to run without termination. For these programs, the exception should be reported in whatever manner is most appropriate, but the program should continue running. If the exceptional condition invalidates the program's computations, then the exception handler should make it clear that the results are tainted.

Programs that can't be stopped

Other programs—such as programs that analyze a large transaction database—should be designed to continue processing after catching such errors. For example, suppose a large airline runs a program once a day to analyze daily ticketing transactions. This kind of program might use exceptions to identify erroneous transactions or transactions that involve invalid data of some sort. Because there are bound to be many errors of this kind in the database, it is not reasonable to stop the program. This kind of program shouldn't stop until it has finished processing all of the transactions. An appropriate action for this kind of program is to log the exceptions into a file and continue processing the transactions.

Suppose a divide-by-zero error happened in one of these programs. In that case, you would override Java's default exception handling to ensure that the program is *not* terminated. More generally, it is important that these types of programs be designed to catch and report such exceptions. This type of exception handling should be built right into the program's design.

> **EFFECTIVE DESIGN: Report and Resume.** If an unfixable exception arises in a program that cannot be terminated reasonably, the exception should be reported and the program should continue executing.

10.5.3 Fix the Error and Resume

Problem statement

As an example of a problem that can be addressed as the program runs, consider the task of inputting an integer into a text field. As you have probably experienced, if a program is expecting an integer and you attempt to input something other than an integer, a Number-FormatException is generated and the program will terminate. For example, if you enter "$55" when prompted to input an integer dollar amount, this will generate an exception when the Integer.parseInt() method is invoked. The input string cannot be parsed into a valid int. However, this is the kind of error that can be addressed as the program is running.

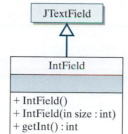

Figure 10.13 An `IntField` is a `JTextField` that accepts only integers.

Let's design a special `IntField` that functions like a normal text field but accepts only integers. If the user enters a value that generates a `NumberFormatException`, an error message should be printed and the user should be invited to try again. As Figure 10.13 shows, we want this special field to be a subclass of `JTextField` and to inherit the basic `JTextField` functionality. It should have the same kind of constructors that a normal `JTextField` has. This leads to the definition shown in Figure 10.14.

Note that the constructor methods use `super` to call the `JTextField` constructor. For now, these two constructors should suffice. However, later in the chapter we will introduce a third constructor that allows us to associate a bound with the `IntField`.

What constructors do we need?

Our `IntField` class needs a method that can return its contents. This method should work like `JTextField.getText()`, but it should return a valid integer. The `getInt()` method takes no parameters and will return an `int`, assuming that a valid integer is typed into the `IntField`. If the user enters "$55," a `NumberFormatException` will be thrown by the `Integer.parseInt()` method. Note that `getInt()` declares that it throws this exception. This is not necessary because a `NumberFormatException` is not a checked exception, but it makes the code clearer.

What methods do we need?

Where and how should this exception be handled? The exception cannot easily be handled within the `getInt()` method. This method has to return an integer value. If the user types in a non-integer, there's no way to return a valid value. Therefore, it's better just to throw the exception to the calling method, where it can be handled more easily.

```java
import javax.swing.*;

public class IntField extends JTextField {
    public IntField () {
        super();
    }
    public IntField (int size) {
        super(size);
    }
    public int getInt() throws NumberFormatException {
        return Integer.parseInt(getText());
    } // getInt()
} // IntField class
```

Figure 10.14 A `NumberFormatException` might be thrown by the `Integer.parseInt()` method in `IntField.getInt()`.

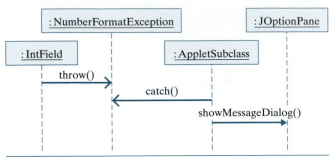

Figure 10.15 If the user types a noninteger into an Int-Field, it will throw a NumberFormatException. The applet will display an error message in a JOptionPane (a dialog window).

In a GUI application or applet, the calling method is likely to be an `actionPerformed()` method, such as the following:

```
public void actionPerformed(ActionEvent e) {
  try {
    userInt = intField.getInt();
    message = "You input " + userInt + " Thank you.";
  } catch (NumberFormatException ex) {
    JOptionPane.showMessageDialog(this,
      "The input must be an integer.   Please re-enter.");
  } finally {
     repaint();
  }
} // actionPerformed()
```

The call to `getInt()` is embedded in a `try/catch` block. This leads to the design summarized in Figure 10.15. The `IntField` throws an exception that is caught by the applet, which then displays an error message.

If the user inputs a valid integer, the program will just report a message that displays the value. A more real-world example would make a more significant use of the value. On the other hand, if the user types an erroneous value, the program will pop up the dialog box shown in Figure 10.16. (See the "From the Library" section of this chapter for more on dialog boxes.) When the user clicks the OK button, the program will resume normal execution, so that when an exception is raised, the enter value is not used, and no harm is done by an erroneous value. The user can try again to input a valid integer. Note that the `finally` clause repaints the GUI. In this case, repainting would display the appropriate message on the applet or the application.

This is an example of what we might call *defensive design*. Defensive design is when we anticipate a possible input error and take steps to ensure that a bad value is not propagated throughout the program.

Defensive design: anticipating an exception

EFFECTIVE DESIGN: Defensive Design.   Well-designed code should anticipate potential problems, especially potential input problems. Effective use of exceptions can help with this task.

Figure 10.16 This exception handler opens a dialog box to display an error message.

Admittedly, the sense in which the error here is "fixed" is simply that the user's original input is ignored and reentered. This is a legitimate and simple course of action for the particular situation. It is far preferable to ignoring the exception. If the program does not handle this exception itself, Java will catch it and will print a stack trace and terminate the program. That would not be a very user-friendly interface!

Clearly, this is the type of exceptional condition that should be anticipated during program design. If this happens to be a program designed exclusively for your own use, then this type of exception handling might be unnecessary. But if the program is meant to be used by others, it is important that it be able to handle erroneous user input without crashing.

Anticipating exceptions

EFFECTIVE DESIGN: Fixing an Exception.   If a method can handle an exception effectively, it should handle it locally. This is both clearer and more efficient.

EFFECTIVE DESIGN: Library Exception Handling.   Many of Java's library classes do not handle their own exceptions. The thinking behind this design is that the user of the class is in a better position to handle the exception in a way that is appropriate for the application.

10.5.4   To Fix or Not to Fix

Let's now consider a problem where it is less clear whether an exception can be successfully fixed "on the fly." Suppose you have a program that contains an array of `String`s initially created with just two elements.

```
String list[] = new String[2];
```

If an attempt is made to add more than two elements to the array, an `ArrayIndexOutOf-BoundsException` will be raised. This exception can be handled by extending the size of the array and inserting the element. Then the program's normal execution can be resumed.

To begin creating such a program, let's first design a method that will insert a string into the array. Suppose that this is intended to be a `private` method that will only be used within the program. Also, let's suppose that the program maintains a variable, `count`, that tracks how many values have been stored in the array. Therefore, it will not be necessary to pass the array as a parameter. So we are creating a `void` method with one parameter, the `String` to be inserted:

```java
private void insertString(String str) {
                                // Might throw ArrayIndexOutOfBoundsException
    list[count] = str;
    ++count;
}
```

The comment notes where an exception might be thrown.

Can we handle this exception? When this exception is raised, we could create a new array with one more element than the current array. We could copy the old array into the new array and then insert the `String` in the new location. Finally, we could set the variable `list`, the array reference, so that it points to the new array. Thus, we could use the following `try/catch` block to handle this exception:

```java
private void insertString(String str) {
    try {
        list[count] = str;
    } catch (ArrayIndexOutOfBoundsException e) {
                                            // Create a new array
        String newList[] = new String[list.length+1];
        for (int k = 0; k < list.length; k++) // Copy array
            newList[k] = list[k];
        newList[count] = str;                 // Insert into new array
        list = newList;                       // Make old point to new
    } finally {                               // Since the exception is now fixed
        count++;                              // Increase the count
    }
} // insertString()
```

The effect of the `catch` clause is to create a new array, still referred to as `list`, but that contains one more element than the original array.

Note the use of the `finally` clause here. For this problem it's important that we increment `count` in the `finally` clause. This is the only way to guarantee that `count` is incremented exactly once whenever an element is assigned to the array.

The design of the `FixArrayBound` class is shown in Figure 10.17. It provides a simple GUI interface that enables you to test the `insertString()` method. This program has a standard Swing interface, using a `JFrame` as the top-level window. The program's components are contained within a `JPanel` that's added to the `JFrame` in the `main()` method.

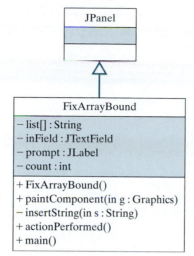

Figure 10.17 The FixArray-Bound class uses exception handling to extend the size of an array each time a new element is inserted.

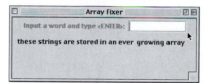

Figure 10.18 The strings displayed are stored in an array that is extended each time a new string is entered.

Each time the user types a string into the text field, the `actionPerformed()` method calls the `insertString()` method to add the string to the array. On each user action, the `JPanel` is repainted. The `paintComponent()` method simply clears the panel and then displays the array's elements (Fig. 10.18).

DEBUGGING TIP: Clearing the JPanel.   Swing components, such as `JPanel`, do not automatically clear their backgrounds. This must be done explicitly in the `paintComponent()` method.

The complete implementation of `FixArrayBound` is given in Figure 10.19. This example illustrates how an exception *can* be handled successfully and the program's normal flow of control resumed. However, the question is whether such an exception *should* be handled this way.

```
import java.awt.*;
import java.awt.event.*;
import javax.swing.*;

public class FixArrayBound extends JPanel implements ActionListener {
    public static final int WIDTH = 350, HEIGHT = 100;
    private JTextField inField = new JTextField(10);
```

Figure 10.19 FixArrayBound increases the size of the array when a ArrayIndexOutOf-BoundsException is raised. (***Continued on next page***)

```java
    private JLabel prompt = new JLabel("Input a word and type <ENTER>: ");
                                             // Initially list has 2 elements
    private String list[] = new String[2];
    private int count = 0;
    public  FixArrayBound() {
      inField.addActionListener(this);
      add(prompt);
      add(inField);
      setSize(WIDTH, HEIGHT);
    } // FixArrayBound()
    public void paintComponent(Graphics g) {
      g.setColor(getBackground());               // Clear the background
      g.fillRect(0, 0, WIDTH, HEIGHT);
      g.setColor(getForeground());
      String tempS = "";
      for (int k = 0; k < list.length; k++)
        tempS = tempS +  list[k] + " ";
      g.drawString(tempS, 10, 50);
    } // paintComponent()

    private void insertString(String str) {
      try {
        list[count] = str;
      } catch (ArrayIndexOutOfBoundsException e) {
        String newList[] = new String[list.length+1]; // New array
        for (int k = 0; k < list.length; k++) // Copy old to new
          newList[k] = list[k];
          newList[count] = str;              // Insert item into new
          list = newList;                    // Make old point to new
      } finally {                            // The exception is now fixed
       count++;                              // so increase the count
      }
    } // insertString()

    public void actionPerformed(ActionEvent evt) {
      insertString(inField.getText());
      inField.setText("");
      repaint();
    } // actionPerformed()

    public static void main( String args[] ) {
        JFrame f = new JFrame("Array Fixer");
        FixArrayBound panel = new FixArrayBound();
        f.getContentPane().add(panel);
        f.setSize(panel.WIDTH, panel.HEIGHT);
        f.setVisible(true);
        f.addWindowListener(new WindowAdapter() {
            public void windowClosing(WindowEvent e) {
                System.exit(0);              // Quit the application
            }
        });
    } // main()
} // FixArrayBound class
```

Figure 10.19 FixArrayBound increases the size of the array when a ArrayIndexOutOf-BoundsException is raised. (*Continued from previous page*)

Unfortunately, this is not a well-designed program. The array's initial size is much too small for the program's intended use. Therefore, the fact that these exceptions arise at all is the result of poor design. In general, exceptions should *not* be used as a remedy for poor design.

Poor program design

> **EFFECTIVE DESIGN: Truly Exceptional Conditions.** A well-designed program should use exception handling to deal with truly exceptional conditions, not to process conditions that arise under normal or expected circumstances.

For a program that uses an array, the size of the array should be chosen so that it can store all the objects required by the program. If the program is a failsafe program, and therefore cannot afford to crash, then something like the previous approach might be justified, provided this type of exception occurs very rarely. Even in that case it would be better to generate a message that alerts the program's user that this condition has occurred. The alert will indicate a need to modify the program's memory requirements and restart the program.

Proper array usage

If it is not known in advance how many objects will be stored in an array, a better design would be to make use of the `java.util.Vector` class (see "From the Java Library" in Chapter 9). Vectors are designed to grow as new objects are inserted. In some ways the exception-handling code in our example mimics the behavior of a vector. However, the `Vector` class makes use of efficient algorithms for extending its size. By contrast, exception-handling code is very inefficient. Because exceptions force the system into an abnormal mode of execution, it takes considerably longer to handle an exception than it would to use a `Vector` for this type of application.

Choosing the correct data structure

> **EFFECTIVE DESIGN: Appropriate Data Structure.** A major component of problem solving is choosing the best way to represent the data. A vector should be used as an array structure whenever the size of the array will grow and shrink dynamically during the program's execution.

SELF-STUDY EXERCISE

EXERCISE 10.13   For each of the following exceptions, determine whether it can be handled in such a way that the program can be resumed or whether the program should be terminated:

a. A computer game program detects a problem with one of its GUI elements and throws a `NullPointerException`.
b. A factory assembly-line control program determines that an important control value has become negative and generates an `ArithmeticException`.
c. A company's Web-based order form detects that its user has entered an invalid `String` and throws a `SecurityException`.

10.6   Creating and Throwing Your Own Exceptions

Like other Java classes, the `Exception` class can be extended to handle cases not already covered by Java's built-in exceptions. Exceptions that you define will be handled the same way by the Java interpreter, but you will have to `throw` them yourself.

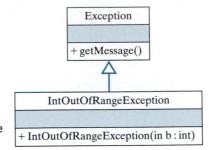

Figure 10.20 The `IntOutOfRange` exception.

For example, Figure 10.20 shows the design of an exception that can be used for validating that an integer is less than or equal to a certain maximum value. It would be coded as follows:

```
/**
 * IntOutOfRangeException reports an exception when
 *     an integer exceeds its bound.
 */
public class IntOutOfRangeException extends Exception {

    public IntOutOfRangeException (int Bound) {
      super("The input value exceeds the bound " + Bound);
    }
}
```

The class extends `Exception` and consists entirely of a constructor method that calls the superclass constructor. The argument passed to the superclass constructor is the message that will be returned by `getMessage()` when an instance of this exception is created.

Now let's consider an example where this new exception will be thrown. Suppose we wish to constrain the `IntField` class that we developed previously (Fig. 10.14) so that it will only accept numbers less than a certain bound. First, let's modify `IntField` so that its bound can be set when an instance is created. We want its bound to be an instance variable with some initial value, and we want to provide a constructor that can be used to override the default (Fig. 10.21).

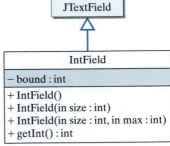

Figure 10.21 The revised `Int-Field` class contains a bound on the size of the numbers that should be entered.

This leads to the following revision of `IntField`:

```java
public class IntField extends JTextField {
    private int bound = Integer.MAX_VALUE;

    public IntField(int size, int max) {
        super(size);
        bound = max;
    }
    // The rest of the class is unchanged for now
} // IntField
```

Our new constructor has the signature `IntField(int,int)`, which does not duplicate any of `JTextField`'s constructors. This is good design, because in extending a class, we want to be careful about the effect our definitions have on the original methods in the superclass. Superclass methods should be overridden by design, not by accident. If a method is redefined inadvertently, it might not function as expected by users of the subclass.

EFFECTIVE DESIGN: Extending a Class.   When extending a class, care must be taken to ensure that the superclass's methods are not inadvertently overridden. A superclass method should only be overridden by design, not by accident.

Note how we have handled the problem of setting the default value of the `bound`. `Integer.MAX_VALUE` is a class constant that sets the maximum value for the `int` type. It is an appropriate value to use, because any valid `int` that the user types should be less than or equal to `MAX_VALUE`. Given these changes to `IntField`, let's now incorporate our new exception into its `getInt()` method (Fig. 10.22).

```java
import javax.swing.*;

public class IntField extends JTextField {
    private int bound = Integer.MAX_VALUE;

    public IntField (int size) {
        super(size);
    }

    public IntField(int size, int max) {
        super(size);
        bound = max;
    }

    public int getInt() throws NumberFormatException, IntOutOfRangeException {
        int num = Integer.parseInt(getText());
        if (num > bound)
            throw new IntOutOfRangeException(bound);
        return num;
    } // getInt()
} // IntField
```

Figure 10.22   The revised `IntField` class containing the revised `getInt()` method.

This new version of `getInt()` throws an exception if the integer entered by the user is greater than the `IntField`'s bound. Here again, it is difficult to handle this exception appropriately in this method. The method would either have to return an erroneous value—because it must return something—or it must terminate. Neither is an acceptable alternative. It is far better to throw the exception to the calling method.

The `IntFieldTester` class (Fig. 10.23) has the design and functionality shown in Figure 10.15. It provides a simple GUI interface to test the `IntField` class. It prompts the user to type an integer less than 100, and then it echoes the user's input. Note how the exception is handled in the `actionPerformed()` method. If an exception is thrown in `IntField.getInt()`, the `actionPerformed()` method pops up an error dialog, and the erroneous input is not used. Instead, the user is given another chance to enter a valid integer.

```java
import java.awt.*;
import java.awt.event.*;
import javax.swing.*;

public class IntFieldTester extends JPanel implements ActionListener {
  public static final int WIDTH = 300, HEIGHT = 300;
  private JLabel prompt = new JLabel("Input an integer <= 100: ");
  private IntField intField = new IntField(12, 100);
  private int userInt;
  private String message = "Hello";

  public IntFieldTester() {
    add(prompt);
    intField.addActionListener(this);
    add(intField);
    setSize(WIDTH, HEIGHT);
  } // IntFieldTester()

  public void paintComponent( Graphics g ) {
    g.setColor(getBackground());                    // Clear the panel
    g.fillRect(0, 0, WIDTH, HEIGHT);
    g.setColor(getForeground());
    g.drawString(message, 10, 70);
  } // paintComponent()

  public void actionPerformed(ActionEvent evt) {
    try {
      userInt = intField.getInt();
      message = "You input " + userInt + " Thank you.";
    } catch (NumberFormatException e) {
      JOptionPane.showMessageDialog(this,
        "The input must be an integer.  Please reenter.");
    } catch (IntOutOfRangeException e) {
      JOptionPane.showMessageDialog(this, e.getMessage());
    } finally {
      repaint();
    }
  } // actionPerformed()
  public static void main(String args[]) {
    JFrame f = new JFrame("IntField Tester");
    IntFieldTester panel = new IntFieldTester();
```

Figure 10.23 An application that uses an `IntField` object to process integers. (*Continued on next page*)

```
    f.getContentPane().add(panel);
    f.setSize(panel.WIDTH, panel.HEIGHT);
    f.setVisible(true);
    f.addWindowListener(new WindowAdapter() {
      public void windowClosing(WindowEvent e) {
        System.exit(0);                           // Quit the application
      }
    });
  } // main()
} // IntFieldTester class
```

Figure 10.23   An application that uses an `IntField` object to process integers. (*Continued from previous page*)

SELF-STUDY EXERCISES

EXERCISE 10.14   Define a new `Exception` named `FieldIsEmptyException` to be thrown if the user forgets to enter a value into a `IntField`.

EXERCISE 10.15   Modify the `IntField.getInt()` method so that it throws and catches the `FieldIsEmptyException`.

10.7   From the Java Library: `javax.swing.JOptionPane`

A **dialog box** is a window that can be opened by a program to communicate in some way with the user. Dialog boxes come in many varieties and have many uses in a GUI environment. You have undoubtedly encountered them when using your own computer.

For example, a *file dialog* is opened whenever you want to open or save a file. It provides an interface that lets you name the file and helps you search through the computer's directory structure to find a file.

A *warning dialog*, or **error dialog**, is opened whenever a program needs to notify or warn you that some kind of error has occurred. It usually presents an error message and an OK button that you click to dismiss the dialog.

java.sun.com/docs

Dialogs are easy to create and use in Java. The Swing component set provides several different kinds of basic dialogs that can be incorporated into your program with one or two lines of code. For example, the `IntFieldTester` class makes use of a simple message dialog to report an input error to the user. This dialog was created by the following code segment in the program (see Figure 10.23):

```
catch (NumberFormatException e) {
  JOptionPane.showMessageDialog(this,
    "The input must be an integer.   Please reenter.");
}
```

This method call displays the window shown in Figure 10.16. It contains the error message and an OK button that is used to close the window. The `showMessageDialog()` method is a `static` method of the `javax.swing.JOptionPane` class. This class provides a collection of similar methods for creating and displaying basic dialog boxes.

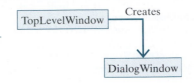

Figure 10.24 A dialog window cannot stand alone. It must be created by a top-level window.

A dialog differs from other kinds of top-level windows—such as JApplet and JFrame—in that it is associated with another window (Fig. 10.24). The first parameter in this version of the showMessageDialog() method is a reference to the dialog's parent window. The second parameter is a String representing the message.

The basic message dialog used in this example is known as a **modal dialog**. This means that once it has been displayed, you can't do anything else until you click the OK button and dismiss the dialog. It's also possible to create *nonmodal* dialogs. These can stay on the screen while you move on to other tasks.

Modal and nonmodal dialogs

Note that the dialog box also contains an *icon* that symbolizes the purpose of the message (Fig. 10.25). The icon is representative of the dialog's message type. Among the basic types available in JOptionPane are the following:

```
JOptionPane.PLAIN_MESSAGE
JOptionPane.INFORMATIONAL_MESSAGE      // Default
JOptionPane.WARNING_MESSAGE
JOptionPane.QUESTION_MESSAGE
JOptionPane.ERROR_MESSAGE
```

To set the dialog to anything other than the default (informational) type, you can use the following version of showMessageDialog():

```
showMessageDialog(Component comp, Object message, String title, int msgType);
```

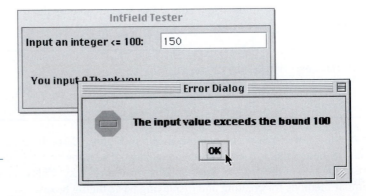

Figure 10.25 An error dialog.

The first parameter is a reference to the parent window. The second is the message string. The third is a string used as the dialog window's title, and the fourth is one of the five dialog types. For example, we can change our dialog to an error dialog with the following statement:

```
catch (IntOutOfRangeException e) {
    JOptionPane.showMessageDialog(this,
            e.getMessage(),
            "Error dialog",
            JOptionPane.ERROR_MESSAGE);
}
```

This would produce the dialog shown in Figure 10.25.

The other kinds of basic dialogs provided by the `JOptionPane` class are listed in Table 10.4. All of the dialogs listed there can be created with a line or two of code. In addition to these, it is also possible to create sophisticated dialogs that can be as customized as any other GUI interface you can build in Java.

Basic Swing dialogs

Table 10.4. Basic dialogs provided by `JOptionPane`

Dialog	Description
Message Dialog	Presents a simple error or informational message
Confirm Dialog	Prompts the user to confirm a particular action
Option Dialog	Lets the user choose from some options
Input Dialog	Prompts and inputs a string

CHAPTER SUMMARY

Technical Terms

catch an exception

`catch` block

checked exception

dialog box

dynamic scope

error dialog

exception

exception handling

`finally` block

method call stack

method stack trace

modal dialog

static scope

throw an exception

`try` block

unchecked exception

Summary of Important Points

- In Java, when an error or exceptional condition occurs, you `throw` an `Exception`, which is caught by a special code known as an *exception handler*. A `throw` statement—`throw new Exception()`—is used to throw an exception.

- A `try` block is a block of statements containing one or more statements that may throw an exception. Embedding a statement in a `try` block indicates your awareness that it might throw an exception and your intention to handle the exception.

- Java distinguishes between *checked* and *unchecked* exceptions. Checked exceptions must either be caught by the method in which they occur or you must declare that the method containing that statement `throws` the exception.

- Unchecked exceptions are those that belong to subclasses of `RuntimeException`. If they are left uncaught, they will be handled by Java's default exception handlers.

- A `catch` block is a block of statements that handles the exceptions that match its parameter. A `catch` block can only follow a `try` block, and there may be more than one `catch` block for each `try` block.

- The `try/catch` syntax allows you to separate the normal parts of an algorithm from special code meant to handle errors and exceptional conditions.

- A *method stack trace* is a trace of the method calls that have led to the execution of a particular statement in the program. The `Exception.printStackTrace()` method can be called by exception handlers to print a trace of exactly how the program reached the statement that threw the exception.

- *Static scoping* refers to how the text of the program is arranged. If a variable is declared within a method or a block, its static scope is confined to that method or block.

- *Dynamic scoping* refers to how the program is executed. A statement is within the dynamic scope of a method or block if it is called from that method or block, or if it is called by some other method that was called from that method or block.

- When searching for a `catch` block to handle an exception thrown by a statement, Java searches upward through the statement's static scope and backward through its dynamic scope until it finds a matching `catch` block. If none is found, the Java Virtual Machine will handle the exception itself by printing an error message and a method stack trace.

- Many Java library methods throw exceptions when an error occurs. These `throw` statements do not appear in the program. For example, Java's integer division operator will throw an `ArithmeticException` if an attempt is made to divide by zero.

- Generally, there are four ways to handle an exception: (1) let Java handle it; (2) fix the problem that led to the exception and resume the program; (3) report the problem and resume the program; and (4) print an error message and terminate the program. Most erroneous conditions reported by exceptions are difficult or impossible to fix.

- A `finally` statement is an optional part of a `try/catch` block. Statements contained in a `finally` block will be executed whether an exception is raised or not.

- A well-designed program should use exception handling to deal with truly exceptional conditions, not as a means of normal program control.

- User-defined exceptions can be defined by extending the `Exception` class or one of its subclasses.

SOLUTIONS TO SELF-STUDY EXERCISES

SOLUTION 10.1

  a. `Integer.parseInt("26.2");` ==> `NumberFormatException`
  b. `String s; s.indexOf('a');` ==> `NullPointerException`
  c. `String s = "hello"; s.charAt(5);` ==> `StringIndexOutOfBoundsException`

SOLUTION 10.2 The unchecked exceptions are `IndexOutOfBoundsException`, `NumberFormatException`, and `NullPointerException`, because these are subclasses of `RuntimeException`. The others are checked exceptions.

SOLUTION 10.3 An `ArrayIndexOutOfBoundsException` could be handled by the handlers in a, c, or d, because their classes are all superclasses of `ArrayIndexOutOfBoundsException`.

SOLUTION 10.4 If `Math.random()` in `MyClass2` returns 0.98 and then 0.44, the program will generate the following output:

```
0.98 is out of range
```

Note that because the out-of-range error occurs in `method1()`, `method2()` is not called at all.

SOLUTION 10.5 If `Math.random()` in `MyClass2` returns 0.98 and then 0.44, the following stack trace would be printed:

```
java.lang.ArithmeticException: 0.98 is out of range
    at MyClass2.method1(MyClass2.java:3)
    at MyClass2.main(MyClass2.java:15)
```

SOLUTION 10.6 If `Math.random()` in `MyClass2` returns 0.44 and then 0.98, the program will generate the following output:

```
Hello 0.44
0.98 is out of range
```

SOLUTION 10.7 If `Math.random()` in `MyClass2` returns 0.44 and then 0.98, the following stack trace would be printed:

```
java.lang.ArithmeticException: 0.98 is out of range
    at MyClass2.method2(MyClass2.java:8)
    at MyClass2.main(MyClass2.java:16)
```

SOLUTION 10.8   The divide-by-zero error in BadDivide occurs in the expression n/d in Method2(). It would generate the following stack trace:

```
java.lang.ArithmeticException: divide by zero
    at BadDivide.method2(BadDivide.java:7)
    at BadDivide.method1(BadDivide.java:3)
    at BadDivide.main(BadDivide.java:13)
```

SOLUTION 10.9   The following version of BadDivide.method2() will handle the divide-by-zero error itself:

```java
public void method2 (int n, int d) {
    try {
        System.out.println(n / d);
    } catch (ArithmeticException e) {
        System.out.println(e.getMessage());
        e.printStackTrace();
        System.exit(0);
    }
}
```

SOLUTION 10.10   If someValue equals 1000, the code segment will print:

```
Entering try block
ERROR: 1000 is too large
```

SOLUTION 10.11   If someValue equals 50, the code segment will print:

```
Entering try block
Exiting try block
```

SOLUTION 10.12

```java
try {
  if (X < 0)
    throw new Exception("ERROR: Negative value in X coordinate");
} catch (Exception e) {
  System.out.println( e.getMessage() );
}
```

SOLUTION 10.13

a. It depends. This is a computer game, so one way to handle this problem would be to generate a message into a log file and resume the game. If the GUI element is crucial to the game, it's hard to see how it could be successfully handled.

b. It depends. You would have to decide whether it would be more harmful or dangerous to continue production than not.

c. The program could report the security violation to the user and the system manager and then keep accepting user input.

SOLUTION 10.14

```java
public class FieldIsEmptyException extends Exception {
    public FieldIsEmptyException () {
        super("The input field is empty ");
    }
}
```

SOLUTION 10.15

```java
public int getInt() {
    int num = 0;
    try {
        String data = getText();
        if (data.equals(""))
            throw new FieldIsEmptyException();
        num = Integer.parseInt( getText() );
        if (num > bound)
            throw new IntOutOfRangeException(bound);
    } catch (FieldIsEmptyException e) {
        System.out.println("Error: " + e.getMessage() );
    } catch (NumberFormatException e) {
        System.out.println("Error: You must input an integer. Please try again.");
    } catch (IntOutOfRangeException e) {
        System.out.println(e.getMessage());
        return 0;
    }
    return num;
}
```

EXERCISES

EXERCISE 10.1 Explain the difference between the following pairs of terms:

a. *Throwing an exception* and *catching an exception*.
b. *Try block* and `catch block`.
c. *Catch block* and `finally block`.
d. *Try block* and `finally block`.
e. *Dynamic scope* and *static scope*.
f. *Dialog box* and *top-level window*.
g. *Checked* and `unchecked` exception.
h. *Method stack* and *method call*.

Note: For programming exercises, **first** draw a UML class diagram describing all classes and their inheritance relationships and/or associations.

EXERCISE 10.2   Fill in the blanks.

a. _____ an exception is Java's way of signaling that some kind of abnormal situation has occurred.

b. The only place that an exception can be thrown in a Java program is within a _____.

c. The block of statements placed within a `catch` block is generally known as an _____.

d. To determine a statement's _____ scope, you have to trace the program's execution.

e. To determine a statement's _____ scope, you can just read its definition.

f. When a method is called, a representation of the method call is placed on the _____.

g. The root of Java's exception hierarchy is the _____ class.

h. A _____ exception must be either caught or declared within the method in which it might be thrown.

i. An _____ exception can be left up to Java to handle.

EXERCISE 10.3   Compare and contrast the four different ways of handling exceptions within a program.

EXERCISE 10.4   Suppose you have a program that asks the user to input a string of no more than five letters. Describe the steps you'd need to take in order to design a `StringTooLongException` to handle cases where the user types in too many characters.

EXERCISE 10.5   Exceptions require more computational overhead than normal processing. Explain.

EXERCISE 10.6   Suppose the following `ExerciseExample` program is currently executing the `if` statement in `method2()`:

```java
public class ExerciseExample {
  public void method1(int M) {
    try {
      System.out.println("Entering try block");
      method2( M );
      System.out.println("Exiting try block");
    } catch (Exception e) {
      System.out.println("ERROR: " + e.getMessage());
    }
  } // method1()
  public void method2(int M) {
    if (M > 100)
      throw new ArithmeticException(M + " is too large");
  }
  public static void main(String argv[]) {
    ExerciseExample ex = new ExerciseExample();
    ex.method1(500);
  }
} // ExerciseExample class
```

Draw a picture of the method call stack that represents this situation.

EXERCISE 10.7   Repeat the preceding exercise for the situation where the program is currently executing the second `println()` statement in `method1()`.

EXERCISE 10.8   Draw a hierarchy chart that represents the static scoping relationships among the elements of the `ExerciseExample` program.

EXERCISE 10.9   What would be printed by the `ExerciseExample` program when it is run?

EXERCISE 10.10   What would be printed by the `ExerciseExample` program, if the statement in its `main()` method were changed to `ex.method1(5)`?

EXERCISE 10.11   Consider again the `ExerciseExample` program. If the exception thrown were `Exception` rather than `ArithmeticException`, explain why we would get the following error message: `java.lang.Exception must be caught, or it must be declared ....`

EXERCISE 10.12   Write a `try/catch` block that throws an `Exception` if the value of variable X is less than zero. The exception should be an instance of `Exception`, and when it is caught, the message returned by `getMessage()` should be "ERROR: Negative value in X coordinate".

EXERCISE 10.13   Look at the `IntFieldTester` program (Fig. 10.23) and the `IntField` class definition (Fig. 10.22). Suppose the user inputs a value that is greater than 100. Show what the method call stack would look like when the `IntField.getInt()` method is executing the `num > bound` expression.

EXERCISE 10.14   As a continuation of the preceding exercise, show what the program's output would be if the user input a value greater than 100.

EXERCISE 10.15   As a continuation of the preceding exercise, modify the `IntOutOfRangeException` handler so that it prints the message call stack. Then show what it would print.

EXERCISE 10.16   Define a subclass of `RuntimeException` named `InvalidPasswordException` that contains two constructors. The first constructor takes no parameters and an exception thrown with it should return "ERROR: invalid password" when its `getMessage()` is invoked. The second constructor takes a single `String` parameter. Exceptions thrown with this constructor should return the constructor's argument when `getMessage()` is invoked.

EXERCISE 10.17   Extend the `IntField` class so that it will constrain the integer `JTextField` to an `int` between a lower and upper bound. In other words, it should throw an exception if the user types in a value lower than the lower bound or greater than the upper bound.

EXERCISE 10.18   Design Issue: One of the preconditions for the `InsertionSort()` method (Fig. 9.15) is that its array parameter not be null. Of course, this precondition would fail if the array were passed a null array reference. In that case, Java would throw a `NullPointerException` and terminate the program. Is this an appropriate way to handle that exception?

EXERCISE 10.19   With respect to the preceding exercise, suppose you decide that it is more appropriate to handle the `NullPointerException` by presenting an error dialog. Modify the method to accommodate this behavior.

EXERCISE 10.20   Design Issue: Another possible way to design the `sequentialSearch()` method (Fig. 9.18) would be to have it throw an exception when its key is not found in the array. Is this a good design? Explain.

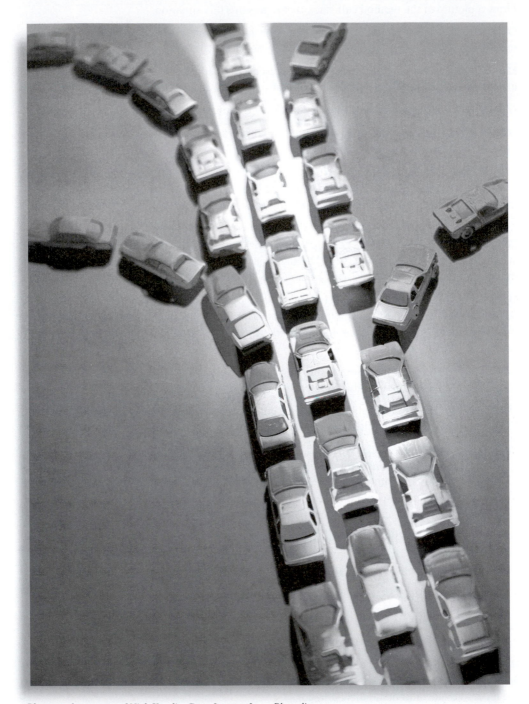

Photograph courtesy of Nick Koudis, Getty Images, Inc. - Photodisc.

11

Files and Streams: Input/Output Techniques

OBJECTIVES

After studying this chapter, you will

- Be able to read and write text files.
- Know how to read and write binary files.
- Understand the use of `InputStream`s and `OutputStream`s.
- Be able to design methods for performing input and output.
- Know how to use the `File` class.
- Be able to use the `JFileChooser` class.

OUTLINE

11.1   Introduction

We have been using input and output in our programs since the very first chapters of the book. In this chapter we will take a closer look at Java's input and output elements.

    Input refers to information or data read from some external source into a running program. We introduced you to working with input in Chapter 4, when we developed the Keyboard-Reader class with methods for reading data from the keyboard into the console window. The chapter also discussed reading data from the keyboard into a JTextField in a GUI interface, as well as reading data from a text file using methods in the Scanner class.

input and output

    Output refers to information or data written from a running program to some external destination. Up to this point, whenever our programs have produced output, it has been sent to either the Java console, a text area, or some other GUI component. These destinations are transitory, in the sense that they reside in the computer's primary memory and exist only so long as the program is running.

    A **file** is a collection of data stored on a disk or on some other relatively permanent storage medium. A file's existence does not depend on a running program. In this chapter, we will learn how to create files and how to perform input and output operations on their data using the Java classes designed specifically for this purpose. Methods from these classes allow us to write data to files and provide greater flexibility in the way we read data from files than the Scanner class offers.

11.2   Streams and Files

As was noted in Chapter 4, all input and output (I/O) in Java is accomplished through the use of input streams and output streams. You are already familiar with input and output streams because we have routinely used the System.out output stream and the System.in input stream (Fig. 11.1) in this text's examples. Recall that System.out usually connects your program (source) to the screen (destination) and System.in usually connects the keyboard (source) to the running program (destination). What you have learned about streams will be a key for connecting files to a program.

I/O streams

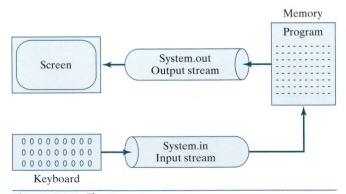

Figure 11.1 The System.out output stream connects your program to the screen, and the System.in input stream connects it to the keyboard.

11.2.1   The Data Hierarchy

The stuff that flows through Java streams or is stored in Java files is known as information or data. All data consist of binary digits, or *bits*. A bit is simply a 0 or a 1, the electronic states that correspond to these values. As we learned in Chapter 5, a bit is the smallest unit of data.

However, it would be tedious if a program had to work with data in units as small as bits. Therefore, most operations involve various-sized aggregates of data, such as an 8-bit `byte`, a 16-bit `short`, a 16-bit `char`, a 32-bit `int`, a 64-bit `long`, a 32-bit `float`, or a 64-bit `double`. As we know, these are Java's primitive numeric types. In addition to these aggregates, we can group together a sequence of `char` to form a `String`.

It is also possible to group data of different types into objects. A **record**, which corresponds closely to a Java object, can have **fields** that contain different types of data. For example, a student record might contain fields for the student's name and address represented by (`Strings`), expected year of graduation (`int`), and current grade-point average represented by (`double`). Collections of these records are typically grouped into *files*. For example, your registrar's office may have a separate file for each of its graduating classes. These are typically organized into a collection of related files called a **database**.

Taken together, the different kinds of data processed by a computer or stored in a file can be organized into a **data hierarchy** (Fig. 11.2).

It is important to recognize that while programmers may group data into various types of abstract entities, the information flowing through an input or output stream is just a sequence of bits. There are no natural boundaries that mark where one byte (or one `int` or one record) ends and the next one begins. Therefore, it will be up to us to provide the boundaries as we process the data.

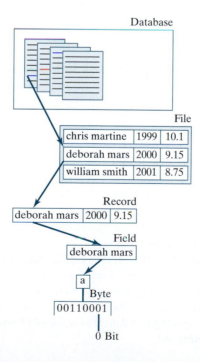

Figure 11.2 A data hierarchy.

11.2.2   Binary Files and Text Files

As we noted in Chapter 4, there are two types of files in Java: binary files and text files. Both kinds store data as a sequence of bits—that is, a sequence of 0's and 1's. Thus, the difference between the two types of files lies in the way they are interpreted by the programs that read and write them. A **binary file** is processed as a sequence of bytes, whereas a *text file* is processed as a sequence of characters.

Text editors and other programs that process text files interpret the file's sequence of bits as a sequence of characters—that is, as a string. Your Java source programs (`*.java`) are text files, and so are the HTML files that populate the World Wide Web. The big advantage of text

Text files are portable

files is their portability. Because their data are represented in the ASCII code (Table 5.13), they can be read and written by just about any text-processing program. Thus, a text file created by a program on a Windows/Intel computer can be read by a Macintosh program.

In non-Java environments, data in binary files are stored as bytes, and the representation used varies from computer to computer. The manner in which a computer's memory stores binary data determines how it is represented in a file. Thus, binary data are not very portable. For example, a binary file of integers created on a Macintosh cannot be read by a Windows/Intel program.

Binary files are platform dependent

One reason for the lack of portability is that each type of computer has its own definition of an integer. On some systems an integer might be 16 bits, and on others it might be 32 bits, so even if you know that a Macintosh binary file contains integers, that still won't make it readable by Windows/Intel programs. Another problem is that even if two computers use the same number of bits to represent an integer, they might use different representation schemes. For example, some computers might use 10000101 as the 8-bit representation of the number 133, whereas other computers might use the reverse, 10100001, to represent 133.

The good news is that Java's designers have made its binary files *platform independent* by carefully defining the exact size and representation that must be used for integers and all other primitive types. Thus, binary files created by Java programs can be interpreted by Java programs on any platform.

> **JAVA LANGUAGE RULE**   **Platform Independence.** Java binary files are platform independent. They can be interpreted by any computer that supports Java.

11.2.3   Input and Output Streams

Java has a wide variety of streams for performing I/O. They are defined in the `java.io` package, which must be imported by any program that does I/O. They are generally organized into the hierarchy illustrated in Figure 11.3. We will cover only a small portion of the hierarchy in this text. Generally speaking, binary files are processed by subclasses of `InputStream`

I/O streams

and `OutputStream`. Text files are processed by subclasses of `Reader` and `Writer`, both of which are streams despite their names.

`InputStream` and `OutputStream` are abstract classes that serve as the root classes for reading and writing binary data. Their most commonly used subclasses are `DataInput-Stream` and `DataOutputStream`, which are used for processing `String` data and data of any of Java's primitive types—`char`, `boolean`, `int`, `double`, and so on. The analogues of these classes for processing text data are the `Reader` and `Writer` classes, which serve as the root classes for all text I/O.

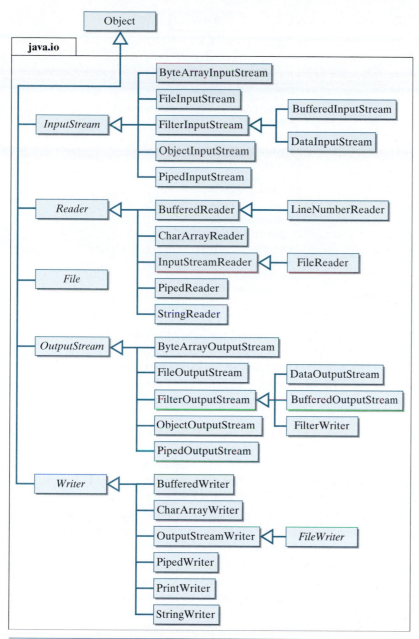

Figure 11.3 Java's stream hierarchy.

JAVA PROGRAMMING TIP: Choosing a Stream. In choosing an appropriate stream for an I/O operation, `DataInputStreams` and `DataOutputStreams` normally are used for binary I/O. `Reader` and `Writer` streams normally are used for text I/O.

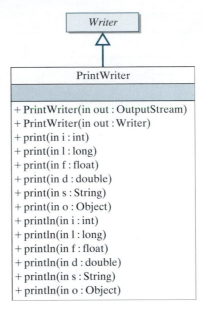

Figure 11.4   `PrintWriter` methods print data of various types.

The subclasses of these root classes perform various specialized I/O operations. For example, `FileInputStream` and `FileOutputStream` perform binary input and output on files. The `PrintStream` class contains methods for outputting certain types of primitive data—integers, floats, and so forth—as text. The `System.out` stream, one of the most widely used output streams, is an object of this type. The `PrintWriter` class, introduced in JDK 1.1, contains the same methods as `PrintStream`, but the methods are designed to support platform independence and internationalized I/O—that is, I/O that works in different languages and alphabets.

The various methods defined in `PrintWriter` are designed to output particular types of primitive data (Fig. 11.4). As you would expect, there are both a `print()` method and `println()` method for each kind of data the programmer wants to output.

Table 11.1 briefly describes Java's most commonly used input and output streams. In addition to the ones we've already mentioned, you are already familiar with methods from the `BufferedReader` and `File` classes, which were used in Chapter 4.

Filtering refers to performing operations on data while the data are being input or output. Methods in the `FilterInputStream` and `FilterReader` classes can be used to filter binary and text data during input. Methods in the `FilterOutputStream` and `FilterWriter` can be used to filter output data. These classes serve as the root classes for various filtering subclasses. They can also be subclassed to perform customized data filtering.

One type of filtering is **buffering**, which is provided by several buffered streams, including `BufferedInputStream` and `BufferedReader`, for performing binary and text input, and `BufferedOutputStream` and `BufferedWriter`, for buffered output operations. As was discussed in Chapter 4, a *buffer* is a relatively large region of memory used to temporarily store data during input or output. When buffering is used, a program will transfer a large number of bytes into the buffer from the relatively slow input device and then transfer them to the program as each read operation is performed. The transfer from the buffer to the program's memory is very fast.

Table 11.1. Some of Java's important stream classes

Class	Description
InputStream	Abstract root class of all binary input streams
FileInputStream	Provides methods for reading bytes from a binary file
FilterInputStream	Provides methods required to filter data
BufferedInputStream	Provides input data buffering for reading large files
ByteArrayInputStream	Provides methods for reading an array as if it were a stream
DataInputStream	Provides methods for reading Java's primitive data types
PipedInputStream	Provides methods for reading piped data from another thread
OutputStream	Abstract root class of all binary output streams
FileOutputStream	Provides methods for writing bytes to a binary file
FilterOutputStream	Provides methods required to filter data
BufferedOutputStream	Provides output data buffering for writing large files
ByteArrayOutputStream	Provides methods for writing an array as if it were a stream
DataOutputStream	Provides methods for writing Java's primitive data types
PipedOutputStream	Provides methods for writing piped data to another thread
PrintStream	Provides methods for writing primitive data as text
Reader	Abstract root class for all text input streams
BufferedReader	Provides buffering for character input streams
CharArrayReader	Provides input operations on char arrays
FileReader	Provides methods for character input on files
FilterReader	Provides methods to filter character input
StringReader	Provides input operations on Strings
Writer	Abstract root class for all text output streams
BufferedWriter	Provides buffering for character output streams
CharArrayWriter	Provides output operations to char arrays
FileWriter	Provides methods for output to text files
FilterWriter	Provides methods to filter character output
PrintWriter	Provides methods for printing binary data as characters
StringWriter	Provides output operations to Strings

Similarly, when buffering is used during output, data are transferred directly to the buffer and then written to the disk when the buffer fills up or when the flush() method is called.

JAVA PROGRAMMING TIP: Buffering. Buffered streams can improve a program's overall efficiency by reducing the amount of time it spends accessing relatively slow input or output devices.

You can also define your own data filtering subclasses to perform customized filtering. For example, suppose you want to add line numbers to a text editor's printed output. To perform this task, you could define a FilterWriter subclass and override its write() methods to perform the desired filtering operation. Similarly, to remove the line numbers from such a file during input, you could define a FilterReader subclass. In that case, you would override its read() methods to suit your goals for the program.

Buffering

Filtering data

There are several classes that provide I/O-like operations on various internal memory structures. ByteArrayInputStream, ByteArrayOutputStream, CharArrayReader, and CharArrayWriter are four classes that take input from or send output to arrays in the program's memory. Methods in these classes can be used for performing various operations on data during input or output. For example, suppose a program reads an entire line of integer data from a binary file into a `ByteArray`. It might then transform the data by, say, computing the remainder modulo N of each value. The program now can read the transformed data by treating the byte array as an input stream. A similar example would apply for some kind of output transformation.

The `StringReader` and `StringWriter` classes provide methods for treating `String`s and `StringBuffer`s as I/O streams. These methods are useful for certain data conversions.

JAVA PROGRAMMING TIP: Integer/String Conversion. An integer can be converted to a `String` by writing it to a `StringBuffer`, which can then be output as an entire line of text. `StringReader` methods can read integer data from an ordinary `String` object.

11.3 CASE STUDY: Reading and Writing Text Files

Let's write a GUI application that will be able to read and write data to and from a text file. To do this, we will need to develop a set of methods to perform I/O on text files.

GUI design

The GUI for this application will contain a `JTextArea`, where text file data can be input and displayed, and a `JTextField`, where the user can enter the file's name. It will also contain two `JButton`s, one for reading a file into the `JTextArea`, and the other for writing the data in the `JTextArea` into a file (Fig. 11.5). Note that even this simple interface will let the user create new files and rename existing files.

11.3.1 Text File Format

End-of-file character

A text file consists of a sequence of characters divided into zero or more lines and ending with a special **end-of-file character**. When you open a new file in a text editor, it contains zero lines and zero characters. After typing a single character, it would contain one character and one line. The following would be an example of a file with four lines of text:

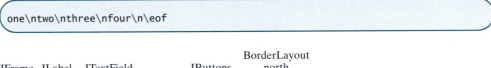

one\ntwo\nthree\nfour\n\eof

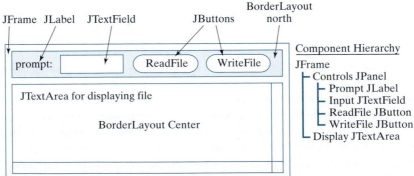

Figure 11.5 The GUI design for a program that reads and writes text files.

Note the use of the end-of-line character, \n, to mark the end of each line, and the use of the end-of-file character, \eof, to mark the end of the file. As we will see, the I/O methods for text files use these special characters to control reading and writing loops. Thus, when the file is read by appropriate Java methods, such as the `BufferedReader.readLine()` and `BufferedReader.read()` methods, one or more characters will be read until either an end-of-line or end-of-file character is encountered. When a line of characters is written using `println()`, the end-of-line character is appended to the characters themselves.

11.3.2   Writing to a Text File

Let's see how to write to a text file. In this program we write the entire contents of the `JTextArea()` to the text file. In general, writing data to a file requires three steps:

1. Connect an output stream to the file.
2. Write text data into the stream, possibly using a loop.
3. Close the stream.

As Figure 11.1 shows, connecting a stream to a file looks like doing a bit of plumbing. The first step is to connect an output stream to the file. The output stream serves as a conduit between the program and a named file. The output stream opens the file and gets it ready to accept data from the program. If the file already exists, then opening the file will destroy any data it previously contained. If the file doesn't yet exist, then it will be created from scratch.   *Output stream*

   Once the file is open, the next step is to write the text to the stream, which passes the text on to the file. This step may require a loop that outputs one line of data on each iteration. Finally, once all the data have been written to the file, the stream should be closed. This also has the effect of closing the file.

> **EFFECTIVE DESIGN: Writing a File.**   Writing data to a file requires a three-step algorithm: (1) connect an output stream to the file, (2) write the data, and (3) close the file.

Code Reuse: Designing an Output Method

Now let's see how these three steps are done in Java. Suppose the text we want to write is contained in a `JTextArea`. Thus, we want a method that will write the contents of a `JTextArea` to a named file.

   What output stream should we use for the task of writing a `String` to a named file? To decide this, we need to use the information in Figure 11.3 and Table 11.1. As we pointed out earlier, we are writing a text file, and therefore we must use a `Writer` subclass. But which subclass should we use? The only way to decide is to consult the Java API documentation, using links at   *Choosing an output stream*

```
http://java.sun.com/j2se/docs/
```

to see what methods are available in the various subclasses. For I/O operations you want to consult the classes in the `java.io` package. Ideally, we would like to be able to create an output stream to a named file, and we would like to be able to write a `String` to the file.

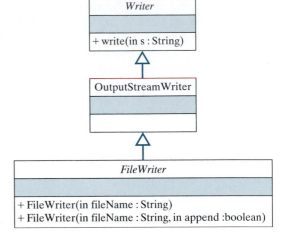

Figure 11.6   To find the right I/O method, it is sometimes necessary to search the Java class hierarchy. This is easy to do with the online documentation.

One likely candidate is the `FileWriter` class (Fig. 11.6). Its name and description (Table 11.1) suggest that it is designed for writing text files. And indeed it contains the kind of constructor we need—that is, one that takes the file name as a parameter. Note that by taking a `boolean` parameter, the second constructor allows us to append data to a file rather than rewrite the entire file, which is the default case.

However, `FileWriter` does not define a `write()` method. This doesn't necessarily mean that it does not contain such a method. Perhaps it has inherited one from its super-classes, `OutputStreamWriter` and `Writer`. Indeed, the `Writer` class contains a method, `write()`, whose signature suggests that it is ideally suited for our task (Fig. 11.6).

Inheritance

Having decided on a `FileWriter` stream, the rest of the task of designing our method is simply a matter of using `FileWriter` methods in an appropriate way:

```
private void writeTextFile(JTextArea display, String fileName) {
                      // Create stream & open file
    FileWriter outStream = new FileWriter(fileName);
                      //  Write the entire display text and close the stream
    outStream.write(display.getText());
    outStream.close();   //  Close the output stream
}
```

We use the `FileWriter()` constructor to create an output stream to the file whose name is stored in `fileName`. In this case, the task of writing data to the file is handled by a single `write()` statement, which writes the entire contents of the `JTextArea` in one operation.

Finally, once we have finished writing the data, we `close()` the output stream. This also has the effect of closing the file. The overall effect of this method is that the text contained in `display` has been output to a file, named `fileName`, which is stored on the disk.

JAVA PROGRAMMING TIP: Closing a File.   Even though Java will close any open files and streams when a program terminates normally, it is good programming practice to close the file yourself with a `close()` statement. This reduces the chances of damaging the file if the program terminates abnormally.

```
private void writeTextFile(JTextArea display, String fileName) {
    try {
        FileWriter outStream =  new FileWriter (fileName);
        outStream.write (display.getText());
        outStream.close();
    } catch (IOException e) {
        display.setText("IOERROR: " + e.getMessage() + "\n");
        e.printStackTrace();
    }
} // writeTextFile()
```

Figure 11.7   A method to write a text file.

Because so many different things can go wrong during an I/O operation, most I/O operations generate some kind of *checked exception*. Therefore, it is necessary to embed the I/O operations within a `try/catch` statement. In this example, the `FileWriter()` constructor, the `write()` method, and the `close()` method may each throw an `IOException`. Therefore, the entire body of this method should be embedded within a `try/catch` block that catches the `IOException` (Fig. 11.7).

11.3.3   Code Reuse: Designing Text File Output

The `writeTextFile()` method provides a simple example of how to write data to a text file. More important, its development illustrates the kinds of choices necessary to design effective I/O methods. Two important design questions we asked and answered were:

- What methods do we need to perform the desired task?
- What streams contain the desired methods?

As in so many other examples we have considered, designing a method to perform a task is   Method design
often a matter of finding the appropriate methods in the Java class hierarchy.

EFFECTIVE DESIGN: Code Reuse.   Developing effective I/O routines is primarily a matter of choosing the right library methods. Start by asking yourself, what methods you need, and then find a stream class that contains the appropriate methods.

As you might expect, there is more than one way to write data to a text file. Suppose we decided that writing text to a file is like printing data to `System.out`. And suppose we chose to use a `PrintWriter` object as our first candidate for an output stream (Fig. 11.3 and Table 11.1). This class (Fig. 11.4) contains a wide range of `print()` methods for writing different types of data as text. So it has exactly the kind of method we need: `print(String)`. However, this stream does not contain a constructor method that allows us to create a stream from the name of a file. Its constructors require either a `Writer` object or an `OutputStream` object.

  This means that we can use a `PrintWriter` to print to a file, but only if we can first construct either an `OutputStream` or a `Writer` object to the file. So we must go back to searching Figure 11.3 and Table 11.1 for an appropriate candidate. Fortunately, the `FileOutputStream` class (Fig. 11.8) has just the constructors we want. We now have an alternative way of

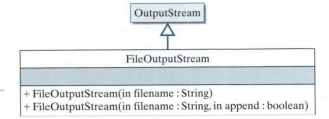

Figure 11.8 The FileOutput-
Stream class.

coding the `writeTextFile()` method, this time using a combination of `PrintWriter` and
`FileOutputStream`:

```
//  Create an output stream and open the file
PrintWriter outStream = new PrintWriter(new FileOutputStream(fileName));
//  Write the display's text and close the stream
outStream.print ( display.getText() );
outStream.close();
```

Note how the output stream is created in this case. First we create a `FileOutputStream` using
the file name as its argument. Then we create a `PrintWriter` using the `FileOutputStream`
as its argument. The reason we can do this is because the `PrintWriter()` constructor takes
a `FileOutputStream` parameter. This is what makes the connection possible.

*Parameter
agreement*

To use the plumbing analogy again, this is like connecting two sections of pipe between the
program and the file. The data will flow from the program through `PrintWriter`, through
the `OutputStream`, to the file. Of course, you can't just arbitrarily connect one stream to
another. They have to "fit together," which means that their parameters have to match.

> **EFFECTIVE DESIGN: Stream/Stream Connections.** Two different kinds of streams
> can be connected if a constructor for one stream takes the second kind of stream as a
> parameter. This is often an effective way to create the kind of object you need to perform
> an I/O task.

java.sun.com/docs

The important lesson here is that we found what we wanted by searching through the `java.io.*`
hierarchy. The same approach can be used to help you design I/O methods for other tasks.

SELF-STUDY EXERCISE

EXERCISE 11.1   Is it possible to perform output to a text file using a `PrintWriter` and a
`FileWriter` stream in combination? If so, write the Java code.

11.3.4   Reading from a Text File

Let's now look at the problem of inputting data from an existing text file, a common operation
that occurs whenever your email program opens an email message or your word processor
opens a document. In general, there are three steps to reading data from a file:

1. Connect an input stream to the file.
2. Read the text data using a loop.
3. Close the stream.

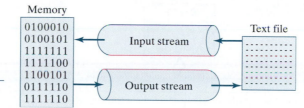

Memory

0100010
0100101
1111111
1111100
1100101
0111110
1111110

Figure 11.9 A stream serves as a pipe through which data flow.

As Figure 11.9 shows, the input stream serves as a kind of pipe between the file and the program. The first step is to connect an input stream to the file. (Of course, the file can only be read if it exists.) The input stream serves as a conduit between the program and the named file. It opens the file and gets it ready for reading. Once the file is open, the next step is to read the file's data. This will usually require a loop that reads data until the end of the file is reached. Finally, the stream is closed once all the data are read.

EFFECTIVE DESIGN: Reading Data   Reading data from a file requires a three-step algorithm: (1) connect an input stream to the file, (2) read the data, and (3) close the file.

Now let's see how these three steps are done in Java. Suppose that we want to put the file's data into a JTextArea. Thus, we want a method that will be given the name of a file and a reference to a JTextArea, and it will read the data from the file into the JTextArea.

What input stream should we use for this task? Here again we need to use the information in Figure 11.3 and Table 11.1. Because we're reading a text file, we should use a Reader subclass. A good candidate is the FileReader, whose name and description suggest that it might contain useful methods.

Choosing an input stream

What methods do we need? As in the preceding example, we need a constructor method that connects an input stream to a file when the constructor is given the name of the file. And, ideally, we'd like to have a method that will read one line at a time from the text file.

What methods should we use?

The FileReader class (Fig. 11.10) has the right kind of constructor. However, it does not contain the readLine() methods that would be necessary for our purposes. Searching upward through its superclasses, we find that InputStreamReader, its immediate parent class, has a method that reads ints:

```
public int read() throws IOException();
```

As shown in Figure 11.10, this read() method is an override of the read() method defined in the Reader class, the root class for text file input streams. Thus, there are no read-Line() methods in the Reader branch of the hierarchy. We have to look elsewhere for an appropriate class.

One class that does contain a readLine() method is BufferedReader (Fig. 11.10). Can we somehow use it? Fortunately, the answer is yes. BufferedReader's constructor takes a

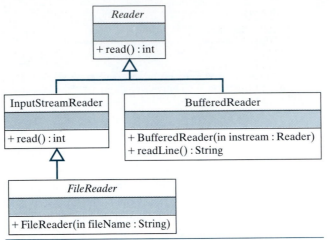

Figure 11.10 FileReader's superclasses contain read() methods but no readLine() methods.

Reader object as a parameter. But a FileReader *is* a Reader—that is, it is a descendant of the Reader class. So, using our plumbing analogy again, to build an input stream to the file, we can join a BufferedReader and a FileReader

```
BufferedReader inStream = new BufferedReader(new FileReader(fileName));
```

Given this sort of connection to the file, the program can use BufferedReader.readLine() to read one line at a time from the file.

We have found a method that reads one line at a time. Now we need an algorithm that will read the entire file. Of course, this will involve a loop, and the key will be to make sure we get the loop's termination condition right.

Using the end-of-file character

An important fact about readLine() is that it will return null as its value when it reaches the end of the file. Recall that text files have a special end-of-file character. When readLine() encounters this character, it will return null. Therefore, we can specify the following while loop:

```
String line = inStream.readLine();
while (line != null) {
    display.append(line + "\n");
    line = inStream.readLine();
}
```

We begin outside the loop by attempting to read a line from the file. If the file happens to be empty (which it might be), then line will be set to null; otherwise it will contain the String that was read. In this case, we append the line to a JTextArea. Note that readLine() *does not* return the end-of-line character with its return value. That is why we add a \n before we append the line to the JTextArea.

```java
private void readTextFile(JTextArea display, String fileName) {
  try {
    BufferedReader inStream                    // Create and open the stream
      = new BufferedReader (new FileReader(fileName));
    String line = inStream.readLine();         // Read one line
    while (line != null) {                     // While more text
        display.append(line + "\n");           // Display a line
        line = inStream.readLine();            // Read next line
    }
     inStream.close();                         // Close the stream
  } catch (FileNotFoundException e) {
    display.setText("IOERROR: "+ fileName +" NOT found\n");
    e.printStackTrace();
  } catch ( IOException e ) {
    display.setText("IOERROR: " + e.getMessage() + "\n");
    e.printStackTrace();
  }
} // readTextFile()
```

Figure 11.11   A method for reading a text file.

JAVA PROGRAMMING TIP: End of Line.   Remember that `readLine()` does not return the end-of-line character as part of the text it returns. If you want to print the text on separate lines, you must append \n.

The last statement in the body of the loop attempts to read the next line from the input stream. If the end of file has been reached, this attempt will return `null` and the loop will terminate. Otherwise, the loop will continue reading and displaying lines until the end of file is reached. Taken together, these various design decisions lead to the definition for `readTextFile()` shown in Figure 11.11.

Note that we must catch both the `IOException`, thrown by `readLine()` and `close()`, **IOException** and the `FileNotFoundException`, thrown by the `FileReader()` constructor. It is important to make sure that the read loop has the following form:

```
try to read one line of data
    and store it in line          // Loop initializer
while ( line is not null ) {       // Loop entry condition
   process the data
   try to read one line of data
      and store it in line         // Loop updater
}
```

When it attempts to read the *end-of-file* character, `readLine()` will return `null`.

EFFECTIVE DESIGN: Reading Text.   In reading text files, the `readLine()` method will return `null` when it tries to read the end-of-file character. This provides a convenient way of testing for the end of file.

EFFECTIVE DESIGN: Reading an Empty File. Loops for reading text files are designed to work even if the file is empty. Therefore, the loop should attempt to read a line *before* testing the loop-entry condition. If the initial read returns `null`, that means the file is empty and the loop body will be skipped.

SELF-STUDY EXERCISE

EXERCISE 11.2 What's wrong with the following loop for reading a text file and printing its output on the screen?

```
String line = null;
do {
    line = inStream.readLine();
    System.out.println ( line );
} while (line != null);
```

11.3.5 Code Reuse: Designing Text File Input

Our last example used `BufferedReader.readLine()` to read an entire line from the file in one operation. But this isn't the only way to do things. For example, we could use the `FileReader` stream directly if we were willing to do without the `readLine()` method. Let's design an algorithm that works in this case.

As we saw earlier, if you use a `FileReader` stream, then you must use the `InputStreamReader.read()` method. This method reads bytes from an input stream and translates them into Java Unicode characters. The `read()` method, for example, returns a single Unicode character as an `int`:

```
public int read() throws IOException();
```

Of course, we can always convert this to a `char` and concatenate it to a `JTextArea`, as the following algorithm illustrates:

```
int ch = inStream.read();           // Init: Try to read a character
while (ch != -1) {                   // Entry-condition: while more chars
    display.append((char)ch + "");   // Append the character
    ch = inStream.read();            // Updater: try to read
}
```

Although the details are different, the structure of this loop is the same as if we were reading one line at a time.

Data conversion

The loop variable in this case is an `int` because `InputStreamReader.read()` returns the next character as an `int`, or returns −1 if it encounters the `end-of-file` character. Because `ch` is an `int`, we must convert it to a `char` and then to a `String` in order to `append()` it to the display.

A loop to read data from a file has the following basic form:

```
try to read data into a variable      // Initializer
while ( read was successful ) {        // Entry condition
    process the data
    try to read data into a variable // Updater
}
```

EFFECTIVE DESIGN: Read Loop Structure. The `read()` and `readLine()` methods have different ways to indicate when a read attempt fails. These differences affect how the loop-entry condition is specified, but the structure of the `read` loop is the same.

JAVA PROGRAMMING TIP: Read Versus Readline. Unless it is necessary to manipulate each character in the text file, reading a whole line at one time is more efficient and, therefore, preferable.

It is worth noting again the point we made earlier: Designing effective I/O routines is largely a matter of searching the `java.io` package for appropriate classes and methods. The methods we have developed can serve as suitable models for a wide variety of text I/O tasks, but if you find that they are not suitable for a particular task, you can design your own method. Just think about what it is you want the program to accomplish, then find the stream classes that contain methods you can use to perform the desired task. Basic reading and writing algorithms will be pretty much the same no matter which read or write method you use.

Reusing existing code

SELF-STUDY EXERCISE

EXERCISE 11.3 What's wrong with the following loop for reading a text file and printing its output on the screen?

```
int ch;
do {
    ch = inStream.read();
    System.out.print((char)ch);
} while (ch != -1)
```

11.3.6 The `TextIO` Application

Given the text I/O methods we wrote in the preceding sections, we can now specify the overall design of our `TextIO` class (Fig. 11.12). In order to complete this application, we need only set up its GUI and write its `actionPerformed()` method.

Setting up the GUI for this application is straightforward. Figure 11.13 shows how the finished product will look. The code is given in Figure 11.14. Pay particular attention to the `actionPerformed()` method, which uses the methods we defined in Section 11.3.5.

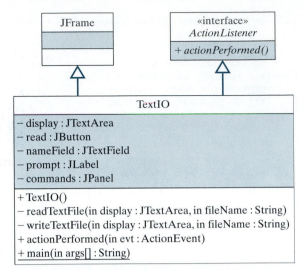

Figure 11.12 The TextIO class.

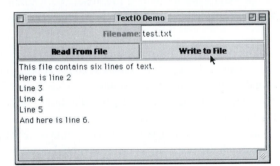

Figure 11.13 An application that performs simple text I/O.

```
import javax.swing.*;          // Swing components
import java.awt.*;
import java.io.*;
import java.awt.event.*;

public class TextIO extends JFrame implements ActionListener{
 private JTextArea display = new JTextArea();
 private JButton read = new JButton("Read From File"),
             write = new JButton("Write to File");
 private JTextField nameField = new JTextField(20);
 private JLabel prompt = new JLabel("Filename:",JLabel.RIGHT);
 private JPanel commands = new JPanel();

 public TextIO() {                              // Constructor
  super("TextIO Demo");                         // Set window title
  read.addActionListener(this);
  write.addActionListener(this);
  commands.setLayout( new GridLayout(2,2,1,1)); // Control panel
  commands.add(prompt);
  commands.add(nameField);
```

Figure 11.14 The TextIO class. (*Continued on next page*)

```java
      commands.add(read);
      commands.add(write);
      display.setLineWrap(true);
      this.getContentPane().setLayout(new BorderLayout());
      this.getContentPane().add("North", commands);
      this.getContentPane().add( new JScrollPane(display));
      this.getContentPane().add("Center", display);
  } // TextIO()
  private void writeTextFile(JTextArea display, String fileName) {
    try {
       FileWriter outStream =  new FileWriter (fileName);
       outStream.write (display.getText());
       outStream.close();
    } catch (IOException e) {
       display.setText("IOERROR: " + e.getMessage() + "\n");
       e.printStackTrace();
    }
  } // writeTextFile()
  private void readTextFile(JTextArea display, String fileName) {
    try {
       BufferedReader inStream             // Create and open the stream
          = new BufferedReader (new FileReader(fileName));
       String line = inStream.readLine();  // Read one line
       while (line != null) {              // While more text
         display.append(line + "\n");      // Display a line
         line = inStream.readLine();       // Read next line
       }
       inStream.close();                   // Close the stream
    } catch (FileNotFoundException e) {
       display.setText("IOERROR: "+ fileName +" NOT found\n");
       e.printStackTrace();
    } catch (IOException e) {
       display.setText("IOERROR: " + e.getMessage() + "\n");
       e.printStackTrace();
    }
  } // readTextFile()
  public void actionPerformed(ActionEvent evt) {
     String fileName = nameField.getText();
     if (evt.getSource()  == read) {
        display.setText("");
        readTextFile(display, fileName);
     }
     else writeTextFile(display, fileName);
  } // actionPerformed()

  public static void main(String args[]) {
     TextIO tio = new TextIO();
     tio.setSize(400, 200);
     tio.setVisible(true);
     tio.addWindowListener(new WindowAdapter() {
        public void windowClosing(WindowEvent e) {
           System.exit(0); // Quit the application
        }
     });
  } // main()
} // TextIO class
```

Figure 11.14   The TextIO class. (*Continued from previous page*)

11.4 The File Class

As we have seen, an attempt to create a FileReader stream may throw a FileNotFoundException. This happens if the user provides a name for a file that either does not exist or is not located where its name says it should be located. Is there any way we can detect these kinds of errors before attempting to read the file?

The java.io.File class provides methods that can be used for this task. The File class provides a representation of the computer's file and directory information in a platform-independent manner. As you know, a file is a collection of data, whereas a **directory** is a collection of files. (To be exact, a directory is a file that stores its files' names and attributes, not the files themselves.) In this section, we will provide details about the File class and how to use the methods available in it.

11.4.1 Names and Paths

In order to correctly specify a file's location, it is necessary to know a little about how files are stored on your computer's disk drive. File systems are organized into a hierarchy. A **path** is a description of a file's location in the hierarchy. For example, consider the hierarchy of files in Figure 11.15. Assume that your Java program is named MyClass.class. The directory of a running program is considered the *current directory*. Any files located in the current directory can be referred to by name alone—for example, MyClass.java. To refer to a file located in a subdirectory of the current directory, you need to provide the name of the subdirectory and the file: datafiles/data.txt. In this case, we are assuming a Unix file system, so we are using the / as the separator between the name of the directory (datafiles) and the name of the file (data.txt). This is an example of a **relative path name**, because we are specifying a file in relation to the current directory.

The file hierarchy

Alternatively, a file can be specified by its **absolute path name**. This would be a name whose path starts at the root directory of the file system. For example,

```
/root/java/examples/datafiles/data.txt
```

would be the absolute path name for the file named data.txt on a Unix system. When you supply the name of a file to one of the stream constructors, you are actually providing a *path* name. If the path consists of just a name, such as data.txt, Java assumes that the file is located in the same directory as the program itself.

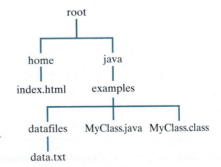

Figure 11.15 A simple hierarchy of directories and files.

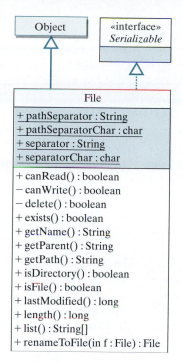

Figure 11.16 The java.io.File class.

11.4.2 Validating File Names

Before reading a file it is often necessary to determine whether the file's name is a valid one and whether the file can be read. The File class (Fig. 11.16) provides platform-independent methods for dealing with files and directories. It contains methods that list the contents of directories, determine a file's attributes, and rename and delete files. Note the several static constants provided. These allow path names to be specified in a platform-independent way. For example, on a Unix system, the File.separator character will be the / and on a Windows system it will be the \. File.separator will be initialized to the appropriate separator for the system being used.

> **JAVA PROGRAMMING TIP: File Separators.** To help make your programs platform independent, use the File.separator constant instead of a literal value whenever you are specifying a path name.

As an example of how you might use some of File's methods, let's write a method that tests whether the file name entered by the user is the name of a valid, readable file.

A file may be unreadable for several differrent reasons. It might be owned by another user and readable only by that user. Or it might be designated as not readable by its owner. We will pass the method the name of the file (a String), and the method will return true if a readable file with that name exists. Otherwise, the method will throw an exception and return false:

Method design

```java
private boolean isReadableFile(String fileName) {
  try {
    File file = new File(fileName);
    if (!file.exists())
        throw (new FileNotFoundException("No such File:" + fileName));
    if (!file.canRead())
        throw (new IOException("File not readable: " + fileName));
    return true;
  } catch (FileNotFoundException e) {
    System.out.println("IOERROR: File NOT Found: " + fileName + "\n");
    return false;
  } catch (IOException e) {
    System.out.println("IOERROR: " + e.getMessage() + "\n");
    return false;
  }
} // isReadableFile()
```

The method simply creates a `File` instance and uses its `exists()` and `canRead()` methods to check whether its name is valid. If either condition fails, an exception is thrown. The method handles its own exceptions, printing an error message and returning false in each case.

Before attempting to write data to a file, we might want to check that the file has been given an appropriate name. For example, if the user leaves the file name blank, we should not write data to the file. Also, a file might be designated as unwriteable in order to protect it from being inadvertently overwritten. We should check that the file is writeable before attempting to write to it:

```java
private boolean isWriteableFile(String fileName) {
  try {
    File file = new File (fileName);
    if (fileName.length() == 0)
        throw (new IOException("Invalid file name: " + fileName));
    if (file.exists() && !file.canWrite())
        throw (new IOException( "IOERROR: File not writeable: " + fileName));
    return true;
  } catch (IOException e) {
    display.setText("IOERROR: " + e.getMessage() + "\n");
    return false;
  }
} // isWriteableFile()
```

The first check in this code determines that the user has not forgotten to provide a name for the output file. It is unlikely that the user wants to name the file with an empty string. We use the `exists()` method to test whether the user is attempting to write to an existing file. If so, we use the `canWrite()` method to test whether the file is writeable. Both kinds of errors result in `IOExceptions`.

SELF-STUDY EXERCISE

EXERCISE 11.4   The other methods of the `File` class are just as easy to use as the ones we have illustrated in this section. Write a method that takes the name of a file as its single parameter and prints the following information about the file: its absolute path, its length, and whether it is a directory or a file.

11.5 Example: Reading and Writing Binary Files

Although text files are extremely useful and often employed, they can't and shouldn't be used for every data-processing application. For example, your college's administrative data system undoubtedly uses files to store student records. Because your student record contains a variety of different types of data—Strings, ints, doubles—it cannot be processed as text. Similarly, a company's inventory files, which also include data of a wide variety of types, cannot be processed as text. Files such as these must be processed as binary data.

Suppose you are asked to write an application that involves the use of a company's employee records. Recall that a record is a structure that combines different types of data into a single entity. It's like an object with no methods, just instance variables.

A binary file is a sequence of bytes. Unlike a text file, which is terminated by a special end-of-file marker, a binary file consists of nothing but data. A binary file doesn't have an end-of-file character because any such character would be indistinguishable from a binary datum.

DEBUGGING TIP: End of Binary File. Because a binary file does not have an end-of-file character, it would be an error to use the same loop-entry conditions we used in the loops we designed for reading text files.

Generally speaking, the steps involved in reading and writing binary files are the same as for text files:

1. Connect a stream to the file.
2. Read or write the data, possibly using a loop.
3. Close the stream.

The difference between text and binary file I/O resides in the Java streams we use.

11.5.1 Writing Binary Data

Let's begin by designing a method that will output employee data to a binary file. As the developer of this program, one thing you'll have to do is build some sample data files. These can't easily be built by hand—remember you can't use a text editor to create them—so you'll want to develop a method that can generate some random data of the sort your application will have to process.

Generating binary data

EFFECTIVE DESIGN: I/O Design. When designing file I/O applications, it is good to design the input and output methods together. This is especially important for binary I/O.

The first thing we need to know is exactly what the data look like. Let's assume that each record contains three individual pieces of data—the employee's name, age, and pay rate. For example, the data in a file containing four records might look like this, once the data is interpreted:

```
Name0 24 15.06
Name1 25 5.09
Name2 40 11.45
Name3 52 9.25
```

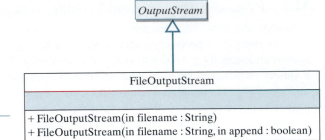

Figure 11.17 The `FileOutput-`
`Stream` class.

As you can see, these data items look as if they were randomly generated, but they resemble the real data in some important respects: they are of the right type—`String`, `int`, `double`—and have the right kind of values. Of course, when these data terms are stored in the file or in the program's memory, they just look like one long string of 0's and 1's.

Our approach to designing this output method will be the same as the approach we used in designing methods for text I/O. That is, we start with two questions:

- What stream classes should I use?
- What methods can I use?

And we find the answers to these by searching through the `java.io` package (Fig. 11.3 and Table 11.1).

Because we are performing binary output, we need to use a subclass of `OutputStream`. Because we're outputting to a file, one likely candidate is `FileOutputStream` (Fig. 11.17). This class has the right kind of constructors, but it only contains `write()` methods for writing `int`s and `byte`s, and we need to be able to write `String`s and `double`s as well as `int`s.

These kinds of methods are found in `DataOutputStream` (Fig. 11.18), which contains a `write()` method for each different type of data. As you can see, there is one method for each

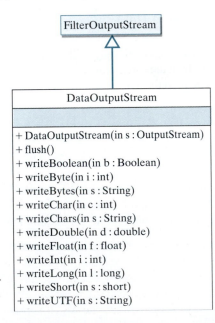

Figure 11.18 The `java.io.Data-`
`OutputStream` class contains methods for writing all types of data.

primitive type. However, note that the `writeChar()` takes an `int` parameter, which indicates that the character is written in binary format rather than as a ASCII or Unicode character. Although you can't tell by just reading its method signature, the `writeChars(String)` method also writes its data in binary format rather than as a sequence of characters. This is the main difference between these `write()` methods and the ones defined in the `Writer` branch of Java's I/O hierarchy.

Now that we've found the appropriate classes and methods, we need to create a pipeline to write data to the file and develop an output algorithm. To construct a stream to use in writing employee records, we want to join together a `DataOutputStream` and a `FileOutputStream`. The `DataOutputStream` gives us the output methods we need, and the `FileOutputStream` lets us use the file's name to create the stream:

```
DataOutputStream outStream
  = new DataOutputStream(new FileOutputStream (fileName));
```

This enables the program to write data to the `DataOutputStream`, which will pass it through the `FileOutputStream` to the file. That settles the first question.

To develop the output algorithm, we need a loop of some kind that involves calls to the appropriate methods. In this case, because we are generating random data, we can use a simple `for` loop to generate, say, five records of employee data. We need one `write()` statement for each of the elements in the employee record: the name (`String`), age (`int`), and pay rate (`double`):

```
for (int k = 0; k < 5; k++) {              // Output 5 data records
  outStream.writeUTF("Name" + k);          // Name
  outStream.writeInt((int)(20 + Math.random() * 25));  // Age
  outStream.writeDouble(Math.random() * 500);  // Payrate
}
```

Within the loop body we have one output statement for each data element in the record. The names of the methods reflect the type of data they write. Thus, we use `writeInt()` to write an `int` and `writeDouble()` to write a `double`. But why do we use `writeUTF` to write the employee's name, a `String`?

The Unicode Text Format (UTF)

There is no `DataOutputStream.writeString()` method. Instead, `Strings` are written using the `writeUTF()` method. **UTF** stands for **Unicode Text Format**, a coding scheme for Java's Unicode character set. Recall that Java uses the Unicode character set instead of the ASCII set. As a 16-bit code, Unicode can represent 8-bit ASCII characters plus a wide variety of Asian and other international characters. However, Unicode is not a very efficient coding scheme if you aren't writing an international program. If your program just uses the standard ASCII characters, which can be stored in 1 byte, you would be wasting 1 byte per character if you stored them as straight Unicode characters. Therefore, for efficiency purposes, Java uses the UTF format. UTF encoding can still represent all of the Unicode characters, but it provides a more efficient way of representing the ASCII subset.

ASCII vs. Unicode

```
private void writeRecords( String fileName ) {
  try {
    DataOutputStream outStream                          // Open stream
      = new DataOutputStream(new FileOutputStream(fileName));
    for (int k = 0; k < 5; k++) {                       // Output 5 data records
      String name = "Name" + k;                         // of name, age, payrate
      outStream.writeUTF("Name" + k);
      outStream.writeInt((int)(20 + Math.random() * 25));
      outStream.writeDouble(5.00 + Math.random() * 10);
    } // for
    outStream.close();                                  // Close the stream
  } catch (IOException e) {
    display.setText("IOERROR: " + e.getMessage() + "\n");
  }
} // writeRecords()
```

Figure 11.19 A method to write a binary file consisting of five randomly constructed records.

It is now time to combine these separate elements into a single method (Fig. 11.19). The `writeRecords()` method takes a single `String` parameter that specifies the name of the file. This is a `void` method. It will output data to a file, but it will not return anything to the calling method. The method follows the standard output algorithm: create an output stream, write the data, close the stream. Note also that the method includes a `try/catch` block to handle any `IOExceptions` that might be thrown.

11.5.2 Reading Binary Data

The steps involved in reading data from a binary file are the same as for reading data from a text file: create an input stream and open the file, read the data, close the file. The main difference lies in the way you check for the end-of-file marker in a binary file.

Let's design a method to read the binary data that were output by the `writeRecords()` method. We'll call this method `readRecords()`. It, too, will consist of a single `String` parameter that provides the name of the file to be read, and it will be a void method. It will just display the data on `System.out`.

The next questions we need to address are: What stream classes should we use, and what methods should we use? For binary input, we need an `InputStream` subclass (Fig. 11.3 and Table 11.1). As you have probably come to expect, the `FileInputStream` class contains constructors that let us create a stream from a file name (Fig. 11.20). However, it does not contain useful `read()` methods. Fortunately, the `DataInputStream` class contains the input counterparts of the methods we found in `DataOutputStream` (Fig. 11.21). Therefore, our

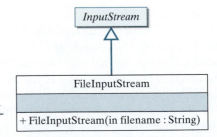

Figure 11.20 The `java.io.File-InputStream` class.

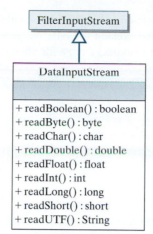

Figure 11.21 The `java.io.Data-InputStream` class contains methods for reading all types of data.

input stream for this method will be a combination of `DataInputStream` and `FileInput-Stream`:

```
DataInputStream inStream = new DataInputStream(new FileInputStream(file));
```

Now that we have identified the classes and methods we'll use to read the data, the most important remaining issue is designing a read loop that will terminate correctly. Unlike text files, binary files do not contain a special end-of-file marker. Therefore, the read methods can't see anything in the file that tells them they're at the end of the file. Instead, when a binary read method attempts to read past the end of the file, an end-of-file exception `EOFException` is thrown. Thus, the binary loop is coded as an infinite loop that is exited when the `EOFException` is raised:

```
try {
  while (true) {                                      // Infinite loop
    String name = inStream.readUTF();                 // Read a record
    int age = inStream.readInt();
    double pay = inStream.readDouble();
    display.append(name + " " + age + " " + pay + "\n");
  } // while
} catch (EOFException e) {}                            // Until EOF exception
```

The read loop is embedded within a `try/catch` statement. Note that the `catch` clause for the `EOFException` does nothing. Recall that when an exception is thrown in a `try` block, the block is exited for good, which is precisely the action we want to take. That is why we needn't do anything when we catch the `EOFException`. We have to catch the exception or else Java will catch it and terminate the program. This is an example of an expected exception.

An expected exception

EFFECTIVE DESIGN: EOFException. An attempt to read past the end of a binary file will cause an `EOFException` to be thrown. Catching this exception is the standard way of terminating a binary input loop.

Note also that the read() statements within the loop are mirror opposites of the write() statements in the method that created the data. This will generally be true for binary I/O routines: the statements that read data from a file should "match" those that wrote the data in the first place.

EFFECTIVE DESIGN: Matching Input to Output.   The statements used to read binary data should match those that wrote the data. If a writeX() method were used to write the data, a readX() should be used to read it.

To complete the method, the only remaining task is to close() the stream after the data are read. The complete definition is shown in Figure 11.22.

It is important to place a close() statement after the catch EOFException clause. If it were placed in the try block, it would never get executed. Note also that the entire method is embedded in an outer try block that catches the IOException thrown by the various read() methods and the FileNotFoundException thrown by the FileInputStream() constructor. These make the method a bit longer, but conceptually they belong in the method.

JAVA PROGRAMMING TIP: The finally **Block.**   In coding a binary read loop, the try block is exited as soon as the EOFException is raised. Therefore, the close() statement must be placed in the finally clause, which is executed after the catch clause.

```java
private void readRecords( String fileName ) {
  try {
    DataInputStream inStream                              // Open stream
      = new DataInputStream(new FileInputStream(fileName));
    display.setText("Name    Age Pay\n");
    try {
      while (true) {                                      // Infinite loop
        String name = inStream.readUTF();                // Read a record
        int age = inStream.readInt();
        double pay = inStream.readDouble();
        display.append(name + " " + age + " " + pay + "\n");
      } // while
    } catch (EOFException e) {                            // Until EOF exception
    } finally {
      inStream.close();                                  // Close the stream
    }
  } catch (FileNotFoundException e) {
    display.setText("IOERROR: "+ fileName + " NOT Found: \n");
  } catch (IOException e) {
    display.setText("IOERROR: " + e.getMessage() + "\n");
  }
} // readRecords()
```

Figure 11.22 A method for reading binary data.

EFFECTIVE DESIGN: Nested Try/Catch.   Nested **try** blocks must be used to perform binary I/O correctly. The outer block encapsulates statements that throw **IOExceptions**. The inner block encapsulates the read loop and catches the **EOFException**. No particular action need be taken when the **EOFException** is caught.

SELF-STUDY EXERCISE

EXERCISE 11.5   Identify the error in the following method, which is supposed to read a binary file of **ints** from a **DataInputStream**:

```java
public void readIntegers(DataInputStream inStream) {
    try {
        while (true) {
            int num = inStream.readInt();
            System.out.println(num);
        }
        inStream.close();
    } catch (EOFException e) {
    } catch (IOException e) {
    }
} // readIntegers()
```

11.5.3   The BinaryIO Application

Given the methods we wrote in the preceding section, we can now specify the overall design of the BinaryIO class (Fig. 11.23). The program sets up the same interface we used in the text file example (Fig. 11.24). It allows the user to specify the name of a data file to read or write. One button allows the user to write random employee records to a binary file, and the other allows the user to display the contents of a file in a JTextArea. The BinaryIO program in Figure 11.25 incorporates both readRecords() and writeRecords() into a complete Java program.

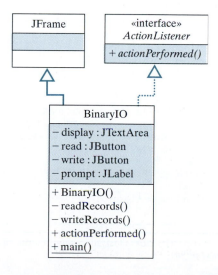

Figure 11.23   Design of the BinaryIO class.

Figure 11.24 A program to read and write binary files.

```java
import javax.swing.*;                                    // Swing components
import java.awt.*;
import java.io.*;
import java.awt.event.*;

public class BinaryIO extends JFrame implements ActionListener{
    private JTextArea display = new JTextArea();
    private JButton read = new JButton("Read Records From File"),
                    write = new JButton("Generate Random Records");
    private JTextField nameField = new JTextField(10);
    private JLabel prompt = new JLabel("Filename:", JLabel.RIGHT);
    private JPanel commands = new JPanel();

    public BinaryIO() {
        super("BinaryIO Demo");                          // Set window title
        read.addActionListener(this);
        write.addActionListener(this);
        commands.setLayout(new GridLayout(2,2,1,1));     // Control panel
        commands.add(prompt);
        commands.add(nameField);
        commands.add(read);
        commands.add(write);
        display.setLineWrap(true);
        this.getContentPane().setLayout(new BorderLayout () );
        this.getContentPane().add("North", commands);
        this.getContentPane().add( new JScrollPane(display));
        this.getContentPane().add("Center", display);
    } // BinaryIO()

    private void readRecords( String fileName ) {
        try {
            DataInputStream inStream                      // Open stream
                = new DataInputStream(new FileInputStream(fileName));
            display.setText("Name     Age Pay\n");
            try {
                while (true) {                            // Infinite loop
                    String name = inStream.readUTF();     // Read a record
                    int age = inStream.readInt();
                    double pay = inStream.readDouble();
                    display.append(name + "   " + age + "   " + pay + "\n");
                } // while
            } catch (EOFException e) {                    // Until EOF exception
            } finally {
                inStream.close();                         // Close the stream
            }
```

Figure 11.25 BinaryIO class illustrating simple input and output from a binary file. (*Continued on next page*)

```
            } catch (FileNotFoundException e) {
                display.setText("IOERROR: File NOT Found: " + fileName + "\n");
            } catch (IOException e) {
                display.setText("IOERROR: " + e.getMessage() + "\n");
            }
        } // readRecords()
    private void writeRecords( String fileName )  {
        try {
            DataOutputStream outStream                          // Open stream
                = new DataOutputStream(new FileOutputStream(fileName));
            for (int k = 0; k < 5; k++) {                        // Output 5 data records
                String name = "Name" + k;                       // of name, age, payrate
                outStream.writeUTF("Name" + k);
                outStream.writeInt((int)(20 + Math.random() * 25));
                outStream.writeDouble(5.00 + Math.random() * 10);
            } // for
            outStream.close();                                  // Close the stream
        } catch (IOException e) {
            display.setText("IOERROR: " + e.getMessage() + "\n");
        }
    } // writeRecords()

    public void actionPerformed(ActionEvent evt) {
        String fileName = nameField.getText();
        if (evt.getSource()  == read)
            readRecords(fileName);
        else
            writeRecords(fileName);
    } // actionPerformed()

    public static void main(String args[]) {
        BinaryIO bio = new BinaryIO();
        bio.setSize(400, 200);
        bio.setVisible(true);
        bio.addWindowListener(new WindowAdapter() {             // Quit
            public void windowClosing(WindowEvent e) {
                System.exit(0);
            }
        });
    } // main()
} // BinaryIO class
```

Figure 11.25 `BinaryIO` class illustrating simple input and output from a binary file.
(*Continued from previous page*)

11.5.4 Abstracting Data from Files

The method to read a binary file must exactly match the order of the write and read statements of the method that wrote the binary file. For example, if the file contains records that consist of a `String` followed by an `int` followed by a `double`, then they must be written in a sequence consisting of

```
writeUTF();
writeInt():
writeDouble();
```

And they must thereafter be read by the sequence of

```
readUTF();
readInt():
readDouble();
```

Attempting to do otherwise would make it impossible to interpret the data in the file.

Portability   This point should make it evident why (non-Java) binary files are not portable, whereas text files are. With text files, each character consists of 8 bits, and each 8-bit chunk can be interpreted as an ASCII character. So even though a text file consists of a long sequence of 0's and 1's, we know how to find the boundaries between each character. That is why any text editor can read a text file, no matter what program created it.

On the other hand, binary files are also just a long sequence of 0's and 1's, but we can't tell where one data element begins and another one ends. For example, the 64-bit sequence

```
0101001100110010010101001100110011000
0101001100110010110101001100110011000
```

could represent two 32-bit `int`s or two 32-bit `float`s or one 64-bit `double` or four 16-bit `char`s or a single `String` of eight ASCII characters. We can't tell what data we have unless we know exactly how the data were written.

DEBUGGING TIP: Interpreting Binary Data.   The fact that you can read the data in a binary file is no guarantee that you are interpreting it correctly. To interpret it correctly, you must read it the same way it was written.

EFFECTIVE DESIGN: Data Abstraction.   A string of binary data is "raw" and has no inherent structure. The programs that read and write the string provide it with structure. A string of 64 0's and 1's can be interpreted as two `int`s or one `long` or even as some kind of object, so an `int`, `long` or an object is an abstraction imposed upon the data by the program.

11.6   Object Serialization: Reading and Writing Objects

The examples in the preceding sections showed how to perform I/O operations on simple binary data or text. The `java.io` package also provides methods for reading and writing objects, a process known as **object serialization**. Objects can be converted into a sequence of bytes, or *serialized*, by using the `ObjectOutputStream` class, and they can be *deserialized*, or converted from bytes into a structured object, by using the `ObjectInputStream` class (Fig. 11.26). Despite the complexity of the serialization/deserialization processes, the methods in these classes make the task just as easy as reading and writing primitive data.

To illustrate object serialization, let's begin by defining a `Student` class (Fig. 11.27). In order to serialize an object, it must be a member of a class that implements the `Serializable` interface. The `Serializable` interface is a *marker interface*, an interface that does not define any methods or constants but just serves to designate whether an object can be serialized.

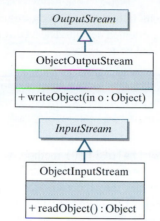

Figure 11.26 Classes used for performing I/O on objects.

```java
import java.io.*;

public class Student implements Serializable {
  private String name;
  private int year;
  private double gpa;

  public Student() {}

  public Student (String nameIn, int yr, double gpaIn) {
    name = nameIn;
    year = yr;
    gpa = gpaIn;
  }

  public void writeToFile(FileOutputStream outStream) throws IOException{
    ObjectOutputStream ooStream = new ObjectOutputStream(outStream);
    ooStream.writeObject(this);
    ooStream.flush();
  } // writeToFile()

  public void readFromFile(FileInputStream inStream)
          throws IOException, ClassNotFoundException {
    ObjectInputStream oiStream = new ObjectInputStream(inStream);
    Student s = (Student)oiStream.readObject();
    this.name = s.name;
    this.year = s.year;
    this.gpa = s.gpa;
  } // readFromFile()

  public String toString() {
    return name + "\t" + year + "\t" + gpa;
  }
} // Student class
```

Figure 11.27 The *serializable* Student class.

The Student class contains its own I/O methods, readFromFile() and writeToFile(). This is an appropriate object-oriented design. The Student class encapsulates all the relevant information needed to read and write its data.

> **EFFECTIVE DESIGN: I/O Design.**   If an object is going to be input and output to and from files, it should define its own I/O methods. An object contains all the relevant information needed to perform I/O correctly.

Object serialization

Note the definition of the writeToFile() method, which performs the output task. This method's FileOutputStream parameter is used to create an ObjectOutputStream, whose writeObject() method writes the object into the file. To output a Student object, we merely invoke the writeObject() method. This method writes out the current values of all the object's public and private fields. In this case, the method would write a String for the object's name, an int for the object's year, and a double for the object's gpa.

Although our example doesn't require it, the writeObject() method can also handle fields that refer to other objects. For example, suppose our Student object provided a field for courses that contained a reference to an array of objects, each of which described a course the student has taken. In that case, the writeObject() method would serialize the array and all its objects (assuming they are serializable). Thus, when a complex object is serialized, the result will be a complex structure that contains all the data linked to the root object.

Object deserialization

Object deserialization, as shown in the readFromFile() method, is simply the reverse of the serialization process. The readObject() method reads one serialized object from the ObjectInputStream. Its result type is Object, so it is necessary to cast the result into the proper type. In our example we use a local Student variable to store the object as it is input. We then copy each field of the local object to this object.

Note that the readFromFile() method throws both the IOException and ClassNotFoundException. An IOException will be generated if the file you are attempting to read does not contain serialized objects of the correct type. Objects that can be input by readObject() are those that were output by writeObject(). Thus, just as in the case of binary I/O, it is best to design an object's input and output routines together so that they are compatible. The ClassNotFoundException will be thrown if the Student class cannot be found. This is needed to determine how to deserialize the object.

> **JAVA PROGRAMMING TIP: Object Serialization.**   Java's serialization classes, ObjectOutputStream and ObjectInputStream, should be used whenever an object needs to be input or output from a stream.

11.6.1   The ObjectIO Class

Given the Student class, let's now write a user interface that can read and write Student objects. We can use the same interface we used in the BinaryIO program. The only things we need to change are the writeRecords() and readRecords() methods. Everything else about this program will be exactly the same as in BinaryIO.

Figure 11.28 provides the full implementation of the ObjectIO class. Note that the writeRecords() method will still write five random records to the data file. The difference in this case is that we will call the writeToFile() method in the Student class to take care of

```java
import javax.swing.*;                                    // Swing components
import java.awt.*;
import java.io.*;
import java.awt.event.*;
public class ObjectIO extends JFrame implements ActionListener{
  private JTextArea display = new JTextArea();
  private JButton read = new JButton("Read From File"),
                  write = new JButton("Write to File");
  private JTextField nameField = new JTextField(10);
  private JLabel prompt = new JLabel("Filename:",JLabel.RIGHT);
  private JPanel commands = new JPanel();

  public ObjectIO () {
    super("ObjectIO Demo");                             // Set window title
    read.addActionListener(this);
    write.addActionListener(this);
    commands.setLayout(new GridLayout(2,2,1,1));
    commands.add(prompt);                               // Control panel
    commands.add(nameField);
    commands.add(read);
    commands.add(write);
    display.setLineWrap(true);
    this.getContentPane().setLayout(new BorderLayout () );
    this.getContentPane().add("North",commands);
    this.getContentPane().add( new JScrollPane(display));
    this.getContentPane().add("Center", display);
  } // ObjectIO()

  public void actionPerformed(ActionEvent evt) {
    String fileName = nameField.getText();
    if (evt.getSource() == read)
        readRecords(fileName);
    else
        writeRecords(fileName);
  } // actionPerformed()

  private void readRecords(String fileName) {
    try {
      FileInputStream inStream = new FileInputStream(fileName); // Open a stream
      display.setText("Name\tYear\tGPA\n");
      try {
        while (true) {                                  // Infinite loop
          Student student = new Student();              // Create a student instance
          student.readFromFile(inStream);              // and have it read an object
          display.append(student.toString() +  "\n"); //  and display it
        }
      } catch (IOException e) {      // Until IOException
      }
      inStream.close();                                 // Close the stream
    } catch (FileNotFoundException e) {
        display.append("IOERROR: File NOT Found: " + fileName + "\n");
    } catch (IOException e) {
        display.append("IOERROR: " + e.getMessage() + "\n");
    } catch (ClassNotFoundException e) {
        display.append("ERROR: Class NOT found " + e.getMessage() + "\n");
    }
  } // readRecords()
```

Figure 11.28 The ObjectIO class provides an interface to read and write files of Students.
(*Continued on next page*)

```
private void writeRecords(String fileName) {
  try {
    FileOutputStream outStream = new FileOutputStream( fileName );// Open stream
    for (int k = 0; k < 5 ; k++) {                    // Generate 5 random objects
      String name = "name" + k;                       // Name
      int year = (int)(2000 + Math.random() * 4);     // Class year
      double gpa = Math.random() * 12;                // GPA
      Student student = new Student(name, year, gpa); // Create the object
      display.append("Output: "+ student.toString() +"\n"); // and display it
      student.writeToFile(outStream) ;                // and tell it to write data
    } // for
    outStream.close();
  } catch (IOException e) {
    display.append("IOERROR: " + e.getMessage() + "\n");
  }
} // writeRecords()
public static void main(String args[]) {
  ObjectIO io = new ObjectIO();
  io.setSize( 400,200);
  io.setVisible(true);
  io.addWindowListener(new WindowAdapter() {
    public void windowClosing(WindowEvent e) {
      System.exit(0);                                 // Quit the application
    }
  });
} // main()
} // ObjectIO class
```

Figure 11.28   The `ObjectIO` class provides an interface to read and write files of Students.
(*Continued from previous page*)

the actual output operations. The revised algorithm will create a new `Student` object, using randomly generated data for its name, year, and GPA and then invoke its `writeToFile()` to output its data. Note how a `FileOutputStream` is created and passed to the `writeToFile()` method in the `Student` class.

The `readRecords()` method (Fig. 11.28) will read data from a file containing serialized `Student` objects. To do so, it first creates a `Student` object and then invokes its `read-FromFile()` method, passing it a `FileInputStream`. Note how the `FileInputStream` is created and, unlike in `BinaryIO`, the inner `try` block is exited by an `IOException` rather than an `EOFException`.

SELF-STUDY EXERCISE

EXERCISE 11.6   Given the following definition, would a binary file consisting of several `SomeObject`s be readable by either the `BinaryIO` or `ObjectIO` program? Explain.

```
public class SomeObject {
    private String str;
    private short n1;
    private short n2;
    private long  n3;
}
```

11.7   From the Java Library: `javax.swing.JFileChooser`

The `javax.swing.JFileChooser` class is useful for dealing with files and directories in a GUI environment. You are probably already familiar with `JFileChooser`s, although you may not have known them by that name. A `JFileChooser` provides a dialog box that enables the user to select a file and a directory when opening or saving a file. Figure 11.30 shows an example.

A `JFileChooser` is designed primarily to be used in conjunction with menu-based programs. The `JFileChooser` class (Fig. 11.29) contains methods that support the *Open File* and *Save As* options which often appear in GUI applications either in a menu or attached to buttons. In this section we provide the basics for using a `JFileChooser`. Options for opening a file or saving a file can be added to the kind of GUI applications that we encountered earlier in the text by using buttons. In Chapter 13, we will discuss the use of `JMenus`, which will provide a more natural means of using the `JFileChooser` dialogs.

A `JFileChooser` is not itself the dialog window, but rather the object that manages the dialog. After a `JFileChooser` instance is created, its **showOpenDialog()** or **showSave-Dialog()** methods are used to open a dialog window. Note that these methods require a `Component` parameter, usually a `JFrame` or a `JApplet`. Thus, `JFileChooser`s can be used only in GUI applications and applets.

To illustrate how to use a `JFileChooser`, let's consider the case where the user has selected an *Open File* menu item or clicked a button labeled *Open File*. In this case, executing the following code will cause an "Open File" dialog to appear:

```java
JFileChooser chooser = new JFileChooser();
int result = chooser.showOpenDialog(this);

if (result == JFileChooser.APPROVE_OPTION) {
    File file = chooser.getSelectedFile();
    // Insert code here to read data from file
    String fileName = file.getName();
    display.setText("You selected " + fileName);
} else
    display.setText("You cancelled the file dialog");
```

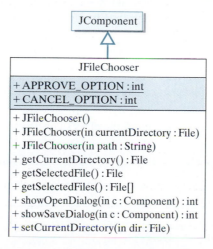

Figure 11.29 The `javax.swing.JFileChooser` class.

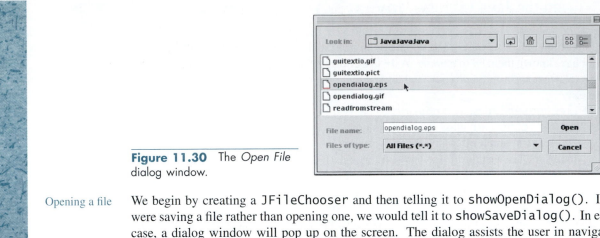

Figure 11.30 The *Open File* dialog window.

Opening a file

We begin by creating a `JFileChooser` and then telling it to `showOpenDialog()`. If we were saving a file rather than opening one, we would tell it to `showSaveDialog()`. In either case, a dialog window will pop up on the screen. The dialog assists the user in navigating through the file system and selecting a file (Fig. 11.30).

The dialog contains two buttons, one labeled Open and the other labeled Cancel. If the user selects a file, that choice will correspond to `APPROVE_OPTION`. If the user cancels the dialog, that will correspond to `CANCEL_OPTION`. After opening a dialog, the code should check which option resulted. In this case, if the user opened a file, the code gets a reference to the file and then simply uses it to print the file's path name to a text area named `display`. In an actual application, code would be inserted at the spot that uses the file reference to read data from the file.

11.8 Using File Data in Programs

This chapter's examples have provided explicit details for several ways of writing data to files and reading data from files. In actual programs, deciding if and how files might be useful in the program are worked out as part of the design process. Choosing between text files, binary files, and reading and writing objects is part of this process.

To illustrate how we can apply what we have learned about file I/O, let's modify the `WordGuess` class (listed in Fig. 8.27) so that it reads a list of possible words for players to guess from a file. The Chapter 8 version of the class contains a method, `getSecret-Word()`, which uses a `switch` statement to randomly choose and return a word from a fixed list of 10 words. Reading the words from a text file would allow a user to modify the list of possible words by adding or changing words without needing to recompile the program.

Modifying WordGuess

We will modify the `WordGuess` class in three ways:

1. Add two new instance variables, an array of type `String` and a variable to store the size of the array;

2. Add code at the beginning of the class's constructor to read words from the file and store them in the array;

3. Rewrite the `getSecretWord()` method so that it randomly chooses a word from the array.

New instance variables

Let us first choose descriptive names for declaring the two new instance variables:

```
private String[] wordArray;
private int arraySize;
```

It will be useful to store the number of words in the file in its first line so that this information can be used to allocate memory for the array. For example, assume that the text file will be named `secretwords.txt`, will be located in the same directory as the `WordGuess` class, will have the same number of words in the file as its first line, and will have a single word per line after that. Thus, a small file might look like:

Format for the text file

```
3
STREAMS
CONDUIT
DIALOGS
```

We can use the body of the `readTextFile()` method of the `TextIO` class as a model for the Java code that needs to be added to the `WordGuess` constructor. Pseudocode for this code will look like:

Code to add to constructor

```
Use file name to open a  BufferedReader stream
Read first line and convert to an integer
Store the integer as the size of the array
Allocate memory for the array
Read second line of file
While a word is read
   Store the word in the next array element
   Read next line of file
Close the BufferedReader stream
```

When this pseudocode is translated into Java and inserted into a `try-catch` statement, we get the code fragment in Figure 11.31.

```java
try{
    FileReader fr = new FileReader("secretwords.txt");
    BufferedReader inStream = new BufferedReader(fr);
    String line = inStream.readLine();
    arraySize = Integer.parseInt(line);
    wordArray = new String[arraySize];
    line = inStream.readLine();
    int k = 0;
    while((line != null) && (k < arraySize)){
        wordArray[k] = line;
        line = inStream.readLine();
        k++;
    } // while
    inStream.close();
} catch(FileNotFoundException e){
    e.printStackTrace();
} catch(IOException e){
    e.printStackTrace();
} // catch
```

Figure 11.31 Code added at beginning of the `WordGuess` constructor.

New code for
getSecretWord

The new `getSecretWord()` method merely needs to generate a random array index and return the corresponding array element:

```java
private String getSecretWord(){
    int num = (int)(Math.random()*arraySize);
    return wordArray[num];
} // getSecretWord()
```

Databases and Personal Privacy

During a typical day we all come in contact with lots of electronic databases that store information about us. If you use a supermarket discount card, every purchase you make is logged against your name in the supermarket's database. When you use your bank card at the ATM machine, your financial transaction is logged against your account. When you charge gasoline or buy dinner, those transactions are logged against your credit card account. If you visit the doctor or dentist, a detailed record of your visit is transmitted to your medical insurance company's database. If you receive a college loan, detailed financial information about you is entered into several different credit service bureaus. And so on.

Should we be worried about how this information is used? Many privacy advocates say yes. With the computerization of medical records, phone records, financial transactions, driving records, and many other records, there is an enormous amount of personal information held in databases. At the same time, there are pressures from many sources for access to this information. Law-enforcement agencies want to use this information to monitor individuals. Corporations want to use it to help them market their products. Political organizations want to use it to help them market their candidates.

Recently there has been pressure from government and industry in the United States to use the social security number (SSN) as a unique identifier. Such an identifier would make it easy to match personal information across different databases. Right now, the only thing your bank records, medical records, and supermarket records may have in common is your name, which is not a unique identifier. If all online databases were based on your SSN, it would be much simpler to create a complete profile. While this might improve services and reduce fraud and crime, it might also pose a significant threat to our privacy.

Online databases serve many useful purposes. They help fight crime and reduce the cost of doing business. They help improve government and commercial services on which we have come to depend. On the other hand, databases can be and have been misused. They can be used by unauthorized individuals or agencies or in unauthorized ways. When they contain inaccurate information, they can cause personal inconvenience or even harm.

A number of organizations have sprung up to address the privacy issues raised by online databases. If you're interested in learning more about this issue, a good place to start would be the Web site maintained by the Electronic Privacy Information Center (EPIC) at

http://www.epic.org/

The only other modification needed to complete the new `WordGuess` class is to add an initial `import java.io.*;` statement so that the file IO classes can be accessed.

The earlier examples in this chapter can be used as models to enhance numerous practical applications. GUI applications that involve a user's choice to load data from a file or save data in a file should make use of the `JFileChooser` dialogs to initiate the file operations.

CHAPTER SUMMARY

Technical Terms

absolute path name	filtering
binary file	input
buffering	object serialization
database	output
data hierarchy	path
directory	record
end-of-file character	relative path name
field	Unicode Text Format (UTF)
file	

Summary of Important Points

- A *file* is a collection of data stored on a disk. A *stream* is an object that delivers data to and from other objects.

- An `InputStream` is a stream that delivers data to a program from an external source, such as the keyboard or a file. `System.in` is an example of an `InputStream`. An `OutputStream` is a stream that delivers data from a program to an external destination, such as the screen or a file. `System.out` is an example of an `OutputStream`.

- Data can be viewed as a hierarchy. From highest to lowest, a *database* is a collection of files. A *file* is a collection of records. A *record* is a collection of fields. A *field* is a collection of bytes. A *byte* is a collection of eight bits. A *bit* is one binary digit, either 0 or 1.

- A *binary file* is a sequence of 0s and 1s that is interpreted as a sequence of bytes. A *text file* is a sequence of 0s and 1s that is interpreted as a sequence of characters. A text file can be read by any text editor, but a binary file cannot. `InputStream` and `OutputStream` are abstract classes that serve as the root classes for reading and writing binary data. `Reader` and `Writer` serve as root classes for text I/O.

- *Buffering* is a technique in which a *buffer*, a temporary region of memory, is used to store data during input or output.

- A text file contains a sequence of characters divided into lines by the \n character and ending with a special *end-of-file* character.

- The standard algorithm for performing I/O on a file consists of three steps: (1) open a stream to the file, (2) perform the I/O, and (3) close the stream.

- Designing effective I/O routines answers two questions: (1) What streams should I use to perform the I/O? (2) What methods should I use to do the reading or writing?

- To prevent damage to files when a program terminates abnormally, streams should be closed when they are no longer needed.

- Most I/O operations generate an IOException that should be caught in the I/O methods.

- Text input uses a different technique to determine when the end of a file has been reached. Text input methods return null or −1 when they attempt to read the special end-of-file character. Binary files do not contain an end-of-file character, so binary read methods throw an EOFException when they attempt to read past the end of the file.

- The java.io.File class provides methods that enable a program to interact with a file system. Its methods can be used to check a file's attributes, including its name, directory, and path.

- Streams can be joined together to perform I/O. For example, a DataOutputStream and a FileOutputStream can be joined to perform output to a binary file.

- A binary file is "raw" in the sense that there are no markers within it that allow you to tell where one data element ends and another begins. The interpretation of binary data is up to the program that reads or writes the file.

- Object serialization is the process of writing an object to an output stream. Object deserialization is the reverse process of reading a serialized object from an input stream. These processes use the java.io.ObjectOutputStream and java.io.ObjectInputStream classes.

- The JFileChooser class provides a dialog box that enables the user to select a file and directory when opening or saving a file.

SOLUTIONS TO SELF-STUDY EXERCISES

SOLUTION 11.1   FileWriter contains a constructor that takes a file name argument, File-Writer(String), so it can be used with PrintWriter to perform output to a text file:

```
PrintWriter outStream =                             //  Create output stream
    new PrintWriter(new FileWriter(fileName));  // Open file
outStream.print (display.getText());                // Display text
outStream.close();                                  // Close output stream
```

SOLUTION 11.2   An empty file doesn't affect this loop. If the file is empty, it will print a null line. The test line != null, should come right after the readLine(), as it does in the while loop.

SOLUTION 11.3   This loop won't work on an empty text file. In that case, ch would be set to −1, and the attempt to cast it into a char would cause an error.

SOLUTION 11.4

```
public void getFileAttributes(String fileName) {
    File file = new File (fileName);
    System.out.println(filename);
    System.out.println("absolute path:" + file.getAbsolutePath());
    System.out.println("length:" + file.length());
    if (file.isDirectory())
        System.out.println("Directory");
    else
        System.out.println("Not a Directory");
} // getFileAttributes()
```

SOLUTION 11.5   The `inStream.close()` statement is misplaced in `readIntegers()`. By placing it inside the same `try/catch` block as the read loop, it will get skipped and the stream will not be closed. The `EOFException` should be caught in a separate `try/catch` block from other exceptions, and it should just cause the read loop to exit.

SOLUTION 11.6   Yes, a binary file containing several `SomeObjects` would be "readable" by the `BinaryIO` program because the program will read a `String` followed by 64 bytes. However, `BinaryIO` would misinterpret the data, because it will assume that `n1` and `n2` together comprise a single `int`, and `n3` (64 bits) will be interpreted as a `double`. A file of `SomeObjects` could not be read by the `ObjectIO` program, because `SomeObject` does not implement the `Serializable` interface.

EXERCISES

EXERCISE 11.1   Explain the difference between each of the following pairs of terms:

a. `System.in` and `System.out`.
b. *File* and *directory*.
c. *Buffering* and *filtering*.
d. *Absolute* and *relative path name*.
e. *Input stream* and *output stream*.

f. *File* and *database*.
g. *Record* and *field*.
h. *Binary file* and *text file*.
i. *Directory* and *database*.

Note: For programming exercises, **first** draw a UML class diagram describing all classes and their inheritance relationships and/or associations.

EXERCISE 11.2   Fill in the blanks.

a. Unlike text files, binary files do not have a special _____ character.
b. In Java, the `String` array parameter in the `main()` method is used for _____.
c. _____ files are portable and platform independent.
d. A _____ file created on one computer can't be read by another computer.

EXERCISE 11.3   Arrange the following kinds of data into their correct hierarchical relationships: `bit`, `field`, `byte`, `record`, `database`, `file`, `String`, `char`.

EXERCISE 11.4   In what different ways can the following string of 32 bits be interpreted?

```
00010101111000110100000110011110
```

EXERCISE 11.5 When reading a binary file, why is it necessary to use an infinite loop that is exited only when an exception occurs?

EXERCISE 11.6 Is it possible to have a text file with 10 characters and 0 lines? Explain.

EXERCISE 11.7 In reading a file, why is it necessary to attempt to read from the file before entering the read loop?

EXERCISE 11.8 When designing binary I/O, why is it especially important to design the input and output routines together?

EXERCISE 11.9 What is the difference between ASCII code and UTF code?

EXERCISE 11.10 Could the following string of bits possibly be a Java object? Explain.

```
000101110001111010101010100001110010000100
110100100101010100101010010000010000000111
```

EXERCISE 11.11 Write a method that could be added to the `TextIO` program to read a text file and print all lines containing a certain word. This should be a `void` method that takes two parameters: the name of the file and the word to search for. Lines not containing the word should not be printed.

EXERCISE 11.12 Write a program that reads a text file and reports the number of characters and lines contained in the file.

EXERCISE 11.13 Modify the program in the preceding exercise so that it also counts the number of words in the file. (*Hint*: The `StringTokenizer` class might be useful for this task.)

EXERCISE 11.14 Modify the `ObjectIO` program so that it allows the user to designate a file and then input `Student` data with the help of a GUI. As the user inputs data, each record should be written to the file.

EXERCISE 11.15 Write a program that will read a file of `ints` into memory, sort them in ascending order, and output the sorted data to a second file.

EXERCISE 11.16 Write a program that will read two files of `ints`, which are already sorted into ascending order, and merge their data. For example, if one file contains 1, 3, 5, 7, 9, and the other contains 2, 4, 6, 8, 10, then the merged file should contain 1, 2, 3, 4, 5, 6, 7, 8, 9, 10.

EXERCISE 11.17 Suppose you have a file of data for a geological survey. Each record consists of a longitude, a latitude, and an amount of rainfall, all represented by `doubles`. Write a method to read this file's data and print them on the screen, one record per line. The method should be `void` and should take the name of the file as its only parameter.

EXERCISE 11.18 Suppose you have the same data as in the preceding exercise. Write a method that will generate 1,000 records of random data and write them to a file. The method should be `void` and should take the file's name as its parameter. Assume that longitudes have values in the range $+/-$ 0 to 180 degrees, latitudes have values in the range $+/-$ 0 to 90 degrees, and rainfalls have values in the range 0 to 20 inches.

EXERCISE 11.19 Design and write a file copy program that will work for either text files or binary files. The program should prompt the user for the names of each file and copy the data from the source file into the destination file. It should not overwrite an existing file, however. (*Hint*: Read and write the file as a file of `byte`.)

EXERCISE 11.20   Design a class, similar to `Student`, to represent an `Address`. It should consist of street, city, state, and zip code and should contain its own `readFromFile()` and `writeToFile()` methods.

EXERCISE 11.21   Using the class designed in the preceding exercise, modify the `Student` class so that it contains an `Address` field. Modify the `ObjectIO` program to accommodate the new definition of `Student` and test your program.

EXERCISE 11.22   Write a program called `Directory`, which provides a listing of any directory contained in the current directory. This program should prompt the user for the name of the directory. It should then print a listing of the directory. The listing should contain the following information: the full path name of the directory, and the file name, length, last-modified date, and a read/write code for each file. The read/write code should be an *r* if the file is readable and a *w* if the file is writeable, in that order. Use a "-" to indicate not readable or not writeable. For example, a file that is readable but not writeable will have the code *r-*. Here is an example listing:

```
Listing for directory: myfiles
  name            length modified    code
  index.html      548    129098      rw
  index.gif       78     129190      rw
  me.html         682    128001      r-
  private.txt     1001   129000      --
```

Note that the `File.lastModified()` returns a `long`, which gives the modification time of the file. This number cannot easily be converted into a date, so just report its value.

EXERCISE 11.23   **Challenge:** Modify the `OneRowNimGUI` class listed in Figure 4.25 so that the user can save the position of the game to a file or open and read a game position from a file. Add two new `JButton`s to the GUI interface. Use the object serialization example as a model for your input and output streams.

EXERCISE 11.24   **Challenge:** In Unix systems, there is a program named `grep` that can list the lines in a text file containing a certain string. Write a Java version of this program that prompts the user for the name of the file and the string to search for.

EXERCISE 11.25   **Challenge:** Write a program in Java named `Copy` to copy one file into another. The program will prompt the user for two file names, `filename1` and `filename2`. Both `filename1` and `filename2` must exist or the program should throw a `FileNotFoundException`. Although `filename1` must be the name of a file (not a directory), `filename2` may be either a file or a directory. If `filename2` is a file, then the program should copy `filename1` to `filename2`. If `filename2` is a directory, then the program should simply copy `filename1` into `filename2`. That is, it should create a new file with the name `filename1` inside the `filename2` directory, copy the old file to the new file, and then delete the old file.

Photograph courtesy of Glen Allison, Creative Eye/MIRA.com.

12

Recursive Problem Solving

OBJECTIVES

After studying this chapter, you will

- Understand the concept of recursion.
- Know how to use recursive programming techniques.
- Have a better understanding of recursion as a problem-solving technique.

OUTLINE

12.1   Introduction

The pattern in Figure 12.1 is known as the Sierpinski gasket. Its overall shape is that of an equilateral triangle. But notice how inside the outer triangle there are three smaller triangles that are similar to the overall pattern. And inside each of those are three even smaller triangles, and so on. The Sierpinski gasket is known as a *fractal* because when you divide it up, you end up with a smaller version of the overall pattern. The overall gasket pattern is repeated over and over, at smaller and smaller scales, throughout the figure.

How would you draw this pattern? If you try to use some kind of nested loop structure, you'll find that it is very challenging. It can be done using loops, but not easily. On the other hand, if you use the approach known as *recursion*, this problem is much easier to solve. It's a little bit like the representation issue we discussed in Chapter 5. Your ability to solve a problem often depends on how you represent the problem. Recursion gives you another way to approach problems that involve repetition, such as the problem of drawing the Sierpinski gasket.

The main goal of this chapter is to introduce recursion as both a problem-solving technique and an alternative to loops (which we discussed in Chapter 6) for implementing repetition. We begin with the notion of a *recursive definition*, a concept used widely in mathematics and computer science. We then introduce the idea of a *recursive method*, which is the way recursion is implemented in a program.

Recursion is a topic taken up in considerable detail in upper-level computer science courses, so our goal here is mainly to introduce the concept and give you some idea of its power as a problem-solving approach. To illustrate recursion, we use a number of simple examples throughout the chapter. One risk in using simple examples, though, is that you might be tempted to think that recursion is only good for "toy problems." Nothing could be further from the truth. Recursion is often used for some of the most difficult algorithms. Some of the exercises at the end of the chapter are examples of more challenging problems.

12.1.1   Recursion as Repetition

A **recursive method** is a method that calls itself. An **iterative method** is a method that uses a loop to repeat an action. In one sense, *recursion* is an alternative to the iterative (looping) control structures we studied in Chapter 6. In this sense, recursion is just another way to repeat an action.

Iterative method   For example, consider the following iterative method for saying "Hello" N times:

```java
public void hello(int N)   {
    for (int k = 0; k < N; k++)
        System.out.println("Hello");
} // hello()
```

Figure 12.1   The Sierpinski gasket.

A recursive version of this method would be defined as follows: Recursive method

```java
public void hello(int N)  {
    if (N > 0) {
        System.out.println("Hello");
        hello(N - 1);                    // Recursive call
    }
} // hello()
```

This method is recursive because it calls itself when *N* is greater than 0. However, note that when it calls itself, it passes *N* − 1 as the value for its parameter. If this method is initially called with *N* equal to 5, the following is a trace of what happens. The indentations indicate each time the method calls itself:

```
hello(5)
    Print "Hello"
    hello(4)
        Print "Hello"
        hello(3)
            Print "Hello"
            hello(2)
                Print "Hello"
                hello(1)
                    Print "Hello"
                    hello(0)
```

Thus, "Hello" will be printed five times, just as it would be in the iterative version of this method.

So in one sense, recursion is just an alternative to iteration. In fact, there are some programming languages, such as the original versions of LISP and PROLOG, that do not have loop structures. In these languages, *all* repetition is done by recursion. In contrast, if a language contains loop structures, it can do without recursion. Anything that can be done iteratively can be done recursively, and vice versa.

Moreover, it is much less efficient to call a method five times than to repeat a `for` loop five times. Method calls take up more memory than loops and involve more **computational over-head** for such tasks as passing parameters, allocating storage for the method's local variables,   Computational and returning the method's results. Therefore, because of its reliance on repeated method calls,   overhead recursion is often less efficient than iteration as a way to code a particular algorithm.

EFFECTIVE DESIGN: Efficiency.   Iterative algorithms and methods are generally more efficient than recursive algorithms that do the same thing.

SELF-STUDY EXERCISES

EXERCISE 12.1 What would be printed if we call the following method with the expression mystery(0)?

```java
public void mystery(int N) {
    System.out.print(N + " ");
    if (N <= 5)
        mystery(N + 1);
} // mystery()
```

What about mystery(100)?

EXERCISE 12.2 What would be printed if we call the following method with the expression mystery(5)?

```java
public void mystery(int N) {
    System.out.print(N + " ");
    if (N <= 5)
        mystery(N - 1);
} // mystery()
```

12.1.2   Recursion as a Problem-Solving Approach

Given that recursion is not really necessary if a programming language has loops, and is not more efficient than loops, why is it so important? The answer is that in a broader sense, recursion is an effective approach to problem solving. It is a way of viewing a problem. It is mostly in this sense that we want to study recursion.

Recursion is based on two key problem-solving concepts: *divide and conquer* and **self-similarity**. In recursive problem solving we use the divide-and-conquer strategy repeatedly to break a big problem into a sequence of smaller and smaller problems until we arrive at a problem that is practically trivial to solve.

Subproblems

What allows us to create this series of subproblems is that each subproblem is similar to the original problem—that is, each subproblem is just a smaller version of the original problem. Look again at the task of saying "Hello" N times. Solving this task involves solving the similar task of saying "Hello" $N - 1$ times, which can be divided into the similar task of saying "Hello" $N - 2$ times. And so on.

Self-similarity

The ability to see a problem as composed of smaller, self-similar problems is at the heart of the recursive approach. And, although you may not have thought about this before, a surprising number of programming problems have this self-similarity characteristic. We will illustrate these ideas with some simple examples.

JAVA PROGRAMMING TIP: Divide and Conquer. Many programming problems can be solved by dividing them into smaller, simpler problems. For recursive solutions, finding the key to the subproblem often holds the solution to the original problem.

12.2   Recursive Definition

One place you may have already seen recursion is in mathematics. A **recursive definition** consists of two parts: a recursive part in which the nth value is defined in terms of the $(n-1)$st value, and a nonrecursive, *boundary*, or **base case**, which defines a limiting condition.

12.2.1   Factorial: $N!$

For example, consider the problem of calculating the factorial of n—that is, $n!$ for $n \geq 0$. As you may recall, $n!$ is calculated as follows:

```
n! = n * (n-1) * (n-2) * ... * 1, for n > 0
```

In addition, 0! is defined as 1. Let's now look at some examples for different values of n:

```
4! = 4 * 3 * 2 * 1 = 24
3! = 3 * 2 * 1 = 6
2! = 2 * 1 = 2
1! = 1
0! = 1
```

As these examples suggest, $n!$ can always be calculated in terms of $(n-1)!$ This relationship might be clearer if we rewrite the previous calculations as follows:

```
4! = 4 * 3 * 2 * 1 = 4 * 3! = 24
3! = 3 * 2 * 1      = 3 * 2! = 6
2! = 2 * 1          = 2 * 1! = 2
1!                  = 1 * 0! = 1
0!                  = 1
```

The only case in which we can't calculate $n!$ in terms of $(n-1)!$ is when n is 0. Otherwise, in each case we see that

```
n! = n * (n-1)!
```

This leads to the following recursive definition:

```
n! = 1            if n = 0     // Boundary (or base) case
n! = n * (n-1)!  if n > 0     // Recursive case
```

Note that if we had omitted the base case, the recursion would have continued to $(-1)!$ and $(-2)!$ and so on.

DEBUGGING TIP: Bounding the Repetition.   An infinite repetition will result if a recursive definition is not properly bounded.

The recursive case uses divide and conquer to break the problem into a smaller problem, but the smaller problem is just a smaller version of the original problem. This combination of self-similarity and divide and conquer is what characterizes recursion. The base case is used to stop or limit the recursion.

EFFECTIVE DESIGN: Recursive Definition. For recursive algorithms and definitions, the base case serves as the bound for the algorithm. The **recursive case** defines the nth case in terms of the $(n - 1)$st case.

12.2.2   Drawing a Nested Pattern

As another example, consider the problem of drawing the nested boxes pattern in Figure 12.2. The self-similarity occurs in the fact that for this pattern, the parts resemble the whole. The basic shape involved is a square, which is repeated over and over at an ever-smaller scale. A recursive definition for this pattern would be

```
Base case:      if side < 5 do nothing
Recursive case: if side >= 5
                    draw a square
                    decrease the side and draw a smaller
                              pattern inside the square
```

This definition uses the length of the square's side to help define the pattern. If the length of the side is greater than or equal to 5, draw a square with dimensions $side \times side$. Then decrease the length of the side and draw a smaller version of the pattern inside that square. In this case, the *side* variable will decrease at each level of the drawing. When the length of the side becomes less than 5, the recursion stops. Thus, the length of the side serves as the limit or bound for this algorithm.

Note that the length of the side functions here like a parameter in a method definition: it provides essential information for the definition, just as a method parameter provides essential data to the method. Indeed, this is exactly the role that parameters play in recursive methods. They provide essential information that determines the method's behavior.

Figure 12.3 illustrates how we would apply the definition. Suppose the side starts out at 20 and decreases by 5 at each level of recursion. As you move from top to bottom across the four patterns, each pattern contains the one below it. A nestedBoxes(20) can be drawn by first drawing a 20 × 20 square and then drawing a nestedBoxes(15) pattern inside it. Similarly, a nestedBoxes(15) can be drawn by first drawing a 15 × 15 square and then drawing a nestedBoxes(10) pattern inside it. And so on.

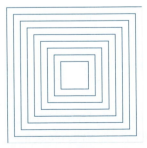

Figure 12.2 The nested squares pattern.

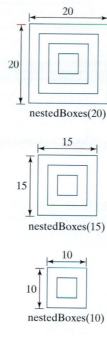

Figure 12.3 A trace of the nested boxes definition starting with a side of 20 and decreasing the side by 5 each time.

These examples illustrate the power of recursion as a problem-solving technique for situations that involve repetition. Like the iterative (looping) control structures we studied in Chapter 6, recursion is used to implement repetition within a bound. For recursive algorithms, the bound is defined by the base case, whereas for loops, the bound is defined by the loop's entry condition. In either case, repetition stops when the bound is reached.

SELF-STUDY EXERCISES

EXERCISE 12.3   You can calculate 2^n by multiplying 2 by itself n times. For example, 2^3 is $2 \times 2 \times 2$. Note also that $2^0 = 1$. Given these facts, write a recursive definition for 2^n, for $n \geq 0$.

EXERCISE 12.4   Generalize your solution to the preceding exercise by giving a recursive definition for x^n, where x and n are both integers ≥ 0.

EXERCISE 12.5   Is the recursive definition given earlier for the nested boxes equivalent to the following recursive definition? Explain.

```
Draw a square.        // In every case
If side > 5
    draw a smaller nested boxes inside the square
```

In this case, the base case ($side <= 5$) is implicit.

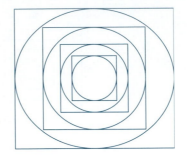

Figure 12.4   Write a recursive
definition for this pattern.

EXERCISE 12.6   Write a recursive definition for the recursive pattern shown in Figure 12.4.

DEBUGGING TIP: Infinite Recursion.   An unbounded or incorrectly bounded recursive
algorithm will lead to infinite repetition. Care must be taken to get the boundary condition
correct.

12.3   Recursive String Methods

Remember that a *recursive method* is a method that calls itself. Like recursive definitions,
recursive methods are designed around the divide-and-conquer and self-similarity principles.
Defining a recursive method involves a similar analysis to the one we used in designing recursive
definitions. We identify a self-similar subproblem of the original problem plus one or more
limiting cases.

The idea of a method calling itself seems a bit strange at first. It's perhaps best understood
in terms of a clone or a copy. When a method calls itself, it really calls a copy of itself, one that
has a slightly different internal state. Usually the difference in state is the result of a difference
How can a in the invoked method's parameters.
method call itself?

12.3.1   Printing a String

To illustrate the concept of a recursive method, let's define a recursive method for printing a
string. This is not intended to be a practical method—we already have the `println()` method
for printing strings. But pretend for a moment that you only have a version of `println()`
that works for characters, and your task is to write a version that can be used to print an entire
string of characters.

A little terminology will help us describe the algorithm. Let's call the first letter of a string
the *head* of the string, and let's refer to all the remaining letters in the string as the *tail* of the
string. Then the problem of printing a string can be solved using a **head-and-tail algorithm**,
Head-and-tail which consists of two parts: printing the head of the string and recursively printing its tail.
algorithm The limiting case here is when a string has no characters in it. Printing the empty string is
trivial—there is nothing to print! This leads to the method definition shown in Figure 12.5.

The base case here provides a limit and bounds the recursion when the length of s is 0—that
is, when the string is empty. The recursive case solves the problem of printing s by solving
the smaller, self-similar problem of printing a substring of s. Note that the recursive case
makes progress toward the limit. On each recursion, the tail will get smaller and smaller until
it becomes the empty string.

```
/**
 * printString() prints each character of the string s
 * Pre: s is initialized (non-null)
 * Post: none
 */
public void printString(String s) {
    if (s.length() == 0)
        return;                              // Base case: do nothing
    else {                                   // Recursive case:
        System.out.print(s.charAt(0));       // Print head
        printString(s.substring(1));         // Print tail
    }
} // printString()
```

Figure 12.5   The recursive `printString()` method.

EFFECTIVE DESIGN: Recursive Progress.   In a recursive algorithm, each recursive call must make progress toward the bound, or base case.

Let's now revisit the notion of a method calling itself. Obviously this is what happens in the recursive case, but what does it mean—what actions does this lead to in the program? Each recursive call to a method is really a call to a *copy* of that method, and each copy has a slightly different internal state. We can define `printString()`'s internal state completely in terms of its recursion parameter, *s*, which is the string that is being printed. A **recursion parameter** is a parameter whose value is used to control the progress of the recursion. In this case, if *s* differs in each copy, then so will `s.substring(1)` and `s.charAt(0)`.

Recursive call

EFFECTIVE DESIGN: Recursion and Parameters.   Recursive methods use a recursion parameter to distinguish between self-similar instances of the method call. The parameter controls the progress of the recursion toward its bound.

Figure 12.6 illustrates the sequence of recursive method calls and the output that results when `printString("hello")` is invoked. Each box represents a separate instance of the `printString()` method with its own internal state. In this illustration, its state is represented by its parameter, `s`. Because each instance has a different parameter, behaviors differ slightly. Each box shows the character that will be printed by that instance (`s.charAt(0)`) and the string that will be passed on to the next instance (`s.substring(1)`).

Self-similar instances

DEBUGGING TIP: Off-by-One Error.   The expressions `s.charAt(0)` and `s.substring(1)` will generate exceptions if *s* is the empty string.

The arrows represent the method calls and returns. The first `return` executed is the one in the base case. Each instance of the method must wait for the instance it called to return before it can return. That is why the instances "pile up" in a cascade-like structure. The arrowless lines trace the order in which the output is produced.

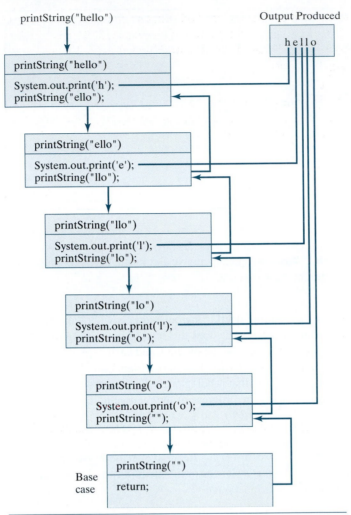

Figure 12.6 A recursive method call invokes a copy of the method. As this is done repeatedly, a stack of method calls is created, each with a slightly different internal state.

Each instance of `printString()` is similar to the next in that each will print one character and then pass on a substring, but each performs its duties on a different string. Note how the string, the recursion parameter in this case, gets smaller in each instance of `printString()`. This represents progress toward the method's base case `s.length() == 0`. When the empty string is passed as an argument, the recursion will stop. If the method does not make progress toward its bound in this way, the result will be an infinite recursion.

Progress toward the bound

EFFECTIVE DESIGN: Bounding the Recursion. For recursive algorithms, the recursion parameter is used to express the algorithm's bound, or base case. In order for the algorithm to terminate, each recursive call should make progress toward the bound.

Note also the order in which things are done in this method. First `s.charAt(0)` is printed, and then `s.substring(1)` is passed to `printString()` in the recursion. This is a typical structure for a head-and-tail algorithm. What makes this work is that the tail is a smaller, self-similar version of the original structure.

Self-similarity

> **EFFECTIVE DESIGN: Head-and-Tail Algorithm.** Many recursive solutions involve breaking a sequential structure, such as a string or an array, into its head and tail. An operation is performed on the head, and the algorithm recurses on the tail.

SELF-STUDY EXERCISE

EXERCISE 12.7 What would be printed by the following version of the `printString2()` method if it is called with `printString2("hello")`?

```java
public void printString2(String s) {
  if (s.length() == 1)
    System.out.print(s.charAt(0));            // Base case:
  else {
    System.out.print(s.charAt(s.length() - 1));  // Print last char
    printString2(s.substring(0, s.length() - 1));  // Print rest of string
  }
} // printString2()
```

12.3.2 Printing the String Backward

What do you suppose would happen if we reversed the order of the statements in the `print-String()` method? That is, what if the recursive call came before `s.charAt(0)` is printed, as in the following method:

```java
/**
 * printReverse() prints each character s in reverse order
 * Pre: s is initialized (non-null)
 * Post: none
 */
public void printReverse(String s) {
  if (s.length() > 0) {                   // Recursive case:
    printReverse(s.substring(1));         // Print tail
    System.out.print(s.charAt(0));        // Print first char
  }
} // printReverse()
```

As its name suggests, this method will print the string in reverse order. The trace in Figure 12.7 shows how this works. Before `printReverse("hello")` can print *h*, it calls `printReverse("ello")` and must wait for that call to complete its execution and return. But `printReverse("ello")` calls `printReverse("llo")` and so must wait for that call to complete its execution and return.

This process continues until `printReverse("")` is called. While the base case is executing, each of the other five instances of `printReverse()` must wait for the instance

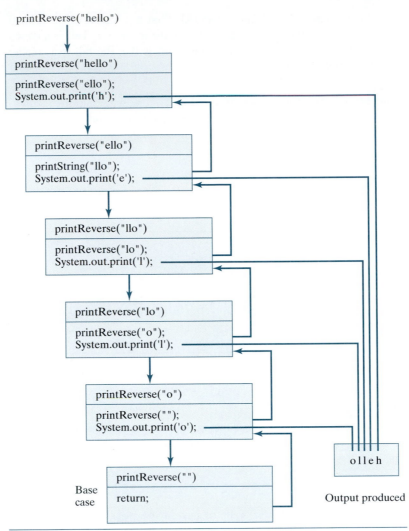

Figure 12.7 A trace of `printReverse(s)`, which prints its string argument in reverse order.

that it called to complete its execution. It is only after the base case returns that `printReverse("o")` can print its first character and return. So the letter *o* will be printed first. After `printReverse("o")` has returned, then `printReverse("lo")` can print its first character. The letter *l* will be printed next, and so on, until the original call to `printReverse("hello")` is completed and returns. Thus, the string will be printed in reverse order.

The method call and return structure in this example follows a **last-in/first-out (LIFO) protocol**. That is, the last method called is always the first method to return. This is the protocol used by all method calls, recursive or otherwise.

Last-in/first-out protocol

| **JAVA LANGUAGE RULE** | **LIFO.** All programming languages, including Java, use a last-in/first-out protocol for procedure call and return. |

For example, compare the order in which things happen in Figure 12.7 with the method stack trace in Figure 10.12. The only real difference between the two figures is that here the method stack is represented as growing downward, whereas in Figure 10.12 it grows upward. As each method call is made, a representation of the method call is placed on the *method call stack*. When a method returns, its block is removed from the top of the stack. The only difference between recursive and nonrecursive method calls is that recursive methods call instances of the same method definition. Of course, as we have seen, the instances are all slightly different from each other.

Method call stack

SELF-STUDY EXERCISES

EXERCISE 12.8   Write a recursive method called `countDown()` that takes a single `int` parameter, $N \geq 0$, and prints a countdown, such as "5, 4, 3, 2, 1, blastoff". In this case, the method would be called with `countDown(5)`.

EXERCISE 12.9   Revise the method in the preceding exercise so that when it is called with `count-Down(10)`, it will print "10 8 6 4 2 blastoff"; if it is called with `countDown(9)`, it prints "9 7 5 3 1 blastoff".

12.3.3   Counting Characters in a String

Suppose you are writing an encryption program and you need to count the frequencies of the letters of the alphabet. Let's write a recursive method for this task.

Problem statement

This method will have two parameters: a `String` to store the string that will be processed and a `char` to store the target character—the one we want to count. The method should return an `int` representing the number of occurrences of the target character in the string:

```
// Goal: count the occurrences of ch in s
public int countChar(String s, char ch) {
    ...
}
```

Here again our analysis must identify a recursive step that breaks the problem into smaller, self-similar versions of itself, plus a base case or limiting case that defines the end of the recursive process. Because the empty string will contain no target characters, we can use it as our base case. So, if it is passed the empty string, `countChar()` should just return 0 as its result.

Base case

For the recursive case, we can divide the string into its head and tail. If the head is the target character, then the number of occurrences in the string is (1 + the number of occurrences in its tail). If the head of the string is not the target character, then the number of occurrences is (0 + the number of occurrences in its tail). Of course, we will use recursion to calculate the number of occurrences in the tail.

Recursive case

This analysis leads to the recursive method shown in Figure 12.8. Note that for both recursive cases the same recursive call is used. In both cases we pass the tail of the original string plus the target character. Note also how the return statement is evaluated:

```
return 1 + countChar(s.substring(1),ch);   // Head = ch
```

```
/**
 * Pre:  s is a non-null String, ch is any character
 * Post: countChar() == the number of occurrences of ch in str
 */
public int countChar(String s, char ch) {
  if (s.length() == 0)                          // Base case: empty string
    return 0;
  else if (s.charAt(0) == ch)                   // Recursive case 1
    return 1 + countChar(s.substring(1), ch);   // Head = ch
  else                                          // Recursive case 2
    return 0 + countChar(s.substring(1), ch);   // Head != ch
} // countChar()
```

Figure 12.8   The recursive countChar() method.

Before the method can return a value, it must receive the result of calling countChar(s.substring(1),ch) and add it to 1. Only then can a result be returned to the calling method. This leads to the following evaluation sequence for countChar("dad",'d'):

Evaluation order is crucial

```
countChar("dad",'d');
1 + countChar("ad",'d');
1 + 0 + countChar("d",'d');
1 + 0 + 1 + countChar("",'d');
1 + 0 + 1 + 0 = 2                // Final result
```

In this way, the final result of calling countChar("dad",'d') is built up recursively by adding together the partial results from each separate instance of countChar(). The evaluation process is shown graphically in Figure 12.9.

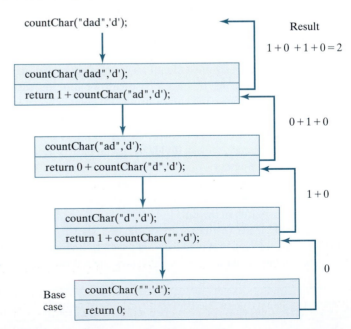

Figure 12.9   A trace of countChar("dad",'d'), which returns the value 2.

DEBUGGING TIP: Return Type. A common error with nonvoid recursive algorithms is forgetting to make sure that return statements that contain a recursive call yield the correct data type.

SELF-STUDY EXERCISE

EXERCISE 12.10   Here is a numerical problem. Write a recursive method to compute the sum of 1 to N, given N as a parameter.

12.3.4   Translating a String

A widely used string-processing task is to convert one string into another string by replacing one character with a substitute throughout the string. For example, suppose we want to convert a Unix path name, which uses the forward slash "/" to separate one part of the path from another, into a Windows path name, which uses the backslash character "\" as a separator. For example, we want a method that can translate the following two strings into one another:

Problem statement

```
/unix_system/myfolder/java
\Windows_system\myfolder\java
```

Thus, we want a method that takes three parameters: a `String`, on which the conversion will be performed, and two `char` variables, the first being the original character in the string and the second being its substitute. The precondition for this method is simply that each of these three parameters has been properly initialized with a value. The post condition is that all occurrences of the first character have been replaced by the second character.

Method design

As in our previous string-processing methods, the limiting case in this problem is the empty string, and the recursive case will divide the string into its head and its tail. If the head is the character we want to replace, we concatenate its substitute with the result we obtain by recursively converting its tail.

Head-and-tail algorithm

This analysis leads to the definition shown in Figure 12.10. This method has more or less the same head-and-tail structure as the preceding example. The difference is that here the operation we perform on the head of the string is concatenation rather than addition.

```java
/**
 * Pre:  str, ch1, ch2 have been initialized
 * Post: the result contains a ch2 everywhere that ch1
 *       had occurred in str
 */
public static String convert(String str, char ch1, char ch2) {
  if (str.length() == 0)                       // Base case: empty string
    return str;
  else if (str.charAt(0) == ch1)               // Recursive 1: ch1 at head

    return ch2 + convert(str.substring(1), ch1, ch2);  // Replace ch1 with ch2
  else                                         // Recursive 2:  ch1 not at head
    return str.charAt(0) + convert(str.substring(1), ch1, ch2);
} // convert()
```

Figure 12.10   The convert() method replaces one character with another in a string.

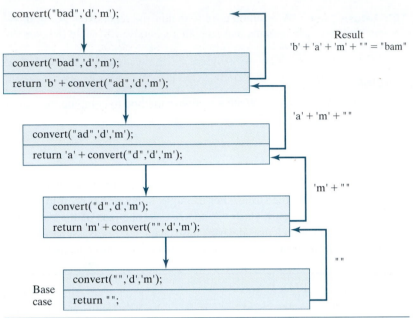

Figure 12.11 A trace of `convert("bad",'d','m')`, which returns "bam".

The base case is still the case in which `str` is the empty string. The first recursive case occurs when the character being replaced is the head of `str`. In that case, its substitute (`ch2`) is concatenated with the result of converting the rest of the string and returned as the result. The second recursive case occurs when the head of the string is *not* the character being replaced. In this case, the head of the string is simply concatenated with the result of converting the rest of the string. Figure 12.11 shows an example of its execution.

SELF-STUDY EXERCISE

EXERCISE 12.11   Write a recursive method that changes each blank in a string into two consecutive blanks, leaving the rest of the string unchanged.

12.3.5   Printing All Possible Outcomes When Tossing N Coins

Suppose that a student who is studying probability wishes to have a Java program that for any positive integer N, will print out a list of all possible outcomes when N coins are tossed. For purposes of analyzing the problem, it is assumed that the coins are numbered 1 through N and are tossed one at a time. An outcome will be represented by a string of Hs and Ts corresponding to heads and tails. Thus, if $N = 2$, the string HT represents a head on the first coin and a tail on the second coin. What we need is a method which, when given the number of coins, will print out all strings of this type. In the case of two coins the output should be:

A coin-tossing experiment

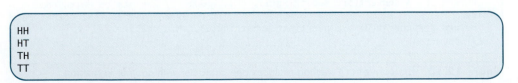
```
HH
HT
TH
TT
```

Let's devise a strategy, given any positive integer N, for printing the strings that correspond to all possible outcomes when tossing N coins. Clearly, for $N = 1$, the method needs to print an H on one line and a T on the next line. For an arbitrary number of coins N, one way to generate all outcomes is to think of two kinds of strings—those that start with an H and those that start with a T. The strings that start with H can be generated by inserting an H in front of each of the outcomes that occur when $N - 1$ coins are tossed. The strings beginning with T can be generated in a similar manner. Thus, using the outcomes for two coins above, we know that the outcomes for three coins for which the first coin is H are:

Designing a recursive algorithm

```
HHH
HHT
HTH
HTT
```

Using an argument similar to the one above, we can generalize this to a description of the recursive case for an algorithm. We want an algorithm that generates all the outcomes for N coins where we are given a string STR representing one particular outcome for all but the last K coins where $0 < K <= N$. To print out all such outcomes, just print all outcomes with a fixed outcome corresponding to STR + "H" for all but the last $K - 1$ coins and then print all outcomes with the fixed outcome STR + "T" for all but the last $K - 1$ coins. The base case is the special case $K = 1$ when you just need STR + "H" on one line and STR + "T" on the next. If you start the algorithm with STR = "" and $K = N$, this algorithm will print out all the outcomes for tossing N coins.

To translate this into Java code, we can create a class called CoinToss which has a single static method called printOutcomes(String str, int N). The above recursive description easily translates into code for the method in Figure 12.12.

```java
/**
 * printOutcomes(str, N) prints out all possible outcomes
 * beginning with str when N more coins are tossed.
 * Pre: str is a string of Hs and Ts.
 * Pre: N is a positive integer.
 * Post: none
 */
public static void printOutcomes(String str, int N){
    if (N == 1){                          // The base case
        System.out.println(str + "H");
        System.out.println(str + "T");
    } else {                              // The recursive case
        printOutcomes(str + "H", N - 1);
        printOutcomes(str + "T", N - 1);
    } // else
} // printOutcomes()
```

Figure 12.12   The method printOutcomes() prints all outcomes given the results on some initial coins.

```
printOutcomes("",3)
  printOutcomes("H",2)
    printOutcomes("HH",1)
      HHH
      HHT
    printOutcomes("HT",1)
      HTH
      HTT
  printOutcomes("T",2)
    printOutcomes("TH",1)
      THH
      THT
    printOutcomes("TT",1)
      TTH
      TTT
```

Figure 12.13   The order in which the recursive calls and output occur when `printOutcomes("",3)` is executed.

To print out all outcomes when tossing, say, seven coins, just make the method call `Coin-Toss.printOutcomes("",7)`. This call would generate the desired output:

```
HHHHHHH
HHHHHHT
.......
TTTTTTH
TTTTTTT
```

To better understand how the recursive method definition generates its output, it might be helpful to trace the order of recursive calls and output to `System.out` that occurs when executing `printOutcomes("",3)`, as shown in Figure 12.13.

Note that the recursive case in the method implementation makes two calls to itself, and as a result it is not so clear how this method would be written using a loop instead of recursion. This example is more typical of the type of problem for which a recursive method is shorter and clearer than a method that solves the same problem without using recursion.

SELF-STUDY EXERCISE

EXERCISE 12.12   Modify the above `printOutcomes()` method so that it will print out all possible outcomes when a chess player plays a series of N games. The outcome of each game is to be represented by a W, L, or D corresponding to the player's winning, losing, or drawing the game.

12.4   Recursive Array Processing

Like strings, arrays also have a recursive structure. Just as each substring of a string is similar to the string as a whole, each portion of an array is similar to the array as a whole. Similarly, just as a string can be divided into a head and a tail, an array can be divided into its *head*, the first element, and its *tail*, the rest of its elements (Fig. 12.14). Because the tail of an array is itself an array, it satisfies the self-similarity principle. Therefore, arrays have all the appropriate characteristics that make them excellent candidates for recursive processing.

Figure 12.14 An array of `int` is a recursive structure whose tail is similar to the array as a whole.

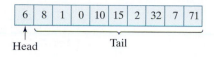

| 6 | 8 | 1 | 0 | 10 | 15 | 2 | 32 | 7 | 71 |

↑
Head   Tail

12.4.1 Recursive Sequential Search

Let's start by developing a recursive version of the sequential search algorithm that we discussed in Chapter 9. Recall that the sequential search method takes two parameters: the array being searched and the *key*, or target value, being searched for. If the key is found in the array, the method returns its index. If the key is not found, the method returns −1, thereby indicating that the key was not contained in the array. The iterative version of this method has the following general form:

Method design

```
/**
 * Performs a sequential search of an integer array
 * @ param arr is the array of integers
 * @ param key is the element being searched for
 * @ return the key's index is returned if the key is
 *   found otherwise -1 is returned
 * Pre:  arr is not null
 * Post: either -1 or the key's index is returned
 */
public int sequentialSearch(int arr[], int key) {
   return -1;               // failure if this is reached
}
```

If we divide the array into its head and tail, then one way to describe a recursive search algorithm is as follows:

```
If the array is empty, return -1
If the array's head matches the key, return its index
If the array's head doesn't match the key,
 return the result of searching the tail of the array
```

This algorithm clearly resembles the approach we used in recursive string processing: perform some operation on the head of the array, and recurse on the tail of the array.

The challenge in developing this algorithm is not so much knowing what to do but knowing how to represent concepts like the head and the tail of the array. For strings, we had methods such as `s.charAt(0)` to represent the head of the string and `s.substring(1)` to represent the string's tail. For an array named `arr`, the expression `arr[0]` represents the head of the array. Unfortunately, we have no method comparable to the `substring()` method for strings that lets us represent the tail of the array.

How do we represent head and tail?

To help us out of this dilemma, we can use an integer parameter to represent the head of the array. Let's have the `int` parameter, *head*, represent the current head of the array (Fig. 12.15). Then *head* + 1 represents the start of the tail, and `arr.length-1` represents the end of the

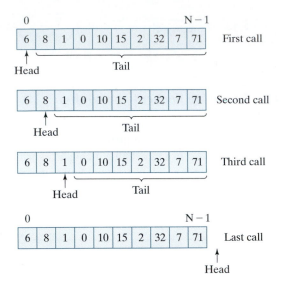

Figure 12.15 A parameter, *head*, can represent the head of some portion of the array.

tail. Our method will always be passed a reference to the whole array, but it will restrict the search to the portion of the array starting at *head*. If we let *head* vary from 0 to `arr.length` on each recursive call, the method will recurse through the array in head/tail fashion, searching for the key. The method will stop when `head = arr.length`.

> **JAVA PROGRAMMING TIP: Subarray Parameter.** For methods that take an array argument, an `int` parameter can be used to designate the portion of the array that should be processed in the method.

This leads to the definition for recursive search shown in Figure 12.16. The recursive search method takes three parameters: the array to be searched, `arr`, the `key` being sought, and an

```java
/**
 * search(arr,head,key)---Recursively search arr for key starting at head
 * Pre:  arr != null and 0 <= head <= arr.length
 * Post: if arr[k] == key for k, 0 <= k < arr.length,
 *       return k else return -1
 */
private int search(int arr[], int head, int key)  {
  if (head == arr.length)                        // Base: empty list - failure
    return -1;
  else if (arr[head] == key)                     // Base: key found---success
    return head;
  else                                           // Recursive: search the tail
    return search(arr, head + 1, key);
}
```

Figure 12.16 The recursive search method takes three parameters. The *head* parameter points to the beginning of the portion of the array that is being searched.

integer `head` that gives the starting location for the search. The algorithm is bounded when
`head = arr.length`. In effect, this is like saying the recursion should stop when we have
reached a tail that contains 0 elements. This underscores the point we made earlier about the
importance of parameters in designing recursive methods. Here the *head* parameter serves as
the *recursion parameter*. It controls the progress of the recursion.

Recursion parameter

Note that we need two base cases for the search algorithm. One represents the successful
case, where the key is found in the array. The other represents the unsuccessful case, which
comes about after we have looked at every possible head in the array and not found the key.
This case will arise through exhaustion—that is, when we have exhausted all possible locations
for the key.

> **DEBUGGING TIP: Recursive Search.** For the recursive search method to work prop-
> erly, it must be called with the correct value for the *head* parameter.

12.4.2 Information Hiding

In order to use the `search()` method, you have to supply a value of 0 as the argument for
the *head* parameter. This is not only awkward but impractical. After all, if we want to search
an array, we just want to pass two arguments, the array and the key we're searching for. It's
unreasonable to expect users of a method to know that they also have to pass 0 as the head in
order to get the recursion started. In addition, this design is prone to error, because it is quite
easy for a mistake to be made when the method is called.

Design issue

For this reason, it is customary to provide a nonrecursive interface to the recursive method.
The interface hides the fact that a recursive algorithm is being used, but this is exactly the
kind of implementation detail that should be hidden from the user. This is an example of the
principle of information hiding introduced in Chapter 0. A more appropriate design would
make the recursive method a `private` method called by the public method, as shown in
Figure 12.17 and implemented in the `Searcher` class (Fig. 12.18).

Hide implementation details

> **EFFECTIVE DESIGN: Information Hiding.** Unnecessary implementation details, such
> as whether a method uses a recursive or iterative algorithm, should be hidden within the
> class. Users of a class or method should be shown only the details they need to know.

SELF-STUDY EXERCISE

EXERCISE 12.13 Write a `main()` method for the `Searcher` class to conduct the following test
of `search()`. Create an `int` array of 10 elements, initialize its elements to the even numbers
from 0 to 18, and then use a `for` loop to search the array for each of the numbers from 0 to 20.

Figure 12.17 The public `search()`
method serves as an interface to the
private recursive method, `search()`.
Note that the methods have different
signatures.

Searcher
+ search(in arr[] : int, in key : int) : int − search(in arr[] : int, in head : int, in key : int) : int

```java
public class Searcher {
  /**
   * search(arr,key) -- searches arr for key.
   * Pre:   arr != null and 0 <= head <= arr.length
   * Post: if arr[k] == key for k,  0 <= k < arr.length,
   *        return k,  else return -1
   */
  public int search(int arr[], int key) {
    return search(arr, 0, key);                  // Call recursive search
  }
  /**
   * search(arr, head, key) -- Recursively search arr for key
   *   starting at head
   * Pre:   arr != null and 0 <= head <= arr.length
   * Post: if arr[k] == key for k,  0 <= k < arr.length, return k
   *        else return -1
   */
  private int search(int arr[], int head, int key)  {
    if (head == arr.length)                   // Base case: empty list - failure
      return -1;
    else if (arr[head] == key)                // Base case: key found -- success
      return head;
    else                                      // Recursive case: search the tail
        return search(arr, head + 1, key);
  } // search()
  public static void main(String args[]) {
    int numbers[] = {0, 2, 4, 6, 8, 10, 12, 14, 16, 18};
    Searcher searcher = new Searcher();
    for (int k = 0; k <= 20; k++) {
        int result = searcher.search(numbers, k);
        if (result != -1)
          System.out.println(k + " found at " + result);
        else
          System.out.println(k + " is not in the array ");
    } // for
  } // main()
} // Searcher class
```

Figure 12.18 Information-hiding principle: The `public search()` method calls the `private`, recursive `search()`, thereby hiding the fact that a recursive algorithm is used.

12.4.3 Recursive Selection Sort

Next we want you to think back to Chapter 9, where we introduced the selection sort algorithm. To review the concept, suppose you have a deck of 52 cards. Lay them out on a table, face up, one card next to the other. Starting at the last card, look through the deck from last to first, find the largest card and exchange it with the last card. Then go through the deck again, starting at the next-to-the-last card, find the next, largest card, and exchange it with the next-to-the-last card. Go to the next card, and so on. If you repeat this process 51 times, the deck will be completely sorted.

Sorting a deck of cards

DEBUGGING TIP: Off-by-One Error. Sorting algorithms are highly susceptible to an off-by-one error. To sort an array with N elements, you generally need to make $N - 1$ passes.

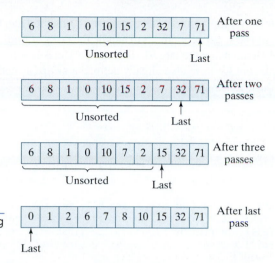

Figure 12.19 Selection sort: using a head-and-tail algorithm in reverse to sort an integer array.

Let's design a recursive version of this algorithm. The algorithm we just described is like a head-and-tail algorithm in reverse, where the last card in the deck is like the head, and the cards before it are like the tail. After each pass or recursion, the last card will be in its proper location, and the cards before it will represent the unsorted portion of the deck. If we use parameter to represent *last*, then it will be moved one card to the left at each level of the recursion.

Figure 12.19 illustrates this process for an array of integers. The base case is reached when the *last* parameter is pointing to the first element in the array. An array with one element in it is already sorted. It needs no rearranging. The recursive case involves searching an ever-smaller portion of the array. This is represented in our design by moving *last* down one element to the left.

Figure 12.20 provides a partial implementation of selection sort for an array of `int`. In this definition, the array is one parameter. The second parameter, `int last`, defines the portion of the array, from right to left, that is yet to be sorted. On the first call to this method, *last* will be `arr.length` $-$ 1. On the second, it will be `arr.length` $-$ 2, and so on. When *last* gets to be 0, the array will be sorted. Thus, in terms of the card-deck analogy, *last* represents the last card in the unsorted portion of the deck.

```java
/**
 * selectionSort(arr,last)--Recursively sort arr starting at last element
 * Pre:  arr != null and 0 <= last < arr.length
 * Post: arr will be arranged so that arr[j] <= arr[k], for any j < k
 */
private void selectionSort(int arr[], int last) {
  if (last > 0) {
    int maxLoc = findMax (arr, last);    // Find the largest
    swap(arr, last, maxLoc);             // Swap it with last
    selectionSort(arr, last - 1);        // Move down the array
  }
} // selectionSort()
```

Figure 12.20 The `selectionSort()` method uses the `findMax()` and `swap()` methods to sort an array.

Task decomposition

Note how simply the `selectionSort()` method can be coded. Of course, this is because we have used separate methods to handle the tasks of finding the largest element and swapping the last element and the largest. This not only makes sense in terms of the divide-and-conquer principle, but we have also already defined a `swap()` method in Chapter 9. So here is a good example of reusing code:

```java
/**
 * swap(arr, el1 el2) swaps el1 and el2 in the array, arr
 * Pre: arr is non null, 0 <= el1 < arr.length,
 *                        0 <= el2 < arr.length
 * Post: the locations of el1 and el2 are swapped in arr
 */
private void swap(int arr[], int el1, int el2)  {
 int temp = arr[el1];   // Assign the first element to temp
 arr[el1] = arr[el2];   // Overwrite first with second
 arr[el2] = temp;       // Overwrite second with first(temp)
} // swap()
```

The definition of the `findMax()` method is left as a self-study exercise.

JAVA PROGRAMMING TIP: Method Decomposition. A task can be simplified by breaking it up into simpler subtasks, especially if you already have methods for solving one or more of the subtasks.

SELF-STUDY EXERCISES

EXERCISE 12.14 As in the case of the `search()` method, we need to provide a public interface to the recursive `selectionSort()` method. We want to enable the user to sort an array just by calling `sort(arr)`, where `arr` is the name of the array to be sorted. Define the `sort()` method.

EXERCISE 12.15 Define an iterative version of the `findMax(arr,N)` method used in `selectionSort()`. Its goal is to return the location (index) of the largest integer between `arr[0]` and `arr[N]`.

12.5 Example: Drawing (Recursive) Fractals

Fractal patterns

A *fractal* is a geometric shape that exhibits a recursive structure. When it is divided into parts, each part is a smaller version of the whole. Fractal patterns occur in many situations and places. For example, if you look at a graph of the Dow Jones Industrial Average (DJIA) over the past year, the graph for each day is similar to the graph of each month, which is similar to the graph of each year, and so on. Each part is a reduced-scale version of the whole. Fractals also occur throughout nature. If you look at a coastline from an airplane, the shape of each part of the coastline, no matter how small the scale, resembles the shape of the whole coastline. If you look at a tree, each branch of the tree is similar in shape to the whole tree.

So fractal patterns are all around us. Because of their self-similarity and divisibility, fractals are well-suited for recursive programming. Drawing recursive patterns is also an excellent way to illustrate how to use parameters to create generality in method design. In this section, we will develop two simple patterns and incorporate them into an applet.

12.5.1   Nested Squares

Earlier in this chapter, we developed a recursive definition for drawing a nested squares pattern (Fig. 12.2). Now let's develop a recursive method that actually draws the pattern. For this pattern, the base case is the drawing of the square. The recursive case, if more divisions are desired, is the drawing of smaller patterns within the square:

```
Draw a square.
If more divisions are desired
    draw a smaller version of pattern within square.
```

An important consideration for this algorithm is to specify precisely what we mean by "if more divisions are desired." In other words, how exactly do we control the recursion? In our earlier definition of the pattern, we used the length of the side to control the algorithm. When $side \geq 5$, we recursed.

Another more general way to do this is to describe the fractal structure in terms of its *levels*. For nested squares, the level-zero pattern would be just the basic square shape (Fig. 12.21). A level-one pattern would be the basic square shape plus an inner square, and so on. The higher the level, the more subdividing we do. Therefore, one way to control the recursion is to use a *level* parameter as the *recursion parameter*—the parameter that controls the recursion:

How should we represent the problem?

Levels of recursion

```
Draw a square.
If the level is greater than 0,
    draw a smaller version of pattern within square.
```

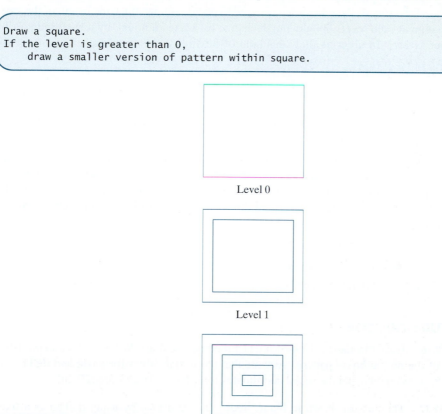

Level 0

Level 1

Level 4

Figure 12.21 Levels 0, 1, and 4 of the nested squares pattern.

```
/**
 * drawBoxes()---recursively draws pattern of nested
 *   squares with top left corner of outer square at
 *   (locX, locY) and dimensions of length side.
 * level (>= 0) is the recursion parameter (base: = 0)
 * delta is used to adjust the length of the side.
 */
private void drawBoxes(Graphics g, int level,
    int locX, int locY, int side, int delta) {
  g.drawRect(locX, locY, side, side );
  if (level > 0) {
    int newLocX = locX + delta;
    int newLocY = locY + delta;
    drawBoxes(g, level - 1, newLocX, newLocY, side - 2 * delta, delta);
  } // if
} // drawBoxes()
```

Figure 12.22   The drawBoxes() method.

What other parameters will we need for this method? If we're going to draw a rectangle, we'll need parameters for its x- and y-coordinates. We'll also need a parameter for the length of the sides of the square. Another issue we need to decide is how much the length of the sides should change at each level. Should length change by a fixed amount, by a fixed ratio, or by some other factor? In order to allow this kind of flexibility, let's use another parameter for this value.

These design considerations suggest the method shown in Figure 12.22. Note that we must also provide a `Graphics` parameter so that the method can use the `drawRect()` method to draw the square. As we decided, the `level` parameter controls the recursion. Its value is decreased by 1 in the recursive call. This ensures that `level` will eventually reach 0, and recursion will stop.

Finally, note the use of the `delta` parameter, which is used to change the length of the sides by a fixed amount, 2 * `delta`, at each level. It is also used to calculate the x- and y-coordinates for the location of the next level of boxes *(locX + delta, locY + delta)*. But `delta`'s value remains constant through all the levels. This will lead to a pattern where the "gap" between nested squares is constant.

 EFFECTIVE DESIGN: Levels of Recursion.   Many recursive algorithms use a *level* parameter as the recursion parameter.

SELF-STUDY EXERCISES

EXERCISE 12.16   Trace through the `drawBoxes()` method and draw the level-four and level-five versions of the nested boxes pattern. Assume that the initial values for `side` and `delta` are 100 and 5, respectively, and the initial coordinates for (`locX`,`locY`) are (20,20).

EXERCISE 12.17   The pattern shown in Figure 12.23 can be drawn by using `delta` as a fixed ratio of the length of the side, for example, 10 percent. Modify the `drawBoxes()` method to use `delta` in this way.

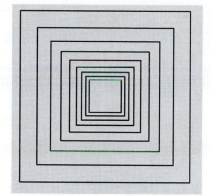

Figure 12.23 This version of nested boxes can be drawn by using delta as a fixed percentage of the length of the side.

EXERCISE 12.18 Write an iterative version of the drawBoxes() method. (*Hint*: On each iteration, you must change the x- and y-coordinates of the square's location and the length of its side.)

12.5.2 The Sierpinski Gasket

Let's return now to the *Sierpinski gasket* pattern that we introduced at the start of the chapter. This is a much more interesting fractal pattern (Fig. 12.24). The overall shape of the pattern is that of a triangle, but note how the outer triangle is divided into three smaller triangles. Then each of these triangles is divided into three smaller triangles. If you continue this process of dividing and shrinking, you get the level-seven pattern shown here.

Let's develop a recursive method to draw this pattern. If we follow the same strategy we used in the nested squares example, we get the following algorithm:

```
Base case:        Draw a triangle.
Recursive Case:   If more divisions are desired,
    draw three smaller gaskets within the triangle.
```

For this pattern the base case is the drawing of the basic triangle. The recursive cases, if more divisions are desired, are the drawing of smaller gaskets within the triangle. Again we will use a level parameter to control the depth of the recursion. The higher the level, the more divisions will be drawn.

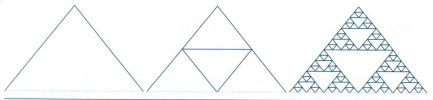

Figure 12.24 Levels 0, 1, and 7 of the Sierpinski gasket fractal pattern.

```
/**
 * drawGasket()---recursively draws the Sierpinski gasket
 *  pattern, with points (p1X, p1Y),(p2X, p2Y),(p3X, p3Y)
 *  representing the vertices of its enclosing triangle.
 * level (>= 0) is the recursion parameter (base: = 0)
 */
private void drawGasket(Graphics g, int lev, int p1X, int p1Y,
                int p2X, int p2Y, int p3X, int p3Y) {
    g.drawLine(p1X, p1Y, p2X, p2Y);        // Draw a triangle
    g.drawLine(p2X, p2Y, p3X, p3Y);
    g.drawLine(p3X, p3Y, p1X, p1Y);
    if (lev > 0) {                          // If more levels, draw 3 smaller gaskets
        int q1X = (p1X + p2X) / 2;    int q1Y = (p1Y + p2Y) / 2;
        int q2X = (p1X + p3X) / 2;    int q2Y = (p1Y + p3Y) / 2;
        int q3X = (p2X + p3X) / 2;    int q3Y = (p2Y + p3Y) / 2;
        drawGasket(g, lev - 1, p1X, p1Y, q1X, q1Y, q2X, q2Y);
        drawGasket(g, lev - 1, p2X, p2Y, q1X, q1Y, q3X, q3Y);
        drawGasket(g, lev - 1, p3X, p3Y, q2X, q2Y, q3X, q3Y);
    } // if
} // drawGasket()
```

Figure 12.25 The drawGasket() method.

What other parameters do we need?

If we're going to draw a triangle shape, we need the coordinates of its three vertices—that is, an x- and y-coordinate for each vertex. Taken together, these design considerations suggest the method definition shown in Figure 12.25.

Levels of recursion

As we described earlier, we use the level parameter as the recursion parameter for this method, which controls the recursion. Each of the three recursive calls decreases the level by 1. This ensures that level will eventually equal 0, and recursion will stop.

Note how the three pairs of coordinates are used. Drawing a triangle is simple. Just draw three lines from (p1X,p1Y) to (p2X,p2Y), from (p2X,p2Y) to (p3X,p3Y), and from (p3X,p3Y) back to (p1X,p1Y). The most complicated part of the method is calculating the vertices for the three inner gaskets. If you look at Figure 12.24 again, you will note that each of the inner triangles uses one of the vertices of the main triangle plus the *midpoints* of the two adjacent sides. Thus, the triangle on the "left" uses the left vertex (p1X,p1Y), and the midpoints of the other two lines from (p1X,p1Y) to (p2X,p2Y) and from (p1X,p1Y) to

Midpoint of a line

(p3X,p3Y). As you may remember from high school math, the formula for computing the midpoint of the line segment $(x1, y1)$ to $(x2, y2)$ is

```
( (x1 + x2) / 2, (y1 + y2) / 2 )
```

This formula is used repeatedly to calculate the vertices of the three smaller gaskets.

12.6 Object-Oriented Design: Tail Recursion

Although the drawBoxes() method is relatively simple to convert into an iterative version (see Self-Study Exercise 12.18), the same cannot be said for the drawGasket() method. It is clearly a case where the recursive approach makes the problem easier to solve.

One difference between drawBoxes() and drawGasket() is that drawBoxes() is an

Tail recursion

example of a tail-recursive method. A method is **tail recursive** if all of its recursive calls occur as the last action performed in the method. You have to be a bit careful about this definition. The recursive call in a tail-recursive method has to be the last *executed* statement. It needn't be the last statement *appearing* in the method's definition.

For example, the following method will print "Hello" *N* times. This method is tail recursive even though its last statement is not a recursive call:

```java
public void printHello(int N) {
  if (N > 1) {
    System.out.println("Hello");
    printHello(N - 1);                // The last executed statement
  } else
    System.out.println("Hello");
} // printHello()
```

This method is tail recursive because the last statement that will be executed, in its recursive cases, is the recursive call.

A tail-recursive method is relatively easy to convert into an iterative method. The basic idea is to make the recursion parameter into a loop variable, taking care to make sure the bounds are equivalent. Thus, the following iterative method will print "Hello" *N* times:

```java
public void printHelloIterative(int N) {
    for (int k = N; k > 0; k--)
        System.out.println("Hello");
}
```

In this case, we use the parameter *N* to set the initial value of the loop variable, *k*, and we decrement *k* on each iteration. This is equivalent to what happens when we decrement the recursion parameter in the recursive call.

EFFECTIVE DESIGN: Tail Recursion. Tail-recursive algorithms are relatively simple to convert into iterative algorithms that do the same thing.

As you can see, recursive methods that are not tail recursive are much more complex. Just compare the drawGasket() and drawBoxes() methods. Yet it is precisely for these non-tail-recursive algorithms that recursion turns out to be most useful. As you might expect, if you can't give a simple tail-recursive solution to a problem, the problem probably doesn't have a simple iterative solution either. Thus, the problems where we most need recursion are those where we can't give a simple tail-recursive or an iterative solution. And there are a lot of such problems, especially when you get into nonlinear data structures such as trees and graphs.

To gain some appreciation for this complexity, consider how difficult it would be to draw the Sierpinski gasket using an iterative approach. We could start by developing an outer for loop to account for the different levels in the pattern:

```java
for (int k = lev; k > 0; k--) {
  drawGasket(g, lev - 1, p1X, p1Y, q1X, q1Y, q2X, q2Y);
  drawGasket(g, lev - 1, p2X, p2Y, q1X, q1Y, q3X, q3Y);
  drawGasket(g, lev - 1, p3X, p3Y, q2X, q2Y, q3X, q3Y);
}
```

But now each of the method calls within the body of this loop would have to be replaced by very complex loops. That would be a daunting task. So the lesson to be drawn from this observation is that recursion is most useful as a problem-solving technique for problems that don't yield to a simple iterative solution.

EFFECTIVE DESIGN: Recursion or Iteration? If you have difficulty designing an iterative solution to a problem, try developing a recursive solution.

SELF-STUDY EXERCISES

EXERCISE 12.19 Trace the `drawGasket()` method for levels two and three. Pick your own values for the three vertices.

EXERCISE 12.20 Is the `printReverse()` method, discussed earlier, tail recursive? Explain.

EXERCISE 12.21 Is the `countChar()` method, discussed earlier, tail recursive? Explain.

12.7   Object-Oriented Design: Recursion or Iteration?

As we mentioned at the outset of this chapter, recursive algorithms require more computational overhead than iterative algorithms. We are now in a good position to appreciate why this is so.

A recursive algorithm incurs two kinds of overhead that are not incurred by an iterative algorithm: memory and CPU time. Both of these are direct results of the fact that recursive algorithms do a lot of method calling.

Method call overhead

As we saw in our various traces, each time a method is called, a representation of the method call is placed on the **method call stack**. These representations often take the form of a *block* of memory locations. Such blocks can be quite large. The block must contain space for the method's local variables, including its parameters. Unless the method is `void`, the block must also contain space for the method's return value. In addition it must contain a reference to the calling method, so that it will know where to go when it is done. Figure 12.26 shows what the method call block would look like for the `search()` method.

Memory overhead

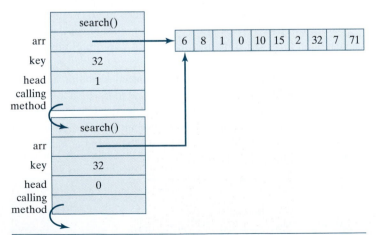

Figure 12.26 A more detailed picture of the method call stack, showing two method blocks for `search()` after two levels of recursion.

In addition to the memory required, a method call also requires extra CPU time. Each time   CPU overhead
a method is called, Java must create a method call block, copy the method call arguments to
the parameters in the block, create initial values for any local variables used by the method,
and fill in the return address of the calling method. All of this takes time, and in the case of a
recursive method, these steps are repeated at each level of the recursion.

Exploring the Mandelbrot Set

The Mandelbrot set is one of the most fascinating fractals. It is named after its discovered,
IBM mathematician Benoit Mandelbrot. The Mandelbrot set itself is the black, heart-
shaped image shown in Figure 12.27. What makes the Mandelbrot set so interesting is
that with the help of a Java applet you can explore the set as if you were taking a trip through
outer space. The most interesting regions to explore are those just along the boundary of
the set. For example, note that the boundary contains numerous circular shapes, each of
which is itself studded with circular shapes. This is an example of the scaled self-similarity
that we found to be so prevalent in recursive structures. By continually expanding the
regions around the boundary, you'll find an infinite recursion of fascinating images and
shapes. In some regions of the set you'll even find miniature replications of the set itself.

The Mandelbrot set is generated by an *iterated function system*. The mathematics
underlying this fascinating object is quite accessible, and there are a number of online
tutorials that explain how the set is generated and how the pictures are produced. Many
of the Mandelbrot and fractal Web sites contain excellent Java applets that let you explore
the Mandelbrot set as well as related sets. An excellent place to start your exploration
would be David Joyce's award-winning Web site,

```
http://aleph0.clarku.edu/~djoyce/julia/
```

which contains references to a number of other good sites. For a tutorial on how the
various Mandelbrot set-generating Java programs work, see

```
http://storm.shodor.org/mteach/
```

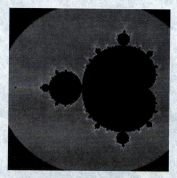

Figure 12.27 The Mandelbrot set.

Compare these memory and CPU requirements with what normally transpires for an iterative algorithm—an algorithm involving a loop. The loop structure usually occurs entirely within a method, so it doesn't incur either the memory or CPU overhead involved in recursion. Therefore, iterative algorithms are generally more efficient than recursive algorithms. Here, then, is a useful guideline: when runtime performance and efficiency are of prime importance, use iteration instead of recursion.

EFFECTIVE DESIGN: Iteration or Recursion?   Use an iterative algorithm instead of a recursive algorithm whenever efficiency and memory usage are important design factors.

On the other hand, for many problems recursive algorithms are much easier to design than the corresponding iterative algorithms. We tried to illustrate this point in our development of the Sierpinski gasket algorithm, but there are many other examples we could have used. Given that programmer and designer time is the most expensive resource involved in software development, a recursive solution may be easier to develop and maintain than a corresponding iterative solution. And given the great cost of software development, a less efficient solution that is easier to develop, easier to understand, and easier to maintain may be preferable to a highly efficient algorithm that is difficult to understand. For some problems, then, such as the Sierpinski gasket, a recursive algorithm may provide the best solution.

Efficiency of development

EFFECTIVE DESIGN: Keep It Simple.   When all other factors are equal, choose the algorithm (recursive or iterative) that is easiest to understand, develop, and maintain.

One final point worth making is that some *optimizing* compilers are able to convert recursive methods into iterative methods when they compile the program. The algorithms for doing this are well known. They are often subjects for study in a data structures course, so we won't go into them here. The resulting runtime programs will be just as efficient, in CPU time and memory, as if you had written iterative methods. The point is that if you have such a compiler, you really get the best of both worlds. You get the advantage of using recursion as a problem-solving and software-development approach, and the compiler takes care of producing an efficient object program.

Optimizing compiler

12.8 From the Java Library: `javax.swing.JComboBox`

java.sun.com/docs

A `JComboBox` is a Swing component that combines a text field and a drop-down list (Fig. 12.28). It lets the user either type in a selection or choose a selection from a list that appears when the user requests it—a `JComboBox`'s drop-down behavior is somewhat similar to a `java.awt.-Choice` box.

A `JComboBox` can be used to represent a *drop-down menu*. When the user clicks on a `JComboBox`, a list of options drops down, and the user can select a particular option stored in the box's internal state (Fig. 12.29). The list of options associated with a `JComboBox` can be built beforehand and inserted into the component in a constructor, or items can be inserted one at a time by repeatedly using its `addItem()` method.

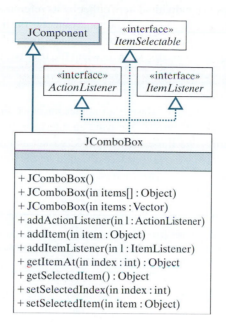

Figure 12.28 A `JComboBox` responds to action events and item events.

As Figure 12.28 shows, either an array or a vector of items can be passed to a constructor method to initialize the box's menu. The items stored in a `JComboBox` box are references to `Object`s, most commonly `String`s that represent the name of a menu item. They are stored in the (zero-indexed) order in which they are added. The `addItem()` method is used to add an individual `Object` to a `JComboBox`. By default, the first item added to a `JComboBox` will be the *selected* item until the user selects another item.

When the user makes a selection in a `JComboBox`, the item selected can be gotten either by its reference (`getSelectedItem()`) or by its position within the menu (`getSelected-Index()`). There are also methods to `setSelectedItem()` and `setSelectedIndex()`

Figure 12.29 Using a `JComboBox` box.

that let you select an individual item either by its reference or its position. The addItemLis-tener() method is used to designate some object as the listener for the ItemEvents generated whenever the user selects a menu option. Alternatively, the addActionListener() method lets you handle action events, such as when the user types a value into the box.

12.8.1 A JComboBox **Example**

As a simple example, let's design an applet interface that can be used to display the fractal patterns we developed earlier. We want an interface that lets the user select from among the available patterns—we'll use the Sierpinski gasket and nested boxes for starters. In addition, the user should also be able to select different levels for the drawings, from 0 to 9. We want to present these options in two menus, with one JComboBox for each menu.

The first step is to declare and instantiate the JComboBoxes as instance variables:

```
private String items[] = {"Sierpinski Gasket","Nested Boxes"};
private JComboBox patterns = new JComboBox(items);
private JComboBox levels = new JComboBox();
```

Note that in this case we pass the constructor for the patterns menu an entire array of items. If we hadn't done it this way, we would add individual items to the combo box in the applet's init() method. In fact, that's how we will initialize the levels menu:

```
for (int k=0; k < 10; k++)         // Add 10 levels
    levels.addItem(k + "" );
levels.setSelectedItem("4");       // Select default level
```

This loop would be placed in the applet's init() method. It adds strings representing levels 0 to 9 to the menu and initializes the box so that level four is showing as the default option.

Our next step is to designate the applet as the ItemListener for both menus—that is, the applet is named as the object that will handle the events that occur in the JComboBoxes. Then we add the JComboBox component to the applet's window:

```
controls.add(levels);                                // Control panel for menus
controls.add(patterns);
getContentPane().add(controls, "North"); // Add the controls
getContentPane().add(canvas, "Center");   // And the drawing panel
levels.addItemListener(this);                    // Register the menus with a listener
patterns.addItemListener(this);
```

Note that we use a separate controls panel (a JPanel) for the two menus and a canvas panel (another JPanel) for the drawings.

The next step is to implement the itemStateChanged() method to handle the user's se-lections. Whenever the user selects an item from a JComboBox menu, an ItemEvent is gener-ated. In order to handle these events, the applet must implement the ItemListener interface,

which consists of the single method `itemStateChanged()`. This method is invoked automatically whenever the user selects an item from one of the `JComboBox`es:

```java
public void itemStateChanged(ItemEvent e) {
    canvas.setPattern(patterns.getSelectedIndex(), levels.getSelectedIndex());
    repaint();
}
```

The `itemStateChanged()` method has the same general form as the `actionPerformed()`
method, except that its parameter is an `ItemEvent`. For this example, the program uses the
`getSelectedIndex()` method to get the selected pattern and the selected level by their
respective item numbers within the menus. It then passes these values along to the `canvas`
object, which takes care of the drawing. Finally, the method invokes the `repaint()` method.
Because the applet is a container, this will cause all of its components to be repainted as well.

Figure 12.30 illustrates the sequence of events that occurs when an item is selected from a
`JComboBox`. The complete implementation for the applet is given in Figure 12.31.

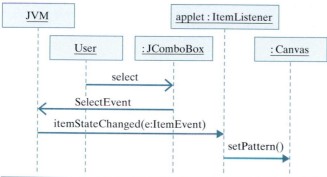

Figure 12.30 This UML sequence diagram shows the interaction between the various objects included in the action of
selecting an item from a `JComboBox`.

```java
import java.awt.*;
import javax.swing.*;
import java.awt.event.*;

public class RecursivePatterns extends JApplet implements ItemListener  {
    private String choices[] = {"Sierpinski Gasket", "Nested Boxes"};
    private JComboBox patterns = new JComboBox(choices); // Pattern choices
    private JComboBox levels = new JComboBox();          // Level choices
    private Canvas canvas = new Canvas();                // Drawing panel
    private JPanel controls = new JPanel();
```

Figure 12.31   The RecursivePatterns applet. (***Continued on next page***)

```java
public void init() {
    for (int k=0; k < 10; k++)                      // Add 10 levels
        levels.addItem(k + "" );
    patterns.setSelectedItem(choices[0]);           // Initialize menus
    levels.setSelectedItem("4");
    canvas.setBorder(BorderFactory.createTitledBorder("Drawing Canvas"));
    controls.add(levels);                           // Control panel for menus
    controls.add(patterns);
    getContentPane().add(controls,"North");         // Add controls
    getContentPane().add(canvas,"Center");          // Add drawing panel
    levels.addItemListener(this);                   // Register menus with listener
    patterns.addItemListener(this);
    setSize(canvas.WIDTH,canvas.HEIGHT+controls.getSize().width);
} // init()

public void itemStateChanged(ItemEvent e) {
    canvas.setPattern(patterns.getSelectedIndex(),levels.getSelectedIndex());
    repaint();                                      // Repaint the applet
} // itemStateChanged()
} // RecursivePatterns class
```

Figure 12.31 The RecursivePatterns applet. (*Continued from previous page*)

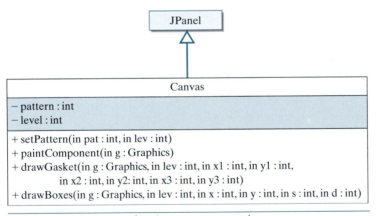

Figure 12.32 Design of a drawing Canvas class.

The actual drawing of the fractal patterns is handled by the `canvas` `JPanel` component. Its design is shown in Figure 12.32, and its implementation is given in Figure 12.33. All of the drawing is done in the `paintComponent()` method. Because the `canvas` is contained within the applet, the `paintComponent()` method is called automatically whenever the applet repaints itself. Note how the `switch` statement uses the pattern that the user chose to call the corresponding drawing method. You can see from this `switch` statement that a `JComboBox`'s items are *zero indexed*.

Zero indexing

```java
import javax.swing.*;
import java.awt.*;

public class Canvas extends JPanel {
  private static final int GASKET = 0, BOXES = 1;
  public static final int WIDTH=400, HEIGHT=400;
  private final int HBOX=10, VBOX=50, BOXSIDE=200, BOXDELTA=10;
  private final int gP1X = 10;  private final int gP1Y = 280; // Initial
  private final int gP2X = 290; private final int gP2Y = 280; // gasket
  private final int gP3X = 150; private final int gP3Y = 110; // points
  private int pattern = 0 ;                      // Current pattern
  private int level = 4;                         // Current level

  public Canvas() {
    setSize(WIDTH, HEIGHT);
  }

  public void setPattern(int pat, int lev) {
    pattern = pat;
    level = lev;
  }

    public void paintComponent(Graphics g) {
        g.setColor(getBackground());   // Redraw the panel's background
        g.drawRect(0, 0, WIDTH, HEIGHT);
        g.setColor(getForeground());
        switch (pattern) {
        case GASKET:
            drawGasket(g, level, gP1X, gP1Y, gP2X, gP2Y, gP3X, gP3Y);
            break;
        case BOXES:
            drawBoxes(g, level, HBOX, VBOX, BOXSIDE, BOXDELTA );
            break;
        } // switch
    } // paintComponent()

  /*
   * drawGasket()---recursively draws the Sierpinski
   * gasket pattern, with points (p1X, p1Y), (p2X, p2Y), (p3X, p3Y)
   * representing the vertices of its enclosing triangle.
   * level (>=0) is the recursion parameter (base case:  level 0)
   */
  private void drawGasket(Graphics g, int lev, int p1X, int p1Y,
                int p2X, int p2Y, int p3X, int p3Y) {
     g.drawLine(p1X, p1Y, p2X, p2Y); // Draw a triangle
     g.drawLine(p2X, p2Y, p3X, p3Y);
     g.drawLine(p3X, p3Y, p1X, p1Y);
     if (lev > 0) {            // If more levels, draw 3 smaller gaskets
         int q1X = (p1X + p2X) / 2;   int q1Y = (p1Y + p2Y) / 2;
         int q2X = (p1X + p3X) / 2;   int q2Y = (p1Y + p3Y) / 2;
         int q3X = (p2X + p3X) / 2;   int q3Y = (p2Y + p3Y) / 2;
         drawGasket(g, lev - 1, p1X, p1Y, q1X, q1Y, q2X, q2Y);
         drawGasket(g, lev - 1, p2X, p2Y, q1X, q1Y, q3X, q3Y);
         drawGasket(g, lev - 1, p3X, p3Y, q2X, q2Y, q3X, q3Y);
     }
  } // drawGasket()
```

Figure 12.33   The Canvas class is a drawing panel. (*Continued on next page*)

```
/*
 * drawBoxes()---recursively draws pattern of nested squares
 *   with (locX, locY) the top left corner of outer the square and
 *   side being the length square's side.
 * level (>= 0) is the recursion parameter (base case: level  0)
 * delta is used to adjust the length of the side.
 */
  private void drawBoxes(Graphics g, int level,
         int locX, int locY, int side, int delta) {
      g.drawRect(locX, locY, side, side );
      if (level > 0) {
          int newLocX = locX + delta; int newLocY = locY + delta;
          drawBoxes(g, level - 1, newLocX, newLocY, side - 2 * delta, delta);
      }
  } // drawBoxes()
} // Canvas class
```

Figure 12.33 The Canvas class is a drawing panel. (*Continued from previous page*)

CHAPTER SUMMARY

Technical Terms

base case	recursion parameter
computational overhead	recursive case
head-and-tail algorithm	recursive definition
iterative method	recursive method
last-in/first-out (LIFO)	self-similarity
method call stack	tail recursive

Summary of Important Points

- A *recursive definition* is one that defines the nth case of a concept in terms of the $(n-1)$st case plus a limiting condition. It is based on the idea of breaking a problem up into smaller, self-similar problems.
- A *recursive method* is one that calls itself. It is usually defined in terms of a *base case*, or limiting case that stops the recursive process and a recursive case, that breaks the method into a smaller, self-similar copy of itself. A *recursion parameter* is generally used to control the recursion.
- An iterative algorithm is one that uses a loop as its control structure. Any algorithm that can be done iteratively can also be done recursively, and vice versa.
- Because method calling is relatively costly in terms of both memory used and CPU time involved, a recursive algorithm is generally less efficient than an iterative one that does the same thing.
- In designing recursive algorithms, the *base case* defines a limit. Each level of recursion should make progress toward the limit, and the algorithm should eventually reach the limit. The limit is usually expressed in terms of the *recursion parameter*.

- A recursive method is *tail recursive* if and only if each of its recursive calls is the last action executed by the method.
- A Swing `JComboBox` component is used to represent a GUI drop-down menu.

SOLUTIONS TO SELF-STUDY EXERCISES

SOLUTION 12.1   The output produced by `mystery(0)` would be 0 1 2 3 4 5 6. The output produced by `mystery(100)` would be 100.

SOLUTION 12.2   The output produced by `mystery(5)` would be: 5 4 3, and so on. In other words, this is an infinite recursion.

SOLUTION 12.3

```
Definition: twoToN(N), N >= 0
   1, if N == 0                    // Base case
   2 * twoToN(N - 1),  N > 0       // Recursive case
```

SOLUTION 12.4   The function x^n is known as the power function:

```
Definition: power(X,N), N >= 0
   1, if N == 0                  // Base case
   X * power(X, N - 1),  N > 0   // Recursive case
```

SOLUTION 12.5   Yes, the two definitions for nested boxes are equivalent. Suppose the square starts out with a side of 20. The definition given in the exercise will also draw squares with sides of 20, 15, 10, 5.

SOLUTION 12.6   A recursive definition for the pattern in Figure 12.3:

```
Draw a square with side, s.
Inscribe a circle with diameter, s.
If s > 5,
  Draw a smaller version of same pattern. // Recursive case
```

SOLUTION 12.7   The `printString2("hello")` method will print "olleh".

SOLUTION 12.8   A definition for `countDown()`:

```
/**
 * countDown(N) recursively prints a countdown beginning at N and ending at 1
 * @ param N >= 1
 * Base case: N == 0
 */
void countDown(int N) {
    if (N == 0)                          // Base case
        System.out.println("blastoff");
    else {
        System.out.print(N + ", ");      // Recursive case
        countDown(N - 1);
    }
} // countDown()
```

SOLUTION 12.9   A revised definition for countDown():

```
/**
 * countDown(N) recursively prints a countdown
 *   beginning at N, counting every other number, 10 8 6 ...
 *   and ending at "blastoff"
 * @ param N >= 1
 * Base case: N <= 0
 */
void countDown(int N) {
    if (N <= 0)                                // Base case
        System.out.println("blastoff");
    else {
        System.out.print(N + ", ");            // Recursive case
        countDown(N - 2 );
    }
} // countDown()
```

SOLUTION 12.10   A method to sum the numbers from 1 to N.

```
int sum(int N) {
    if (N == 0)
        return 0;
    else
        return N + sum(N-1);
}
```

SOLUTION 12.11   A method to change each blank within a string to two blanks.

```
String addBlanks(String s) {
    if (s.length() == 0)
        return "";
    else if (s.charAt(0) == ' ')
        return ' ' + s.charAt(0) + addBlanks(s.substring(1));
    else
        return s.charAt(0) + addBlanks(s.substring(1));
}
```

SOLUTION 12.12   A method to print out all possible outcomes for a chess player playing N games. printOutcomes(str, N) will print all outcomes for the next N games given that results for previous games are stored in the string named str.

```
public static void printOutcomes(String str, int N){
    if (N = 1){                                // Base case: win, lose, or draw one game
        System.out.println(str + "W");
        System.out.println(str + "L");
        System.out.println(str + "D");
    } else {                                   // Recursive case
        printOutcomes(str + "W", N - 1);
        printOutcomes(str + "L", N - 1);
        printOutcomes(str + "D", N - 1);
    } // else
} // printOutcomes()
```

SOLUTION 12.13

```java
public static void main(String args[]) {
   int numbers[] = {0, 2, 4, 6, 8, 10, 12, 14, 16, 18};
   Searcher searcher = new Searcher();
   for (int k = 0; k <= 20; k++) {
      int result = searcher.search(numbers, k);
      if (result != -1)
         System.out.println(k + " found at " + result);
      else
         System.out.println(k + " is not in the array ");
   } // for
} // main()
```

SOLUTION 12.14   The `sort()` method is used as a public interface to the recursive `selectionSort()` method:

```java
/**
 * sort(arr) sorts the int array, arr
 *   Pre: arr is not null
 *   Post: arr will be arranged so that arr[j] <= arr[k]
 *       for any j < k
 */
public void sort(int arr[]) {
    selectionSort(arr, arr.length - 1);
            // Just call the recursive method
}
```

SOLUTION 12.15   An iterative version of `findMax()`:

```java
/**
 * findMax (arr,N) returns the index of the largest
 *   value between arr[0] and arr[N], N >= 0.
 *   Pre: 0 <= N <= arr.length -1
 *   Post: arr[findMax()]>= arr[k] for k between 0 and N.
 */
private int findMax(int arr[], int N) {
   int maxSoFar = 0;
   for (int k = 0; k <= N; k++)
      if (arr[k] > arr[maxSoFar])
            maxSoFar = k;
   return maxSoFar;
} // findMax()
```

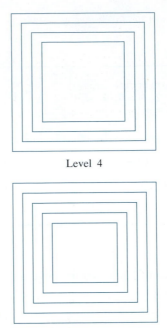

Level 4

Level 5

Figure 12.34 Levels four and five of the nested boxes pattern.

SOLUTION 12.16 Levels four and five of the nested boxes pattern are shown in Figure 12.34.

SOLUTION 12.17 The following method will reduce the length of the side by `delta` percent at each level of recursion. The spacing between the boxes will vary by a constantly decreasing amount.

```
private void  drawBoxes(Graphics g, int level, int locX,
                  int locY, int side, int delta) {
    g.drawRect(locX, locY, side, side );
    if (level > 0) {
      int dside = side * delta / 100; // Percent delta
      int newLocX = locX + dside;
      int newLocY = locY + dside;
      drawBoxes(g, level - 1, newLocX, newLocY, side - 2 * dside, delta);
    }
} // drawBoxes()
```

SOLUTION 12.18

```
private void drawBoxesIterative(Graphics g, int level,
            int locX, int locY, int side, int delta) {
  for (int k = level; k >= 0; k--) {
    g.drawRect(locX, locY, side, side );   // Draw a square
    locX += delta;                         // Calculate new location
    locY += delta;
    side -= 2 * delta;                     // Calculate new side length
  }
} // drawBoxes()
```

SOLUTION 12.19   The level-two and -three gaskets are shown in Figure 12.35.
topfloat

SOLUTION 12.20   The `printReverse()` method is not tail recursive because in that method the recursive call is not the last statement executed.

SOLUTION 12.21   The `countChar()` method is tail recursive. The recursive calls are not the last statements in the method definition. However, each of the recursive calls would be the last statement executed by the method.

EXERCISES

EXERCISE 12.1   Explain the difference between the following pairs of terms:

  a. *Iteration* and *recursion*.
  b. *Recursive method* and *recursive definition*.
  c. *Base case* and *recursive case*.
  d. *Head* and *tail*.
  e. *Tail* and *nontail* recursive.

EXERCISE 12.2   Describe how the *method call stack* is used during a method call and return.

EXERCISE 12.3   Why is a recursive algorithm generally less efficient than an iterative algorithm?

EXERCISE 12.4   A tree, such as a maple tree or pine tree, has a recursive structure. Describe how a tree's structure displays *self-similarity* and *divisibility*.

EXERCISE 12.5   Write a recursive method to print each element of an array of `double`.

EXERCISE 12.6   Write a recursive method to print each element of an array of `double` from the last to the first element.

EXERCISE 12.7   Write a recursive method that will concatenate the elements of an array of `String` into a single `String` delimited by blanks.

EXERCISE 12.8   Write a recursive method that is passed a single `int` parameter, $N \geq 0$, and prints all the odd numbers between 1 and N.

EXERCISE 12.9   Write a recursive method that takes a single `int` parameter $N \geq 0$ and prints the sequence of even numbers from N down to 0.

EXERCISE 12.10   Write a recursive method that takes a single `int` parameter $N \geq 0$ and prints the multiples of 10 between 0 and N.

*Note: For programming exercises, **first** draw a UML class diagram describing all classes and their inheritance relationships and/or associations.*

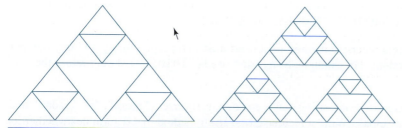

Figure 12.35 Levels two and three of the Sierpinski gasket.

EXERCISE 12.11   Write a recursive method to print the following geometric pattern:

```
#
# #
# # #
# # # #
# # # # #
```

EXERCISE 12.12   Write recursive methods to print each of the following patterns.

```
# # # # # # # #     # # # # # # # #
  # # # # # # #     # # # # # # #
    # # # # # #     # # # # # #
      # # # # #     # # # # #
        # # # #     # # # #
          # # #     # # #
            # #     # #
              #     #
```

EXERCISE 12.13   Write a recursive method to print all multiples of M up to $M * N$.

EXERCISE 12.14   Write a recursive method to compute the sum of the grades stored in an array.

 EXERCISE 12.15   Write a recursive method to count the occurrences of a substring within a string.

EXERCISE 12.16   Write a recursive method to remove the HTML tags from a string.

EXERCISE 12.17   Implement a recursive version of the `Caesar.decode()` method from Chapter 8.

 EXERCISE 12.18   The Fibonacci sequence (named after the Italian mathematician Leonardo of Pisa, ca. 1200) consists of the numbers $0,1,1,2,3,5,8,13,\ldots$ in which each number (except for the first two) is the sum of the two preceding numbers. Write a recursive method `fibonacci(N)` that prints the first N Fibonacci numbers.

 EXERCISE 12.19   Write a recursive method to rotate a `String` by N characters to the right. For example, `rotateR("hello," 3)` should return "llohe".

EXERCISE 12.20   Write a recursive method to rotate a `String` by N characters to the left. For example, `rotateL("hello," 3)` should return "lohel".

EXERCISE 12.21   Write a recursive method to convert a `String` representing a binary number to its decimal equivalent. For example, `binTodecimal("101011")` should return the `int` value 43.

EXERCISE 12.22   A palindrome is a string that is equal to its reverse—"mom", "i", "radar", and "able was i ere i saw elba". Write a recursive `boolean` method that determines whether its `String` parameter is a palindrome.

Figure 12.36 A level-four binary
tree pattern.

EXERCISE 12.23   Challenge: Incorporate a `drawBinaryTree()` method into the `RecursivePatterns` program. A level-one binary tree has two branches. At each subsequent level, two smaller branches are grown from the endpoints of every existing branch. The geometry is easier if you use 45-degree angles for the branches. Figure 12.36 shows a level-four binary tree drawn upside down.

EXERCISE 12.24   Challenge: Towers of Hanoi. According to legend, some Buddhist monks were given the task of moving 64 golden disks from one diamond needle to another needle, using a third needle as a backup. To begin with, the disks were stacked one on top of the other from largest to smallest (Fig. 12.37). The rules were that only one disk could be moved at a time and that a larger disk could never go on top of a smaller one. The end of the world was supposed to occur when the monks finished the task!

Write a recursive method, `move(int N, char A, char B, char C)`, that will print out directions the monks can use to solve the towers of Hanoi problem. For example, here's what it should output for the three-disk case, `move(3, "A", "B","C")`:

```
Move 1 disk from A to B.
Move 1 disk from A to C.
Move 1 disk from B to C.
Move 1 disk from A to B.
Move 1 disk from C to A.
Move 1 disk from C to B.
Move 1 disk from A to B.
```

Figure 12.37 The towers of Hanoi
problem. Move all the disks from
needle A to needle B. Only one
disk can be moved at a time, and
a larger disk can never go on top of
a smaller one.

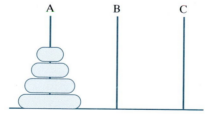

Photograph courtesy of Cindy Charles, PhotoEdit.

13

Graphical User Interfaces

OBJECTIVES

After studying this chapter, you will

- Gain more experience with the Swing component set.
- Understand the relationship between the AWT and Swing.
- Learn more about Java's event model.
- Be able to design and build useful Graphical User Interfaces (GUIs).
- Appreciate how object-oriented design principles were used to extend Java's GUI capabilities.

OUTLINE

13.1   Introduction

As we have seen, a *Graphical User Interface* (GUI) creates a certain way of interacting with a program. It is what gives a program its *look and feel*. In preceding chapters, we have already used the basic components from which GUIs are created, including buttons, text fields, labels, and text areas. Throughout this chapter, we will focus on designing and building GUIs that are easy for users to navigate. However, Java's GUI libraries are so large that we will concentrate on only a handful of additional components, including containers, check boxes, radio buttons, and menus.

We will try to identify design principles that can be applied to the design of more advanced interfaces. Also, because Java's GUI classes provide an excellent example of object-oriented design, we will highlight some of the important design decisions and principles that have influenced the development of Java's GUI classes in both the AWT and Swing. Let's begin with a brief history Java's GUI libraries.

13.2   Java GUIs: From AWT to Swing

Ever since the release of version 1.2 of the Java Development Kit (JDK) in 2000, Java has contained two distinct libraries of GUI components. The *Abstract Windowing Toolkit* (AWT) has been part of Java since the original 1.0 version of the JDK 1.0. The more advanced *Swing component set* was first introduced in JDK 1.1 and was extensively revised in JDK 1.2.

Although the original version of the AWT was suitable for developing Java applets, it wasn't powerful enough to support full-fledged applications. Commonly used programs, such as word processors and spreadsheets, have GUI requirements that were just too much for the original AWT. The main problem was that the AWT was dependent on the underlying operating system. This meant that Java GUI programs were forced to rely on GUI elements that were part of the underlying operating system. A Java GUI program running on a Windows platform had to depend on Windows code for implementations of its buttons and text fields. A Java program running on Unix depended upon underlying Unix code for its GUI components. Such dependence on the underlying operating system made the AWT less portable and less efficient.

In contrast, the Swing GUI components are part of the *Java Foundation Classes* (JFC), a collection of classes that do not depend as much on the underlying platform. The Swing library makes it possible to write GUI programs entirely in Java. Because they are rendered entirely by Java code, Swing components make it possible to design GUIs that are truly platform independent. Such programs are much more portable than those that rely on AWT components and the underlying platform. A program that uses Swing components will have the same look and feel on a Mac, Windows, or Unix platform.

13.2.1   Heavyweight Versus Lightweight Components

AWT components are based on the **peer model**, a design in which every AWT component has a corresponding class (a *peer*) written in the underlying system's code. For example, the `java.awt.Button` class has a peer named `java.awt.peer.Button`. The peer class serves as the interface between the Java code and the computer's underlying windowing system. The methods in the peer class are written in so-called *native* code—that is, the non-Java code of the underlying operating system. Therefore, AWT components are inherently platform dependent.

AWT components are called *heavyweight* because they depend on the native (peer) system for their drawing and rendering. Since every AWT component has an associated peer com-

The AWT peer model

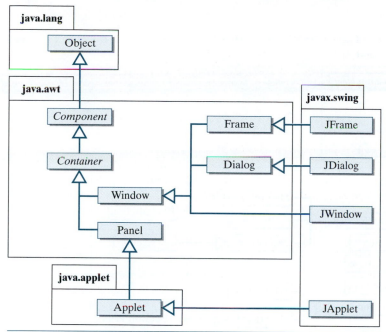

Figure 13.1 Swing classes, part 1: Relationship between the AWT and the top-level Swing windows.

ponent, a Java AWT component would look just like the peer component. This is why an AWT button on a Windows platform looks just like a Windows button. In effect, the AWT button, via its peer, creates and uses a Windows button. When you change the Java button's label, it must call a method in the peer class that changes the label of the peer button. This interaction between Java and the native windowing system requires a good deal of overhead, thereby affecting the overall efficiency of the system.

By contrast, a **lightweight component** is one written entirely in Java. Instead of depending on a native component for its rendering, a lightweight component is drawn and rendered entirely by Java code. Because they do not depend on underlying system code, Swing components are more efficient and more portable than corresponding AWT components.

Lightweight components

Figures 13.1 and 13.2 show the relationship between AWT and Swing classes. The top-level Swing classes—`JApplet`, `JDialog`, `JFrame`, and `JWindow`—are direct subclasses of their corresponding AWT counterparts. These are the top-level GUI windows. The remaining Swing components (Fig. 13.2) are subclasses of `java.awt.Component` and `java.awt.Container`. As you can see, the names of Swing and AWT components are very similar. Swing components that have corresponding AWT components have names that begin with "J."

One might think that because Swing components are superior to their AWT counterparts, the AWT package will eventually be dropped. However, this is not likely. Even if a Java program uses Swing components exclusively, that will still not break the dependence on the AWT.

There are several reasons for this dependence. First, Swing's top-level window classes—`JApplet`, `JDialog`, `JFrame`, and `JWindow`—are defined as extensions to their AWT counterparts. This means that Swing-based GUIs are still dependent on the AWT. Java programs

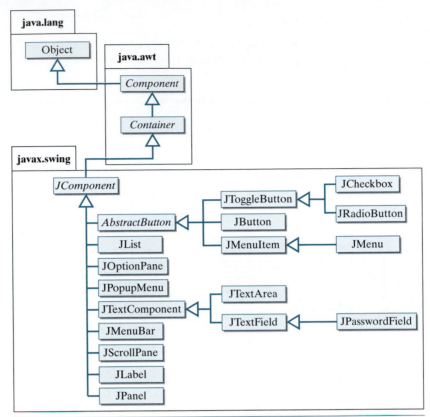

Figure 13.2 Swing classes, part 2: Swing GUI components are derived from the JComponent class.

need to have some way to map their windows to the windowing system used on the native (Windows, Unix, or Macintosh) platform. The AWT's top-level windows—Window, Frame, Dialog, and Panel—provide that mapping.

Second, the JComponent class, which is the basis for all Swing components, is derived from java.awt.Container. There are many more such dependencies. Fundamentally, Swing components are based on the AWT.

Finally, all GUI applications and applets use layout managers (java.awt.FlowLayout), fonts (java.awt.Font), colors (java.awt.Color), and other noncomponent classes that are defined in the AWT. There is just no way to design a GUI without using AWT classes. Therefore, the programs presented in this and subsequent chapters will use Swing components instead of corresponding AWT components, but they also will use layouts and other elements from the AWT.

JAVA PROGRAMMING TIP: Swing Documentation. Complete documentation of the Swing classes is available for downloading or browsing on Sun's Web site at http://java.sun.com/docs/.

13.3 The Swing Component Set

Java's Swing components are defined in a collection of packages named `javax.swing.*`, which is imported by the code shown in this and subsequent chapters. Swing packages include the following:

```
javax.swing.event.*
javax.swing.text.*
javax.swing.plaf.*
```

The `javax.swing.event` package defines the various Swing events and their listeners, such as the `MenuEvent` and the `MenuListener`. (In the AWT, the AWT events and listeners are defined in `java.awt.event`.)

The `javax.swing.text` package contains the classes for `JTextField` and `JTextComponent`. The Swing text components are more complex than their AWT counterparts. For example, one of their important features is the ability to undo changes made to the text they contain. This feature is crucial for building sophisticated word-processing applications.

The `javax.swing.plaf` package contains Swing's look-and-feel classes. The term *plaf* is an acronym for **pluggable look and feel**. It refers to the fact that changing an application's look and feel is a simple matter of "plugging in" a different plaf model. Changing how a program looks does not change what it does.

Swing's platform-independent look and feel is achieved by placing all the code responsible for drawing a component in a class that is separate from the component itself. For example, in addition to `JButton`, the class that defines the button control, there will be a separate class responsible for drawing the button on the screen. The drawing class will control the button's color, shape, and other characteristics of its appearance.

There are several look-and-feel packages built into Swing. For example, the `javax.swing.plaf.motif` package contains the classes that implement the Motif interface, a common Unix-based interface. The `javax.swing.plaf.windows` packages contains classes that support a Windows look and feel, and the `javax.swing.plaf.metal` package provides classes that support the Metal interface, a Java look and feel. These classes know how to draw each component and how to react to mouse, keyboard, and other events associated with these components.

> Look and feel

13.4 Object-Oriented Design: Model-View-Controller Architecture

Java's Swing components have been implemented using an object-oriented design known as the **model-view-controller (MVC)** model. Any Swing component can be considered in terms of three independent aspects: what state it is in (its model), how it looks (its view), and what it does (its controller).

For example, a button's role is to appear on the interface waiting to be clicked. When it is clicked, the button's appearance changes. It looks pushed in or it changes color briefly, and then it changes back to its original (unclicked) appearance. In the MVC model, this aspect of the button is its **view**. If you were designing an interface for a button, you would need visual representations for both the clicked and the unclicked button (as well as other possible states).

When you click a button, its internal state changes from pressed to unpressed. You have also probably seen buttons that were disabled—that is, in a state where they just ignore your

> View

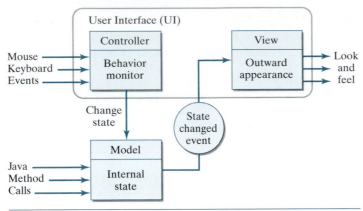

Figure 13.3 The model-view-controller architecture.

Model

clicks. Whether a button is enabled or disabled and whether it is pressed or not are properties of its internal state. Taken together, such properties constitute the button's **model**. Of course, a button's view—how it looks—depends on its model. When a button is pressed, it has one appearance, and when it is disabled, it has another.

Controller

Because a button's state will change when it is clicked or when it is enabled by the program, some object needs to keep track of these changes. That part of the component is its **controller**.

Figure 13.3 shows how the button's model, view, and controller interact with each other. Suppose the user clicks the button. This action is detected by the controller. Whenever the mouse button is pressed, the controller tells the model to change into the pressed state. The model, in turn, generates an event that is passed to the view. The event tells the view that the button needs to be redrawn to reflect its change in state.

When the mouse button is released, a similar sequence of events occurs. The model is told to change to the unpressed state. It in turn generates an event, handled by the view, which changes the button's appearance.

A change in the button's appearance does not necessarily depend on direct action by the user. For example, the program itself could call a method that disables the button. In this case, the program issues a command directly to the model, which in turn generates an event that causes the view to change the object's appearance.

For some Swing components, such as the text components, this three-part model is implemented almost exactly as we just described. For others, such as `JButton`, one class is used to implement both the view and the controller. The `JButton` model is defined in the `Default-ButtonModel` class, and its view and controller are defined in the `BasicButtonUI` class (UI stands for User Interface). The point is that for some components, Swing has organized the view and control—the look and the feel—into a single class.

13.4.1   Pluggable Look and Feel

The MVC model uses a clear division of labor to implement a GUI component. The main advantage of this design is the independence between the model, the view, and the controller. If you want to give a button a different look and feel, you can redefine its view and its controller.

By combining the view and controller into a single class, Swing makes it even easier to change a component's look and feel. For example, to design your own look and feel for a `JBut-`

Figure 13.4 The same Java application using the Motif, Windows, and Metal look and feel styles.

ton, you would define a class that implemented all of the methods in the `BasicButtonUI`. Of course, this is a job for an experienced software developer.

However, if you just want to set your program to use one of the pre-defined look-and-feel models, you can simply use the `UIManager.setLookAndFeel()` method:

```java
public static void main (String args[]){
  try{
     UIManager.setLookAndFeel("javax.swing.plaf.metal.MetalLookAndFeel");
  }catch (Exception e) {
     System.out.err("Exception: " + e.getMessage());
  }
} // main()
```

Java's default, the *Metal* look and feel, has been designed specifically for Java applications. For a Windows look, you can use the following argument:

```java
com.sun.java.swing.plaf.windows.WindowsLookAndFeel
```

Figure 13.4 shows how the simple application would appear under the three different look-and-feel styles.

SELF-STUDY EXERCISE

EXERCISE 13.1   The MVC architecture is a model of object-oriented design. But if a `JButton` is really composed of three separate parts, how can we still call it a component? Isn't it really three things?

13.5   The Java Event Model

As we saw in Chapter 4, whatever happens while the computer is running is classified as an event. Every keystroke and mouse click, every time a disk is inserted into a disk drive, an event is generated. The handling of events is an important element of GUI programming. Therefore, before we begin discussing how to design GUIs, it will be useful to review the main concepts of Java's **event model**.

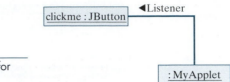

Figure 13.5 The GUI listens for action events on the JButton.

When a Java program is running, events generated by the hardware are passed up through the operating system (and through the browser, for applets) to the program. Events that belong to the program must be handled by the program (refer to Fig. 4.18). For example, if you click your browser's menu bar, that event will be handled by the browser itself. If you click a button contained in the Java program, that event should be handled by the program.

In Java, whenever something happens within a GUI component, an event object is generated and passed to the *event listener* registered to handle the component's events. You have seen numerous examples of this process in earlier chapters, but we've included a simple example to serve as a reminder.

Suppose you create a `JButton` in a GUI as follows:

```java
private JButton clickme = new JButton("ClickMe");
```

Whenever the user clicks the `JButton`, an `ActionEvent` is generated. In order to handle these events, the GUI must register the `JButton` with a listener object that listens for action events. This can be done in an applet's `init()` method or in an application's constructor method, as in this example:

```java
public MyGUI() {

  add(clickme);   // Add clickme to the GUI and assign it a listener
  clickme.addActionListener(this);
}
```

In this case, we have designated the GUI itself (`this`) as an `ActionListener` for `clickme` (Fig. 13.5). A **listener** is any object that implements a *listener interface*, which is one of the interfaces derived from `java.util.EventListener`. An `ActionListener` is an object that listens for and receives `ActionEvents`.

In order to complete the event-handling code, the GUI must implement the `ActionListener` interface. As Figure 13.6 shows, implementing an interface is a matter of declaring the interface in the class heading and implementing the methods contained in the interface, in this case the `actionPerformed()` method.

Now that we have implemented the code in Figure 13.6, whenever the user clicks `clickme`, that action is encapsulated within an `ActionEvent` object and passed to the `actionPerformed()` method. This method contains Java code that will handle the user's action in an appropriate way. For this example, it modifies the button's label by appending an asterisk to it each time it is clicked. Figure 13.7 depicts the sequence of actions and events that occur when the user clicks a button.

```
import javax.swing.*;
import java.awt.event.*;

public class MyGUI extends JFrame
                            implements ActionListener {
    private JButton clickme = new JButton("ClickMe");

    public MyGUI() {
                            // Add clickme to the GUI and assign it a listener
        getContentPane().add(clickme);
        clickme.addActionListener(this);
        setSize(200,200);
        setVisible(true);
    } // init()
    public void actionPerformed(ActionEvent e) {
        if (e.getSource() == clickme) {
            clickme.setText(clickme.getText()+"*");
        }
    } // actionPerformed()
    public static void main(String args[]) {
        MyGUI gui = new MyGUI();
    }
} // MyGUI class
```

Figure 13.6 A simple GUI application that handles action events on a JButton.

The methods used to handle the ActionEvent are derived from the java.util.EventObject class, the root class for all events (Fig. 13.8). Our example (Fig. 13.6) uses the getSource() method to get a reference to the object that generated the event. To see what

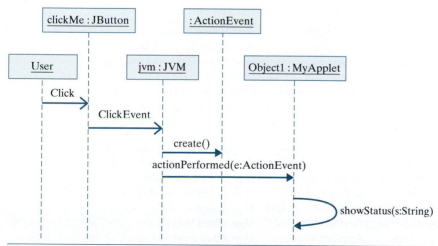

Figure 13.7 A UML depiction of the sequence of actions and events that take place when a button is clicked. The vertical lines represent time lines, with time running from top to bottom. The arrows between lines represent messages passing between objects.

EventObject
+ EventObject(in src : Object) + getSource() : Object + toString() : String

Figure 13.8   An EventObject. The getSource() method is used to get the object that caused the event.

information is contained in an event object, we can use the toString() method to print a string representation of the event that was generated. Here's what it displays:

```
java.awt.event.ActionEvent[ACTION_PERFORMED,cmd=ClickMe]
  on javax.swing.JButton[,58,5,83x27,
  layout=javax.swing.OverlayLayout]
```

As you can see, the event generated was an ACTION_PERFORMED event, in response to the ClickMe command. The source of the event was the JButton.

13.5.1   Event Classes

Although the event model is the same for both AWT and Swing classes, the Swing package introduces many additional events. Table 13.1 lists the events generated by both AWT and Swing components. You worked with some of these when we wrote GUIs that handled ActionEvents for JButtons and JTextFields in preceding chapters.

In viewing Table 13.1, remember that the classes it lists are arranged in a hierarchy. This will affect the events any given object can generate. For example, a JButton is a JComponent (Fig. 13.2), so in addition to generating ActionEvents when the user clicks on it, it can

Table 13.1. Java's AWTEvents for each Component type

Component	Event	Description
Button, JButton	ActionEvent	User clicked button
CheckBox, JCheckBox	ItemEvent	User toggled a checkbox
CheckboxMenuItem, JCheckboxMenuItem	ItemEvent	User toggled a checkbox
Choice, JPopupMenu	ItemEvent	User selected a choice
Component, JComponent	ComponentEvent	Component was moved or resized
	FocusEvent	Component acquired or lost focus
	KeyEvent	User typed a key
	MouseEvent	User manipulated the mouse
Container, JContainer	ContainerEvent	Component added/removed from container
List, JList	ActionEvent	User double-clicked a list item
	ItemEvent	User clicked a list item
Menu, JMenu	ActionEvent	User selected menu item
Scrollbar, JScrollbar	AdjustmentEvent	User moved scrollbar
TextComponent, JTextComponent	TextEvent	User edited text
TextField, JTextField	ActionEvent	User typed Enter key
Window, JWindow	WindowEvent	User manipulated window

Original source: David Flanagan, *Java in a Nutshell*, 2d ed., O'Reilly Associates, 1997. Modified for Swing components.

Table 13.2. Some of the events defined in the Swing library

Component	Event	Description
JPopupMenu	PopupMenuEvent	User selected a choice
JComponent	AncestorEvent	Event occurred in an ancestor
JList	ListSelectionEvent	User double-clicked a list item
	ListDataEvent	List's contents were changed
JMenu	MenuEvent	User selected menu item
JTextComponent	CaretEvent	Mouse clicked in text
	UndoableEditEvent	Undoable edit occurred
JTable	TableModelEvent	Items added/removed from table
	TableColumnModelEvent	Table column was moved
JTree	TreeModelEvent	Items added/removed from tree
	TreeSelectionEvent	User selected a tree node
	TreeExpansionEvent	User expanded or collapsed a tree node
JWindow	WindowEvent	User manipulated window

also generate MouseEvents when the user moves the mouse over it. Similarly, because a JTextField is also a JComponent, it can generate KeyEvents as well as ActionEvents.

Note that the more generic events, such as those that involve moving, focusing, or resizing a component, are associated with the more generic components. For example, the JComponent class contains methods that are used to manage ComponentEvents. Because they are sub-classes of JComponent, JButtons and JTextFields can also use these methods. Defining the more generic methods in the JComponent superclass is another example of the effective use of inheritance.

EFFECTIVE DESIGN: Inheritance.   The higher a method is defined in the inheritance hierarchy, the broader is its use.

Table 13.2 lists events that are new with the Swing classes. Some of the events apply to new components. For example, JTable and JTree do not have AWT counterparts. Other events provide Swing components with capabilities not available in their AWT counterparts. For example, a CaretEvent allows the programmer to have control over mouse clicks that occur within a text component.

Tables 13.1 and 13.2 provide only a brief summary of these classes and Swing components. For further details, consult the JDK online documentation at

http://java.sun.com/docs/

SELF-STUDY EXERCISES

EXERCISE 13.2   Is it possible to register a component with more than one listener?

EXERCISE 13.3   Is it possible for a component to have two different kinds of listeners?

13.6   CASE STUDY: Designing a Basic GUI

What elements make up a basic user interface? If you think about all of the various interfaces you have encountered—and don't limit yourself to computers—they all have the following elements:

- Some way to provide help/guidance to the user.
- Some way to allow input of information.
- Some way to allow output of information.
- Some way to control the interaction between the user and the device.

Think about the interface on a beverage machine. Printed text on the machine will tell you what choices you have, where to put your money, and what to do if something goes wrong. The coin slot is used to input money. There's often some kind of display to tell you how much money you've inserted. And there's usually a bunch of buttons and levers that let you control the interaction with the machine.

The same kinds of elements make up the basic computer interface. Designing a Graphical User Interface is primarily a process of choosing components that can effectively perform the tasks of input, output, control, and guidance.

EFFECTIVE DESIGN: User Interface.   A user interface must effectively perform the tasks of input, output, control, and guidance.

In the programs we designed in the earlier chapters, we used two different kinds of interfaces. In the *command-line* interface, we used printed prompts to inform the user, typed commands for data entry and user control, and printed output to report results. Our GUI interfaces used JLabels to guide and prompt the user, JTextFields and JTextAreas as basic input and output devices, and either JButtons or JTextFields for user control.

Let's begin by building a basic GUI in the form of a Java application. To keep the example as close as possible to the GUIs we have already used, we will build it out of the following Swing components: JLabel, JTextField, JTextArea, and JButton.

13.6.1   The Metric Converter Application

Suppose the coach of the cross-country team asks you to write a Java application that can be used to convert miles to kilometers. The program should let the user input a distance in miles and should report the equivalent distance in kilometers.

Before we design the interface for this, let's first define a MetricConverter class that can be used to perform the conversions (Fig. 13.9). For now at least, this class's only task will be to convert miles to kilometers, for which it will use the formula that 1 kilometer equals 0.62 miles:

```
public class MetricConverter {
    public static double milesToKm(double miles) {
        return miles / 0.62;
    }
}
```

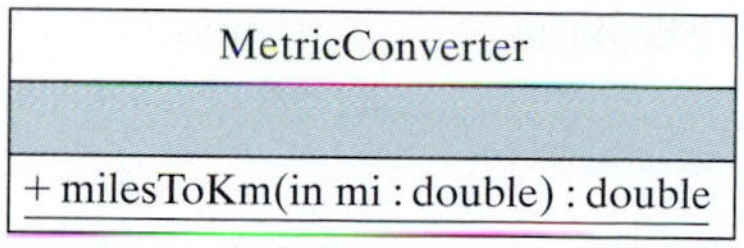

Figure 13.9 The `MetricConverter` class has a single method to convert miles to kilometers.

Note that the method takes a `double` as input and returns a `double`. Also, by declaring the method `static`, we make it a class method, so it can be invoked simply by

```
MetricConverter.milesToKm(10);
```

Choosing the Components

Let's now design a GUI to handle the interaction with the user. First, we choose Swing components for each of the four interface tasks of input, output, control, and guidance. For each component, it might be useful to refer back to Figure 13.2 to note its location in the Swing hierarchy.

Which components do we need?

- A `JLabel` is a display area for a short string of text, an image, or both. Its AWT counterpart, the `Label`, cannot display images. A `JLabel` does not react to input. Therefore, it is used primarily to display a graphic or small amounts of static text. It is perfectly suited to serve as a prompt, which is what we will use it for in this interface.
- A `JTextField` is a component that allows the user to edit a single line of text. It is identical to its AWT counterpart, the `TextField`. By using its `getText()` and `setText()` methods, a `JTextField` can be used for either input or output, or both. For this problem, we'll use it to perform the interface's input task.
- A `JTextArea` is a multiline text area that can be used for either input or output. It is almost identical to the AWT `TextArea` component. One difference, however, is that a `JTextArea` does not contain scrollbars by default. For this program, we'll use the `JTextArea` for displaying the results of conversions. Because it is used solely for output in this program, we'll make it *uneditable* to prevent the user from typing in it.
- A `JButton` will be our main control for this interface. By implementing the `ActionListener` interface we will handle the user's action events.

Choosing the Top-Level Window

The next issue is what kind of top-level window to use for this interface. For applet interfaces, the top-level component would be a `JApplet`. For Java applications, you would typically use a `JFrame` as the top-level window. Both of these classes are subclasses of `Container`, so they are suitable for holding the components that make up the interface (Fig. 13.1).

What top-level window to use?

As noted earlier, `JApplet`s and `JFrame`s are both examples of heavyweight components, so they both have windows associated with them. To display a `JFrame` we just have to give it a size and make it visible. Because a frame runs as a standalone window, not within a browser context, it should also be able to exit the application when the user closes the frame.

Designing a Layout

The next step in designing the interface is deciding how to arrange the components so that they will be visually appealing and comprehensible, as well as easy to use.

How should the components be arranged?

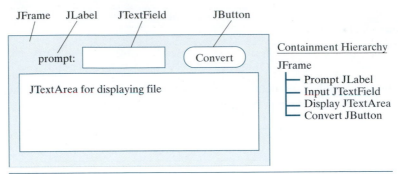

Figure 13.10 A design and layout for the Metric Converter GUI. The *containment hierarchy* (also called a *widget hierarchy*) shows the containment relationships among the components.

Figure 13.10 shows a design for the layout. The largest component is the output text area, which occupies the center of the JFrame. The prompt, input text field, and control button are arranged in a row above the text area. This is a simple and straightforward layout.

Figure 13.10 provides a **containment hierarchy**, also called a **widget hierarchy**, which shows the containment relationships among the various components. Although it may not be apparent for this simple layout, the containment hierarchy plays an important role in showing how the various components are grouped in the interface. For this design, we have a relatively simple hierarchy, with only one level of containment. All of the components are contained directly in the JFrame.

Figure 13.11 shows the design of the Converter class, which extends the JFrame class and implements the ActionListener interface. As a JFrame subclass, a Converter can contain GUI components. As an implementor of the ActionListener interface, it also will be able to handle action events through the actionPerformed() method.

Figure 13.12 gives the implementation of the Converter class. Note the three packages that are imported. The first contains definitions of the Swing classes, and the other two contain definitions of AWT events and layout managers used in the program.

We have to do all the initializing tasks in the constructor. First, we have to set the JFrame's layout to FlowLayout. A **layout manager** is the object responsible for sizing and arranging

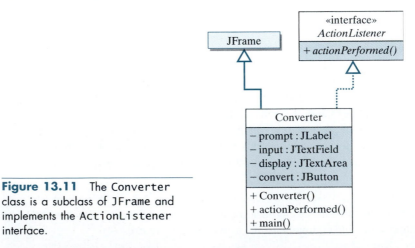

Figure 13.11 The Converter class is a subclass of JFrame and implements the ActionListener interface.

```java
import javax.swing.*;                              // Packages used
import java.awt.*;
import java.awt.event.*;

public class Converter extends JFrame implements ActionListener{
    private JLabel prompt = new JLabel("Distance in miles: ");
    private JTextField input = new JTextField(6);
    private JTextArea display = new JTextArea(10,20);
    private JButton convert = new JButton("Convert!");

    public Converter() {
        getContentPane().setLayout(new FlowLayout());
        getContentPane().add(prompt);
        getContentPane().add(input);
        getContentPane().add(convert);
        getContentPane().add(display);
        display.setLineWrap(true);
        display.setEditable(false);
        convert.addActionListener(this);
    } // Converter()

    public void actionPerformed( ActionEvent e ) {
        double miles =  Double.valueOf(input.getText()).doubleValue();
        double km = MetricConverter.milesToKm(miles);
        display.append(miles + " miles equals " + km + " kilometers\n");
    } // actionPerformed()

    public static void main(String args[]) {
        Converter f = new Converter();
        f.setSize(400, 300);
        f.setVisible(true);
        f.addWindowListener(new WindowAdapter() {
            public void windowClosing(WindowEvent e) {
                System.exit(0);                      // Quit the application
            }
        });
    } // main()
} // Converter class
```

Figure 13.12   The Converter class implements a simple GUI interface.

the components in a container so that the elements are organized in the best-possible manner. A flow layout is the simplest arrangement: the components are arranged left to right in the window, wrapping around to the next "row" if necessary.

Second, note the statements used to set the layout and to add components directly to the JFrame. Instead of adding components directly to the JFrame, we must add them to its content pane:

```java
getContentPane().add(input);
```

A **content pane** is a JPanel that serves as the working area of the JFrame. It contains all of the frame's components. Java will raise an exception if you attempt to add a component directly to a JFrame.

DEBUGGING TIP: Content Pane   A `JFrame` cannot directly contain GUI elements. Instead, they must be added to its content pane, which can be retrieved using the `getContentPane()` method.

The `JFrame` and all the other top-level Swing windows have an internal structure made up of several distinct objects that can be manipulated by the program. Because of this structure, GUI elements can be organized into different layers within the window to create many types of sophisticated layouts. One layer of the structure makes it possible to associate a menu with the frame.

Finally, note how the `Converter` frame is instantiated, made visible, and eventually exited in the application's `main()` method:

```java
public static void main(String args[]) {
    Converter f = new Converter();
    f.setSize(400, 300);
    f.setVisible(true);
    f.addWindowListener(new WindowAdapter() {

        public void windowClosing(WindowEvent e) {
            System.exit(0);    // Quit the application
        }
    });
} // main()
```

It is necessary to set both the size and visibility of the frame, since these are not set by default. Because we are using a `FlowLayout`, it is especially important to give the frame an appropriate size. Failure to do so can cause the components to be arranged in a confusing way and might even cause some components to not appear in the window. These are limitations we will fix when we learn how to use some of the other layout managers.

13.6.2 Inner Classes and Adapter Classes

In this section we introduce two new language features, *inner classes* and *adapter classes*, which are used in the `main()` method shown above to handle the closing of the `Converter` application's window when the program is exited:

```java
f.addWindowListener(new WindowAdapter() {
    public void windowClosing(WindowEvent e) {
        System.exit(0);
    }
});
```

Inner classes

This code segment provides a listener that listens for window closing events. When such an event occurs, it exits the application by calling `System.exit()`.

The syntax used here is an example of an *anonymous inner class*. An **inner class** is a class defined within another class. The syntax is somewhat ugly, because it places the class definition right where a reference to a window listener object would go. In effect, the code is defining a subclass of `WindowAdapter` and creating an instance of it to serve as a listener for window-closing events.

Anonymous inner classes provide a useful way of creating classes and objects on the fly to handle just this kind of listener task. The syntax used actually enables us to write one expression that both defines a class and creates an instance of it to listen for window-closing events. The new subclass has local scope limited here to the main() method. It is anonymous, meaning that we aren't giving it a name, and therefore you can't create other instances of it in the program. Note that the body of the class definition is placed right after the new keyword, which takes the place of the argument to the addWindowListener() method. For more details on the inner and anonymous classes, see Appendix F.

> **JAVA LANGUAGE RULE**   **Inner Class.** An inner class is a class defined within another class. Inner classes are mostly used to handle a task that supports the work of the containing class.

An **adapter class** is a wrapper class that implements trivial versions of the abstract methods that make up a particular interface. (Remember from Chapter 4 that a wrapper class contains methods for converting primitive data into objects and for converting data from one type to another.)

Adapter class

The WindowAdapter class implements the methods of the WindowListener interface. When you implement an interface, such as ActionListener, you must implement all the abstract methods defined in the interface. For ActionListener there is just one method, the actionPerformed() method, so we can implement it as part of our applet or frame class. However, we want to use only one of the seven methods available in the WindowListener interface, the windowClosing() method, which is the method implemented in the anonymous inner class:

```java
public void windowClosing(WindowEvent e) {
    System.exit(0);
}
```

The WindowAdapter is defined simply as

```java
public abstract class WindowAdapter implements WindowListener {
    public void windowActivated(WindowEvent e) {}
    public void windowClosed(WindowEvent e) {}
    ...
    // Five other window listener methods
}
```

Note that each method is given a trivial implementation ({ }). To create a subclass of WindowAdapter, you must override at least one of its trivially implemented methods.

Another way to manage the application's window-closing event is to define a subclass of `WindowAdapter`:

```
import javax.swing.*;
import java.awt.*;
import java.awt.event.*;
public class WindowCloser extends WindowAdapter {
    public void windowClosing(WindowEvent e) {
        System.exit(0);
    }
}
```

Given this class, we can then place the following statement in `Converter`'s `main()` method:

```
f.addWindowListener(new WindowCloser());
```

This is somewhat more familiar looking than the inner class construct. If you prefer this way of handling things, you can use this method in place of the inner classes here and in other examples.

EFFECTIVE DESIGN: Anonymous Adapter Classes.   Anonymous adapter classes provide a useful way of creating an object to handle one specific kind of event within a program.

13.6.3   GUI Design Critique

Figure 13.13 shows the converter interface. Although our basic GUI design satisfies the demands of input, output, control, and guidance, it has a few significant design flaws.

First, it forces the user to manually clear the input field after each conversion. Unless it is important for the input value to remain displayed until another value is entered, this is just an inconvenience to the user. In this case, the user's input value is displayed along with the result in the `JTextArea`, so there's no reason not to clear the input text field:

```
input.setText("");  // Clear the input field
```

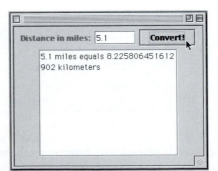

Figure 13.13 The first version of the metric converter GUI.

EFFECTIVE DESIGN: Reduce the User's Burden. A GUI should aim to minimize the responsibility placed on the user. In general, the program should perform any task it can perform, unless, of course, there is a compelling reason that the user should do the task.

A second problem with our design is that it forces the user to switch between the keyboard (for input) and the mouse (for control). Experienced users will find this annoying. An easy way to fix this problem is to make both the `JTextField` and the `JButton` serve as controls. That way, to get the program to do the conversion, the user can just press the Enter key after typing a number into the text field.

To give the interface this type of control, we only need to add an `ActionListener` to the `JTextField` during the initialization step:

```
input.addActionListener(this);
```

A `JTextField` generates an `ActionEvent` whenever the Enter key is pressed. We don't even need to modify the `actionPerformed()` method, since both controls will generate the same action event. This will allow users who prefer the keyboard to use just the keyboard.

EFFECTIVE DESIGN: User Interface. A GUI should aim to minimize the number of different input devices (mouse, keyboard) the user has to manipulate to perform a particular task.

Given that the user can now interact with the interface with just the keyboard, a question arises over whether we should keep the button at all. In this case, it seems justifiable to keep both the button and the text field controls. Some users dislike typing and prefer to use the mouse. Also, having two independent sets of controls is a desirable form of redundancy. You see it frequently in menu-based systems that allow menu items to be selected either by mouse or by special control keys.

EFFECTIVE DESIGN: Desirable Redundancy. Certain forms of redundancy in an interface, such as two sets of independent controls (mouse and keyboard), make it a more flexible or more widely usable program.

SELF-STUDY EXERCISES

EXERCISE 13.4 Another deficiency in the converter interface is that it doesn't round off its result, leading sometimes to numbers with 20 or so digits. Develop Java code to fix this problem.

EXERCISE 13.5 Give an example of desirable redundancy in automobile design.

13.6.4 Extending the Basic GUI: Button Array

Suppose the coach likes our program but complains that some of the folks in the office are terrible typists and would prefer not to have to use the keyboard at all. Is there some way we could modify the interface to accommodate these users?

What components do we need?

This gets back to the point we were just making about incorporating redundancy into the interface. One way to satisfy this requirement would be to implement a numeric keypad for input, similar to a calculator keypad. Regular JButtons can be used as the keypad's keys. As a user clicks keypad buttons, their face values—0 through 9—are inserted into the text field. The keypad will also need a button to clear the text field and one to serve as a decimal point.

How should the components be organized?

This new feature will add 12 new JButton components to our interface. Instead of inserting them into the JFrame individually, it will be better to organize them into a separate panel and insert the entire panel into the frame as a single unit. This will help reduce the complexity of the display, especially if the keypad buttons can be grouped together visually. Instead of having to deal with 16 separate components, the user will see the keypad as a single unit with a unified function. This is an example of the abstraction principle, similar to the way we break long strings of numbers (1-888-889-1999) into subgroups to make them easier to remember.

EFFECTIVE DESIGN: Reducing Complexity. Organizing elements into distinct groups by function helps to reduce the GUI's complexity.

Figure 13.14 shows the revised converter interface design. The containment hierarchy shows that the 12 keypad JButtons are contained within a JPanel. In the frame's layout, the entire panel is inserted just after the text area.

Incorporating the keypad into the interface requires several changes in the program's design. Because the keypad has such a clearly defined role, let's make it into a separate object by defining a KeyPad class (Fig. 13.15). The KeyPad will be a subclass of JPanel and will handle its own ActionEvents. As we saw in Chapter 4, a JPanel is a generic container. It is a subclass of Container via the JComponent class (Fig. 13.2). Its main purpose is to contain and organize components that appear together on an interface.

In this case, we will use a JPanel to hold the keypad buttons. As you might recall from Chapter 4, to add elements to a JPanel, you use the add() method, which is inherited from Container. (A JApplet is also a subclass of Container via the Panel class.)

As a subclass of JPanel, the KeyPad will take care of holding and organizing the JButtons in the visual display. We also need some way to organize and manage the 12 keypad buttons

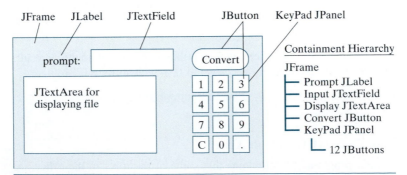

Figure 13.14 A widget hierarchy showing the containment relationships among the components.

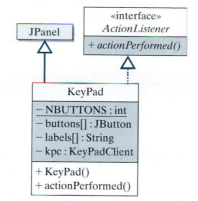

Figure 13.15 A KeyPad is a `JPanel` of `JButtons` that handles its own action events.

within the program's memory. Clearly, this is a good job for an array. Actually, two arrays would be even better, one for the buttons and one for their labels:

```
private JButton buttons[];
private String labels[] =        // An array of button labels
          { "1","2","3",
            "4","5","6",
            "7","8","9",
            "C","0","." };
```

The `label` array stores the strings that we will use as the buttons' labels. The main advantage of the array is that we can use a loop to instantiate the buttons:

```
buttons = new JButton[NBUTTONS];        // Create the array
                                        // For each labeled button
for(int k = 0; k < buttons.length; k++) {
  buttons[k] = new JButton(labels[k]);  // Create button
  buttons[k].addActionListener(this);   // and a listener
  add(buttons[k]);                      // and add it to the panel
} // for
```

This code should be placed in the `KeyPad()` constructor. It begins by instantiating the array itself. It then uses a `for` loop, bounded by the size of the array, to instantiate each individual button and insert it into the array. Note how the loop variable here, k, plays a dual role. It serves as the index into both the button array (`buttons`) and the array of strings that serves as the buttons' labels (`labels`). In that way the labels are assigned to the appropriate buttons. Note also how each button is assigned an `ActionListener` and added to the panel:

Algorithm design

```
buttons[k].addActionListener(this);  // Add listener
add(buttons[k]);                     // Add button to panel
```

An important design issue for our `KeyPad` object concerns how it will interact with the `Converter` that contains it. When the user clicks a keypad button, the key's label has to be displayed in the `Converter`'s text area. But because the text area is private to the converter,

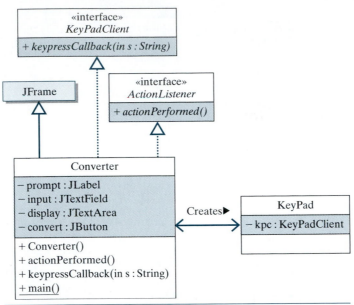

Figure 13.16 In a callback design, the `Converter` implements the `KeyPadClient` interface. It passes a reference to itself when it creates the `KeyPad` object. The `KeyPad` object can then invoke the `keypressCallback()` method whenever a keypad button is pressed, and the `Converter` can display the result of the keypress.

Callback design

the `KeyPad` does not have direct access to it. To address this problem, we will use a Java interface to implement a **callback design**. In this design, whenever a `KeyPad` button is pressed, the `KeyPad` object calls a method in the `Converter` that displays the key's label in the text area.

Figure 13.16 provides a summary of the callback design. Note that the association between the `Converter` and the `KeyPad` is bi-directional. This means that each object has a reference to the other and can invoke the other's public methods. This will be effected by having the `Converter` pass a reference to itself when it constructs the `KeyPad`:

```
private KeyPad keypad = new KeyPad(this);
```

Another important design issue is that the `KeyPad` needs to know the name of the callback method and the `Converter` needs to have an implementation of that method. This is a perfect job for an abstract interface:

```
public abstract interface KeyPadClient {
    public void keypressCallback(String s);
}
```

The `KeyPad` can interact with any class that implements the `KeyPadClient` interface. Note that the `KeyPad` has a reference to the `KeyPadClient`, which it will use to invoke the `keypressCallback()` method.

```
import java.awt.*;
import java.awt.event.*;
import javax.swing.*;

public class KeyPad extends JPanel implements ActionListener{

  private final static int NBUTTONS = 12;
  private KeyPadClient kpc;                    // Owner of the KeyPad
  private JButton buttons[];
  private String labels[] =                    // An array of button labels
              { "1","2","3",
                "4","5","6",
                "7","8","9",
                "C","0","." };

  public KeyPad(KeyPadClient kpc) {
    this.kpc = kpc;
    buttons = new JButton[NBUTTONS];            // Create the array
    for(int k = 0; k < buttons.length; k++) {   // For each button
      buttons[k] = new JButton(labels[k]);      // Create a button
      buttons[k].addActionListener(this);       // and a listener
      add(buttons[k]);                          // and add it to panel
    } // for
  } // KeyPad()

  public void actionPerformed(ActionEvent e) {
    String keylabel = ((JButton)e.getSource()).getText();
    kpc.keypressCallback(keylabel);
  } // actionPerformed()
} // KeyPad class
```

Figure 13.17   The KeyPad object implements a 12-key keypad in a JPanel. It has a reference to the KeyPadClient that contains the keypad.

The implementation of KeyPad is shown in Figure 13.17. Note that its constructor takes a reference to a KeyPadClient and saves it in an instance variable. Its actionPerformed() method then passes the key's label to the KeyPadClient's callback method.

Given the KeyPad design, we need to revise our design of the Converter class (Fig. 13.16). The Converter will now implement the KeyPadClient interface, which means it must provide an implementation of the keypressCallback() method:

```
public void keypressCallback(String s) {
    if (s.equals("C"))
        input.setText("");
    else
        input.setText(input.getText() + s);
}
```

Recall that whenever the KeyPad object calls the keypressCallback() method, it passes the label of the button that was pressed. The Converter object simply appends the key's label to the input text field, just as if the user typed the key in the text field.

The complete implementation of this revised version of the interface is shown in Figure 13.18. The appearance of the interface is shown in Figure 13.19.

```java
import javax.swing.*;        // Packages used
import java.awt.*;
import java.awt.event.*;

public class Converter extends JFrame    // Version 2
                implements ActionListener, KeyPadClient {
  private JLabel prompt = new JLabel("Distance in miles: ");
  private JTextField input = new JTextField(6);
  private JTextArea display = new JTextArea(10,20);
  private JButton convert = new JButton("Convert!");
  private KeyPad keypad = new KeyPad(this);

  public Converter () {
    getContentPane().setLayout(new FlowLayout());
    getContentPane().add(prompt);
    getContentPane().add(input);
    getContentPane().add(convert);
    getContentPane().add(display);
    getContentPane().add(keypad);
    display.setLineWrap(true);
    display.setEditable(false);
    convert.addActionListener(this);
    input.addActionListener(this);
  } // Converter()

  public void actionPerformed(ActionEvent e) {
    double miles =  Double.valueOf(input.getText()).doubleValue();
    double km = MetricConverter.milesToKm(miles);
    display.append(miles + " miles equals " + km + " kilometers\n");
    input.setText("");
  } // actionPerformed()

  public void keypressCallback(String s) {
    if (s.equals("C"))
        input.setText("");
     else
        input.setText(input.getText() + s);
  } // keypressCallback()

  public static void main(String args[]) {
    Converter f = new Converter();
    f.setSize(400, 300);
    f.setVisible(true);
    f.addWindowListener(new WindowAdapter() {
      public void windowClosing(WindowEvent e) {
        System.exit(0);  // Quit the application
      }
    });
  } // main()
} // Converter class
```

Figure 13.18 The second version of the Converter class implements the GUI shown in Figure 13.19.

13.6.5 GUI Design Critique

Figure 13.19 shows that despite our efforts to group the keypad into a rectangular array, it doesn't appear as a single entity in the interface, thereby indicating a layout problem. The default layout for our KeyPad (a JPanel) is FlowLayout, which is not appropriate for a

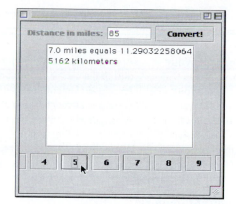

Figure 13.19 The second version of the metric converter GUI uses a set of keypad buttons for input, but they are not properly arranged.

numeric keypad that needs to be arranged into a two-dimensional grid pattern, the kind of layout our design called for (Fig. 13.14).

Fortunately, this flaw can easily be fixed by using an appropriate layout manager from the AWT. In the next version of the program, we employ the `java.awt.GridLayout`, which is perfectly suited for a two-dimensional keypad layout (Section 13.7.2).

The lesson to be learned from this example is that screen layout is an important element of an effective GUI. If not done well, it can undermine the GUI's effort to guide the user toward the appointed tasks. If done poorly enough, it can even keep the user from doing the task at all.

EFFECTIVE DESIGN: Layout Design. The appropriate layout and management of GUI elements is an important part of interface design. It contributes to the interface's ability to guide the user's action toward the interface's goals.

13.7 Containers and Layout Managers

A `Container` is a component that can contain other components. Because containers can contain other containers, it is possible to create a hierarchical arrangement of components, as we did in the second version of our `Converter` interface. In its present form, the hierarchy for `Converter` consists of a `JFrame` as the top-level container (Fig. 13.14). Contained within the frame is a `KeyPad` (subclass of `JPanel`) that contains 12 `JButton`s. Most GUIs will have a similar kind of containment hierarchy.

A `Container` is a relatively simple object whose main task is primarily to hold its components in a particular order. It has methods to add and remove components (Fig. 13.20). As you can see from these methods, a container keeps track of the order of its elements, and it is possible to refer to a component by its index order.

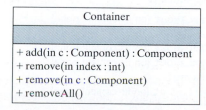

Figure 13.20 A `Container` contains `Component`s.

Table 13.3. Some of Java's AWT and Swing layout managers

Manager	Description
java.awt.BorderLayout	Arranges elements along the north, south, east, west, and in the center of the container.
java.swing.BoxLayout	Arranges elements in a single row or single column.
java.awt.CardLayout	Arranges elements like a stack of cards, with one visible at a time.
java.awt.FlowLayout	Arranges elements left to right across the container.
java.awt.GridBagLayout	Arranges elements in a grid of variably sized cells (complicated).
java.awt.GridLayout	Arranges elements into a two-dimensional grid of equally sized cells.
java.swing.OverlayLayout	Arranges elements on top of each other.

13.7.1 Layout Managers

The hard work of organizing and managing the elements within a container is the task of the layout manager. Among other tasks, the layout manager determines

- The overall size of the container.
- The size of each element in the container.
- The spacing between elements.
- The positioning of the elements.

Although it is possible to manage your own layouts, it is not easy. For most applications you are much better off by learning to use one of the AWT's built-in layouts. Table 13.3 gives a brief summary of the available layouts. We will show examples of FlowLayout, GridLayout, and BorderLayout. Some of the widely used Swing containers have a default layout manager assigned to them (Table 13.4).

To override the default layout for any of the JApplet, JDialog, JFrame, and JWindow containers, you must remember to use the getContentPane(). The correct statement is

```
getContentPane().setLayout(new FlowLayout());
```

DEBUGGING TIP: Content Pane. Attempting to add a component directly to a JApplet or a JFrame will cause an exception. For these top-level containers, components must be added to their content panes.

Table 13.4. Default layouts for some of the common Swing containers

Container	Layout Manager
JApplet	BorderLayout (on its content pane)
JBox	BoxLayout
JDialog	BorderLayout (on its content pane)
JFrame	BorderLayout (on its content pane)
JPanel	FlowLayout
JWindow	BorderLayout (on its content pane)

Figure 13.21 This version of the metric converter GUI uses a keypad for mouse-based input. It has an attractive overall layout.

13.7.2 The GridLayout Manager

It is simple to remedy the layout problem that affected the keypad in the most recent version of the Converter program. The problem was caused by the fact that as a subclass of JPanel, the KeyPad uses a default FlowLayout, which causes its buttons to be arranged in a row. A more appropriate layout for a numeric keypad would be a two-dimensional grid, exactly the kind of layout supplied by the java.awt.GridLayout. Therefore, to fix this problem, we need only set the keypad's layout to a GridLayout. This takes a single statement, which should be added to the beginning of the KeyPad() constructor:

```
setLayout(new GridLayout(4,3,1,1));
```

This statement creates a GridLayout object and assigns it as the layout manager for the keypad. It ensures that the keypad will have four rows and three columns of buttons (Fig. 13.21). The last two arguments in the constructor affect the relative spacing between the rows and the columns. The higher the number, the larger the spacing. As components are added to the keypad, they will automatically be arranged by the manager into a 4 × 3 grid.

Note that for a JPanel, the setLayout() method applies to the panel itself. Unlike the top-level containers, such as JFrame, other containers do not have content panes. The same point would apply when adding components to a JPanel. They are added directly to the panel, not to a content pane. Confusion over this point could be the source of bugs in your programs.

> **DEBUGGING TIP: Content Pane.** Top-level containers, such as JFrame, are the only ones that use a content pane. For other containers, such as JPanel, components are added directly to the container.

As its name suggests, the GridLayout layout manager arranges components in a two-dimensional grid. When components are added to the container, the layout manager starts inserting elements into the grid at the first cell in the first row and continues left to right across row 1, then row 2, and so on. If there are not enough components to fill all the cells of the grid, the remaining cells are left blank. If an attempt is made to add too many components to the grid, the layout manager will try to extend the grid in some reasonable way in order to accommodate the components. However, despite its effort in such cases, it usually fails to achieve a completely appropriate layout.

JAVA PROGRAMMING TIP: Grid Layout.   Make sure the number of components added to a `GridLayout` is equal to the number of rows times the number of columns.

13.7.3 GUI Design Critique

Although the layout in Figure 13.21 is much improved, there are still some deficiencies. One problem is that the `convert` button seems to be misplaced. It would make more sense if it were grouped with the keypad rather than with the input text field.

A more serious problem results from the fact that we are still using a `FlowLayout` for the program's main window, the `JFrame`. Among all of Java's layouts, `FlowLayout` gives you the least amount of control over the arrangement of the components. Also, `FlowLayout` is most sensitive to changes in the size and shape of its container.

13.7.4 The `BorderLayout` Manager

One way to fix these problems is to use a `BorderLayout` to divide the frame into five areas, north, south, east, west, and center, as shown in Figure 13.22. The `BorderLayout` class contains two constructors:

```
public BorderLayout();
public BorderLayout(int hgap, int vgap);
```

The two parameters in the second version of the constructor allow you to insert spacing between the areas.

Components are added to a `BorderLayout` by using the `add(Component, String)` method found in the `Container` class. For example, to set the application window to a border layout and add the keypad to its east area, we would use the following statements:

```
getContentPane().setLayout(new BorderLayout(2, 2));
getContentPane().add(keypad,"East");
```

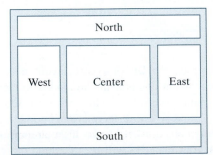

Figure 13.22 Arrangement of components in a border layout. The relative sizes of the areas will vary.

In this version of the add() method, the second parameter must be a capitalized String with one of the names "North", "South", "East", "West", or "Center". The order in which components are added does not matter.

One limitation of the BorderLayout is that only one component can be added to each area. That means that if you want to add several components to an area, you must first enclose them within a JPanel and then add the entire panel to the area. For example, let's create a panel to contain the prompt and the text field and place it at the north edge of the frame:

Containment hierarchy

```
JPanel inputPanel = new JPanel();              // Create panel
inputPanel.add(prompt);                        // Add label
inputPanel.add(input);                         // Add textfield
getContentPane().add(inputPanel,"North");      // Add the panel to the frame
```

The same point would apply if we want to group the keypad with the convert button and place them at the east edge. There are several ways these elements could be grouped. In this example, we give the panel a border layout and put the keypad in the center and the convert button at the south edge:

```
JPanel controlPanel= new JPanel(new BorderLayout(0,0));
controlPanel.add(keypad,"Center");
controlPanel.add(convert, "South");
getContentPane.add(controlPanel,"East");   // Add the panel to the frame
```

Given these details about the BorderLayout, a more appropriate design for the converter application is shown in Figure 13.23. Note that the border layout for the top-level JFrame uses only the center, north, and east areas. Similarly, the border layout for the control panel uses just the center and south areas.

In a BorderLayout, when one or more border areas are not used, one or more of the other areas will be extended to fill the unused area. For example, if West is not used, then North, South, and Center will extend to the left edge of the Container. If North is not used,

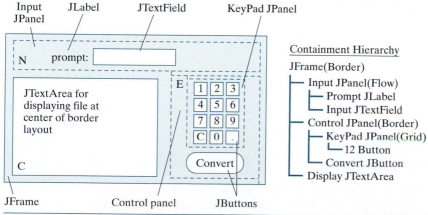

Figure 13.23 A border layout design for the metric converter program. The dotted lines show the panels.

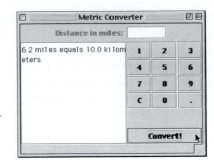

Figure 13.24 The metric converter, showing its appearance when a border design is used.

then West, East, and Center will extend to the top edge. This is true for all areas except Center. If Center is unused, it is left blank.

Figure 13.24 shows the results we get when we incorporate these changes into the program. The only changes to the program itself occur in the constructor method, which in its revised form is defined as follows:

```java
public Converter() {
  getContentPane().setLayout(new BorderLayout());
  keypad = new KeyPad(this);

  JPanel inputPanel = new JPanel();                        // Input panel
  inputPanel.add(prompt);
  inputPanel.add(input);
  getContentPane().add(inputPanel,"North");

  JPanel controlPanel= new JPanel(new BorderLayout(0,0));
  controlPanel.add(keypad, "Center");                      // Control panel
  controlPanel.add(convert, "South");
  getContentPane().add(controlPanel, "East");
  getContentPane().add(display,"Center");                  // Output display
  display.setLineWrap(true);
  display.setEditable(false);

  convert.addActionListener(this);
  input.addActionListener(this);
} // Converter()
```

This layout divides the interface into three main panels, an input panel, display panel, and control panel, and gives each its own layout. The control panel contains the keypad panel. Thus, the containment hierarchy for this design is much more complex than in our original design.

SELF-STUDY EXERCISES

EXERCISE 13.6 The border layout for the top window uses the north, center, and east regions. What other combinations of areas might be used for these three components?

EXERCISE 13.7 Why wouldn't a flow layout be appropriate for the control panel?

13.8   Checkboxes, Radio Buttons, and Borders

Suppose you are the software developer for Acme Software Titles, a software business specializing in computer games. You want to develop an applet-based order form that customers can use to order software over the Web. At the moment you have three software titles—a chess game, a checkers game, and a crossword puzzle game. The assumption is that the user will choose one or more of these titles from some kind of menu. The user must also indicate a payment option—either E-cash, credit card, or debit card. These options are mutually exclusive—the user can choose one and only one.

Let's design an applet interface for this program. Unlike the previous problem, where the input was a numeric value, in this problem the input will be the user's selection from a menu. The result will be the creation of an order. Let's suppose that this part of the task happens behind the scenes—that is, we don't have to worry about creating an actual order. The output the user sees will simply be an acknowledgment that the order was successfully submitted.

There are several kinds of controls needed for this interface. A conventional way to have users indicate their purchase decisions is to have them click a Submit button. They should also have the option to cancel the transaction at any time.

In addition to these button controls, a couple of menus must be presented, one for the software titles, and one for the payment choices. The Swing and AWT libraries provide many options for building menus.

One key requirement for this interface is the mutually exclusive payment options. A conventional way to handle this kind of selection is with a `JRadioButton`—a button that belongs to a group of mutually exclusive alternatives. Only one button from the group may be selected at one time. The selection of software titles could be handled by a collection of checkboxes. A `JCheckbox` is a button that can be selected and deselected, and that always displays its current state to the user. Using a checkbox will make it obvious to the user exactly what software has been selected.

To complete the design, let's use a `JTextArea` again to serve as something of a printed order form. It will confirm the user's order and display other messages needed during the transaction.

Given these decisions, we arrive at the design shown in Figure 13.25. In this case, our design uses a `JPanel` as the main container instead of using the top window itself. The reason for this

Problem statement

Interface design

What components do we need?

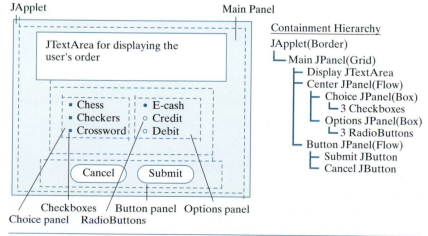

Figure 13.25 A design for an online order form interface.

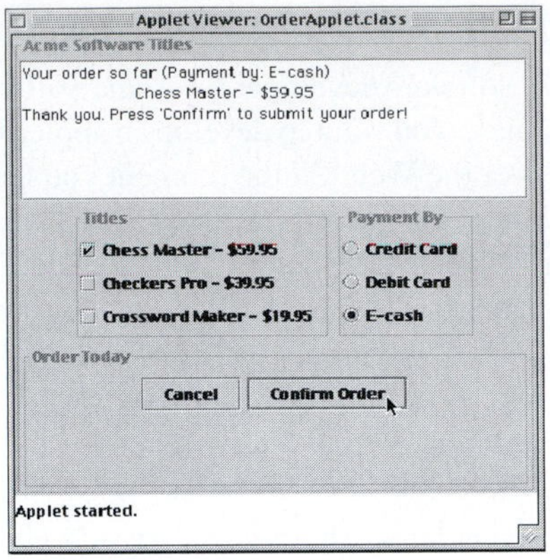

Figure 13.26 Borders around containers help make them stand out more.

decision is that we want to use Swing Borders around the various JPanels to enhance the overall visual appeal of the design. The borders will have titles that help explain the purpose of the various panels.

What top-level windows do we use?

Note that the top-level window in this case is a JApplet. By default it will have a border layout. For the main JPanel we are using a 3 × 1 GridLayout. The components in the main panel are the JTextArea and two other JPanels. The GridLayout will take care of sizing these so that they will all be of equal size.

Component layout

The center panel, which uses a flow layout, contains panels for the checkboxes and the radio buttons. These elements are grouped within their own panels. Again, we can put a border around them in the final implementation (Fig. 13.26). The button panels use a BoxLayout, which we will discuss later. This design leads to the most complex containment hierarchy thus far.

Containment hierarchy

13.8.1 Checkbox and Radio Button Arrays

What data structures do we need?

Because we will need three checkboxes, one for each title, and three radio buttons, one for each payment option, it will be useful again to use arrays to store both the buttons and their titles:

```
private ButtonGroup optGroup = new ButtonGroup();
private JCheckBox titles[] = new JCheckBox[NTITLES];
private JRadioButton options[] = new JRadioButton[NOPTIONS];
private String titleLabels[] =
    {"Chess Master — $59.95", "Checkers Pro — $39.95",
                     "Crossword Maker — $19.95"};
private String optionLabels[] = {"Credit Card", "Debit Card", "E-cash"};
```

Again, the advantage of this design is that it simplifies the instantiation and initialization of the buttons:

```
for(int k = 0; k < titles.length; k++) {
    titles[k] = new JCheckBox(titleLabels[k]);
    titles[k].addItemListener(this);
    choicePanel.add(titles[k]);
}
```

The only difference between this array of checkboxes and the keypad array of buttons used in the `Converter` program is that checkboxes generate `ItemEvents` instead `ActionEvents`. Therefore, each checkbox must be registered with an `ItemListener` (and, of course, the applet itself must implement the `ItemListener` interface). We'll show how `ItemEvents` are handled later.

The code for instantiating and initializing the radio buttons is almost the same:

```
for(int k = 0; k < options.length; k++) {
    options[k] = new JRadioButton(optionLabels[k]);
    options[k].addItemListener(this);
    optionPanel.add(options[k]);
    optGroup.add(options[k] );
}
options[0].setSelected(true); // Set first button 'on'
```

Radio buttons also generate `ItemEvents`, so they too must be registered with an `ItemListener`. Note that the first button is set on, which represents a default payment option for the user.

The difference between checkboxes and radio buttons is that radio buttons must be added to a `ButtonGroup`—here named `optGroup`—in order to enforce mutual exclusion among them. A `ButtonGroup` is an object whose sole task is to enforce mutual exclusion among its members. Whenever you click one radio button, the `ButtonGroup` will automatically be notified of this event and will turn off whatever other button was turned on. As Figure 13.27 illustrates, radio buttons are monitored by two different objects, a `ButtonGroup`, which manages the radio buttons' states, and an `ItemListener`, which listens for clicks on the buttons and takes appropriate actions.

Note the effective division of labor in the design of the various objects to which a radio button belongs. The `optionPanel` is a GUI component (a `JPanel`) that contains the button within the visual interface. Its role is to help manage the graphical aspects of the button's behavior. The `ButtonGroup` is just an `Object`, not a GUI component. Its task is to monitor the button's relationship to the other buttons in the group. Each object has a clearly delineated task.

Divide and conquer

This division of labor is a key feature of object-oriented design. It is clearly preferable to giving one object broad responsibilities. For example, a less effective design might have given the task of managing a group of buttons to the `JPanel` that contains them. However, this would lead to all kinds of problems, not least of which is the fact that not everything in the container belongs to the same button group. So a clear division of labor is a much preferable design.

EFFECTIVE DESIGN: Division of Labor. In good object-oriented design, objects are specialists (experts) for very narrow, clearly defined tasks. If a new task needs doing, design a new object to do it.

Figure 13.27 The ButtonGroup object tracks each radio button's state, ensuring that only one is selected at a time. The ItemListener listens for events on each button.

13.8.2   Swing Borders

The Swing `Border` and `BorderFactory` classes can place borders around virtually any GUI element. Using borders is an effective way to make the grouping of components more apparent. Borders can have titles that enhance the GUI's ability to guide and inform the user. They can also have a wide range of styles and colors, thereby helping to improve the GUI's overall appearance.

A border occupies some space around the edge of a `JComponent`. For the Acme Software Titles interface, we place titled borders around four of the panels (Fig. 13.26). The border on the main panel serves to identify the company again. The one around the button panel serves to group the two control buttons. The borders around both the checkbox and the radio button menus set them apart from other elements of the display and identify the purpose of the buttons.

Attaching a titled border to a component—in this case to a `JPanel`—is very simple. It takes one statement:

```
choicePanel.setBorder(BorderFactory.createTitledBorder("Titles"));
```

The `setBorder()` method is defined in `JComponent`, is inherited by all Swing components, and takes a `Border` argument. In this case, we use the `BorderFactory` class to create a border and assign it a title. There are several versions of the static `createTitledBorder()` method. This version lets us specify the border's title. It uses default values for the type of border (etched), the title's position (sitting on the top line), justification (left), and the font's type and color.

As you would expect, the `Border` and `BorderFactory` classes contain methods that let you exert significant control over the border's look and feel. You can even design and create your own custom borders.

13.8.3   The `BoxLayout` Manager

Another type of layout to use is the `BoxLayout`. This can be associated with any container, and it comes as the default with the Swing `Box` container. We use it in this example to arrange the checkboxes and radio buttons (Fig. 13.25).

A `BoxLayout` is like a one-dimensional grid layout. It allows multiple components to be arranged either vertically or horizontally in a row. The layout will not wrap around, as does the `FlowLayout`. Unlike the `GridLayout`, the `BoxLayout` does not force all its components to be the same size. Instead, it tries to use each component's preferred width (or height) in arranging them horizontally (or vertically). (Every Swing component has a preferred size that is used by the various layout managers in determining the component's actual size in the interface.) The `BoxLayout` manager also tries to align its components' heights (for horizontal layouts) or widths (for vertical layouts).

Once again, to set the layout manager for a container you use the `setLayout()` method:

```
choicePanel.setLayout(new BoxLayout(choicePanel,BoxLayout.Y_AXIS));
```

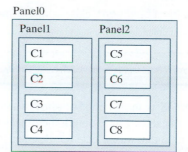

Panel0

Panel1   Panel2

C1   C5

C2   C6

C3   C7

C4   C8

Figure 13.28 Complex layouts can be achieved by nesting containers that use the BoxLayout.

The BoxLayout() constructor has two parameters. The first is a reference to the container being managed, and the second is a constant that determines whether horizontal (x-axis) or vertical (y-axis) alignment is used.

One nice feature of the BoxLayout is that it can be used in combinations to imitate the look of the very complicated GridBoxLayout. For example, Figure 13.28 shows an example with two panels (Panel1 and Panel2) arranged horizontally within an outer box (Panel0), each containing four components arranged vertically. The three panels all use the BoxLayout.

13.8.4   The ItemListener Interface

In this section, we will describe how to handle menu selections. Whenever the user makes a menu selection, or clicks a check box or radio button, an ItemEvent is generated. Item-Events are associated with items that make up menus, including JPopupMenus, JCheck-boxes, JRadioButtons, and other types of menus. Item events are handled by the Item-Listener interface, which consists of a single method, the itemStateChanged() method:

```
public void itemStateChanged(ItemEvent e) {
  display.setText("Your order so far (Payment by: ");
  for (int k = 0; k < options.length; k++ )
    if (options[k].isSelected())
      display.append(options[k].getText() + ")\n");
  for (int k = 0; k < titles.length; k++ )
    if (titles[k].isSelected())
      display.append("\t" + titles[k].getText() + "\n");
} // itemStateChanged()
```

This version of the method handles item changes for both the checkbox menu and the radio buttons menu. The code uses two consecutive for loops. The first iterates through the options menu (radio buttons) to determine what payment option the user has selected. Since only one option can be selected, only one title will be appended to the display. The second loop iterates through the titles menu (checkboxes) and appends each title the user selected to the display. Thus the complete status of the user's order is displayed after every selection. The isSelected() method is used to determine whether a checkbox or radio button is selected or not.

In this example, we have no real need to identify the item that caused the event. No matter what item the user selected, we want to display the entire state of the order. However, like the

`ActionEvent` class, the `ItemEvent` class contains methods that can retrieve the item that caused the event:

```
getItem();  // Returns a menu item within a menu
```

The `getItem()` method is the `ItemListener`'s analogue to the `ActionEvent`'s `get-Source()` method. It enables you to obtain the object that generated the event but returns a representation of the item that was selected or deselected.

13.8.5 The `OrderApplet`

The design of the `OrderApplet` is summarized in Figure 13.29, and its complete implementation is given in Figure 13.30. There are several important points to make about this program. First, five `JPanel`s are used to organize the components into logical and visual groupings. This conforms to the design shown in Figure 13.25.

Second, note the use of titled borders around the four internal panels. These reinforce that the components within the border are related by function.

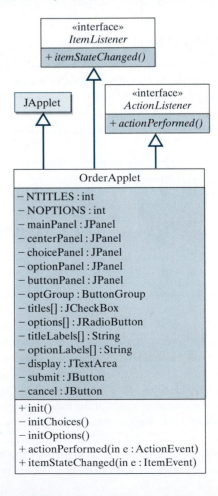

Figure 13.29 The `OrderApplet` makes extensive use of GUI components.

```java
import javax.swing.*;
import javax.swing.border.*;
import java.awt.*;
import java.awt.event.*;
public class OrderApplet extends JApplet
                      implements ItemListener, ActionListener {
  private final int NTITLES = 3, NOPTIONS = 3;
  private JPanel mainPanel = new JPanel(),
                 centerPanel = new JPanel(),
                 choicePanel = new JPanel(),
                 optionPanel = new JPanel(),
                 buttonPanel = new JPanel();
  private ButtonGroup optGroup = new ButtonGroup();
  private JCheckBox titles[] = new JCheckBox[NTITLES];
  private JRadioButton options[] = new JRadioButton[NOPTIONS];
  private String titleLabels[] =
    {"Chess Master — $59.95", "Checkers Pro — $39.95",
                            "Crossword Maker — $19.95"};
  private String optionLabels[] = {"Credit Card", "Debit Card", "E-cash"};
  private JTextArea display = new JTextArea(7, 25);
  private JButton submit = new JButton("Submit Order"),
                  cancel = new JButton("Cancel");

  public void init() {
    mainPanel.setBorder(BorderFactory.createTitledBorder(
                                "Acme Software Titles"));
    mainPanel.setLayout(new GridLayout(3, 1, 1, 1));
    cancel.addActionListener(this);
    submit.addActionListener(this);
    initChoices();
    initOptions();
    buttonPanel.setBorder(BorderFactory.createTitledBorder("Order Today"));
    buttonPanel.add(cancel);
    buttonPanel.add(submit);
    centerPanel.add(choicePanel);
    centerPanel.add(optionPanel);

    mainPanel.add( display);
    mainPanel.add(centerPanel);
    mainPanel.add( buttonPanel);
    getContentPane().add(mainPanel);
    setSize(400,400);
  } // init()

  private void initChoices() {
    choicePanel.setBorder(
            BorderFactory.createTitledBorder("Titles"));
    choicePanel.setLayout(
            new BoxLayout(choicePanel, BoxLayout.Y_AXIS));
    for (int k = 0; k < titles.length; k++) {
      titles[k] = new JCheckBox(titleLabels[k]);
      titles[k].addItemListener(this);
      choicePanel.add(titles[k]);
    }
  } // initChoices()
```

Figure 13.30   The `OrderApplet` class. (*Continued on next page*)

```
private void initOptions() {
  optionPanel.setBorder(
          BorderFactory.createTitledBorder("Payment By"));
  optionPanel.setLayout(
          new BoxLayout(optionPanel, BoxLayout.Y_AXIS));
  for (int k = 0; k < options.length; k++) {
    options[k] = new JRadioButton(optionLabels[k]);
    options[k].addItemListener(this);
    optionPanel.add(options[k]);
    optGroup.add(options[k]);
  }
  options[0].setSelected(true);
} // initOptions()

public void itemStateChanged(ItemEvent e) {
  display.setText("Your order so far (Payment by: ");
  for (int k = 0; k < options.length; k++ )
    if (options[k].isSelected())
      display.append(options[k].getText() + ")\n");
  for (int k = 0; k < titles.length; k++ )
    if (titles[k].isSelected())
      display.append("\t" + titles[k].getText() + "\n");
} // itemStateChanged()

public void actionPerformed(ActionEvent e){
  String label = submit.getText();
  if (e.getSource() == submit) {
    if (label.equals("Submit Order")) {
      display.append(
      "Thank you. Press 'Confirm' to submit your order!\n");
      submit.setText("Confirm Order");
    } else {
      display.append(
        "Thank you. You will receive your order tomorrow!\n");
      submit.setText("Submit Order");
    }
  } else
    display.setText(
      "Thank you. Maybe we can serve you next time!\n");
} // actionPerformed()
} // OrderApplet class
```

Figure 13.30   The `OrderApplet` class. (*Continued from previous page*)

The applet `init()` method is used to initialize the interface. This involves setting the layouts for the various containers and filling the containers with their components. Because their initializations are relatively long, the checkboxes and radio buttons are initialized in separate methods, the `initChoices()` and `initOptions()` methods, respectively.

Finally, note how the `actionPerformed()` method creates a mock order form in the display area. This allows the user to review the order before it is submitted. Also note that the algorithm used for submittal requires the user to confirm an order before it is actually submitted. The first time the user clicks the Submit button, the button's label is changed to "Confirm Order", and the user is prompted in the display area to click the Confirm button to submit the order. This design allows the interface to catch inadvertent button clicks.

A user interface should anticipate errors by the user. When a program involves an action that can't be undone—such as placing an order—the program should make sure the user really wants to take the action before carrying it out.

EFFECTIVE DESIGN: Anticipate the User. A well-designed interface should make it difficult for the user to make errors and should make it easy to recover from mistakes when they do happen.

SELF-STUDY EXERCISE

EXERCISE 13.8 What is your favorite interface horror story? How would you have remedied the problem? The interface need not be a computer interface.

13.9 Menus and Scroll Panes

Pop-up and pull-down menus allow an application or applet to grow in complexity and functionality without cluttering its interface. Menus are hierarchical in nature. A menu is divided into a number of menu items, which can themselves be further subdivided. Java makes it simple to implement menus.

A JMenuBar is an implementation of a menu bar—a horizontal list of names that appears at the top of a window (Fig. 13.31).

Almost all applications have a menu bar. To construct a menu, you add JMenu objects to a JMenuBar. A JMenu is essentially a clickable area on a menu bar that is associated with a JPopupMenu, a small window that pops up and displays the menu's JMenuItems. A menu can also contain JSeparators—dividers that can be placed between menu items to organize them into logical groupings.

13.9.1 Adding a Menu Bar to an Application

It is easy to create menus in Swing. The process involves three steps, although you need not perform them in this order:

1. Create the individual JMenuItems.

2. Create a JMenu and add the JMenuItems to it.

3. Create a JMenuBar and add the JMenus to it.

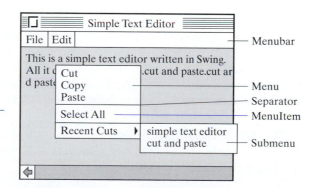

Figure 13.31 An application with a menu bar that is showing its edit menu. The edit menu contains a cascading drop-down menu that can show recent cuts.

For example, suppose you're building the interface for a text editor. A text editor typically contains at least two standard menus. The file menu is used to create new documents, open and close files, save your document, and so on. The edit menu is used to cut and paste selected text from the document.

Here's how you would create the file menu for this program. First you create a menu bar and make it the menu bar for the application's JFrame or for the JApplet. This is usually done in the application's constructor or in the applet's init() method:

```
JMenuBar mBar = new JMenuBar();   // Create menu bar
this.setMenuBar(mBar);            // Add it to this window
```

The next step involves creating and adding menus and menu items to the menu bar. This is also usually done in the constructor or the init() method. If the menu is large, you should break this task into subtasks and define a method for each subtask.

EFFECTIVE DESIGN: Method Size. A method that gets longer than 20 to 25 lines is probably trying to do too much and should be divided into separate methods, each with a clearly defined task.

Here is the definition of the file menu for our simple text editor:

```
private void initFileMenu() {
    fileMenu = new JMenu("File");          // Create menu
    mBar.add(fileMenu);                    // Add it to menu bar

    openItem = new JMenuItem("Open");      // Open item
    openItem.addActionListener( this );
    openItem.setEnabled(false);
    fileMenu.add(openItem);

    saveItem = new JMenuItem("Save");      // Save item
    saveItem.addActionListener(this);
    saveItem.setEnabled(false);
    fileMenu.add(saveItem);
    fileMenu.addSeparator();               // Logical separator

    quitItem = new JMenuItem("Quit");      // Quit item
    quitItem.addActionListener(this);
    fileMenu.add(quitItem);
} // initFileMenu()
```

The first two statements in the method create the file menu and add it to the menu bar. The rest of the statements create the individual menu items that make up the file menu. Note the use of a *separator* item after the save item. This has the effect of grouping the file-handling items (open and save) into one logical category and distinguishing them from the quit item. A separator is represented as a line in the menu (Fig. 13.31).

EFFECTIVE DESIGN: Logical Design. In designing interfaces, an effort should be made to use visual cues, such as menu item separators and borders, to group items that are logically related. This will help to orient the user.

Each menu item is given an `ActionListener`. As we will see shortly, action events for menu items are handled the same way as action events for buttons. Finally, note how the `setEnabled()` method is used to disable both the open and save menu items. Implementation of these actions is left as an exercise.

13.9.2   Menu Hierarchies

Menus can be added to other menus to create a hierarchy. For example, the edit menu will include the standard cut, copy, and paste menu items. Some edit menus also contain an "Undo" item, which can be used to undo the last editing operation performed. In other words, if you cut a piece of text, you can undo the operation and get the cut back. Many editors allow just a single undo. If you cut two pieces of text, the capability to undo the first piece is lost to the user. This can be an issue, especially if you didn't mean to do the first cut.

To remedy this situation, let's add a feature to our editor that will keep track of cuts by storing them in a `Vector`. This function will be like an "Unlimited Undo" operation for cuts. For this example, we won't place any limit on the size of the vector. Every cut the user makes will be inserted at the beginning of the vector. To go along with this feature we need a menu that can grow dynamically during the program. Each time the user makes a cut, the string that was cut will be added to the menu.

This kind of menu should occur within the edit menu, but it will have its own items. This is a menu within a menu (Fig. 13.31), an example of a *cascading* drop-down menu. The edit menu itself drops down from the menu bar, and the recent-cuts menu drops down and to the right of where its arrow points. The following method was used to create the edit menu:

```
private void initEditMenu() {
  editMenu = new JMenu("Edit");              // Create edit menu
  mBar.add(editMenu);                        // Add to menu bar

  cutItem = new JMenuItem ("Cut");           // Cut item
  cutItem.addActionListener(this);
  editMenu.add(cutItem);
  copyItem = new JMenuItem("Copy");          // Copy item
  copyItem.addActionListener(this);
  editMenu.add(copyItem);
  pasteItem = new JMenuItem("Paste");        // Paste item
  pasteItem.addActionListener(this);
  editMenu.add(pasteItem);
  editMenu.addSeparator();
  selectItem = new JMenuItem("Select All");  // Select
  selectItem.addActionListener(this);
  editMenu.add(selectItem);
  editMenu.addSeparator();
  cutsMenu = new JMenu("Recent Cuts");       // Cuts submenu
  editMenu.add(cutsMenu);
} // initEditMenu()
```

The main difference between this method and the one used to create the file menu is that here we insert an entire submenu as one of the items in the edit menu. The `cutsMenu` will be used to hold the strings that are cut from the document. Initially, it will be empty.

13.9.3 Handling Menu Actions

Handling `JMenuItem` actions is no different from handling `JButton` actions. Whenever a user makes a menu selection, an `ActionEvent` is generated. Programs that use menus must implement the `actionPerformed()` method of the `ActionListener` interface. In the text editor example, there are a total of six enabled menu items, including the recent-cuts menu. This translates into a large `if-else` structure, with each clause handling a single menu item.

The following `actionPerformed()` method is used to handle the menu selections for the text editor:

```java
public void actionPerformed(ActionEvent e) {
    JMenuItem m  = (JMenuItem)e.getSource();         // Get selected menu item
    if ( m == quitItem ) {                           // Quit
        dispose();}
    } else if (m == cutItem) {                       // Cut the selected text
        scratchPad = display.getSelectedText();      // Copy text to scratchpad
        display.replaceRange("",                     // and delete
            display.getSelectionStart(),             // from the start of selection
            display.getSelectionEnd());              // to the end
        addRecentCut(scratchPad);                    // Add text to the cuts menu
    } else if (m == copyItem)                        // Copy text to scratchpad
        scratchPad = display.getSelectedText();
    } else if (m == pasteItem) { // Paste scratchpad to document at caret
        display.insert(scratchPad, display.getCaretPosition()); // position
    } else if ( m == selectItem ) {
        display.selectAll();                         // Select the entire document
    } else {
        JMenuItem item = (JMenuItem)e.getSource();   // Default is cutsMenu
        scratchPad = item.getActionCommand();        // Put cut back in scratchpad
    }
} // actionPerformed()
```

The method begins by getting the source of the `ActionEvent` and casting it into a `JMenuItem`. It then checks each case of the `if-else` structure. Because the actions taken by this program are fairly short, they are mostly coded within the `actionPerformed()` method. However, for most programs it will be necessary to write a separate method corresponding to each menu item and then call the methods from `actionPerformed()`.

Our text editor's main task is to implement the cut/copy/paste functions, which are simple to do in Java. The text being edited is stored in a `JTextArea`, which contains instance methods that make it very easy to select, insert, and replace text. To copy a piece of text, the program need only get the text from the `JTextArea` (`getSelectedText()`) and assign it to the `scratchpad`, which is represented as a `String`. To paste a piece of text, the program inserts the contents of the `scratchpad` into the `JTextArea` at the location marked by the *caret*, a cursor-like character in the document that marks the next insertion point.

The structure of this `if-else` statement is significant. Note how the default case of the `if-else` is designed. We are using the last `else` clause as a "catch-all" condition to catch and handle selections from the `cutsMenu`. All of the other menu items can be referred to by name. However, the menu items in the `cutsMenu` are just snippets of a string that the user has previously cut from the text, so they can't be referenced by name. Luckily, we don't really

Default logic

need to. For any `JMenuItem`, the `getActionCommand()` method returns its text, which in this case is the previously cut text. So we just assign the cut text from the menu to the `scratchpad`.

> **JAVA PROGRAMMING TIP: Default Cases.**   Although the order of the clauses in an `if-else` structure is usually not important, the default clause can sometimes be used to handle cases that can't be referenced by name.

Handling Previously Cut Text

The most difficult function in our program is the cut operation. Not only must the selected text be removed from the document and stored in the `scratchpad`, but it must also be inserted into the vector that is storing all the previous cuts. The `addRecentCut()` method takes care of this last task. The basic idea here is to take the cut string and insert it at the beginning of the vector, so that cuts will be maintained in a last-in/first-out order. Then the `cutsMenu` must be completely rebuilt by reading its entries out of the vector, from first to last. That way the most recent cut will appear first in the menu:

Algorithm design

```
private void addRecentCut(String cut) {
  recentCuts.insertElementAt(cut,0);
  cutsMenu.removeAll();
  for (int k = 0; k < recentCuts.size(); k++) {
    JMenuItem item =
     new JMenuItem((String)recentCuts.elementAt(k));
    cutsMenu.add( item );
    item.addActionListener(this);
  }
} // addRecentCut()
```

The `recentCuts Vector` stores the cut strings. Note the use of the `insertElementAt()` method to insert strings into the vector and the `elementAt()` method to get strings from the vector. (You may find it helpful to review the section on vectors in Chapter 9.)

Note also how menu items are removed and inserted in menus. The `cutsMenu` is reinitialized, using the `removeAll()` method. Then the `for` loop iterates through the strings stored in the vector, making new menu items from them, which are then inserted into the `cutsMenu`. In this way, the `cutsMenu` is changed dynamically each time the user cuts a piece of text from the document.

13.9.4   Adding Scrollbars to a Text Area

The design of the `SimpleTextEditor` class is summarized in Figure 13.32, and its complete implementation is shown in Figure 13.33. It uses a `BorderLayout` with the `JTextArea` placed at the center. Note how simple it is to add scrollbars to the text area:

Scrollbars

```
this.getContentPane().add(new JScrollPane(display));
```

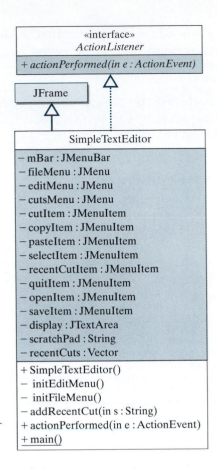

Figure 13.32 Design of the
`SimpleTextEditor`.

This statement creates a `JScrollPane` and adds it to the application's container. A `JScroll-Pane` is one of Swing's scrollbar classes. Its function is to manage the viewing and scrolling of a scrollable component, such as a `JTextArea`. A `JScrollPane` is actually a container, which is why it takes the `display` as an argument. The `display` is being added to the `JScrollPane`.

Just about any `Component` can be added to a `JScrollPane`. Once a component is added, the scroll pane will manage the scrolling functions for the component. The default constructor used in this example takes a single `Component` parameter. This refers to the scrollable component—in this case to the `JTextArea`. Another constructor that you might use takes the following form:

```
public JScrollPane(Component comp, int vsbPolicy, int hsbPolicy);
```

The two integers refer to the vertical and horizontal scrolling policies. These cover properties such as whether the scrollbars are always present or just as needed. The default policy is to attach scrollbars to the component only when needed. Thus, to see the scrollbars in the

```java
import javax.swing.*;
import java.awt.*;
import java.awt.event.*;
import java.util.Vector;
public class SimpleTextEditor extends JFrame implements ActionListener{
  private JMenuBar mBar = new JMenuBar();        // Create the menu bar
  private JMenu fileMenu, editMenu, cutsMenu;    // Menu references and items
  private JMenuItem cutItem, copyItem, pasteItem, selectItem,recentcutItem;
  private JMenuItem quitItem, openItem, saveItem; // File items
  private JTextArea display = new JTextArea();   // Here's where the editing occurs
  private String scratchPad = "";                // Scratch pad for cut/paste
  private Vector recentCuts = new Vector();

  public SimpleTextEditor() {
    super("Simple Text Editor");                 // Set the window title
    this.getContentPane().setLayout(new BorderLayout());
    this.getContentPane().add("Center", display);
    this.getContentPane().add(new JScrollPane(display));
    display.setLineWrap(true);
    this.setJMenuBar(mBar);                       // Set this program's menu bar
    initFileMenu();                               // Create the menus
    initEditMenu();
  } // SimpleTextEditer()

  private void initEditMenu() {
    editMenu = new JMenu("Edit");                 // Create the edit menu
    mBar.add(editMenu);                           // and add it to menu bar
    cutItem = new JMenuItem ("Cut");              // Cut item
    cutItem.addActionListener(this);
    editMenu.add(cutItem);
    copyItem = new JMenuItem("Copy");             // Copy item
    copyItem.addActionListener(this);
    editMenu.add(copyItem);
    pasteItem = new JMenuItem("Paste");           // Paste item
    pasteItem.addActionListener(this);
    editMenu.add(pasteItem);
    editMenu.addSeparator();
    selectItem = new JMenuItem("Select All");     // Select item
    selectItem.addActionListener(this);
    editMenu.add(selectItem);
    editMenu.addSeparator();
    cutsMenu = new JMenu("Recent Cuts");          // Recent cuts submenu
    editMenu.add(cutsMenu);
  } // initEditMenu()

  private void initFileMenu() {
    fileMenu = new JMenu("File");                 // Create the file menu
    mBar.add(fileMenu);                           // and add it to the menu bar
    openItem = new JMenuItem("Open");             // Open item
    openItem.addActionListener( this );
    openItem.setEnabled(false);
```

Figure 13.33 A menu-based `SimpleTextEditor` application. (*Continued on next page*)

```
      fileMenu.add(openItem);
      saveItem = new JMenuItem("Save");          // Save item
      saveItem.addActionListener(this);
      saveItem.setEnabled(false);
      fileMenu.add(saveItem);
      fileMenu.addSeparator();                    // Logical separator
      quitItem = new JMenuItem("Quit");           // Quit item
      quitItem.addActionListener(this);
      fileMenu.add(quitItem);
    } // initFileMenu()
    public void actionPerformed(ActionEvent e) {
      JMenuItem m = (JMenuItem)e.getSource(); // Get selected menu item
      if ( m == quitItem ) {                      // Quit
        dispose();
      } else if (m == cutItem) {                  // Cut the selected text
        scratchPad = display.getSelectedText();// Copy text to scratchpad
        display.replaceRange("",                  // and delete
            display.getSelectionStart(),          // from the start of the selection
            display.getSelectionEnd());           // to the end
        addRecentCut(scratchPad);                 // Add the cut text to the cuts menu
      } else if (m == copyItem) {  // Copy the selected text to the scratchpad
        scratchPad = display.getSelectedText();
      } else if (m == pasteItem) { // Paste the scratchpad to the document at caret
        display.insert(scratchPad, display.getCaretPosition()); // position
      } else if ( m == selectItem ) {
        display.selectAll();                      // Select the entire document
      } else {
        JMenuItem item = (JMenuItem)e.getSource();// Default is cutsMenu
        scratchPad = item.getActionCommand();   // Put cut back in the scratchpad
      }
    } // actionPerformed()
    private void addRecentCut(String cut) {
      recentCuts.insertElementAt(cut,0);
      cutsMenu.removeAll();
      for (int k = 0; k < recentCuts.size(); k++) {
        JMenuItem item =
            new JMenuItem((String)recentCuts.elementAt(k));
        cutsMenu.add( item );
        item.addActionListener(this);
      }
    } // addRecentCut()

    public static void main(String args[]) {
      SimpleTextEditor f = new SimpleTextEditor();
      f.setSize(300, 200);
      f.setVisible(true);
      f.addWindowListener(new WindowAdapter() {
        public void windowClosing(WindowEvent e) {
          System.exit(0);                         // Quit the application
        }
      });
    } // main()
} // SimpleTextEditor class
```

Figure 13.33 A menu-based `SimpleTextEditor` application. (*Continued from previous page*)

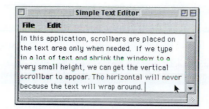

Figure 13.34 The scrollbars appear on the text area only when they are needed. In this case, only a vertical scrollbar is necessary.

`SimpleTextEditor`, you would have to shrink the window to the point where all of the text cannot be viewed (Fig. 13.34). Because the text area in this example is wrapping the text, the horizontal scrollbar will never be needed.

SELF-STUDY EXERCISES

EXERCISE 13.9 Modify the `addRecentCut()` method so that it limits the cuts stored in the vector to the last 10 cuts.

EXERCISE 13.10 Modify the `addRecentCut()` method so that it does not duplicate cuts already stored in the vector. (*Hint*: Use the `indexOf(String)` method in the `Vector` class.)

Are Computers Intelligent?

Contemporary computer interfaces are largely visual and graphical, and many things we use a computer for, such as word processing, still require us to type. Will there come a day when instead of typing a letter or e-mail message, we'll be able to dictate it to our computer? Will computers eventually have the same kind of interface we have—that is, will we someday be able to carry on conversations with our computers? Clearly, a "conversational interface" would require substantial intelligence on the part of the computer. Do computers have any chance of acquiring such intelligence?

The question of machine intelligence, or *artificial intelligence* (AI), has been the subject of controversy since the very first computers were developed. In 1950, in an article in the journal *Mind*, Alan Turing proposed the following test to settle the question of whether computers could be intelligent. Suppose you put a person and a computer in another room, and you let a human interrogate both with any kind of question whatsoever. The interrogator could ask them to parse a Shakespearian sonnet, or solve an arithmetic problem, or tell a joke. The computer's task would be to try to fool the interrogator into thinking that it was the human. And the (hidden) human's task would be to try to help the interrogator see that he or she was the human.

Turing argued that someday computers would be able to play this game so well that interrogators would have no better than a 50/50 chance of telling which was which. When that day came, he argued, we would have to conclude that computers were intelligent.

This so-called *Turing test* has been the subject of controversy ever since. Many of the founders of AI and many of its current practitioners believe that computation and human thinking are basically the same kind of process, and that eventually computers will develop enough capability that we will have to call them intelligent. Skeptics argue that even if

continued

computers could mimic our intelligence, there is no way they will be self-conscious, and therefore they can never be truly intelligent. According to the skeptics, merely executing programs, no matter how clever the programs are, will never add up to intelligence.

Computers have made some dramatic strides lately. In 1997, an IBM computer named Deep Blue beat world chess champion Gary Kasparov in a seven-game chess match. In 1998, a computer at Los Alamos National Laboratory proved a mathematical theorem that some of the best mathematicians had been unable to prove for the past 40 years.

However, despite these achievements, most observers would agree that computers are not yet capable of passing the Turing test. One area where computers fall short is in natural-language understanding. Although computers are good at understanding Java and other computer languages, human languages are still too complex and require too much common-sense knowledge for computers to understand them perfectly. Another area where computers still fall somewhat short is in speech recognition. However, an American company recently demonstrated a telephone that could translate between English and German (as well as some other languages) in real time. The device's only limitation was that its discourse was limited to the travel domain. As computer processing speeds improve, this limitation is expected to be only temporary. Thus, we may be closer than we think to having our "conversational user interface."

Natural-language understanding, speech recognition, learning, perception, chess playing, and problem solving are the kinds of problems addressed in AI, one of the major applied areas of computer science. Almost every major research group in AI has a Web site that describes its work. To find some of these, just do a search for "artificial intelligence" and then browse through the links that are returned.

CHAPTER SUMMARY

Technical Terms

adapter class	lightweight component
callback design	listener
content pane	model
containment hierarchy	model-view-controller (MVC)
controller	peer model
event model	pluggable look and feel
inner class	view
layout manager	widget hierarchy

Summary of Important Points

- Java provides two sets of Graphical User Interface (GUI) components, the Abstract Windowing Toolkit (AWT), which was part of Java 1.0, and the Swing component set, the GUI part of the Java Foundation Classes (JFC), introduced in JDK 1.1.

- Unlike their AWT counterparts, Swing components are written entirely in Java. This allows programs written in Swing to have a platform-independent look and feel. There are three built-in look-and-feel packages in Swing: a Windows style, a Unix-like Motif style, and a purely Java Metal style.

- Swing components are based on the *model-view-controller* (MVC) architecture, in which the component is divided into three separate objects: how it looks (*view*), what state it's in (*model*), and what it does (*controller*). The view and controller parts are sometimes combined into a single *user interface* class, which can be changed to create a customized look and feel.

- AWT components are based on the *peer model*, in which every AWT component has a peer in the native windowing system. This model is less efficient and more platform dependent than the MVC model.

- Java's *event model* is based on *event listeners*. When a GUI component is created, it is registered with an appropriate event listener, which takes responsibility for handling the component's events.

- A user interface combines four functions: guidance/information for the user, input, output, and control.

- Components in a GUI are organized into a *containment hierarchy* rooted at the top-level window. `JPanel`s and other `Container`s can be used to organize the components into a hierarchy according to function or some other criterion.

- The top-level Swing classes—`JApplet`, `JDialog`, `JFrame`, and `JWindow`—use a *content pane* as their component container.

- A GUI should minimize the number of input devices the user needs to manipulate, as well as the complexity the user needs to deal with. Certain forms of redundancy—such as two independent but complete sets of controls—are desirable because they make the interface more flexible and more widely applicable.

- A *layout manager* is an object that manages the size and arrangement of the components in a container. The AWT and Swing provide a number of built-in layouts, including flow, border, grid, and box layouts.

- A *radio button* is a toggle button that belongs to a group in which only one button from the group may be selected at the same time. A *checkbox* is a toggle button that always displays its state.

- A well-designed interface should reduce the chance of user error and should make it as easy as possible to recover from errors when they occur.

SOLUTIONS TO SELF-STUDY EXERCISES

SOLUTION 13.1   How can a button still be considered a component under the MVC model? This is a good question. The `JButton` class acts as a wrapper class and hides the model-view-controller details (Fig. 13.35). When you instantiate a `JButton`, you still get a single instance. Think of it this way: Your body consists of several systems that interact (internally) with each other, but it's still one body that other bodies interact with as a single object.

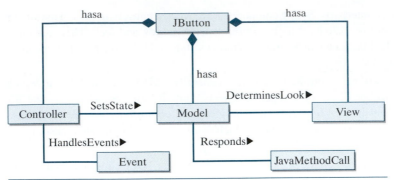

Figure 13.35 A JButton has internal model-view-controller components that interact with each other to produce the button's overall behavior.

SOLUTION 13.2   A component can indeed be registered with more than one listener. For example, the ToggleButton defined in Chapter 4 has two listeners. The first is the button itself, which takes care of toggling the button's label. The second is the applet in which the button is used, which takes care of handling whatever action the button is associated with.

SOLUTION 13.3   Some components can have two different kinds of listeners. For example, imagine a "sticky button" that works like this. When you click and release the button, it causes some action to take place, just like a normal button. When you click and hold the mouse button down, the button "sticks" to the cursor and you can then move it to a new location. This button would need listeners for ActionEvents, MouseEvents, and MouseMotionEvents.

SOLUTION 13.4   To round a double you could use the Math.round() method. For example, suppose the number you want to round is d. Then the expression Math.round(100 * d) /100.0 will round to two decimal places. Alternatively, you could use the java.text.NumberFormat class. Both of these approaches were covered in Chapter 5.

SOLUTION 13.5   Many cars today have cruise control as an alternative way to control the accelerator. Push buttons, usually located on the steering wheel, are used to speed up and slow down, so you can drive with your foot or your hand.

SOLUTION 13.6   As an alternative, a north-west-center border layout for the top-level window in the Converter might work. So might center-south-east and center-south-west. What makes these possible is the fact that the layout manager will use up space in any edge area that is not assigned a component.

SOLUTION 13.7   A flow layout would not be appropriate for the control panel because you would have little control of where the convert button would be placed relative to the keypad.

SOLUTION 13.8   Interface design disaster: My car uses the same kind of on/off switch for the headlights and the windshield wipers. One is on a stem on the left side of the steering wheel, and the other is on a stem on the right side of the steering wheel. On more than one occasion, I've managed to turn off the headlights when I intended to turn on the wipers.

SOLUTION 13.9   Modify the addRecentCut() method so it limits the cuts stored in the vector to the last 10 cuts. Solution: Check the size of the vector after inserting the cut. If it exceeds 10, remove the last element in the vector.

```
private void addRecentCut(String cut) {
  recentCuts.insertElementAt(cut, 0);
  if (recentCuts.size() > 10) {                    // If more than 10 cuts
    recentCuts.removeElementAt(10);                // remove oldest cut
  }
  cutsMenu.removeAll();
  for (int k = 0; k < recentCuts.size(); k++) {
    JMenuItem item =
      new JMenuItem((String) recentCuts.elementAt(k));
    cutsMenu.add(item);
    item.addActionListener(this);
  }
} // addRecentCut()
```

SOLUTION 13.10   Modify the addRecentCut() method so that it does not duplicate cuts stored in the vector. Solution: Use the indexOf() method to search for the cut in the vector. If it's already there, don't insert the cut.

```
private void addRecentCut(String cut) {
  if (recentCuts.indexOf(cut) == -1) {             // If not already cut
    recentCuts.insertElementAt(cut,0);
    if (recentCuts.size() > 10) {                  // If more than 10 cuts
      recentCuts.removeElementAt(10);              // remove oldest
    }
    cutsMenu.removeAll();
    for (int k = 0; k < recentCuts.size(); k++) {
      JMenuItem item =
        new JMenuItem((String) recentCuts.elementAt(k));
      cutsMenu.add(item);
      item.addActionListener(this);
    }
  }                                                // if not already cut
} // addRecentCut()
```

EXERCISES

EXERCISE 13.1   Explain the difference between the following pairs of terms:

a. A *model* and a *view*.
b. A *view* and a *controller*.
c. A *lightweight* component and a *heavyweight* component.
d. A JButton and a Button.
e. A *layout manager* and a *container*.
f. A *containment hierarchy* and an *inheritance hierarchy*.
g. A *content pane* and a JFrame.

Note: For programming exercises, **first** draw a UML class diagram describing all classes and their inheritance relationships and/or associations.

EXERCISE 13.2   Fill in the blanks.

a. A GUI component that is written entirely in Java is known as a _____ component.

b. The AWT is not platform independent because it uses the _____ model to implement its GUI components.

c. The visual elements of a GUI are arranged in a _____.

d. A _____ is an object that takes responsibility for arranging the components in a container.

e. The default layout manager for a `JPanel` is _____.

f. The default layout manager for a `JApplet` is _____.

EXERCISE 13.3   Describe in general terms what you would have to do to change the standard look and feel of a Swing `JButton`.

EXERCISE 13.4   Explain the differences between the model-view-controller design of a `JButton` and the design of an AWT `Button`. Why is MVC superior?

EXERCISE 13.5   Suppose you have an applet that contains a `JButton` and a `JLabel`. Each time the button is clicked, the applet rearranges the letters in the label. Using Java's event model as a basis, explain the sequence of events that happens in order for this action to take place.

EXERCISE 13.6   Draw a containment hierarchy for the most recent GUI version of the `OneRowNim` program.

EXERCISE 13.7   Create a GUI design, similar to the one shown in Figure 13.25, for a program that would be used to buy tickets online for a rock concert.

EXERCISE 13.8   Create a GUI design, similar to the one shown in Figure 13.25, for an online program that would be used to play musical recordings.

EXERCISE 13.9   Design and implement a GUI for the `BankCD` program in Self-Study solution 5.20. The program should let the user input the interest rate, principal, and period and should accumulate the value of the investment.

EXERCISE 13.10   Design and implement a GUI for the `Temperature` class (Fig. 5.5). One challenge of this design is to find a good way for the user to indicate whether a Fahrenheit or Celsius value is being input. This should also determine the order of the conversion: F to C or C to F.

EXERCISE 13.11   Design an interface for a 16-button integer calculator that supports addition, subtraction, multiplication, and division. Implement the interface so that the label of the button is displayed in the calculator's display—that is, it doesn't actually do the math.

EXERCISE 13.12   Challenge: Design and implement a `Calculator` class to go along with the interface you developed in the preceding exercise. It should function the same way as a hand calculator except that it only handles integers.

EXERCISE 13.13   Modify the `Converter` application so that it can convert in either direction: from miles to kilometers or from kilometers to miles. Use radio buttons in your design to let the user select one or the other alternative.

Figure 13.36 A basic JOption-
Pane error dialog.

EXERCISE 13.14   Here's a design problem for you. A biologist needs an interactive program that calculates the average of some field data represented as real numbers. Any real number could be a data value, so you can't use a sentinel value, such as 9999, to indicate the end of the input. Design and implement a suitable interface for this problem.

EXERCISE 13.15   **Challenge:** A dialog box is a window associated with an application that appears only when needed. Dialog boxes have many uses. An error dialog is used to report an error message. A file dialog is used to help the user search for and open a file. Creating a basic error dialog is very simple in Swing. The JOptionPane class has class methods that can be used to create the kind of dialog shown in Figure 13.36. Such a dialog box can be created with a single statement:

```
JOptionPane.showMessageDialog(this, "Sorry, your number is out of range.");
```

Convert the Validate program (Fig. 6.12) to a GUI interface, and use the JOptionPane dialog to report errors.

EXERCISE 13.16   **Challenge:** Design and implement a version of the game *Memory*. In this game you are given a two-dimensional grid of boxes that contain pairs of matching images or strings. The object is to find the matching pairs. When you click a box, its contents are revealed. You then click another box. If its contents match the first one, their contents are left visible. If not, the boxes are closed up again. The user should be able to play multiple games without getting the same arrangement every time.

EXERCISE 13.17   **Challenge:** Extend the SimpleTextEditor program by adding methods to handle the opening, closing, and saving of text files.

Photograph courtesy of Don Farrall Getty Images, Inc. - Photodisc.

14

Threads and Concurrent Programming

OBJECTIVES

After studying this chapter, you will

- Understand the concept of a thread.
- Know how to design and write multithreaded programs.
- Be able to use the `Thread` class and the `Runnable` interface.
- Understand the life cycle of a thread.
- Know how to synchronize threads.

OUTLINE

14.1   Introduction

This chapter is about doing more than one thing at a time. Doing more than one thing at once is commonplace in our everyday lives. For example, let's say your breakfast today consists of cereal, toast, and a cup of java. You have to do three things at once to have breakfast: eat cereal, eat toast, and drink coffee.

Actually, you do these things "at the same time" by alternating among them: you take a spoonful of cereal, then a bite of toast, and then sip some coffee. Then you have another bite of toast, or another spoonful of cereal, more coffee, and so on, until breakfast is finished. If the phone rings while you're having breakfast, you will probably answer it—and continue to have breakfast, or at least to sip the coffee. This means you're doing even more "at the same time." Everyday life is full of examples where we do more than one task at the same time.

The computer programs we have written so far have performed one task at a time. But there are plenty of applications where a program needs to do several things at once, or **concurrently**. For example, if you wrote an Internet chat program, it would let several users take part in a discussion group. The program would have to read messages from several users at the same time and broadcast them to the other participants in the group. The reading and broadcasting tasks would have to take place concurrently. In Java, concurrent programming is handled by *threads*, the topic of this chapter.

14.2   What Is a Thread?

A **thread** (or *thread of execution* or *thread of control*) is a single sequence of executable statements within a program. For Java applications, the flow of control begins at the first statement in `main()` and continues sequentially through the program statements. For Java applets, the flow of control begins with the first statement in `init()`. Loops within a program cause a certain block of statements to be repeated. `If-else` structures cause certain statements to be selected and others to be skipped. Method calls cause the flow of execution to jump to another part of the program, from which it returns after the method's statements are executed. Thus, within a single thread, you can trace the sequential flow of execution from one statement to the next.

Visualizing a thread

One way to visualize a thread is to imagine that you could make a list of the program's statements as they are executed by the computer's central processing unit (CPU). Thus, for a particular execution of a program with loops, method calls, and selection statements, you could list each instruction that was executed, beginning at the first, and continuing until the program stopped, as a single sequence of executed statements. That is a thread!

Now imagine that we break a program up into two or more independent threads. Each thread will have its own sequence of instructions. Within a single thread, the statements are executed one after the other, as usual. However, by alternately executing the statements from one thread and another, the computer can run several threads *concurrently*. Even though the CPU executes one instruction at time, it can run multiple threads concurrently by rapidly alternating among them. The main advantage of concurrency is that it allows the computer to do more than one task at a time. For example, the CPU could alternate between downloading an image from the Internet and running a spreadsheet calculation. This is the same way you ate toast and cereal and drank coffee in our earlier breakfast example. From our perspective, it might look as if the computer had several CPUs working in parallel, but that's just the illusion created by effectively scheduling threads.

> **JAVA LANGUAGE RULE**   **JVM Threads.** The Java Virtual Machine (JVM) is itself an example of a multithreaded program. JVM threads perform tasks that are essential to the successful execution of Java programs.

> **JAVA LANGUAGE RULE**   **Garbage Collector Thread.** One of the JVM threads, the *garbage collector thread*, automatically reclaims memory taken up by objects that are not used in your programs. This happens at the same time that the JVM is interpreting your program.

14.2.1   Concurrent Execution of Threads

The technique of concurrently executing several tasks within a program is known as **multi-tasking**. A **task** in this sense is a computer operation of some sort, such as reading or saving a file, compiling a program, or displaying an image on the screen. Multitasking requires the use of a separate thread for each of the tasks. The methods available in the Java `Thread` class make it possible (and quite simple) to implement **multithreaded** programs.

Multitasking

Most computers, including personal computers, are *sequential* machines that consist of a single CPU capable of executing one machine instruction at a time. In contrast, *parallel computers*, used primarily for large-scale scientific and engineering applications, are made up of multiple CPUs working in tandem.

Today's personal computers, running at clock speeds over 1 gigahertz (i.e., more than 1 billion cycles per second) are capable of executing millions of machine instructions per second. Despite its great speed, however, a single CPU can process only one instruction at a time.

A CPU uses a **fetch-execute cycle** to retrieve the next instruction from memory and execute it. Since CPUs can execute only one instruction at a time, multithreaded programs are made possible by dividing the CPU's time and sharing it among the threads. The CPU's schedule is managed by a **scheduling algorithm**, which is an algorithm that schedules threads for execution on the CPU. The choice of a scheduling algorithm depends on the platform on which the program is running. Thus, thread scheduling is handled differently on Unix, Windows, and Macintosh systems.

One common scheduling technique is known as **time slicing**, in which each thread alternately gets a slice of the CPU's time. For example, suppose we have a program that consists of two threads. Using this technique, the system would give each thread a small **quantum** of CPU time—say, one thousandth of a second (1 *millisecond*)—to execute its instructions. When its quantum expires, the thread would be *preempted* and the other thread would be given a chance to run. The algorithm would then alternate in this **round-robin** fashion between one thread and the other (Fig. 14.1). During each millisecond on a 300-megahertz CPU, a thread can execute 300,000 machine instructions. One *megahertz* equals 1 million cycles per second. Thus, within each second of real time, each thread will receive 500 time slices and will be able to execute something like 150 million machine instructions.

CPUs are sequential

Time slicing

Under **priority scheduling**, threads of higher priority are allowed to run to completion before lower-priority threads are given a chance. An example of a high-priority thread would

Priority scheduling

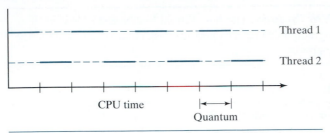

Figure 14.1 Each thread gets a slice of the CPU's time.

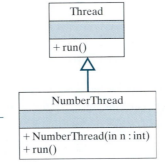

Figure 14.2 The NumberThread class overrides the inherited run() method.

be one that is processing keyboard input or any other interactive input from the user. If such tasks were given low priority, users would experience noticeable delays in their interaction, which would be quite unacceptable.

The only way a high-priority thread can be preempted is if a thread of still higher priority becomes available to run. In many cases, higher-priority threads can complete their task within a few milliseconds, so they can be allowed to run to completion without starving the lower-priority threads. An example would be processing a user's keystroke, a task that can begin as soon as the key is struck and can be completed very quickly. Starvation occurs when one thread is repeatedly preempted by other threads.

JAVA LANGUAGE RULE **Thread Support.** Depending on the hardware platform, Java threads can be supported by assigning different threads to different processors, by time slicing a single processor, or by time slicing many hardware processors.

14.2.2 Multithreaded Numbers

Let's consider a simple example of a threaded program. Suppose we give every individual thread a unique ID number, and each time it runs, it prints its ID 10 times. For example, when the thread with ID 1 runs, the output produced would just be a sequence of 10 1's: 1111111111.

As shown in Figure 14.2, the NumberThread class is defined as a subclass of Thread and overrides the run() method. To set the thread's ID number, the constructor takes a single parameter that is used to set the thread's ID number. In the run() method, the thread simply executes a loop that prints its own number 10 times:

```
public class NumberThread extends Thread {
    int num;

    public NumberThread(int n) {
        num = n;
    }
    public void run() {
        for (int k=0; k < 10; k++) {
            System.out.print(num);
        } // for
    } // run()
} // NumberThread class
```

Now let's define another class whose task will be to create many `NumberThread`s and get them all running at the same time (Fig. 14.3). For each `NumberThread`, we want to call its constructor and then `start()` it:

Thread subclass

```
public class Numbers {
  public static void main(String args[]) {
                                  // 5 threads
    NumberThread number1, number2, number3, number4, number5;

                                  // Create and start each thread
    number1 = new NumberThread(1); number1.start();
    number2 = new NumberThread(2); number2.start();
    number3 = new NumberThread(3); number3.start();
    number4 = new NumberThread(4); number4.start();
    number5 = new NumberThread(5); number5.start();
  } // main()
} // Numbers class
```

When a thread is started by calling its `start()` method, it automatically calls its `run()` method. The output generated by this version of the `Numbers` application is as follows:

Starting a thread

```
111111111122222222223333333333444444444455555555555
```

From this output, it appears that the individual threads were run in the order in which they were created. In this case, each thread was able to run to completion before the next thread started running.

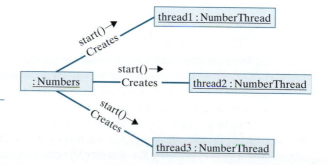

Figure 14.3 The Numbers object creates several instances of Number-Thread and tells each one to start().

What if we increase the number of iterations that each thread performs? Will each thread still run to completion? The following output was generated for 200 iterations per thread:

```
11111111111111111111111111111111111111111111111111111111111111111111
11111111111111111111111111111111111111111111111111111111111111111111
111111111111111111111111111111111111111111111111111111111112222222
22222222222222222222222222222222222222222222222222222222222222222222
22222222222222222222222222222222222222222222222222222222222222222222
222222222222222222222222222222222222222223333333333333333333333333
33333333333333333333333333333333333333333333333333333333333333333333
333333333333333333333333333344444444444444444444444444444444444444444
444444444444444444444444444444444444444444444444444444444444444444
44444444445555555555555555555555555555555555555555555555555555555555
5555555555555555555555555555555555555555555555555555555552222222
22223333333333333333333333333333333333333333333333333333333333333333
333333333333344444444444444444444444444445555555555555555555555555
5555555555555555555555555555555555555555555555555544444444444444444
444444444444444444444444444444444444
```

In this case, only thread 1 managed to run to completion. Threads 2, 3, 4, and 5 did not. As this example illustrates, the order and timing of a thread's execution are highly unpredictable. The example also serves to illustrate one way of creating a multithreaded program:

- Create a subclass of the `Thread` class.
- Within the subclass, implement a method with the signature `void run()` that contains the statements to be executed by the thread.
- Create several instances of the subclass and start each thread by invoking the `start()` method on each instance.

> **JAVA LANGUAGE RULE**   **Thread Creation.** One way to create a thread in Java is to define a subclass of `Thread` and override the default `run()` method.

14.3   From the Java Library: `java.lang.Thread`

The `java.lang.Thread` class contains some of the public methods shown in Figure 14.4. Note that `Thread` implements the `Runnable` interface, which consists simply of the `run()` method. As we will now see, another way to create a thread is to instantiate a `Thread` object and pass it a `Runnable` object that will become its body. This approach allows you to turn an existing class into a separate thread.

A `Runnable` object is any object that implements the `Runnable` interface—that is, any object that implements the `run()` method (Fig. 14.5). The following example provides an alternative way to implement the `NumberThread` program:

```java
public class NumberPrinter implements Runnable {
    int num;

    public NumberPrinter(int n) {
        num = n;
    }

    public void run() {
        for (int k=0; k < 10; k++)
            System.out.print(num);
    } // run()
} // NumberPrinter class
```

Given this definition, we would then pass instances of this class to the individual threads as we create them:

```java
public class Numbers {
    public static void main(String args[]) {

        Thread number1, number2, number3, number4, number5;
        // Create and start each thread
        number1 = new Thread(new NumberPrinter(1)); number1.start();
        number2 = new Thread(new NumberPrinter(2)); number2.start();
        number3 = new Thread(new NumberPrinter(3)); number3.start();
        number4 = new Thread(new NumberPrinter(4)); number4.start();
        number5 = new Thread(new NumberPrinter(5)); number5.start();
    } // main()
} // Numbers class
```

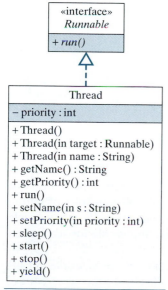

Figure 14.4 The `java.lang.Thread` class.

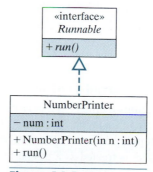

Figure 14.5 Any object that implements the `Runnable` interface can be run as a separate thread.

The NumberPrinter class implements Runnable by defining exactly the same run() that was used in the NumberThread class. We then pass instances of NumberPrinter when we create the individual threads. Doing things this way gives exactly the same output as earlier. This example illustrates another way of creating a multithreaded program:

- Implement the Runnable interface for an existing class by implementing the void run() method, which contains the statements to be executed by the thread.
- Create several Thread instances by first creating instances of the Runnable class and passing each instance as an argument to the Thread() constructor.
- Start each thread instance by invoking the start() method on it.

JAVA LANGUAGE RULE   **Thread Creation.**   A thread can be created by passing a Runnable object to a new Thread instance. The object's run() method will be invoked automatically as soon as the thread's start() method is called.

EFFECTIVE DESIGN: Converting a Class to a Thread.   Using the Runnable interface to create threads enables you to turn an existing class into a thread. For most applications, using the Runnable interface is preferable to redefining the class as a Thread subclass.

SELF-STUDY EXERCISE

EXERCISE 14.1   Use the Runnable interface to convert the following class into a thread. You want the thread to print all the odd numbers up to its bound:

```java
public class PrintOdds {
    private int bound;
    public PrintOdds(int b) {
        bound = b;
    }
    public void print() {
        for (int k = 1; k < bound; k+=2)
            System.out.println(k);
    }
} // PrintOdds class
```

14.3.1   Thread Control

Controlling threads

The various methods in the Thread class (Fig. 14.4) can be used to exert some control over a thread's execution. The start() and stop() methods play the obvious roles of starting and stopping a thread. These methods will sometimes be called automatically. For example, an applet is treated as a thread by the browser, or appletviewer, responsible for starting and stopping it.

As we saw in the NumberThread example, the run() method encapsulates the thread's basic algorithm. It is usually not called directly. Instead, it is called by the thread's start() method, which handles any system-dependent initialization tasks before calling run().

14.3.2   Thread Priority

The `setPriority(int)` method lets you set a thread's priority to an integer value between `Thread.MIN_PRIORITY` and `Thread.MAX_PRIORITY`, the bounds defined as constants in the `Thread` class. Using `setPriority()` gives you some control over a thread's execution. In general, higher-priority threads get to run before, and longer than, lower-priority threads.

> **JAVA LANGUAGE RULE**   **Preemption.** A higher-priority thread that wants to run will *preempt* any threads of lower priority.

To see how `setPriority()` works, suppose we change `NumberThread`'s constructor to the following:

```java
public NumberThread(int n) {
    num = n;
    setPriority(n);
}
```

In this case, each thread sets its priority to its ID number. So thread five will have priority five, a higher priority than all the other threads. Suppose we now run 2 million iterations of each of these threads. Because 2 million iterations will take a long time if we print the thread's ID on each iteration, let's modify the `run()` method, so that the ID is printed every 1 million iterations:

Thread priority

```java
for (int k = 0; k < 2000000; k++)
    if (k % 1000000 == 0)
        System.out.print(num);
```

Given this modification, we get the following output when we run `Numbers`:

```
5544332211
```

It appears from this output that the threads ran to completion in priority order. Thus, thread five completed 2 million iterations before thread four started to run, and so on. This shows that, on my system at least, the Java Virtual Machine supports priority scheduling.

JAVA PROGRAMMING TIP: Platform Dependence.   Thread implementation in Java is platform dependent. Adequate testing is necessary to ensure that a program will perform correctly on a given platform.

EFFECTIVE DESIGN: Thread Coordination.   One way to coordinate the behavior of two threads is to give one thread higher priority than another.

DEBUGGING TIP: Starvation.   A high-priority thread that never gives up the CPU can starve lower-priority threads by preventing them from accessing the CPU.

14.3.3   Forcing Threads to Sleep

Sleep versus yield

The `Thread.sleep()` and `Thread.yield()` methods also provide some control over a thread's behavior. When executed by a thread, the `yield()` method causes the thread to yield the CPU, allowing the thread scheduler to choose another thread. The `sleep()` method causes the thread to yield and not be scheduled until a certain amount of real time has passed.

JAVA LANGUAGE RULE   **Sleep Versus Yield.** The `yield()` and `sleep()` methods both yield the CPU, but the `sleep()` method keeps the thread from being rescheduled for a fixed amount of real time.

The `sleep()` method can halt a running thread for a given number of milliseconds, allowing other waiting threads to run. The `sleep()` method throws an `InterruptedException`, which is a checked exception. This means that the `sleep()` call must be embedded within a `try/catch` block or the method it is in must throw an `InterruptedException`. `Try/catch` blocks were covered in Chapter 10.

```java
try {
    sleep(100);
} catch (InterruptedException e) {
    System.out.println(e.getMessage());
}
```

For example, consider the following version of the `NumberPrinter.run()`:

```java
public void run() {
    for (int k=0; k < 10; k++) {
        try {
            Thread.sleep((long)(Math.random() * 1000));
        } catch (InterruptedException e) {
            System.out.println(e.getMessage());
        }
        System.out.print(num);
    } // for
} // run()
```

In this example, each thread is forced to sleep for a random number of milliseconds between 0 and 1,000. When a thread sleeps, it gives up the CPU, which allows one of the other waiting threads to run. As you would expect, the output we get from this example will reflect the randomness in the amount of time each thread sleeps:

```
14522314532143154232152423541243235415523113435451
```

As we will see, the `sleep()` method provides a rudimentary form of thread synchronization, in which one thread yields control to another.

SELF-STUDY EXERCISES

EXERCISE 14.2   What happens if you run five NumberThreads of equal priority through 2 million iterations each? Run this experiment and note the output. Don't print after every iteration! What sort of scheduling algorithm (round-robin, priority scheduling, or something else) was used to schedule threads of equal priority on your system?

EXERCISE 14.3   Try the following experiment and note the output. Let each thread sleep for 50 milliseconds (rather than a random number of milliseconds). How does this affect the scheduling of the threads? To make things easier to see, print each thread's ID after every 100,000 iterations.

EXERCISE 14.4   The purpose of the Java garbage collector is to recapture memory that was used by objects no longer being used by your program. Should its thread have higher or lower priority than your program?

14.3.4   The Asynchronous Nature of Threaded Programs

Threads are **asynchronous**. This means that the order of execution and the timing of a set of threads are unpredictable, at least from the programmer's point of view. Threads are executed under the control of the scheduling algorithm used by the operating system and the Java Virtual Machine. In general, unless threads are explicitly synchronized, it is impossible for the programmer to predict when and for how long an individual thread will run. In some systems, under some circumstances, a thread may run to completion before any other thread can run. In other systems, or under different circumstances, a thread may run for a short time and then be suspended while another thread runs. Of course, when a thread is preempted by the system, its state is saved so that its execution can be resumed without losing any information.

Thread preemptions are unpredictable

One implication of a thread's asynchronicity is that it is not generally possible to determine where in its source code an individual thread might be preempted. You can't even assume that a thread will be able to complete a simple Java arithmetic operation once it has started it. For example, suppose a thread had to execute the following operation:

```
int N = 5 + 3;
```

This operation computes the sum of 5 and 3 and assigns the result to N. It is tempting to think that once the thread starts this operation, it will be able to complete it, but that is not necessarily so. You have to remember that Java code is compiled into a rudimentary bytecode, which is translated still further into the computer's machine language. In machine language, this operation would break down into something like the following three steps:

An arithmetic operation can be interrupted

```
Fetch 5 from memory and store it in register A.
Add 3 to register A.
Assign the value in register A to N.
```

Although none of the individual machine instructions can be preempted, the thread could be interrupted between any two machine instructions. The point here is that not even a single Java language instruction can be assumed to be indivisible or unpreemptible. Therefore, it is

Threads are asynchronous

impossible to make any assumptions about when a particular thread will run and when it will give up the CPU. This suggests the following important principle of multithreaded programs:

> **JAVA LANGUAGE RULE**   **Asynchronous Thread Principle.** Unless they are explicitly prioritized or synchronized, threads behave in a completely *asynchronous* fashion.

> **JAVA PROGRAMMING TIP: Thread Timing.**   Unless they are explicitly synchronized, you cannot make any assumptions about when, or in what order, individual threads will execute, or where a thread might be interrupted or preempted during its execution.

As we will see, this principle plays a large role in the design of multithreaded programs.

14.4   Thread States and Life Cycle

Every thread has a **life cycle** that consists of several different states, as summarized in Fig-

Ready, running, and sleeping

ure 14.6 and Table 14.1. Thread states are represented by labeled ovals, and transitions between states are represented by labeled arrows. Much of a thread's life cycle is under the control of the operating system and the Java Virtual machine. Transitions represented by method

Controlling a thread

names—such as start(), stop(), wait(), sleep(), notify()—can be controlled by the program. Of these methods, the stop() method has been deprecated in JDK 1.2 because it is inherently unsafe to stop a thread in the middle of its execution. Other transitions—such as *dispatch, I/O request, I/O done, time expired, done sleeping*—are under the control of the CPU scheduler. When first created, a thread is in the ready state, which means that it is ready to run. In the ready state, a thread is waiting in the **ready queue**, perhaps with other threads, for its turn on the CPU. A **queue** is like a waiting line. When the CPU becomes available, the

The ready queue

first thread in the ready queue will be **dispatched**—that is, it will be given the CPU. It will then be in the running state.

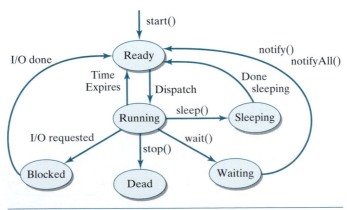

Figure 14.6 A thread's life cycle.

Table 14.1. Summary of thread states

State	Description
Ready	The thread is ready to run and waiting for the CPU.
Running	The thread is executing on the CPU.
Waiting	The thread is waiting for some event to happen.
Sleeping	The thread has been told to sleep for a time.
Blocked	The thread is waiting for I/O to finish.
Dead	The thread is terminated.

Transitions between the ready and running states happen under the control of the CPU scheduler, a fundamental part of the Java runtime system. The job of scheduling many threads in a fair and efficient manner is a little like sharing a single bicycle among several children. Children who are ready to ride the bike wait in line for their turn. The grown-up (scheduler) lets the first child (thread) ride for a period of time before the bike is taken away and given to the next child in line. In round-robin scheduling, each child (thread) gets an equal amount of time on the bike (CPU). CPU scheduler

When a thread calls the `sleep()` method, it voluntarily gives up the CPU, and when the sleep period is over, it goes back into the ready queue. This would be like one of the children deciding to rest for a moment during his or her turn. When the rest is over, the child gets back in line.

When a thread calls the `wait()` method, it voluntarily gives up the CPU, but this time it won't be ready to run again until it is notified by some other thread. Threads can give up the CPU

This would be like one child giving his or her turn to another child. When the turn is up, the second child notifies the first child, who will then get back in line.

The system also manages transitions between the **blocked** and ready states. A thread is put into a blocked state when it does some kind of I/O operation. I/O devices, such as disk drives, modems, and keyboards, are very slow compared to the CPU. Therefore, I/O operations are handled by separate processors known as *controllers*. For example, when a thread wants to read data from a disk drive, the system will give this task to the disk controller, telling it where to place the data. The thread is blocked because it can't do anything until the data are read, so another thread is allowed to run. When the disk controller completes the I/O operation, the blocked thread is unblocked and placed back in the ready queue. Threads block on I/O operations

In terms of the bicycle analogy, blocking a thread would be like giving the bicycle to another child when the rider has to stop to tie a shoe. Instead of letting the bicycle just sit there, we let another child ride it. When the shoe is tied, the first child is ready to ride again and goes back into the ready line. Letting other threads run while one thread is waiting for an I/O operation to complete improves the overall utilization of the CPU.

SELF-STUDY EXERCISE

EXERCISE 14.5 Round-robin scheduling isn't always the best idea. Sometimes *priority scheduling* leads to a better system. Can you think of ways that priority scheduling—higher-priority threads go to the head of the line—can be used to improve the responsiveness of an interactive program?

14.5   Using Threads to Improve Interface Responsiveness

One good use for a *multithreaded* program is to help make a more responsive user interface. In a single-threaded program, a program that is executing statements in a long (perhaps even infinite) loop remains unresponsive to the user's actions until the loop is exited. Thus, the user will experience a noticeable and sometimes frustrating delay between the time an action is initiated and the time it is actually handled by the program.

14.5.1   Single-Threaded Design

It is always a good idea to make an interface responsive to user input, but sometimes it is crucial to an application. For example, suppose a psychology experiment is trying to measure how quickly a user responds to a certain stimulus presented by a program. Obviously, the program should take action as soon as the user clicks a button to indicate a response to the stimulus. Let's work through an appropriate program design for the experiment. We will begin by formally stating the situation and describing what the program should do. Then we will examine the components that would make up an effective program.

Problem Statement

A psychologist is conducting a psychometric experiment to measure user response to a visual cue and asks you to create the following program. The program should have two buttons. When the Draw button is clicked, the program begins drawing thousands of black dots at random locations within a rectangular region of the screen (Fig. 14.7). After a random time interval, the program begins drawing red dots. This change corresponds to the presentation of the stimulus. As soon as the stimulus is presented, the user is supposed to click on a Clear button, which clears the drawing area. To provide a measure of the user's reaction time, the program should report how many red dots were drawn before the user clicked the Clear button.

Problem specification

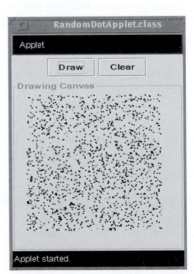

Figure 14.7 Random dots are drawn until the user clicks the Clear button.

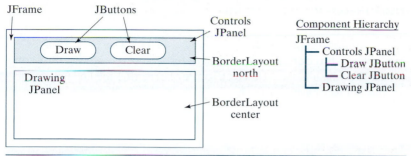

Figure 14.8 GUI design for the dot-drawing program.

Figure 14.8 shows a design for the program's GUI. It contains a control `JPanel` that contains the two `JButton`s. The dots are drawn on a `JPanel`, positioned in the center of a `BorderLayout` design. *GUI design*

Problem Decomposition

This program should be decomposed into two classes, a GUI to handle the user interface and a drawing class to manage the drawing. The main features of its classes are as follows: *Interface class and drawing class*

- `RandomDotGUI` Class: This class manages the user interface, responding to user actions by calling methods of the `Dotty` class (Fig. 14.9).
- `Dotty` Class: This class contains `draw()` and `clear()` methods for drawing on the GUI's drawing panel (Fig. 14.10).

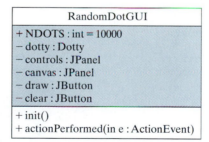

Figure 14.9 The `RandomDotGUI`.

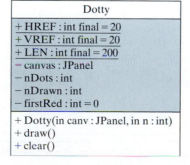

Figure 14.10 The `Dotty` class manages the drawing actions.

The RandomDotGUI Class

The implementation of RandomDotGUI is shown in Figure 14.11. The GUI arranges the control and drawing panels in a BorderLayout and listens for action events on its JButtons. When the user clicks the Draw button, the GUI's actionPerformed() method will create a new Dotty instance and call its draw() method:

```java
dotty = new Dotty(canvas, NDOTS);
dotty.draw();
```

```java
import java.awt.*;
import javax.swing.*;
import java.awt.event.*;
public class RandomDotGUI extends JFrame implements ActionListener  {
  public final int NDOTS = 10000;
  private Dotty dotty;          // The drawing class
  private JPanel controls = new JPanel();
  private JPanel canvas = new JPanel();
  private JButton draw = new JButton("Draw");
  private JButton clear = new JButton("Clear");

  public RandomDotGUI() {
    getContentPane().setLayout(new BorderLayout());
    draw.addActionListener(this);
    clear.addActionListener(this);
    controls.add(draw);
    controls.add(clear);
    canvas.setBorder(
      BorderFactory.createTitledBorder("Drawing Canvas"));
    getContentPane().add("North", controls);
    getContentPane().add("Center", canvas);
    getContentPane().setSize(400, 400);
  } // RandomDotGUI()
  public void actionPerformed(ActionEvent e) {
    if (e.getSource() == draw) {
      dotty = new Dotty(canvas, NDOTS);
      dotty.draw();
    } else {
      dotty.clear();
    }
  } // actionPerformed()
  public static void main(String args[]){
    RandomDotGUI gui = new RandomDotGUI();
    gui.setSize(400,400);
    gui.setVisible(true);
  } // main()
} // RandomDotGUI
```

Figure 14.11 The RandomDotGUI class.

Note that `Dotty` is passed a reference to the drawing `canvas` as well as the number of dots to be drawn. When the user clicks the Clear button, the GUI should call the `dotty.clear()` method. Of course, the important question is, How responsive will the GUI be to the user's action?

The `Dotty` Class

The purpose of the `Dotty` class is to draw the dots and report how many red dots were drawn before the canvas was cleared. Because it will be passed a reference to the drawing panel and the number of dots to draw, the `Dotty` class will need instance variables to store these two values. It will also need a variable to keep track of how many dots were drawn. Finally, since it will be drawing within a fixed rectangle on the panel, the reference coordinates and dimensions of the drawing area are declared as class constants.

The `Dotty()` constructor method will be passed a reference to a drawing panel as well as the number of dots to be drawn and will merely assign these parameters to its instance variables. In addition to its constructor method, the `Dotty` class will have public `draw()` and `clear()` methods, which will be called from the GUI. The `draw()` method will use a loop to draw random dots. The `clear()` method will clear the canvas and report the number of dots drawn.

The complete implementation of `Dotty` is shown in Figure 14.12. Note how its `draw()` method is designed. The drawing loop is bounded by the number of dots to be drawn. On each iteration, the `draw()` method picks a random location within the rectangle defined by the coordinates (HREF, VREF) and (HREF+LEN, VREF+LEN) and draws a dot there. On each iteration it also generates a random number. If the random number is less than 0.001, it changes the drawing color to red and keeps track of the number of dots drawn up to that point.

The problem with this design is that as long as the `draw()` method is executing, the program will be unable to respond to the GUI's Clear button. In a single-threaded design, both the GUI and `dotty` are combined into a single thread of execution (Fig. 14.13). When the user clicks the Draw button, the GUI's `actionPerformed()` method is invoked. It then invokes `Dotty`'s `draw()` method, which must run to completion before anything else can be done. If the user clicks the Clear button while the dots are being drawn, the GUI won't be able to get to this until all the dots are drawn.

If you run this program with `nDots` set to 10,000, the program will not clear the drawing panel until all 10,000 dots are drawn, no matter when the Clear button is pressed. Therefore, the values reported for the user's reaction time will be wrong. Obviously, since it is so unresponsive to user input, this design completely fails to satisfy the program's specifications.

JAVA LANGUAGE RULE   **Single-Threaded Loop.** In a single-threaded design, a loop that requires lots of iterations will completely dominate the CPU during its execution, which forces other tasks, including user I/O tasks, to wait.

SELF-STUDY EXERCISE

EXERCISE 14.6   Suppose the Java Virtual Machine was single threaded and your program got stuck in an infinite loop. Would you be able to break out of the loop by typing a special command (such as Control-C) from the keyboard?

```java
import java.awt.*;
import javax.swing.*;                         // Import Swing classes

public class Dotty {
                                              // Coordinates
  private static final int HREF = 20, VREF = 20, LEN = 200;
  private JPanel canvas;
  private int nDots;                          // Number of dots to draw
  private int nDrawn;                         // Number of dots drawn
  private int firstRed = 0;                   // Number of the first red dot

  public Dotty(JPanel canv, int dots) {
    canvas = canv;
    nDots = dots;
  }
  public void draw() {
    Graphics g = canvas.getGraphics();
    for (nDrawn = 0; nDrawn < nDots; nDrawn++) {
      int x = HREF + (int)(Math.random() * LEN);
      int y = VREF + (int)(Math.random() * LEN);
      g.fillOval(x, y, 3, 3);                 // Draw a dot

      if ((Math.random() < 0.001) && (firstRed == 0)) {
        g.setColor(Color.red);               // Change color to red
        firstRed = nDrawn;
      }
    } // for
  } // draw()
  public void clear() {                       // Clear screen and report result
    Graphics g = canvas.getGraphics();
    g.setColor(canvas.getBackground());
    g.fillRect(HREF, VREF, LEN + 3, LEN + 3);
    System.out.println(
      "Number of dots drawn since first red = " + (nDrawn-firstRed));
  } // clear()
} // Dotty class
```

Figure 14.12 The Dotty class, single-threaded version.

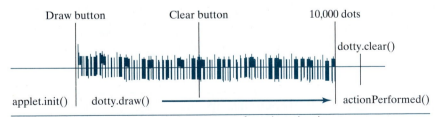

Figure 14.13 A single-threaded execution of random dot drawing.

14.5.2 Multithreaded Drawing: The Dotty Thread

One way to remedy this problem is to create a second thread (in addition to the GUI itself) to do the drawing. The drawing thread will be responsible just for drawing, while the GUI thread will be responsible for handling user actions in the interface. The trick to making the user interface more responsive will be to interrupt the drawing thread periodically so that the GUI thread has a chance to handle any events that have occurred.

Multithreaded design: interrupt the drawing loop

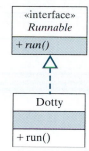

Figure 14.14 In a multithreaded design, the Dotty class implements Runnable.

As Figure 14.14 illustrates, the easiest way to convert `Dotty` into a thread is to have it implement the `Runnable` interface:

```java
public class Dotty implements Runnable {

    // Everything else remains the same

    public void run() {
        draw();
    }
}
```

This version of `Dotty` will perform the same task as before except that it will now run as a separate thread of execution. Note that its `run()` method just calls the `draw()` method defined in the previous version. When the `Dotty` thread is started by the `RandomDotGUI`, we will have a multithreaded program.

However, the fact that this program has two threads does not necessarily mean that it will be any more responsive to the user. There is no guarantee that the drawing thread will stop as soon as the Clear button is clicked. On most systems, if both threads have equal priority, the GUI thread won't run until the drawing thread finishes drawing all *N* dots.

Thread control

> **DEBUGGING TIP: Thread Control.** Just breaking a program into two separate threads won't necessarily give you the desired performance. It might be necessary to *coordinate* the threads.

Therefore, we have to modify our design in order to guarantee that the GUI thread will get a chance to handle the user's actions. One good way to do this is to have `Dotty` sleep for a short instance after it draws each dot. When a thread sleeps, any other threads that are waiting their turn will get a chance to run. If the GUI thread is waiting to handle the user's click on Clear, it will now be able to call `Dotty`'s `clear()` method.

Using sleep() to interrupt the drawing

The new version of `draw()` is shown in Figure 14.15. In this version of `draw()`, the thread sleeps for 1 millisecond on each iteration of the loop. This makes it possible for the GUI to run on every iteration, so that it can handle user actions immediately.

Another necessary change is that once the `clear()` method is called, the `Dotty` thread should stop running (drawing). The correct way to stop a thread is to use some variable whose value will cause the run loop (or in this case the drawing loop) to exit, so the new version of

```java
import java.awt.*;
import javax.swing.*;                              // Import Swing classes

public class Dotty implements Runnable {
                                                   // Coordinates
  private static final int HREF = 20, VREF = 20, LEN = 200;
  private JPanel canvas;
  private int nDots;                               // Number of dots to draw
  private int nDrawn;                              // Number of dots drawn
  private int firstRed = 0;                        // Number of the first red dot
  private boolean isCleared = false;               // Panel is cleared

  public void run() {
    draw();
  }
  public Dotty(JPanel canv, int dots) {
    canvas = canv;
    nDots = dots;
  }
  public void draw() {
    Graphics g = canvas.getGraphics();
    for (nDrawn = 0; !isCleared && nDrawn < nDots; nDrawn++) {
      int x = HREF + (int)(Math.random() * LEN);
      int y = VREF + (int)(Math.random() * LEN);
      g.fillOval(x, y, 3, 3);                      // Draw a dot

      if (Math.random() < 0.001 && firstRed == 0) {
        g.setColor(Color.red);                     // Change color to red
        firstRed = nDrawn;
      }
      try {
        Thread.sleep(1);                           // Sleep for an instant
      } catch (InterruptedException e) {
        System.out.println(e.getMessage());
      }
    } // for
  } // draw()
  public void clear() {
    isCleared = true;
    Graphics g = canvas.getGraphics();
    g.setColor( canvas.getBackground() );
    g.fillRect(HREF,VREF,LEN+3,LEN+3);
    System.out.println("Number of dots drawn since first red = "
                                  + (nDrawn-firstRed));
  } // clear()
} // Dotty class
```

Figure 14.15   By implementing the Runnable interface, this version of Dotty can run as a separate thread.

Dotty uses the boolean variable isCleared to control when drawing is stopped. Note that the variable is initialized to false and then set to true in the clear() method. The for loop in draw() will exit when isCleared becomes true. This causes the draw() method to return, which causes the run() method to return, which causes the thread to stop in an orderly fashion.

EFFECTIVE DESIGN: Threaded GUIs.   Designing a multithreaded GUI involves creating a secondary thread that will run concurrently with the main GUI thread. The GUI thread handles the user interface, while the secondary thread performs CPU-intensive calculations.

JAVA PROGRAMMING TIP: Threading a GUI.   Creating a second thread within a GUI requires three steps: (1) define the secondary thread to implement the `Runnable` interface, (2) override its `run()` method, and (3) incorporate some mechanism, such as a `sleep()` state, into the thread's run algorithm so that the GUI thread will periodically have a chance to run.

Modifications to RandomDotGUI

We don't need to make many changes in `RandomDotGUI` to get it to work with the new version of `Dotty`. The primary change comes in the `actionPerformed()` method. Each time the Draw button was clicked in the original version of this method, we created a `dotty` instance and then called its `draw()` method. In the revised version we must create a new `Thread` and pass it an instance of `Dotty`, which will then run as a separate thread:

Starting the drawing thread

```java
public void actionPerformed(ActionEvent e) {
    if (e.getSource() == draw) {
        dotty = new Dotty(canvas, NDOTS);
        dottyThread = new Thread(dotty);
        dottyThread.start();
    } else {
        dotty.clear();
    }
} // actionPerformed()
```

In addition to a reference to `dotty`, we also have a reference to a `Thread` named `dottyThread`. This additional variable must be declared within the GUI.

Remember that when you call the `start()` method, it automatically calls the thread's `run()` method. When `dottyThread` starts to run, it will immediately call the `draw()` method and start drawing dots. After each dot is drawn, `dottyThread` will sleep for an instant.

Note how the GUI stops the drawing thread. In the new version, `Dotty.clear()` will set the `isCleared` variable, which will cause the drawing loop to terminate. Once again, this is the proper way to stop a thread. Thus, as soon as the user clicks the Clear button, the `Dotty` thread will stop drawing and report its result.

DEBUGGING TIP: Stopping a Thread.   The best way to stop a thread is to use a `boolean` control variable whose value can be set to true or false to exit the `run()` loop.

14.5.3   Advantages of Multithreaded Design

By creating a separate thread for `Dotty`, we have turned a single-threaded program into a multithreaded program. One thread, the GUI, handles the user interface. The second thread

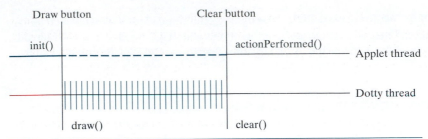

Figure 14.16 Two independent threads: one for drawing, the other for the GUI.

Divide and conquer!

handles the drawing task. By forcing the drawing to sleep on each iteration, we guarantee that the GUI thread will be responsive to the user's actions. Figure 14.16 illustrates the difference between the single- and multithreaded designs. Note that the GUI thread starts and stops the drawing thread, and also executes `dotty.clear()`. The drawing thread simply executes its `draw()` method. In the single-threaded version, all of these actions are done by one thread.

Trade-off: speed vs. responsiveness

The trade-off involved in this design is that it will take longer to draw *N* random dots, since `dottyThread.draw()` will sleep for an instant on each iteration. However, the extra time is hardly noticeable. By breaking the program into two separate threads of control, one to handle the drawing task and one to handle the user interface, the result is a much more responsive program.

EFFECTIVE DESIGN: Responsive Interfaces. In order to give a program a more responsive user interface, divide it into separate threads of control. Let one thread handle interactive tasks, such as user input, and let the second thread handle CPU-intensive computations.

SELF-STUDY EXERCISES

EXERCISE 14.7 Someone might argue that because the Java Virtual Machine uses a round-robin scheduling algorithm, it's redundant to use the `sleep()` method, since the GUI thread will get its chance to run. What's wrong with this argument for interface responsiveness?

EXERCISE 14.8 Instead of sleeping on each iteration, another way to make the interface more responsive would be to set the threaded `Dotty`'s priority to a low number, such as 1. Make this change, and experiment with its effect on the program's responsiveness. Is it more or less responsive than sleeping on each iteration? Why?

14.6 CASE STUDY: Cooperating Threads

For some applications it is necessary to synchronize and coordinate the behavior of threads to enable them to carry out a cooperative task. Many cooperative applications are based on the **producer/consumer model**. According to this model, two threads cooperate at producing and consuming a particular resource or piece of data. The producer thread creates some message or result, and the consumer thread reads or uses the result. The consumer has to wait for a result to be produced, and the producer has to take care not to overwrite a result that has not yet been consumed. Many types of coordination problems fit the producer/consumer model.

One example of an application for this model would be to control the display of data that is read by your browser. As information arrives from the Internet, it is written to a buffer by the producer thread. A separate consumer thread reads information from the buffer and displays it in your browser window. Obviously, the two threads must be carefully synchronized.

Producer and consumer threads

14.6.1 Problem Statement

To illustrate how to address the sorts of problems that can arise when you try to synchronize threads, let's consider a simple application in which several threads use a shared resource. You're familiar with the take-a-number devices used in bakeries to manage a waiting line. Customers take a number when they arrive, and the clerk announces who's next by looking at the device. As customers are called, the clerk increments the "next customer" counter by one.

Simulating a waiting line

There are some obvious potential coordination problems here. The device must keep proper count and can't skip customers. Nor can it give the same number to two different customers. Nor can it allow the clerk to serve nonexistent customers.

Our task is to build a multithreaded simulation that uses a model of a take-a-number device to coordinate the behavior of customers and a (single) clerk in a bakery waiting line. To illustrate the various issues involved in trying to coordinate threads, we will develop more than one version of the program.

Problem Decomposition

This simulation will use four classes of objects. Figure 14.17 provides a UML representation of the interactions among the objects. The TakeANumber object will serve as a model of a

What classes do we need?

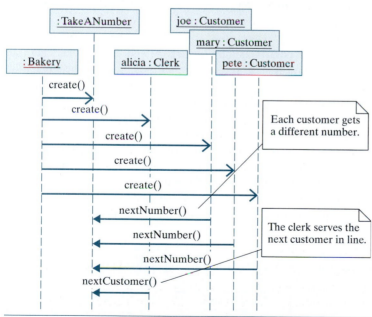

Figure 14.17 The Bakery creates the Customer and Clerk threads and the TakeANumber gadget. Then Customers request and receive waiting numbers, and the Clerk requests and receives the number of the next customer to serve.

take-a-number device. This is the resource that will be shared by the threads, but it is not itself a thread. The Customer class, a subclass of Thread, will model the behavior of a customer who arrives on line and takes a number from the TakeANumber device. There will be several Customer threads created that then compete for a space in line. The Clerk thread, which simulates the behavior of the store clerk, should use the TakeANumber device to determine who the next customer is and should serve that customer. Finally, there will be a main program that will have the task of creating and starting the various threads. Let's call this the Bakery class, which gives us the following list of classes:

- Bakery—creates the threads and starts the simulation.
- TakeANumber—represents the gadget that keeps track of the next customer to be served.
- Clerk—uses the TakeANumber to determine the next customer and then serves the customer.
- Customer—represents the customers who will use the TakeANumber to take their place in line.

14.6.2 Design: The TakeANumber Class

The TakeANumber class must track two things: which customer will be served next, and which waiting number the next customer will be given. This suggests that it should have at least two public methods: nextNumber(), which will be used by customers to get their waiting numbers, and nextCustomer(), which will be used by the clerk to determine who should be served (Fig. 14.18). Each of these methods will simply retrieve the values of the instance variables, next and serving, which keep track of these two values. As part of the object's state, these variables should be private.

How should we make this TakeANumber object accessible to all of the other objects—that is, to all of the customers and to the clerk? The easiest way is to have the main program pass a reference to TakeANumber when it constructs the Customers and the Clerk. They can each store the reference as an instance variable. In this way, all the objects in the simulation can share a TakeANumber object as a common resource. Our design considerations lead to the definition of the TakeANumber class shown in Figure 14.19.

Note that the nextNumber() method is declared synchronized. As we will discuss in more detail, this ensures that only one customer at a time can take a number. Once a thread begins executing a synchronized method, no other thread can execute that method until the first thread finishes. This is important because otherwise, several Customers could call the nextNumber method at the same time. It is important that the customer threads have access only one at a time, also called *mutually exclusive access*, to the TakeANumber object. This form of **mutual exclusion** is important for the correctness of the simulation.

*Passing a
reference to a
shared object*

*Synchronized
methods*

SELF-STUDY EXERCISE

EXERCISE 14.9   What is the analogue to mutual exclusion in the real-world bakery situation?

TakeANumber
− next : int − serving : int
+ nextNumber() : int + nextCustomer() : int

Figure 14.18 The TakeANumber object keeps track of numbers and customers.

```
public class TakeANumber {
    private int next = 0;               // Next place in line
    private int serving = 0;            // Next customer to serve

    public synchronized int nextNumber() {
        next = next + 1;
        return next;
    } // nextNumber()

    public int nextCustomer() {
        ++serving;
        return serving;
    } // nextCustomer()
} // TakeANumber class
```

Figure 14.19 Definition of the TakeANumber class, Version 1.

14.6.3 Java Monitors and Mutual Exclusion

An object that contains synchronized methods has a **monitor** associated with it. A monitor is a widely used synchronization mechanism that ensures that only one thread at a time can execute a synchronized method. When a synchronized method is called, a **lock** is acquired on that object. For example, if one of the Customer threads calls nextNumber(), a lock will be placed on that TakeANumber object. No other synchronized method can run in an object that is *locked*. Other threads must wait for the lock to be released before they can execute a synchronized method.

The monitor concept

While one Customer is executing nextNumber(), all other Customers will be forced to wait until the first Customer is finished. When the synchronized method is exited, the lock on the object is released, allowing other Customer threads to access their synchronized methods. In effect, a synchronized method can be used to guarantee mutually exclusive access to the TakeANumber object among the competing customers.

Mutually exclusive access to a shared object

JAVA LANGUAGE RULE   Synchronized. Once a thread begins to execute a synchronized method in an object, the object is *locked* so that no other thread can gain access to the object's synchronized methods.

EFFECTIVE DESIGN: Synchronization.   In order to restrict access of a method or set of methods to one object at a time (mutual exclusion), declare the methods synchronized.

A cautionary note here is that a synchronized method blocks access to other synchronized methods, but not to nonsynchronized methods. This could cause problems. We will return to this issue in the next part of our case study when we discuss the testing of our program.

14.6.4 The Customer Class

A Customer thread should model the behavior of taking a number from the TakeANumber gadget. For the sake of the simulation, let's suppose that after taking a number, the Customer object just prints it out. This will serve as a simple model of "waiting on line." What about the Customer's state? To distinguish one customer from another, let's give each customer a

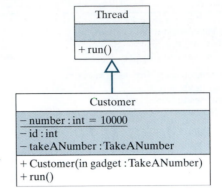

Figure 14.20 The Customer thread.

unique ID number starting at 10001, which will be set in the constructor method. As we noted earlier, each `Customer` also needs a reference to the `TakeANumber` object, which is passed as a constructor parameter (Fig. 14.20). This leads to the definition of `Customer` shown in Figure 14.21. Note that before taking a number, the customer sleeps for a random interval of up to 1,000 milliseconds. This will introduce a bit of randomness into the simulation.

Another important feature of this definition is the use of the `static` variable `number` to assign each customer a unique ID number. Remember that a `static` variable belongs to the class itself, not to its instances. Therefore, every `Customer` that is created can share this variable. By incrementing it and assigning its new value as the `Customer`'s ID, we guarantee that each customer has a unique ID number.

Static (class) variables

JAVA LANGUAGE RULE **Static (Class) Variables.** Static variables are associated with the class itself and not with its instances.

```java
public class Customer extends Thread {

  private static int number = 10000;                    // Initial ID number
  private int id;
  private TakeANumber takeANumber;

  public Customer( TakeANumber gadget ) {
    id = ++number;
    takeANumber = gadget;
  }

  public void run() {
    try {
      sleep( (int)(Math.random() * 1000 ) );
      System.out.println("Customer " + id +
        " takes ticket " + takeANumber.nextNumber());
    } catch (InterruptedException e) {
      System.out.println("Exception " + e.getMessage());
    }
  } // run()
} // Customer class
```

Figure 14.21 Definition of the `Customer` class, Version 1.

EFFECTIVE DESIGN: Unique IDs. Static variables are often used to assign a unique ID number or a unique initial value to each instance of a class.

14.6.5 The Clerk Class

The Clerk thread should simulate the behavior of serving the next customer in line, so it will repeatedly access TakeANumber.nextCustomer() and then serve that customer. For the sake of the simulation, we'll just print a message to indicate which customer is being served. Because there is only one clerk in this simulation, the only variable in its internal state will be a reference to the TakeANumber object (Fig. 14.22). In addition to the constructor, all we really need to define for this class is the run() method. This leads to the definition of Clerk shown in Figure 14.23. In this case, the sleep() method is necessary to allow the Customer threads to run. The Clerk will sit in an infinite loop serving the next customer on each iteration.

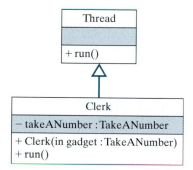

Figure 14.22 The Clerk thread.

```java
public class Clerk extends Thread {
  private TakeANumber takeANumber;

  public Clerk(TakeANumber gadget) {
    takeANumber = gadget;
  }

  public void run() {
    while (true) {
      try {
        sleep( (int)(Math.random() * 50));
        System.out.println("Clerk serving ticket" +takeANumber.nextCustomer());
      } catch (InterruptedException e) {
        System.out.println("Exception " + e.getMessage() );
      }
    } // while
  } // run()
} // Clerk class
```

Figure 14.23 Definition of Clerk, Version 1.

```
public class Bakery {
  public static void main(String args[]) {
    System.out.println("Starting clerk and customer threads");
    TakeANumber numberGadget = new TakeANumber();
    Clerk clerk = new Clerk(numberGadget);
    clerk.start();
    for (int k = 0; k < 5; k++) {
      Customer customer = new Customer(numberGadget);
      customer.start();
    }
  } // main()
} // Bakery class
```

Figure 14.24 Definition of the Bakery class.

14.6.6 The Bakery Class

The main
program

Finally, Bakery is the simplest class to design. It contains the main() method, which gets the whole simulation started. As we said, its role will be to create one Clerk thread and several Customer threads, and get them all started (Fig. 14.24). Note that the Customers and the Clerk are each passed a reference to the shared TakeANumber gadget.

Problem: Nonexistent Customers

Now that we have designed and implemented the classes, let's run several experiments to test whether everything works as intended. Except for the synchronized nextNumber() method, we have made little attempt to ensure that the Customer and Clerk threads can work together cooperatively, without violating the real-world constraints that should be satisfied by the simulation. If we run the simulation as presently coded, it will generate five customers and the clerk will serve all of them. But we get something like the following output:

Testing and
debugging

```
Starting clerk and customer threads
  Clerk serving ticket 1
  Clerk serving ticket 2
  Clerk serving ticket 3
  Clerk serving ticket 4
  Clerk serving ticket 5
Customer 10004 takes ticket 1
Customer 10002 takes ticket 2
  Clerk serving ticket 6
Customer 10005 takes ticket 3
  Clerk serving ticket 7
  Clerk serving ticket 8
  Clerk serving ticket 9
  Clerk serving ticket 10
Customer 10001 takes ticket 4
Customer 10003 takes ticket 5
```

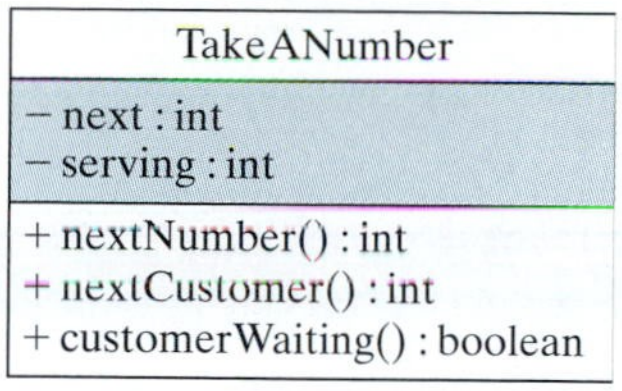

TakeANumber
− next : int − serving : int
+ nextNumber() : int + nextCustomer() : int + customerWaiting() : boolean

Figure 14.25 The revised TakeANumber class.

Our current solution violates an important real-world constraint: you can't serve customers before they enter the line! How can we ensure that the clerk doesn't serve a customer unless there is actually a customer waiting?

Problem: the clerk thread doesn't wait for customer threads

The wrong way to address this issue would be to increase the amount of sleeping the Clerk does between serving customers. This would allow more customer threads to run, so it might seem to have the desired effect, but it doesn't truly address the main problem: a clerk cannot serve a customer if no customer is waiting.

The correct way to solve this problem is to have the clerk check that there are customers waiting before taking the next customer. One way to model this would be to add a customerWaiting() method to our TakeANumber object. This method would return true whenever next is greater than serving. That will correspond to the real-world situation in which the clerk can see customers waiting in line. Thus we make the following modification to Clerk.run():

The clerk checks the line

```java
public void run() {
  while (true) {
    try {
      sleep((int)(Math.random() * 50));
      if (takeANumber.customerWaiting())
        System.out.println("Clerk serving ticket " +takeANumber.nextCustomer());
    } catch (InterruptedException e) {
      System.out.println("Exception " + e.getMessage());
    }
  } // while
} // run()
```

And we add the following method to TakeANumber (Fig. 14.25):

```java
public boolean customerWaiting() {
    return next > serving;
}
```

In other words, the Clerk won't serve a customer unless there are customers waiting—that is, unless next is greater than serving. Given these changes, we get the following type of output when we run the simulation:

```
Starting clerk and customer threads
Customer 10003 takes ticket 1
  Clerk serving ticket 1
Customer 10005 takes ticket 2
  Clerk serving ticket 2
Customer 10001 takes ticket 3
  Clerk serving ticket 3
Customer 10004 takes ticket 4
  Clerk serving ticket 4
Customer 10002 takes ticket 5
  Clerk serving ticket 5
```

This example illustrates that when application design involves cooperating threads, the algorithm used must ensure the proper cooperation and coordination among the threads.

EFFECTIVE DESIGN: Thread Coordination. When two or more threads must behave cooperatively, their interaction must be carefully coordinated by the algorithm.

14.6.7 Problem: Critical Sections

Thread interruptions are unpredictable

It is easy to forget that thread behavior is asynchronous. You can't predict when a thread will be interrupted or may have to give up the CPU to another thread. In designing applications that involve cooperating threads, it's important for the design to incorporate features that guard against problems caused by asynchronicity. To illustrate this problem, consider the following statement from the `Customer.run()` method:

```
System.out.println("Customer " + id +
      " takes ticket " + takeANumber.nextNumber());
```

Even though this is a single Java statement, it breaks up into several Java bytecode statements. A `Customer` thread could certainly be interrupted between getting the next number back from `TakeANumber` and printing it out. We can simulate this by breaking `println()` into two statements and putting a `sleep()` between them:

```
public void run() {
  try {
    int myturn = takeANumber.nextNumber();
    sleep( (int)(Math.random() * 1000 ) );
    System.out.println("Customer " + id + " takes ticket " + myturn);
  } catch (InterruptedException e) {
    System.out.println("Exception " + e.getMessage());
  }
} // run()
```

If this change is made in the simulation, you might get the following output:

```
Starting clerk and customer threads
   Clerk serving ticket 1
   Clerk serving ticket 2
   Clerk serving ticket 3
Customer 10004 takes ticket 4
   Clerk serving ticket 4
   Clerk serving ticket 5
Customer 10001 takes ticket 1
Customer 10002 takes ticket 2
Customer 10003 takes ticket 3
Customer 10005 takes ticket 5
```

Because the `Customer` threads are now interrupted in between taking a number and reporting their number, it looks as if they are being served in the wrong order. Actually, they are being served in the correct order. It's their reporting of their numbers that is wrong!

The problem here is that the `Customer.run()` method is being interrupted in such a way that it invalidates the simulation's output. A method that displays the simulation's state should be so designed that once a thread begins reporting its state, it will be allowed to finish reporting before another thread can start reporting its own state. Accurate reporting of a thread's state is a critical element of the simulation's overall integrity.

Problem: an interrupt in a critical section

A **critical section** is any section of a thread that should not be interrupted during its execution. In the bakery simulation, all of the statements that report the simulation's progress are critical sections. Even though it is very unlikely that a thread will be interrupted in the midst of a `println()` statement, the faithful reporting of the simulation's state should not be left to chance. Therefore, we must design an algorithm that prevents the interruption of critical sections.

Creating a Critical Section

The correct way to address this problem is to treat the reporting of the customer's state as a critical section. As we saw earlier when we discussed the concept of a monitor, a `synchronized` method within a shared object ensures that once a thread starts the method, it will be allowed to finish it before any other thread can start it. Therefore, one way out of this dilemma is to redesign the `nextNumber()` and `nextCustomer()` methods in the `TakeANumber` class so that they report which customer receives a ticket and which customer is being served (Fig. 14.26). In this version all of the methods are `synchronized`, so all the actions of the `TakeANumber` object are treated as critical sections.

Making a critical section uninterruptible

Note that the reporting of both the next number and the next customer to be served are now handled by `TakeANumber` in Figure 14.26 . Because the methods that handle these actions are `synchronized`, they cannot be interrupted by any threads involved in the simulation. This guarantees that the simulation's output will faithfully report the simulation's state.

```
public class TakeANumber {
  private int next = 0;                            // Next place in line
  private int serving = 0;                         // Next customer to serve

  public synchronized int nextNumber(int custId) {
    next = next + 1;
    System.out.println( "Customer " + custId + " takes ticket " + next );
    return next;
  } // nextNumber()
  public synchronized int nextCustomer() {
    ++serving;
    System.out.println("   Clerk serving ticket " + serving );
    return serving;
  } // nextCustomer()
  public synchronized boolean customerWaiting() {
    return next > serving;
  } // customerWaiting()
} // TakeANumber class
```

Figure 14.26 Definition of the TakeANumber class, Version 2.

Given these changes to TakeANumber, we must remove the `println()` statements from the `run()` methods in Customer:

```
public void run() {
  try {
    sleep((int)(Math.random() * 2000));
    takeANumber.nextNumber(id);
  } catch (InterruptedException e) {
    System.out.println("Exception: "+ e.getMessage());
  }
} // run()
```

and from the `run()` method in Clerk:

```
public void run() {
  while (true) {
    try {
      sleep( (int)(Math.random() * 1000));
      if (takeANumber.customerWaiting())
        takeANumber.nextCustomer();
    } catch (InterruptedException e) {
      System.out.println("Exception: "+e.getMessage());
    }
  } // while
} // run()
```

Rather than printing their numbers, these methods now just call the appropriate methods in TakeANumber. Given these design changes, our simulation now produces the following correct output:

```
Starting clerk and customer threads
Customer 10001 takes ticket 1
  Clerk serving ticket 1
Customer 10003 takes ticket 2
Customer 10002 takes ticket 3
  Clerk serving ticket 2
Customer 10005 takes ticket 4
Customer 10004 takes ticket 5
  Clerk serving ticket 3
  Clerk serving ticket 4
  Clerk serving ticket 5
```

The lesson to be learned from this is that in designing multithreaded programs, it is important to assume that if a thread *can* be interrupted at a certain point, it *will* be interrupted at that point. The fact that an interrupt is unlikely to occur is no substitute for the use of a critical section. This is something like "Murphy's Law of Thread Coordination."

Preventing undesirable interrupts

EFFECTIVE DESIGN: The Thread Coordination Principle. Use critical sections to coordinate the behavior of cooperating threads. By designating certain methods as synchronized, you can ensure their mutually exclusive access. Once a thread starts a synchronized method, no other thread will be able to execute the method until the first thread is finished.

In a multithreaded application, the classes and methods should be designed so that undesirable interrupts will not affect the correctness of the algorithm.

JAVA PROGRAMMING TIP: Critical Sections. Java's monitor mechanism will ensure that while one thread is executing a synchronized method, no other thread can gain access to it. Even if the first thread is interrupted, when it resumes execution again it will be allowed to finish the synchronized method before other threads can access synchronized methods in that object.

SELF-STUDY EXERCISE

EXERCISE 14.10 Given the changes we have described, the bakery simulation should now run correctly regardless of how slow or fast the Customer and Clerk threads run. Verify this by placing different-sized sleep intervals in their run() methods. (*Note*: You don't want to put a sleep() in the synchronized methods because that would undermine the whole purpose of making them synchronized in the first place.)

14.6.8   Using `wait/notify` to Coordinate Threads

The examples in the preceding sections were designed to illustrate the issue of thread asynchronicity and the principles of mutual exclusion and critical sections. Through the careful design of the algorithm and the appropriate use of the `synchronized` qualifier, we have managed to design a program that correctly coordinates the behavior of the `Customer`s and `Clerk` in this bakery simulation.

The Busy-Waiting Problem

Busy waiting

One problem with our current design of the Bakery algorithm is that it uses *busy waiting* on the part of the `Clerk` thread. **Busy waiting** occurs when a thread, while waiting for some condition to change, executes a loop instead of giving up the CPU. Because busy waiting is wasteful of CPU time, we should modify the algorithm.

As presently designed, the `Clerk` thread sits in a loop that repeatedly checks whether there is a customer to serve:

```java
public void run() {
  while (true) {
    try {
      sleep( (int)(Math.random() * 1000));
      if (takeANumber.customerWaiting())
        takeANumber.nextCustomer();
    } catch (InterruptedException e) {
      System.out.println("Exception: " + e.getMessage());
    }
  } // while
} // run()
```

A far better solution would be to force the `Clerk` thread to wait until a customer arrives without using the CPU. Under such a design, the `Clerk` thread can be notified and enabled to run as soon as a `Customer` becomes available. Note that this description views the customer/clerk relationship as one-half of the producer/consumer relationship. When a customer takes a number, it *produces* a customer in line that must be served (i.e., *consumed*) by the clerk.

Producer/consumer

This is only half the producer/consumer relationship because we haven't placed any constraint on the size of the waiting line. There is no real limit to how many customers can be produced. If we did limit the line size, customers might be forced to wait before taking a number if, say, the tickets ran out, or the bakery filled up. In that case, customers would have to wait until the line resource became available, and we would have a full-fledged producer/consumer relationship.

The `wait/notify` Mechanism

Let's use Java's `wait/notify` mechanism to eliminate busy waiting from our simulation. As noted in Figure 14.6, the `wait()` method puts a thread into a waiting state, and `notify()` takes a thread out of waiting and places it back in the ready queue. To use these methods in the program, we need to modify the `nextNumber()` and `nextCustomer()` methods. If there is no customer in line when the `Clerk` calls the `nextCustomer()` method, the `Clerk` should be made to `wait()`:

```java
public synchronized int nextCustomer() {
  try {
    while (next <= serving)
      wait();
  } catch(InterruptedException e) {
    System.out.println("Exception: " + e.getMessage());
  } finally {
    ++serving;
    System.out.println(" Clerk serving ticket " + serving);
    return serving;
  }
}
```

Note that the `Clerk` still checks whether there are customers waiting. If there are none, the `Clerk` calls the `wait()` method. This removes the `Clerk` from the CPU until some other thread notifies it, at which point it will be ready to run again. When it runs again, it should check that there is in fact a customer waiting before proceeding. That is why we use a `while` loop here. In effect, the `Clerk` will wait until there is a customer to serve. This is not busy waiting because the `Clerk` thread loses the CPU and must be notified each time a customer becomes available.

A waiting thread gives up the CPU

When and how will the `Clerk` be notified? Clearly, the `Clerk` should be notified as soon as a customer takes a number. Therefore, we put a `notify()` in the `nextNumber()` method, which is the method called by each `Customer` as it gets in line:

```java
public synchronized int nextNumber( int custId) {
  next = next + 1;
  System.out.println("Customer " + custId + " takes ticket " + next);
  notify();
  return next;
}
```

Thus, as soon as a `Customer` thread executes the `nextNumber()` method, the `Clerk` will be notified and allowed to proceed.

What happens if more than one `Customer` has executed a `wait()`? In that case, the JVM will maintain a queue of waiting `Customer` threads. Then, each time a `notify()` is executed, the JVM will take the first `Customer` out of the queue and allow it to proceed.

If we use this model of thread coordination, we no longer need to test `customerWaiting()` in the `Clerk.run()` method. It will be tested in the `TakeANumber.nextCustomer()`. Thus, the `Clerk.run()` can be simplified to

```java
public void run() {
  while (true) {
    try {
      sleep((int)(Math.random() * 1000));
      takeANumber.nextCustomer();
    } catch (InterruptedException e) {
      System.out.println("Exception: "+ e.getMessage());
    }
  } // while
} // run()
```

TakeANumber
− next : int
− serving : int
+ nextNumber() : int<<synchronized>>
+ nextCustomer() : int<<synchronized>>

Figure 14.27 In the final design of TakeANumber, its methods are synchronized.

The Clerk thread may be forced to wait when it calls the nextCustomer method.

Because we no longer need the customerWaiting() method, we end up with the new definition of TakeANumber shown in Figures 14.27 and 14.28.

Given this version of the program, the following kind of output will be generated:

```
Starting clerk and customer threads
Customer 10004 takes ticket 1
Customer 10002 takes ticket 2
  Clerk serving ticket 1
  Clerk serving ticket 2
Customer 10005 takes ticket 3
Customer 10003 takes ticket 4
  Clerk serving ticket 3
Customer 10001 takes ticket 5
  Clerk serving ticket 4
  Clerk serving ticket 5
  Clerk waiting
```

```java
public class TakeANumber {
  private int next = 0;
  private int serving = 0;

  public synchronized int nextNumber(int custId) {
    next = next + 1;
    System.out.println( "Customer " + custId + " takes ticket " + next);
    notify();
    return next;
  } // nextNumber()

  public synchronized int nextCustomer() {
    try {
      while (next <= serving)  {
        System.out.println("    Clerk waiting ");
        wait();
      }
    } catch(InterruptedException e) {
        System.out.println("Exception " + e.getMessage());
    } finally {
        ++serving;
        System.out.println("    Clerk serving ticket " + serving);
        return serving;
    }
  } // nextCustomer()
} // TakeANumber class
```

Figure 14.28 The TakeANumber class, Version 3.

JAVA PROGRAMMING TIP: Busy Waiting. Java's wait/notify mechanism can be used effectively to eliminate busy waiting from a multithreaded application.

EFFECTIVE DESIGN: Producer/Consumer The producer/consumer model is a useful design for coordinating the wait/notify interaction.

SELF-STUDY EXERCISE

EXERCISE 14.11   An interesting experiment to try is to make the Clerk a little slower by making it sleep for up to 2,000 milliseconds. Take a guess at what would happen if you ran this experiment. Then run the experiment and observe the results.

The wait/notify Mechanism

There are a number of important restrictions that must be observed when using the wait/notify mechanism:

Wait/notify go into synchronized methods

- Both wait() and notify() are methods of the Object class, not the Thread class. This enables them to lock objects, which is the essential feature of Java's monitor mechanism.
- A wait() method can be used within a synchronized method. The method doesn't have to be part of a Thread.
- You can only use wait() and notify() within synchronized methods. If you use them in other methods, you will cause an IllegalMonitorStateException with the message "current thread not owner."
- When a wait() or a sleep() is used within a synchronized method, the lock on that object is released so that other methods can access the object's synchronized methods.

DEBUGGING TIP: Wait/Notify.   It's easy to forget that the wait() and notify() methods can only be used within synchronized methods.

14.7   CASE STUDY: The Game of Pong

The game of Pong was one of the first computer video games and was all the rage in the 1970s. The game consists of a ball that moves horizontally and vertically within a rectangular region, and a single paddle, located at the right edge of the region, that can be moved up and down by the user. When the ball hits the top, left, or bottom wall or the paddle, it bounces off in the opposite direction. If the ball misses the paddle, it passes through the right wall and re-emerges at the left wall. Each time the ball bounces off a wall or the paddle, it emits a pong sound.

14.7.1   A Multithreaded Design

Let's develop a multithreaded applet to play the game of Pong. Figure 14.29 shows how the game's GUI should appear. There are three objects involved in this program: the applet, which serves as the GUI, the ball, which is represented as a blue circle in the applet, and the paddle, which is represented by a red rectangle along the right edge of the applet. What cannot be seen in the figure is that the ball moves autonomously, bouncing off the walls and paddle. The paddle's motion is controlled by the user by pressing the up- and down-arrow keys on the keyboard.

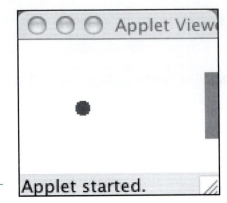

Figure 14.29 The UI for Pong.

We will develop class definitions for the ball, paddle, and applet. Following the example of our dot-drawing program earlier in the chapter, we will employ two independent threads, one for the GUI and one for the ball. Because the user will control the movements of the paddle, the applet will employ a listener object to listen for and respond to the user's key presses.

Figure 14.30 provides an overview of the object-oriented design of the Pong program. The `PongApplet` class is the main class. It uses instances of the `Ball` and `Paddle` classes. `PongApplet` is a subclass of `JApplet` and implements the `KeyListener` interface. This is another of the several event handlers provided in the `java.awt` library. This one han-

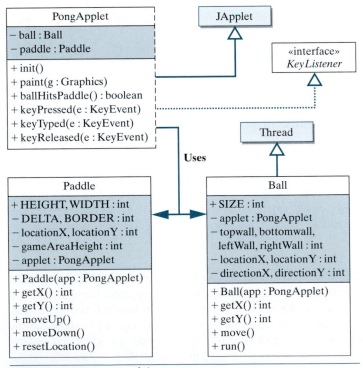

Figure 14.30 Design of the Pong program.

dles KeyEvents, and the KeyListener interface consists of three abstract methods, key-Pressed(), keyTyped(), and keyReleased(), all of which are associated with the act of pressing a key on the keyboard. All three of these methods are implemented in the Pong-Applet class. A key-typed event occurs when a key is pressed down. A key-release event occurs when a key that has been pressed down is released. A key-press event is a combination of both of these events.

The Ball class is a Thread subclass. Its data and methods are designed mainly to keep track of its motion within the applet's drawing panel. The design strategy employed here leaves the drawing of the ball up to the applet. The Ball thread itself just handles the movement within the applet's drawing panel. Note that the Ball() constructor takes a reference to the PongApplet. As we will see, the Ball uses this reference to set the dimensions of the applet's drawing panel. Also, as the Ball moves, it will repeatedly call the applet's repaint() method to draw the ball.

The Paddle class is responsible for moving the paddle up and down along the drawing panel's right edge. Its public methods, moveUP() and moveDown(), will be called by the applet in response to the user pressing the up and down arrows on the keyboard. Because the applet needs to know where to draw the applet, the paddle class contains several public methods, getX(), getY(), and resetLocation(), whose tasks are to report the paddle's location or to adjust its location in case the applet is resized.

The PongApplet controls the overall activity of the program. Note in particular its ball-HitsPaddle() method. This method has the task of determining when the ball and paddle come in contact as the ball continuously moves around in the applet's drawing panel. As in the ThreadedDotty example earlier in the chapter, it is necessary for the Ball and the applet to be implemented as separated threads so that the applet can be responsive to the user's key presses.

14.7.2   Implementation of the Pong Program

We begin our discussion of the program's implementation with the Paddle class implementation (Fig. 14.31).

Class constants HEIGHT and WIDTH are used to define the size of the Paddle, which is represented on the applet as a simple rectangle. The applet will use Graphics fillRect() method to draw the paddle:

```
g.fillRect(pad.getX(),pad.getY(),Paddle.WIDTH,Paddle.HEIGHT);
```

Note how the applet uses the paddle's getX() and getY() methods to get the paddle's current location.

The class constants DELTA and BORDER are used to control the paddle's movement. DELTA represents the number of pixels that the paddle moves on each move up or down, and BORDER is used with gameAreaHeight to keep the paddle within the drawing area. The moveUp() and moveDown() methods are called by the applet each time the user presses an up- or down-arrow key. They change the paddle's location by DELTA pixels up or down.

```
public class Paddle {
    public static final int HEIGHT = 50;         // Paddle size
    public static final int WIDTH = 10;
    private static final int DELTA = HEIGHT/2;   // Move size
    private static final int BORDER = 0;
    private int gameAreaHeight;
    private int locationX, locationY;
    private PongApplet applet;

    public Paddle (PongApplet a) {
        applet = a;
        gameAreaHeight  = a.getHeight();
        locationX = a.getWidth()-WIDTH;
        locationY = gameAreaHeight/2;
    } // Paddle()
    public void resetLocation() {
        gameAreaHeight  = applet.getHeight();
        locationX = applet.getWidth()-WIDTH;
    }
    public int getX() {
        return locationX;
    } // getX()
    public int getY() {
        return locationY;
    } // getY()
    public void moveUp () {
        if (locationY > BORDER )
            locationY -= DELTA;
    } // moveUp()
    public void moveDown() {
        if (locationY + HEIGHT < gameAreaHeight - BORDER)
            locationY += DELTA;
    } // moveDown()
} // Paddle class
```

Figure 14.31   Definition of the Paddle class.

The Ball class (Fig. 14.32) uses the class constant SIZE to determine the size of the oval that represents the ball, drawn by the applet as follows:

```
g.fillOval(ball.getX(),ball.getY(),ball.SIZE,ball.SIZE);
```

As with the paddle, the applet uses the ball's getX() and getY() method to determine the ball's current location.

Unlike the paddle, however, the ball moves autonomously. Its run() method, which is inherited from its Thread superclass, repeatedly moves the ball, draws the ball, and then sleeps for a brief interval (to slow down the speed of the ball's apparent motion). The run() method itself is quite simple because it consists of a short loop. We will deal with the details of how the ball is painted on the applet when we discuss the applet itself.

```java
import javax.swing.*;
import java.awt.Toolkit;
public class Ball extends Thread {
  public static final int SIZE = 10;              // Diameter of the ball
  private PongApplet applet;                       // Reference to the applet
  private int topWall, bottomWall, leftWall, rightWall;  // Boundaries
  private int locationX, locationY;                // Current location of the ball
  private int directionX = 1, directionY = 1;      // x- and y-direction (1 or −1)
  private Toolkit kit = Toolkit.getDefaultToolkit(); // For beep() method

  public Ball(PongApplet app) {
    applet = app;
    locationX = leftWall + 1;                       // Set initial location
    locationY = bottomWall/2;
  } // Ball()
  public int getX() {
    return locationX;
  } // getX()
  public int getY() {
    return locationY;
  } // getY()
  public void move() {
    rightWall = applet.getWidth() - SIZE;          // Define bouncing region
    leftWall = topWall = 0;                         // And location of walls
    bottomWall = applet.getHeight() - SIZE;
    locationX = locationX + directionX;            // Calculate a new location
    locationY = locationY + directionY;

    if (applet.ballHitsPaddle()){
      directionX = -1;                              // move toward left wall
      kit.beep();
    }                                               // if ball hits paddle
    if (locationX <= leftWall){
      directionX = + 1;                             // move toward right wall
      kit.beep();
    }                                               // if ball hits left wall
    if (locationY + SIZE >= bottomWall || locationY <= topWall){
      directionY = -directionY;                     // reverse direction
      kit.beep();
    }                                               // if ball hits top or bottom walls
    if (locationX  >= rightWall + SIZE) {
      locationX = leftWall + 1;                     // jump back to left wall
    }                                               // if ball goes through right wall
  } // move()
  public void run() {
    while (true) {
      move();                                       // Move
      applet.repaint();
      try {  sleep(15);
      } catch (InterruptedException e) {}
    } // while
  } // run()
} // Ball class
```

Figure 14.32 Definition of the Ball class.

The most complex method in the `Ball` class is the `move()` method. This is the method that controls the ball's movement within the boundaries of the applet's drawing area. This method begins by moving the ball one pixel left, right, up, or down by adjusting the values of its `locationX` and `locationY` coordinates:

```
locationX = locationX + directionX;  // Calculate location
locationY = locationY + directionY;
```

The `directionX` and `directionY` variables are set to either $+1$ or -1, depending on whether the ball is moving left or right, up or down. After the ball is moved, the method uses a sequence of `if` statements to check whether the ball is touching one of the walls or the paddle. If the ball is in contact with the top, left, or bottom wall or the paddle, its direction is changed by reversing the value of the `directionX` or `directionY` variable. The direction changes depend on whether the ball has touched a horizontal or vertical wall. When the ball touches the right wall, having missed the paddle, it passes through the right wall and re-emerges from the left wall going in the same direction.

Note how the applet method `ballHitsPaddle()` is used to determine whether the ball has hit the paddle. This is necessary because only the applet knows the locations of both the ball and the paddle.

14.7.3   The `KeyListener` Interface

The implementation of the `PongApplet` class is shown in Figure 14.33. The applet's main task is to manage the drawing of the ball and paddle and to handle the user's key presses. Handling keyboard events is a simple matter of implementing the `KeyListener` interface. This works in much the same way as the `ActionListener` interface, which is used to handle button clicks and other `ActionEvents`. Whenever a key is pressed, it generates `KeyEvents`, which are passed to the appropriate methods of the `KeyListener` interface.

There is a bit of redundancy in the `KeyListener` interface in the sense that a single key press and release generates three `KeyEvents`: a key-typed event, when the key is pressed, a key-released event when the key is released, and a key-pressed event when the key is pressed and released. While it is important for some programs to be able to distinguish between key-typed and key-released events, for this program we will take action whenever either of the arrow keys is pressed (typed and released). Therefore, we implement the `keyPressed()` method as follows:

```
public void keyPressed( KeyEvent e) {  // Check arrow keys
    int keyCode = e.getKeyCode();
    if (keyCode == e.VK_UP)               // Up arrow
        pad.moveUp();
    else if (keyCode == e.VK_DOWN)        // Down arrow
        pad.moveDown();
} // keyReleased()
```

```java
import javax.swing.*;
import java.awt.*;
import java.awt.event.*;

public class PongApplet extends JApplet implements KeyListener {
    private Ball ball;
    private Paddle pad;

    public void init() {
        setBackground(Color.white);
        addKeyListener(this);
        pad = new Paddle(this);             // Create the paddle
        ball = new Ball(this);              // Create the ball
        ball.start();
        requestFocus();                     // Required to receive key events
    } // init()

    public void paint (Graphics g ) {
        g.setColor(getBackground());        // Erase the drawing area
        g.fillRect(0,0,getWidth(),getHeight());

        g.setColor(Color.blue);             // Paint the ball
        g.fillOval(ball.getX(),ball.getY(),ball.SIZE,ball.SIZE);

        pad.resetLocation();                // Paint the paddle
        g.setColor(Color.red);
        g.fillRect(pad.getX(),pad.getY(),Paddle.WIDTH,Paddle.HEIGHT);
    } // paint()

    public boolean ballHitsPaddle() {
        return ball.getX() + Ball.SIZE >= pad.getX()
            && ball.getY() >= pad.getY()
            && ball.getY() <= pad.getY() + Paddle.HEIGHT;
    } // ballHitsPaddle()

    public void keyPressed( KeyEvent e) {   // Check for arrow keys
        int keyCode = e.getKeyCode();
        if (keyCode == e.VK_UP)             // Up arrow
            pad.moveUp();
        else if (keyCode == e.VK_DOWN)      // Down arrow
            pad.moveDown();
    } // keyReleased()
    public void keyTyped(KeyEvent e) {}     // Unused
    public void keyReleased( KeyEvent e) {} // Unused
} // PongApplet class
```

Figure 14.33 Definition of the PongApplet class.

Each key on the keyboard has a unique code that identifies it. The key's code is gotten from the KeyEvent object by means of the getKeyCode() method. Then it is compared with the codes for the up-arrow and down-arrow keys, which are implemented as class constants, VK_UP and VK_DOWN, in the KeyEvent class. If either of these keys is typed, the appropriate paddle method, moveUP() or moveDown(), is called.

Even though we are not using the keyPressed() and keyReleased() methods in this program, it is still necessary to provide implementations for them in the applet. In order to implement an interface, such as the KeyListener interface, you must implement *all* the abstract methods in the interface. That is why we provide trivial implementations of the keyPressed() and keyReleased() methods.

14.7.4   Animating the Bouncing Ball

Computer animation is accomplished by repeatedly drawing, erasing, and redrawing an object at different locations on the drawing panel. The applet's `paint()` method is used for drawing the ball and the paddle at their current locations. The `paint()` method is never called directly. Rather, it is called automatically after the `init()` method, when the applet is started. It is then invoked indirectly by the program by calling the `repaint()` method, which is called in the `run()` method of the `Ball` class. The reason that `paint()` is called indirectly is because Java needs to pass it the applet's current `Graphics` object. Recall that in Java all drawing is done using a `Graphics` object.

In order to animate the bouncing ball, we first erase the current image of the ball, then we draw the ball in its new location. We also draw the paddle in its current location. These steps are carried out in the applet's `paint()` method. First the drawing area is cleared by painting its rectangle in the background color. Then the ball and paddle are painted at their current locations. Before painting the paddle, we first call its `resetLocation()` method. This causes the paddle to be relocated in case the user has resized the applet's drawing area. There is no need to do this for the ball because the ball's drawing area is updated within the `Ball.move()` method every time the ball is moved.

Double buffering One problem with computer animations of this sort is that the repeated drawing and erasing of the drawing area can cause the screen to flicker. In some drawing environments a technique known as *double buffering* is used to reduce the flicker. In double buffering, an invisible, off-screen, buffer is used for the actual drawing operations and is then used to replace the visible image all at once when the drawing is done. Fortunately, Java's Swing components, including `JApplet` and `JFrame`, perform an automatic form of double buffering, so we need not worry about it. Some graphics environments, including Java's AWT environment, do not perform double buffering automatically, in which case the program itself must carry it out.

Like the other examples in this chapter, the game of Pong provides a simple illustration of how threads are used to coordinate concurrent actions in a computer program. As computer game fans will realize, most modern interactive computer games utilize a multithreaded design. The use of threads allows our interactive programs to achieve a responsiveness and sophistication that is not possible in single-threaded programs. One of the great advantages of Java is that it simplifies the use of threads, thereby making thread programming accessible to programmers. However, one of the lessons illustrated in this chapter is that multithreaded programs must be carefully designed in order to work effectively.

SELF-STUDY EXERCISE

EXERCISE 14.12   Modify the `PongApplet` program so that it contains a second ball that starts at a different location from the first ball.

CHAPTER SUMMARY

Technical Terms

asynchronous	concurrent
blocked	critical section
busy waiting	dispatched

fetch-execute cycle

lock

monitor

multitasking

multithreaded

mutual exclusion

priority scheduling

producer/consumer model

quantum

queue

ready queue

round-robin scheduling

scheduling algorithm

task

thread

thread life cycle

time slicing

Summary of Important Points

- *Multitasking* is the technique of executing several tasks at the same time a single program. In Java we give each task a separate *thread of execution*, thus resulting in a *multithreaded* program.

- A *sequential* computer with a single *central processing unit* (CPU) can execute only one machine instruction at a time. A *parallel* computer uses multiple CPUs operating simultaneously to execute more than one instruction at a time.

- A CPU uses a *fetch-execute cycle* to retrieve the next machine instruction from memory and execute it. The cycle is under the control of the CPU's internal clock, which typically runs at several hundred *megahertz*—where 1 megahertz (MHz) is 1 million cycles per second.

- *Time slicing* is the technique whereby several threads can share a single CPU over a given time period. Each thread is given a small slice of the CPU's time under the control of a scheduling algorithm.

- In *round-robin scheduling*, each thread is given an equal slice of time in first-come/first-served order. In *priority scheduling*, higher-priority threads are allowed to run before lower-priority threads.

- There are generally two ways of creating threads in a program. One is to create a subclass of `Thread` and implement a `run()` method. The other is to create a `Thread` instance and pass it a `Runnable` object—that is, an object that implements `run()`.

- The `sleep()` method removes a thread from the CPU for a determinate length of time, giving other threads a chance to run.

- The `setPriority()` method sets a thread's priority. Higher-priority threads have more and longer access to the CPU.

- Threads are *asynchronous*. Their timing and duration on the CPU are highly sporadic and unpredictable. In designing threaded programs, you must be careful not to base your algorithm on any assumptions about the threads' timing.

- To improve the responsiveness of interactive programs, you could give compute-intensive tasks, such as drawing a large number of dots, to a lower-priority thread or to a thread that sleeps periodically.

- A thread's life cycle consists of ready, running, waiting, sleeping, and blocked states. Threads start in the ready state and are dispatched to the CPU by the scheduler, an operating system program. If a thread performs an I/O operation, it blocks until the I/O is completed. If it voluntarily sleeps, it gives up the CPU.

- According to the *producer/consumer* model, two threads share a resource, one serving to produce the resource and the other to consume the resource. Their cooperation must be carefully synchronized.

- An object that contains `synchronized` methods is known as a *monitor*. Such objects ensure that only one thread at a time can execute a synchronized method. The object is *locked* until the thread completes the method or voluntarily sleeps. This is one way to ensure mutually exclusive access to a resource by a collection of cooperating threads.

- The `synchronized` qualifier can also be used to designate a method as a *critical section*, whose execution should not be preempted by one of the other cooperating threads.

- In designing multithreaded programs, it is useful to assume that if a thread *can* be interrupted at a certain point, it *will* be interrupted there. Thread coordination should never be left to chance.

- One way of coordinating two or more cooperating threads is to use the `wait/notify` combination. One thread waits for a resource to be available, and the other thread notifies when a resource becomes available.

SOLUTIONS TO SELF-STUDY EXERCISES

SOLUTION 14.1

```java
public class PrintOdds implements Runnable {
  private int bound;
  public PrintOdds(int b) {
    bound = b;
  }

  public void print() {
    for (int k = 1; k < bound; k+=2)
      System.out.println(k);
  }

  public void run() {
    print();
  }
}
```

SOLUTION 14.2 On my system, the experiment yielded the following output, if each thread printed its number after every 100,000 iterations:

```
1111112222222211111111133333332222222111111333333
2222244444444333333344444445555555544445555555555555
```

This suggests that round-robin scheduling is being used.

SOLUTION 14.3   If each thread is given 50 milliseconds of sleep on each iteration, they tend to run in the order in which they were created:

```
123451234512345...
```

SOLUTION 14.4   The garbage collector runs whenever the available memory drops below a certain threshold. It must have higher priority than the application, since the application won't be able to run if it runs out of memory.

SOLUTION 14.5   To improve the responsiveness of an interactive program, the system could give a high priority to the threads that interact with the user and a low priority to those that perform noninteractive computations, such as number crunching.

SOLUTION 14.6   If the JVM were single threaded, it wouldn't be possible to break out of an infinite loop, because the program's loop would completely consume the CPU's attention.

SOLUTION 14.7   If round-robin scheduling is used, each thread will get a portion of the CPU's time, so the GUI thread will eventually get its turn. But you don't know how long it will be before the GUI gets its turn, so there might still be an unacceptably long wait before the user's actions are handled. Thus, to *guarantee* responsiveness, it is better to have the drawing thread sleep on every iteration.

SOLUTION 14.8   If `Dotty`'s priority is set to 1, a low value, this does improve the responsiveness of the interface, but it is significantly less responsive than using a `sleep()` on each iteration.

SOLUTION 14.9   In a real bakery only one customer at a time can take a number. The take-a-number gadget "enforces" mutual exclusion by virtue of its design: There is room for only one hand to grab the ticket, and there is only one ticket per number. If two customers got "bakery rage" and managed to grab the same ticket, it would rip in half and neither would benefit.

SOLUTION 14.10   One experiment to run would be to make the clerk's performance very slow by using large sleep intervals. If the algorithm is correct, this should not affect the order in which customers are served. Another experiment would be to force the clerk to work fast but the customers to work slowly. This too should not affect the order in which the customers are served.

SOLUTION 14.11   You should observe that the waiting line builds up as customers enter the bakery, but the clerk should still serve the customers in the correct order.

SOLUTION 14.12   A two-ball version of Pong would require the following changes to the original version:

1. A new `Ball()` constructor that has parameters to set the initial location and direction of the ball.

2. The `PongApplet` should create a new `Ball` instance, start it, and draw it.

EXERCISES

Note: For programming exercises, **first** draw a UML class diagram describing all classes and their inheritance relationships and/or associations.

EXERCISE 14.1   Explain the difference between the following pairs of terms:

a. *Blocked* and *ready*.

b. *Priority scheduling* and *round-robin scheduling*.

c. *Producer* and *consumer*.

d. *Monitor* and *lock*.

e. *Concurrent* and *time slicing*.

f. *Mutual exclusion* and *critical section*.

g. *Busy waiting* and *nonbusy waiting*.

EXERCISE 14.2   Fill in the blanks.

a. _____ happens when a CPU's time is divided among several different threads.

b. A method that should not be interrupted during its execution is known as a _____.

c. The scheduling algorithm in which each thread gets an equal portion of the CPU's time is known as _____.

d. The scheduling algorithm in which some threads can preempt other threads is known as _____.

e. A _____ is a mechanism that enforces mutually exclusive access to a synchronized method.

f. A thread that performs an I/O operation may be forced into the _____ state until the operation is completed.

EXERCISE 14.3   Describe the concept of *time slicing* as it applies to CPU scheduling.

EXERCISE 14.4   What's the difference in the way concurrent threads would be implemented on a computer with several processors and on a computer with a single processor?

EXERCISE 14.5   Why are threads put into the *blocked* state when they perform an I/O operation?

EXERCISE 14.6   What's the difference between a thread in the sleep state and a thread in the ready state?

EXERCISE 14.7   **Deadlock** is a situation that occurs when one thread is holding a resource that another thread is waiting for, while the other thread is holding a resource that the first thread is waiting for. Describe how deadlock can occur at a four-way intersection with cars entering from each branch. How can it be avoided?

EXERCISE 14.8   **Starvation** can occur if one thread is repeatedly preempted by other threads. Describe how starvation can occur at a four-way intersection and how it can be avoided.

EXERCISE 14.9   Use the Runnable interface to define a thread that repeatedly generates random numbers in the interval 2 through 12.

 EXERCISE 14.10   Create a version of the Bakery program that uses two clerks to serve customers.

EXERCISE 14.11   Modify the `Numbers` program so that the user can interactively create `NumberThreads` and assign them a priority. Modify the `NumberThreads` so that they print their numbers indefinitely (rather than for a fixed number of iterations). Then experiment with the system by observing the effect of introducing threads with the same, lower, or higher priority. How do the threads behave when they all have the same priority? What happens when you introduce a higher-priority thread into the mix? What happens when you introduce a lower-priority thread into the mix?

EXERCISE 14.12   Create a bouncing-ball simulation in which a single ball (thread) bounces up and down in a vertical line. The ball should bounce off the bottom and top of the enclosing frame.

EXERCISE 14.13   Modify the simulation in the preceding exercise so that more than one ball can be introduced. Allow the user to introduce new balls into the simulation by pressing the space bar or clicking the mouse.

EXERCISE 14.14   Modify your solution to the preceding problem by having the balls bounce off the wall at a random angle.

EXERCISE 14.15   Challenge: One type of producer/consumer problem is the *reader/writer* problem. Create a subclass of `JTextField` that can be shared by threads, one of which writes a random number to the text field, and the other reads the value in the text field. Coordinate the two threads so that the overall effect of the program will be to print the values from 0 to 100 in the proper order. In other words, the reader thread should not read a value from the text field until there is a value to be read. The writer thread should not write a value to the text field until the reader has read the previous value.

EXERCISE 14.16   Challenge: Create a streaming banner thread that moves a simple message across a panel. The message should repeatedly enter at the left edge of the panel and exit from the right edge. Design the banner as a subclass of `JPanel` and have it implement the `Runnable` interface. That way it can be added to any user interface. One of its constructors should take a `String` argument that lets the user set the banner's message.

EXERCISE 14.17   Challenge: Create a slide-show applet that repeatedly cycles through an array of images. The action of displaying the images should be a separate thread. The applet thread should handle the user interface. Give the user some controls that let it pause, stop, start, speed up, and slow down the images.

EXERCISE 14.18   Challenge: Create a horse-race simulation, using separate threads for each of the horses. The horses should race horizontally across the screen, with each horse having a different vertical coordinate. If you don't have good horse images to use, just make each horse a colored polygon or some other shape. Have the horses implement the `Drawable` interface introduced in Chapter 8.

EXERCISE 14.19   Challenge: Create a multithreaded digital-clock application. One thread should keep time in an endless `while` loop. The other thread should be responsible for updating the screen each second.

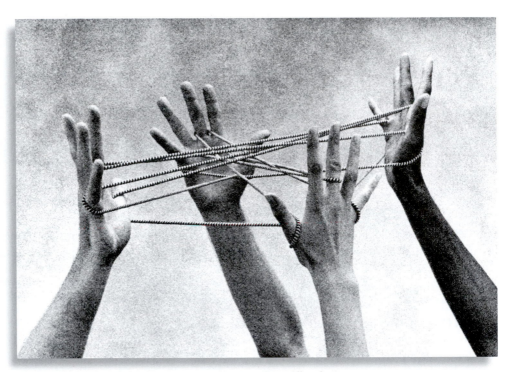

Photograph courtesy of Ray Massey, Getty Images, Inc. - Stone Allstock

15

Sockets and Networking

OBJECTIVES

After studying this chapter, you will

- Understand some basics about networks.
- Know how to use Java's URL class to download network resources from an applet or application.
- Be able to design networking applications, using the client/server model.
- Understand how to use Java's `Socket` and `ServerSocket` classes.

OUTLINE

15.1   Introduction

One of the key strengths of Java is the support it provides for the Internet and client/server programming. In Chapter 11, we saw how to make Java programs transfer information to and from external files. Although files are external to the programs that process them, they are still located on the same computer. In this chapter, we learn how to transfer information to and from files that reside on a network. This enables programs to communicate with programs running on other computers. With networking, we can communicate with computers anywhere in the world.

15.2   An Overview of Networks

Networking is a broad and complex topic. In a typical computer science curriculum, it is covered in one or more upper-level courses. Nevertheless, in this chapter you can learn enough about networking to be able to use network resources and to design simple Java networking applications.

15.2.1   Network Size and Topology

Computer networks come in a variety of sizes and shapes. A *local area network* (LAN) is usually a privately owned network located within a single office or a single organization. Your campus network would be an example of a LAN. A *wide area network* (WAN) spans a wide geographical distance like a country or a continent. It may use a combination of public, private, and leased communication devices. Some of the large commercial networks, such as MCI and Sprint, are examples of WANs.

Network topology   The computers that make up a network can be arranged in a variety of *topologies*, or shapes, some of the most common of which are shown in Figures 15.1 and 15.2. As you would expect, different topologies use different techniques for transmitting information from computer to computer.

In a star network (Fig. 15.1), a central computer functions as a hub to which every other computer in the network is connected. Each computer can communicate with the others but

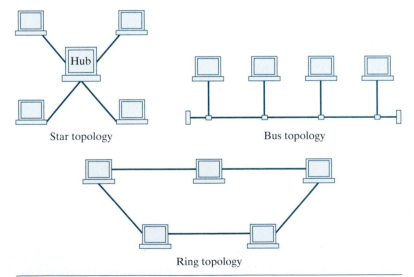

Star topology   Bus topology

Ring topology

Figure 15.1 Star, bus, and ring topologies.

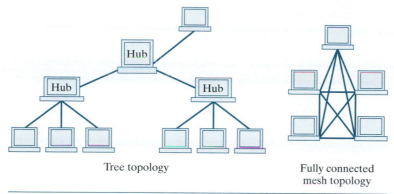

Figure 15.2 Tree and fully connected mesh topologies.

only through the hub. The bus topology doesn't have a hub computer. Instead, each node looks at each message sent on the bus to find those that are addressed to it. In sending a message, a node waits until the bus is free and then transmits the message.

A ring network (Fig. 15.1) also has no host, and the computers are connected in a loop through which they exchange information. The tree topology (Fig. 15.2) is organized into a hierarchy, with each level (trunk of the tree, major branch of the tree) controlled by a hub. The fully connected mesh network directly connects all points to all points, eliminating the "middleman." Here there is no need to go through one or more other computers in order to communicate with a particular computer in the network.

Network topologies differ quite a bit in the expense of the wiring they require, their efficiency, their susceptibility to failure, and the types of protocols they use. These differences are beyond the scope of this chapter.

15.2.2 Internets

An **internet** (lowercase *i*) is a collection of two or more distinct networks joined by devices called **routers** (Fig. 15.3). An internet is like a meeting of the United Nations. Each country

An internet vs. the Internet

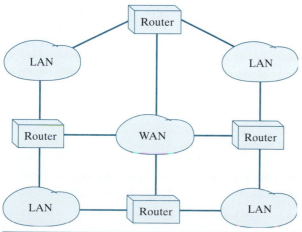

Figure 15.3 An internet is a collection of networks joined together by routers.

sends a delegation whose members all speak that country's language. A national delegation is like a single computer network. Language interpreters take on the task of translating one language to another so that any two delegations, say, the United States and China, can communicate. The routers play a similar translation role within an internet. The UN conference, composed of communicating delegations from all the different countries of the world, is like a worldwide internet.

The United Nations is an apt analogy for the **Internet** (uppercase *I*), which is an example of a worldwide internet. Internets, in the generic sense, should not be confused with the Internet. It is quite likely that your campus LAN is itself composed of several smaller networks, each of which uses its own "language."

SELF-STUDY EXERCISES

EXERCISE 15.1   In a network of 10 computers, which topology would require the most cables?

EXERCISE 15.2   Which topology would be most resistant to having one of its computers crash?

EXERCISE 15.3   Which topology would be least resistant to having one of its computers crash?

15.2.3   Network Protocols

Network
protocols

A **protocol** is a set of rules that governs the communication of information. For example, the **World Wide Web** is based on the **HyperText Transfer Protocol** (HTTP). HTTP describes how information is to be exchanged between a Web browser, such as Internet Explorer or Netscape Navigator, and a Web server that stores an individual's or company's Web pages. Web pages are encoded in the *HyperText Markup Language* (HTML). Among other things, the HTTP protocol can interpret HTML pages.

Similarly, the **Simple Mail Transfer Protocol** (SMTP) is a set of rules that governs the transfer of *e-mail*. And the **File Transfer Protocol** (FTP) is the protocol that governs the transfer of files across the Internet.

Application Protocols

HTTP, SMTP, and FTP are examples of application protocols. They are relatively high-level protocols that support and govern a particular network application, such as e-mail or WWW access. Among other things, they determine how we address different computers on the network. For example, the HTTP protocol specifies Web addresses by using a **Uniform Resource Locator** (URL). A URL specifies three necessary bits of information: the method used to transfer information (e.g., HTTP or FTP), the address of the host computer (e.g., `www.prenhall.com`), and the path describing where the file is located on the host (`/morelli/index.html`):

```
METHOD:   // HOST/PATH
HTTP:     // www.prenhall.com/morelli/index.html
```

Similarly, an e-mail address is specified by the SMTP protocol to consist of a local mailbox address (`George.W.Bush`) followed by the address of the computer (`mail.whitehouse.gov`):

```
LOCAL_MAILBOX@COMPUTER
George.W.Bush@mail.whitehouse.gov
```

Another good example of an application protocol is the Internet's *Domain Name System* (DNS), which is the system that governs how names, such as `whitehouse.gov` and `java.trin-coll.edu`, can be translated into numeric addresses. In the DNS, each host computer on the Internet is identified with a unique host name—for example, `mail`, `java`—which is usually made up by the network administrator whose job it is to manage an organization's network. The DNS divides the entire Internet into a hierarchy of *domains* and *subdomains*. The generic domains are names like `com`, `edu`, and `mil`, which refer to the type of organization—commercial, educational, and military, respectively. In addition, there are country domains, such as `fr`, `au`, and `nz`, for France, Australia, and New Zealand. Finally, individuals and organizations can buy their own **domain names**, such as `whitehouse`, `microsoft`, and `trincoll`.

Internet domain names

What makes the whole system work is that certain computers within the network are designated as DNS servers. It is their role to translate names such as `java.trincoll.edu` to numeric addresses whenever they are requested to do so by clients such as the SMTP or the HTTP server. The DNS servers must also communicate among themselves to make sure that their databases of names and addresses are up-to-date.

SELF-STUDY EXERCISE

EXERCISE 15.4 What is the URL of the Web server at Prentice Hall? Identify its component parts—host name, domain name, Internet domain.

15.2.4 Client/Server Applications

The HTTP, FTP, SMTP, and DNS protocols are examples of **client/server protocols**, and the applications they support are examples of client/server applications. In general, a client/server application is one in which the task at hand has been divided into two subtasks, one performed by the **client** and one performed by the **server** (Fig. 15.4).

For example, in the HTTP case, the Web browser plays the role of a client by requesting a Web page from a Web (HTTP) server. A Web server is just a computer that runs HTTP software—a program that implements the HTTP protocol. For e-mail, the program you use to read your e-mail—Eudora, Pine, or Outlook—is an e-mail client. It requests certain services, such as send mail or get mail, from an e-mail (SMTP) server, which is simply a computer that runs SMTP software. In the FTP case, to transfer a program from one computer to another, you would use an FTP client, such as Fetch. Finally, in the DNS case, the DNS servers handle requests for name to address translations that come from HTTP, FTP, and SMTP servers, acting in this case like clients.

So we can say that a client/server application is one that observes the following protocol:

```
Server: Set up a service on a particular host computer.
Client: Contact the server and request the service.
Server: Accept a request from a client and provide the service.
```

Figure 15.4 Client/server application.

As these examples illustrate, many Internet applications are designed as client/server applications.

EFFECTIVE DESIGN: Divide and Conquer. The client/server protocol is an example of the effective use of the divide-and-conquer strategy.

SELF-STUDY EXERCISE

EXERCISE 15.5   Many of our everyday interactions fit into the client/server model. Suppose you are the client in the following services:

• Buying a piece of software at a bookstore.
• Buying a piece of software over the phone.
• Buying a piece of software over the Internet.

Identify the server and then describe the basic protocol.

15.2.5   Lower-Level Network Protocols

Modern computer networks, such as the Internet, are organized into a number of levels of software and hardware. Each level has its own collection of protocols (Fig. 15.5).

The application level, which contains the HTTP, FTP, SMTP, and DNS protocols, is the highest level. Underlying the application-level protocols are various *transmission protocols*, such as the *Transfer Control Protocol* (TCP) and the *User Datagram Protocol* (UDP). These protocols govern the transfer of large blocks of information, or **packets**, between networked computers. All of the applications we have mentioned—WWW, e-mail, and file transfer— involve data transmission and, therefore, rely on one or more of the transmission protocols.

Packet transfer

At the very lowest end of this hierarchy of protocols are those that govern the transmission of bits, or electronic pulses, over wires and those that govern the delivery of data from node to node. Most of these protocols are built right into the hardware—the wires, connectors, transmission devices—that networks use. On top of these are protocols, such as the **ethernet protocol** and the *token ring protocol*, that govern the delivery of packets of information on a local area network. These too may be built right into the network hardware.

Application level: Provide services. (HTTP, SMTP, DNS)

Transport layer: Deliver packets; error recovery. (TCP, UDP)

Network layer: Move packets; provide internetworking. (IP)

Physical and data link layers: Transmit bits over a medium from one address to another. (ETHERNET)

Figure 15.5   Levels of network protocols.

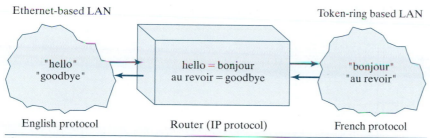

Figure 15.6 Routers between individual networks use the IP protocol to translate one network protocol to another.

As you might expect, these lower-level protocols are vastly different from each other. An ethernet network cannot talk directly to a token ring network. How can we connect such disparate networks together? Think again of our United Nations analogy. How do we get French-speaking networks to communicate with English-speaking networks? The answer supplied by the Internet is to use the **Internetworking Protocol** (IP), which governs the task of translating one network protocol to a common format (Fig. 15.6).

To push the UN analogy a bit further, the Internet's IP is like a universal language built into the routers that transmit data between disparate networks. On one end of a transmission, a router takes a French packet of information received from one of the delegates in its network. The router translates the French packet into an IP packet, which it then sends on through the network to its destination. When the IP packet gets close to its destination, another router takes it and translates it into an English packet before sending it on to its destination on its network.

Disparate protocols

The Internet protocol

15.2.6 The `java.net` Package

As we have seen, networks are glued together by a vast array of protocols. Most of these protocols are implemented in software that runs on general-purpose computers. You can install software on your personal computer to turn it into a Web server, an FTP server, or an e-mail server. Some of the lower-level protocols are implemented in software that runs on special-purpose computers, the routers. Still other protocols, such as the ethernet protocol, are implemented directly in hardware.

Fortunately, we don't have to worry about the details of even the highest-level protocols in order to write client/server applications in Java. The `java.net` (Fig. 15.7) package supplies a powerful and easy-to-use set of classes that supports network programming.

The `java.net.URL` class provides a representation of the Internet's Uniform Resource Locator that we described earlier. We will show how to use its methods to download WWW pages. We will also look at an example that uses a URL and an input stream so that files stored on the Web can be used as input files to a Java applet or application program.

`java.net.*`

The `Socket` and `ServerSocket` classes provide methods that let us develop our own networking applications. They enable us to make a direct connection to an Internet host, and read and write data through `InputStream`s and `OutputStream`s. As we will see, this is no more difficult than reading and writing data to and from files. The `DatagramPacket` and `DatagramSocket` classes provide support even for lower-level networking applications, based on Internet packets.

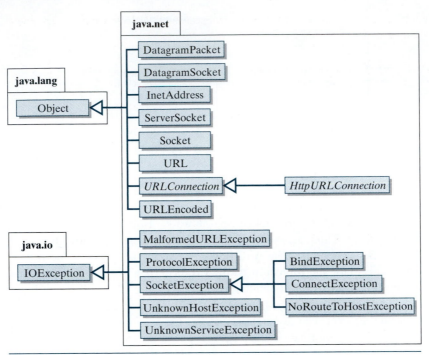

Figure 15.7 The `java.net` package.

15.3   Using Network Resources from an Applet

Suppose you want to write an applet that will automatically display a slide show consisting of images or documents that you have prepared and stored on your Web site. Perhaps you can use such an applet to give people who visit your site a tour of your campus (Fig. 15.8). Or perhaps a company might use such an applet to advertise its products. In addition to making the slide show available through its main Web site, you can imagine it running continuously on a computer kiosk in the company's lobby.

Problem statement

In order to solve this problem we have to be able to download and display Web resources. As you know, Web resources are multimedia. That is, they could be documents, images, sounds, video clips, and so on. All Web resources are specified in terms of their Uniform Resource Locators (URLs). Thus, to download an image (or an HTML file or audio clip), we usually type its URL into a Web browser. We want our program to know beforehand the URLs of the

Specifying Web resources

Figure 15.8 An applet that continuously displays slides downloaded from the Web.

images it will display so that there will be no need to input the URL. We want to implement something like the following algorithm:

```
repeat forever
    Generate the URL for the next slide.
    Use the URL to download the image or document.
    Display the image or document.
```

A URL specification is just a `String`, such as

```
http://starbase.trincoll.edu:80/~jjjava/slideshow/slide1.gif
```

which describes how to retrieve the resource. First it specifies the protocol or method that should be used to download the resource (`http`). Then it provides the domain name of the server that runs the protocol and the port number where the service is running (`starbase.trincoll.edu:80`). Next the URL specifies the resource's file name (`jjjava/slideshow/slide1.gif`).

15.4 From the Java Library: `java.net.URL`

Given such a URL specification, how can we download its associated resource? Are there Java classes that can help us solve this problem? Fortunately, there are. First, the `java.net.URL` class contains methods to help retrieve the resource associated with a particular URL (Fig. 15.9). The URL class represents a Uniform Resource Locator. The `URL()` constructor shown here (there are others) takes a URL specification as a `String` and, assuming it specifies a valid URL, creates a URL object. If the URL specification is invalid, a `MalformedURLException` is thrown. A URL would be invalid if the protocol were left off or if it is not a known protocol. The following simple code creates a URL for the home page of our companion Web site:

java.sun.com/docs

```
URL url;
try {
  url = new URL("http://www.prenhall.com:80/morelli/index.html");
} catch (MalformedURLException e) {
  System.out.println("Malformed URL: " + url.toString());
}
```

URL
+ URL(in urlSpec : String)
+ openConnection() : URLConnection
+ openStream() : InputStream

Figure 15.9 The `java.net.URL` class.

Note how we catch the `MalformedURLException` when we create a new URL.

Once we have a valid URL instance, it can be used to download the data or object associated with it. There are different ways to do this. The `openConnection()` method creates a `URLConnection`, which can then be used to download the resource. You would only use this method if your application required extensive control over the download process. A much simpler approach would use the `openStream()` method. This method will open an `InputStream`, which you can then use to read the associated URL data the same way you would read a file. This method is especially useful for writing Java applications (rather than applets). As you might guess, downloading Web resources is very easy from a Java applet. Now let's search around for other methods that we can use.

URLs and streams

15.4.1 Code Reuse: The `java.applet.Applet` Class

The `java.applet.Applet` class itself contains several useful methods for downloading and displaying Web resources. These methods are inherited by `javax.swing.JApplet`:

```java
public class Applet extends Panel {
    public AppletContext getAppletContext();
    public AudioClip getAudioClip(URL url);
    public Image getImage(URL url);
    public void play(URL url);
    public void showStatus(String msg);
}
```

As you can see, the `getImage()` and `getAudioClip()` methods both use a URL to download a resource. An `AudioClip` is a sound file encoded in AU format, a special type of encoding for sound files. The `getImage()` method can return files in either GIF or JPEG format, two popular image file formats. The `play()` method downloads and plays an audio file in one easy step. For example, to download and play an audio clip in an applet requires just two lines of code:

```java
URL url;
try {
    url = new URL("http://starbase.trincoll.edu/~jjjava/slideshow/sound.au");
    play(url);
} catch (MalformedURLException e) {
    System.out.println("Malformed URL: " + url.toString()) ;
}
```

Similarly, to download (and store a reference to) an image is just as simple:

```java
URL url;
try {
    url = new URL("http://starbase.trincoll.edu/~jjjava/slideshow/slide0.gif") ;
    imgRef = getImage(url);
} catch (MalformedURLException e) {
    System.out.println( "Malformed URL: " + url.toString()) ;
}
```

It looks as if we have found the methods we need to implement our slide-show applet. We'll use the URL() constructor to create a URL from a `String`, and we'll use the `Applet.getImage(URL)` method to retrieve the images from the Web.

What methods can we use?

15.5   The Slide-Show Applet

Problem Specification

Let's suppose our slide show will repeatedly display a set of images named "slide0.gif", "slide1.gif", and "slide2.gif". Suppose these images are stored on a Web site at `star-base.trincoll.edu` and are stored in a directory named in-`jjjava/slideshow`. This means that our program will have to load the following three URLs:

```
http://starbase.trincoll.edu/~jjjava/slideshow/slide0.gif
http://starbase.trincoll.edu/~jjjava/slideshow/slide1.gif
http://starbase.trincoll.edu/~jjjava/slideshow/slide2.gif
```

We want our show to cycle endlessly through these images, leaving about 5 seconds after each slide.

User Interface Design

The user interface for this applet does not contain any GUI components. It just needs to display an image every 5 seconds. It can use a simple `paint()` method to display an image each time it is repainted:

```java
public void paint(Graphics g) {
    if (currentImage != null)
        g.drawImage(currentImage, 10, 10, this);
}
```

The assumption here is that the `currentImage` instance variable will be set initially to `null`. Each time an image is downloaded, it will be set to refer to that image. Because `paint()` is called before the applet starts downloading the images, it is necessary to guard against attempting to draw a `null` image, which would lead to an exception.

Problem Decomposition

One problem we face with this applet is getting it to pause after each slide. One way to do this is to set up a loop that does nothing for about 5 seconds:

```java
for (int k = 0; k < 1000000; k++ ) ;   // Busy waiting
```

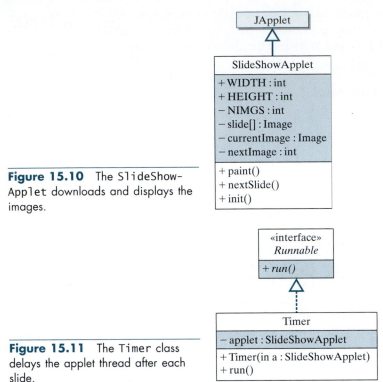

Figure 15.10   The SlideShow-Applet downloads and displays the images.

Figure 15.11   The Timer class delays the applet thread after each slide.

However, this isn't a very good solution. As we saw in Chapter 14, this is a form of *busy waiting* that monopolizes the CPU, making it very difficult to break out of the loop. Another problem with this loop is that we don't really know how many iterations to do to approximate 5 seconds of idleness.

 A much better design would be to use a separate timer thread that can `sleep()` for 5 seconds after each slide. So our program will have two classes: one to download and display the slides, and one to serve as a timer (Figs. 15.10 and 15.11).

- `SlideShowApplet`. This `JApplet` subclass will take care of downloading and displaying the images and starting the timer thread.
- `Timer`. This class will implement the `Runnable` interface so that it can run as a separate thread. It will repeatedly sleep for 5 seconds and then tell the applet to display the next slide.

EFFECTIVE DESIGN: Busy Waiting.   Instead of busy waiting, a thread that sleeps for a brief period on each iteration is a better way to introduce a delay into an algorithm.

15.5.1   The SlideShowApplet class

What should we do with the images we download? Should we repeatedly download and display them, or should we just download them once and store them in memory? The second of these alternatives seems more efficient. If an image has already been downloaded, it would be wasteful to download it again.

EFFECTIVE DESIGN: Network Traffic.   In general, a design that minimizes network traffic is preferable.

So we will need an array to store the images. Our slide show will then consist of retrieving the next image from the array and displaying it. To help us with this task, let's use a `nextImg` variable as an array index to keep track of the next image. Even though it isn't absolutely necessary, we could use a third variable here, `currentImage`, to keep track of the current image being displayed. Thus, our applet needs the following instance variables:

What data do we need?

```java
private static final int NIMGS = 3;
private Image[] slide = new Image[NIMGS];
private Image currentImage = null;
private int nextImg = 0;
```

Given these variables, let's now write a method to take care of choosing the next slide. Recall that the `paint()` method is responsible for displaying `currentImage`, so all this method needs to do is to update both `currentImage` and `nextImg`. This method should be designed so that it can be called by the `Timer` thread whenever it is time to display the next slide, so it should be a `public` method. It can be a `void` method with no parameters, because the applet already contains all the necessary information to display the next slide. Thus, there's no need for information to be passed back and forth between `Timer` and this method:

Method design

```java
public void nextSlide() {
    currentImage = slide[nextImg];
    nextImg = (nextImg + 1) % NIMGS;
    repaint();
} // nextSlide()
```

The method's algorithm is very simple. It sets `currentImage` to whatever `slide` is designated by `nextImg`, and it then updates `nextImg`'s value. Note here the use of modular arithmetic to compute the value of `nextImg`. Given that NIMGS is 3, this algorithm will cause `nextImg` to take on the repeating sequence of values 0, 1, 2, 0, 1, 2, and so forth. Finally, the method calls `repaint()` to display the image.

JAVA PROGRAMMING TIP: Modular Arithmetic.   Modular arithmetic (x % N) is useful for cycling repeatedly through the values 0, 1, ..., $N - 1$.

The applet's `init()` method will have two tasks:

- Download and store the images in `slide[]`.
- Start the `Timer` thread.

Figure 15.12 Timer uses the nextSlide() method to *call back* the applet to remind it to switch to the next slide.

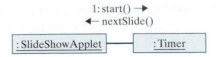

As we discussed, downloading Web resources requires the use of the getImage() method. Here we just place these method calls in a loop:

```
for (int k=0; k < NIMGS; k++)
    slide[k] = getImage(getCodeBase(), "gifs/demo" + k + ".gif");
```

Note here how we convert the loop variable *k* into a String and concatenate it right into the URL specification. This allows us to have URLs containing "slide0.gif", "slide1.gif", and "slide2.gif". This makes our program easily extensible should we later decide to add more slides to the show. Note also the use of the class constant NIMGS as the loop bound. This too adds to the program's extensibility.

JAVA PROGRAMMING TIP: Concatenation. Concatenating an integer value (k) with a string lets you create file names of the form file1.gif, file2.gif, and so on.

The task of starting the Timer thread involves creating an instance of the Timer class and calling its start() method:

```
Thread timer = new Thread(new Timer(this));
timer.start();
```

Note that Timer is passed a reference to this applet. This enables Timer to call the applet's nextSlide() method every 5 seconds. This programming technique is known as *callback*, and the nextSlide() method is an example of a **callback method** (Fig. 15.12).

JAVA PROGRAMMING TIP: Callback. Communication between two objects can often be handled using a callback technique. One object is passed a reference to the other object. The first object uses the reference to call one of the public methods of the other object.

This completes our design and development of SlideShowApplet, which is shown in Figure 15.13.

15.5.2 The Timer Class

The timer thread

The Timer class is a subclass of Thread and therefore must implement the run() method. Recall that we never directly call a thread's run() method. Instead, we call its start() method, which automatically calls run(). This particular thread has a very simple and singular function. It is to call the nextSlide() method of the SlideShowApplet class and then sleep for 5 seconds. So its main algorithm will be:

```
import java.awt.*;
import javax.swing.*;
import java.net.*;

public class SlideShowApplet extends JApplet  {
    public static final int WIDTH=300, HEIGHT=200;
    private static final int NIMGS = 3;
    private Image[] slide = new Image[NIMGS];
    private Image currentImage = null;
    private int nextImg = 0;

    public void paint(Graphics g) {
        g.setColor(getBackground());
        g.fillRect(0, 0, WIDTH, HEIGHT);
        if (currentImage != null)
            g.drawImage(currentImage, 10, 10, this);
    } // paint()

    public void nextSlide() {
        currentImage = slide[nextImg];
        nextImg = (nextImg + 1) % NIMGS;
        repaint();
    } // nextSlide()

    public void init() {
        for (int k=0; k < NIMGS; k++)
            slide[k] = getImage(getCodeBase(), "gifs/demo" + k + ".gif");
        Thread timer = new Thread(new Timer(this));
        timer.start();
        setSize( WIDTH, HEIGHT );
    } // init()
} // SlideShowApplet class
```

Figure 15.13 The SlideShowApplet class.

```
while (true) {
    applet.nextSlide();
    sleep( 5000 );
}
```

However, recall that `Thread.sleep()` throws the `InterruptedException`. This means that we will have to embed this `while` loop in a `try/catch` block.

To call the applet's `nextSlide()` method, we also need a reference to the `SlideShowApplet`, so we need to give it a reference, such as an instance variable, as well as a constructor that allows the applet to pass `Timer` a reference to itself.

Given these design decisions, the complete implementation of `Timer` is shown in Figure 15.14. To see how it works, download it from the *Java, Java, Java* Web site and run it.

SELF-STUDY EXERCISE

EXERCISE 15.6 Describe the design changes you would make to `SlideShowApplet` if you wanted to play a soundtrack along with your slides. Assume that the sounds are stored in a sequence of files, "sound0.au", "sound1.au", and so forth, on your Web site.

```
public class Timer implements Runnable {
    private SlideShowApplet applet;

    public Timer( SlideShowApplet app ) {
        applet = app;
    }

    public void run() {
        try {
            while ( true ) {
                applet.nextSlide();
                Thread.sleep( 5000 );
            }
        } catch (InterruptedException e) {
            System.out.println(e.getMessage());
        }
    } // run()
} // Timer class
```

Figure 15.14 The Timer class.

15.6 Using Network Resources from an Application

The `SlideShowApplet` illustrates the ease of downloading Web resources from an applet. However, applets have limited use in this regard, because they come with rather severe security restrictions that would make them a poor choice for most networking applications (see Section 15.10). For example, applets cannot save files that they download, because they cannot access the host computer's file system. Similarly, an applet can only download files from the same host from which it was downloaded. This would not be a problem for the slide-show applet, since we can simply store the slides in the same directory as the applet itself. So we want to learn how to download Web resources from a Java application. The next example illustrates a solution to this problem.

Applet restrictions

Problem Specification

Problem statement

Suppose a realtor asks you to write a Java application that will allow customers to view pictures and descriptions of homes from an online database. The application should allow the customer to select a home and should then display both an image of the home and a text description of its features, such as square footage, asking price, and so on.

Suppose that the database of image and text files is kept at a fixed location on the Web, but the names of the files themselves may change. This will enable the company to change the database as it sells the homes. The company will provide a text file that contains the names of the files for the current selection of homes to input into the program. To simplify matters, both image and text files have the same name but different extensions—for example, `ranch.txt` and `ranch.gif`. The data file will store just the names of the files, one per line, giving it the following format:

```
beautifulCape
handsomeRanch
lovelyColonial
```

15.6.1   Downloading a Text File from the Web

This application requires us to solve three new problems:

1. How do we download a text file of names that we want to use as menu items?
2. How do we download a text file and display it in a JTextArea?
3. How do we download and display an image file?

The third problem is very similar to the problem we solved in SlideShowApplet, but here we can't use the Applet.getImage() method. However, as we shall see, we can find a Java library method to perform this task for us. Therefore, the most challenging part of this program is the task of downloading a Web file and using its data in the program.

For this program we must make use of two types of data downloaded from the Web. The first will be the names of the image and document files. We'll want to read these names and use them as menu items that the user can select. Second, once the user has selected a home to view, we must download and display an image and a text description of the home. Downloading the text is basically the same as downloading the file of names. The only difference is that we need to display this text in a JTextArea. Downloading the image file can be handled in more or less the same way that it was handled in the SlideShowApplet— by using a special Java method to download and display the image file.

Clearly, the problems of downloading a file from the Web and reading a file from the disk are quite similar. Recall that we used streams to handle the I/O operation when reading disk files. The various InputStream and OutputStream classes contained the read() and write() methods needed for I/O. The situation is the same for downloading Web files.

Recall that the URL class contains the openStream() method, which opens an Input-Stream to the resource associated with the URL. Once the stream has been opened, you can read data from the stream just as if it were coming from a file. The program doesn't care whether the data are coming from a file on the Internet or a file on the disk. It just reads data from the stream. Thus, to download a data file from the Internet, regardless of whether it's a text file, image file, audio file, or whatever, you would use the following general algorithm:

(margin note) Understanding the problem

(margin note) File-download algorithm

```
URL url;
InputStream data;
try {
    url = new URL(fileURL);              // Create a URL
    data = url.openStream();             // Open a stream to URL
    // read the file into memory         // Read data
    data.close();                        // Close the stream
} catch (MalformedURLException e) {      // Thrown by URL()
    System.out.println(e.getMessage());
} catch( IOException e ) {
    System.out.println(e.getMessage());
}
```

The algorithm consists of four basic steps:

- Create a URL instance.
- Open an InputStream to it.
- Read the data.
- Close the stream.

Step 3 of this algorithm—read the data—involves many lines of code and has, therefore, been left as a subtask suitable for encapsulation within a method.

Reading the Data

Text or binary data?

As we saw in Chapter 11, the algorithm for step 3 will depend on the file's data. If it is a text file, we would like to read one line at a time, storing the input in a `String`. If it is an image or an audio file, we would read one `byte` at a time.

What library methods can we use?

Because our data are contained in a text file, we want to read one line at a time. The `BufferedReader` class contains a `readLine()` method that returns either a `String` storing the line or the value `null` when it reaches the end of file. The following method shows how you would read a text file into the program's `JTextArea`, which is named `display`:

```java
private void readTextIntoDisplay(URL url) throws IOException {
    BufferedReader data
        = new BufferedReader(new InputStreamReader(url.openStream()));
    display.setText("");              // Reset the text area
    String line = data.readLine();
    while (line != null)  {           // Read each line
        display.append(line + "\n");  // Add to display
        line = data.readLine();
    }
    data.close();
} // readTextIntoDisplay()
```

I/O exceptions

The method is passed the file's URL and uses the `URL.openStream()` method to open the input stream. Note that the method throws `IOException`, which means that any I/O exceptions that are raised will be handled by the calling method.

In this example, the input algorithm reads each line of the file and adds it to the `display`. For our real estate application, the same basic algorithm can be used to read the names of the data files and store them in a menu from which a user makes selections. For example, if we use a `JComboBox` menu named `homeChoice`, we would simply add each line to it:

```java
String line = data.readLine();
while (line != null) {
    homeChoice.addItem(line);
    line = data.readLine();
}
```

Interface Design

The interface for this application is very important. It should provide some means to display a text file and an image. The text file can be displayed in a `JTextArea`, and the image can be drawn on a `JPanel`.

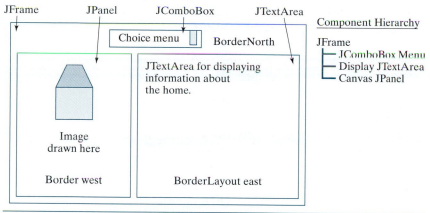

Figure 15.15 User interface design for the real estate application.

Next, let's consider the types of controls a user might need. The customer should be allowed to select a home to view from a menu of options. Because the program will have the list of available homes, it can provide the options in a JComboBox pull-down menu.

To create an appropriate layout, we want to make sure that the controls, the image, and JTextArea all have their own region of the application's window. This suggests a BorderLayout, which is the default layout for a JFrame. We can put the JComboBox menu at the "North" border, and the image and text on the "West" and "East" borders, respectively. Figure 15.15 illustrates these design decisions.

Problem Decomposition: RealEstateViewer

The task of downloading and displaying information from the Internet is best handled by two separate classes: one to perform the downloading and user interface tasks, and the other to take care of displaying the image.

The task of downloading the image and text files from the Web can be handled by the program's main class, the RealEstateViewer, which will also handle the user interface (Fig. 15.16). As the application's top-level window, RealEstateViewer is a subclass of JFrame. Because its controls will include a JComboBox, it must implement the itemState Changed() method of the ItemListener interface.

What components and other instance variables will we need for this class? According to our interface design, it will need a JComboBox, a JTextArea, and the ImagePanel. Because it will be downloading images, it will need an Image variable.

The constants used by this application include the URL string for the data file. Also, because all the images and data files will start with the same prefix,

```
http://java.trincoll.edu/~jjjava/homes/
```

we should make this a constant in the program. These preliminary decisions lead to the initial version of RealEstateViewer shown in Figure 15.17. Note that the main() method merely creates an instance of the application and shows it. Note also that the currentImage variable is declared public. This will let the ImagePanel have direct access to currentImage whenever it needs to display a new image.

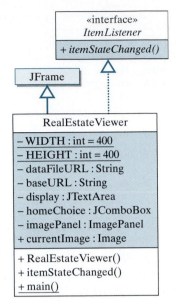

Figure 15.16 The RealEstate-Viewer class defines the user interface.

```
import java.awt.*;
import java.awt.event.*;
import java.net.*;
import java.io.*;
import javax.swing.*;
public class RealEstateViewer extends JFrame implements ItemListener {
    public static final int WIDTH=400,HEIGHT=200;
    private final String dataFileURL =
        "http://java.trincoll.edu/~jjjava/homes/homes.txt";
    private final String baseURL = "http://java.trincoll.edu/~jjjava/homes/";
    private JTextArea display = new JTextArea(20,20);
    private JComboBox homeChoice = new JComboBox();
    private ImagePanel imagePanel = new ImagePanel(this);
    public Image currentImage = null;

    public RealEstateViewer () { }              // Stub Constructor
                                                // ItemListener interface
    public void itemStateChanged(ItemEvent evt) { }  // Stub

    public static void main(String args[]) {
      RealEstateViewer viewer = new RealEstateViewer();
      viewer.setSize(viewer.WIDTH,viewer.HEIGHT);
      viewer.setVisible(true);
      viewer.addWindowListener(new WindowAdapter() {
        public void windowClosing(WindowEvent e) {
          System.exit(0);                       // Quit the application
        }
      });
    } // main()
} // RealEstateViewer class
```

Figure 15.17 The RealEstateViewer, Version 1.

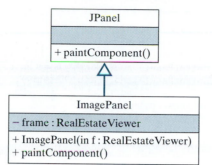

Figure 15.18 An overview of the ImagePanel class.

```
import javax.swing.*;
import java.awt.*;

public class ImagePanel extends JPanel {

    private RealEstateViewer frame;

    public ImagePanel(RealEstateViewer parent) {
        frame = parent;
    }

    public void paintComponent(Graphics g) {
        if (frame.currentImage != null)
            g.drawImage(frame.currentImage, 0, 0, this);
    }
} // ImagePanel class
```

Figure 15.19 The ImagePanel class.

The ImagePanel Class

We'll use a second class, the ImagePanel, to handle displaying the image (Figs. 15.18 and 15.19). The reason we use a separate class for this task is that we want the image to appear in its own panel (which appears on the West border of the main window). In addition to its constructor, the only method needed in this class is the paintComponent() method. This method will be called automatically whenever the main window is repainted. Its task is simply to get the current image from its parent frame and display it. Note that a reference to the parent frame is passed to the object in its constructor.

Method Decomposition

The stub methods listed in the initial version of RealEstateViewer (Fig. 15.17) outline the main tasks required by the application. Some of these methods are very simple and even trivial to implement. Others should be broken up into subtasks.

The constructor method should be responsible for creating the user interface, most of which will involve the routine tasks of registering a listener for the homeChoice menu and setting up an appropriate layout that implements the design we developed for the user interface:

```
public RealEstateViewer () {
    super("Home Viewer Application");              // Set window title
    homeChoice.addItemListener( this);
    this.getContentPane().add("North",homeChoice);
    this.getContentPane().add("East",display);
    this.getContentPane().add("Center",imagePanel);
    display.setLineWrap(true);
    initHomeChoices();                             // Set up choice box
    showCurrentSelection();                        // Display current home
}
```

Note the last two statements of the method. The first sets up the JComboBox by reading its contents from a file stored in the company's database. That task will require several statements, so we define it as a separate method, initHomeChoices(), and defer its development for now. Similarly, the task of displaying the current menu choice has been organized into the showCurrentSelection() method, whose development we also defer for now.

ItemListener   The itemStateChanged() method is called automatically when the user selects a home from the JComboBox menu. Its task is to download and display information about the current menu selection. To do this, it can simply call the showCurrentSelection() method:

```
public void itemStateChanged(ItemEvent evt) {
    showCurrentSelection();
}
```

Downloading the Menu Items

According to our specification, the real estate firm stores its current listing of homes in a text file, one home per line. The initHomeChoices() method downloads the text and uses its contents to set up the items in the homeChoice JComboBox menu:

```
private void initHomeChoices() {
  try {
    URL url = new URL(dataFileURL);
    BufferedReader data = new BufferedReader(
        new InputStreamReader(url.openStream()));
    String line = data.readLine();
    while (line != null) {
      homeChoice.addItem(line);
      line = data.readLine();
    }
    data.close();
  } catch (MalformedURLException e) {
    System.out.println( "ERROR: " + e.getMessage());
  } catch (IOException e) {
    System.out.println( "ERROR: " + e.getMessage());
  }
} // initHomeChoices()
```

It uses the algorithm we developed earlier for downloading a text file. Each line of the text file represents a menu item, so, as each line is read by `data.readLine()`, it is added to the `JComboBox` menu.

Downloading and Displaying Home Information

The `showCurrentSelection()` method is responsible for downloading and displaying images and text files whenever the user selects a home to view. Recall that our specification called for using the name of the menu item as a basis for constructing the name of its corresponding text file and image file. Therefore, the basic algorithm we need is

- Get the user's home choice.
- Create a URL for the associated text file.
- Download and display the associated text file.
- Create a URL for the associated GIF file.
- Download and display the image.

Because downloading a text document requires stream processing, we should handle that in a separate method. The task of downloading an image file is also a good candidate for a separate method. Both of these methods will use a URL, so we can leave that task up to `showCurrentSelection()` itself. The `showCurrentSelection()` method will create the URLs and then invoke the appropriate methods to download and display the resources:

Method decomposition

```java
private void showCurrentSelection() {
  URL url = null;
                                       // Get user's choice
  String choice = homeChoice.getSelectedItem().toString();
  try {                                // Create url and download file
    url = new URL(baseURL + choice + ".txt");
    readTextIntoDisplay(url);
                                       // Create url and download image
    url = new URL(baseURL + choice + ".gif");
    currentImage = Toolkit.getDefaultToolkit().getImage(url);
    Toolkit.getDefaultToolkit().beep();        // Beep user
    repaint();
  } catch (MalformedURLException e) {
    System.out.println( "ERROR: " + e.getMessage()) ;
  } catch (IOException e) {
    System.out.println("ERROR: " + e.getMessage()) ;
  } // Try/catch block
} // showCurrentSelection()
```

Note that we have also elected to handle both the `MalformedURLException` and `IOException` in this method. The advantage of this design is that it separates exception handling from the normal algorithm and organizes it into one method. Finally, note how string concatenation is used to build the URL specifications, each of which consists of three parts: the `baseURL`, the user's `choice`, and the file extension.

The task of reading the text file and displaying its contents has been encapsulated into the `readTextIntoDisplay()` method. This `private` utility method performs a standard file-reading algorithm using the `readLine()` method that we developed earlier. Figure 15.20 provides a view of the program's appearance as it is displaying information to a user. Figure 15.21 provides the complete implementation of this program.

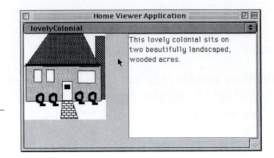

Figure 15.20 The RealEstate-Viewer program downloads images and documents over the Web.

```
import java.awt.*;
import java.awt.event.*;
import java.net.*;
import java.io.*;
import javax.swing.*;

public class RealEstateViewer extends JFrame implements ItemListener {
    public static final int WIDTH=400,HEIGHT=200;
    private final String dataFileURL =
        "http://java.trincoll.edu/~jjjava/homes/homes.txt";
    private final String baseURL = "http://java.trincoll.edu/~jjjava/homes/";
    private JTextArea display = new JTextArea(20,20);
    private JComboBox homeChoice = new JComboBox();
    private ImagePanel imagePanel = new ImagePanel(this);
    public Image currentImage = null;

    public RealEstateViewer () {
        super("Home Viewer Application");            // Set window title
        homeChoice.addItemListener( this);
        this.getContentPane().add("North",homeChoice);
        this.getContentPane().add("East",display);
        this.getContentPane().add("Center",imagePanel);
        display.setLineWrap(true);
        initHomeChoices();                           // Set up the choice box
        showCurrentSelection();                      // Display the current home
    } // RealEstateViewer()

    private void initHomeChoices() {
        try {
            URL url = new URL(dataFileURL);
            BufferedReader data = new BufferedReader(
                    new InputStreamReader(url.openStream()));
            String line = data.readLine();
            while (line != null) {
                homeChoice.addItem(line);
                line = data.readLine();
            } data.close();
        } catch (MalformedURLException e) {
            System.out.println("ERROR: " + e.getMessage()) ;
        } catch (IOException e) {
            System.out.println("ERROR: " + e.getMessage()) ;
        }
    } // initHomeChoices()
```

Figure 15.21 The RealEstateViewer class. (*Continued on next page*)

```java
private void readTextIntoDisplay(URL url) throws IOException {
  BufferedReader data
    = new BufferedReader(new InputStreamReader(url.openStream()));
  display.setText("");                          // Reset the text area
  String line = data.readLine();
  while (line != null)  {                       // Read each line
    display.append(line + "\n");                // And add it to the display
    line = data.readLine();
  } data.close();
} // readTextIntoDisplay()

private void showCurrentSelection() {
  URL url = null;                               // Get user's choice
  String choice = homeChoice.getSelectedItem().toString();
  try {
    url = new URL(baseURL + choice + ".txt") ;   // Create URL
    readTextIntoDisplay(url); // Download and display text file
    url = new URL(baseURL + choice + ".gif");   // Create URL
                                                // Download image
    currentImage = Toolkit.getDefaultToolkit().getImage(url);
    Toolkit.getDefaultToolkit().beep();         // Alert the user
    repaint();
  } catch (MalformedURLException e) {
      System.out.println( "ERROR: " + e.getMessage()) ;
  } catch (IOException e) {
      System.out.println("ERROR: " + e.getMessage()) ;
  }
} // showCurrentSelection()

public void itemStateChanged(ItemEvent evt) {
  showCurrentSelection();
} // itemStateChanged()

public static void main(String args[]) {
  RealEstateViewer viewer = new RealEstateViewer();
  viewer.setSize(viewer.WIDTH,viewer.HEIGHT);
  viewer.setVisible(true);
  viewer.addWindowListener(new WindowAdapter() {
    public void windowClosing(WindowEvent e) {
      System.exit(0);                           // Quit the application
    }
  });
} // main()
} // RealEstateViewer class
```

Figure 15.21 The `RealEstateViewer` class. (*Continued from previous page*)

15.6.2 Reusing Code

As in other examples we have developed, our discovery and use of the `getImage()` method of the `Toolkit` class and other classes from the Java class library illustrate an important principle of object-oriented programming.

EFFECTIVE DESIGN: Code Reuse.   Before writing code to perform a particular task, search the available libraries to see if there is already code that performs the task.

An important step in designing object-oriented programs is making appropriate use of existing classes and methods. In some cases, you want to directly instantiate a class and use its methods to perform the desired tasks. In other cases, it is necessary to create a subclass (inheritance) or implement an interface (inheritance) in order to gain access to the methods you need.

Of course, knowing what classes exist in the libraries is something that comes with experience. There is no way that a novice Java programmer would know about, say, the `getImage()` method of the `Toolkit` class. However, one skill or habit you should try to develop is always to ask yourself the question: "Is there a method that will do what I'm trying to do here?" This question should be the first question on your search through the libraries and reference books.

```
http://java.sun.com/docs/
```

15.7   Client/Server Communication via `Sockets`

As we said earlier, many networking applications are based on the client/server model. According to this model, a task is viewed as a service that can be requested by clients and handled by servers. In this section, we develop a simple client/server framework based on a *socket* connection between the client and the server.

A **socket** is a simple communication channel through which two programs communicate over a network. A socket supports two-way communication between a client and a server, using a well-established protocol. The protocol simply prescribes rules and behavior that both the server and client must follow in order to establish two-way communication.

Sockets and ports   According to this protocol, a server program creates a socket at a certain port and waits until a client requests a connection. A **port** is a specific address or entry point on the host computer, which typically has hundreds of potential ports. It is usually represented as a simple integer value. For example, the standard port for an HTTP (Web) server is 80. Once the connection is established, the server creates input and output streams to the socket and begins sending messages to and receiving messages from the client. Either the client or the server can close the connection, but it is usually done by the client.

> **DEBUGGING TIP: Reserved Port Numbers.**   Port numbers below 1024 are reserved for system use and should not be used by an application program.

Client/server protocol   To clarify this protocol, think of some service performed by a human using a telephone connection. The "server" waits for the phone to ring. When it rings, the server picks it up and begins communicating with the client. A socket, combined with input and output streams, is something like a two-way phone connection.

From the client's side, the protocol goes as follows: The client creates a socket and attempts to make a connection to the server. The client has to know the server's URL and the port at which the service exists. Once a connection has been established, the client creates input and output streams to the socket and begins exchanging messages with the server. The client can close the connection when the service is completed.

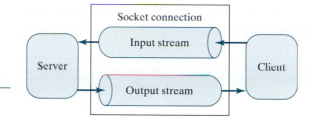

Figure 15.22 A socket is a two-channel communication link.

Think again of the telephone analogy. A human client picks up the phone and dials the number of a particular service. This is analogous to the client program creating a socket and making a connection to a server. Once the service agent answers the phone, two-way communication between the client and the server can begin.

Figure 15.22 provides a view of the client/server connection. Note that a socket has two channels. Once a connection has been established between a client and a server, a single two-way channel exists between them. The client's output stream is connected to the server's input stream. The server's output stream is connected to the client's input stream.

Sockets and channels

JAVA PROGRAMMING TIP: Socket Streams. A socket has two streams, one for input and one for output.

15.7.1 The Server Protocol

Let's now see how a client/server application would be coded in Java. The template in Figure 15.23 shows the code that is necessary on the server side. The first step the server takes is to create a `ServerSocket`. The first argument to the `ServerSocket()` method is the port at which the service will reside. The second argument specifies the number of clients that can be backlogged, waiting on the server, before a client will be refused service. If more than one client at a time requests service, Java will establish and manage a waiting list, turning away clients when the list is full.

```
Socket socket;                          // Reference to the socket
ServerSocket port;                      // The port where the server will listen
try {
    port = new ServerSocket(10001, 5);  // Create a port
    socket = port.accept();             // Wait for client to call

                                        // Communicate with the client

    socket.close();
} catch (IOException e) {
    e.printStackTrace();
}
```

Figure 15.23 Template for the server protocol.

The next step is to wait for a client request. The `accept()` method will *block* until a connection is established. The Java system is responsible for waking the server when a client request is received.

Once a connection is established, the server can begin communicating with the client. As we have suggested, a socket connection is like a two-way telephone conversation. Client and server can "talk" back and forth to each other. The details of this step are not shown here. As we will see, the two-way conversation is managed by connecting both an input and an output stream to the socket.

Once the conversation between client and server is finished—once the server has delivered the requested service—the server can close the connection by calling `close()`. Thus, there are four steps involved on the server side:

- Create a `ServerSocket` and establish a port number.
- Listen for and accept a connection from a client.
- Converse with the client.
- Close the socket.

What distinguishes the server from the client is that the server establishes the port and accepts the connection.

15.7.2   The Client Protocol

The client protocol (Fig. 15.24) is just as easy to implement. Indeed, on the client side there are only three steps involved. The first step is to request a connection to the server. This is done in the `Socket()` constructor by supplying the server's URL and port number. Once the connection is established, the client can carry out two-way communication with the server. This step is not shown here. Finally, when the client is finished, it can simply `close()` the connection. Thus, from the client side, the protocol involves just three steps:

- Open a socket connection to the server, given its address.
- Converse with the server.
- Close the connection.

What distinguishes the client from the server is that the client initiates the two-way connection by requesting the service.

```java
Socket connection;                                    // Reference to the socket
try {                                                 // Request a connection
    connection = new Socket("java.cs.trincoll.edu", 10001);

                                                      // Carry on a two-way communication

    connection.close();                               // Close the socket
} catch (IOException e ) {
    e.printStackTrace();
}
```

Figure 15.24 Template for the client protocol.

15.7.3   A Two-Way Stream Connection

Now that we have seen how to establish a socket connection between a client and server, let's look at the actual two-way communication that takes place. Because this part of the process will be exactly the same for both client and server, we develop a single set of methods, `writeToSocket()` and `readFromSocket()`, that may be called by either.

The `writeToSocket()` method takes two parameters, the `Socket` and a `String`, which will be sent to the process on the other end of the socket:

Output routine

```
protected void writeToSocket(Socket sock, String str) throws IOException {
    oStream = sock.getOutputStream();
    for (int k = 0; k < str.length(); k++)
        oStream.write(str.charAt(k));
} // writeToSocket()
```

If `writeToSocket()` is called by the server, then the string will be sent to the client. If it is called by the client, the string will be sent to the server.

The method is declared `protected` because we will define it in a superclass so that it can be inherited and used by both the client and server classes. Note also that the method declares that it throws an `IOException`. There is no way to fix an `IOException`, so we will just let this exception be handled elsewhere, rather than handle it within the method.

Protected methods

In order to write to a socket we need only get the socket's `OutputStream` and then write to it. For this example, `oStream` is an instance variable of the client/server superclass. We use the `getOutputStream()` method of the `Socket` class to get a reference to the socket's output stream. Note that we are not creating a new output stream here. We are just getting a reference to an existing stream, which was created when the socket connection was accepted. Note also that we do not close the output stream before exiting the method. This is important. If you close the stream, you will lose the ability to communicate through the socket.

JAVA LANGUAGE RULE   **Socket Streams.** When a socket is created, it automatically creates its own streams. To use one you just need to get a reference to it.

DEBUGGING TIP: Socket Streams.   After writing to or reading from a socket I/O stream, do not close the stream. That would make the socket unusable for subsequent I/O.

Given the reference to the socket's output stream, we simply write each character of the string using the `write()` method of the `OutputStream` class. This method writes a single `byte`. Therefore, the input stream on the other side of the socket must read bytes and convert them back into characters.

EFFECTIVE DESIGN: Designing a Protocol.   In designing two-way communication between a client and a server, you are designing a protocol that each side must use. Failure to design and implement a clear protocol will cause the communication to break down.

Input routine

The `readFromSocket()` method takes a `Socket` parameter and returns a `String`:

```
protected String readFromSocket(Socket sock)throws IOException {
    iStream = sock.getInputStream();
    String str="";
    char c;
    while (  ( c = (char) iStream.read() ) != '\n')
        str = str + c + "";
    return str;
}
```

It uses the `getInputStream()` method of the `Socket` class to obtain a reference to the socket's input stream, which has already been created. So here again it is important not to close the stream in this method. A socket's input and output streams will be closed automatically when the socket connection itself is closed.

The `read()` method of the `InputStream` class reads a single byte at a time from the input stream until an end-of-line character is received. For this particular application, the client and server will both read and write one line of characters at a time. Note the use of the cast operator `(char)` in the `read()` statement. Because `byte`s are being read, they must be converted to `char` before they can be compared to the end-of-line character or concatenated to the `String`. When the read loop encounters an end-of-line character, it terminates and returns the `String` that was input.

DEBUGGING TIP: Bytes and Chars.   It is a syntax error to compare a `byte` and a `char`. One must be converted to the other using an explicit cast operator.

15.8   CASE STUDY: Generic Client/Server Classes

Problem statement

Suppose your boss asks you to set up generic client/server classes that can be used to implement a number of related client/server applications. One application that the company has in mind is a query service in which the client would send a query string to the server, and the server would interpret the string and return a string that provides the answer. For example, the client might send the query `"Hours of service"`, and the client would respond with the company's business hours.

Another application the company wants will enable the client to fill out an order form and transmit it as a string to the server. The server will interpret the order, fill it, and return a receipt, including instructions as to when the customer will receive the order.

All of the applications to be supported by this generic client/server will communicate via strings, so something very much like the `readFromSocket()` and `writeToSocket()` methods can be used for their communication. Of course, you want to design classes that can be easily extended to support byte-oriented, two-way communications should that type of service be needed.

The echo service

In order to test the generic models, we will subclass them to create a simple echo service. This service will echo back to the client any message the server receives. For example, we'll have the client accept keyboard input from the user and then send the user's input to the server and simply report what the server returns. The following shows the output generated by a typical client session:

```
CLIENT: connected to 'java.cs.trincoll.edu'
SERVER: Hello, how may I help you?
CLIENT: type a line or 'goodbye' to quit
INPUT: hello
SERVER: You said 'hello'
INPUT: this is fun
SERVER: You said 'this is fun'
INPUT: java java java
SERVER: You said 'java java java'
INPUT: goodbye
SERVER: Goodbye
CLIENT: connection closed
```

On the server side, the client's message will be read from the input stream and then simply echoed back (with some additional characters attached) through the output stream. The server does not display a trace of its activity other than to report when connections are established and closed. We will code the server in an infinite loop so that it will accept connections from a (potentially) endless stream of clients. In fact, most servers are coded in this way. They are designed to run forever and must be restarted whenever the host they are running on needs to be rebooted. The output from a typical server session is as follows:

```
Echo server at java.cs.trincoll.edu/157.252.16.21 waiting for connections
Accepted a connection from java.cs.trincoll.edu/157.252.16.21
Closed the connection

Accepted a connection from java.cs.trincoll.edu/157.252.16.21
Closed the connection
```

EFFECTIVE DESIGN: Infinite Loop. A server is an application designed to run in an infinite loop. The loop should be exited only when some kind of exception occurs.

15.8.1 Object-Oriented Design

A suitable solution for this project will make extensive use of object-oriented design principles. We want `Server` and `Client` classes that can easily be subclassed to support a wide variety of services. The solution should make appropriate use of *inheritance* and *polymorphism* in its design. Perhaps the best way to develop our generic class is first to design the echo service as a typical example and then generalize it.

The Threaded Root Subclass: `ClientServer`

One lesson we can draw at the outset is that both clients and servers use basically the same socket I/O methods. Thus, as we have seen, the `readFromSocket()` and `writeToSocket()` methods could be used by both clients and servers. Because we want all clients and servers to inherit these methods, they must be placed in a common superclass. Let's name this the `ClientServer` class.

Where should we place this class in the Java hierarchy? Should it be a direct subclass of `Object`, or should it extend some other class that would give it appropriate functionality? One feature that would make our clients and servers more useful is if they were independent threads. That way they could be instantiated as part of another object and given the subtask of communicating on behalf of that object.

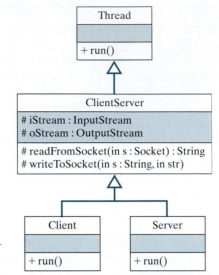

Figure 15.25 Overall design of a client/server application.

Therefore, let's define the **ClientServer** class as a subclass of **Thread** (Fig. 15.25). Recall from Chapter 14 that the typical way to derive functionality from a **Thread** subclass is to override the **run()** method. The **run()** method will be a good place to implement the client and server protocols. Because they are different, we will define **run()** in both the **Client** and **Server** subclasses.

For now, the only methods contained in **ClientServer** (Fig. 15.26) are the two I/O

```java
import java.io.*;
import java.net.*;

public class ClientServer extends Thread {

  protected InputStream iStream;   // Instance variables
  protected OutputStream oStream;

  protected String readFromSocket(Socket sock)throws IOException {
    iStream = sock.getInputStream();
    String str="";
    char c;
    while ( ( c = (char) iStream.read() ) != '\n')
      str = str + c + "";
    return str;
  }

  protected void writeToSocket(Socket sock, String str)throws IOException {
    oStream = sock.getOutputStream();
    if (str.charAt( str.length() - 1 ) != '\n')
      str = str + '\n';
    for (int k = 0; k < str.length() ; k++)
      oStream.write(str.charAt(k));
  } // writeToSocket()
} // ClientServer class
```

Figure 15.26 The ClientServer class serves as the superclass for client/server applications.

methods we designed. The only modification to the methods occurs in the `writeToSocket()` method, where we have added code to make sure that any strings written to the socket are terminated with an end-of-line character.

This is an important enhancement, because the read loop in the `readFromSocket()` method expects to receive an end-of-line character. Rather than rely on specific clients to guarantee that their strings end with \n, our design takes care of this problem for them. This ensures that every communication between one of our clients and servers will be line oriented.

> **EFFECTIVE DESIGN: Defensive Design.** Code that performs I/O, whether across a network or otherwise, should be designed to anticipate and remedy common errors. This will lead to more robust programs.

15.8.2 The EchoServer Class

Let's now develop a design for the echo server. This class will be a subclass of `ClientServer` (Fig. 15.27). As we saw in discussing the server protocol, one task that echo server will do is create a `ServerSocket` and establish a port number for its service. Then it will wait for a `Socket` connection, and once a connection is accepted, the echo server will communicate with the client. This suggests that our server needs at least two instance variables. It also suggests that the task of creating a `ServerSocket` would be an appropriate action for its constructor method. This leads to the following initial definition:

What data do we need?

```java
import java.net.*;
import java.io.*;

public class EchoServer extends ClientServer {

    private ServerSocket port;
    private Socket socket;

    public EchoServer(int portNum, int nBacklog)  {
      try {
        port = new ServerSocket (portNum, nBacklog);
      } catch (IOException e) {
        e.printStackTrace();
      }
    }

    public void run() { }  // Stub method
} // EchoServer class
```

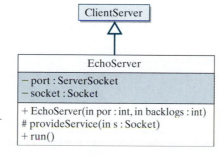

Figure 15.27 Design of the EchoServer class.

Note that the constructor method catches the IOException. Note also that we have included a stub version of run(), which we want to define in this class.

Once EchoServer has set up a port, it should issue the port.accept() method and wait for a client to connect. This part of the server protocol belongs in the run() method. As we have said, most servers are designed to run in an infinite loop. They don't just handle one request and then quit. Instead, once started (usually by the system), they repeatedly handle requests until deliberately stopped by the system. This leads to the following run algorithm:

The server algorithm

```java
public void run() {
    try {
        System.out.println("Echo server at " + InetAddress.getLocalHost()
                        + " waiting for connections ");
        while(true) {
            socket = port.accept();
            System.out.println("Accepted a connection from "
                                + socket.getInetAddress());
            provideService(socket);
            socket.close();
            System.out.println("Closed the connection\n");
        }
    } catch (IOException e) {
        e.printStackTrace();
    }
} // run()
```

For simplicity, we are printing the server's status messages on System.out. Ordinarily these should go to a log file. Note also that the details of the actual service algorithm are hidden in the provideService() method.

As described earlier, the provideService() method consists of writing a greeting to the client and then repeatedly reading a string from the input stream and echoing it back to the client via the output stream. This is easily done using the writeToSocket() and readFromSocket() methods we have developed. The implementation of this method is shown, along with the complete implementation of EchoServer, in Figure 15.28.

The protocol used by EchoServer's provideService() method starts by saying "hello" and loops until the client says "goodbye". When the client says "goodbye", the server responds with "goodbye". In all other cases it responds with "You said X", where X is the string received from the client. Note the use of the toLowerCase() method to convert client messages to lowercase. This simplifies the task of checking for "goodbye" by removing the necessity of checking for different spellings of "Goodbye".

EFFECTIVE DESIGN: Defensive Design. Converting I/O to lowercase helps to minimize miscommunication between client and server and leads to a more robust protocol.

This completes the design of the EchoServer. We have deliberately designed it in a way that will make it easy to convert into a generic server. Hence, we have the motivation for using `provideService()` as the name of the method that provides the echo service. In order to turn `EchoServer` into a generic `Server` class, we can simply make `provideService()` an abstract method, leaving its implementation to the `Server` subclasses. We will discuss the details of this change later.

Designing for extensibility

```java
import java.net.*;
import java.io.*;
public class EchoServer extends ClientServer {
    private ServerSocket port;
    private Socket socket;
    public EchoServer( int portNum, int nBacklog)  {
        try {
            port = new ServerSocket (portNum, nBacklog);
        } catch (IOException e) {
            e.printStackTrace();
        }
    } // EchoServer()
    public void run() {
        try {
            System.out.println("Echo server at " +
                InetAddress.getLocalHost() + " waiting for connections ");
            while(true) {
                socket = port.accept();
                System.out.println("Accepted a connection from " +
                                        socket.getInetAddress());
                provideService(socket);
                socket.close();
                System.out.println("Closed the connection\n");
            } // while
        } catch (IOException e) {
            e.printStackTrace();
        } // try/catch
    } // run()
    protected void provideService (Socket socket) {
        String str="";
        try {
            writeToSocket(socket, "Hello, how may I help you?\n");
            do {
                str = readFromSocket(socket);
                if (str.toLowerCase().equals("goodbye"))
                    writeToSocket(socket, "Goodbye\n");
                else
                    writeToSocket( socket, "You said '" + str + "'\n");
            } while (!str.toLowerCase().equals("goodbye"));
        } catch (IOException e) {
            e.printStackTrace();
        } // try/catch
    } // provideServer()
    public static void main(String args[]) {
        EchoServer server = new EchoServer(10001,3);
        server.start();
    } // main()
} // EchoServer class
```

Figure 15.28 EchoServer simply echoes the client's message.

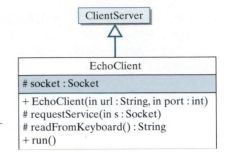

Figure 15.29   Design of the `EchoClient` class.

15.8.3   The `EchoClient` Class

The `EchoClient` class is just as easy to design (Fig. 15.29). It, too, will be a subclass of `ClientServer`. It needs an instance variable for the `Socket` it will use, and its constructor should be responsible for opening a socket connection to a particular server and port. The main part of its protocol should be placed in the `run()` method. The initial definition is as follows:

```java
import java.net.*;
import java.io.*;

public class EchoClient extends ClientServer {

    protected Socket socket;

    public EchoClient(String url, int port) {
      try {
        socket = new Socket(url, port);
        System.out.println("CLIENT: connected to " + url + ":" + port);
      } catch (Exception e) {
        e.printStackTrace();
        System.exit(1);
      }
    } // EchoClient()

    public void run() { }   // Stub method
} // EchoClient class
```

The constructor method takes two parameters that specify the URL and port number of the echo server. By making these parameters, rather than hard coding them within the method, we give the client the flexibility to connect to servers on a variety of hosts.

As with other clients, `EchoClient`'s `run()` method will consist of requesting some kind of service from the server. Our initial design called for `EchoClient` to repeatedly input a line from the user, send the line to the server, and then display the server's response. Thus, for this particular client, the service requested consists of the following algorithm:

The client algorithm

```
Wait for the server to say "hello".
Repeat
     Prompt and get and line of input from the user.
     Send the user's line to the server.
     Read the server's response.
     Display the response to the user.
until the user types "goodbye"
```

With an eye toward eventually turning `EchoClient` into a generic client, let's encapsulate this procedure into a `requestService()` method that we can simply call from the `run()` method. As in the case of the `provideService()` method, this design is another example of the encapsulation principle:

> **EFFECTIVE DESIGN: Encapsulation.**   Encapsulating a portion of the algorithm into a separate method makes it easy to change the algorithm by overriding the method.

The `requestService()` method will take a `Socket` parameter and perform all the I/O for this particular client:

```java
protected void requestService(Socket socket) throws IOException {
    String servStr = readFromSocket(socket);        // Check for "Hello"
    System.out.println("SERVER: " + servStr);       // Report the server's response
    System.out.println("CLIENT: type a line or 'goodbye' to quit"); // Prompt
    if (servStr.substring(0,5).equals("Hello")) {
        String userStr = "";
        do {
            userStr = readFromKeyboard();           // Get input
            writeToSocket(socket, userStr + "\n");   // Send it to server
            servStr = readFromSocket(socket);        // Read the server's response
            System.out.println("SERVER: " + servStr); // Report server's response
        } while (!userStr.toLowerCase().equals("goodbye")); // Until 'goodbye'
    }
} // requestService()
```

Although this method involves several lines, they should all be familiar to you. Each time the client reads a message from the socket, it prints it on `System.out`. The first message it reads should start with the substring "Hello". This is part of its protocol with the client. Note how the `substring()` method is used to test for this. After the initial greeting from the server, the client begins reading user input from the keyboard, writes it to the socket, then reads the server's response and displays it on `System.out`.

Note that the task of reading user input from the keyboard has been made into a separate method that we have used before:

```java
protected String readFromKeyboard() throws IOException {
    BufferedReader input = new BufferedReader(new InputStreamReader(System.in));
    System.out.print("INPUT: ");
    String line = input.readLine();
    return line;
} // readFromKeyboard()
```

The only method remaining to be defined is `run()`, which is shown with the complete definition of `EchoClient` in Figure 15.30. The `run()` method can simply call the `request-Service()` method. When control returns from the `requestService()` method, `run()` closes the socket connection. Because `requestService()` might throw an `IOException`, the entire method must be embedded within a `try/catch` block that catches the exception.

```java
import java.net.*;
import java.io.*;

public class EchoClient extends ClientServer {

    protected Socket socket;

    public EchoClient(String url, int port) {
        try {
            socket = new Socket(url, port);
            System.out.println("CLIENT: connected to " + url + ":" + port);
        } catch (Exception e) {
            e.printStackTrace();
            System.exit(1);
        }
    } // EchoClient()

    public void run() {
        try {
            requestService(socket);
            socket.close();
            System.out.println("CLIENT: connection closed");
        } catch (IOException e) {
            System.out.println(e.getMessage());
            e.printStackTrace();
        }
    } // run()

    protected void requestService(Socket socket) throws IOException {
        String servStr = readFromSocket(socket);        // Check for "Hello"
        System.out.println("SERVER: " + servStr);       // Report the server's response
        System.out.println("CLIENT: type a line or 'goodbye' to quit");// Prompt user
        if (servStr.substring(0,5).equals("Hello")) {
            String userStr = "";
            do {
                userStr = readFromKeyboard();            // Get input from user
                writeToSocket(socket, userStr + "\n");   // Send it to server
                servStr = readFromSocket(socket);        // Read server's response
                System.out.println("SERVER: " + servStr);// Report server's response
            } while (!userStr.toLowerCase().equals("goodbye"));// Until 'goodbye'
        }
    } // requestService()

    protected String readFromKeyboard( ) throws IOException {
        BufferedReader input = new BufferedReader(new InputStreamReader(System.in));
        System.out.print("INPUT: ");
        String line = input.readLine();
        return line;
    } // readFromKeyboard()

    public static void main(String args[]) {
        EchoClient client = new EchoClient("java.trincoll.edu",10001);
        client.start();
    } // main()
} // EchoClient class
```

Figure 15.30 The EchoClient class prompts the user for a string and sends it to the EchoServer, which simply echoes it back.

Testing the Echo Service

Both `EchoServer` and `EchoClient` contain `main()` methods (Figs. 15.28 and 15.30). In order to test the programs, you would run the server on one computer and the client on another computer. (Actually they can both be run on the same computer, although they wouldn't know this and would still access each other through a socket connection.)

The `EchoServer` must be started first, so that its service will be available when the client starts running. It also must pick a port number. In this case it picks 10001. The only constraint on its choice is that it cannot use one of the privileged port numbers—those below 1024—and it cannot use a port that is already in use.

```
public static void main(String args[]) {
    EchoServer server = new EchoServer(10001,3);
    server.start();
} // main()
```

When an `EchoClient` is created, it must be given the server's URL (`java.trincoll.edu`) and the port that the service is using:

```
public static void main(String args[]) {
    EchoClient client = new EchoClient("java.trincoll.edu",10001);
    client.start();
} // main()
```

As they are presently coded, you will have to modify both `EchoServer` and `EchoClient` to provide the correct URL and port for your environment. In testing this program, you might wish to experiment by introducing various errors into the code and observing the results. When you run the service, you should observe something like the following output on the client side:

```
CLIENT: connected to java.trincoll.edu:10001
SERVER: Hello, how may I help you?
CLIENT: type a line or 'goodbye' to quit
 INPUT: this is a test
SERVER: You said 'this is a test'
 INPUT: goodbye
SERVER: Goodbye
CLIENT: connection closed
```

15.9 Playing One-Row Nim Over the Network

In the preceding section we developed and tested a generic echo service. It is based on a common root class, `ClientServer`, which is a subclass of `Thread`. Both `EchoServer` and `EchoClient` extend the root class, and each implements its own version of `run()`. In this section, we will generalize this design so that it can support a wide range of services. To illustrate the effectiveness of the design, we will use it as the basis for a program that plays One-Row Nim over the Internet.

In order to generalize our design, we begin by identifying the elements common to all servers and clients and what is particular to the echo service and client. Clearly, the general

Designing for extensibility

server and client protocols defined here in their respective `run()` methods are something that all servers and clients have in common. What differs from one application to another is the particular service provided and requested, as detailed in their respective `provideService()` and `requestService()` methods. In this example, the service provided will be One-Row Nim. The clients that use this service will be (human) players of the game.

Abstract service methods

Therefore, the way to generalize the application is to define the `run()` method in the generic `Server` and `Client` classes. The overall design of the One-Row Nim service will now consist of five classes organized into the hierarchy shown in Figure 15.31. At the root of the hierarchy is the `ClientServer` class, which contains nothing but I/O methods used by both clients and servers. The abstract `Server` and `Client` classes contain implementations of `Thread`'s `run()` method, which defines the basic protocols for servers and clients, respectively. The details of the particular service are encoded in the `provideService()` and `requestService()` methods. Because the `run()` methods defined in `Client` and `Server`

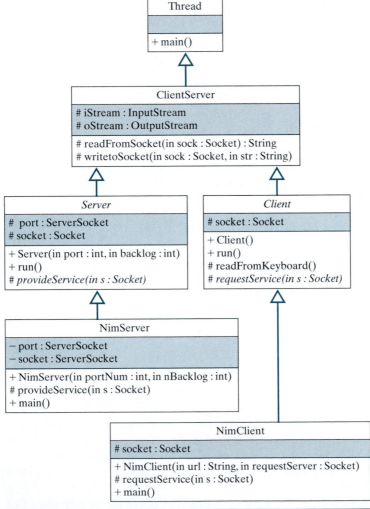

Figure 15.31 Class hierarchy for a generic client/server application.

call `provideService()` and `requestService()`, respectively, these methods must be declared as `abstract` methods in the `Server` and `Client` classes. Any class that contains an `abstract` method must itself be declared `abstract`.

Note that we have left the `readFromSocket()` and `writeToSocket()` methods in the `ClientServer` class. These methods are written in a general way and can be used, without change, by a wide range of clients and servers. If necessary, they can also be overridden by a client or server. In fact, as we will see, the `NimServer` class does override the `writeToSocket()` method. Similarly, note that the `readFromKeyboard()` method is defined in the `Client` superclass. This is a general method that can be used by a large variety of clients, so it is best if they don't have to redefine it themselves.

These design decisions lead to the definitions of `Server` and `Client` shown in Figures 15.32 and 15.33, respectively. Note that `provideService()` and `requestService()` are left unimplemented. Subclasses of `Server`, such as `NimServer`, and subclasses of `Client`, such as `NimClient`, can implement `provideService()` and `requestService()` in a way that is appropriate for the particular service they are providing.

```java
import java.net.*;
import java.io.*;
public abstract class Server extends ClientServer {
    protected ServerSocket port;
    protected Socket socket;

    public Server(int portNum, int nBacklog)  {
        try {
            port = new ServerSocket (portNum, nBacklog);
        } catch (IOException e) {
            e.printStackTrace();
        } // try/catch
    } // Server()

    public void run() {
        try {
            System.out.println("Server at " + InetAddress.getLocalHost() +
                        " waiting for connections ");
            while (true) {
                socket = port.accept();
                System.out.println("Accepted a connection from "
                                + socket.getInetAddress());
                provideService(socket);
                socket.close();
                System.out.println("Closed the connection\n");
            } // while
        } catch (IOException e) {
            e.printStackTrace();
        } // try/catch
    } // run()

                                        // Implemented in subclass
    protected abstract void provideService(Socket socket);
} // Server class
```

Figure 15.32 The abstract Server class.

```
import java.net.*;
import java.io.*;

public abstract class Client extends ClientServer {
   protected Socket socket;

   public Client(String url, int port) {
      try {
         socket = new Socket(url,port);
         System.out.println("CLIENT: connected to " + url + ":" + port);
      } catch (Exception e) {
         e.printStackTrace();
         System.exit(1);
      } // try/catch block
   } // Client()

   public void run() {
      try {
         requestService(socket);
         socket.close();
         System.out.println("CLIENT: connection closed");
      } catch (IOException e) {
         System.out.println(e.getMessage());
         e.printStackTrace();
      } // try/catch block
   } // run()

                                          // Implemented in subclass
   protected abstract void requestService(Socket socket)throws IOException;

   protected String readFromKeyboard() throws IOException {
      BufferedReader input = new BufferedReader
                    (new InputStreamReader(System.in));
      System.out.print("INPUT: ");
      String line = input.readLine();
      return line;
   } // readFromKeyboard()
} // Client class
```

Figure 15.33   The abstract Client class.

EFFECTIVE DESIGN: Polymorphism.   Defining a method as abstract within a super-class, and implementing it in various ways in subclasses, is an example of polymorphism. Polymorphism is a powerful object-oriented design technique.

15.9.1   The NimServer Class

Given the abstract definition of the Server class, defining a new service is simply a matter of extending Server and implementing the provideService() method in the new subclass. We will name the subclass NimServer.

Extensibility

Figure 15.34 provides a definition of the NimServer subclass. Note how its implementation of provideService() uses an instance of the OneRowNim class from Chapter 8. The play() method, which encapsulates the game-playing algorithm, similarly uses an instance of NimPlayer from Chapter 8. As you will recall, OneRowNim is a TwoPlayerGame, and

```java
import java.net.*;
import java.io.*;

public class NimServer extends Server {
    public NimServer(int port, int backlog) {
        super(port, backlog);
    }
    protected void provideService (Socket socket) {
        OneRowNim nim = new OneRowNim();
        try {
            writeToSocket(socket, "Hi Nim player. You're Player 1 and I'm Player 2. "
                    + nim.reportGameState()  + " " + nim.getGamePrompt() + "\n");
            play(nim, socket);
        } catch (IOException e) {
            e.printStackTrace();
        } // try/catch
    } // provideService()

    private void play(OneRowNim nim, Socket socket) throws IOException {
        NimPlayer computerPlayer = new NimPlayer(nim);
        nim.addComputerPlayer(computerPlayer);
        String str="", response="";
        int userTakes = 0, computerTakes = 0;
        do {
            str = readFromSocket(socket);
            boolean legalMove = false;
            do {
                userTakes = Integer.parseInt(str);
                if (nim.takeSticks(userTakes)) {
                    legalMove = true;
                    nim.changePlayer();
                    response = nim.reportGameState() + " ";
                    if (!nim.gameOver()) {
                        computerTakes = Integer.parseInt(computerPlayer.makeAMove(""));
                        response = response + " My turn. I take " + computerTakes
                                                            + " sticks. ";
                        nim.takeSticks(computerTakes);
                        nim.changePlayer();
                        response = response + nim.reportGameState() + " ";
                        if (!nim.gameOver())
                            response = response + nim.getGamePrompt();
                    } // if not game over
                    writeToSocket(socket, response);
                } else {
                    writeToSocket(socket, "That's an illegal move. Try again.\n");
                    str = readFromSocket(socket);
                } // if user takes
            } while (!legalMove);
        }  while (!nim.gameOver());
    } // play

    // Overriding writeToSocket to remove \n from str
    protected void writeToSocket(Socket soc, String str) throws IOException {
```

Figure 15.34 The NimServer class. (*Continued on next page*)

```
      StringBuffer sb = new StringBuffer();
      for (int k = 0; k < str.length(); k++)
        if (str.charAt(k) != '\n')
          sb.append(str.charAt(k));
      super.writeToSocket(soc, sb.toString() + "\n");

  }
  public static void main(String args[]) {
    NimServer server = new NimServer(10001,5);
    server.start();
  } // main()
} // NimServer class
```

Figure 15.34 The NimServer class. (*Continued from previous page*)

NimPlayer defines methods that allow a computer to play an optimal game of One-Row Nim. In this example, the server acts as one of the players and uses a NimPlayer to manage its playing strategy. Thus, clients that connect to NimServer will be faced by a computer that plays an optimal game.

If you compare the details of the NimServer's play() method with the play() method from the implementation of OneRowNim, you will see that they are very similar. In this implementation, we use public methods of the OneRowNim object to manage the playing of the game. Thus, addComputerPlayer() adds an instance of NimPlayer to the game. The take-Sticks(), changePlayer(), and gameOver() methods are used to manage the moves made by both itself and the client. And the getGamePrompt() and reportGameState() methods are used to manage the interaction and communication with the client. Note that whenever it is the server's turn to move, it uses the NimPlayer's makeAMove() method to determine the optimal move to make.

Although the programming logic employed in the play() method looks somewhat complex, it is very similar to the logic employed in the Chapter 8 version of the game. The main difference here is that the server uses the writeToSocket() and readFromSocket() methods to manage the communication with the client. In this regard, this instance of provideService() is no different than the provideService() method we used in the EchoServer class.

Overriding a method

Finally, note that NimServer provides an implementation of the writeToSocket() method. This method is implemented in the ClientServer() class and is inherited by NimServer. However, the default implementation assumes that the client will use a carriage return (\n) to determine the end of a particular message in the socket. Because OneRowNim's methods, getGamePrompt() and reportGameState(), contain embedded carriage returns, it is necessary to filter these. The new version of writeToSocket() performs this filtering and calls the default method, super.writeToSocket(), after it has finished its filtering task.

15.9.2 The NimClient Class

The NimClient class is even easier to implement. As its task is simply to manage the communication between the human user and the NimServer, it is very similar to the re-questService() method we used in EchoClient. The relationship between the abstract Client class (Fig. 15.33) and its extension in NimClient (Fig. 15.35) is very similar to the relationship between Server and NimServer. The requestService() method is called by Client.run(). It is implemented in NimClient. In this way, the Client class can

```java
import java.net.*;
import java.io.*;

public class NimClient extends Client {
    private KeyboardReader kb = new KeyboardReader();
    public NimClient( String url, int port) {
        super(url,port);
    }

    protected void requestService(Socket socket) throws IOException {
        String servStr = readFromSocket(socket);        // Get server's response
        kb.prompt("NIM SERVER: " + servStr +"\n");       // Report server's response
        if ( servStr.substring(0,6).equals("Hi Nim") ) {
            String userStr = "";
            do {
                userStr = kb.getKeyboardInput();          // Get user's move
                writeToSocket(socket, userStr + "\n");     // Send it to server
                servStr = readFromSocket(socket);          // Read server's response
                kb.prompt("NIM SERVER: " + servStr + "\n"); // Report response
            } while(servStr.indexOf("Game over!") == -1);  // Until game over
        }
    } // requestService()

    public static void main(String args[]) {
        NimClient client = new NimClient("localhost", 10001);
        client.start();
    } // main()
} // NimClient class
```

Figure 15.35 The derived `NimClient` class.

serve as a superclass for any number of clients. New clients for new services can be derived from `Client` by simply implementing their own `requestService()` method.

Creating new clients

> **EFFECTIVE DESIGN: Inheritance.** By placing as much functionality as possible into a generic client/server superclass, you can simplify the creation of new services. This is an effective use of Java's inheritance mechanism.

15.9.3 Testing the Nim Service

Testing the One-Row Nim service will be no different than testing the Echo service. To test the service, you want to run both `NimServer` and `NimClient` at the same time and preferably on different computers. As they are currently coded, you will have to modify the `main()` methods of both `NimServer` and `NimClient` to provide the correct URL and port for your environment.

SELF-STUDY EXERCISES

EXERCISE 15.7 The design of the client/server hierarchy makes it easy to create a new service by extending the `Server` and `Client` classes. Describe how you would implement a scramble service with this model. A scramble service can be used to solve the daily scramble puzzles found in many newspapers. Given a string of letters, the scramble service will return a string containing all possible letter combinations. For example, given "cat", the scramble service will return "act atc cat cta tac tca".

EXERCISE 15.8 Describe what happens when each of the following errors is introduced into the EchoClient or EchoServer program:

- Specify the wrong host name when running EchoClient.
- Specify the wrong port number when running EchoClient.
- Remove the reference to \n in the writeToSocket() call in requestService().

15.10 Java Network Security Restrictions

One of the most attractive features of Java is the extensive effort to make it a *secure* language. This is especially important for a language that makes it so easy to implement networking applications. After all, nobody wants to download a Java applet that proceeds to erase the hard disk. Such an applet might be written by a cyber-terrorist deliberately aiming to cause severe damage, or it might be written by a cyber-doofus who inadvertently writes code that does severe damage.

Code verification

What are some of Java's techniques for guarding against deliberate or inadvertent insecure code? One level of security is Java's *bytecode verification* process, which the Java Virtual Machine performs on any "untrusted" code it receives. Java checks every class that it loads into memory to make sure it doesn't contain illegal or insecure code. Another line of defense is the so-called **sandbox security model**, which refers to the practice of restricting the kinds

Limited privileges

of things that certain programs can do. For example, the "sandbox" environment for Java applets restricts them from having any access whatsoever to the local file system.

Another restriction imposed on applets limits their networking capabilities. For example, a Java applet cannot create a network connection to any computer except the one from which

Limited network access

its code was downloaded. Also, a Java applet cannot listen for, or accept, connections on privileged ports—those numbered 1024 or lower. Together, these two restrictions severely limit the kinds of client/server programs that can be built as applets.

Java sets aside certain locations as repositories for **trusted code**. The Java class libraries are placed in such a location, as are the directories where your Java programs are stored. Any class loaded from some other directory is considered *untrusted*. By this definition, applets downloaded over the Internet would be considered untrusted code.

Trusted code

In addition to the restrictions for applets, which apply to all untrusted code, Java defines a number of other limitations:

- Untrusted code cannot make use of certain system facilities, such as System.exit() and classes in the java.security package.
- Untrusted code cannot make use of certain AWT methods, such as methods that access the system clipboard. Another AWT restriction is that any window created by untrusted code must display a message informing the user that it is untrusted. You may have seen such messages on windows opened from applets.
- Untrusted code is limited in the kinds of threads it can create.

JDK 1.2 introduced security enhancements based on the concepts of "permission" and "policy." Code is assigned "permissions" based on the security policy currently in effect. Each permission specifies the type of access allowed for a particular resource (such as "read" and "write" access to a specified file or directory, or "connect" access to a given host and port). The policy that controls permissions can be initialized from an external configurable policy file. Unless a permission is explicitly granted to code, it cannot access the resource guarded by the permission. These new enhancements offer a more fine-grained and extensible approach to security for both applets and applications.

As this brief overview illustrates, the Java Virtual Machine is designed with security as one of its primary issues. This does not guarantee 100 percent security, but it is a big improvement over some of the languages and systems that preceded Java. Moreover, security is an ongoing concern of the Java development process. Flaws in the existing security system are fixed very quickly. Advanced methods are constantly being developed and incorporated into the system. One such enhancement is the use of encryption to guarantee the integrity of classes transferred over the network.

15.11   Java Servlets and Java Server Pages

In this chapter we have been discussing the client/server model of computing. Thus far we have learned how to implement client/server applications using socket connections between programs running on different computers. Because it requires the programmer to directly create and manage the socket protocol, this socket-level approach is a low-level approach. It is important to know about sockets and how they are used, but most client/server applications are programmed at a much higher level by using Java library classes.

Our focus in this section will be to give you a brief sense of how Java programs can be integrated into Web pages. We will discuss two approaches: *Java Server Pages* (JSP) and *Java servlets*. As Web-based approaches, both of these require the use of HTML (HyperText Markup Language) code, the language used for coding Web pages. This means that in order to write your own servlets and JSPs you would really have to learn a little about HTML code. Fortunately, learning HTML code is not difficult, and although it doesn't fit within the scope of this book, you can easily find books or Web sites that cover basic HTML coding. Moreover, in order for servlets and JSPs to work, they must be associated with a Web server specially configured to understand Java code. At the end of this section we will provide links to a Web site where you can learn more about HTML and about how to set up your own JSPs and servlets.

15.11.1   Java Server Pages

A Java Server Page (JSP) is a Web page that contains small snippets of Java code. The simple example discussed here was downloaded from an online tutorial at

```
http://developer.apple.com/internet/java/tomcat1.html
```

The Java code on a JSP is embedded within <% ... %> brackets and interspersed among the page's HTML tags. The Java code can extend over one or more lines. Figure 15.36 shows the complete sourcecode for a simple JSP.

In this example we see two uses of Java code. In the first case, a JSP expression tag is used to display the current date on the Web page:

```
Current time: <%= new java.util.Date() %>
```

A JSP expression element begins with <%= and ends with %>. The expression contained within the tag is evaluated, converted into a Java `String`, and inserted into the Web page. In this case the `Date` object is evaluated and its string value is displayed on the Web page (Fig. 15.37).

```
<html><head><title>Very Simple JSP Example</title></head>
<body bgcolor="white">

<h1>Very Basic JSP</h1>

Current time:  < %= new java.util.Date() %>
<br><br>

Reload this page to watch the greeting change.
<br><br><b>
<!-- including lines of Java code in an HTML page -->
<%
    int um = (int)( Math.random() * 5 );
    switch ( um )
    {
       case 0:  out.println("Welcome"); break;
       case 1:  out.println("Bienvenidos"); break;
       case 2:  out.println("Bienvenue"); break;
       case 3:  out.println("Bienvenuti"); break;
       case 4:  out.println("Willkommen"); break;
       default:  out.println("Huh? " + um);
    }
    out.println("<br>");
%>
</b>
</body>
</html>
```

Figure 15.36   A simple JavaServer Page (JSP).

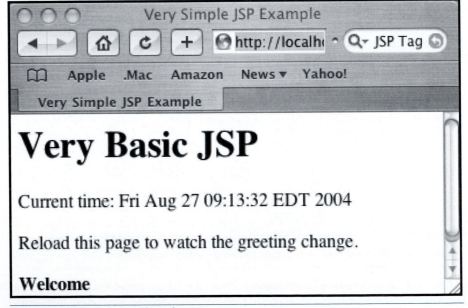

Figure 15.37   A screen shot of a JSP.

In the second case, a *scriptlet* of Java code uses the `Math.random()` method to display a random greeting on the Web page. A **scriptlet** extends over several lines and is contained within the `<% ... %>` tag (Fig. 15.36). Note the use of the output statement, `out.println()`. The `out` object is a built-in output stream. Anything written to `out` will be transmitted as part of the HTML code sent to the Web page. In this case, one of the greetings is displayed each time the page is reloaded.

Obviously, this simple example only scratches the surface of what you can do with JSP. If you want to learn more about JSP, there are many helpful online tutorials available, such as `http://www.jsptut.com/`. However, remember that in order to experiment with JSP, it will be necessary to have access to a JSP-aware Web server either on your own computer or on one provided by your service provider.

15.11.2 Java Servlets

A Java *servlet* is another high-level approach to developing client/server applications. A **servlet** is a Java program that runs on a Web server and processes Web pages using the HyperText Transfer Protocol (HTTP). In a Web application, the browser serves as the client.

Many URLs that we access on the Web are pure HTML files that are simply transmitted back to the browser by the Web server. For example, the URL for a simple HTML document on the author's Web site is:

```
http://starbase.cs.trincoll.edu/~jjjava/hello.html
```

If you type that URL into a Web browser, the Web server at `starbase.cs.trincoll.edu` would transmit the following text file to your browser, which would then render and display the document.

```
<HTML>
<HEAD>
    <TITLE>Very Simple HTML Document</TITLE>
</HEAD>
<BODY>
    <CENTER><H1>Hello</H1></CENTER>
</BODY>
</HTML>
```

If we want the server to do some processing and submit the results of the processing to the browser, we could use a Java servlet. A servlet can perform a processing task and return the results to the browser in the form of an HTML document.

The difference between a Java servlet and a Java applet is that an applet performs all of its processing on the client side of the client/server connection. A servlet performs its processing on the server side. When you load a Java applet into a browser, the Web server downloads the applet's bytecode into the browser. The browser then runs the byte code, assuming, of course, that it is equipped with a plugin for the Java Virtual Machine (JVM). When you access a Java servlet from a browser, the Web server performs some computation and transmits just the results to the browser.

Servlets vs. applets

Servlets have several advantages over applets. First, servlets cut down significantly on the amount of data that has to be transmitted to the browser. Second, because the servlet returns an HTML-encoded page, there are many fewer platform-related problems. All browsers can interpret HTML code, but not all browsers have the right plugins for interpreting Java applets. Third, servlets are not subject to the same security and privacy restrictions as Java applets, which, as we saw earlier in the chapter, must be run as untrusted code. Finally, Java servlets can directly access large databases and other resources stored on the server. Access to such resources via an applet would be very difficult and inefficient.

In short, servlets have many advantages over applets. Because of these advantages they have quickly become an industry standard for developing client/server applications on the Web.

15.11.3   A Simple Servlet Example

To illustrate the difference between a Java servlet and a simple HTML page, Figure 15.38 shows a servlet that creates a Web page that says "Hello". As you can see, a servlet is a Java program. In addition to libraries that you are already familiar with, such as `java.io`, it also imports names from two new libraries: `javax.servlet` and `javax.servlet.http`. The program defines a single class, the `HelloServlet` class, which is a subclass of `HttpServlet`, the standard superclass for all Java servlets.

The servlet defines the `doGet()` method. This is a method defined in the `HttpServlet` superclass. Our `HelloServlet` is overriding `doGet()`. In general, Web browsers make two types of requests when they request a Web page, a **get** or a **post**. We won't go into the differences between these requests. The result in either case is that the Web server will respond to the request by transmitting some text data to the browser. When a browser makes a get request, the server will automatically call the servlet's `doGet()` method. That's why we have to override it. The `HttpServlet` class also has a default `doPost()` method, which is called automatically to handle *post* requests.

```java
import java.io.*;
import java.text.*;
import java.util.*;
import javax.servlet.*;
import javax.servlet.http.*;

public class HelloServlet extends HttpServlet {

    public void doGet(HttpServletRequest request, HttpServletResponse response)
        throws IOException, ServletException
    {
        response.setContentType("text/html");
        PrintWriter out = response.getWriter();

        out.println("<HTML>");
        out.println("<HEAD>");
        out.println("<TITLE>Simple Servlet</TITLE>");
        out.println("</HEAD>");
        out.println("<BODY>");
        out.println("<H1> Hi, from a Java Servlet.</H1>");
        out.println("</BODY>");
        out.println("</HTML>");
    }
}
```

Figure 15.38   A simple Java servlet.

Note the two parameters in the `doGet()` method: the `HttpServletRequest` and the `HttpServletResponse`. The `doPost()` method has the same two parameters. These are the objects used to hold the data communicated between the client and the server. When the client (browser) makes a get request, the `HttpServletRequest` objects hold the data contained in the request. The data might include data that a user has typed into an HTML form. We will see an example of how to extract such data in the next section.

The `HttpServletResponse` object is where the servlet will write its response. As you can see from examining the code, the `HttpServletResponse` object has an associated output stream, a `PrintWriter`, and it is a simple matter to write text to that output stream. Note that the text we write is HTML code that is practically identical to the code contained in the previous HTML example.

15.11.4   The Nim Servlet

The simple servlet in the preceding section illustrates how the servlet communicates with the client—by writing HTML code to the `HttpServletResponse` object. Let's now look at an example that uses two-way communication between the client and server. To keep the example simple, we will once again revisit our One-Row Nim game. In this application the servlet will manage the One-Row Nim game and will play against a human player who will access the game through a Web browser.

The browser interface for this version of the game is shown in Figure 15.39. As you can see, it is a simple Web page. The sticks in this instance are replaced by pennies. In addition to reporting the total number of pennies left, the page displays images of pennies. This Web page is itself organized as a simple HTML form that contains one text field for the user's input. Each time the user hits the RETURN key in the text field, the user's input is transmitted to the servlet where it is processed. The servlet then transmits a new page to the user's browser, which shows the updated state of the game.

Let's now look at the servlet program itself, whose code is shown in Figures 15.40 and 15.41. This servlet program is quite a bit longer than the simple hello server, but it is not really any more complex or difficult. The `NimServlet` extends the `HttpServlet` superclass and overrides the `doGet()` method. Note that it also overrides the `doPost()` method by simply having that method call the `doPost()` method. So this servlet will work for both *get* and *post* requests.

`NimServlet` uses two other objects: a `OneRowNim` object and a `NimPlayer` object. You should be familiar with these from Chapter 8, so we won't go over their internal details here. The `OneRowNim` object manages the playing of the game, and the `NimPlayer` object acts as a computer-based player of the game. Note that variable references for these two objects are declared in the beginning of the class definition, but the objects themselves are declared in the `doGet()` method.

One of the tricky parts of `NimServlet` is how we declare the `OneRowNim` object. As you might already know, the HTTP protocol is said to be a *stateless* protocol, which means that each time a browser submits a request to a Web server, the Web server sees the request as a completely independent communication. The server does not, in and of itself, maintain an internal state that keeps track of a series of transactions with a particular browser session. For example, consider shopping for books on Amazon. Each time you go to a new page, the Amazon Web server treats that request as a completely independent action. Web applications use various techniques to get around the stateless nature of the HTTP protocol. One technique is to use *cookies* to record the progress of a session. A **cookie** is a small text file containing

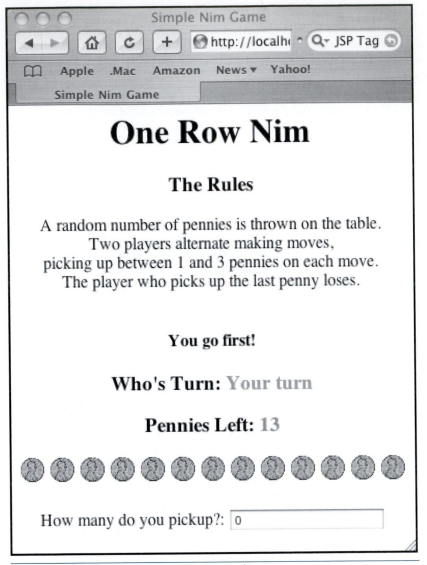

Figure 15.39 The interface for the Nim servlet.

```
import java.io.*;
import java.util.*;
import javax.servlet.*;
import javax.servlet.http.*;
public class NimServlet extends HttpServlet {

    private OneRowNim nim = null;
    private NimPlayer nimPlayer = null;
```

Figure 15.40 Java code for the NimServlet minus the doGet() method. (*Continued on next page*)

```java
    public void doPost(HttpServletRequest request,
                        HttpServletResponse response)
      throws IOException, ServletException
    {
        doGet(request, response);
    }

    //  The doGet() method goes here.
} // NimServlet class
```

Figure 15.40 Java code for the NimServlet minus the doGet() method. (*Continued from previous page*)

```java
public void doGet(HttpServletRequest request, HttpServletResponse response)
      throws IOException, ServletException
{
   response.setContentType("text/html");
   PrintWriter out = response.getWriter();
   HttpSession session = request.getSession(true);

   out.println("<html>");
   out.println("<body>");
   out.println("<head>");
   out.println("<title>Simple Nim Game</title>");
   out.println("</head>");
   out.println("<body>");

   out.println("<center><h1>One Row Nim</h1></center>");
   out.println("<center><h3>The Rules</h3>");
   out.println("A random number of pennies is thrown on the table.<BR>");
   out.println("Two players alternate making moves,<BR>");
   out.println("picking up between 1 and 3 pennies on each move.<BR>");
   out.println("The player who picks up the last penny loses.<BR><BR>");

   if (nim == null) {
      nim = new OneRowNim(7 + (int)(Math.random() * 11));
      nimPlayer = new NimPlayer(nim);
      out.println("<h4>You go first!</h4></center>");
   } else {
      int userTakes = Integer.parseInt(request.getParameter("pickup"));
      if (!nim.takeSticks(userTakes)) {
         out.println("<h4><font color='red'>Woops. That's an illegal move!. "
                                +"Try again. </font><h4>");
      } else if (!nim.gameOver()) {
         nim.changePlayer();
         out.println("<h4>So, you took <font color='blue'>" + userTakes
                                + "</font><BR>");
         out.println("That leaves me with <font color='blue'>" + nim.getSticks()
                                + "</font><BR>");
         int iTake = nimPlayer.move();
         out.println("OK. I take <font color='red'>" + iTake
                                + " </font>pennies.<BR></h4>");
         nim.takeSticks(iTake);
         nim.changePlayer();
      } // if not gameover
   } // else nim != null
```

Figure 15.41 Java code for the NimServlet's doGet() method. (*Continued on next page*)

```
    if (!nim.gameOver()) {
      if (nim.getPlayer() == 1)
        out.println("<center><h3>Who's Turn: <font color='magenta'> "
                            + "Your turn </font><h3></center>");
      else
        out.println("<center><h3>Who's Turn: <font color='magenta'> "
                            + "My turn </font><h3></center>");
      out.println("<center><h3>Pennies Left: <font color='red'>"
                            + nim.getSticks() + "</font><h3></center>");
      out.println("<center>");
      for (int k=0; k < nim.getSticks(); k++)
        out.println("<img src='http://xroads.virginia.edu/€AP/LINCOLN/cent.jpg' "
                            + "width='25' height='25'>");
      out.println("</center><br>");

      out.println("<center>");
      out.println("<form action='/jjj3e/NimServlet' method='POST'>");
      out.println("<table border='0'>");
      out.println("<tr><td>How many do you pickup?: </td>" +
          "<td><input type='text' name='pickup' value='0'></td></tr>");
      out.println("</table>");
      out.println("</center>");
      out.println("</form>");
    } else {
      out.println("<h3><font color='red'>Game over!</font><h3>");
      if (nim.getPlayer() == 1)
        out.println("<center><h4>And the winner is : <font color='magenta'> "
                            + "Me.</font><h4></center>");
      else
        out.println("<center><h4>And the winner is: <font color='magenta'> "
                            + "You.</font><h4></center>");
      out.println("<center><h4><font color='magenta'> "
                            + "Nice game!</font><h4></center>");
      out.println("<center><h4>To play again, "
                            + "just reload the page.<h4></center>");
      nim = null;
    } // else game over
    out.println("</body>");
    out.println("</html>");
} // doGet()
```

Figure 15.41 Java code for the NimServlet's doGet() method. (*Continued from previous page*)

data that the server uses to keep track of a user's session. Data that identifies the user and the state of the transaction—for example, buying a book—are passed back and forth between the browser and the server each time the user visits the Amazon Web site.

Java's servlet library contains methods and objects that support the use of cookies. But rather than use cookies, we will use the OneRowNim object itself to keep track of the state of the Nim game. The first time the user submits a request to Nim servlet—that is, when the user first visits the servlet's URL—the servlet will create an instance of the OneRowNim object. Creating a OneRowNim object will have the effect of initializing the game, including the creation of a NimPlayer to play the server's moves. The OneRowNim object will persist throughout the playing of the game and will handle all of the user's subsequent moves. When the game is over, the `NimServlet` will, in effect, dispose of the `OneRowNim` object by setting its reference to `null`. Thus, in outline form, the code for creating and disposing of the `OneRowNim` object goes as follows:

```
                                    // First request: Start a new Nim game
if (nim == null) {
    nim = new OneRowNim(7 + (int)(Math.random() * 11));
    nimPlayer = new NimPlayer(nim);
                                    // Code deleted here.
else {
                                    // Code for playing the game goes here.
}
if (!nim.gameOver()) {
                                    // Code for playing the game goes here.
} else {
                                    // Code deleted here.
    nim = null;
}
```

The places where code has been deleted in this segment would contain Java code for responding to the user's input and deciding how many pennies to take.

Unlike the `HelloServlet`, the `NimServlet` accepts input from the client. The code for handling user input is as follows:

```
int userTakes = Integer.parseInt(request.getParameter("pickup"));
```

This statement reads the user's input from the text field on the Web page by using the `request.getParameter()` method. This is one of the public methods of the `HttpServletRequest` object. The name of the text field is 'pickup,' which is provided as an argument in this method call. As we noted above, the text field itself is an element of the HTML form contained in the servlet's Web page. The HTML code for creating the form element is also generated by the servlet:

```
out.println("<form action='/jjj3e/NimServlet' method='POST'>");
out.println("<table border='0'>");
out.println("<tr><td>How many do you pick up?: </td>" +
    "<td><input type='text' name='pickup' value='0'></td></tr>");
```

Unless you already know something about HTML, you won't completely understand this code. We will give a minimal explanation. In HTML, a text field is known as an input element of type 'text'. Note that this code segment names the element 'pickup', which allows our program to refer to it by that name.

The remaining details in the servlet have to do with managing the game and repeat concepts that were covered in Chapter 8. We won't repeat them here, other than to note that any output sent to the client must be in the form of HTML statements, hence the appearance throughout the code of HTML tags, which are the elements in the angle brackets.

15.11.5   Setting Up and Using Java Servlets

Java servlets can only run on a Web server that is specially configured to interpret them. To experiment with the servlets discussed in this chapter, just go to the following URL:

```
http://starbase.cs.trincoll.edu/~jjjava/servlets
```

That Web page contains links to both `HelloServlet` and `NimServlet`. It also contains links to Web sites where you can learn more about creating servlets. In order to create and run your own servlets, you will need access to a Web server specially configured to run servlets. There are several very good free servers that support Java servlets. You can download one of them onto your own computer and follow the directions on how to set it up. Links to Java servlet sites are also provided on our servlets page.

CHAPTER SUMMARY

Technical Terms

busy waiting	port
callback method	post
client	protocol
client/server protocols	router
domain name	sandbox security model
ethernet protocol	scriptlet
File Transfer Protocol (FTP)	server
get	servlet
HyperText Transfer Protocol (HTTP)	Simple Mail Transfer Protocol (SMTP)
internet	socket
Internet	trusted code
Internetworking Protocol (IP)	Uniform Resource Locator (URL)
Java Server Page (JSP)	World Wide Web (WWW)
packet	

Summary of Important Points

- An *internet* is a collection of two or more distinct networks joined by *routers*, which have the task of translating one network's language to the other's. The *Internet* is a network of networks that uses the *Internet Protocol* (IP) as the translation medium.

- A *protocol* is a set of rules that controls the transfer of information between two computers in a network. The *HyperText Transfer Protocol* (HTTP) governs information exchange on the World Wide Web (WWW). The *Simple Mail Transfer Protocol* controls mail service on the Internet. The *File Transfer Protocol* (FTP) controls the transfer of files between Internet computers. The *Domain Name System* (DNS) governs the use of names on the Internet.

- A *client/server* application is one that divides its task between a client, which requests service, and a server, which provides service. Many Internet applications and protocols are based on the client/server model.

- Lower-level protocols, such as the *ethernet protocol* and *token ring protocol*, govern the transmission of data between computers on a single network. The *Internet Protocol* (IP) translates between such protocols.

- A *Uniform Resource Locator* (URL) is a standard way of specifying addresses on the Internet. It consists of several parts separated by slashes and colons: `method://host:port/-path/file`. The `java.net.URL` class is used to represent URLs.

- Files of text or data (images, audio files) on the Internet or Web can be downloaded using the same `InputStream`s and `OutputStream`s as files located on a disk. To read or write a resource located on a network, you need to connect its URL to an input or output stream.

- The `java.awt.Toolkit` class contains useful methods for downloading `Image`s into an application.

- A *socket* is a two-way communication channel between two running programs on a network. The `java.net.Socket` class can be used to set up communication channels for client/server applications. The *server* process listens at a socket for requests from a client. The *client* process requests service from a server listening at a particular socket. Once a connection exists between client and server, input and output streams are used to read and write data over the socket.

SOLUTIONS TO SELF-STUDY EXERCISES

SOLUTION 15.1   The fully connected mesh topology requires the most cables.

SOLUTION 15.2   The fully connected mesh topology would have the most potential to use alternative routes if one of the host computers crashed.

SOLUTION 15.3   The star topology would be rendered completely useless if its central hub crashed.

SOLUTION 15.4   Prentice Hall's Web server is located at

```
http://www.prenhall.com
```

The protocol is `http`. The host computer is named `www`. Prentice Hall's domain name is `prenhall`, and it is part of the `com` (commercial) Internet domain.

SOLUTION 15.5

- For buying a piece of software at a bookstore, the server would be the sales clerk. The protocol would be to select the software from off the shelf, bring it to the checkout counter, give the sales clerk money, and get a receipt.
- For buying a piece of software over the phone, the server would be the telephone sales clerk. The protocol would be to select from a catalog, provide the sales clerk with your credit card information, and say goodbye.
- For buying a piece of software over the Internet, the server would be the computer that handles the transaction. The protocol would be to select the item from a Web-based form, provide the form with personal and payment information, and click on the Buy button.

SOLUTION 15.6   To play sounds along with slides in the `SlideShowApplet`, you would make the following modifications to the code:

```
private URL soundURL[] = new URL[NIMGS];
```

Declare an array of URLs to store the URLs of the audio files you want to play.

Assign URLs to the array at the same time you input the images:

```
for (int k=0; k < NIMGS; k++) {
  url = new URL( "http://starbase.trincoll.edu/~jjjava/slide" + k + ".gif");
  slide[k] = getImage( url );
  soundURL[k]
      = new URL("http://starbase.trincoll.edu/~jjjava/sound" + k + ".au");
}
```

Each time an image is displayed in `paint()`, play the corresponding sound by using the URL from the array:

```
public void paint(Graphics g) {
    if (currentImage != null) {
        g.drawImage(currentImage,10,10,this);
        play( soundURL[currentImage] );
    }
}
```

SOLUTION 15.7   The scramble service would be implemented by defining two new classes: The `ScrambleServer` class is a subclass of `Server`, and the `ScrambleClient` class is a subclass of `Client`. The `ScrambleClient` would implement the `requestService()` method, and the `ScrambleServer` would implement the `provideService()` method.

SOLUTION 15.8

- If you specify the wrong host name or port, you will get the following exception: `java.net.ConnectException: Connection refused`.
- If you leave off the `\n` in the `writeToSocket()` call, nothing will go wrong because the `writeToSocket()` method will catch this error and add the end-of-line character to the string before sending it to the server. The server reads lines from the client, so every communication must end with `\n` or the protocol will break down.

EXERCISES

EXERCISE 15.1   Explain the difference between each of the following pairs of terms:

a. *Stream* and *socket*.
b. *Internet* and *internet*.
c. *Domain name* and *port*.

d. *Client* and *server*.
e. *Ethernet* and *Internet*.
f. *URL* and *domain name*.

Note: For programming exercises, **first** draw a UML class diagram describing all classes and their inheritance relationships and/or associations.

EXERCISE 15.2   What is a *protocol*? Give one or two examples of protocols used on the Internet.

EXERCISE 15.3   What service is managed by the HTTP protocol?

EXERCISE 15.4   Give examples of client applications that use the HTTP protocol.

EXERCISE 15.5   Why is it important that applets be limited in terms of their network and file system access? Describe the various networking restrictions that apply to Java applets.

EXERCISE 15.6   What does the `Internet Protocol` do? Describe how it would be used to join an ethernet and a token ring network.

EXERCISE 15.7   Describe one or two circumstances under which a `ConnectException` would be thrown.

EXERCISE 15.8   Modify the `SlideShowApplet` so that it plays an audio file along with each slide.

EXERCISE 15.9   Design and implement a Java applet that downloads a random substitution cryptogram and provides an interface that helps the user try to solve the cryptogram. The interface should enable the user to substitute an arbitrary letter for the letters in the cryptogram. The cryptogram files should be stored in the same directory as the applet.

EXERCISE 15.10   Design and implement a Java application that displays a random message (or a random joke) each time the user clicks a `GetMessage` button. The messages should be stored in a set of files in the same directory as the applet. Each time the button is clicked, the applet should download one of the message files.

EXERCISE 15.11   Write a client/server application of the message or joke service described in the preceding exercise. Your implementation should extend the `Server` and `Client` classes.

EXERCISE 15.12   Write an implementation of the scramble service. Given a word, the scramble service will return a string containing all possible permutations of the letter combinations in the word. For example, given "man", the scramble service will return "amn, anm, man, mna, nam, nma". Use the `Server` and `Client` classes in your design. (See the Self-Study Exercises for a description of the design.)

EXERCISE 15.13   **Challenge:** Modify the Nim server game in this chapter so that the client and server can negotiate the rules of the game, including how many sticks, how many pick-ups per turn, and who goes first.

Photograph courtesy of RH Productions, Robert Harding World Imagery.

16

Data Structures: Lists, Stacks, and Queues

OBJECTIVES

After studying this chapter, you will

- Understand the concepts of a dynamic data structure and an Abstract Data Type (ADT).
- Be able to create and use dynamic data structures such as linked lists and binary search trees.
- Understand the stack, queue, set, and map ADTs.
- Be able to use inheritance to define extensible data structures.
- Know how to use the TreeSet, TreeMap, HashSet, and HashMap library classes.
- Be able to use the Java generic type construct.

OUTLINE

16.1   Introduction

A **data structure** is used to organize information that a computer can access and process easily and efficiently. You are already familiar with one type of data structure—arrays, which we discussed in Chapter 9. If you remember, an array is an example of a data structure in which all of the data are of the same type or class and in which individual elements are accessed by their position (index or subscript). An array is an example of a **static structure**, because its size is fixed for the duration of the program's execution. (This is a different meaning of *static* than the Java keyword `static`.)

The `Vector` class from Chapter 9 is another example of a data structure. Like an array, individual vector elements are accessed by their position. However, unlike arrays, a vector is an example of a **dynamic structure**—that is, one that can grow and shrink during a program's execution.

These are only two of the many data structures developed by computer scientists. For more advanced problems, it is often necessary to develop specialized structures to store and manipulate information. Some of these structures—linked lists, stacks, queues, binary trees, hash tables—have become classic objects of study in computer science.

This chapter describes how to implement a linked list and how to use inheritance to extend the list to implement the stack and queue structures. Then the Java Collections Framework implementation of numerous data structures in the `java.util` package will be described. The data structure classes in this library make use of a new Java construct called *generic types*. Finally, the binary tree data structure used in the Java Collections Framework will be studied briefly.

16.2   The Linked List Data Structure

Static vs. dynamic

A *static* data structure is one whose size is fixed during a program's execution—a static structure's memory is allocated at compile time. By contrast, a *dynamic* structure is one that can grow and shrink as needed. In this section, we will develop a dynamic **list**, a data structure whose elements are arranged in a linear sequence. The list has a first element, a second element, and so on. Lists are quite general and, as we will discuss later, they have a broad range of applications. Depending on how elements are inserted and removed, a list can be used for a range of specialized purposes.

16.2.1   Using References to Link Objects

Referring to objects

As you know from earlier chapters, when you create an object using the `new` operator you get back a **reference** to the object that you then can assign to a reference variable. In the following example, *b* is a reference to a `JButton`:

```
JButton b = new JButton();
```

We have defined many classes that contained references to other objects:

```
public class Student {
    private String name;
}
```

In this example, `name` is a reference to a `String` object.

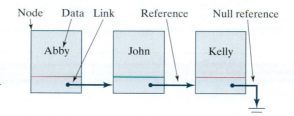

Node Data Link Reference Null reference

Abby John Kelly

Figure 16.1 A linked list of Nodes terminated by a `null` link.

A **linked list** is a list in which a collection of nodes are linked together by references from one node to the next. To make a linked list, we will define a class of self-referential objects. A **self-referential object** is an object that contains a reference to an object of the same class. The convention is to name these objects Nodes:

Self-referential objects

```java
public class Node {
    private String name;
    private Node next;
}
```

In addition to the reference to a `String` object, each `Node` object contains a reference to another `Node` object. The `next` variable is often called a **link** because it is used to link together two `Node` objects. For example, Figure 16.1 provides an illustration of a linked list of `Node`s.

By assigning references to the `next` variables in each `Node`, we can chain together arbitrarily long lists of objects. Therefore, we will want to add methods to our `Node` class that enable us to manipulate a `Node`'s next variable (Fig. 16.2). By assigning it a reference to another `Node`, we can link two `Node`s together. By retrieving the link's value, we can find the next `Node` in the list.

JAVA LANGUAGE RULE **Self-Referential Object.** A *self-referential object* is one that contains an instance variable that refers to an object of the same class.

In addition to the link variable, each `Node` stores some data. In this example, the data is a single `String`. But there is no real limit to the amount and type of data that can be stored in a

Linking objects together

Node
− data : Object
− next : Node
+ Node(in o : Object)
+ setData(in o : Object)
+ getData() : Object
+ setNext(in link : Node)
+ getNext() : Node

Figure 16.2 The Node class.

linked list. Therefore, in addition to methods that manipulate a `Node`'s link, we will also want methods to manipulate its data. These points suggest the following basic design for a `Node`:

```
public class Node {
    private Object data;
    private Node next;

    public Node(Object obj);          // Constructor

    public void setData(Object obj);  // Data access
    public Object getData();

    public void setNext(Node link);   // Link access
    public Node getNext();
} // Node class
```

We have defined the `Node`'s data in the most general possible way: as a reference to an `Object`. Because the `Object` class is the root of Java's entire class hierarchy, an `Object` can encompass any kind of data. By using Java's wrapper classes, such as `Integer` and `Double`, a `Node`'s data can even include primitive data.

The important point is that regardless of its type of data, a `Node` will have data access methods and link access methods. The data access methods differ, depending on the type of data, but the link access methods will generally be the same.

Divide and conquer

EFFECTIVE DESIGN: Link Versus Data. Making a clear distinction between an object's data and the elements used to manipulate the object is an example of the divide-and-conquer principle.

SELF-STUDY EXERCISES

EXERCISE 16.1 Write a statement to create a new `Node` whose data element consists of the `String` "Hello".

EXERCISE 16.2 Write a statement to create a new `Node` whose data element consists of the `Student` named "William". Assume that the `Student` class has a constructor with a `String` parameter for the student's name.

16.2.2 Example: The Dynamic Phone List

Let's define a `PhoneListNode` class that can be used to implement a phone list (Fig. 16.3). This definition will be a straightforward specialization of the generic `Node` list defined in the preceding section. Each element of the phone list will consist of a person's name and phone number. These will be the node's data and can be stored in two `String` variables. To access these data, we will provide a constructor and a basic set of access methods. Thus, we have the definition shown in Figure 16.4.

Accessing a list's data

The constructor and data access methods should be familiar to you. Note that the constructor sets the initial value of `next` to `null`, which means that it refers to no object.

DEBUGGING TIP: Null Reference. A common programming error is the attempt to use a `null` reference to refer to an object. This usually means the reference has not been successfully initialized.

PhoneListNode
− name : String − phone : String − next : PhoneListNode
+ PhoneListNode(in name : String, in phone : String) + setData(in name : String, in phone : String) + getName() : String + getData() : String + toString() : String + setNext(in next : PhoneListNode) + getNext() : PhoneListNode

Figure 16.3 Design of the Phone-ListNode class.

Let's discuss the details of the link access methods—the `setNext()` and `getNext()` methods—which are also simple to implement. Because this is a `PhoneListNode`, these methods take `PhoneListNode` as a parameter and return type, respectively. Given a reference to a `PhoneListNode`, the `setNext()` method assigns it to `next`. The `getNext()` method simply returns the value of its `next` link.

Manipulating a list's nodes

```java
public class PhoneListNode {
    private String name;
    private String phone;
    private PhoneListNode next;
    public PhoneListNode(String s1, String s2) {
        name = s1;
        phone = s2;
        next = null;
    } // PhoneListNode()
    public void setData(String s1, String s2) {
        name = s1;
        phone = s2;
    } // setData()
    public String getName() {
        return name;
    } // getName()
    public String getData() {
        return name + " " + phone;
    } // getData()
    public String toString() {
        return name + " " + phone;
    } // toString()
    public void setNext(PhoneListNode nextPtr) {
        next = nextPtr;
    } // setNext()
    public PhoneListNode getNext() {
        return next;
    } // getNext()
} // PhoneListNode class
```

Figure 16.4 The PhoneListNode class.

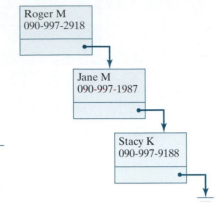

Figure 16.5 The phone list: a linked list of nodes, each of which contains a person's name and phone number.

Let's now see how we would use these methods to construct a list. The following statements create three nodes:

```
PhoneListNode node1 = new PhoneListNode("Roger M","090-997-2918");
PhoneListNode node2 = new PhoneListNode("Jane M","090-997-1987");
PhoneListNode node3 = new PhoneListNode("Stacy K","090-997-9188");
```

The next two statements chain the nodes together into the list shown in Figure 16.5:

```
node1.setNext(node2);
node2.setNext(node3);
```

If we wanted to add a fourth node to the end of this list, we could use the following statements:

```
PhoneListNode node4 = new PhoneListNode("gary g","201-119-8765");
node3.setNext(node4);
```

Although this example illustrates the basic technique for inserting nodes at the end of the list, it depends too much on our knowledge of the list. In order to be truly useful we will have to develop a more general set of methods to create and manipulate a list of nodes. As we will see, a better design would be able to find the end of the list without knowing anything about the list's data.

EFFECTIVE DESIGN: Generality.   In a well-designed list data structure, you should be able to manipulate its elements without knowing anything about its data.

SELF-STUDY EXERCISE

EXERCISE 16.3   Suppose you know that `nodeptr` is a reference to the last element of a linked list of `PhoneListNode`s. Create a new element for "Bill C" with phone number "111-202-3331" and link it into the end of the list.

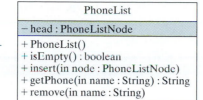

Figure 16.6 The PhoneList class has a reference to the first node of the list (head) and methods to insert, remove, and look up information.

16.2.3 Manipulating the Phone List

In addition to the Nodes that make a list, we must define a class containing methods to manipulate the list. This class will include the insert, access, and remove methods. It must also contain a reference to the list itself. This leads to the basic design shown in Figure 16.6. Because this is a list of PhoneListNodes, we need a PhoneListNode reference to point to the list, which is the purpose of the head variable.

A preliminary coding of the PhoneList class is shown in Figure 16.7. As you can see there, when a new PhoneList instance is constructed, head is initialized to null, meaning that the list is initially empty. Since we will frequently want to test whether the list is empty, we define the boolean isEmpty() method for that purpose. As you can see, its definition says that a list is empty when the reference to the head of the list is null.

An empty list

> **JAVA PROGRAMMING TIP: The null Reference.** A null reference is useful for defining limit cases, such as an empty list or an uninstantiated object.

Inserting Nodes into a List

The insert() method will have the task of inserting new PhoneListNodes into the list. There are a number of ways to do this. The node could be inserted at the beginning or end of the list, or in alphabetical order, or possibly in other ways. As we will see, it is easiest to insert a new node at the head of the list. But for this example, let's develop a method that inserts the node at the end of the list.

There are two cases we need to worry about for this algorithm. First, if the list is empty, we can insert the node by simply setting head to point to the node, as can be seen in Figure 16.8(a).

Insertion algorithm

```java
public class PhoneList {
    private PhoneListNode head;

    public PhoneList() {
        head = null;                       // Start with empty list
    }
    public boolean isEmpty() {             // Defines an empty list
        return head == null;
    }
    public void insert(PhoneListNode node) { }
    public String getPhone(String name) { }
    public String remove(String name) { }
    public void print() { }
} // PhoneList class
```

Figure 16.7 A preliminary version of the PhoneList class.

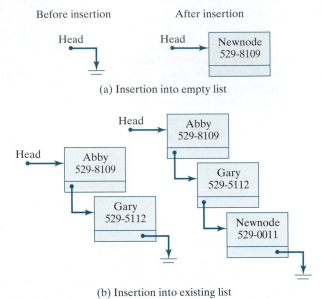

Figure 16.8 Two cases. (a) The list is empty before the insertion, which takes place at head. (b) The list is not empty, so the insertion takes place at the end of the list.

Second, if the list is not empty, we must move through, or **traverse**, the links of the list until we find the last node and insert the new node after it, as shown in Figure 16.8(b). In this case, we want to set the `next` variable of the last node to point to the new node. This gives us the following algorithm:

```
public void insert(PhoneListNode newNode) {
    if (isEmpty())
        head = newNode;                      // Insert at head of list
    else {
        PhoneListNode current = head;        // Start traversal at head
        while (current.getNext() != null)    // While not last node
            current = current.getNext();     // go to next node
            current.setNext( newNode );      // Do the insertion
    }
} // insert()
```

Recall that when nodes are linked, their `next` variables are non-`null`. So when a node's `next` variable is `null`, that indicates the end of the list—there is no next node. Thus, our algorithm begins by checking whether the list is empty. If so, we assign `head` the reference to `newNode`, the `PhoneListNode` that is being inserted.

Traversing a list   If the list is not empty, then we need to find the last node. In order to traverse the list, we will need a temporary variable, `current`, which will always point to the current node. It is important to understand the `while` loop used here:

```
PhoneListNode current = head;        // Initializer
while (current.getNext() != null)    // Entry condition
    current = current.getNext();     // Updater
```

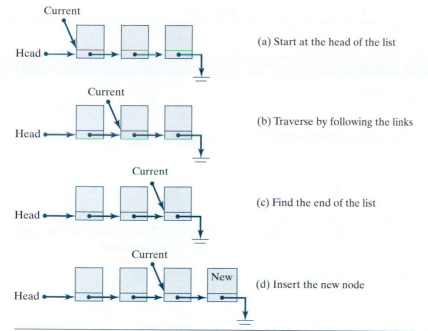

Current

Head

(a) Start at the head of the list

Current

Head

(b) Traverse by following the links

Current

Head

(c) Find the end of the list

Current

New

Head

(d) Insert the new node

Figure 16.9 The temporary variable `current` traverses the list to find its end.

The loop variable, `current`, is initialized by setting it to point to the head of the list. The entry condition tests whether the `next` link, leading out of `current`, is `null` (Fig. 16.9). That is, when the link coming out of a node is `null`, then that node is the last node in the list, as in Figure 16.9(c). Inside the `while` loop, the update expression simply assigns the next node to `current`. In that way, `current` will point to each successive node until the last node is found. It is very important that the loop exit when `current.getNext()` is `null`—that is, when the next pointer of the current node is null. That way `current` is pointing to the last node and can be used to set its `next` variable to the node being inserted, as in Figure 16.9(d). Thus, after the loop is exited, `current` still points to the last node. At that point, the `setNext()` method is used to link `newNode` into the list as the new last node.

Loop-exit
condition

DEBUGGING TIP: List Traversal.   A common error in designing list-traversal algorithms is an erroneous loop-entry or loop-exit condition. One way to avoid this error is to hand trace your algorithm to make sure your code is correct.

Printing the Nodes of a List

The `print()` method also uses a traversal strategy to print the data from each node of the list. Here again it is necessary to test whether the list is empty. If so, we must print an error message. (This would be a good place to throw a programmer-defined exception, such as an

List traversal

EmptyListException.) If the list is not empty, then we use a temporary variable to traverse the list, printing each node's data along the way:

```java
public void print() {
    if (isEmpty())
        System.out.println("Phone list is empty");
    PhoneListNode current = head;                 // Start traversal at head
    while (current != null) {                      // While not end of list
        System.out.println( current.toString() );  // print data
        current = current.getNext();               // go to next node
    }
} // print()
```

Note the differences between this while loop and the one used in the insert() method. In this case, we exit the loop when current becomes null; there is no action to be taken after the loop is exited. The printing takes place within the loop. Thus, in this case, the entry condition, (current != null), signifies that the task has been completed.

JAVA PROGRAMMING TIP: Terminating a Traversal.   In designing list-traversal algorithms where the reference, p, points to the nodes in the list, your exit condition should be p.getNext() == null if you need to refer to the last node in the list after the traversal loop exits. If you have finished processing the nodes when the loop exits, your exit condition should be p == null.

Looking up a Node in a List

List traversal

Because the record associated with a person can be located anywhere in the list, the traversal strategy must also be used to look up someone's phone number in the PhoneList. Here again we start at the head of the list and traverse through the next links until we find the node containing the desired phone number. This method takes the name of the person as a parameter. There are three cases to worry about: (1) the list is empty, (2) the normal case where the person named is found in the list, and (3) the person named is not in the list. Because the method returns a String, we can return error messages in the first and third cases:

```java
public String getPhone(String name) {
    if (isEmpty())                                            // Case 1: Empty list
        return "Phone list is empty";
    else {
        PhoneListNode current = head;
        while ((current.getNext() != null) && (!current.getName().equals(name)))
            current = current.getNext();
        if (current.getName().equals(name))
            return current.getData();                         // Case 2: Found name
        else                                                  // Case 3: No such person
            return ("Sorry.   No entry for " + name);
    }
} // getPhone()
```

Note the while loop in this case. As in the insert() method, when the loop exits, we need a reference to the current node so that we can print its phone number, current.getData(). But here there are three ways to exit the loop: (1) we reach the end of the list without finding the named person, (2) we find the named person in the interior of the list, or (3) we find the named person in the last node of the list. In any case, it is necessary to test whether the name was found or not after the loop is exited. Then appropriate action can be taken.

Compound exit condition

SELF-STUDY EXERCISE

EXERCISE 16.4 What if the exit condition for the `while` loop in `getPhone()` were stated as shown below.

```
((current.getNext() != null) || (!current.getName().equals(name)))
```

Removing a Node from a List

By far the most difficult task is that of removing a node from a list. In the `PhoneList` we use the person's name to identify the node, and we return a `String` that can be used to report either success or failure. There are four cases to worry about in designing this algorithm: (1) the list is empty, (2) the first node is being removed, (3) some other node is being removed, and (4) the named person is not in the list. The same traversal strategy we used in `getPhone()` is used here, with the same basic `while` loop for cases 3 and 4.

Node-removal algorithm

As Figure 16.10 shows, the first two cases are easily handled. If the list is empty, we just return an error message. We use `current` as the traversal variable. If the named node is the first node, we simply need to set `head` to `current.getNext()`, which has the effect of making `head` point to the second node in the list, as seen in Figure 16.11(a). Once the node is cut out from the chain of links, there will be no further reference to it. In this case, Java will recapture the memory it uses when it does garbage collection.

```java
public String remove(String name) {              // Remove an entry by name
  if (isEmpty())                                  // Case 1: empty list
    return "Phone list is empty";
  PhoneListNode current = head;
  PhoneListNode previous = null;
  if (current.getName().equals(name)) {           // Case 2: remove first node
    head = current.getNext();
    return "Removed " + current.toString() ;
  }
  while ((current.getNext() != null) && (!current.getName().equals(name))) {
    previous = current;
    current = current.getNext();
  }
  if (current.getName().equals(name)) {           // Case 3: remove named node
    previous.setNext(current.getNext());
    return "Removed " + current.toString();
  } else
    return ("Sorry.  No entry for " + name);      // Case 4: node not found
} // remove()
```

Figure 16.10 The `remove()` method.

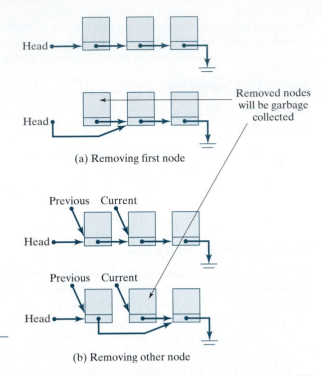

(a) Removing first node

Removed nodes will be garbage collected

(b) Removing other node

Figure 16.11 Removing different nodes from a linked list.

> **JAVA LANGUAGE RULE** **Garbage Collection.** Java's garbage collector handles the disposal of unused objects automatically. This helps to simplify linked-list applications. In languages such as C++, the programmer would have to *dispose* of the memory occupied by the deleted node.

In order to remove some other node besides the first, two traversal variables are needed: `previous` and `current`. They proceed together down the list, with `previous` always pointing to the node just before the `current` node. The reason, of course, is that to remove the `current` node, you need to adjust the link pointing to it contained in the `previous` node, as seen in Figure 16.11(b). That is, the new value of `previous.next` will be the current value of `current.next`. We use the `getNext()` and `setNext()` methods to effect this change:

Tandem traversal

```
previous.setNext(current.getNext());
```

Testing the List

In developing list-processing programs, it is important to design good test data. As we have seen, both the insertion and removal operations involve several distinct cases. Proper testing of these methods ideally would test every possible case. The `main()` program in Figure 16.12 illustrates the kinds of tests that should be performed. This method could be incorporated directly into the `PhoneList` class, or it could be made part of a separate class.

Designing test data

```
public static void main(String argv[]) {
                    // Create list and insert nodes
    PhoneList list = new PhoneList();
    list.insert( new PhoneListNode("Roger M", "997-0020"));
    list.insert( new PhoneListNode("Roger W", "997-0086"));
    list.insert( new PhoneListNode("Rich P", "997-0010"));
    list.insert( new PhoneListNode("Jane M", "997-2101"));
    list.insert( new PhoneListNode("Stacy K", "997-2517"));
                    // Test whether insertions worked
    System.out.println( "Phone Directory" );
    list.print();
                    // Test whether lookups work
    System.out.println("Looking up numbers by name");
    System.out.println(list.getPhone("Roger M"));
    System.out.println(list.getPhone("Rich P"));
    System.out.println(list.getPhone("Stacy K"));
    System.out.println(list.getPhone("Mary P"));
    System.out.println(list.remove("Rich P"));

    System.out.println("Phone Directory");
    list.print();
        // Test removals, printing list after each removal
    System.out.println(list.remove("Roger M"));
    System.out.println("Phone Directory");
    list.print();
    System.out.println(list.remove("Stacy K"));
    System.out.println("Phone Directory");
    list.print();
    System.out.println(list.remove("Jane M"));
    System.out.println("Phone Directory");
    list.print();
    System.out.println(list.remove("Jane M"));
    System.out.println("Phone Directory");
    list.print();
    System.out.println(list.remove("Roger W"));
    System.out.println("Phone Directory");
    list.print();
    System.out.println(list.remove("Roger W"));
    System.out.println("Phone Directory");
    list.print();
} // main()
```

Figure 16.12 A main() method containing a set of tests for the PhoneList class.

Of course, there are often so many combinations of list operations that exhaustive testing might not be feasible. At the very least, you should design test data that test each of the different conditions identified in your algorithms. For example, in testing removals from a list, you should test all four cases that we discussed. In testing insertions or lookups, you should test all three cases that we identified.

EFFECTIVE DESIGN: Test Data.   Test data for validating list-processing algorithms should (at least) test each of the cases identified in each of the removal and insertion methods.

SELF-STUDY EXERCISES

EXERCISE 16.5 Trace through the `main()` method line by line and predict its output.

EXERCISE 16.6 Design a test of `PhoneList` that shows that new elements can be inserted into a list after some or all of its previous nodes have been removed.

16.3 Object-Oriented Design: The List Abstract Data Type (ADT)

The `PhoneList` example from the preceding section illustrates the basic concepts of the linked list. Keep in mind that there are other implementations that could have been described. For example, some linked lists use a reference to both the first and last elements of the list. Some lists use nodes that have two pointers, one to the next node and one to the previous node. This enables traversals in two directions—front to back and back to front—and, as well, makes it easier to remove nodes from the list. The example we showed was intended mainly to illustrate the basic techniques involved in list processing.

A generic list structure

Also, the `PhoneList` example is limited to a particular type of data—namely, a `PhoneListNode`. Let's develop a more general linked list class and a more general node class that can be used to store and process lists of any kind of data.

An **Abstract Data Type (ADT)** involves two components: the data that are being stored and manipulated and the methods and operations that can be performed on the data. For example, an `int` is an ADT. The data are the integers ranging from some `MININT` to some `MAXINT`. The operations are the various integer operations: addition, subtraction, multiplication, and division. These operations prescribe the ways that `int`s can be used. There are no other ways to manipulate integers.

Information hiding

In designing an ADT, it is important to hide the implementation of the operations from the users of the operations. Thus, our programs have used all of these integer operations on `int`s, but we have no real idea how they are implemented—that is, what exact algorithm they use.

Objects can be designed as ADTs, because we can easily distinguish an object's use from its implementation. Thus, the `private` parts of an object—its instance variables and private methods—are hidden from the user, while the object's interface—its `public` methods—are available. As with the integer operators, the object's public methods prescribe just how the object can be used.

Design specifications

So let's design a list ADT. We want it to be able to store any kind of data, and we want to prescribe the operations that can be performed on the data—the insert, delete, and so on. Also, we want to design the ADT so that it can be extended to create more specialized kinds of lists.

The Node Class

> **EFFECTIVE DESIGN: Generalizing a Type.** An effective strategy for designing a list abstract data type is to start with a specific list and generalize it. The result should be a more abstract version of the original list.

Our approach will be to generalize the classes we created in the `PhoneList` example. Thus, the `PhoneListNode` will become a generic `Node` that can store any kind of data (Fig. 16.13). Some of the changes are merely name changes. Thus, wherever we had `PhoneListNode`, we now have just `Node`. The link access methods have not changed significantly. What has

```
                 Node
  ─ data : Object
  ─ next : Node
  + Node(in o : Object)
  + setData(in o : Object)
  + getData() : Object
  + setNext(in link : Node)
  + getNext() : Node
  + toString() : String
```

Figure 16.13 The Node class is a generalization of the PhoneList-Node class.

changed is that instead of instance variables for the name, phone number, and so on, we now have just a single data reference to an Object. This is as general as you can get, because, as we pointed out earlier, data can refer to any object, even to primitive data.

The implementation of the Node class is shown in Figure 16.14. Note that the data access methods, getData() and setData(), use references to Object for their parameter and return type. Note also how we have defined the toString() method. It just invokes data.toString(). Because toString() is defined in Object, every type of data will have this method. And because toString() is frequently overridden in defining new objects, it is useful here.

The List Class

Let's now generalize the PhoneList class (Fig. 16.15). The List class will still contain a reference to the head of the list, which will now be a list of Nodes. It will still define its constructor, its isEmpty() method, and its print() method in the same way as in the PhoneList.

```java
public class Node {
    private Object data;                    // Stores any kind of data
    private Node next;

    public Node(Object obj) {               // Constructor
        data = obj;
        next = null;
    }                                       // Data access methods
    public void setData(Object obj) {
        data = obj;
    }
    public Object getData() {
        return data;
    }
    public String toString() {
        return data.toString();
    }                                       // Link access methods
    public void setNext( Node nextPtr ) {
        next = nextPtr;
    }
    public Node getNext() {
        return next;
    }
} // Node class
```

Figure 16.14 The Node class is a more abstract version of the PhoneListNode class.

List
– head : Node
+ List() + isEmpty() : boolean + print() + insertAtFront(in o : Object) + insertAtRear(in o : Object) + removeFirst() : Object + removeLast() : Object

Figure 16.15 The List class contains a pointer to the head of the list and public methods to insert and remove objects from both the front and rear of the list.

However, in designing a generic List class, we want to design some new methods, particularly because we want to use this class as the basis for more specialized lists. The PhoneList.insert() method was used to insert nodes at the end of a list. In addition to this method, let's design a method that inserts at the head of the list. Also, PhoneList had a method to remove nodes by name. However, now that we have generalized our data, we don't know if the list's Objects have a name field, so we'll scrap this method in favor of two new methods that remove a node from the beginning or end of the list, respectively.

We already know the basic strategies for implementing these new methods, which are shown in the definition in Figure 16.16. We have renamed the insertAtRear() method, which otherwise is very similar to the PhoneList.insert() method. The key change is that now its parameter must be an Object, because we want to be able to insert any kind of object into our list. At the same time, our list consists of Nodes, so we have to use the Object to create a Node in our insert methods:

```
head = new Node(obj);
```

Recall that the Node constructor takes an Object argument and simply assigns it to the data reference. So when we insert an Object into the list, we make a new Node and set its data variable to point to that Object. Note that we check whether the list is empty *before* traversing to the last node.

The new insertAtFront() method (Fig. 16.16) is simple to implement, since no traversal of the list is necessary. You just need to create a new Node with the Object as its data element and then link the new node into the head of the list:

```
Node newnode = new Node(obj);
newnode.setNext(head);
head = newnode;
```

See Figure 16.8a for a graphical representation of this type of insertion.

The new removeFirst() method is also quite simple to implement. In this case, you want to return a reference to the Object stored in the first node, but you need to adjust head so that it points to whatever the previous head.next was pointing to before the removal. This requires the use of a temporary variable, as shown in the method.

The new removeLast() method is a bit more complicated. It handles three cases: (1) the empty list case, (2) the single node list, and (3) all other lists. If the list is empty, it returns null. Obviously, it shouldn't even be called in this case. In designing subclasses of List we will first invoke isEmpty() before attempting to remove a node.

```java
public class List {
  private Node head;
  public List() { head = null; }
  public boolean isEmpty() { return head == null; }
  public void print() {
    if (isEmpty())
      System.out.println("List is empty");
    Node current = head;
    while (current != null) {
      System.out.println(current.toString());
      current = current.getNext();
    }
  } // print()
  public void insertAtFront(Object obj) {
    Node newnode = new Node(obj);
    newnode.setNext(head);
    head = newnode;
  } // insertAtFront()
  public void insertAtRear(Object obj) {
    if (isEmpty())
      head = new Node(obj);
    else {
      Node current = head;                    // Start at head of list
      while (current.getNext() != null)       // Find the end of the list
        current = current.getNext();
        current.setNext(new Node(obj));       // Create and insert newNode
    }
  } // insertAtRear()
  public Object removeFirst() {
    if (isEmpty())                            // Empty List
      return null;
    Node first = head;
    head = head.getNext();
    return first.getData();
  } // removeFirst()
  public Object removeLast() {
    if (isEmpty())                            // empty list
      return null;
    Node current = head;
    if (current.getNext() == null) {          // Singleton list
      head = null;
      return current.getData();
    }
    Node previous = null;                     // All other cases
    while (current.getNext() != null) {
      previous = current;
      current = current.getNext();
    }
    previous.setNext(null);
    return current.getData();
  } // removeLast()
} // List class
```

Figure 16.16 The List ADT.

```java
public static void main( String argv[] ) {
        // Create list and insert heterogeneous nodes
    List list = new List();
    list.insertAtFront(new PhoneRecord("Roger M", "997-0020"));
    list.insertAtFront(new Integer(8647));
    list.insertAtFront(new String("Hello World"));
    list.insertAtRear(new PhoneRecord("Jane M", "997-2101"));
    list.insertAtRear(new PhoneRecord("Stacy K", "997-2517"));

                                    // Print the list
    System.out.println("Generic List");
    list.print();
                                    // Remove objects and print resulting list
    Object o;
    o = list.removeLast();
    System.out.println(" Removed " + o.toString());
    System.out.println("Generic List:");
    list.print();
    o = list.removeLast();
    System.out.println(" Removed " + o.toString());
    System.out.println("Generic List:");
    list.print();
    o = list.removeFirst();
    System.out.println(" Removed " +o.toString());
    System.out.println("Generic List:");
    list.print();
} // main()
```

Figure 16.17 A series of tests for the List ADT.

If the list contains a single node, we treat it as a special case and set head to null, thus resulting in an empty list. In the typical case, case 3, we traverse the list to find the last node, again using the strategy of maintaining both a previous and a current pointer. When we find the last node, we must adjust previous.next so that it no longer points to it.

Testing the List ADT

Testing the list ADT follows the same strategy used in the PhoneList example. However, one of the things we want to test is that we can indeed create lists of heterogeneous types—lists that include Integers mixed with Floats, mixed with other types of objects. The main() method in Figure 16.17 illustrates this feature.

Heterogeneous lists

EFFECTIVE DESIGN: The List ADT. One advantage of defining a List ADT is that it lets you avoid having to write the relatively difficult list-processing algorithms each time you need a list structure.

The list we create here involves various types of data. The PhoneRecord class is a scaled-down version of the PhoneListNode we used in the previous example (Fig. 16.18). Its definition is shown in Figure 16.19. Note how we use an Object reference to remove objects from the list in main(). We use the Object.toString() method to display the object that was removed.

	PhoneRecord
− name : String − phone : String	
+ PhoneRecord(in name : String, in phone : String) + toString() : String + getName() : String + getPhone() : String	

Figure 16.18   The PhoneRecord class stores data for a phone directory.

```java
public class PhoneRecord {
    private String name;
    private String phone;

    public PhoneRecord(String s1, String s2) {
        name = s1;
        phone = s2;
    }
    public String toString() {
        return name + " " + phone;
    }
    public String getName( ) {
        return name;
    }
    public String getPhone( ) {
        return phone;
    }
} // PhoneRecord class
```

Figure 16.19   A PhoneRecord class.

SELF-STUDY EXERCISES

EXERCISE 16.7   Trace through the main() method line by line and predict its output.

EXERCISE 16.8   Design a test of the List program that shows that it is possible to insert new elements into a list after some or all of its previous nodes have been removed.

16.4   The Stack ADT

A **stack** is a special type of list that allows insertions and removals to be performed only to the front of the list. Therefore, it enforces **last-in/first-out (LIFO)** behavior on the list. Think of a stack of dishes at the salad bar. When you put a dish on the stack, it goes onto the top of the stack. When you remove a dish from the stack, it comes from the top of the stack (Fig. 16.20).

The stack operations are conventionally called **push**, for insert, and **pop**, for remove. Thus, the stack ADT stores a list of data and supports the following operations:

- Push: Inserts an object onto the top of the stack.
- Pop: Removes the top object from the stack.
- Empty: Returns true if the stack is empty.
- Peek: Retrieves the top object without removing it.

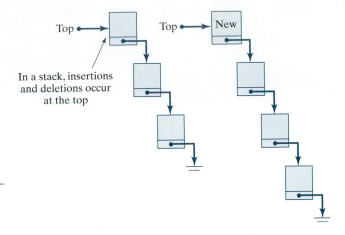

Figure 16.20 A stack is a list that permits insertions and removals only at its top.

Stacks are useful for a number of important computing tasks. For example, during program execution, method call and return happens in a LIFO fashion. The last method called is the first method exited. Therefore, a stack structure known as the *runtime stack* is used to manage method calls during program execution. When a method is called, an activation block is created, which includes the method's parameters, local variables, and return address. The activation block is pushed onto the stack. When the method call returns, the return address is retrieved from the activation block and the whole block is popped off the stack. The `Exception.printStackTrace()` method uses the runtime stack to print a trace of the method calls that led to an exception.

16.4.1 The `Stack` Class

Given our general definition of `List` and `Node`, it is quite easy to define the stack ADT as a subclass of `List` (Fig. 16.21). As a subclass of `List`, a `Stack` will inherit all of the public and protected methods defined in `List`. Therefore, we can simply use the `insertAtFront()` and `removeFirst()` methods for the push and pop operations, respectively (Fig. 16.22).

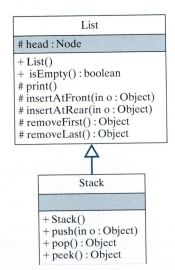

Figure 16.21 As a subclass of `List`, a `Stack` inherits all of its public (+) and protected (#) elements. Therefore, push() can be defined in terms of `insertAtFront()`, and pop() can be defined in terms of `removeFirst()`.

```
public class Stack extends List {
    public Stack() {
        super();                    // Initialize the list
    }
    public void push( Object obj ) {
        insertAtFront( obj );
    }
    public Object pop() {
        return removeFirst();
    }
} // Stack class
```

Figure 16.22 The Stack ADT.

Because the isEmpty() method is defined in List, there is no need to override it in Stack. In effect, the push() and pop() methods merely rename the insertAtFront() and removeFirst() methods. Note that the Stack() constructor calls the superclass constructor. This is necessary so that the list can be initialized.

Do we have to make any changes to the List class in order to use it this way? Yes. We want to change the declaration of head from private to protected, so that it can be accessed in the Stack class. And we want to declare List's public access methods, such as insertAtFront() and removeFirst(), as protected. That will allow them to be used in Stack, and in any classes that extend List, but not in other classes. This is essential. Unless we do this we haven't really restricted the stack operations to push and pop, and therefore we haven't really defined a stack ADT. Remember, an ADT defines the data and operations on the data. A stack ADT must restrict access to the data to just the push and pop operations.

JAVA LANGUAGE RULE   **Protected Elements.** An object's protected elements are hidden from all other objects except instances of the same class or its subclasses.

EFFECTIVE DESIGN: Information Hiding.   Use the private and protected qualifiers to hide an ADT's implementation details from other objects. Use public to define the ADT's interface.

SELF-STUDY EXERCISE

EXERCISE 16.9   Define the peek() method for the Stack class. It should take no parameters and return an Object. It should return the Object on the top of the stack.

16.4.2   Testing the Stack Class

Now let's test our stack class by using a stack to reverse the letters in a String. The algorithm is this: Starting at the front of the String, push each letter onto the stack until you reach the end of the String. Then pop letters off the stack and concatenate them, left to right, into another String, until the stack is empty (Fig. 16.23).

Reversing a string

Because our Nodes store Objects, we must convert each char into a Character, using the wrapper class. We can use the toString() method to convert from Object to String as we are popping the stack.

```
public static void main( String argv[] ) {
    Stack stack = new Stack();
    String string = "Hello this is a test string";

    System.out.println("String: " + string);
    for (int k = 0; k < string.length(); k++)
        stack.push(new Character( string.charAt(k)));

    Object o = null;
    String reversed = "";
    while (!stack.isEmpty()) {
        o  = stack.pop();
        reversed = reversed + o.toString();
    }
    System.out.println("Reversed String: " + reversed);
} // main()
```

Figure 16.23   A method to test the Stack ADT, which is used here to reverse a String of letters.

16.5   The Queue ADT

A **queue** is a special type of list that limits insertions to the end of the list and removals to the front of the list. Therefore, it enforces **first-in/first-out (FIFO)** behavior on the list. Think of the waiting line at the salad bar. You enter the line at the rear and you leave the line at the front (Fig. 16.24).

The queue operations are conventionally called **enqueue**, for insert, and **dequeue**, for remove. Thus, the queue ADT stores a list of data and supports the following operations:

- Enqueue: Insert an object onto the rear of the list.
- Dequeue: Remove the object at the front of the list.
- Empty: Return true if the queue is empty.

Queues are useful for several computing tasks. For example, the ready, waiting, and blocked queues used by the CPU scheduler all use a FIFO protocol. Queues are also useful in implementing certain kinds of simulations. For example, the waiting line at a bank or a bakery can be modeled using a queue.

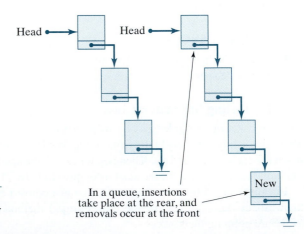

Figure 16.24   A queue is a list that permits insertions only at the rear and removals only at the front.

In a queue, insertions take place at the rear, and removals occur at the front

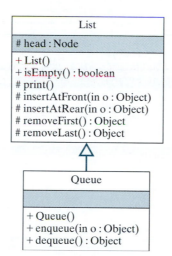

Figure 16.25 The Queue's en-queue() and dequeue() methods can use the List's insert-AtRear() and removeFirst() methods, respectively.

16.5.1 The Queue Class

The Queue class can also easily be derived from List (Fig. 16.25). Here we just restrict operations to the `insertAtRear()` and `removeFirst()` methods (Fig. 16.26). To test the methods of this class, we replace the **push()** and **pop()** operations of the last example to **enqueue()** and **dequeue()**, respectively (Fig. 16.27). In this case, the letters of the test string will come out of the queue in the same order they went in—FIFO.

> **EFFECTIVE DESIGN: ADTs.** ADTs encapsulate and manage the difficult tasks involved in manipulating the data structure. But because of their extensibility, they can be used in a wide range of applications.

SELF-STUDY EXERCISE

EXERCISE 16.10   Define a `peekLast()` method for the Queue class. It should take no parameters and return an **Object**. It should return a reference to the **Object** stored in the last **Node** of the list without removing it.

```
public class Queue extends List {
    public Queue() {
        super();          // Initialize the list
    }
    public void enqueue(Object obj) {
        insertAtRear( obj );
    }
    public Object dequeue() {
        return removeFirst();
    }
} // Queue class
```

Figure 16.26 The Queue ADT.

```
public static void main(String argv[]) {
    Queue queue = new Queue();
    String string = "Hello this is a test string";
    System.out.println("String: " + string);
    for (int k = 0; k < string.length(); k++)
        queue.enqueue( new Character(string.charAt(k)));
    System.out.println("The current queue:");
    queue.print();

    Object o = null;
    System.out.println("Dequeuing:");
    while (!queue.isEmpty()) {
        o = queue.dequeue();
        System.out.print( o.toString() );
    }
} // main()
```

Figure 16.27 A method to test the Queue ADT. Letters inserted in a queue come out in the same order they went in.

The LISP Language

One of the very earliest computer languages, and the one that is most often associated with artificial intelligence (AI), is LISP, which stands for *LISt* Processor. LISP has been, and still is, used to build programs for human learning, natural-language processing, chess playing, human vision processing, and a wide range of other applications.

The earliest (pure) versions of LISP had no control structures, and the only data structure they contained was the list structure. Repetition in the language was done by recursion. Lists are used for everything in LISP, including LISP programs themselves. LISP's unique syntax is simple. A LISP program consists of symbols, such as *5* and *x*, and lists of symbols, such as *(5)*, *(1 2 3 4 5)*, and *((this 5) (that 10))*, where a list is anything enclosed within parentheses. The null list is represented by *()*.

Programs in LISP are like mathematical functions. For example, here is a definition of a function that computes the square of two numbers:

```
(define (square x) (* x x) )
```

The expression *(square x)* is a list giving the name of the function and its parameter. The expression *(* x x)* gives the body of the function.

LISP uses *prefix notation* in which the operator is the first symbol in the expression, as in *(* x x)*. This is equivalent to *(x * x)* in Java's *infix notation*, where the operator occurs between the two operands. To run this program, you would simply input an expression like *(square 25)* to the LISP interpreter, and it would evaluate it to 625.

LISP provides three basic list operators. The expression *(car x)* returns the first element of the (nonempty) list x. The expression *(cdr x)* returns the tail of the list x. Finally, *(cons z x)* constructs a list by making z the head of the list and x its tail. For example, if x is the list *(1 3 5)*, then *(car x)* is 1, *(cdr x)* is *(3 5)*, and *(cons 7 x)* is *(7 1 3 5)*.

continued

Given these basic list operators, it is easy to define a stack in LISP:

```
(define (push x stack) (cons x stack))
(define (pop stack)(setf stack (cdr stack))(car stack))
```

The push operation creates a new stack by forming the *cons* of the element *x* and the previous version of the stack. The pop operation returns the *car* of the stack but first changes the stack (using `setf`) to the tail of the original stack.

These simple examples show that you can do an awful lot of computation using just a simple list structure. The success of LISP, particularly its success as an AI language, shows the great power and generality inherent in recursion and lists.

16.6 From the Java Library: The Java Collections Framework and Generic Types

java.sun.com/docs

The Java class library contains implementations of some abstract data types. The Java utility package, `java.util.*`, contains a good number of classes and interfaces designed to facilitate storing and manipulating groups of objects. This family of related interfaces and classes is called the **Java Collections Framework**. It contains structures that correspond to the ADTs we have just discussed, plus other data structures. Java 5.0 has reimplemented the Java Collections Framework using **generic types** that allow a programmer to specify a type for the objects stored in the structure.

16.6.1 Generic Types in Java

Generic types

Declaring classes that use the generic type construct introduced in Java 5.0 involves using new syntax to refer to the class name. Such classes and interfaces, including those in the collections framework, use angle brackets containing one or more variables (separated by commas) to refer to unspecified type names. For example, you would use <E> or <K,V> to refer to unspecified type names. Thus, names of classes or interfaces implemented with generic types are written with the syntax `ClassName<E>`.

Let's reconsider the `Vector` class, which was introduced in Chapter 9. The `Vector` class, which is part of the Java collections framework, has a generic type implementation in Java 5.0. Figure 16.28 describes the `Vector<E>` class. Note that the E refers to an unspecified type name, that is, the name of a class or interface. This type is specified when a corresponding variable is declared. The type must also be included after a constructor's type name when an object is instantiated and assigned to the variable. The following code demonstrates how to create a `Vector<E>` object for storing `String` objects.

```
Vector<String> strVec = new Vector<String>();
strVec.addElement("alpha");
strVec.addElement("beta");
String str = strVec.elementAt(0);
```

Vector\<E>
+ Vector()
+ Vector(in size : int)
+ addElement(in o : E)
+ elementAt(in index : int) : E
+ insertElementAt(in o : E, in x : int)
+ indexOf(in o : Object) : int
+ lastIndexOf(in o : Object) : int
+ removeElementAt(in index : int)
+ size() : int

Figure 16.28 The `java.util.` Vector class is implemented with a generic type in Java 5.0.

In effect, the \<E> serves as parameter for the type of objects that will be stored in the Vector. Java 5.0 still allows the use of the unparameterized Vector class which is equivalent to instantiating a Vector\<Object> object. If you use a Vector object, the code shown above would be written as follows.

```
Vector strVec = new Vector();
strVec.addElement("alpha");
strVec.addElement("beta");
String str = (String)strVec.elementAt(0);
```

One benefit a generic type provides is type checking of method arguments at compile time. If strVec is a Vector\<String> object, then the statement

```
strVec.addElement(new Integer(57));
```

will generate a compile-time error. By contrast, if strVec was just a plain Vector object, no error would be found at compile time. Thus, if a programmer wishes to create an array of String objects, using generic types will help guarantee that the objects stored are actually of type String. In this way, using generic types helps to reduce the number of programming errors and thereby makes programs safer and more robust.

A second benefit of using generic types is that the return type of objects retrieved from the data structure will be of the specified type rather than of type Object. If you compare the last statement in each of the two code segments above, you can see that using a generic type eliminates the need to cast an Object to a String. This is a big convenience for the programmer, because forgetting to cast objects from one type to another is a common programming error.

The `java.util.Stack<E>` class

The Java collections framework includes the Stack\<E> class, implemented as a subclass of the Vector\<E> class. It contains the methods shown in Figure 16.29. For the most part, its methods provide the same functionality as the methods we developed earlier in this chapter.

Note that the methods provide the functionality of a stack ADT but the details of its implementation are hidden from the user. An object of this class can be declared, instantiated, and used in much the same manner as the Vector\<E> code.

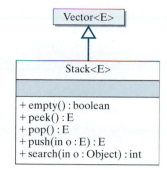

Figure 16.29 The `java.util.Stack<E>` class is a subclass of `Vector<E>`.

```
Stack<String> stk = new Stack<String>();
stk.push("alpha");
stk.push("beta");
String str = stk.pop();
```

SELF-STUDY EXERCISE

EXERCISE 16.11   Write a class with only a `main()` method that modifies Figure 16.23 so that it uses the parameterized `java.util.Stack<E>` class instead of the `Stack` class used there.

16.6.2   The `List<E>` Interface and the `LinkedList<E>` Class

The `java.util.LinkedList<E>` is an implementation of a linked list (Fig. 16.30). Like our implementation earlier in this chapter, it contains methods that can be used to define the standard stack and queue methods.

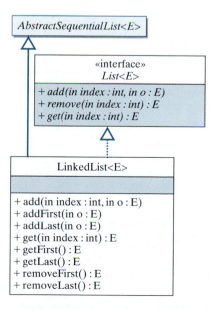

Figure 16.30 The `LinkedList<E>` class implements the `List<E>` interface. Only a partial list of methods is shown.

Many of the standard list-processing methods are defined as part of the `java.util-.List<E>` interface. The advantage of defining list operations as an interface is that they can be implemented by a number of data structures. Code for using the list methods can be written to work independently of the data structure being used.

For example, the collections framework contains `LinkedList<E>` and `ArrayList<E>`, both of which implement the `List<E>` interface. In this section, we will demonstrate how to make appropriate use of the `List<E>` interface and data structures that implement it.

Suppose that a programmer is developing an application to track the activities of employees working at a small company's phone-in help desk. The programmer has decided to use the `LinkedList<E>` data structure to store objects of the `PhoneRecord` class that was defined earlier in this chapter and will use methods of the `List<E>` interface to manipulate the data. A list seems to be an appropriate structure for this problem because—

- An unknown (but relatively small) amount of data will be involved.
- The company wants the data stored in the order it is generated.
- The main use of the data will be to print out the list's phone records.

The programmer might write a short method like the one in Figure 16.31 to demonstrate how the `List<E>` and `LinkedList<E>` structures will be used.

Note that the statement

```
List<PhoneRecord> theList = new LinkedList<PhoneRecord>();
```

declares a variable `theList` of interface type `List<E>` but assigns an object of class type `LinkedList<E>`. This is appropriate because the class implements the interface and the code only uses methods from the interface. The class `ArrayList<E>` in the collections framework also implements the `List<E>` interface. It uses an array rather than a linked list to store elements and has a constructor with an `int` parameter that sets the size of the array. If the programmer knew that `theList` would contain close to, but always less than, 100 elements, then it might be better to declare:

```
List<PhoneRecord> theList = new ArrayList<PhoneRecord>(100);
```

```java
public static void testList() {
    List<PhoneRecord> theList = new LinkedList<PhoneRecord>();
    // new ArrayList?phonerecord?(); could also be used.
    theList.add(new PhoneRecord("Roger M", "090-997-2918"));
    theList.add(new PhoneRecord("Jane M", "090-997-1987"));
    theList.add(new PhoneRecord("Stacy K", "090-997-9188"));
    theList.add(new PhoneRecord("Gary G", "201-119-8765"));
    theList.add(new PhoneRecord("Jane M", "090-997-1987"));
    System.out.println("Testing a LinkedList List");
    for (PhoneRecord pr : theList)
        System.out.println(pr);
} // testList()
```

Figure 16.31 A method that demonstrates the interface `List<E>` and the class `LinkedList<E>`.

The unusual-looking `for` loop at the end of the method is a new feature of Java 5.0 that simplifies the coding of loops that iterate through every object in a collection of objects. The statement

The for--each loop

```
for (PhoneRecord pr : theList) { ***  }
```

should be thought of as executing the enclosed statements *for each* **PhoneRecord** object, pr, in the **theList** data structure. In previous versions of Java, an interface named **Iterator** had to be used to enumerate all the elements in a collection. The **Iterator** approach is more flexible—for example, it allows you to iterate through just some of the members of the collection—and will therefore still have to be used for more complex loops.

The output of the method will be:

```
Roger M 090-997-2918
Jane M 090-997-1987
Stacy K 090-997-9188
Gary G 201-119-8765
Jane M 090-997-1987
```

In the next section we will examine two other structures in the collections framework, the Set interface and the Map interface.

EFFECTIVE DESIGN: Code Reuse.   Given the relative difficulty of writing correct and efficient list-processing algorithms, applications that depend on lists should make use of library classes whenever possible.

16.7   Using the Set and Map **Interfaces**

The Set and Map interfaces are similar to the List interface in that there are multiple classes in the collections framework that implement them.

16.7.1   Using the Set **Interface**

The Set interface is modeled after the *set theory* principles taught in mathematics. In mathematics, sets are groups of elements with a clearly defined algorithm for deciding whether any given element is in any given set. Elements can be added to sets and removed from sets. Sets cannot have duplicate elements; if an element is added to a set that already contains an element equal to it, the new set still has a single such element. The elements of a set have no natural order; two sets that have the same elements listed in different orders are considered to be the same set.

In computer science and in Java, data structures that model sets are designed for large collections of data. Such data structures have a method that determines whether an object is in a given set with an efficient algorithm. For large data sets, using such a method is much faster than iterating through a list. Whether you can list the elements of a set data structure in some natural order depends on how the data structure is implemented. An incomplete listing of the methods of the Set<E> interface is given in the UML diagram in Figure 16.32.

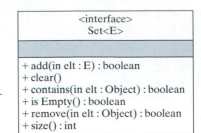

Figure 16.32 A partial list of methods of the Set<E> interface.

TreeSet<E> and HashSet<E> are two classes in the collections framework that implement the Set<E> interface. They both provide fast operations to check whether an element is in a set. They also provide quick insertion of an element into the set or removal of an element from a set. For large sets—those with at least several thousand elements—where there are large numbers of insertions, deletions, and tests for whether elements are in a set, linked lists would be much slower.

Overriding methods

When using the Set<E> interface for a user-defined class E, you will likely want to override the definition of the equals() method from the Object class in E because that method is used when computing the value of aSet.contains(anElement). When using the TreeSet<E> class for a user-defined class E, you should implement the compareTo() method of the Comparable interface because it is used to order the elements of E. In the next section, we will discuss the specific manner in which elements are ordered. Finally, when using the HashSet<E> class for a user-defined class E, you should override the hashCode() method of the Object class because it is used in HashSet<E>. *Hash codes* are indexes computed from the particular object stored in the HashSet. Given an object's hash code, the object can be retrieved directly, as we do with objects stored in an array. However, we will not discuss hash codes in any detail in this text.

Problem Statement

Let's think about a simple example for using a set data structure. Suppose that a programmer is developing an application for a large company for maintaining a *no-call* list. The programmer has decided to use the TreeSet<E> data structure to store objects of the PhoneRecord class defined earlier in this chapter and will use methods of the Set<E> interface to manipulate the data.

A TreeSet seems to be an appropriate structure for this problem because—

- A large amount of data will be involved.
- The company wants the PhoneRecord data stored in alphabetical order.
- The main use of the data will be to test whether names are in the set.

The programmer might write a short method like the one in Figure 16.33 to demonstrate how the Set<E> and TreeSet<E> structures will be used.

In order for the testSet() method to work as we would like, we need to have the PhoneRecord class implement the Comparable interface and override the equals() method. For this example, it is reasonable to assume that the name field of PhoneRecord objects should be unique so that it can be used to decide whether two PhoneRecord objects are equal. The

```
public static void testSet() {
    Set<PhoneRecord> theSet = new TreeSet<PhoneRecord>();
    // new HashSet?phonerecord?(); could also be used.
    theSet.add(new PhoneRecord("Roger M", "090-997-2918"));
    theSet.add(new PhoneRecord("Jane M", "090-997-1987"));
    theSet.add(new PhoneRecord("Stacy K", "090-997-9188"));
    theSet.add(new PhoneRecord("Gary G", "201-119-8765"));
    theSet.add(new PhoneRecord("Jane M", "090-987-6543"));

    System.out.println("Testing TreeSet and Set");
    PhoneRecord ph1 = new PhoneRecord("Roger M", "090-997-2918");
    PhoneRecord ph2 = new PhoneRecord("Mary Q", "090-242-3344");
    System.out.print("Roger M contained in theSet is ");
    System.out.println(theSet.contains(ph1));
    System.out.print("Mary Q contained in theSet is ");
    System.out.println(theSet.contains(ph2));
    for (PhoneRecord pr :   theSet)
        System.out.println(pr);
} // testSet()
```

Figure 16.33   A method that demonstrates use of the interface Set<E> and the class TreeSet<E>.

name field of PhoneRecord can also be used to define the other two methods discussed above. Thus, add the following code to the PhoneRecord class.

```
public boolean equals(Object ob){
    return name.equals(((PhoneRecord)ob).getName());
} // equals()
public int compareTo(Object ob){
    return name.compareTo(((PhoneRecord)ob).getName());
} // compareTo()
public int hashCode(){
    return name.hashCode();
} // hashCode()
```

The output of the TestSet() method is listed below:

```
Testing TreeSet and Set
Roger M is contained in theSet is true
 Mary Q is contained in theSet is false
 Gary G 201-119-8765
 Jane M 090-997-1987
Roger M 090-997-2918
Stacy K 090-997-9188
```

Note that Jane M PhoneRecord appears only once in the listing of elements in the set.

16.7.2   Using the Map<K,V> Interface

The Map<K,V> interface is modeled after looking up definitions for words in a dictionary. In computer science, maps are considered to be a collection of pairs of elements. A pair

```
                              <interface>
                              Map<K,V>

                          + clear()
                          + containsKey(in key : Object) : boolean
                          + get(in key : Object) : V
                          + is Empty() : boolean
                          + put(in key : K, in value : V) : V
                          + remove(in key : Object) : V
                          + size() : int
```

Figure 16.34 A partial list of methods of Map<K,V>.

consists of a **key** that corresponds to a word being looked up, and a **value** corresponds to the definition of the word. Pairs can be added to maps and can be removed from maps. Maps cannot have distinct pairs with the same keys; if you attempt to add a pair to a map that already contains a pair with the same key, the second pair will replace the first. An incomplete listing of the methods of the Map<K,V> interface is given in the UML diagram in Figure 16.34. TreeMap<K,V> and HashMap<K,V> are two classes in the collections framework that implement the Map<K,V> interface.

Let's now consider a simple example of using a map data structure. Suppose that our programmer has been hired by a large company to develop an application that maintains an electronic phone list for company employees. The programmer has decided to use the TreeMap<E> data structure to store pairs of names and telephone numbers, and will use methods of the Map<V,K> interface to manipulate the data. A TreeMap seems like an appropriate data structure for this problem because—

- A large amount of data will be involved.
- The company wants the PhoneRecord data stored in alphabetical order.
- The main use of the data will be to use names to access telephone numbers.

The programmer might write a short method like the one in Figure 16.35 to demonstrate how the Map<K,V> and TreeMap<K,V> structures will be used.

```java
public static void testMap() {
    Map<String, String> theMap = new TreeMap<String,String>();
    // new  HashMap<K,V>(); could also be used
    theMap.put("Roger M", "090-997-2918");
    theMap.put("Jane M", "090-997-1987");
    theMap.put("Stacy K", "090-997-9188");
    theMap.put("Gary G", "201-119-8765");
    theMap.put("Jane M", "090-233-0000");
    System.out.println("Testing TreeMap and Map");
    System.out.print("Stacy K has phone ");
    System.out.print(theMap.get("Stacy K"));
    System.out.print("Jane M has phone ");
    System.out.print(theMap.get("Jane M"));
} // testMap()
```

Figure 16.35 A method that demonstrates use of the interface Map<K,V> and the class TreeMap<K,V>.

The output for this test program is:

```
Stacy K has phone 090-997-9188
Jane M has phone 090-233-0000
```

Note that the second phone number for `Jane M` is the one stored in the data structure.

16.8   The Binary Search Tree Data Structure

To provide some appreciation of what binary search trees are and why they are useful in implementing the `Set` and `Map` interfaces, we will briefly discuss implementing very simple versions of these structures.

Like a linked list, a *binary tree* is a data structure consisting of a collection of nodes that are linked together by references from one node to another. However, unlike a linked list, each node in a binary tree contains references to two other nodes, (`left` and `right`), corresponding to the left- and right-subtrees growing out of a particular node. A *subtree* is a tree that is part of larger tree. This creates a tree-like structure, as shown in Figure 16.36. Note that some of the references to other nodes may be null. The trunk of the tree corresponds to the node labeled `root`. In computer science, trees are almost always drawn upside down. Thus the trunk of the tree, `root`, is at the top of the figure.

If we assume that the objects contained in a tree are from a class that implements the `Comparable` interface, then a **binary search tree** is a binary tree in which the objects are ordered so that the object at any given node is greater than the objects stored in its left subtree and less than the objects stored in its right subtree.

Figure 16.36 shows a binary search tree with the phone list data that we have used throughout the chapter. Objects are compared by comparing the names alphabetically. From the figure it is easy to see that searching for a object should start at the root of the tree. At each node, examining the name at the node will tell you whether you have found the object there. Otherwise, by checking the name at the node, you can decide which subtree the data could be in, and you can traverse either left or right through each level of the tree. One can deduce that if the tree is balanced—that is, if at most nodes the size of the left subtree is about the same size as the right subtree—searching the tree would be much faster than searching a linked list. This is one of the main advantages of using a binary search tree over a linked list.

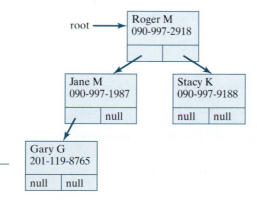

Figure 16.36   A binary search tree of PhoneTreeNodes.

The `TreeSet` and `TreeMap` classes implement sophisticated algorithms for inserting and removing data from a tree. These algorithms guarantee that the tree remains relatively balanced. The details are beyond the scope of this book, but would be a subject of study in a standard data structures and algorithms course.

We will conclude this subsection by giving a brief outline of an implementation of a simple binary search tree that stores our phone list data. Like our `LinkedList` example, you need to define a node class and a tree class. The node class with unimplemented methods, would look like:

```java
public class PhoneTreeNode {
    private String name;
    private String phone;
    private PhoneTreeNode left;
    private PhoneTreeNode right;

    public PhoneTreeNode(String nam, String pho){ }
    public void setData(String nam, String pho){ }
    public String getName(){ }
    public boolean contains(String nam, String pho){ }
    public void insert(String nam, String pho){ }
    // other methods
} // PhoneTreeNode class
```

The tree structure itself contains a reference to a node:

```java
public class PhoneTree {
    private PhoneTreeNode root;

    public PhoneTree(){ }
    public boolean contains(String nam, String pho){ }
    public void insert(String nam, String pho){ }
    // other methods
} // PhoneTreeNode class
```

We will implement only the two `contains()` methods. The `PhoneTree` version is very simple:

```java
public boolean contains(String nam, String pho){
    if (root == null) return false;
    else return root.contains(nam, pho);
} // contains() in PhoneTree
```

The implementation of the `contains()` method of `PhoneTreeNode` is only slightly more involved.

```
public boolean contains(String nam, String pho){
    if (name.equals(nam))
        return true;
    else if(name.compareTo(nam) < 0) {        // name < nam
        if (right == null) return false;
        else return right.contains(nam, pho);
    } else {                                  // name > nam
        if (left == null) return false;
        else return left.contains(nam, pho);
    }
} // contains() in PhoneTreeNode
```

CHAPTER SUMMARY

In this chapter, we have given a brief introduction to dynamic data structures and tried to illustrate how they work and why they are useful for organizing and managing large amounts of data. We also discussed an important new language feature introduced in Java 5.0, the concept of generic types. Obviously, we have only scratched the surface of the important topic of data structures and the algorithms used to manage them. For a broader and deeper treatment of this subject, you will have to take a data structures and algorithms course, which is a fundamental course in most computer science curricula.

Technical Terms

Abstract Data Type (ADT)	linked list
binary search tree	list
data structure	pop
dequeue	push
dynamic structure	queue
enqueue	reference
first-in/first-out (FIFO)	self-referential object
generic type	stack
Java collections framework	static structure
key	traverse
last-in/first-out (LIFO)	value
link	

Summary of Important Points

- A *data structure* is used to organize data and make them more efficient to process. An array is an example of a *static structure* because its size does not change during a program's execution. A vector is an example of a *dynamic structure*, one whose size can grow and shrink during a program's execution.

- A *linked list* is a linear structure in which the individual nodes of the list are joined together by references. A *reference* is a variable that refers to an object. Each node in the list has a *link* variable that refers to another node. An object that can refer to the same kind of object is said to be *self-referential*.

- The `Node` class is an example of a self-referential class. It contains a link variable that refers to a `Node`. By assigning references to the link variable, `Node`s can be chained together into a linked list. In addition to their link variables, `Node`s contain data variables that should be accessible through public methods.

- Depending on the use of a linked list, nodes can be inserted at various locations in the list: at the head, the end, or in the middle of the list.

- Traversal algorithms must be used to access the elements of a singly linked list. To traverse a list, you start at the first node and follow the links of the chain until you reach the desired node.

- Depending on the application, nodes can be removed from the front, rear, or middle of a linked list. Except for the front node, traversal algorithms are used to locate the desired node.

- In developing list algorithms, it is important to test them thoroughly. Ideally, you should test every possible combination of insertions and removals that the list can support. Practically, you should test every independent case of insertions and removals that the list supports.

- An *Abstract Data Type* (ADT) combines two elements: a collection of data, and the operations that can be performed on the data. For a list ADT, the data are the values (`Object`s or `int`s) contained in the nodes that make up the list, and the operations are insertion, removal, and tests of whether the list is empty.

- In designing an ADT, it is important to provide a public interface that can be used to access the ADT's data. The ADT's implementation details should not matter to the user and therefore should be hidden. A Java class definition, with its `public` and `private` aspects, is perfectly suited to implement an ADT.

- A *stack* is a list that allows insertions and removals only at the front of the list. A stack insertion is called a *push*, and a removal is called a *pop*. The first element in a stack is usually called the top of the stack. The `Stack` ADT can easily be defined as a subclass of `List`. Stacks are used for managing the method call and return in most programming languages.

- A *queue* is a list that only allows insertions at the rear and removals from the front. A queue insertion is called *enqueue*, and a removal is called *dequeue*. The `Queue` ADT can easily be defined as a subclass of `List`. Queues are used for managing the various lists used by the CPU scheduler—such as the ready, waiting, and blocked queues.

- A *binary search tree* is a binary tree in which the ordered data stored at any node is greater than all the data stored in the left subtree and less than all the data stored in the right subtree.

SOLUTIONS TO SELF-STUDY EXERCISES

SOLUTION 16.1

```
Node node = new Node(new String("Hello"));
```

SOLUTION 16.2

```
Node node = new Node(new Student("William"));
```

SOLUTION 16.3

```
PhoneListNode newNode = new PhoneListNode("Bill C", "111-202-3331");
nodeptr.setNext(newNode);
```

SOLUTION 16.4   The following condition is too general. It will cause the loop to exit as soon as a non-null node is encountered, whether or not the node matches the one being sought.

```
((current.getNext() != null) || (!current. getName().equals(name)))
```

SOLUTION 16.5   The PhoneList program will generate the following output, which has been edited slightly to improve its readability:

```
Phone Directory
---------------
Roger M 997-0020     Roger W 997-0086     Rich P   997-0010
Jane M   997-2101    Stacy K 997-2517
Looking up numbers by name
    Roger M 997-0020
    Rich P 997-0010
    Stacy K 997-2517
    Sorry. No entry for Mary P
Removed Rich P   997-0010
Phone Directory
---------------
Roger M 997-0020     Roger W 997-0086     Jane M   997-2101
Stacy K 997-2517
Removed Roger M 997-0020
Phone Directory
---------------
```

```
Roger W 997-0086    Jane M  997-2101    Stacy K 997-2517
Removed Stacy K 997-2517
Phone Directory
---------------
Roger W 997-0086    Jane M  997-2101
Removed Jane M  997-2101
Phone Directory
---------------
Roger W 997-0086
Sorry. No entry for Jane M
Phone Directory
---------------
Roger W 997-0086
Removed Roger W 997-0086
Phone Directory
---------------
Phone list is empty
```

SOLUTION 16.6   Executing the following method calls will test whether it is possible to insert items into a list after items have been removed:

```
      // Create and insert some nodes
PhoneList list = new PhoneList();
list.insert(new PhoneListNode("Roger M", "997-0020"));
list.insert(new PhoneListNode("Roger W", "997-0086"));
System.out.println(list.remove("Roger M") );
list.insert(new PhoneListNode("Rich P", "997-0010"));
System.out.println(list.remove("Roger W"));
list.insert(new PhoneListNode("Jane M", "997-2101"));
list.insert(new PhoneListNode("Stacy K", "997-2517"));
System.out.println(list.remove("Jane M"));
System.out.println(list.remove("Stacy K"));
list.print();
      // List should be empty
```

SOLUTION 16.7   The List ADT program will produce the following output:

```
Generic List
---------------
Hello World
8647
Roger M 997-0020
Jane M 997-2101
Stacy K 997-2517
   Removed Stacy K 997-2517
```

```
Generic List:
Hello World
8647
Roger M 997-0020
Jane M 997-2101
    Removed Jane M 997-2101
Generic List:
Hello World
8647
Roger M 997-0020
    Removed Hello World
Generic List:
8647
Roger M 997-0020
```

SOLUTION 16.8 Executing the following method calls will test whether it is possible to insert items into a List after items have been removed:

```
                                        // Create and insert some nodes
List list = new List();
list.insertAtFront(new PhoneRecord("Roger M", "997-0020"));
list.insertAtFront(new PhoneRecord("Roger W", "997-0086"));
System.out.println("Current List Elements");
list.print();
Object o = list.removeLast();           // Remove last element
list.insertAtFront(o);                  // Insert at the front of the list
System.out.println("Current List Elements");
list.print();
o = list.removeFirst();
System.out.println("Removed " + o.toString());
o = list.removeFirst();
System.out.println("Removed " + o.toString());
list.insertAtRear(o);
System.out.println("Current List Elements");
list.print();                           // List should have one element
```

SOLUTION 16.9 The peek() method should just return the first node without deleting it:

```
public Object peek() {
    return head;
}
```

SOLUTION 16.10   The `peekLast()` method can be modeled after the `List.removeLast()` method:

```java
public Object peekLast() {
    if (isEmpty())
        return null;
    else {
        Node current = head;                  // Start at head of list
        while (current.getNext() != null)     // Find end of  list
            current = current.getNext();
            return  current;                   // Return last node
        }
} // peekLast()
```

SOLUTION 16.11   The following class tests the `java.util.Stack<E>` class:

```java
import java.util.*;
public class StackTest{
    public static void main( String argv[] ) {
    Stack<Character> stack = new Stack<Character>();
        String string = "Hello this is a test string";
            System.out.println("String: " + string);
        for (int k = 0; k < string.length(); k++)
            stack.push(new Character(string.charAt(k)));

        Character ch = null;
        String reversed = "";
        while (!stack.empty()) {
            ch  = stack.pop();
            reversed = reversed + ch.charValue();
        }
      System.out.println("Reversed String: " + reversed);
    } // main()
} // StackTest class
```

EXERCISES

Note: For programming exercises, **first** draw a UML class diagram describing all classes and their inheritance relationships and/or associations.

EXERCISE 16.1   Explain the difference between each of the following pairs of terms:

a. *Stack* and *queue*.

b. *Static structure* and *dynamic structure*.

c. *Data structure* and *Abstract Data Type*.

d. *Push* and *pop*.

e. *Enqueue* and *dequeue*.

f. *Linked list* and *node*.

EXERCISE 16.2   Fill in the blanks.

a. An *Abstract Data Type* consists of two main parts: _____ and _____.

b. An object that contains a variable that refers to an object of the same class is a _____.

c. One application for a _____ is to manage the method call and returns in a computer program.

d. One application for a _____ is to balance the parentheses in an arithmetic expression.

e. A _____ operation is one that starts at the beginning of a list and processes each element.

f. A vector is an example of a _____ data structure.

g. An array is an example of a _____ data structure.

h. By default, the initial value of a reference variable is _____.

EXERCISE 16.3   Add a `removeAt()` method to the `List` class to return the object at a certain index location in the list. This method should take an `int` parameter, specifying the object's position in the list, and it should return an `Object`.

EXERCISE 16.4   Add an `insertAt()` method to the `List` class that will insert an object at a certain position in the list. This method should take two parameters, the `Object` to be inserted, and an `int` to designate where to insert it. It should return a `boolean` to indicate whether the insertion was successful.

EXERCISE 16.5   Add a `removeAll()` method to the `List` class. This `void` method should remove all the members of the list.

EXERCISE 16.6   Write an `int` method named `size()` that returns the number of elements in a `List`.

EXERCISE 16.7   Write an `boolean` method named `contains(Object o)` that returns `true` if its `Object` parameter is contained in the list.

EXERCISE 16.8   The *head* of a list is the first element in the list. The *tail* of a list consists of all the elements except the head. Write a method named `tail()` that returns a reference to the tail of the list. Its return value should be `Node`.

EXERCISE 16.9   Write a program that uses the `List` ADT to store a list of 100 random floating-point numbers. Write methods to calculate the average of the numbers.

EXERCISE 16.10   Write a program that uses the `List` ADT to store a list of `Student` records, using a variation of the Student class defined in Chapter 11. Write a method to calculate the mean grade point average for all students in the list.

EXERCISE 16.11   Write a program that creates a copy of a List. It is necessary to copy each node of the list. This will require you to create new nodes that are copies of the nodes in the original list. To simplify this task, define a copy constructor for your node class and then use it to make copies of each node of the list.

EXERCISE 16.12   Write a program that uses a Stack ADT to determine whether a string is a palindrome—spelled the same way backward and forward.

EXERCISE 16.13   Design and write a program that uses a Stack to determine whether a parenthesized expression is well-formed. Such an expression is well-formed only if there is a closing parenthesis for each opening parenthesis.

EXERCISE 16.14   Design and write a program that uses Stacks to determine whether an expression involving both parentheses and square brackets is well-formed.

EXERCISE 16.15   Write a program that links two lists together, appending the second list to the end of the first list.

EXERCISE 16.16   Design a Stack class that uses a Vector instead of a linked list to store its elements. This is the way Java's Stack class is defined.

EXERCISE 16.17   Design a Queue class that uses a Vector instead of a linked list to store its elements.

EXERCISE 16.18   Write a program that uses the List<E> and LinkedList<E> classes to store a list of Student records, using a variation of the Student class defined in Chapter 11. Write a method to calculate the mean grade point average for all students in the list.

EXERCISE 16.19   Write an implementation of the insert() method of the PhoneTree class described at the end of this chapter.

EXERCISE 16.20   Write an implementation of the insert() method of the PhoneTreeNode class described at the end of this chapter.

EXERCISE 16.21   **Challenge:** Design a List class, similar in functionality to the one we designed in this chapter, that uses an *array* to store the list's elements. Set it up so that the middle of the array is where the first element is placed. That way you can still insert at both the front and rear of the list. One limitation of this approach is that, unlike a linked list, an array has a fixed size. Allow the user to set the initial size of the array in a constructor, but if the array becomes full, don't allow any further insertions.

EXERCISE 16.22   **Challenge:** Add a method to the program in the preceding exercise that lets the user increase the size of the array used to store the list.

EXERCISE 16.23   Challenge: Recursion is a useful technique for list processing. Write recursive versions of the `print()` method and the look-up-by-name method for the `PhoneList`. (*Hint*: The base case in processing a list is the empty list. The recursive case should handle the head of the list and then recurse on the tail of the list. The tail of the list is everything but the first element.)

EXERCISE 16.24   Challenge: Design an `OrderedList` class. An ordered list is one that keeps its elements in order. For example, in an ordered list of integers, the first integer is less than or equal to the second, the second is less than or equal to the third, and so on. In an ordered list of employees, the employees might be stored in order according to their social security numbers. The `OrderedList` class should contain an `insert(Object o)` method that inserts its object in the proper order. One major challenge in this project is designing your class so that it will work for any kind of object. (*Hint:* Define an `Orderable` interface that defines an abstract `precedes()` method. Then define a subclass of `Node` that implements `Orderable`. This will let you compare any two `Node`s to see which one comes before the other.)

APPENDIX A

Coding Conventions

This appendix covers various aspects of programming style and coding conventions. It follows the conventions suggested in the Java Language Specification (`http://java.sun.com/docs/books/jls/`), which is summarized on Sun's Java Web site (`http://java.sun.com/docs/`). The conventions have been modified somewhat to fit the needs of an academic programming course. For further details, see:

> `http://java.sun.com/docs/codeconv/index.html`

Coding conventions improve the readability and maintainability of the code. Because maintenance is often done by programmers who did not have a hand in designing or writing the original code, it is important that the code follow certain conventions. For a typical piece of commercial software, much more time and expense are invested in maintaining the code than in creating the code.

Comments

Java recognizes two types of comments. *C-style* comments use the same syntax found in C and C++. They are delimited by `/* ... */` and `//`. The first set of delimiters is used to delimit a multiline comment. The Java compiler will ignore all text that occurs between `/*` and `*/`. The second set of delimiters is used for a single-line comment. Java will ignore all the code on the rest of the line following a double slash (`//`). C-style comments are called *implementation comments* and are mainly used to describe the implementation of your code.

Documentation comments are unique to Java. They are delimited by `/** ... */`. These are used mainly to describe the specification or design of the code rather than its implementation. When a file containing documentation comments is processed by the *javadoc* tool that comes with the Java Development Kit (JDK), the documentation comments will be incorporated into an HTML document. This is how online documentation has been created for the Java library classes.

Implementation Commenting Guidelines

Implementation (C-style) comments should be used to provide an overview of the code and to provide information that is not easily discernible from the code itself. They should not be used as a substitute for poorly written or poorly designed code.

In general, comments should be used to improve the readability of the code. Of course, readability depends on the intended audience. Code that is easily readable by an expert programmer may be completely indecipherable to a novice. Our commenting guidelines are aimed at someone who is just learning to program in Java.

Block Comments

A *block comment* or *comment block* is a multiline comment used to describe files, methods, data structures, and algorithms:

```
/*
 * Multiline comment block
 */
```

Single-Line Comments

A single-line comment can be delimited either by // or by /* ... */. The // is also used to *comment out* a line of code that you want to skip during a particular run. The following example illustrates these uses:

```
/* Single line comment */
System.out.println("Hello");     // End of line comment
// System.out.println("Goodbye");
```

Note that the third line is commented out and would be ignored by the Java compiler.

In this text, we generally use slashes for single-line and end-of-line comments. And we frequently use end-of-line comments to serve as a running commentary on the code itself. These types of comments serve a pedagogical purpose—to teach you how the code works. In a "production environment" it would be unusual to find this kind of running commentary.

Java Documentation Comments

Java's online documentation has been generated by the javadoc tool that comes with the Java Development Kit (JDK). To conserve space, we use documentation comments only sparingly in the programs listed in this textbook. However, javadoc comments are used more extensively to document the online source code that accompanies the textbook.

Documentation comments are placed before classes, interfaces, constructors, methods, and fields. They generally take the following form:

```
/**
 * The Example class blah blah
 * @author J. Programmer
 */
public class Example { ...
```

Note how the class definition is aligned with the beginning of the comment. Javadoc comments use special tags, such as *author* and *param*, to identify certain elements of the documentation. For details on javadoc, see:

```
http://java.sun.com/docs/tooldocs/
```

Indentation and White Space

The use of indentation and white space helps to improve the readability of the program. *White space* refers to the use of blank lines and blank space in a program. It should be used to separate one program element from another, in order to draw attention to the important elements of the program.

- Use a blank line to separate method definitions and to separate a class's instance variables from its methods.
- Use blank spaces within expressions and statements to enhance their readability.
- Be consistent in the way you use white space in your program.

Code should be indented in a way that shows the logical structure of the program. You should use a consistent number of spaces as the size of the indentation tab. The Java Language Specification recommends four spaces.

In general, indentation should represent the *contained in* relationships within the program. For example, a class definition contains declarations for instance variables and definitions of methods. The declarations and definitions should be indented by the same amount throughout the class definition. The statements contained in the body of a method definition should be indented:

```java
public void instanceMethod() {
    System.out.println("Hello");
    return;
}
```

An `if` statement contains an `if` clause and an `else` clause, which should be indented:

```java
if (condition)
    System.out.println("If part");    // If clause
else
    System.out.println("Else part"); // Else clause
```

The statements contained in the body of a loop should be indented:

```java
for (int k = 0; k < 100; k++) {
    System.out.println("Hello " + 'k'); // Loop body
}
```

Finally, indentation should be used whenever a statement or expression is too long to fit on a single line. Generally, lines should be no longer than 80 characters.

Naming Conventions

The choice of identifiers for various elements within a program can help improve the readability of the program. Identifiers should be descriptive of the element's purpose. The name of a class should be descriptive of the class's role or function. The name of a method should be descriptive of what the method does.

Table A.1. Naming rules for Java identifiers

Identifier Type	Naming Rule	Example
Class	Nouns in mixed case with the first letter of each internal word capitalized.	OneRowNim TextField
Interfaces	Same as class names. Many interface names end with the suffix "able."	Drawable ActionListener
Method	Verbs in mixed case with the first letter in lowercase and the first letter of internal words capitalized.	actionPerformed() sleep() insertAtFront()
Instance Variables	Same as method names. The name should be descriptive of how the variable is used.	maxWidth isVisible
Constants	Constants should be written in uppercase with internal words separated by _.	MAX_LENGTH XREF
Loop Variables	Temporary variables, such as loop variables, may have single character names: i, j, k.	int k; int i;

The way names are spelled can also help improve a program's readability. Table A.1 summarizes the various conventions recommended by the Java Language Specification and followed by professional Java programmers.

Use of Braces

Curly braces { } are used to mark the beginning and end of a block of code. They are used to demarcate a class body, a method body, or simply to combine a sequence of statements into a single code block. There are two conventional ways to align braces, and we have used both in the text. The opening and closing brace may be aligned in the same column with the enclosed statements indented:

```java
public void sayHello()
{
    System.out.println("Hello");
}
```

This is the style that is used in the first part of the book, because it is easier for someone just learning the syntax to check that the braces match up.

Alternatively, the opening brace may be put at the end of the line where the code block begins, with the closing brace aligned under the beginning of the line where the code block begins:

```java
public void sayHello() {
    System.out.println("Hello");
}
```

This is the style that is used in the second half of the book, and it seems to be the style preferred by professional Java programmers.

Sometimes, even with proper indentation, it is difficult to tell which closing brace goes with which opening brace. In those cases, you should put an end-of-line comment to indicate what the brace closes:

```java
public void sayHello() {
    for (int k=0; k < 10; k++) {
        System.out.println("Hello");
    } // for loop
} // sayHello()
```

File Names and Layout

Java source files should have the `.java` suffix, and Java bytecode files should have the `.class` suffix. A Java source file can only contain a single `public` top-level class. Private classes and interfaces associated with a `public` class can be included in the same file.

Source File Organization Layout

All source files should begin with a comment block that contains important identifying information about the program, such as the name of the file, author, date, copyright information, and a brief description of the classes in the file. In the professional software world, the details of this "boilerplate" comment will vary from one software house to another. For the purposes of an academic computing course, the following type of comment block would be appropriate:

```java
/*
 * Filename: Example.java
 * Author: J. Programmer
 * Date:  April, 20 1999
 * Description: This program illustrates basic
 *   coding conventions.
 */
```

The beginning comment block should be followed by any package and import statements used by the program:

```java
package java.mypackage;
import java.awt.*;
```

The *package* statement should only be used if the code in the file belongs to the package. None of the examples in this book use the package statement. The *import* statement allows you to use abbreviated names to refer to the library classes used in your program. For example, in a program that imports `java.awt.*` we can refer to the `java.awt.Button` class as simply `Button`. If the import statement were omitted, we would have to use the fully qualified name.

The `import` statements should be followed by the class definitions contained in the file. Figure A.1 illustrates how a simple Java source file should be formatted and documented.

```
/*
 * Filename: Example.java
 * Author: J. Programmer
 * Date:   April, 20 1999
 * Description: This program illustrates basic
 *      coding conventions.
 */
import java.awt.*;


  /**
   * The Example class is an example of a simple
   * class definition.
   * @author J. Programmer
   */
public class Example {
    /** Doc comment for instance variable, var1*/
    public int var1;

 /**
  * Constructor method document at comment describes
  * what the constructor does.
  */
    public Example () {
     // ...    method implementation goes here
    }
 /**
  * An instanceMethod() documentation comment describes
  * what the method does.
  * @param N is a parameter than ....
  * @return This method returns blah blah
  */
    public int instanceMethod( int N ) {
      // ...    method implementation goes here}
    }
} // Example class
```

Figure A.1   A sample Java source file.

Statements

Declarations

There are two kinds of declaration statements: field declarations, which include a class's instance variables, and local variable declarations.

- Put one statement per line, possibly followed by an end-of-line comment if the declaration needs explanation.
- Initialize local variables when they are declared. Instance variables are given default initializations by Java.

- Place variable declarations at the beginning of the code blocks in which they are used rather than interspersing them throughout the code block.

The following class definition illustrates these points:

```java
public class Example {
    private int size = 0;        // Window length and width
    private int area = 0;        // Window's current area

    public void myMethod() {
        int mouseX = 0;          // Beginning of method block

        if (condition) {
            int mouseY = 0;      // Beginning of if block
        ...
        } // if
    } // myMethod()
} // Example class
```

Executable Statements

Simple statements, such as assignment statements, should be written one per line and should be aligned with the other statements in the block. Compound statements are those that contain other statements. Examples would include if statements, for statements, while statements, and do-while statements. Compound statements should use braces and appropriate indentation to highlight the statement's structure. Here are some examples of how to code several kinds of compound statements:

```java
    if (condition) {                           // A simple if statement
        statement1;
        statement2;
    } // if
    if (condition1) {                          // An if-else statement
        statement1;
    } else if (condition2) {
        statement2;
        statement3;
    } else {
        statement4;
        statement5;
    } // if/else
for (initializer; entry-condition; updater) {  // For loop
        statement1;
        statement2;
} // for
while (condition) {                            // While statement
        statement1;
        statement2;
} // while
do {                                           // Do-while statement
        statement1;
        statement2;
} while (condition);
```

Preconditions and Postconditions

A good way to design and document loops and methods is to specify their preconditions and postconditions. A *precondition* is a condition that must be true before the method (or loop) starts. A *postcondition* is a condition that must be true after the method (or loop) completes. Although the conditions can be represented formally—using boolean expressions—this is not necessary. It suffices to give a clear and concise statement of the essential facts before and after the method (or loop).

Chapter 6 introduces the use of preconditions and postconditions, and Chapters 6 through 8 provide numerous examples of how to use them. It may be helpful to reread some of those examples and model your documentation after them.

Sample Programs

For specific examples of well-documented programs used in the text, see the online source code that is available on the accompanying Web site at

```
http://www.prenhall.com/morelli
```

APPENDIX B

The Java Development Kit

The Java Development Kit (JDK) for Java® 2 Platform Standard Edition is a set of command-line tools for developing Java programs. It is available for free in versions for recent editions of Microsoft Windows, Linus, Macintosh OS X, and Solaris (Sun Microsystems).

Download information and documentation are available for the entire range of products associated with the Java® 2 Platform, Standard Edition (J2SE) at:

    http://java.sun.com/j2se/

This appendix summarizes some of the primary tools available in the JDK. For more detailed information, consult Sun's Web site.

Table B.1 provides a summary of some of the JDK tools.
Sun Microsystems provides detailed instructions on how to install JDK for J2SE on computers running any of the above operating systems, including how to set the system's PATH and CLASSPATH variables. Installation instructions can be located using the above link to downloading information.

The Java Compiler: javac

The Java compiler (javac) translates Java source files into Java bytecode. A Java source file must have the .java extension. The javac compiler will create a bytecode file with the same name but with the .class extension. The javac command takes the following form:

    javac   [options]   sourcefiles   [files]

Table B.1. Tools included in the Java Development Kit

Tool Name	Description
javac	Java compiler. Translates source code into bytecode.
java	Java interpreter. Translates and executes bytecode.
javadoc	Java documentation generator. Creates HTML pages from documentation comments embedded in Java programs.
appletviewer	Appletviewer. Used instead of a browser to run Java applets.
jar	Java archive manager. Manages Java archive (JAR) files.
jdb	Java debugger. Used to find bugs in a program.
javap	Java disassembler. Translates bytecode into Java source code.

The brackets in this expression indicate optional parts of the command. Thus, *options* is an optional list of command-line options (including the `-classpath` option), and *files* is an optional list of files, each of which contains a list of Java source files. The *files* option would be used if you were compiling a very large collection of files, too large to list each file individually on the command line.

Most of the time you would simply list the *sourcefiles* you are compiling immediately after the word `javac`, as in the following example:

```
javac MyAppletClass.java MyHelperClass.java
```

Given this command, `javac` will read class definitions contained in `MyAppletClass.java` and `MyHelperClass.java` in the current working directory and translate them into bytecode files named `MyAppletClass.class` and `MyHelperClass.class`.

If a Java source file contains inner classes, these would be compiled into separate class files. For example, if `MyAppletClass.java` contained an inner class named `Inner`, `javac` would compile the code for the inner class into a file named `MyAppletClass$Inner.class`.

If you are writing a program that involves several classes, it is not necessary to list each individual class on the command line. You must list the main class—that is, the class where execution will begin. The compiler will perform a search for all the other classes used in the main class. For example, if `MyAppletClass` uses an instance of `MyHelperClass`, you can compile both classes with the following command:

```
javac MyAppletClass.java
```

In this case, `javac` will perform a search for the definition of `MyHelperClass`.

How Java Searches for Class Definitions

When compiling a file, `javac` needs a definition for every class or interface used in the source file. For example, if you are creating a subclass of `java.applet.Applet`, `javac` will need definitions for all of `Applet`'s superclasses, including `Panel`, `Container`, and `Component`. The definitions for these classes are contained in the `java.awt` package. Here is how `javac` will search for these classes.

Javac will first search among its library files for definitions of classes, such as `Applet` and `Panel`. Next, `javac` will search among the files and directories listed on the user's *class path*. The class path is a system variable that lists all the user directories and files that should be searched when compiling a user's program. JDK no longer requires a class path variable. The class path can be set either by using the environment variable CLASSPATH or by using the `-classpath` option when invoking `javac`. By default, JDK will check in the current working directory for user classes. It does not require that the CLASSPATH variable be set. If this variable **is** set, it must include the current directory. The preferred way to set the classpath is by using `-classpath` option. For example,

The Classpath

```
javac -classpath ../source:. MyApplet.java
```

will tell `javac` to search in both the current directory (.) and in the `../source` directory for user source files. Because the details for setting the CLASSPATH variable are system dependent, it is best to consult the online installation documentation to see exactly how this is done on your system.

During a successful search, `javac` may find a source file, a class file, or both. If it finds a class file but not a source file, `javac` will use the class file. This would be the case for Java library code. If `javac` finds a source file but not a class file, it will compile the source and use the resulting class file. This would be the case for the first compilation of one of your source programs. If `javac` finds both a source and a class file, it determines whether the class file is up-to-date. If so, it uses it. If not, it compiles the source and uses the resulting class file. This would be the case for all subsequent compilations of one of your source programs.

As noted earlier, if your application or applet uses several source files, you need only provide `javac` with the name of the main application or applet file. It will find and compile all the source files, as long as they are located in a directory listed in the class path.

The Java Interpreter: `java`

The `java` interpreter launches a Java application. This command takes one of the following forms:

```
java     [ options]   classname    [ argument ...]
java     [ options]   -jar         file.jar    [ argument ...]
```

If the first form is used, `java` starts a Java runtime environment. It then loads the specified *classname* and runs that class's `main()` method, which must be declared as follows:

```
public static void main(String args[])
```

The `String` parameter `args[]` is an array of strings used to pass any *argument*s listed on the command line. Command-line arguments are optional.

If the second form of the `java` command is used, `java` will load the classes and resources from the specified *Java archive (JAR)*. In this case, the special `-jar` option flag must be specified. The **options** can also include many other command-line options, including the `-classpath` option.

The `appletviewer`

The `appletviewer` tool lets you run Java applets without using a Web browser. This command takes the following form:

```
appletviewer    [ threads flag]    [ options]   url ...
```

The optional *threads flag* tells Java which of the various threading options to use. This is system dependent. For details on this feature and the command-line *options*, refer to Sun's Web site.

The appletviewer will connect to one or more HTML documents specified by their *Uniform Resource Locators* (URLs). It will display each applet referenced in these documents in a separate window. Some example commands would be:

```
appletviewer http://www.domain.edu/~account/myapplet.html
appletviewer myapplet.html
```

AppletViewer tags

In the first case, the document's full path name is given. In the second case, since no host computer is mentioned, `appletviewer` will assume that the applet is located on the local host and will search the class path for `myapplet.html`.

Once `appletviewer` retrieves the HTML document, it will find the applet by looking for either the `object`, `embed`, or `applet` tag within the document. The `appletviewer` ignores all other HTML tags. It just runs the applet. If it cannot find one of these tags, the appletviewer will do nothing. If it does locate an applet, it starts a runtime environment, loads the applet, and then runs the applet's `init()` method. The applet's `init()` must have the following method signature:

```
public void init()
```

The `applet` Tag

The `applet` tag is the original HTML 3.2 tag used for embedding applets within an HTML document. If this tag is used, the applet will be run by the browser, using the browser's own implementation of the Java Runtime Environment (JRE).

Note, however, that if your applet uses the latest Java language features and the browser is not using the latest version of JRE, the applet may not run correctly. For example, this might happen if your applet makes use of Swing features that are not yet supported in the browser's implementation of the JRE. In that case, your applet won't run under that browser.

To ensure that the applet runs with the latest version of the JRE—the one provided by Sun Microsystems—you can also use the `object` or `embed` tags. These tags are used to load the appropriate version of the JRE into the browser as a *plugin* module. A plugin is a helper program that extends the browser's functionality.

The `applet` tag takes the following form:

```
<applet
    code="yourAppletClass.class"
    object="serializedObjectOrJavaBean"
    codebase="classFileDirectory"
    width="pixelWidth"
    height="pixelHeight"
>
    <param name="..." value="...">
    ...
    alternate-text
</applet>
```

You would use only the **code** or **object** attribute, not both. For the programs in this book, you should always use the **code** tag. The **code** tag specifies where the program will begin execution—that is, in the applet class.

The optional **codebase** attribute is used to specify a relative path to the applet. It may be omitted if the applet's class file is in the same directory as the HTML document.

The **width** and **height** attributes specify the initial dimensions of the applet's window. The values specified in the applet tag can be overridden in the applet itself by using the **setSize()** method, which the applet inherits from the **java.awt.Component** class.

The **param** tags are used to specify arguments that can be retrieved when the applet starts running (usually in the applet's **init()** method). The methods for retrieving parameters are defined in the **java.applet.Applet** class.

Finally, the **alternative-text** portion of the applet tag provides text that would be displayed on the Web page if the appletviewer or browser is unable to locate the applet.

Here is a simple example of an applet tag:

```
<applet
    code="HelloWorldApplet.class"
    codebase="classfiles"
    width="200"
    height="200"
>
    <param name="author" value="Java Java Java">
    <param name="date" value="May 1999">
    Sorry, your browser does not seem to be able to
    locate the HelloWorldApplet.
</applet>
```

In this case, the applet's code is stored in a file name **HelloWorldApplet.class**, which is stored in the **classfiles** subdirectory—that is, a subdirectory of the directory containing the HTML file. The applet's window will be 200 × 200 pixels. And the applet is passed the name of the program's author and the date it was written. Finally, if the applet cannot be located, the "Sorry . . . " message will be displayed instead.

The object Tag

The **object** tag is the HTML 4.0 tag for embedding applets and multimedia objects in an HTML document. It is also an Internet Explorer (IE) 4.x extension to HTML. It allows IE to run a Java applet using the latest JRE plugin from Sun. The **object** tag takes the following form:

```
<object
    classid="name of the plugin program"
    codebase="url for the plugin program"
    width="pixelWidth"
    height="pixelHeight"
>
    <param name="code" value="yourClass.class">
    <param name="codebase" value="classFileDirectory">
    ...
    alternate-text
</object>
```

Note that parameters are used to specify your applet's code and codebase. In effect, these are parameters to the plugin module. An example tag that corresponds to the `applet` tag for the `HelloWorldApplet` might be as follows:

```
<object
    classid="clsid:8AD9C840-044E-11D1-B3E9-00805F499D93"
    codebase="http://java.sun.com/products/plugin/"
    width="200"
    height="200"
>
    <param name="code" value="HelloWorldApplet.class">
    <param name="codebase" value="classfiles">
    <param name="author" value="Java Java Java">
    <param name="date" value="May 1999">
    Sorry, your browser does not seem to be able to
    locate the HelloWorldApplet.
</object>
```

If the browser has an older version of the plugin than shown in the `codebase` attribute, the user will be prompted to download the newer version. If the browser has the same or a newer version, that version will run. In theory Netscape 6 should also work the same as IE. For further details on how to use the `object` tag, see Sun's plugin site at:

```
http://java.sun.com/products/plugin/
```

The embed Tag

The embed tag is Netscape's version of the `applet` and `object` tags. It is included as an extension to HTML 3.2. It can be used to allow a Netscape 4.x browser to run a Java applet using the latest Java plugin from Sun. It takes the following form:

```
<embed
    type="Type of program"
    code="yourAppletClass.class"
    codebase="classFileDirectory"
    pluginspage="location of plugin file on the web"
    width="pixelWidth"
    height="pixelHeight"
>
    <noembed>
    Alternative text
    </noembed>
</embed>
```

The `type` and `pluginspage` attributes are not used by the appletviewer, but they are necessary for browsers. They would just be ignored by the appletviewer.

For example, an embed tag for `HelloWorldApplet` would be as follows:

```
<EMBED
    type="application/x-java-applet;version=1.4"
    width="200"
    height="200"
    code="HelloWorldApplet.class"
    codebase="classfiles"
    pluginspage="http://java.sun.com/products/plugin/"
>
    <NOEMBED>
        Sorry.  This page won't be able to run this applet.
    </NOEMBED>
</EMBED>
```

It may be possible to combine the `applet`, `embed`, and `object` tags in the same HTML file. Sun provides much more information, as well as demo programs, on its plugin Web site:

```
http://java.sun.com/products/plugin/
```

The Java Archiver jar Tool

The `jar` tool can be used to combine multiple files into a single JAR archive file. Although the `jar` tool is a general-purpose archiving and compression tool, it was designed mainly to facilitate the packaging of Java applets and applications into a single file.

The main justification for combining files into a single archive and compressing the archive is to improve download time. The `jar` command takes the following format:

```
jar        [ options] destination-file    input-file  [input-files]
```

For an example of its usage, let's use it to archive the files involved in the `WordGuess` example in Chapter 9. As you may recall, this example used classes, such as `TwoPlayerGame`, and interfaces, such as `IGame`, that were developed in earlier sections of the chapter. To help manage the development of `WordGuess`, it would be useful to have a library containing the files that must be linked together when we compile `WordGuess`.

This is a perfect use of a `jar` file. Let's name our library `nplayerlib.jar`. We choose this name because the library can be used to create game programs that have *N* players, including two-player games.

For the two-player game, `WordGuess`, we want to combine all the `.class` files needed by `WordGuess.java` into a single jar file. Here is a list of the files we want to archive:

```
CLUIPlayableGame.class
ComputerGame.class
GUIPlayableGame.class
IGame.class
KeyboardReader.class
Player.class
TwoPlayerGame.class
UserInterface.class
```

Assuming that all of these files are contained in a single directory (along with other files, perhaps), then the command we use from within that directory is as follows:

```
jar cf nplayerlib.jar *.class
```

In this case, the `cf` options specify that we are creating a jar file named `nplayerlib.jar` that will consist of all the files having the `.class` suffix. To list the contents of this file, you can use the following command:

```
jar tf nplayerlib.jar
```

Once we have created the jar file, we can copy it into the directory that contains our source code for the `WordGuess` program. We would then use the following commands to include the code contained in the library when we compile and run `WordGuess.java`:

```
javac -classpath nplayerlib.jar:. WordGuess.java
java -classpath nplayerlib.jar:. WordGuess
```

These commands, which use the `-classpath` option, tell `javac` and `java` to include code from the `nplayerlib.jar`. The notation `:.`, links code in the current directory (`.`) with the library code.

Once we have created a library, we can also use it for Java applets. For example, suppose we have developed an applet version of the `WordGuess` game and linked all of the applet's code into a jar file named `wordguessapplet.jar`. The following HTML file would allow users to download the applet from their Web browser:

```
<html>
    <head><title>WordGuess Applet</title></head>
    <body>
    <applet
        archive="wordguessapplet.jar"
        code="WordGuessApplet.class"
        width=350 height=350
    >
        <parameter name="author" value="Java Java Java">
        <parameter name="date" value="April 2005">
    </applet>
    </body>
</html>
```

When specified in this way, the browser will take care of downloading the archive file and extracting the individual files needed by the applet. Note that the `code` attribute must still designate the file where the program will start execution.

The Java Documentation Tool: javadoc

The javadoc tool parses the declarations and documentation comments in a Java source file and generates a set of HTML pages that describes the following elements: public and protected classes, inner classes, interfaces, constructors, methods, and fields.

The javadoc tool can be used on a single file or an entire package of files. Recall that a Java documentation comment is one that begins with /** and ends with */. These are the comments that are parsed by javadoc.

The javadoc tool has many features, and it is possible to use Java *doclets* to customize your documentation. For full details on using the tool, it is best to consult Sun's Web site. To illustrate how it might be used, let's just look at a simple example.

The FirstApplet program from Chapter 1 contains documentation comments. It was processed using the following command:

```
javadoc FirstApplet.java
```

javadoc generated the following HTML documents:

```
FirstApplet.html        -The main documentation file
allclasses-frame.html   -Names and links to all the classes used in
                            FirstApplet
overview-tree.html      -A tree showing FirstApplet's place
                         in the class hierarchy
packages.html           -Details on the packages used in FirstApplet
index.html              -Top-level HTML document for
                            FirstApplet documentation
index-all.html          -Summary of all methods and variables in
                            FirstApplet
```

To see how the documentation appears, review the FirstApplet.java source file and the documentation it generated. Both are available at:

```
http://www.prenhall.com/morelli/
```

The ASCII and Unicode Character Sets

Java uses version 2.0 of the Unicode character set for representing character data. The Unicode set represents each character as a 16-bit unsigned integer. It can, therefore, represent $2^{16} = 65,536$ different characters. This enables Unicode to represent characters from not only English but also a wide range of international languages. For details about Unicode, see:

> http://www.unicode.org

Unicode supersedes the ASCII character set (American Standard Code for Information Interchange). The ASCII code represents each character as a 7-bit or 8-bit unsigned integer. A 7-bit code can represent only $2^7 = 128$ characters. In order to make Unicode backward compatible with ASCII, the first 128 characters of Unicode have the same integer representation as the ASCII characters.

Table C.1 shows the integer representations for the *printable* subset of ASCII characters. The characters with codes 0 through 31 and code 127 are *nonprintable* characters, many of which are associated with keys on a standard keyboard. For example, the delete key is represented by 127, the backspace by 8, and the return key by 13.

Table C.1. ASCII codes for the printable characters

Code	32	33	34	35	36	37	38	39	40	41	42	43	44	45	46	47
Char	SP	!	"	#	$	%	&	"	(	)	*	+	,	-	.	/
Code	48	49	50	51	52	53	54	55	56	57						
Char	0	1	2	3	4	5	6	7	8	9						
Code	58	59	60	61	62	63	64									
Char	:	;	<	=	>	?	@									
Code	65	66	67	68	69	70	71	72	73	74	75	76	77			
Char	A	B	C	D	E	F	G	H	I	J	K	L	M			
Code	78	79	80	81	82	83	84	85	86	87	88	89	90			
Char	N	O	P	Q	R	S	T	U	V	W	X	Y	Z			
Code	91	92	93	94	95	96										
Char	[	\	]	^	_	"										
Code	97	98	99	100	101	102	103	104	105	106	107	108	109			
Char	a	b	c	d	e	f	g	h	i	j	k	l	m			
Code	110	111	112	113	114	115	116	117	118	119	120	121	122			
Char	n	o	p	q	r	s	t	u	v	w	x	y	z			
Code	123	124	125	126												
Char	{			}	~												

APPENDIX D

Java Keywords

The words shown in Table D.1 are reserved for use as Java *keywords* and cannot be used as identifiers. The keywords `const` and `goto` are C++ keywords. They are not actually used in Java but were included to enable better error messages to be generated when they are mistakenly used in a Java program.

The words `true`, `false`, and `null` may look like keywords but are technically considered *literals*. They too cannot be used as identifiers.

Table D.1. Java keywords cannot be used as names for identifiers

abstract	continue	for	new	switch
assert	default	goto	package	synchronized
boolean	do	if	private	this
break	double	implements	protected	throw
byte	else	import	public	throws
case	enum	instanceof	return	transient
catch	extends	int	short	try
char	final	interface	static	void
class	finally	long	strictfp	volatile
const	float	native	super	while

APPENDIX E

Operator Precedence Hierarchy

Table E.1 summarizes the precedence and associativity relationships for Java operators. Within a single expression, an operator of order m would be evaluated before an operator of order n if $m < n$. Operators having the same order are evaluated according to their association order. For example, the expression

```
25 + 5 * 2 + 3
```

would be evaluated in the order shown by the following parenthesized expression:

```
(25 + (5 * 2)) + 3   ==> (25 + 10) + 3 ==> 35 + 3   ==> 38
```

In other words, because * has higher precedence than +, the multiplication operation is done before either of the addition operations. And because addition associates from left to right, addition operations are performed from left to right.

Table E.1. Java operator precedence and associativity.

Order	Operator	Operation	Association
0	( )	*Parentheses*	
1	++ -- .	*Postincrement, Postdecrement, Dot Operator*	*L to R*
2	++ -- + - !	*Preincrement, Predecrement*	*R to L*
		Unary plus, Unary minus, Boolean NOT	
3	(type) new	*Type Cast, Object Instantiation*	*R to L*
4	* / %	*Multiplication, Division, Modulus*	*L to R*
5	+ - +	*Addition, Subtraction, String Concatenation*	*L to R*
6	< > <= >=	*Relational Operators*	*L to R*
7	== !=	*Equality Operators*	*L to R*
8	∧	*Boolean XOR*	*L to R*
9	&&	*Boolean AND*	*L to R*
10	∧∧	*Boolean OR*	*L to R*
11	= += -= *= /= %=	*Assignment Operators*	*R to L*

Most operators associate from left to right, but note that assignment operators associate from right to left. For example, consider the following code segment:

```
int i, j, k;
i = j = k = 100;        // Equivalent to i = (j = (k = 100));
```

In this case, each variable will be assigned 100 as its value. But it is important that this expression be evaluated from right to left. First, k is assigned 100. Then it's value is assigned to j. And finally j's value is assigned to i.

For expressions containing mixed operators, it is always a good idea to use parentheses to clarify the order of evaluation. This will also help avoid subtle syntax and semantic errors.

Java Inner Classes

This appendix describes basic features of some advanced elements of the Java language. There are details and subtleties involved in using these features that are not covered here. For further details, consult Sun's online references or other references for a more comprehensive description.

What Are Inner Classes?

Inner classes were introduced in Java 1.1. This features lets you define a class as part of another class, just as fields and methods are defined within classes. Inner classes can be used to support the work of the class in which they are contained.

Java defines four types of inner classes. A *nested top-level* class or interface is a *static* member of an enclosing top-level class or interface. Such classes are considered top-level classes by Java.

A *member class* is a nonstatic inner class. It is not a top-level class. As a full-fledged member of its containing class, a member class can refer to the fields and methods of the containing class, even the `private` fields and methods. Just as you would expect for the other instance fields and methods of a class, all instances of a member class are associated with an instance of the enclosing class.

A *local class* is an inner class defined within a block of Java code, such as within a method or within the body of a loop. Local classes have local scope—they can only be used within the block in which they are defined. Local classes can refer to the methods and variables of their enclosing classes. They are used mostly to implement *adapters*, which are used to handle events.

When Java compiles a file containing a named inner class, it creates separate class files for them with names that include the nesting class as a qualifier. For example, if you define an inner class named `Metric` inside a top-level class named `Converter`, the compiler will create a class file named `Converter$Metric.class` for the inner class. If you wanted to access the inner class from some other class (besides `Converter`), you would use a qualified name: `Converter.Metric`.

An *anonymous class* is a local class whose definition and use are combined into a single expression. Rather than defining the class in one statement and using it in another, both operations are combined into a single expression. Anonymous classes are intended for one-time use. Therefore, they do not contain constructors. Their bytecode files are given names like `ConverterFrame$1.class`.

Nested Top-Level Versus Member Classes

The `Converter` class (Fig. F.1) shows the differences between a nested top-level class and a member class. The program is a somewhat contrived example that performs various kinds of

```java
public class Converter {
    private static final double INCH_PER_METER = 39.37;
    private final double LBS_PER_KG = 2.2;

    public static class Distance {                      // Nested Top-level class
        public double metersToInches(double meters) {
            return meters * INCH_PER_METER;
        }
    } // Distance class

    public class Weight {                               // Member class
        public double kgsToPounds(double kg) {
            return kg * LBS_PER_KG;
        }
    } // Weight class
} // Converter class
public class ConverterUser {
    public static void main(String args[]) {
        Converter.Distance distance = new Converter.Distance();
        Converter converter = new Converter();
        Converter.Weight weight = converter.new Weight();
        System.out.println( "5 m = " + distance.metersToInches(5) + " in");
        System.out.println( "5 kg = " + weight.kgsToPounds(5) + " lbs");
    } // main()
} // ConverterUser class
```

Figure F.1   A Java application containing a top-level nested class.

metric conversions. The outer `Converter` class serves as a container for the inner classes, `Distance` and `Weight`, which perform specific conversions.

The `Distance` class is declared `static`, so it is a top-level class. It is contained in the `Converter` class. Note the syntax used in `ConverterUser.main()` to create an instance of the `Distance` class:

```java
Converter.Distance distance = new Converter.Distance();
```

A fully qualified name is used to refer to the `static` inner class via its containing class.

The `Weight` class is not declared `static`. It is, therefore, associated with *instances* of the `Converter` class. Note the syntax used to create an instance of the `Weight` class:

```java
Converter converter = new Converter();
Converter.Weight weight = converter.new Weight();
```

Before you can create an instance of `Weight`, you have to declare an instance of `Converter`. In this example, we have used two statements to create the `weight` object, which requires using the temporary variable, `converter`, as a reference to the `Converter` object. We could also have done this with a single statement by using the following syntax:

```java
Converter.Weight weight = new Converter().new Weight();
```

In either case, the qualified name `Converter.Weight` must be used to access the inner class from the `ConverterUser` class.

There are a couple of other noteworthy features in this example. First, an inner top-level class is really just a programming convenience. It behaves just like any other top-level class in Java. One restriction on top-level inner classes is that they can only be contained within other top-level classes, although they can be nested one within the other. For example, we could nest additional converter classes within the `Distance` class. Java provides special syntax for referring to such nested classes.

Unlike a top-level class, a member class is nested within an instance of its containing class. Because of this, it can refer to instance variables (`LBS_PER_KG`) and instance methods of its containing class, even to those declared `private`. By contrast, a top-level inner class can only refer to class variables (`INCH_PER_METER`)—that is, to variables declared `static`. So you would use a member class if it were necessary to refer to instances of the containing class.

There are many other subtle points associated with member classes, including special language syntax that can be used to refer to nested member classes and rules that govern inheritance and scope of member classes. For these details, consult the *Java Language Specification*, which can be accessed online at

> `http://java.sun.com/docs/books/jls/html/index.html`

Local and Anonymous Inner Classes

In this next example, `ConverterFrame`, a local class, is used to create an `ActionEvent` handler for the application's two buttons (Fig. F.2).

As we have seen, Java's event-handling model uses predefined interfaces, such as the `ActionListener` interface, to handle events. When a separate class is defined to implement an interface, it is sometimes called an *adapter* class. Rather than defining adapter classes as top-level classes, it is often more convenient to define them as local or anonymous classes.

The key feature of the `ConverterFrame` program is the `createJButton()` method. This method is used instead of the `JButton()` constructor to create buttons and to create action listeners for the buttons. It takes a single `String` parameter for the button's label. It begins by instantiating a new `JButton`, a reference to which is passed back as the method's `return` value. After creating an instance button, a local inner class named `ButtonListener` is defined.

The local class merely implements the `ActionListener` interface by defining the `actionPerformed` method. Note how `actionPerformed()` uses the containing class's `converter` variable to acquire access to the `metersToInches()` and `kgsToPounds()` methods, which are inner class methods of the `Converter` class (Fig. F.1). A local class can use instance variables, such as `converter`, that are defined in its containing class.

After defining the local inner class, the `createJButton()` method creates an instance of the class (`listener`) and registers it as the button's action listener. When a separate object is created to serve as listener in this way, it is called an *adapter*. It implements a listener interface and thereby serves as adapter between the event and the object that generated the event. Any action events that occur on any buttons created with this method will be handled by this adapter. In other words, for any buttons created by the `createJButton()` method, a

```
import javax.swing.*;
import java.awt.*;
import java.awt.event.*;
public class ConverterFrame extends JFrame {
    private Converter converter = new Converter();        // Reference to app
    private JTextField inField = new JTextField(8);
    private JTextField outField = new JTextField(8);
    private JButton metersToInch;
    private JButton kgsToLbs;

    public ConverterFrame() {
        metersToInch = createJButton("Meters To Inches");
        kgsToLbs = createJButton("Kilos To Pounds");
        getContentPane().setLayout( new FlowLayout() );
        getContentPane().add(inField);
        getContentPane().add(outField);
        getContentPane().add(metersToInch);
        getContentPane().add(kgsToLbs);
    } // ConverterFram()

    private JButton createJButton(String s) {   // A method to create a JButton
        JButton jbutton = new JButton(s);
        class ButtonListener implements ActionListener {        // Local class

            public void actionPerformed(ActionEvent e) {
                double inValue = double.valueOf(inField.getText()).doubleValue();
                JButton button = (JButton) e.getSource();
                if (button.getText().equals("Meters To Inches"))
                    outField.setText(""+ converter.new
                        Distance().metersToInches(inValue));
                else
                    outField.setText(""+ converter.new Weight().kgsToPounds(inValue));
            } // actionPerformed()
        } // ButtonListener class

        ActionListener listener = new ButtonListener();        // Create a listener
        jbutton.addActionListener(listener);       // Register buttons with listener
        return jbutton;
    } // createJButton()

    public static void main(String args[]) {
        ConverterFrame frame = new ConverterFrame();
        frame.setSize(200,200);
        frame.setVisible(true);
    } // main()
} // ConverterFrame class
```

Figure F.2 The use of a local class as an `ActionListener` adapter.

listener object is created and assigned as the button's event listener. The use of local classes makes the code for doing this much more compact and efficient.

Local classes have some important restrictions. Although an instance of a local class can use fields and methods defined within the class or inherited from its superclasses, it cannot use local variables and parameters defined within its scope unless these are declared `final`. The reason for this restriction is that `final` variables receive special handling by the Java compiler. Because the compiler knows that the variable's value won't change, it can replace uses of the variable with their values at compile time.

Anonymous Inner Classes

An anonymous inner class is just a local class without a name. Instead of using two separate statements to define and instantiate the local class, Java provides syntax that lets you do it in one expression. The following code illustrates how this is done:

```java
private JButton createJButton(String s) {          // A method to create a JButton
    JButton jbutton = new JButton(s);

    jbutton.addActionListener( new  ActionListener() {        // Anonymous class
      public void actionPerformed(ActionEvent e) {
        double inValue = double.valueOf(inField.getText()).doubleValue();
        JButton button = (JButton) e.getSource();
        if (button.getLabel().equals("Meters To Inches"))
          outField.setText("" + converter.new
          Distance().metersToInches(inValue));
        else
          outField.setText("" + converter.new Weight().kgsToPounds(inValue));
      } // actionPerformed()
    }); // ActionListener class
    return jbutton;
} // createJButton()
```

Note that the body of the class definition is put right after the new operator. The result is that we still create an instance of the adapter object, but we define it on the fly. If the name following new is a class name, Java will define the anonymous class as a subclass of the named class. If the name following new is an interface, the anonymous class will implement the interface. In this example, the anonymous class is an implementation of the ActionListener interface.

Local and anonymous classes provide an elegant and convenient way to implement adapter classes that are intended to be used once and have relatively short and simple implementations. The choice of local versus anonymous should largely depend on whether you need more than one instance of the class. If so, or if it is important that the class have a name for some other reason (readability), then you should use a local class. Otherwise, use an anonymous class. As in all design decisions of this nature, you should use whichever approach or style makes your code more readable and more understandable.

APPENDIX G

Java Autoboxing and Enumeration

This appendix describes some basic properties of *autoboxing* and *enumeration*, two of the features added to the Java language with the release of Java 5.0. As is true for many language features, there are details and subtleties involved in using these features that are not covered here. For further details, consult Sun's online references or other references for a more comprehensive description.

Autoboxing and Unboxing

Autoboxing refers to the automatic storing of a value of primitive type into an object of the corresponding wrapper class. Before autoboxing, it was necessary to explicitly box values into wrapper class objects with code like:

```java
Integer iObj = new Integer(345);
double num = -2.345;
Double  dObj = new Double(num);
```

Java 5.0 automatically creates a wrapper class object from a value of primitive type in many situations where a wrapper class object is expected. The assignments shown above can be accomplished with the simpler code:

```java
Integer iObj = 345;
double num = -2.345;
Double  dObj = num;
```

There is a corresponding feature in Java 5.0 which automatically performs the **unboxing** of primitive values from wrapper class objects. Instead of the explicit unboxing in:

```java
int m = iObj.intValue();
double x = dObj.doubleValue();
```

Java 5.0 allows the simpler:

```java
int m = iObj;
double x = dObj;
```

Java 5.0 provides autoboxing of primitive values and automatic unboxing of wrapper class objects in expressions or in arguments of methods where such a conversion is needed to complete a computation. Beginning programmers are unlikely to encounter many problems that require such conversions. One situation which often requires boxing and unboxing are applications that involve data structures. The generic type data structures of Chapter 16 must store objects, but the data to be stored might be represented as values of a primitive type. The code segment below should give you some idea of the type of situation where autoboxing and unboxing can be a genuine help in simplifying one's code:

```java
Stack<Integer> stack = new Stack<Integer>();
for(int k = -1; k > -5; k--)
    stack.push(k);
while (!stack.empty())
    System.out.println(Math.abs(stack.pop()));
```

Note that the `stack.push(k)` method is expecting an `Integer` object, so the `int` value stored in k will be autoboxed into such an object before the method is executed. Also note that the `Math.abs()` method in the last line of the code fragment is expecting a value of primitive type, so the `Integer` value returned by `stack.pop()` must be automatically unboxed before the `Math.abs()` method can be applied.

Sun's online Java 5.0 documentation can be consulted for a more precise description of where autoboxing and unboxing takes place and a list of some special situations where code allowing autoboxing can lead to confusion and problems.

Enumeration

A new **enumeration** construct was included in Java 5.0 to make it simpler to represent a finite list of named values as a type. The **enum** keyword was added as part of this construct. Standard examples of lists of values appropriate for enumerations are the days of the week, the months of the year, the four seasons, the planets, the four suits in a deck of cards, and the ranks of cards in a deck of cards. The following declaration of `Season` enumerated type is an example used by the Sun online documentation.

```java
public enum Season {spring, summer, fall, winter}
```

Compiling a file that contains only this statement will create a `Season.class` file that defines a Java type in the same way that compiling class definitions does. The variables and values of type `Season` can be referred to in other classes just like other types and values. For example, the following statements are valid statements in a method definition in another class:

```java
Season s1 = winter;
if (s1 == spring)
    System.out.println(s1);
```

Note that the values of enumerated types can be used in assignment statements and equality relations, and will be printed out exactly as declared in the `enum` statement.

The enum declaration could also occur inside the definition of a class and be declared as either public or private. In this case, the visibility of the type would be determined in a manner similar to inner classes.

A standard way to represent such a finite list of values in Java before the enum construct was to create a list of constants of type int. For example, to represent the four seasons, you had to do it inside a definition of a class, say of a class named Calendar. Such a representation might look like:

```java
public class Calendar {
    public static final int SPRING = 0;
    public static final int SUMMER = 1;
    public static final int FALL = 2;
    public static final int WINTER = 3;

    // Other Calendar definitions

} // Calendar
```

In addition to being a lengthier declaration, other classes that wished to refer to this representation would have to use notation something like:

```java
int s1 = Calendar.WINTER;
if (s1 == Calendar.SPRING)
    System.out.println(s1);
```

In addition to being more awkward, note that the println() call will print out an integer in this case. Some additional code would have to be written to be able to print the names of the seasons from the int values used to represent them. It is the case that for methods in the Calendar class, the names of the constants look very much like the values of the enum type.

To illustrate a couple of additional advantages of the enum structure, let's consider using the int representation shown above in a method definition that describes the start date of a given season. Code for such a method would look something like:

```java
public static String startDate(int s){
    switch(s){
    case SPRING  :  return "Vernal Equinox";
    case SUMMER  :  return "Summer Solstice";
    case FALL  :  return "Autumnal Equinox";
    case WINTER  :  return "Winter Solstice";
    } // switch
    return "error";
} // startDate()
```

This method has a problem referred to as not being **typesafe**. We would want the start-Date() method to be called only with an argument equal to an int value of 0, 1, 2, or 3. There is no way to tell the compiler to make sure that other int values are not used as an argument to this method.

```
public class Calendar {
    public static String startDate(Season s){
        switch(s){
        case spring  :  return "Vernal Equinox";
        case summer  :  return "Summer Solstice";
        case fall  :  return "Autumnal Equinox";
        case winter  :  return "Winter Solstice";
        } // switch
        return "error";
    } // startDate()

    public static void printDates(){
        for (Season s :  Season.values())
            System.out.println(s + " − " + startDate(s));
    } // printDates()
} // Calendar class
```

Figure G.1 A Calendar class using the Season.

Contrast this with a similar `startDate()` method that can refer to the `Season` enumerated type defined above. The `Calendar` class (Figure G.1) shows the definition of a `startDate()` method as well as a method to print a list of seasons with corresponding starting dates. Note that the parameter of `startDate()` is of type `Season`, and so the Java compiler can check that calls to this method have an argument of this type. This time the `startDate()` is typesafe.

The `printDates()` method illustrates another feature of the enumeration structure. The `for` loop in this method is the `for-in` loop which was added to Java 5.0. The expression `Season.values()` denotes a list of the elements of the type in the order they were declared. The `for-in` loop iterates through all the values of the type in the correct order and, in this case, prints out the type name, followed by a dash, followed by the `String` computed by the `startDate()` method. The output when the `printDates()` method is called is given below:

```
spring - Vernal Equinox
summer - Summer Solstice
fall - Autumnal Equinox
winter - Winter Solstice
```

The `for-in` loop provides a very nice way to iterate through the values of any enumerated type. You may wish to write a corresponding method for the earlier `int` representation of the seasons for a comparison.

Sun's online Java 5.0 documentation provides a more precise definition of enumerated types and describes quite a number of other features that we have not alluded to.

APPENDIX H

Java and UML Resources

Reference Books

- David Flanagan, *Java in a Nutshell Edition 5*, 5th ed., O'Reilly and Associates 2005. Part of the O'Reilly Java series, this book provides a concise desktop reference to Java and the API.
- James Gosling, Bill Joy, and Guy Steele, *The Java Language Specification*, 3d ed., Addison-Wesley, 2005. This book, which is part of Addison-Wesley's Java Series, provides a detailed description of the Java language. An online version is available at

> http://java.sun.com/docs/books/jls

- Martin Fowler, *UML Distilled*, 3d ed., Addison-Wesley, 2003. This book, which is part of Addison-Wesley's Object Technology Series, provides a concise introduction to UML.

Online References

- http://www.omg.org/ contains good information on UML.
- http://java.sun.com/j2se is one of the Sun Microsystems Java Web sites. From this page you can find links to downloads of JDK, API specifications, and documentation on all of Java, including Swing, AWT, and new features of Java 5.0.
- http://java.sun.com/docs/codeconv/ provides a description of coding conventions suggested by the *Java Language Specification* and followed by the Java programming community. (These are summarized in Appendix A.)
- http://java.sun.com/tutorial provides an online Java tutorial.
- http://www.JARS.com provides reviews and ratings of the best Java applets.
- http://www.java-news-center.org/ is a clearinghouse for Java news, programming examples, debugging tips, and many other useful resources.

Index

Index